THE SPECTACLE OF WOMEN

THE SPECTACLE
OF WOMEN

Imagery of the Suffrage Campaign
1907–14

LISA TICKNER

The University of Chicago Press

Lisa Tickner is Reader in Art and Design
at Middlesex Polytechnic.

The University of Chicago Press, Chicago 60637
Chatto and Windus, London

Printed in Great Britain

97 96 95 94 93 92 91 90 89 88   54321

Library of Congress Cataloging-in-Publication Data

Tickner, Lisa.
    The spectacle of women: imagery of the suffrage campaign, 1907-14
Lisa Tickner.
        p.   cm.
    Bibliography: p.
    Includes index.
    ISBN 0-226-80245-0
    1. Women—Suffrage—Great Britain—History—20th century.
    2. Art—Political aspects—Great Britain—History—20th century.
    I. Title.
    JN979.T53 1988   87-30255
    324.6'23'0941—dc 19   CIP

CONTENTS

Acknowledgements, vi
Introduction, ix

1 PROLOGUE, 1

2 PRODUCTION

Women Artists and the Suffrage Campaign, 13
    The Artists' Suffrage League
    The Suffrage Atelier
    Alfred Pearse, Sylvia Pankhurst and the
        WSPU
Pictorial Resources, 30
Finance, 42
Circulation, 45

3 SPECTACLE

Spectacle, 55
Banners and Banner-Making, 60
The Major Processions in the Suffrage
    Campaign, 73
    The 'Mud March': 9 February 1907
    The NUWSS demonstration: 13 June 1908
    WSPU 'Woman's Sunday': 21 June 1908
    The Pageant of Women's Trades and
        Professions: 27 April 1909
    'From Prison to Citizenship': 18 June 1910
    WSPU demonstration: 23 July 1910
    The 'Women's Coronation Procession':
        17 June 1911
    Emily Wilding Davison's Funeral: 14 June
        1913
    The NUWSS 'Women's Pilgrimage': June and
        July 1913

4 REPRESENTATION

Propaganda and Representation, 151
Pro- and Anti-Suffrage Arguments, 153
Women and Suffragists in Edwardian
    Illustration and Caricature, 160
Why Types?, 167
    The Working Woman
    The Modern Woman
    The Hysterical Woman and the Shrieking
        Sisterhood
    The Militant Woman
    The Womanly Woman

5 EPILOGUE, 227

Appendix 1: The Suffrage Atelier: Constitution
    and Addresses, 241
Appendix 2: A Checklist of Artists, 243
Appendix 3: A Checklist of Surviving Posters,
    250
Appendix 4: A Checklist of Surviving Banners,
    254
Appendix 5: 'Banners and Banner-Making' by
    M. Lowndes, 262
Appendix 6: Suffrage Colours, 265
Appendix 7: The Impact of British Propaganda
    Techniques in America, 266
Selected Bibliography, 268
Notes, 274
List of Illustrations, 325
Index, 329

ACKNOWLEDGEMENTS

I have incurred many debts in the course of my research and it would not be possible to list here all those who have answered letters, offered advice or otherwise smoothed my path. I hope they will understand. Anyone working at the Fawcett Library has reason to be grateful to its Librarian, Catherine Ireland, and to David Doughan for his knowledge, enthusiasm and unflagging energies. Veronica Perkins at the Fawcett Library and Valerie Cumming at the Museum of London were particularly helpful with photographic arrangements and permissions. I owe thanks to the staff of various libraries – the British Library, the Bodleian Library, the New York Public Library and the library of Middlesex Polytechnic above all – and to individuals in other institutions, particularly Di Atkinson at the Museum of London, Pamela Burroughs at Street Public Library, Peter Cormack at the William Morris Gallery, Ann Phillips at Newnham College, Cambridge, and Betty Reid at the Communist Party Archives. Private collectors of papers and memorabilia have been unfailingly helpful and kind, among them Frank Corbeil, Jill Craigie, Hunter Davies, John Fraser, John Gorman, Rosemary Hards, Patricia Leeming and Phyllis Wood.

Mrs M. R. Bernard lent me designs by her mother, Catherine Courtauld; Richard Shone helped in tracking down Duncan Grant's designs for 'Handicapped'; Lord (Fenner) Brockway shared with me his memories of the Edwardian suffrage movement; and Barbara Day Jenkinson gave me information on her sister, Sylvia Pankurst's friend Amy Browning. Mary Lowndes's 'On Banners and Banner Making' is reprinted by kind permission of her nephew, M. W. Lowndes. Ben Johnson took most of the photographs that were not supplied by institutions or taken by me. Jon Bird, Barry Curtis, Mike Dawney, Frank Mort, Claire Pajaczkowska and Adrian Rifkin read parts of the manuscript in earlier drafts but are of course not responsible for any errors and deficiencies that remain. I owe thanks to Andrew Motion who commissioned the book, to Ron Costley who designed it, and to Allegra Huston for the tact and rigour of her editing. Most of all I am indebted to Sandy Nairne. His support and encouragement sustained me through bereavement, exhaustion and the birth of two children, and his belief in the book – and in the possibility of finishing it – appeared never to waver (unlike my own).

In memory of my mother,
DORIS ELIZABETH WARTON
1908–1984

Women make their own history, but they do not make it just as they please; they do not make it under circumstances chosen by themselves, but under circumstances directly encountered, given and transmitted from the past.

KARL MARX[1]

INTRODUCTION

In 1908 Emmeline Pethick-Lawrence, treasurer of the Women's Social and Political Union, promised the donors of seven large processional banners for the suffrage demonstration in Hyde Park that they would 'one day be historic possessions to the women of the country'.[1] Alas, she was wrong. What becomes 'historic' is not just a question of accident – of letters and diaries lost and conversations unrecorded – but also a question of power: not the power of open coercion, but the power invested in particular institutions and discourses, and the forms of knowledge that they produce.[2]

The women's suffrage campaign was for many years marginal to the interests of political historians, and its use of posters, postcards and large-scale public spectacle – that 'agitation by symbol'[3] which is the subject of this book – fell victim to what John Gorman has called 'a common myopia with regard to the visual past'.[4] Too 'artistic' for the interests of political history, it was too political (and too ephemeral) for the history of art. Women's work has been traditionally 'hidden from history', but this work is absent even from the two contexts in which it might have found a place: the history of political posters and propaganda on the one hand, and a developing history of women's work as artists and designers on the other.[5] In the first instance, then, this book is intended as an act of reclamation. But it is also a contribution to a 'history of the present', in so far as it attempts to answer a question posed by contemporary feminism: How did we get here?[6]

My first task is to sketch the infrastructure of suffrage propaganda – its organisation, production, circulation and finance – to the extent that that is now possible. (Its importance was often acknowledged but such matters were not publicly discussed.) I have a particular interest here in the Artists' Suffrage League, founded in 1907 'to further the cause of Women's Suffrage by the work and professional help of artists'; and the Suffrage Atelier, formed in 1909 as an 'Arts and Crafts Society composed of suffragists, whose object it is to help any and every Suffrage Society through their arts'.[7] But beyond this I have the more general aim of locating this imagery in its 'intertextuality': in that density of contemporary argument and representation which has drained off from it in more than seventy years. Like the imagery of the Edwardian labour movement it was not a footnote or an illustration to the 'real' political history going on elsewhere, but an integral part of the fabric of social conflict with its own contradictions and ironies and its own power to shape thought, focus debates and stimulate action. It is in this more generous sense that I have taken suffrage imagery as the subject matter of this book. The training and employment of women as artists, the division of labour in the home and at work, the place of women in the family, community, state and empire, the definition and regulation of female sexuality, women's special claims to moral virtue, the consequences of increased educational and employment opportunities for women: all these were part of the political and cultural moment in which suffrage imagery was produced and first received, a moment which was not that of the specific struggle for the vote alone, but also of a broader debate about definitions of femininity and women's place in public life.

Such questions were vigorously argued in the suffrage campaign and invoked in its imagery, where they were not so much reflected as *reworked*. They determined both the conditions of its production and the content of what it produced. At the same time this process – of political argument in visual form – entailed a necessary negotiation of available pictorial genres and styles. Two histories, two practices, converged: that of the political campaign, and that of the artists who brought their particular skills and proclivities to its aid. Women, trained as artists in the late nineteenth century in larger numbers than ever before, still lacked the cultural power to shape the world to their own image. They moved into the practices of representation, but not on terms of their own making. The arguments of the political campaign which fuelled the suffrage imagery were themselves inflected by the themes and modes of representation in that imagery; those in turn were subject to the pressure of precedent in genre and style. Representations of the ethereal feminine, for instance, borrowed from Pre-Raphaelite painting and art-nouveau illustration, were adapted with difficulty to the needs of a militant campaign. But they lent credence to the argument that 'womanly' women needed the vote, and that the emancipation of feminine virtues into public life was a necessary condition of social reform.

Clearly the relations between politics and representation, between dominant and dissident ideologies, and between women's aspirations and their self-perception are complicated here. The terms of modern class politics – radical or conservative, left or right – are insufficiently nuanced for use on historical components which refuse to be sorted in this way, and can only be used with caution in relation to women, whose oppression is not only economic and ideological but domestic, sexual, and therefore intimate. We might do better to borrow from Antonio Gramsci, and in referring to a sexual 'hegemony' understand it as threaded through the hegemony of class like weft through warp, pulling now this way and now that, the interests of dominant groups and the interests of men in general operating together in untidy ways.[8]

*

Something needs to be said about the status of this work, first as the product of minor and sometimes amateur artists, and secondly as propaganda. These attributes, which would exclude it from serious attention by the criteria of orthodox art history, are in fact the source of its significance. The usual distinctions between amateur and professional, art and politics, are blurred in the history of suffrage imagery, which cannot be understood if they are brought back as the principal terms in its analysis. Arguments can be made for the vigorous and even avant-garde elements in this work – which includes some splendid material unjustly neglected – but at the same time as these are worth acknowledging, they are not, in another sense, the point. The historical significance of suffrage propaganda is not determined, but distorted, by a careful sifting of those examples that will fit a modernist history of the poster, detached from the original circumstances of its production and circulation.

I have therefore resisted the temptation to exclude all 'amateurish' examples, because to do so would be to obscure the political significance of the Suffrage Atelier as an organisation that placed the importance of the campaign above the reputations of individual artists, and made a context in which women could share their skills and work collectively. Both the Atelier and the Artists' Suffrage League drew in different ways on women's traditional accomplishments – drawing, stencilling and needlework – and the Atelier set out to train women in the printing techniques it was still difficult for them formally to acquire. To isolate those aspects of its representations which seem aesthetically the most 'progressive' can only be done at the cost of losing sight of those aspects of its *organisation* that were most challenging and ingenious.

As regards propaganda (and printed ephemera) I make no apology for focusing on material that is not in the conventional sense 'art', and I should emphasise that I have no investment in attempting to elevate or integrate it as such. (It was of course *produced* by artists, in so far as the modern profession of graphic designer had scarcely emerged by this period.) 'Used in the same sentence with "art" propaganda finds its historical enemy.'[9] But the art/propaganda divide is itself a kind of propaganda for art: it secures the category of art as something complex, humane and ideologically pure, through the operation of an alternative category of propaganda as that which is crude, institutional and partisan.[10]

We can reject this distinction to the extent that we choose to recognise art as a cultural activity, and culture as the arena in which a society produces those representations that make sense of its world. These sense-making proclivities are active in art as well as propaganda since both are productive of meaning. How specifically those meanings are tied down and whose interests they serve is another matter, but art and propaganda are not mutually exclusive categories. Edwardian painting for instance, distinct as a practice from contemporary anti-suffrage propaganda in its authorship, medium, circulation and intent, was quite as capable of legitimating conservative views on female 'nature' and the proper social place of women – in other words, of serving a common ideological interest. 'Art' and 'propaganda' may be distinguished at any given moment through their modes of address, their links with particular institutions and the different relations between visual practice and social and political interests which they effect; not by a crude division between the ideologically saturated and the ideologically pure. Such a distinction obscures the processes by which signs *circulate*, and hegemony operates, in consequence, through a range of related cultural practices.[11]

That said, it is clear that suffrage imagery is political in the very specific sense that it was designed to meet the needs of a particular campaign, with the aim of bringing about short-term political and, in consequence, long-term social change. Sylvia Pankhurst was probably right to suggest that in this context 'the creation of a Michael Angelo would have ranked low in the eyes of the WSPU members beside a term served in Holloway.'[12] (It was her misfortune to be pulled between the demands of art and politics, of art and propaganda, at a time when the tensions between them were real enough to her.) Suffrage imagery is propaganda in the original sense; it meant to 'propagate' a belief, a position and a set of arguments, in a climate that had proved unfavourable for more than forty years.[13] And to that end it was inextricably bound up in countering other, sometimes heterogeneous but always more dominant and conventional, representations of middle-class femininity. Those representations were for several reasons rather durable. They were often self-fulfilling. Women excluded from public life might indeed appear less suited for it, and women kept out of higher education be judged inferior by the intellectual standards of the day. Ideas about women were not the private mental property of individual women and men. They permeated the legal, political and social institutions and practices that perpetuated them, and they were effective at several different levels of legal prescription, institutional discrimination and social decorum. (By law certain possibilities were closed to women, by precedent certain institutions excluded them, by custom certain activities were not ladylike.) 'We are not governed by armies and police, we are governed by ideas,' as Mona Caird wrote in 1892.[14] Ideas are powerful when they are disseminated and take effect in this way, the more so when they pass as a natural state of affairs, something which it is difficult to question. And it has to be said that ideas about women were productive as well as repressive. They answered, not always adequately perhaps, to a whole panoply of social and psychic needs – repressions, anxieties, projections and desires – which served the interests of the status quo and were not easily unsettled, at least to the extent that they had won women's consent or overridden it, and were woven into the very fabric of their identities. Such unconscious investments imply that we cannot always take suffrage imagery at its face value, although it is the purpose of propaganda to fix its meanings and refuse ambivalence.

Powerful as they were, however, neither the representations nor the practices that together secured women in subordinate positions were immutable. Even long-cherished beliefs were subject to fatigue, and social and ideological contradictions could be exploited by those organised in the desire for change. (It was increasingly clear in the Victorian period, for instance, that the ideal of domestic femininity was attainable neither by the numbers of 'surplus' women, who exceeded the men of marriageable age, nor by most working-class women whose families could not afford for them to emulate the economic dependence of the female bourgeoisie.) The period of the last phase of the women's suffrage campaign was also a period of broader social friction and upheaval in which the values of pre-war liberal England were crumbling under the impact of new industrial, economic and political forces. The *belle époque*, the long summer garden party of the Edwardian afternoon, when there was a lightness in the air, when 'the fruit was ripe and we were eating it':[15] all that was a class-based, wishful misremembering across the chasm of 1914–18. It obscures the struggle for Home Rule, the revolt of the Tories, the constitutional crisis over the power of the House of Lords, labour unrest and intense industrial activity by the increasingly powerful trade unions, as well as the history of the militant and constitutional suffrage campaigns. The Edwardian years were not simply those of the afterglow of Empire, but in essential respects the years of the formation of modern British culture.

The focus of my attention is on the period from about 1906 until the outbreak of war in 1914, at which point the suffrage campaign was, to all intents and purposes, suspended. Some kind of resumé of events from the beginnings of the campaign in 1867 is necessary to explain the point it had reached when WSPU militancy (from 1905) and the landslide victory of a Liberal government (in 1906) injected fresh vigour into a weary cause. It was this last phase of the campaign that Cicely Hamilton had in mind when she claimed that there 'were two respects in which the Woman Suffrage Movement differed from the general run of political strife. It was not a class movement; every rank and grade took part in it. And it was the first political agitation to organise the arts in its aid . . .'[16]

Her point is critical, since this was the moment at which the artists (mostly women but some men) engaged themselves in something remarkable: the first highly organised mass movement of cultural and ideological struggle for political ends; the first to exploit new publicity methods made possible by the rise of national, daily, penny and halfpenny newspapers; the first, or among the first, to adapt the traditional broadsheet or the contemporary advertising poster into a new political instrument; and the first to develop a pictorial rhetoric which drew on, but also challenged, the terms of bourgeois Edwardian femininity. The chapters that follow attempt to map that history.

1 · PROLOGUE

The Women's Suffrage Campaign in 1906

Beginnings are hard to find. People don't see themselves as beginners. How are they to know what comes ahead? They can see behind them not in front. There is no 'beginning' of feminism in the sense that there is no beginning to defiance in women. But there is a beginning of feminist possibility – even before it is conceived as such. Female resistance has taken several historical shapes. SHEILA ROWBOTHAM[1]

The origins of nineteenth-century feminism[2] lay in the period between 1780 and 1830, within the complex of social, economic and political upheavals that accompanied the industrial revolution and England's counter-revolutionary war against France. These were the years of a major social transformation, that of an aristocratic and mercantile capitalist society into an industrial capitalist society, in the course of which the industrial bourgeoisie emerged as the dominant class and consolidated its hold on political power. The development of nineteenth-century feminism took place in a series of political contexts and across a number of reforming campaigns, which often diverged in their general perspectives and in the particular positions they adopted on the nature of femininity and the proper social role of women. Contradictions arose not only between feminist and anti-feminist positions, but within feminism itself, a heterogeneous phenomenon to which the struggle for the vote was later to provide a temporary semblance of unity. Contemporary labels such as 'The Woman Question' or 'Women's Rights' were generously inexact. They did not so much contain as allude to a range of conflicting ideals, expectations and demands that touched on the emancipation of women.

Three main strands have been identified within this ensemble of political positions, strategies and allegiances: that of Enlightenment feminism linking Mary Wollstonecraft with Harriet and John Stuart Mill, that of Evangelicalism (which had a very different notion of women's place and duties) and that of the feminist component in utopian socialism and early Chartism.[3] Most suffrage writers recognised Mary Wollstonecraft's *A Vindication of the Rights of Women* as the founding text of modern feminism, and its publication in 1792 as 'the real date for the beginning of the movement'.[4] Writing as a Jacobin and against the backdrop of the French Revolution, Wollstonecraft had stressed the connection between feudal and domestic tyranny, and in the name of natural rights (for women, as for male bourgeois citizens) had condemned the divine right of husbands, as well as that of kings.[5] Her arguments were broadly compatible with those of utopian socialism and Chartism, but by the time they resurfaced in the mid-nineteenth-century women's movement – purged of their more radical elements[6] – they had become uncomfortably mixed with elements from the Evangelical, political and religious conservatism that had first worked to displace them. The Evangelical movement was anti-Jacobin, anti-aristocratic, patriotic, sexually conservative and very influential indeed on the formation of Victorian society and bourgeois ideology.[7] Evangelicals were utterly opposed to any notion of women's 'equality' with middle-class men, but on their ideology of 'separate spheres' and women's moral mission it was nevertheless possible to construct a different set of arguments for female emancipation.[8]

From the 1850s we are on more familiar ground, with the emergence of an autonomous but heterogeneous women's movement built on the liberal, equal-rights tradition, and organised around a series of campaigns addressed to what Millicent Fawcett described as 'the successful removal of intolerable grievances'.[9] Such campaigns, often linked by their overlapping membership, were directed at the reform of specific instances of social and economic discrimination in the fields of law, employment and education. The vote was the last 'intolerable grievance' to be systematically addressed.

Before the Reform Act of 1832 women had not voted, but then neither had most men. (Mary Wollstonecraft had feared she would 'excite laughter' by hinting that 'women ought to have representatives, instead of being arbitrarily governed,'[10] but she recognised that they were in this respect no worse off than most of the community.) The 1832 Act, in a double movement, had created the middle-class franchise and, by employing the term 'male person', excluded women from it. One of the first liberal acts of a reforming age had as its corollary the effective limitation of women's rights *as women*. But between 1832 and 1867 it was still the case that only one out of five Englishmen possessed the vote, which helps to explain why the leading feminist campaigns of the period were directed at other targets. The Acts of 1867 and 1884, however, enfranchised whole new sections of the community, gave the majority of men the vote for the first time, and in the process left sex as the principal ground for disqualification. Women were thus more isolated at the end of the century than they had been at the beginning. After 1884 the debates around 'fitness' for citizenship that had previously taken place in terms of wealth, class, literacy and education were conducted exclusively in terms of gender. When unfavourable comparisons were made – as they often were in suffrage propaganda – between the respectable and educated but voteless middle-class woman and the feckless labourer, anti-suffragists replied that women's place was in the home. Voting was a

public and political and hence masculine activity, and questions of class and respectability did not come into it. Women were left out of the process of democratisation on the grounds of their proper exclusion from public life. Their different 'natures' rendered them ineligible for 'natural rights'.

The suffrage campaign is usually dated from 1865, when the question of the women's vote was raised within the Langham Place circle (already concerned for a decade with women's rights in education, employment and legal reform)[11] and John Stuart Mill included it in his election address as MP for Westminster. In 1866 Barbara Bodichon, Emily Davies and Jessie Boucherett drafted a petition, eventually signed by 1499 women householders, which was presented by Mill and Henry Fawcett to the House of Commons in June. In 1867 Mill moved a women's amendment to the Reform Act which was defeated, but the organised suffrage campaign grew out of that defeat and the first women's suffrage committees were founded in 1867 and 1868.

The question was debated in Parliament almost every year throughout the 1870s. After the general election of 1880 more than 40 per cent of the returned MPs were pledged in its support, and suffragists, encouraged, pinned their hopes on the 1884 Reform Bill. Gladstone, however, dished their chances: loyalty to the prime minister took precedence over election promises and the women's amendment was defeated by 271 votes to 135. One hundred and four Liberal members who were pledged supporters voted against it.

With most men enfranchised and no immediate prospect of universal suffrage it was clear both that women would have to fight for a Bill that would emancipate them specifically and that the Liberal Party was not to be trusted. (The Pankhursts left the party in disgust in 1884.) From then on interest waned, both in Parliament where MPs talked out proposals without division, and in a disheartened suffrage movement for which these were, in Lady Frances Balfour's phrase, the 'doldrum years'.

But at the same time as the parliamentary vote seemed further away than ever, two other important political opportunities opened up for women: in local government and as party activists. The municipal franchise was granted (or restored) to single women ratepayers by a clause in the Municipal Franchise Act of 1869. Propertied women could vote for school boards (1870), poor law boards (1875), county councils (1888) and parish and district councils (1894). Even anti-suffragists accepted that municipal affairs were the concern of women ratepayers and a legitimate extension of women's domestic concerns for health, education and welfare. The parliamentary electorate had increased as a result of the Reform Acts of 1867 and 1884 (in some seats it had trebled), while the Corrupt Practices Act of 1883 had placed a limit on the authorised expenditure of parliamentary candidates. There was more work to be done by constituency canvassers, fund-raisers and organisers than ever before, and less money to pay for it. 'What more natural,' as Ray Strachey drily remarks, 'than to discover that, after all, it was women's work?'[12] A new structure of electoral machinery was established, underpinned by voluntary women workers who took over from paid male organisers. The Women's Council of the Primrose League (1885), the Women's Liberal Association (1886) and the Women's Liberal Unionist Association (1888) were formed as auxiliaries to the main political parties. (The Times suggested in 1910 that some 50,000 women had 'engaged in the delicate task of converting and convincing the electorate' before the January election.)[13] This was a contradiction that suffragists were quick to identify. Women were 'held competent to form the opinions of electors, and incompetent to give effect to their own'.[14] The conviction that women were sullied in the rough and tumble of political life, or that they were emotionally unstable and unsuited to it, could not long be upheld in the face of their participation in municipal affairs and their evident usefulness as cogs in the party machine. As Milli-

cent Fawcett insisted in mid-campaign, 'short of the vote itself this is one of the most important political weapons that can possibly have been put in our hands.'[15]

*

The franchise in 1906 (and indeed until 1918) was still governed by the provisions of the third Reform Act of 1884.[16] The Act allowed seven franchise qualifications, of which the most important was that of being a male householder with twelve months' continuous residence at one address. In 1914 about seven million men were enfranchised under this heading, and a further million by virtue of one of the other six types of qualification. This eight million – weighted towards the middle classes but with a substantial proportion of working-class voters – represented about 60 per cent of adult males. But of the remainder only a third were excluded from the register by legal provision; the others were left off because of the complexity of the registration system or because they were temporarily unable to fulfil the residency qualification. Of greater concern to Liberal and Labour reformers than the question of adult male suffrage was the issue of plural voting (half a million men had two or more votes) and the question of constituency boundaries. The parliamentary franchise was no longer the central issue that it had been at many points in the nineteenth century (except for the women), because in other respects it was seen to be broadly representative, and because franchise reform was overtaken as a parliamentary issue by a series of apparently more pressing political concerns: the Boer War (between 1899 and 1902), the problems of Home Rule, labour disputes, the licensing laws, imperial issues, and the struggle for power between the House of Commons and the House of Lords.

Any question of democratic principle was in practice undercut by one of political expediency. The non-party issue of women's suffrage split each party – in Philip Snowden's phrase – 'like a flash of crooked lightning'.[17] The Conservative leadership was sympathetic but its rank and file were not. The Liberal Party was broadly favourable but its leaders – Asquith above all – were strongly opposed. Neither of the two main parties was interested in passing a bill that would benefit the electoral chances of the other, and no one could agree on how the women's vote would affect the balance of power. Liberals believed, despite some evidence to the contrary, that it would duplicate or enhance the anomalies and bias of the existing register.[18] There was insufficient support for adult suffrage, but MPs feared that a more limited measure would damage their party and could not be considered unless it had been 'put before the country' at a general election.

The infant Labour Party, like the trade-union and labour movement generally, was divided over the principle of adult versus women's suffrage. The goal of adult suffrage had been little spoken of since 1884, but it was hastily mobilised to meet the demand for women's suffrage as it was raised at the Trades Union Congresses of 1901 and 1902. Between early 1900 and 1906 working-class suffragists in the north of England (termed 'Radical Suffragists' by their historians) ran an impressive campaign among the Lancashire textile workers, and succeeded in making an impact on the older and more middle-class suffrage societies, and on the labour movement through such organisations as the TUC and the growing Labour Representation Committee.[19] Like the National Union of Women's Suffrage Societies and the Women's Social and Political Union, they were prepared to formulate their demand for the vote on the same terms 'as it is, or may be' granted to men. This stopped short of adult suffrage but held several advantages. It helped prevent class divisions and party affiliations from splintering support for the principle of women's suffrage; it was more likely to find support than a broader measure that would put women into the electoral majority, and it might

nevertheless play the part of the thin end of the wedge. The usefulness of such a tactic was accepted by Labour supporters and MPs such as Keir Hardie and Philip Snowden, but some socialists were not prepared to support a limited measure: those like H. M. Hyndman and E. Belfort Bax of the Social Democratic Federation because they believed with many trade unionists that women's place was voteless and in the home,[20] some because they feared that such a move would damage Labour's electoral chances, and others because they refused on principle to countenance anything short of universal suffrage.[21]

Three organisations dominated the Edwardian suffrage campaign. The first and largest was the National Union of Women's Suffrage Societies (the NUWSS), consolidated from sixteen constituent societies under the presidency of Millicent Fawcett from 1897. It was non-party and non-militant and its paper was the *Common Cause*. The second was the Women's Social and Political Union (the WSPU), founded by Emmeline Pankhurst in 1903 but significant on the political stage only from 1905. It was the principal militant society and its paper was *Votes for Women* until the departure in 1912 of the editors, the Pethick-Lawrences, led to its replacement with the *Suffragette*. The third was the Women's Freedom League (the WFL), the result of a split within the WSPU in 1907. It also described itself as a militant society although its tactics were non-violent (e.g. picketing, tax resistance), and its paper was the *Vote*. Each of these had regional and metropolitan branches, and there were hundreds of other groups (including notably Sylvia Pankhurst's East London Federation) organised by social, political, local or professional affiliation.[22] Such unity as these enjoyed was the consequence of their common goal: the vote. There was otherwise no necessary agreement between suffrage societies, either about the strategies through which that goal was best pursued or on the benefits that it would bring. But the intransigence of the opposition brought this reward, that it strengthened their common purpose and tempered the fragile links that bound them. Independently or in concert, the principal societies attempted to extend the activities of the Victorian pressure group into a new kind of political campaign. In doing so, they faced difficulties that were peculiar to their situation as women.

The traditional women's suffrage societies, incorporated into the NUWSS in 1897, had much in common with other Victorian pressure groups, with which they shared an overlapping, liberal and non-conformist membership.[23] They engaged in the same kinds of educational and electoral activities: founding journals, petitioning, lobbying, raising funds, holding meetings, writing pamphlets and establishing a network of local branches. Like other reformers they were the residuary beneficiaries of allied campaigns. (Philanthropists in particular came to see the vote as a necessary tool with which to bring about social reforms.) And yet their weapons were pitifully few. Working-class men could afford to flirt with the spectre of mass violence, which their supporters believed had helped to secure the Reform Bills of 1832 and 1867. Women had no comparable means to force concessions. As a sex they were without political or economic power, without a common base as workers, strung out across the social system and isolated in their private spheres. They had no forum in which to formulate demands, and no means of compelling attention that did not 'unsex' them. Even public speaking in the early years threatened the cause for which they spoke (although it was hardly conceivable that women could win the vote solely through the intercession of men). Because they were women they were confined to the most decorous of pressure-group techniques, which when performed by women were scarcely decorous at all. It was inconceivable in the 1860s, or even at the turn at the century, that they might mount the kind of demonstrations that had influenced the passage of the great Reform Acts. At the same time they were taunted for failing

to do what men had done, and caught in the circuit of two related propositions: that respectable women did not want the vote and organised women did not deserve it. For pressure from without to be effective it needed to be taken up 'within'. As the two-party system crystallised after 1867, the parties came to adopt particular causes and ideologies as part of their political platforms, but neither party adopted the women, and their supporters inside the House, where by definition they could not represent their own interests, were insufficiently powerful or committed to carry their cause. As Mrs Fawcett remarked in exasperation, if women had votes it would be easy to get votes.[24] Without them it was hard to see how public opinion was best organised or changed, and how it could be brought to bear on parliamentary debate. And in so far as exclusion from the franchise had come since 1884 to rest on grounds of sex alone, the success or failure of the women's cause was intimately bound up with deep-seated and cherished beliefs about the nature of femininity and the proper role of women in the family and the state. This meant taking on more than public opinion as an expression of collective feeling or belief; it meant attempting to intervene in a proliferation of contemporary discourses that gave authority to those beliefs (including those of medicine, psychology, education and law), and into the representation of femininity which they secured.

The largest organisation working for a specific bill (and preferably a government measure) on women's suffrage was the NUWSS.[25] Its executive committee included some of the most distinguished women in England, mainly middle-class, middle-aged and non-conformist, Quaker or Evangelical. A considerable proportion of its leadership had engaged in feminist campaigns in higher education, moral reform or local government, and in attempts to improve the industrial condition of working women. Like Millicent Fawcett herself they were eminently respectable, often active in the women's party auxiliaries and outsiders only because of their sex. They were closely related, often literally, to the Victorian establishment.[26] They were competent, caring and intelligent, and they believed their cause was just. They believed in civic rights as well as civic obligations, in reason and progress, and they were initially confident that men of their own class would grant them the vote. Not unnaturally, their tactics before 1906 reflected their social standing, their estimation of the problem, their sense of themselves as women and their experience of other pressure-group campaigns. They organised petitions and public meetings, circulated MPs, created a network of local branches to give themselves a national basis and worked to create a parliamentary lobby and an enlightened public opinion that would support it. The prospect of a general election appears to have spurred them into a new and more assertive phase even before the impact of militant tactics employed by the Women's Social and Political Union in 1905 and 1906.[27]

The WSPU was founded in Manchester by Emmeline Pankhurst in 1903. Mrs Pankhurst was the widow of the radical barrister Dr Richard Pankhurst, with whom she had worked in the Manchester women's suffrage campaign. Both had been active as Liberals until Gladstone effected the exclusion of women from the third Reform Act of 1884, after which they moved to the left and entered the Independent Labour Party in 1894. Their daughters Christabel, Sylvia and Adela were also active in the suffrage movement. Christabel and Emmeline were both members of the North of England Society (which was affiliated to the NUWSS), but they resigned in 1905 and the WSPU moved to London. Until this point it had remained a small and provincial grouping centred on the Pankhurst family in Manchester which did nothing to attract national attention. (Even after it had become notorious the WSPU never enjoyed the mass membership of the NUWSS or established anything comparable to its network of regional branches.)[28] During the autumn of 1905 and the

early months of 1906, however, the WSPU transformed itself. Having moved to London, it began to break with the Labour Party and adopted the militant tactics that were to make a tremendous if highly controversial impact on the campaign as a whole.

In October 1905, in what subsequently came to be regarded as the first militant act, Christabel Pankhurst and Annie Kenney disrupted an election meeting at the Free Trade Hall. Hustled outside, they attempted to address the audience as it left, were arrested and, since they refused to pay their fines, imprisoned. This was the first of many jail sentences suffered in 'the cause' and an outcome apparently intended by Christabel, who had made arrangements to cover her absence and promised her sister, 'I shall sleep in prison tonight.'[29]

Militancy in this first phase consisted of minor insurgencies on this pattern: the heckling of politicians, attempts to enter the House of Commons, the refusal to pay fines, the courting of imprisonment and a dramatic scenario of release. Petitions, drawing-room meetings and the lobbying of MPs continued (during the winter of 1907–08 3000 public meetings were held, 80,000 publications sold and government candidates contested at eight by-elections).[30] But it was militant activity that brought the WSPU into prominence and made of the women's cause a newly topical political issue. The *Daily Mail* coined the term 'suffragette' to distinguish the militants from the constitutional suffragists, and it came into general currency in the months following its first appearance in print on 10 January 1906. The WSPU embraced it, despite the disparaging diminutive.[31] Their motto was 'Deeds not Words', and they were dismissive of the missionary methods of the established societies ('all very polite and very tame')[32] and of the constitutional movement generally, which Emmeline Pethick-Lawrence described in 1906 as 'like a beetle on its back that cannot turn itself over and get on its legs to pursue its path'.[33] The purpose of militancy was to break the stalemate caused by public apathy and press indifference, and to force the hand of a Liberal Party sympathetic in principle but dilatory in practice. That, at least, was the WSPU diagnosis of the situation and the reason for militant activities which took place before the general election of 1906, in the belief that the Liberals would be returned to power and in the hope of influencing a programme of reform.

The landslide Liberal victory of 1906 was the greatest electoral triumph in the party's history. The number of Liberal MPs was almost doubled and a majority of members from all parties in the new House had pledged support for the women's cause. Even though many may have hoped to escape that obligation, and although women's suffrage had not been a major election issue, there was every cause for optimism in the suffrage ranks. But in the event the women's vote was not a priority. Out of office for a decade, the new government was preoccupied with other issues and refused to allow time for a government measure. Sir Henry Campbell-Bannerman, the prime minister, was a lukewarm supporter and Asquith, who succeeded him in 1908, was a long-standing and intransigent opponent. In the face of what they perceived as Liberal vacillation or indifference, the WSPU increased the scope of militant activity. They were, Mrs Pankhurst believed, at a crossroads. 'We had exhausted argument. Therefore, either we had to give up our agitation altogether, as the suffragists of the early eighties virtually had done, or else we must act, and go on acting, until the selfishness and obstinacy of the government was broken down, or the government themselves destroyed.'[34]

Such a strategy depended upon a particular analysis of the power of the government in relation to the convictions of individual MPs (in Mrs Pankhurst's opinion, 'even an overwhelming majority of private members are powerless to enact law in the face of a hostile government of eleven cabinet ministers')[35] and on the assumption that a government with an enormous parliamentary majority

could be threatened, and threatened by voteless women. Mrs Pankhurst argued that radical change had to be wrested from those in power on the model of civil insurgence as it had accompanied the Reform Acts of 1832 and 1867. War had to be waged 'not only on all anti-suffrage forces, but on all neutral and non-active forces'.[36] It had to be made more difficult for Parliament to resist than to concede. The goal was to 'create an impression upon the public throughout the country, to set everyone talking about votes for women, to keep the subject in the press, to leave the government no peace from it'.[37]

In all this the WSPU leaders conceived of themselves as a 'suffrage army in the field', which justified their militant methods and their lack of a democratic organisation. In a series of splits they forfeited the allegiance first of the Women's Cooperative Guild, and then of the radical suffragists who recoiled from the scuffles that attended the WSPU demonstration at the opening of Parliament on 23 October 1906.[38] In 1907 relations with the Independent Labour Party, already strained, ended in conflict over the WSPU by-election policy, and with the resignation of Christabel and her mother from the ILP the last links between the WSPU and northern socialism were broken. These differences served to highlight internal uncertainties as to the authority of the constitution and the nature of the WSPU's leadership.[39] All major decisions were effectively in the hands of the Pankhursts and Mrs and Mrs Pethick-Lawrence. Friction had arisen over Charlotte Despard's and Annie Cobden Sanderson's support for the Labour Party at by-elections in contravention of the WSPU's non-party policy. A rapid expansion of the Union's membership in the summer of 1907, possibly exacerbated by a quarrel between Christabel and Teresa Billington-Greig, seems to have produced a demand for democratic accountability that the Pankhursts were not prepared to tolerate. Christabel had conceived the militant campaign and in Emmeline Pethick-Lawrence's words, 'could not trust her mental offspring to the mercies of politically untrained minds'.[40] The 1907 annual conference was cancelled, the constitution suspended and a new committee elected by a majority of those on the old one, with two dissenters. Mrs Despard, Mrs How-Martyn, Teresa Billington-Greig and a proportion of the membership seceded and became the Women's Freedom League under the presidency of Mrs Despard.[41] Teresa Billington-Greig later pointed to the absurdity of women fighting for votes in an organisation that refused them a voice in their own campaign, but the WSPU defended its structure. 'Autocratic? Quite so . . . The WSPU is not hampered by a complexity of rules. We have no constitution and no bye-laws; nothing to be amended or tinkered with or quarrelled over at an annual meeting . . . It is purely a volunteer army, and no one is obliged to remain in it.'[42]

Both the constitutionalists and the militants had vital contributions to make, at least until the closing stages of the campaign. At crucial moments the tensions between them threatened to pull the suffrage movement apart, but in its early years there is no doubt that the WSPU gave new life to the movement, attracted publicity and large numbers of new recruits to a flagging cause and provoked the traditional societies into a reassessment of the methods of their own campaign. What linked the constitutionalists and the militants, who were united on ends but not on means, was the use of a new kind of political spectacle, and the production of an iconography of their own. For the WSPU it complemented and rehearsed their acts of militancy. For the NUWSS, who needed to revitalise their campaign without resort to force, it took the place of militancy. Pictorial leaflets, cartoons, posters and postcards, like processions and banners, were used by suffragists of all complexions on a scale unprecedented in any Victorian pressure group. Together they made up that 'agitation by symbol', commended by the *Common Cause* for its 'object-lessons, by signs and emblems and pictures, by procession, and many other visible and audible displays', which could offer 'imaginative insight into the minds of others and the reconstruction of suffering which is not felt'.[43]

2 · PRODUCTION

1 Sylvia Pankhurst in her studio.

Women Artists and the Suffrage Campaign

The role, attainments and expectations of the woman artist were fiercely debated in the late Victorian and Edwardian period, in ways that touched on the suffrage campaign and surfaced in its periodicals. Larger numbers of women than ever before were trained in the new public art schools of the late nineteenth century, in the workshops of the arts and crafts movement, in an expanding network of private institutions and in ateliers abroad.[1] Thousands of women were trying to make a living as artists by the turn of the century,[2] but the *idea* of the woman artist, if increasingly familiar, was uncomfortable and contested. On the one hand the 'profession of a woman painter is now consecrated, enrolled, and amiably regarded', as Octave Uzanne put it in *The Modern Parisienne*; on the other (and in the same breath), 'a perfect army' of women artists threatened 'to become a veritable plague, a fearful confusion, and a terrifying stream of mediocrity'.[3] Art was a suitable accomplishment for middle-class women.[4] It might even be an acceptable solution to the problems of the 'redundant' and impecunious since it could be carried on discreetly and at home.[5] But it was understood that the serious pursuit of art was incompatible with the demands of marriage and domesticity – it unsexed women and made them 'irritable, restless, egotistical'[6] – just as the attributes of womanliness were incompatible with the production of good art.[7]

It cannot be coincidence that a flurry of books devoted to women artists, the first exhibitions that grouped them together *as* women, the first serious opportunities for their equal education and employment and the first attempts to demonstrate 'what woman has done, with the general conditions favourable or unfavourable to her efforts',[8] accompanied the rise and influence of the Victorian women's movement and the development of the suffrage campaign. Membership of the Royal Academy and access to its schools had been closed to women since Mary Moser and Angelica Kauffman – both memorialised on suffrage banners – were among its founders in the eighteenth century. What Virginia Woolf called the 'battle of the Royal Academy' was one among many (the battle of Westminster, the battle of Whitehall, the battle of Harley Street), all fought by the same combatants, 'that is by professional men *v.* their sisters and daughters'.[9] And it was a cruel and not insignificant irony that women gained entry to the academic curriculum only at the point at which the power of academic institutions was being challenged by avant-garde developments elsewhere;[10] and that women were often no better placed in these alternatives to the Academy than in the Academy itself. (Vanessa Bell complained of the supposedly radical New English Art Club that its members 'seemed somehow to have the secret of the art universe within their grasp, a secret one was not worthy to learn, especially if one was that terrible low creature, a female painter'.)[11]

It was not just the structures of production, the teaching and exhibiting institutions, that positioned women artists in particular ways, but also the criticism to which they were subject. Giles Edgerton claimed that reviewers 'dipped their pens in treacle' and went forth to women's exhibitions as knights errant 'with powers of analysis laved in chivalry'.[12] This condescension was further complicated by the call for a specifically feminine art, one which would reproduce the values ascribed to women in the dominant discourses on femininity.

Women artists were caught in a paradox produced out of the clash between ideologies of femininity and of art: good-for-a-woman was all that a woman could be, but that in itself would never produce good *art*.[13]

Women artists, whether they were aware of it or not, were engaged in a struggle with the incompatible terms of their identity.[14] They were subject not only to the institutional discrimination they recognised and fought against, but also to its less evident corollary: their powerlessness in the production of social meanings, including social meanings related to the roles of artists and of women. 'Art' was itself complicit in the regulation of sexualities, and in the constructions of femininity which underpinned the identity of the woman artist. (Think of Alma-Tadema's Roman nudes, Pre-Raphaelite Ophelias, the harem scenes of nineteenth-century Orientalism and a whole category of Victorian narrative painting devoted to the troubling sexuality of women: Rossetti's 'Found', Augustus Egg's 'Past and Present', Alfred Elmore's 'On the Brink', George Elgar Hicks's 'Woman's Mission' and hundreds more.)[15]

Suffragists were interested in the woman artist because she was a type of the skilled and independent woman, with attributes of autonomy, creativity and professional competence, which were still unconventional by contemporary criteria.[16] But she was also of interest because the question of women's *cultural* creativity was constantly raised by their opponents as a reason for denying them the vote. 'How many times,' as Mary Lowndes asked in the *Common Cause*, 'have women been reminded – in season and out of season, in conversation, by platform speakers, in print – that their sex has produced no Michael Angelo, and that Raphael was a man? These facts are indisputable; and they are supposed, as a rule, to demonstrate clearly to the meanest capacity that creatures so poorly endowed collectively with creative genius should have no voice in determining the destiny of the threepence weekly which they contribute to the National

Insurance, or in influencing decisions on household economy, or the training of midwives as they arise in Parliament.'[17]

There were several ways of dealing with this. One was to borrow the high-flown rhetoric of masculine genius, and use it to hail the corresponding identities of the avant-garde artist and the modern suffragette. The effect is slightly ludicrous but we are impressed by the attempt, as when Ethel Ducat praises A. E. Rice in *Votes for Women* 'as a possessor of her own soul who has hewn out her individual path to well-deserved fame – as an admitted Genius'.[18] Another was to play down art altogether, or at least, men's practice of it as the guarantee of their social and sexual pre-eminence. Vida Levering, the heroine of Elizabeth Robins's suffragette novel *The Convert*, is heckled by an art student in the crowd who demands to know, 'Where's their Michael Angelo? ... where's their Beethoven? Where's their Plato? Where's the woman Shakespeare?' She refuses the bait and asks instead, 'How many Platos are there in this crowd? ... Not one ... Yet that doesn't keep you men off the register. How many Shakespeares are there in all England today? Not one. Yet the State doesn't tumble to pieces. Railroads and ships are built, homes are kept going, and babies are born. The world goes on ... *by virtue of its common people* ... I am not concerned that you should think we women could paint great pictures or compose immortal music, or write good books. I am content ... that we should be classed with the common people, who keep the world going.'[19] Women were not free and had never been free, Mary Lowndes argued, anticipating Virginia Woolf in *A Room of One's Own*.[20] They would progress towards 'equality' as they were given the opportunity to do so, but more importantly, they might have something different to say. 'Womanliness' would then lie not in its refraction of the feminine body or of female attributes, socially defined, but in its potential for the expression of hitherto oppressed or repressed meanings; or, as Cicely Hamilton put it, 'the men will have only the old ideas to work on, but they will every one of them be new to us.'[21]

Experience of the difficulties and contradictions in their situation made many women artists feminists. They needed citizenship as women (it was degrading to be in a position of inferiority, as the sculptor Edith Downing argued). They were well aware of the outside pressures that shaped their private time in the studio, and of the remaining restrictions on their careers. The 'swift response of the woman artist to the Women's Movement' was not the mystery that it first appeared.[22] Seventy-six painters endorsed the claim for women's suffrage in a list of supporters published by the Central Committee of the National Society for Women's Suffrage in 1897, among them Barbara Bodichon of the Langham Place circle, well-known exhibitors at the Royal Academy (Lady Butler, Mrs Swynnerton, Henrietta Rae, Mrs Stanhope Forbes), several women on the fringes of the Pre-Raphaelite Brotherhood (Lucy Madox Rossetti, Mrs Perugini and Evelyn Pickering, wife of William de Morgan) and three women subsequently active in the twentieth-century suffrage campaign (Louise Jopling Rowe, Bessie Wigan and Emily Ford).[23]

As the campaign progressed so women artists made their contributions as individuals. Marion Wallace Dunlop, illustrator of *Fairies, Elves and Flower Babies* and *The Magic Fruit Garden*, was the first hunger-striker and an accomplice who furnished 'hammers, or black bags filled with flints' to window-breakers later in the campaign.[24] The sisters Marie and Georgina Brackenbury were prominent speakers, and their mother's house in Campden Hill Square became a refuge for women temporarily released from prison under the terms of the 'Cat and Mouse' Act. Olive Hockin's studio was found to contain a small arsenal when it was raided by police in 1913. But from 1907, with the founding of the Artists' Suffrage League (followed by the Suffrage Atelier in 1909), women were able to organise collectively and contribute their

2 Marion Wallace Dunlop (artist, WSPU member and the first hunger-striker) carrying the stamp with which she printed part of the Bill of Rights on the wall inside the House of Commons, 21 June 1909.

professional skills to the suffrage campaign. They designed, printed and embroidered all manner of political material; they taught each other the requisite skills from hand-printing to needlework; they designed major demonstrations and took part in them in their own contingents; they lent their studios for meetings and contributed to exhibitions, bazaars and fund-raising activities; they even turned pavement artists and put out collection boxes after sending their paintings into the Royal Academy.[25] Recognising the role of popular imagery in the maintenance and reproduction of anti-feminism, they threw themselves into that 'agitation by symbol' the *Common Cause* called for, and by its means contested the representation of women, and their association with all those attributes, high or low, serious or comic, moral or depraved, that were used to argue their exclusion from the franchise and from public life.

The Artists' Suffrage League

The Artists' Suffrage League – the first of the suffrage societies of professional women – was founded in January 1907 to help with the NUWSS demonstration the following month.[26] Its object was 'to further the cause of Women's enfranchisement by the work and professional help of artists'; and to this end it produced posters, postcards and illustrative leaflets that were used both in Great Britain and the United States.[27] It participated in the general elections of 1910 and all the by-elections held after 1907; its members designed and executed an enormous number and a very wide range of banners for NUWSS branches and specialised groups; and it organised the decorative schemes for major demonstrations and important public meetings. Looking back on its efforts in the *Suffrage Annual and Women's Who's Who* in 1913, it claimed to have 'done much to popularize the cause of Woman's Suffrage by bringing in an attractive manner before the public eye the long-continued demand for the vote'.[28]

Its beginnings were modest. By the end of 1907, according to the National Union's *Annual Report*, it had contributed two posters which had since been printed, participated in the Wimbledon by-election, coloured a number of designs by hand to save the expense of colour printing, and cooperated in the organisation of a poster and postcard competition. (The first prize was awarded to Dora Meeson Coates for 'Political Help', subsequently published by the NUWSS.)[29]

From this point the Artists' League organised competitions on behalf of the National Union, which was probably only too relieved to hand over the responsibility.[30] There is some suggestion that competitors needed help in formulating their ideas, and designers were encouraged to send in thumbnail sketches in advance. Even trained artists could be ignorant of the particular requirements of a picture poster, and good designs that would make an impact and reproduce efficiently were difficult to come by.

In February 1909 a prize of four pounds (later increased to five pounds), together with several smaller prizes of one pound each, was offered by the Artists' League for 'the best design for a poster, suitable for use at elections'.[31] From among thirty entries, the first prize was awarded jointly to W. F. Winter's 'Votes for Workers' and Duncan Grant's 'Handicapped'.[32] Winter, a Dutchman, remains elusive. Duncan Grant's name, familiar now from his association with the Bloomsbury group and a lifetime as a distinguished British painter, is unexpected in this context. He was twenty-four in 1909 and had been living in Paris, studying at Jacques-Emile Blanche's studio La Palette after a period at the Westminster School of Art, in Italy and at the Slade. His parents lived abroad and he had spent much of his childhood with the Strachey family. He was connected with the suffrage movement through his aunt, Lady Julia Strachey, and her daughters Philippa (Secretary of the London Society for Women's Suffrage) and Pernel. The theme of 'Handicapped' – described in the *Com-*

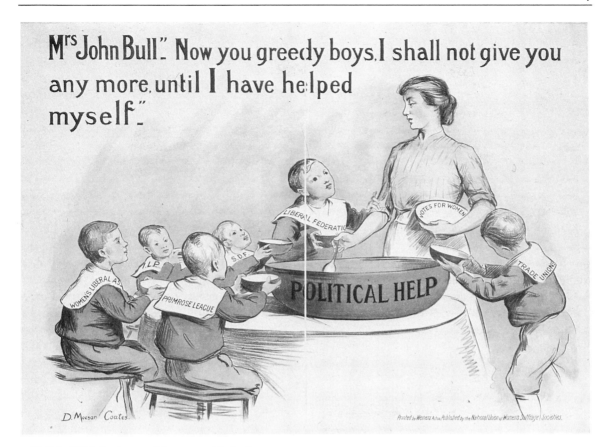

Mrs John Bull: "Now you greedy boys, I shall not give you any more, until I have helped myself."

3 'Political Help': winner of the NUWSS/Artists' Suffrage League poster competition in 1907. Designed by Dora Meeson Coates, published by the NUWSS in 1908.
The six groups clamouring for more 'political help' are the Primrose League, the Women's Liberal Federation, the Independent Labour Party, the Social Democratic Federation, the Women's Liberal Association and the Trade Unions. The Times *Woman's Supplement for 19 November 1910 carried a revealing article on 'How to Help your Party', which concluded that: 'At a modest computation some 50,000 women, voluntary workers all, were engaged in the delicate task of converting and convincing the electorate, either by personal canvass or platform persuasion, at the last General Election.'*

4 Drawing for 'Handicapped': one of a series in Duncan Grant's sketchbook for 1909. See also colour plate 1.

mon Cause as featuring 'a stalwart young woman of the Grace Darling type'[33] – seems to have been proposed by the League's secretary, Barbara Forbes. On the strength of a satisfactory submission in the 1907 competition Grant was encouraged to send in again, and with some diffidence ('good ones are so difficult to find') Barbara Forbes suggested the subject: 'A man in a *sailing* boat, (the sail represents the Vote). A woman with only *oars* – out in the sea *of Labour*.' A caption to underline the moral – 'Britons why handicap the weaker vessel' – was to have run below, but must have seemed redundant and was never used. The preparatory studies in Grant's sketchbook are more vigorous than the final print, which may have been redrawn on the stone by a commercial lithographer, but 'Handicapped' remains one of the most successful and striking of suffrage designs.[34]

Information on the League's output as a whole is both scant and contradictory.[35] Its most substantial contribution in 1907 was to the 'Mud March' in February. Several further posters and postcards were issued in 1908, and in the months leading up to the NUWSS procession on 13 June the League was responsible for the design and execution of seventy to eighty embroidered banners, which were obviously shared out between a large number of women beyond the membership of the League itself. In 1909 they brought out four posters, one meeting's bill, six postcards and two Christmas cards. The Pageant of Women's Trades and Professions for the International Suffrage Alliance in April 1909 was a substantial undertaking, and thirty-four members of the League and their friends decorated the Albert Hall and provided the props for the lamplight procession. With the even greater pressure of two general elections in January and December 1910, the League was at full stretch, sending thousands of postcards, posters and pictorial leaflets around the country. By the end of the year they had published altogether eleven posters, as well as a number of postcards, and with some difficulty the list can be

reconstructed.[36] All the posters were coloured lithographs, designed by known (if minor) artists and professionally printed by firms such as Weiners of Acton, David Allen or Carl Hentschel of Fleet Street. The sizes ranged from 20 by 30 inches to 40 by 30 inches, most were in editions of 1000 copies, and the retail cost (with no profit to the artist) was generally fourpence.[37]

The exact membership of the League remains hazy, as does what might actually have counted as membership in terms of informal affiliation, subscription or the publication of finished designs. Prize-winning drawings submitted to competitions open to women and men were not necessarily the work of members of the League that published them, all of whom were women. No list of members survives, although the published accounts give 'donations and subscriptions' under a separate heading.[38] *The Suffrage Annual and Women's Who's Who* gives only the League's chairman, Mary Lowndes, and the membership of the 1913 committee.[39]

Mary Lowndes's album of designs for posters, postcards and banners, many of them by her, is in the Fawcett Collection. It is clear from this and other evidence (including the minutes and correspondence of the NUWSS and the London Society) that she was the chief instigator of the Artists' Suffrage League, its mainstay and organiser. She is an intriguing if elusive figure. She was born in 1857 (and was therefore fifty when the League was founded in 1907), the daughter of Richard Lowndes, rector of Sturminster Newton in Dorset, which contains her earliest window. In the late 1880s or early 1890s she trained with the arts and crafts designer Henry Holiday, after a brief period of study at the Slade in 1883, and had become a free-lance designer herself by 1896 when the *Art Journal* illustrated her work in a short article on 'Women Workers in the Art Crafts'.[40] Together with Alfred Drury, who left the Southwark firm of Britten and Gilson to join her, she founded Lowndes and Drury in 1897, which became the centre for most of the best British stained-glass artists before 1914. Otherwise, there is little information on these women, most of them artists who exhibited in a range of venues around the turn of the century. Barbara Forbes, the secretary, was Mary Lowndes's companion and associate at Brittany Studios in the King's Road – their own address, but also that printed on the official notepaper of the Artists' Suffrage League.[41] Emily Ford, the vice-chairman, was the artist sister of Isabella Ford, a prosperous Quaker suffragist and member of the Independent Labour Party in Leeds. (Isabella Ford was also on the executive committee of the NUWSS and an active supporter of the Women's Trade Union League.) Sara Anderson, the treasurer, had exhibited since the 1880s. Bertha Newcombe was a painter and illustrator who was a member of the New English Art Club. Mary Wheelhouse was also established as a book illustrator. Dora Meeson Coates had trained in Melbourne, at the Slade and at Julian's in Paris. On Violet Garrard, Bethia Shore and Bessie Wigan there is little information. Other regular contributors included Joan Harvey Drew, a designer and embroiderer trained at Westminster School of Art, and Mary Sargant Florence, a noted mural painter trained at the Slade and at Colarossi's in Paris, who was a member of the New English Art Club and the woman who taught Stanley Spencer how to paint in fresco.[42]

Most of these artists were middle-aged, and all the members of the committee who can be traced turn out to have lived within walking distance of each other in Chelsea. The structure that suggests itself is one of a loose association of women, bound together by shared professional and political interests and ties of friendship, meeting under the aegis and usually at the studio of Mary Lowndes. A number of formal and informal organisations catered to the specific needs and concerns of women artists in the Edwardian period.[43] Questions of identity and community were important to them both pragmatically and psychologically. They

complained of being poorly hung, badly reviewed, excluded from facilities that were crucial to their livelihoods, and they did not like being condescended to. Some insight into this sense of female community, as it straddled the worlds of the studio and of suffrage politics, can be found in Dora Meeson Coates's biography of her husband George.

Dora Meeson was born in New Zealand and had studied in Melbourne, Paris and at the Slade. Some time after she married the painter George Coates in 1903, they rented 9 Trafalgar Studios from Augustus John. (She remarked that John did not remember her from the Slade, 'though he had a compelling stare when he looked at a woman that I much resented'.) Trafalgar Studios in Manresa Road, Chelsea, was 'a nest of busy workers' that included Ambrose McEvoy at number 10, Charles Conder at number 6 and Florence Haig – later a member of the local WSPU – at number 4. Before moving into their own studio the Coateses held a private view of their work in one of the others. Mary Sargant Florence wandered into their exhibition by mistake, looking for the studio where a suffrage meeting was taking place, and through the friendship which they struck up Dora met other women and suffragists in the locality. She made many friends in the movement and remembered particularly Mary Lowndes and Emily Ford, whose cottage and studio at 44 Glebe Place provided the meeting ground for 'artists, suffragists, people who *did* things'. She was introduced to Cicely Hamilton at a meeting in Florence Haig's studio at which Mrs Pankhurst spoke, and lent her own for a gathering addressed by Charlotte Despard of the Women's Freedom League; the artist's studio, spacious, central and convenient, was a useful alternative to the cramped intimacy of the private drawing room and the expense of the public hall.

Dora Meeson Coates became a member of the WFL and designed a number of suffrage posters and a banner for the Commonwealth of Australia. Her husband George joined the Men's League for

Women's Suffrage, walked with her in processions and held the paste-pot, keeping watch while she fly-posted pillar boxes and hoardings at night. In this he was not typical. As his wife recalled, the 'Chelsea men artists – always conservative – were not partisans of the women's suffrage movement ... It was the women-artists, not the men, who welcomed us as new-comers to Chelsea.'[44]

At moments like this we glimpse a different set of relations behind the familiar narratives of the pre-war art world which centre on the activities of men: the controversies stirred by Roger Fry's Post-Impressionist exhibitions of 1910 and 1911; the acrimony surrounding the secession of certain members of the Omega Workshop in 1913; the bohemian rompings of Augustus John. Women were artists, and political activists; they were not only models, mistresses and muses in this scenario. But it would be sentimental to suggest that all was sweetness and sisterhood among them, or that their political commitments did not cause difficulties for their art. 'Oh! my odious Committee!!' Mary Lowndes complained privately to Philippa Strachey. 'They were here till nearly 11 last night – cross, quarrelsome, undecided and prolix – A team of artists is an *awful* team to drive.'[45] And the conflict between paid and unpaid commitments plagued women trying to square a political contribution with a professional career. Referring to them in shorthand as 'suffrage artists' is in this sense misleading, since it unites them under a label they would have recognised for only part of their work at one point in their lives. Suffrage imagery was not their true vocation (it was not something they had set out to do), and it could prove a real drain on their time and energy and interfere with their capacity to earn an independent living. Barbara Forbes once complained that she could not deputise for Mary Lowndes because 'we have a *lot* of work, and as she spends all her time on suffrage I must do what little I can for the despised customer.'[46] Sylvia Pankhurst's suffrage commitments effectively terminated her artistic career.

The Suffrage Atelier

The Suffrage Atelier began with a group of artists meeting from February 1909 'with the special object of training in the arts and crafts of effective picture propaganda for the Suffrage', and of forwarding 'the women's movement by supplying pictorial Advertisements, Banners and Decorations'.[47] In this their general aims were parallel to those of the Artists' Suffrage League (which might have been surprised to learn from the *Vote* that 'little had been done in the way of pictorial propaganda'),[48] but they differed in several important respects.

Most of the Artists' Suffrage League had been trained, and exhibited, as fine artists; they turned to illustration, as many contemporary artists did, to earn a living or to help the cause. The Atelier advertised itself specifically as 'An Arts and Crafts Society Working for the Enfranchisement of Women'.[49] A number of its members had been trained in the crafts, and were familiar with printing processes such as engraving. Unlike the League they held exhibitions of their art and design work as well as their propaganda, advertising their broader skills and offering to sell their services in aid of the suffrage movement.[50]

They saw themselves as aiding the women's movement by a whole variety of means. An early note from Miss E. B. Willis, the Honorary Secretary, lists seventeen ways of forwarding the cause. These included sending in designs for propaganda, or fine art and craft work for exhibition; helping with secretarial work; selling posters and postcards or getting them placed in the press; contributing to pageants and decorative schemes; collecting funds and obtaining more members; forming local branches (there is no evidence that these existed); contributing cuttings, including photographs, illustrations and cartoons for general reference; providing hospitality in studios or drawing rooms for meetings, exhibitions and social occasions; and in two further ways that were at the heart of the Atelier enterprise, by 'supplying the Society with hand-printed publications – made from wood blocks, etchings, stencil plates etc.' and by 'organising Local Meetings for the encouragement of Stencilling, Wood Engraving etc., in order that members may learn or improve themselves in the art of printing by hand'.[51]

In June they held their first public meeting at Caxton Hall with Laurence Housman in the chair, and the *Common Cause* reported their activities. 'Weekly cartoon-meetings are held for illustrations, with practical demonstrations of the methods of drawing required for the various processes of pictorial reproduction, so that members may be properly qualified to turn out work adapted to reproduction as cartoons, posters etc. Hand-printing is also practised, so that the society can produce some of its own publications. By this latter process fresh cartoons could be got out at very short notice and very little expense. This should be particularly valuable at election times, when something topical is often needed at once. The Society would be glad to send trained workers to take the pictorial and decorative work off the hands of organisers and speakers during elections, when their time and energy are otherwise fully occupied.'[52]

Two things are significant here. The first is the emphasis, not just on the general usefulness of visual propaganda and skilled artists to take responsibility for it, but on the importance of cheapness, immediacy, appropriate reproductive skills and access to a hand-printing press (all of which differs from League policy), since the Atelier printed its own designs.[53] This enabled its members to avoid some of the difficulties the League faced in getting images that would reproduce well and in raising the money to have them commercially lithographed in colour. Most Atelier posters and postcards are block prints such as wood or lino-cuts, available in a range of sizes, and in black and white or hand-coloured. In 1912 they published their first broadsheet, which reproduced

twenty-nine available designs in miniature (almost three times as many as the Artists' Suffrage League produced in the same period),[54] and despite their ephemeral nature over forty different posters and about fifty postcards still survive. Compared with the League, they produced a larger number of designs over a longer period: a rougher but livelier and more unorthodox *oeuvre*.

The second significant point of difference between them lay in the Atelier's educational activities. The members of the Artists' Suffrage League were professional artists, and although their competitions were not framed to exclude amateurs, only work that reached their professional standards was acknowledged with prizes or publication. They sometimes had difficulty in acquiring designs that were appropriate, effective, and suitable to reproduce. The Atelier – which also solicited contributions and offered prizes for successful designs – tried to reconcile two aims at the same time: to be of use to suffrage societies in the campaign, but also to afford women artists 'opportunities to experiment and ... to become acquainted with the processes of reproduction'.[55] It functioned as an educational and social centre with a regular programme of activities that mixed instruction, criticism, designing, printing, banner-making and life drawing with exhibitions, guest speakers, and a speakers' class. This was the curriculum in February 1910 when the Atelier resumed its normal programme after the general election in January: 'Tuesdays. – Decorative painting and stencilling. Wednesdays. – Designers' day, 10 am, model posed; 1.30, Criticism of designs; 2.45, Address; 4.30, Committee meeting. Thursdays. – Demonstration of printing processes. Fridays. – Banner-making and embroidery ... The office and workshop ... is open every week-day from 10 am to 4 pm.'[56]

'Membership', and the status of membership, is hard to define here too. The Atelier had a formal constitution and, apparently, weekly committee meetings. Its constitution required that its commit-

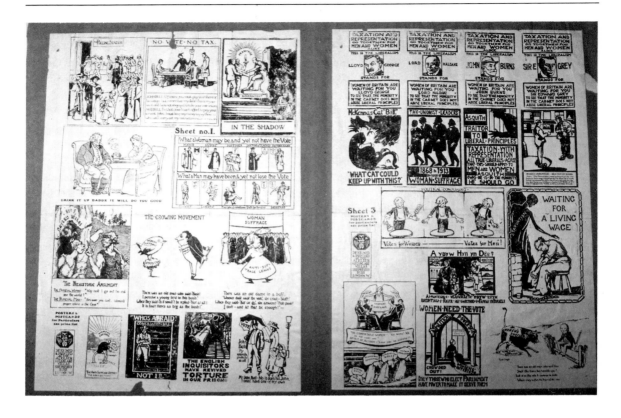

5 The Suffrage Atelier Broadsheet, 1913.
There are three surviving Atelier broadsheets which reproduce available designs in miniature so that prospective customers could make their selection. They help to identify and date Atelier products.

tee of eight members, together with the officials of the society, be elected annually at a general meeting. For that meeting to be quorate, a quarter of the full membership had to be present.[57] The minimum subscription was one shilling and sixpence, which suggests that all subscribers were officially members of the Atelier, although presumably some supporters did not necessarily contribute designs. There seem to have been in practice, if not constitutionally, different kinds of membership. Contributions were drawn from men and women all over the country,[58] but the *Vote* emphasised that the Atelier itself was run entirely by women, 'who make their own designs, cut blocks and do the printing,' dressed in a uniform of 'a bright blue workmanlike coat, a black skirt, and a big black bow like that beloved of the artists who dwell near the Luxembourg'.[59] If its programme is any guide, we should perhaps imagine the Atelier as a central core of women members (their blue coats and floppy bows in honour of Parisian ateliers or Rosa Bonheur) who produced designs and also printed them, together with a floating periphery of subscribers who contributed in one of the seventeen ways recommended by the honorary secretary, coming to take classes, attend discussions or use the life model. Beyond them lay that section of the general public which took an interest in the Atelier's work, bought its products and attended open meetings and social engagements.

The address given over the honorary secretary's name until 1912 – 1, Pembroke Cottages, Edwardes Square – was actually that shared by Laurence and Clemence Housman, with others the co-founders of the Atelier in 1909.[60] Probably its nucleus had been formed the year before, as a by-product of preparations for the WSPU demonstration of 21 June, when members of the Kensington branch came together to make up Laurence Housman's 'From Prison to Citizenship' banner in the studio at the bottom of his garden.[61]

Laurence and Clemence Housman were two of the seven children of a Bromsgrove solicitor, brought up in rural Worcestershire. The poet A. E. Housman was one of their brothers.[62] Their mother died when Laurence was five and Clemence, four years older, promised her that she would look after him. Together they studied at the local art school and then, with the help of a small legacy, established themselves in London in 1883.[63] They enrolled at an art school near their lodgings in Kennington which taught wood engraving, taking classes at the same time at the Miller's Lane School in South Lambeth. Here they met Charles Ricketts and Charles Shannon, and through them Laurence met Oscar Wilde and was encouraged to read Ruskin and contribute drawings to *The Yellow Book*. He established himself as an influential illustrator and brought out a book of poems, *The Green Arras*, in 1896.[64]

From 1885 Clemence had earned her living (and Laurence's too to begin with) as a commercial

engraver for weekly papers like the *Graphic* and the *Illustrated London News*. She was employed by an office in Chancery Lane, but as the introduction of photo-mechanical 'process' engraving displaced the craftsman's skill she found herself redundant and turned to the private presses for work. At the same time as process work met the public appetite for illustrated journalism (saving the publishers money but putting skilled engravers out of business), the private presses of the 1890s set out to preserve or revive the art of fine printing. Clemence Housman cut most of the blocks for her brother's designs, and worked for James Guthrie at the Pear Tree Press and C. R. Asbee at the Essex House Press, as well as for Kegan Paul, Grant Richards and John Lane. Her work was very highly respected and scholars of fine printing consider her the last great exponent of the English tradition of wood engraving that had flourished in the 1860s.[65]

Both she and Laurence worked tirelessly for the suffrage cause in the Edwardian period. Laurence, who claimed he had not been a political animal in the 1890s, found himself converted by a speech of Emmeline Pankhurst's and possessed in consequence of 'that most uncomfortable thing a social conscience'. It interfered with his writing, he said, and he would far rather have done without it. But he credited the women's suffrage movement with bringing him 'into active sympathy with the aims and doings of my own generation' and involving him in the 'political problems and controversies of the present day'.[66] From 1895 he had been art critic of the *Manchester Guardian*, in succession to R. A. M. Stevenson, and during this period he published more than a dozen books and a number of controversial plays; but at the same time he was active in the Men's League for Women's Suffrage, designed banners and demonstrations, wrote pamphlets and mounted platforms in parks and on street corners, and lent his studio for the Suffrage Atelier where 'presently Clemence became chief worker'.[67]

6 Edith Craig.

Clemence was a member of the WSPU and a committed supporter of the Women's Tax Resistance League, in whose cause she spent a week in Holloway prison in October 1911.[68] The Housmans approved of militancy in its early stages, but like others parted company with the Pankhursts over the arson campaign of 1913. Laurence described the 'stab in the back given to the Rokeby Venus' as hurting his artistic feelings. 'After that came the burning of churches; and I felt myself obliged to cease subscribing to WSPU funds.'[69]

Edith Craig, daughter of the architect E. W. Godwin and the actress Ellen Terry, was a principal member of the Atelier too, although in quite what capacity is unclear. (She claimed to have belonged to at least eight different suffrage societies – 'when one considers all the cause means, one cannot belong to too many' – and to have ended up organising for all of them.) Perhaps it was her mother's influence, since she was herself an ardent suffragist, or the result of the school that Edith went to, where the 'interminable addressing of envelopes' for suffrage petitions was a regular duty. Edith Craig was a costume designer who had worked for Henry Irving, and a theatre director by profession. This makes it unlikely that she was responsible for any of the Atelier's graphic material, but she was indispensable for pageants and processions. She was just the sort of person, with exactly the kind of skills, that the suffrage movement needed to turn a political argument into a carefully orchestrated spectacle. She designed a number of banners (which have not survived) and decorative schemes for the processions of 1910. She produced Cicely Hamilton's Pageant of Great Women in 1909, appearing as Rosa Bonheur, and her mother as the actress Nancy Oldfield. And she was the major link, as a prominent member of all three, between the Suffrage Atelier, the Actresses' Franchise League and the Women's Freedom League.[70]

The Suffrage Atelier had been founded as a non-party organisation that would 'work as far as possible for all the Women's Suffrage Societies impartially'.[71] In practice it was affiliated with the Women's Freedom League, for which it designed processional schemes and with which it embarked on the joint venture of a 'pictorial supplement' to the *Vote* in 1912. These coloured inserts (almost always missing from surviving copies) were also issued as posters and postcards.[72] The scheme was intended to prove mutually beneficial. The Atelier had embarked on a special poster campaign at the beginning of 1912 and its regular appearance in the *Vote* was intended to bring it publicity and perhaps new supporters and subscribers. On its part the *Vote*, which had as Charlotte Despard put it 'weathered many a storm',[73] hoped to attract new readers and improve its circulation.

Mrs Despard's editorial introducing the supplement emphasised that it would bring the Atelier's work 'into more intimate relation' with the movement and the public as a whole, while at the same time illustrating 'the advance of the Cause and the fluctuations of the political barometer'.[74] What she also stressed was the Atelier's role in relation to 'the definite campaign on foot to drive women out of the printing trades'. This referred to the development of photographic methods which had displaced skilled engravers like Clemence Housman from commercial publishing. The main question was how to train women in the new mechanical methods and the kinds of drawing appropriate to them, while preserving for the arts and crafts tradition the hand-printing skills that were being replaced. The editorial is fascinating for the glimpse it offers of 'the real work and scope of the Atelier', its 'inner working, the aim and ideals of the artists'. 'The printing and publishing of pictorial matter in black and white, or colours, and the training of pupils who have passed through the Art schools in the work, mechanical and otherwise, of this branch of the artistic profession, is what the Suffrage Atelier has attempted, with a very large measure of success. It is obvious that this opens up a vast field for energy and enterprise, both manual

and imaginative. It is common knowledge that in journalistic, advertising, and poster illustrative work, the artist, on leaving the schools, frequently has so little real knowledge of the style and subject lending itself most effectively to printing work, that the idea for his work has to be chosen and planned for him before he can execute it. Too little attention is paid to a practical side of the training, viz., the consideration of the market value of certain forms of work, so as to provide art pupils not only with an art training, but with a working career which will have a definite commercial value. This is the line on which the Atelier has struck out boldly. Training in subject as well as in craftsmanship is part of its curriculum; and an exceptionally interesting feature of the work is the inventive ability which has been brought out, in designing and constructing plant, which shall in most inexpensive fashion best serve the purpose of the working artist ... The advantage to our organ in obtaining a pictorial supplement is too patent to require comment. The interest which will be evoked in the artist world will also bring a new element into action, greatly to the advantage of the Cause.'[75]

Charlotte Despard's editorial, which we may be confident was written or informed by the Suffrage Atelier, argues that artists are not fitted by their training for the demands of reproductive work. The Atelier appears to have been offering classes in drawing for process work (that is, photomechanical reproduction). Laurence Housman mourned the passing of hand-engraving and Clemence lost her livelihood in it. But process was a method with its own demands and some of the younger and less orthodox artists – pre-eminently Aubrey Beardsley – adapted their drawing styles to its possibilities and did not try to imitate the appearance of hand-engraving. There was no room for sentiment where women's employment was concerned and process methods were clearly triumphant commercially. What this meant was that the Suffrage Atelier was training women in drawing for sophisticated reproductive processes it

7 'Votes for Women (Bogies)': anon., Suffrage Atelier.
Petticoat government, the unwashed babe, and woman unsexed.

could not itself employ, and at the same time, and with some ingenuity, in much simpler hand-printing methods that it could. Process had replaced hand wood engraving as wood engraving had replaced the woodcut, for commercial purposes, by the mid-nineteenth century.[76] The Artists' Suffrage League (and artists designing for the WSPU) were more conventional and up-to-date in sending their designs to commercial lithographers for printing.

The woodcut was in technical terms an archaic method when the Suffrage Atelier adopted it, presumably for ease of production, cheapness, speed and boldness of effect. But this carried certain stylistic consequences. The woodcut poster in the Edwardian period would have been sufficiently unusual to stand out against the technically more refined products that had largely superseded it. Its archaic technique and the associations it aroused could be exploited for impact and urgency, and for the sense of the popular they now invoked. Atelier posters are with hindsight curiously attractive in their ability to face both ways: back to the woodcut poster of the turn of the eighteenth century, an era before the commercial application of wood engraving or lithography, and forward to the political poster of the twentieth century (lino-cut or silk-screen), which suffers the same constraints on its production but holds the same desire for the accumulated associations of hand-prints as popular, expressive and self-consciously unrefined.

Alfred Pearse, Sylvia Pankhurst and the WSPU

Unlike the National Union, which could call on the Artists' Suffrage League, or the Women's Freedom League which developed a special relationship with the Suffrage Atelier, the WSPU was not served by any organised group of artists. It seems to have relied instead on a small number of individuals: most notably Sylvia Pankhurst, but also Marion Wallace Dunlop and Edith Downing who provided schemes for processions, and Alfred Pearse, who as 'A Patriot' provided illustrations to *Votes for Women* and designs for posters and post-cards over many years.

Alfred Pearse (1856–1933) had studied wood engraving in the early 1870s and was a prolific illustrator for family journals (*Punch*, *Cassell's Magazine*, the *Strand Magazine*, the *Illustrated London News*), with a particular penchant for boys' adventure stories such as those by G. A. Henty. He worked as a special artist for *Pictorial World* (1879–86) and for the *Sphere* on the royal colonial tour of 1901–03, and for forty-five years contributed illustrations to the *Boy's Own Paper* (1878–1923). He seems to have given his services free to the WSPU, presumably as an act of political sympathy, and they were indeed fortunate in finding an engraver who would reproduce his designs without charge.[77] Pearse was a highly competent illustrator, and his cartoons for *Votes for Women* – pithy and apt – helped give the paper its attractive and professional tone. (It compared favourably with its rivals in this respect, and put to shame the uninviting print of the *Anti-Suffrage Review*.)

Most of the WSPU posters that survive are signed by Pearse or in his style, with the exception of those advertising *Votes for Women* or the *Suffragette*, which are the work of Hilda Dallas and M. Bartels. The single best known suffrage image, the WSPU's 'Cat and Mouse' poster, remains anonymous, but Pearse is the closest candidate for it. (The style of draughtsmanship is fairly conventional, but this in its own way serves to heighten an image of dream-like intensity.)[78]

The notoriety of the WSPU campaign and the fame of particular images like the 'Cat and Mouse' poster have obscured the fact that the WSPU published very few designs. This was not because militancy displaced other kinds of propaganda in its campaign – at least not until its final years – but because the WSPU seems to have concentrated on photographic postcards and on spectacle. Its motto required it, after all, to place a priority on 'Deeds Not Words', and as the militant campaign intensified so did its rhetoric of crusade and martyrdom. The WSPU relied a great deal on the charismatic personalities of its leaders, particularly Christabel, and these factors helped to determine its concentration on public spectacle, the production of large numbers of photographic postcards which recorded the major processions, and portrait photographs which took their place in a kind of martyrology of the campaign. (Other societies produced these too, but not in the same numbers or with the same kind of emphasis.)

Sylvia Pankhurst was the trained artist most prominent in the suffrage movement, by reason of her political sympathies and family connections. But she was not consistently active in it *as* an artist and it is thus an exaggeration to describe her as 'virtually the official artist'[79] of the campaign, despite some influential designs and two ambitious decorative schemes. The richly blended politico-aesthetic ambience of her childhood was not untypical of radical middle-class homes in the 1880s and 1890s. Her parents owned wallpapers by William Morris and books from his Kelmscott Press, together with reproductions of Walter Crane's Cartoons for the Cause.[80] Under their influence she conceived 'the longing to be a painter and draughtsman in the service of the great movements for social betterment': 'I would decorate halls where people would foregather in the movement to win the new world, and make banners for the meetings and processions. I had been with my parents to meetings of the Social Democratic Federation in dingy rooms in back streets, and to drab and dreary demonstrations in Hyde Park; I wanted to make these beautiful.'[81]

She studied first at Manchester Art School, where in 1902 she won a National Silver Medal for mosaic designs, a Primrose Medal and the Proctor Travelling Studentship (which took her to Florence and Venice to study frescoes and mosaics). In 1904 she won a scholarship to the Royal College of

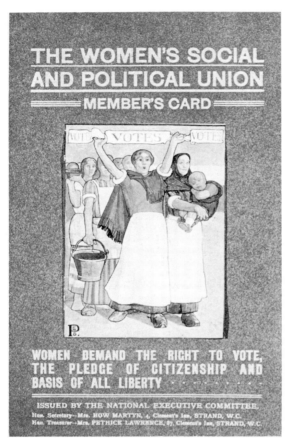

8 Sylvia Pankhurst, WSPU membership card, *c.* 1905.
*Sylvia Pankhurst's design, so different from the allegorical
style of her murals for the Prince's Skating Rink Exhibition
in 1909, reflects the origins of the WSPU in the Manchester
labour movement in 1903, and her work for Keir Hardie's
proposed poster campaign for the unemployed in 1905. By
1905–06 it was already in conflict with Christabel's desire
to sever the WSPU's ties with the ILP and recruit more
middle-class women into the movement.*

Art, heading the list of competitors for the whole
country. ('I was surprised, but not elated; the
standard is not very high, I concluded.')[82] External
scholarships were conducted anonymously. At the
Royal College she encountered a level of discrimination against the women students that
disturbed her, and fighting it only increased the
hostility she faced. In 1906 her award ended and
she took two rooms in Cheyne Walk.[83] For some
time she had been combining her studies with paid
work and political activity; now she became the
focal point for WSPU activity as it shifted from
Manchester to London.

At the end of 1906 or early in 1907 she designed
the WSPU membership card – the exclusively
working-class women it portrays were at just this
point ceasing to find a place in the militant campaign – and published a series of prison sketches
from Holloway in the *Pall Mall Magazine* in the first
half of 1907. Her 'trumpeting angel' design was
widely adopted on printed ephemera, for banners,
on the bound volumes of *Votes for Women* and even
on a tea service. Her allegorical scheme decorating
the interior of the Prince's Skating Rink Exhibition
in 1909 (reused in the Portman Rooms in 1911)
was much admired. But despite her skills and her
political sympathies she was subject to several
different conflicts that together prevented her from
making a more substantial contribution to the
pictorial propaganda of the campaign. She was
increasingly divided from her mother and Christabel over questions of allegiance and strategy. She
deplored what she saw as their neglect of the needs
of working-class women, and the severing of ties
with the socialist movement. In her working life,
she was torn between her political commitments
and those of the artist she wanted to be. And as an
artist, her work is itself divided between two kinds
of pictorial vocabulary: the embryonic socialist
realism of her paintings of working-class women,
and that dilute Pre-Raphaelite allegory, derived
from Walter Crane, which is her chief contribution
to suffrage iconography.

In the summer of 1907, the year the Artists' Suffrage League was founded, Sylvia Pankhurst was painting the women chainmakers in Cradley Heath and studying the conditions in which they worked. She was active in various by-elections on the WSPU's behalf, and then left for the border counties to paint 'the neat, quiet women farm labourers of the locality, and the casual potato-pickers imported by the day from the slums of Berwick-on-Tweed'.[84] Art and politics pulled stubbornly apart for her: the project of working as an artist in the cause of the suffrage and of social-ism was hard to realise. She had no inclination for commercial work, and little desire to sell to private patrons, but there was no market for the large-scale decorative schemes she had hoped to pro-duce. She was deprecatory of the National Union's 'Mud March' in February – 'Its authors were so proud of it that they forgot such efforts were already habitual in the WSPU'[85] – but it was in fact the constitutionalists and the Artists' Suffrage League which led the way in suffrage propaganda, in part because they did not enjoy the equivocal publicity gained by the WSPU's militancy.

For Sylvia Pankhurst public struggles and pri-vate aims proved less and less reconcilable. 'As a speaker, a pamphlet-seller, a chalker of pavements, a canvasser on doorsteps, you are wanted: as an artist the world has no real use for you.'[86] The idea of giving up the artist's life for the platform and the street corner was 'a prospect too tragically barren to endure',[87] but at the same time she doubted 'whether it was worthwhile to fight one's individual struggle . . . to make one's way as an artist, to bring out of oneself the best possible, and to induce the world to accept one's creations, and give one in return one's daily bread, when all the time the great struggles to better the world for humanity demand other service'.[88] Within a couple of years she had made her decision and given up her painting. 'Mothers came to me with their wasted little ones. I saw starvation look at me from patient eyes. I knew then that I should never return to my art.'[89]

9 Sylvia Pankhurst working on the murals for the Prince's Skating Rink Exhibition, 1909.

Pictorial Resources

The suffrage artists drew on a repertoire of pictorial components which were not only technical, but stylistic and thematic. Different styles coexisted among different groups in the campaign, and some of the same resources were drawn on by their opponents and by other artists including those working for the labour movement. As combinations of thematic, formal and technical elements, styles embody values that relate to the interests of particular ideologies and social groups, but they are essentially mobile and open to a degree of co-option and adaptation by others. A group does not generate spontaneously the style or 'visual ideology' appropriate to its needs.[90] (And women, whose images were everywhere disseminated in this period, were peculiarly placed in deciding what their needs were and how they might best be pictured.)

To trace the processes by which elements are gathered or discarded, emptied or refilled, coaxed and manipulated to new ends, we need to refer to suffrage artists as social subjects with particular skills and resources at their disposal. They were not a homogenous group with a unified ideology – any more than were suffragists at large – but some generalisations can be made about their position. They were almost all women. They were middle class. They were trained in the liberalising art-educational institutions of the later nineteenth century. Their class politics, when specifically articulated, appear to have leaned towards the radical end of liberalism and socialism (there were links with the Fabians, and the socialist side of the arts and crafts movement). Many of them had independent careers at a time when this was still unusual for women. They were all by definition feminists and actively committed to the furtherance of women's suffrage 'by the work and professional help of artists' in the production of 'effective picture propaganda' for the cause.[91]

Many of the artists were trained illustrators or engravers, some specialising in children's books. (The self-consciously coy style of C. Hedley Charlton, adapted to the suffrage context, was calculated to render innocent, humorous and domestic a campaign characterised by its opponents as dangerously subversive and grim.) Both suffragists and their opponents drew on the iconography of woman in a late and dilute Pre-Raphaelitism, and in the contemporary advertising and magazine illustration that surrounded them, much of it influenced by art nouveau. These styles were aesthetically and ideologically congruent with the image of womanliness they wished to convey – the suffragists to assume its mantle, the anti-suffragists to argue that 'real' women had no need of the vote. On the other hand, some of the Atelier artists were influenced by a more avant-garde style of illustration, derived from the 'chapbook' or broadsheet style popularised by the Beggarstaff Brothers (William Nicholson and James Pryde) and Edward Gordon Craig. Craig (who was Edith Craig's brother) had learned the rudiments of wood engraving from Nicholson and Pryde, whose bold outlines and massed shadows were influenced by old ballad-sheets and *fin-de-siècle* posters by artists such as Toulouse-Lautrec. Heavier cutting of the wood and a certain calculated primitivism were common to a number of artists and printers in the 1890s, especially those influenced by the arts and crafts movement, and including women like the Atelier's Pamela Coleman Smith.[92] Her illustrations to Craig's *The Page* in 1901 anticipate art-deco designs of the 1920s and 1930s. Not all, but some, of the most interesting Atelier posters were produced in this style, which was partly derived from, and certainly appropriate to, the rather primitive methods of hand-printing they employed. The broadsheet manner, reminiscent at the same time of something archaic and something very avant-garde in its striking contours and vigorous cutting, was particularly apt to the visual impact that suffrage imagery needed to make. Atelier posters are technically primitive but 'modern' in

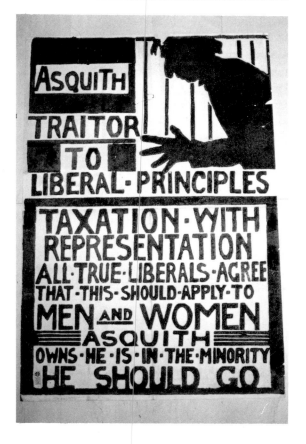

10 'Franchise Villa': anon., Suffrage Atelier.

11 'Asquith, Traitor to Liberal Principles': designed by Jessica Walters of the Suffrage Atelier, *c.* 1913. *Suffragists regularly appealed to the liberal tenet of 'No Taxation without Representation' as the American colonists had done before them. The Women's Tax Resistance League was founded in October 1909, suspended on the outbreak of war, and wound up in 1917. Active members (including Clemence Housman, who spent a week in Holloway for non-payment of taxes in 1911) had their goods seized and auctioned by the authorities. The aims, objects and methods of the League are set out in* The Tax Resistance Movement in Great Britain *by Margaret Kineton Parkes (c. 1919).*

12 Walter Crane, 'A Garland for May Day 1895'.

their forcefulness and economy. In this they carry us away from the influence of artists like Walter Crane, and forward to hand-printed political posters from twentieth-century Russia, Mexico, Cuba, China and France. League posters, on the other hand, which are chromolithographed, derive mainly from contemporary fine art and illustrational styles which match the gentle symbolism of a helpmeet for John Bull. The Atelier's 'Inquisitors' makes no stylistic compromises; its 'look', theme and inscription alike are welded into its confrontational and deeply uncomfortable politics.

The influence of Walter Crane (1845–1915), which was considerable, was strongest in the WSPU through the work of Sylvia Pankhurst. Crane was a leading figure in the arts and crafts movement, a follower of William Morris, and the amalgamation in his own work of elements from Pre-Raphaelitism, medieval illumination and Japanese prints made him a significant part of the aesthetic ambience in which Sylvia Pankhurst and Edith Craig grew up.[93] He was an influential figure in art education in the 1890s and 1900s (as were several other members of the arts and crafts movement), and the impact of his style is evident in a great deal of art-school work of the period.[94] He was also a socialist, a member of the Social Democratic Federation, the Hammersmith Socialist League, and for a period of the Fabian Society, and almost single-handed he shaped the imagery of the British labour movement for more than thirty years. His illustrations permeated the labour press, and banner-makers seem to have used *Cartoons for the Cause* (1894) as a pattern book. His 1885 'Angel of Freedom' was widely copied, and he was chiefly responsible for revitalising the ideal woman of Pre-Raphaelite imagery and adapting her to the iconography of socialism. Tutill's, the major source of trade-union banners, were quick to systematise Crane's motifs and reproduce them in an imagery adequate to the aspirations of the organised working class – an imagery, however, forged out of elements that were from some perspectives

not altogether appropriate for the task.

Crane's socialist cartoons, particularly his 'Triumph of Labour', had inspired Sylvia Pankhurst as a child with the longing to be a 'draughtsman in the service of the great movements for social betterment'.[95] Her first large decorative scheme was produced for the lecture hall in a building erected by the Independent Labour Party in memory of her father. Its Pre-Raphaelite and Crane-like symbolism, further elaborated, reappeared in her decorations for the WSPU exhibition at the Prince's Skating Rink in 1909 (reused for the Suffrage Bazaar in the Portman Rooms in 1911). These were scaled up on to canvas 20 feet high from quarter-sized cartoons, and painted and stencilled in the suffragette colours of purple, white and green. The central figure was a 13-foot-high female sower with blossoming almond trees on either side, accompanied by a text from the Psalms: 'They that sow in tears shall reap in joy. He that goeth forth and weepeth, bearing precious seed, shall doubtless come again with rejoicing, bringing his sheaves with him.' Crane had opened the ILP hall, and this is a version of Crane's socialist imagery of springtime and harvest, of women in flowing draperies and Ceres as the goddess of socialism. Surrounding the central figure, and emphasising by their other connotations the switch from the masculine gender of the Psalms, were further emblems of sacrifice, triumph and harvest: a pelican piercing its breast to feed its young; a dove with the olive branch of peace; and a suffrage symbol synthesised from two motifs in popular currency, a gilded prison arrow enclosed in the laurel wreath of victory (a straight appropriation of the sign of the reprobate to represent virtue).[96]

Variations on Sylvia Pankhurst's female sower and trumpeting angel appeared everywhere in the militant movement: on suffrage literature, calendars and greetings cards, on banners and teacups, on the embossed covers of bound volumes of *Votes for Women* and the illuminated addresses accorded to WSPU prisoners from 1908. Her decorative

13 Sylvia Pankhurst's designs for the walls of the WSPU
exhibition at the Prince's Skating Rink in 1909.

schemes, often carried out in a hurry with assistants or by groups of people working together, had
to draw on an available symbolism since they would
have been useless if obscure. Their agricultural
and Old Testament imagery endorsed the moral
authority of the suffrage claim in the face of anti-
suffrage arguments that feminism was against the
laws of religion and nature. Curiously, her paintings of rural and urban working women are not
reflected in her work for the suffrage movement,
except in the WSPU membership card (*c.* 1905–06)
and an early banner that has not survived.[97] This
may be because the WSPU was already severing its
links with the labour movement by 1906, and
preferred an imagery which was more neutral in
party political terms. The trumpeting angel can be
seen as a pictorial equivalent to the heightened
religiose rhetoric of Emmeline Pethick-Lawrence,
Emmeline and Christabel Pankhurst, and the
militant campaign.

The principal themes in official and unofficial
anti-suffrage imagery have to do with browbeaten
husbands and neglected homes; suffragists as
spinsters, viragos or men; suffragists and Parliament; men, children or animals dressed up as
militants; suffragettes and policemen; suffragettes
and sex. The principal themes in suffrage imagery
are more complex and extensive, largely because
they deal with questions of detail, where anti-
suffrage imagery offers blanket condemnation or
paints the disastrous outcome of women's enfranchisement in sweeping strokes.

They relate to particular figures and incidents in
the campaign: petitions and demonstrations, tax
and census resistance, arrests, forcible feeding,
and the 'Cat and Mouse' Act. They also refer to
developments in Parliament including the Conciliation Bill, the Insurance Bill, and the tussle
between the Lords and the Commons with which
the fortunes of women's suffrage were bound up.
In 1912 the artist Louisa Jopling Rowe gave a
speech 'on the value of pictorial art in political
propaganda' in which she stressed 'the great value

of caricature in political work' and urged her colleagues to 'hold up to ridicule the Members of
Parliament who think that women, having no sense
of humour, cannot register votes'.[98] Asquith, an
obvious and prominent target as prime minister, as
a leading opponent and because of his physical
characteristics, was eminently caricaturable. H. G.
Wells chided the suffragists for turning him into
'the State Husband, the Official Wretch of the
Woman Movement, the Depository of Feminine
Repartee, the Public Hen Peckee',[99] but he did
rather offer himself for the purpose, and caricature
does not lend itself to structural conflicts unless
they can be depicted through the physiognomies of
the chief participants. The problem for suffragists
was one of ethics. Antis had no qualms about
slandering their opponents, and Sir Almroth
Wright, a leading medical anti-feminist, characterised the women's male supporters as 'intel-

Inmate of Lunatic Asylum to Visitor
"What! you a Militant Suffragette!
Pooh! you've no business here you're
not mad. You're only a fool!"

14 'Is your Wife a Suffragette?', Burlesque Series, postmarked 1908.

15 Lunatic Asylum visitor: designed by Lawson Wood.

16 'A Bird in the Hand': poster and postcard designed by Pamela Coleman Smith for the Suffrage Atelier. *The Conciliation Bill is the 'Bird in the Hand'. Asquith and Lloyd George offer instead something 'in the dim and speculative future' (the possibility of an amendment to the Reform Bill).*

17 'In the Dim and Speculative Future': designed by Gladys Letcher of the Suffrage Atelier, 1909. *Sylvia Pankhurst (1931, p. 282) records that on 26 May 1908 Asquith, having promised electoral reform with the possibility of a women's suffrage amendment before the end of the parliamentary session, was asked by a Liberal anti-suffragist what would happen should such an amendment be carried. He replied: 'My honourable friend has asked me a contingent question with regard to a remote and speculative future.'*

C.E. Marshall.

"THE COMMON CAUSE." FEBRUARY 3, 1910.

The Common Cause.
The Organ of the Women's Movement for Reform.

VOL. I. No. 48.   Registered as a Newspaper.   FEBRUARY 3, 1910.   ONE PENNY.

"D——n! Get out of my way!"

"Woman's place is the home."

"Go home and learn your manners."

"Tut! Tut!"

"I'm afraid it's a subject that doesn't interest me."

"Not likely!"

"What would my old woman say?"

"Women haven't sufficient strength of character."

E. BLINCOE
"I'd rather give you six months' hard."

**Some types of Electors who did NOT sign the Petition, drawn from
the description of a woman in charge of a Polling Station.**

lectuals', cranks and sentimental idealists.[100] Feminists were regularly caricatured as over- or under-sexed, ugly, hysterical, masculine or incompetent. But the editor of the *Common Cause* had to defend Louisa Thomson Price's cartoons of antis to a correspondent who described herself as 'shocked and distressed' at such a descent 'to the level of the worst of the Yellow Press'.[101]

The related theme of woman 'with her political peers' was apparently less controversial, since it is a staple of suffrage imagery to play up the stigma of being categorised with lunatics, criminals, paupers and aliens. The antis refuted this argument, claiming that suffragists placed themselves in a category of their own making,[102] but it was an effective one in pictorial form, where a certain nobility of feature in the woman graduate could be contrasted to telling effect with the lascivious or stupid or degenerate expressions of the men. The enfranchisement of large groups of urban working-class men in 1867 and of agricultural labourers in 1884 produced the temptation, not always resisted, to exploit the very moral superiority of women on which the antis insisted by contrasting it with the inferior status and moral capacity ascribed in conservative arguments to working-class men. Women were keenly attuned to the implications of an exclusion that denied them a right and a responsibility enjoyed even by working-class alcoholics and illiterate farm labourers. Judging by the Artists' Suffrage League competition of 1907 this was at a grass roots level a popular theme ('It may be mentioned that this subject was a favourite one with competitors'), if not an entirely legitimate one ('from the point of view of propaganda, it was considered that the representation of a working man given to drink as a typical voter as contrasted with worthier types of women was not a perfectly fair comparison').[103] The politically tactless argument of the 'franchise drunk' was seen by the more principled as an undignified descent to the level of the opposition, and Mary Lowndes's letter soliciting contributions in the *Common Cause*

19 '*This* is Allowed to Vote': postcard designed by Edwyn Llewellyn, 1907.
A postcard produced apparently independently of any of the women's suffrage organisations, this is the nearest surviving British equivalent to the directly racist appeal of certain American imagery, which contrasts the political status of the educated, middle-class white woman with that of immigrants, Indians, and the newly enfranchised American Negro (Paula Harper, 1975, reproduces a good example).

opposite page
18 The *Common Cause*, 3 February 1910 (anti-suffrage 'types' by the suffragists).
Louisa Thomson-Price produced a series of twelve 'Types of Anti-Suffragists' (male and female) for the Vote, *between 25 November 1909 and 5 March 1910. They were separately issued as postcards.*

in 1910 ends with the terse postscript: 'We do not depict drunken men.'[104]

For different reasons it was dangerous to show woman as man's victim, as the voteless, helpless female of the WSPU representations centred around forcible feeding and the Cat and Mouse Act.[105] Such imagery was very powerful – many people were incensed at the way women were treated in prison and by the police – but it was double-edged. There was a sado-masochistic element in WSPU posters which was intended to heighten a sense of outrage at women's suffering, but which might equally invite a covert pleasure in its spectacle. Anti-suffragists were inclined to believe that the militants had so far degraded themselves that they could scarcely claim to be victims innocent of any part in the circumstances in which they found themselves. Constitutionalists and even militants from the Women's Freedom League were uneasy about what Teresa Billington-Greig called the 'double shuffle' between violent activity and injured innocence. The emphasis on women as helpless victims was all too familiar, and it risked occluding their active and rational role in the conduct of the campaign. The WSPU wanted martyrs, and to prove that men's 'chivalry' to women was conditional on a certain class relation and a prescribed form of feminine behaviour. There seems little doubt that some women were brutally treated in prison, but it is also the case that an imagery which emphasised abuse and assault sorted well with an increasing emphasis in WSPU rhetoric on men's sexual exploitation of women as prostitutes or wives.

Many of the suffrage arguments based on 'expediency' found pictorial form in widespread representations of the sweated labour, the legal discrimination or the 'white slave traffic' in which men had vested interests, but which the women's vote would cure. Others simply emphasised the responsibilities and burdens of the state which women would gladly share. Most suffragists took the 'separate spheres' argument sufficiently

seriously to exploit the notion of complementarity to their own ends, and to suggest that the boundary between them had become displaced in the exigencies of modern life. In return for an umbrella, a horse, a seat (a vote) of her own, Mrs John Bull would help her husband out; and since his burdens are presented via the domestic metaphors of shopping and housework her offer can be understood as involving merely an extension of wifely duties and not an act of trespass into the public sphere.

The verbal arguments were closely bound up with the iconographic and narrative themes that were used to develop them in pictorial form. The imagery of the crusading angel and the dawn of a new day, derived from earlier religious and political vocabularies, was common to socialism and the suffrage campaign (partly through the shared influence of Walter Crane). What Stephen Yeo terms the 'language and style of religiosity' surrounded the altruism of both in the late Victorian and Edwardian period, presumably because it was the most obvious resource to the prophets and activists of social regeneration. It was often mingled with organic metaphors of springtime and harvest which were themselves already loaded with religious significance: where neither socialism nor feminism could be precise on the detailed programme or outcome of revolutionary change, religious metaphors could at least disclose its potential. As Eleanor Marx Aveling argued in urging the Council of the Socialist League to adopt a Christmas tree in 1885: 'Is not socialism the real "new birth", and with its light will not the old darkness of the earth disappear?'[106]

Allegorical figures were also popular, particularly of Justice or other feminine virtues; so were diverse representations of different kinds of working women, and sometimes the two were combined as in 'Justice demands the Vote', where she does so on behalf of the lady and the worker at her feet. Justice is in a sense John Bull's counterpart (although Jane Bull is sometimes used). If he stands for the selfish, or more frequently for the

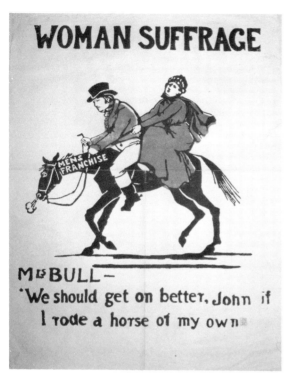

WOMAN SUFFRAGE

Mr BULL –
'We should get on better, John if
I rode a horse of my own'

20 'John Bull's Horse': postcard, anon., Suffrage
Atelier.
*One of a large category of suffrage images in which the
woman pleads with John Bull for a horse, an umbrella, a seat
– a vote – of her own.*

burdened male, she – disabled, locked up or shut
out – stands for the fettered partner who cannot
help.[107] Her use in this context involves a re-
identification of the abstract and allegorical with
the concrete (the commonality of voteless women).
It reclaims her from being a symbol of the Law, and
makes her a symbol of women subject to the
operations of the law. It is a tricky procedure, but
no less paradoxical than that which conventionally
assigns to women a central signifying, but a
subordinate social, role.

Suffrage artists had recourse in addition to such
familiar themes and narratives as those from
proverbs, fables, myths and children's stories: the
Goose and the Gander (Aesop was popular), the
pot calling the kettle black, Alice in Wonderland,
Edward Lear's nonsense rhymes, Canute failing to
turn back the tide.[108] These did not have to have a
female protagonist, they only had to be applicable
to moments in the suffrage campaign. 'What's
sauce for the goose' gained a new resonance during
Asquith's struggle with the House of Lords. (If it
was undemocratic for the Lords to veto the budget,
what about the suffrage majority of 110 for the
Conciliation Bill for which parliamentary facilities
had been denied?) Reference to Lewis Carroll or
Edward Lear was a means of invoking the looking-
glass nature of a topsy-turvy world: a world in
which the logic of things was obscured and where
what seemed natural was, in fact, nonsensical.
Canute was the easiest point of reference for the
inevitability of the campaign.[109] This kind of association, which could be summoned up in a frag-
ment of phrase or image, was a kind of shorthand
language that crossed the boundaries of both. The
Suffrage Atelier could put Canute on a postcard,
and Lord Lytton could argue in favour of the
Conciliation Bill that the 'tide behind this movement has for many years been rising with increasing force'.[110] When Frederick Pethick-Lawrence
christened the Prisoners' Temporary Discharge
for Ill Health Act the Cat and Mouse Act, everyone
understood the image invoked and the terms in

opposite page

21 'Justice Demands the Vote': anon., published by the Brighton and Hove Society for Women's Suffrage and available from the Artists' Suffrage League in 1909.

22 'Votes for Women' ('The People, not the Commons . . .'): poster and postcard designed by A. Patriot (Alfred Pearse) on behalf of the WSPU who used it in the General Election of December 1910. It was based on a well-known advertisement for Ripolin paint, as *Votes for Women* acknowledged when it was reproduced on 2 December 1910.

The general elections of 1910 were chiefly fought on the right of the House of Lords to veto Lloyd George's Budget of 1909. Asquith writes on the back of the peer that the Lords must bow to the will of the people, as expressed through their elected representatives in the Commons. Suffragists took the opportunity to point out that Asquith had, in their view, effectively vetoed the Conciliation Bill, despite a majority of 110, and that women had no elected representatives in the House of Commons. It was WSPU election policy always to vote against the Liberal candidate.

23 'Mrs Partington' ('Coming in with the Tide'): designed by Emily J. Harding Andrews, published by the Artists' Suffrage League.

Mrs Partington was a Canute-like figure – said to have tried to sweep back the ocean after a storm – whose story had already been used in debates on the 1832 Reform Bill to suggest the futility of trying to stem the tide of social progress.

which it cast its characters (law-enforcement agents including judges, the Home Secretary, police and prison officers on the one hand, suffragettes on the other). The force of such a metaphor was extended and developed in the imagery to which it gave rise.

All kinds of rhetorical devices were employed in this process: metaphor and simile, syntagmatic and paradigmatic substitution, in plainer terms the fragmentation, extension and manipulation which are the means by which ideas are pictured and produced. This infuriated the anti-suffragists. Almroth Wright specifically condemned the 'undefined general principles, apothegms set out in the form of axioms, formulae which are vehicles for fallacies, ambiguous abstract terms, and "question-begging" epithets' which he claimed suffragists used. 'Your ordinary unsophisticated man and woman,' he argued, 'stand almost helpless against arguments of this kind.'[111] But if this is not necessarily how political debate must be conducted, it is certainly how political imagery operates as the long history of English caricature demonstrates, and it is certainly how points are scored in the heat of the hustings. Almroth Wright's fastidious distaste for the non sequitur is not borne out in his own prose, which with its anti-libertarian and misogynist flavour has a much nastier tang to it. In the age of popular politics and mass communication it is the telling image, epigram or formula that wins.

Finance

All the main suffrage organisations enjoyed substantial growth, both in membership and revenue, in the years after 1907. This expansion was partly stimulated by a range of propaganda activities which gave their cause a new public visibility in the Edwardian period; but propaganda on this scale was expensive. What did all this cost, and how was it paid for?

The WSPU exhibition in 1909 raised almost £6000 and in addition to its propaganda effect helped, as Emmeline Pethick-Lawrence put it, 'to furnish one other thing that is necessary in political warfare, the money'.[112] The WSPU had expanded rapidly and was by any standards a wealthy organisation. Its annual income of £2705 for the year ending February 1907 had risen to £7081 by February 1908; the Pethick-Lawrences had founded *Votes for Women*; the premises had been doubled in size; and the staff had trebled. A year later receipts and expenditure stood at £20,232 and *Votes for Women* had become a weekly with circulation figures rising towards 20,000. The WSPU now employed seventy-five people, spent £2800 on salaries, and occupied nineteen rooms in its London offices with premises in eleven provincial centres. By 1914 its income had risen to £36,535.[113] Well might Christabel claim that 'our treasurer excites the envy of the entire political world'; and others refer to her as 'the most persuasive beggar in London'.[114]

The other societies were less affluent, but they were scarcely poor. The income of the Women's Freedom League for the year ending 31 December 1909 was £6103 compared with the WSPU's £31,686 for approximately the same period.[115] The NUWSS raised over £20,000 in 1910. What proportion of this was spent on propaganda is impossible to say, at least in any detail. Little survives by way of published accounts from the artists' groups, and the itemisation of accounts by the main suffrage societies is too broad and too variable to provide a clear picture of what was probably a rather confused and muddy kind of subsidy.

The principal costs were those of raw materials, the labour involved in designing and producing posters, banners and postcards where this was not volunteered, and the cost of distribution. Appeals were often made for donations towards the cost of banners, which were expensive items required *en masse* to make an impression at a demonstration.[116] The WSPU Report for the year ending 28 February

1909 gives a long list of women who donated or collected for banners for the Hyde Park demonstration of 21 June 1908. But the suspicion in all cases is that artists were not generally paid. Sylvia Pankhurst, who worked sometimes for 'modest sums' and sometimes for nothing, received 30 shillings a week for very long hours on the Skating Rink decorations, and her (male) assistants got tenpence an hour. Dependent on her work as her only source of income, she notes with a trace of bitterness in her autobiographical account that WSPU organisers were paid the same amount for their subsistence alone in 1914.[117] (On the other hand, in another context she herself gives the average wage of the highest-paid women textile operatives as fifteen shillings and ninepence a week in the same period.) She wrote later that she was always 'torn between the economic necessities of the immediate moment ... and the urging of conscience to assist the movement'.[118] In 1910 the WSPU had 110 salaried officials, but the bulk of its propaganda was carried out by volunteers.

The Artists' Suffrage League accounts survive for the years 1909 and 1910 and show their turnover to have been modest, as one might expect, compared with the suffrage organisations for which they worked: approximately £145 for 1909 and £205 for 1910. Their income was made up from subscriptions and donations, and from 'League Industries' (which presumably involved the sale of posters, postcards, badges and related material). Their outgoings included a salary for the secretary of £24 10s. rising to £25 in 1910; competitions; postage, stationery and advertisements; badges and sundries; and printing costs, by far the largest item, rising from £63 10s. 6d. in 1909 to more than £110 in 1910, the year of two general elections.[119]

It may have been the case that the NUWSS, the WSPU and the WFL were more appreciative of the cost and labour involved in producing banners for their processions and decorations for their public meetings, because these things touched them more

immediately, than they were of the resources necessary to the reproduction of posters and postcards. Certainly they helped to raise money through their periodicals for the subsidy of banners and processional schemes, while there are no instances of an appeal for contributions toward printing costs. Even during 1910, when the general elections impelled propaganda activity to a new pitch of intensity, posters may have seemed less urgent a medium, and because they could be mass-produced they seemed (probably wrongly) to be self-financing. The Artists' Suffrage League, which sold its posters at a price calculated on printing costs with no fee to the artists, had difficulty raising the money on current sales to publish more than one new design in 1910, and that, presumably, is why they produced little after this date. Virtually all their posters were produced in the first four years of their existence. They were caught in an economic circuit constrained by the costs of commercial printing and the limited market (if not audience) for their work. Mary Lowndes wrote to the *Common Cause* to explain at the end of 1910.

The Artists' Suffrage League has published in all ten of these [posters] and I can quite believe people are pretty tired of many of them, as, indeed, we are ourselves. I have been asked why we did not issue new ones for this last general election; it is this question that I want to answer. I need not dwell on the unexpectedness of the election when it finally burst on us, and the hurry with which the whole matter has been conducted. Such haste, however, affects nothing more than placards, as all observers may have noted for themselves. Apart from this our Society cannot well issue many posters till it disposes of the old ones. Coloured posters are expensive. To be able to sell them at fourpence each (without making any profit) we are obliged to have at least 1000 copies printed at the same time. Now, these copies sell off very slowly. When a society has ordered six of each sort it feels it has sent a large order, and that particular society probably wants no more for six months. But six copies of one design makes a very small inroad into a thousand. It takes us from one to two years to sell 1000 copies. We have laid out on this design ten to fifteen pounds, say, and this sum comes back in driblets. We cannot print new posters till our money returns, or till we have amassed large profits on selling postcards, or other objects.

If people would purchase posters in hundreds and really post them on the hoardings we should soon get through our 10,000 copies, and I think then we should not be remiss about producing new designs. One or two generous people sent the Artists' League money for posting 200+ posters in East St Pancras. I think myself this money was well bestowed – people look a great deal at the pictures on the hoardings. For the information of anyone who may meditate a like extravagance, I may say that a quad-crown poster (price fourpence) costs in a general way fourpence a week to post. It is known to your readers that the Artists' League issued one new poster for their election, 'Votes for Mothers'. It was rather an expensive one to produce, and we were obliged to have 2000 copies at once to enable us to sell it at fourpence. We hope very much it will be bought up quickly.[120]

The WSPU produced new and topical posters for the 1910 elections and only charged twopence for them (presumably because they were in fewer colours and subsidised from Union funds). For the Artists' League the problem of printing costs, compounded by the fact that there was no point producing material if hoardings had not been hired for it, continued into 1912. Once again they were asked if they would be publishing any new posters, and once again the answer was, effectively, if you buy up our stocks and thus provide us with the money. The League had actually 'got a design ready which it would be willing to publish if there should be sufficient demand to cover the cost of production . . . The price at which the posters are sold to societies barely covers the printing and paper if the whole issue is sold. The designs representing so much labour and thought, are generously given by the Artists, and if more are produced than can be sold the posters are an actual loss to the League . . .'[121] (This design may have been Mary Lowndes's 'Justice at the Door', described by the *Common Cause* in November 1912, and significantly published not by the League but directly by the NUWSS.)

A guest speaker at the Suffrage Atelier in 1912

remarked that theirs was 'the worst sweated labour she knew',[122] and appealed for money to pay a secretary and a traveller to take posters to all branches of every society, so that they might have at least one on a hoarding near their offices.

Atelier posters, if coloured and as large as the League's commercially printed and technically sophisticated lithographs, might cost as much or even more. (In 1912 the three-colour 40-by-30-inch version of 'The Anti-Suffrage Ostrich' cost fivepence.) But they came also in black and white and in a range of sizes on cheaper paper, so that an uncoloured 15-by-20-inch 'posterette' was only a penny, the same price as a postcard.[123] The Atelier may have enjoyed larger sales. In any case it was in a position to raise money by other means. In 1910, for example, it organised a fund-raising fair to which all the major societies contributed. There was every kind of stall, from those selling suffrage designs and literature to Christmas gifts and roast chestnuts, an exhibition of work by Laurence Housman and Walter Crane and entertainments by the Actresses' Franchise League directed by Edith Craig. Tactfully, the fair was opened on successive days by Mrs Pethick-Lawrence of the WSPU, Mrs Despard of the WFL and Miss Edith Palliser of the NUWSS, their disagreements over militant tactics temporarily buried in their common duty – as Mrs Despard expressed it – of supporting the Suffrage Atelier which never failed them in their need for banners and decorations.[124]

By such means, and perhaps through tuition fees as well as their subscriptions, the Atelier kept its workshop running through to 1914. But it was in financial difficulties by this point, as a letter from an Atelier organiser to Maud Arncliffe-Sennett (who had ordered new banners for the Northern Men's League for Women's Suffrage) makes clear. 'You are indeed a generous woman. The finances of the Atelier are a tragedy, people get used to me managing to get through somehow but it is an awful strain . . . Thank you for offering help in the way of an appeal . . . In this movement we have to deal with a good many who do not understand what an unfinanced business is like to work. I do not wish to infer that our members do not help, they all do their best but artists are not wealthy and most of them have trouble enough to get through. We want more subscribers and more members who are determined to do something towards getting subscribers. We can manage if we get £120 – for the year on top of what we earn.'[125]

Both the League and the Atelier, although in other respects their circumstances were different, limped along where money was concerned.[126] For the League, having their posters commercially printed meant that the gap between the cost of production and money recouped from sales became *their* loss: no matter how appreciative in principle, the NUWSS does not seem to have stepped in, in practice, with any of its £20,000. The suffrage organisations valued the artists' labour and gratefully exploited their pictorial skills and their organising abilities. Individual artists working for the WSPU might (like Sylvia Pankhurst after the event) complain of being meanly treated, but there were certain advantages in the central administration of subsidy and distribution. The NUWSS and the WFL apparently assumed that the artists would raise whatever money they needed for material and printing costs, for distribution and posting on hoardings. Only in the case of processions did they recognise a need to contribute towards expenses, or appeal through their newspapers for donors to help do so. As an unwanted corollary, perhaps, of forming themselves into organisations at all, the Artists' Suffrage League and the Suffrage Atelier found themselves with a larger brief than they were either inclined or equipped to fulfil.

Circulation

Suffrage posters were distributed in particular contexts to particular audiences (on hoardings, in shops, at railway stations), and among other images competing for public attention for commercial or political ends. They circulated, we might say, in the real space of the physical environment, and in the imaginary space of all other pictorial representations. The best images were witty and concise. They did not so much illustrate suffrage arguments – aspiring designers were castigated in poster competitions if they were 'wordy' or literal-minded – as rehearse and embody them in pictorial form.

The purpose of suffrage propaganda was to rouse the public to the existence of the cause and bring pressure to bear on Parliament through public opinion, and with the aid of cooperative MPs. It was necessary as part of this process, first, to make a substantial case for the extent and influence of public support; second, for the absurdity or injustice of existing legislation; and third, for the moral, social or political benefits that change would bring. Posters were designed to reach those parts of the public that suffrage oratory failed to reach: partly because they could reach a broad and mobile audience ('the homes, the halls, the hoardings throughout the land'),[127] and partly because they were thought to make a different, but complementary impact. A section of the community too busy, lazy or tired 'to try to understand what the Suffrage really means to women and, reflexly, to men,' would have the points brought home to them by the pictorial poster that supplemented 'the eloquent and never-tiring voice of the leaders of the Suffrage Cause'. Posters were recommended for 'soundness of pictorial argument' and for 'the great saving likely to be effected in the outlay of vocal power'.[128]

Some images were used at meetings, exhibitions and 'at homes' – that is, in spaces appropriate to respectable middle-class femininity. In these private contexts they seem to have been much admired, but they can scarcely have found an unconverted audience. Others were displayed in branch shops and meeting-places. The WSPU alone had thirty-six London branches by the end of 1911, ten of them with shops, and another eighty-six branches with seventeen shops in the rest of

the country.[129] Three London branches of the NUWSS rented premises together in 1908 and filled the windows with banners and posters for the three weeks preceding the demonstration of 13 June. Three or four meetings were held there every day, and the one addressed by Mrs Fawcett was so successful that chairs had to be borrowed from all the neighbouring shopkeepers. The window display and the meetings advertised both the cause in general and the forthcoming demonstration in particular. 'From the first hour a kaleidoscopic crowd has gazed at our posters and derived instruction and amusement from them. Where should we be without our Artists' League who has made this method of conversion possible? . . . No small part of the educative value of our effort lies in the conversations which we hold on our doorstep. The mistaken ideas which we are able to correct are amazing, and show the need of further propaganda.'[130]

Some posters were fly-posted, although this probably applied to more ephemeral notices advertising particular meetings. This was risky but cheap. The Women's Freedom League issued detailed instructions which entailed arriving at the office late on a Sunday evening and bringing a hip-flask of water with which to dampen gummed posters, biscuits or sandwiches, together with a man (if reliable) to allay suspicion. Commercial sites were also used but these were expensive, and since political posters were easily swamped by advertisements, they needed choosing with care. Donors were invited to rent railway sites at 25 shillings per year. Newsagents were prepared to display *Votes for Women* posters free of charge if twelve customers undertook to buy a copy weekly.

24 Advertising *Votes for Women* in Kingsway.

25 Mrs Fawcett opening the Suffrage Shop in Kensington before the 1908 march (the 'Bugler Girl' and other posters are visible in the window, and the lettering is by Mary Lowndes).

Supporters were urged to leave posters and copies of the *Suffragette* wherever they went on holiday: at hotels and boarding houses, in almshouses and hospitals, in cab shelters and station waiting rooms.[131]

Poster parades (recommended by the Women's Freedom League as 'easy and health-giving')[132] used schemes of posters in organised sandwich-board demonstrations. They demanded more skill and courage than the WFL acknowledged, however, both because sandwich-men had been drawn traditionally from the ranks of the destitute residuum, and because carrying heavy boards in the gutter was more difficult than it at first appeared. Laurence Housman and a 'noble array of martyrs' from the Men's League discovered that the 'carrying of sandwich-boards is a skilled trade; unable to see your own feet, you have to walk in the gutter without falling over the kerb in your anxiety to escape collision with the traffic: also, to make your advertising effective, you should keep a five-yards distance between yourself and the one in front of you'. That was where they failed: 'like Adam and Eve in the garden in search of fig-leaves, we closed up telescopically one against another to hide our nakedness, and to get nearer to the wished-for goal – release from the awful ordeal to which we had committed ourselves.'[133] Women replaced the wooden boards with lighter cardboard sheets (although in volunteering to be a 'sandwich' an American expatriate found her knees banged black and blue with every step),[134] and stepped out with the dignity of shared conviction in a political cause. But it was still something of an ordeal, and in conventional eyes the conflation of radical politics with common advertising declassed and unsexed them. ('You are the very latest thing / In modern femininity; / You pass – a parti-coloured string – / Down West, and the vicinity, / With sandwich boards that soil the wing / Of womanhood's divinity.')[135]

In entering the more abstract space of 'representation', suffrage posters were exploiting a situation in which they were also obliged to compete. They were the beneficiaries of a range of technical, educational and political developments in the nineteenth century (such as improved literacy rates, changes in printing techniques, the facilitation of communication by the expanding railway network and developments in the postal services), but so too were their competitors. From about 1850 colour printing by lithography was cheap enough to popularise the production of all kinds of cards, packaging and printed ephemera, and to displace earlier methods as the standard process for the printing of posters. By the end of the nineteenth century public advertising had shifted from a predominantly verbal to a predominantly visual means of representation, a development facilitated by refinements in colour reproduction and registration, and accelerated by a parallel shift from indiscriminate bill-posting to a more orderly display.

By the Edwardian period picture posters had become a ubiquitous and seemingly natural part of the urban environment, as, in the West, they have remained; at the same time a commercial phenomenon and an artistic one. The suffrage artists were heirs to both aspects of this new tradition. They could not but be familiar with advertising imagery on the hoardings around them, and some women found work in this area, although significantly fewer than in illustration. Artists' Suffrage League and WSPU posters were printed by commercial lithographers, one of which was David Allen's, a firm that reflects in microcosm the whole history of commercial picture posters, modern methods of advertising, and bill-posting.[136] On the other hand, as trained artists, they would have been aware of posters as objects of connoisseurship. The first exhibitions had been held in New York, Paris and London in the 1890s, and it has been estimated that in the United States alone there were more than 6000 collections of posters by 1896.[137] Influential publications appeared in the same period, including Charles Hiatt's seminal

article in the first volume of the *Studio*.[138]

It was their partial exploitation of the 'artistic' canon – especially in certain Atelier examples – which set the suffrage posters apart from the bulk of the commercial advertising around them. Nevertheless, since they were relatively few, they needed to be carefully placed. All posters needed street legibility, for which the requirements included a bold image, not too much text, a large enough typeface and, in the case of suffrage posters, something harder to define and achieve: political lucidity. (This was why parody and role reversal were popular, since they lent themselves to a rapid but comprehensive reading.)

Posters were aimed specifically at targets in the political machinery – the more politicised the context, the more productive their display: critical parliamentary debates, general and by-elections. By-elections occurred more frequently before 1919, when an MP appointed to a government post was normally obliged to stand for re-election, and they provided a crucial opportunity for pressure-group activity, in this case for suffragists to intervene in an electoral process that excluded them as voters: holding public meetings, opening committee rooms, interrogating candidates and generally advertising the cause and soliciting support in an atmosphere of heightened political debate. For the NUWSS, elections were educational opportunities. They provided a chance to form new societies, support the suffrage candidate and propagandise to the electorate. The WSPU strategy, on the other hand, more subtle or more perverse depending on one's point of view, was to 'Keep the Liberal Out'. They opposed the Liberal candidate whatever his views on the suffrage question, and by doing so attempted to put pressure on the government to bring in a women's measure. At general elections, which means particularly at the elections of January and December 1910, both suffrage organisations faced competition from other interest groups in the electorate, as well as from the propaganda produced by the political parties themselves.[139]

26 The NUWSS committee rooms during the Oldham by-election.

The Times observed that the January election 'was characterised by a greater output of campaign publications of all kinds, posters, pamphlets and leaflets, than any which has occurred since the passing of the Reform Bill of 1832'.[140] 'Never in the annals of our country,' the *Common Cause* remarked in February, 'have pictures played so large a part in politics as during the general election of 1910, and enormous sums of money have been spent by both Liberals and Conservatives in this pictorial warfare.'[141] For the first time political posters covered the advertisement hoardings, and the *Daily Mail* estimated that by early January the posters originating from London alone would take up 2 million square feet of display space. The Liberal Publication Department issued 662,000 posters and more than 3 million booklets and leaflets; the Conservative and Unionist Party 1,147,000 posters and 2,844,590 postcards; and even the Labour Party, with modest and hard-pressed resources, managed 50,000 picture posters and 800,000 copies of the party manifesto.[142] Through the agency of the Artists' Suffrage League and the Atelier the suffrage cause had its posters too, although spending on the party political scale was impossible for them. (The Labour Party, on a limited budget, paid up to five guineas for a design. The suffrage artists were unpaid, the Atelier printed its own material, and the cost of production limited the League's posters to eleven designs.) In the weeks immediately preceding the January election Barbara Forbes, the Artists' League secretary, sent out 2708 posters, 6488 postcards and 65,000 pictorial leaflets which were used in suffrage committee rooms all over the country.[143]

Generalisations about Edwardian party political and pressure-group posters, and about their relation to suffrage imagery, must be made with caution.[144] The designs are various, and there is no way of knowing how representative are those that survive. But while the suffrage posters held no monopoly on political advertising at this date, in certain respects they were more accomplished and more challenging. Most of the party posters from the 1906 election are like scaled-up cartoons. The images are weaker, the draughtsmanship poorer, and they have neither the competent drawing and organisation of the Artists' Suffrage League nor the vigour and bite of the best Atelier designs. In content and reference both suffrage and non-suffrage political posters have recourse to the same pictorial vocabulary. Everybody uses John Bull, who is dismayed in turn at unemployment, socialism, free trade, or the pressure of business to attend to with no help from the women's vote. In January 1910 pride of place in the Liberal gallery (as Neal Blewett puts it) went to the peers. 'Coroneted, ermined, gartered and robed, the peer capered across the hoardings of the country'[145] (and appeared on WSPU posters for the second election in December). Unionists concentrated on the pathetic figure of the unemployed workman at

the mercy of free trade (the most widely reproduced poster in both elections was T. B. Kennington's portrayal of poverty and unemployment under free trade, published by the National Union, i.e. the Conservative and Unionist Party). The depiction of the British workman in Unionist posters was criticised in the press as feeble and inadequate, and from inside the party J. L. Garvin, editor of the *Observer* and the most influential Tory journalist, attacked its campaign literature as pictorially inept: 'the British workman must appear in all our pictures as a fine fellow, not the debased, and uncouth and grotesque person that he seems in some of our pictures.'[146] All groups used the image of the working-class woman as the figure most oppressed by the policies of their opponents. In Conservative posters she sits at the knee of her unemployed husband to demonstrate the iniquity of foreigners taking his work. In January 1910 she cried out from a tariff reform poster, 'Don't let them tax our food!', spurring the suffragists to a counter-image inscribed: 'Give me a vote and let me speak for myself.'[147]

Like other political groups, especially at election time, the suffragists published a large number of propaganda postcards. The last phase of the suffrage campaign coincided with what is often called the 'golden age' of the picture postcard, specifically with the boom period of postcard production and circulation between about 1904 and 1910. (By 1910 866 million cards were sent through the post each year, and by 1913 more than 900 million.) John Fraser has suggested that the pictorial postcard was 'possibly the great vehicle for messages of the new urban proletariat between 1900 and 1914' (it was cheap to buy and to post, simple to use, and quick to arrive in an age of frequent postal deliveries).[148] At the same time it was avidly collected by middle-class enthusiasts who formed postcard clubs and subscribed to postcard journals (the same kind of people who had collected posters in the 1890s).[149] The British Post Office was finally obliged to relax its monopoly on the postcard

Published by the Artists' Suffrage League. Carl Hentschel Ltd. 182, 183 & 184 Fleet St. E.C.

VOTES

HANDICAPPED!

1 'Handicapped': the joint winner with W. F. Winter of the ASL poster competition in 1909. Designed by Duncan Grant, published by the Artists' Suffrage League.
The Common Cause *(4 November 1909) praised the* poster's sense of humour and drew attention to the 'stalwart young woman of the Grace Darling type' who has only a pair of sculls in heavy seas, 'while a nonchalant young man in flannels glides gaily by, with the wind inflating his sail – the vote'.

The poster reads:

VOTES FOR WORKERS

CARL HENTSCHEL LTD. 182, 183 & 184 FLEET ST E.C.   PUBLISHED BY ARTISTS' SUFFRAGE LEAGUE.

W.F. Winter

11 'Votes for Workers': joint winner with Duncan Grant of the ASL poster competition in 1909. Designed by W. F. Winter, published by the Artists' Suffrage League.

The exploitation of domestic servants was variable, and often invisible to the middle class that depended on them. Factory women were thought of as coarse and independent. But ever since Thomas Hood's popular ballad 'The Song of the Shirt' (published in Punch, December 1843*), the sweated seamstress had been sentimentalised in the press, paintings and popular prints as the most oppressed (but womanly) of female workers ('It is not linen you're wearing out, / But human creatures' lives!'). Winter's is no consumptive heroine but a sturdy, if impoverished, middle-aged outworker: an image closer in style and tone to the work of Käthe Kollwitz in Germany than to the more sentimental traditions of British illustration.*

"THEY **HAVE** A CHEEK **I**'VE NEVER BEEN ASKED".

PRINTED BY WEINERS, ACTON. PUBLISHED BY THE ARTIST'S SUFFRAGE LEAGUE.

III 'Factory Acts' ('They've a Cheek'): designed by Emily Ford, published by the Artists' Suffrage League, 1908.
Between 1847 and 1901 eleven acts were passed restricting the hours and conditions of women's work in factories and workshops. Protective legislation was supposed to be in the women's own interests (not always the case), but suffragists argued that without the vote women had no say in the passage of laws that affected their livelihoods. The clogs and shawl are those of a North of England mill girl (Annie Kenney kept hers, and sometimes wore them on suffrage processions).

IV 'Convicts and Lunatics': designed by Emily Harding Andrews, published by the Artists' Suffrage League, c. 1908.
The theme was a popular one, at least since Frances Power Cobbe's 'Criminals, Idiots, Women, Minors, is the *classification sound?' in* Fraser's Magazine, *vol. 78, 1868. The point is sharpened physiognomically: the woman graduate is given the idealised and regular features of the eugenically superior, while the prisoner and lunatic are clearly portrayed as 'degenerate' types.*

v 'Justice at the Door': designed by Mary Lowndes, published by the NUWSS, 1912.
The Common Cause *(8 November 1912) commented: 'Those who see it will perhaps be reminded that it is not possible for those in power to exclude all women from the [Reform] Bill without excluding also the cardinal virtue who, like her sisters, has been symbolised from time immemorial by a woman's form.'*

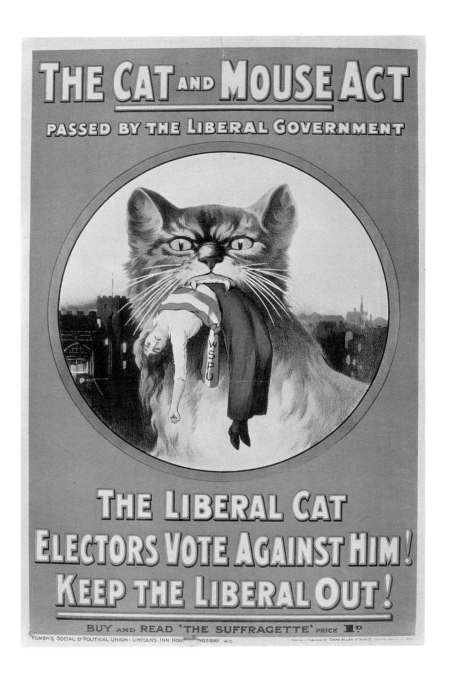

VI 'Cat and Mouse': anon., for the WSPU, 1914. *Reginald McKenna, as Home Secretary, was responsible for the Prisoners' Temporary Discharge for Ill-Health Act (1913), popularly known as the Cat and Mouse Act. It allowed for the temporary release of suffrage prisoners weakened by hunger strikes and forcible feeding, and their rearrest without remission of sentence. See also the Suffrage Atelier poster 'McKenna's Cat "Bill"'.*

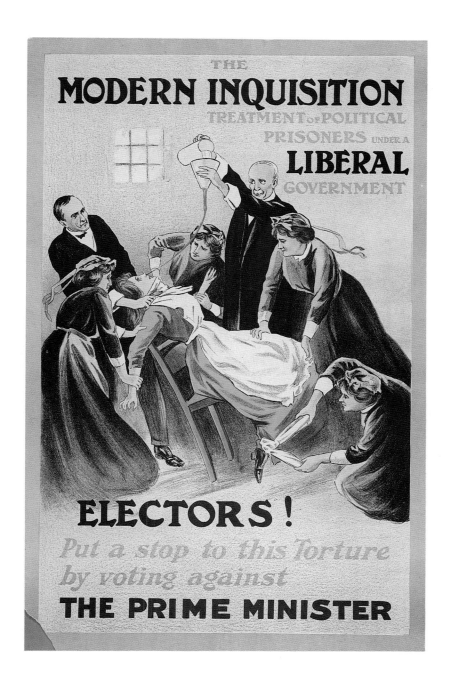

VII 'Modern Inquisition': designed by A. Patriot (Alfred Pearse) and published by the WSPU for the January 1910 General Election.

Forcible feeding of hunger-striking prisoners, by mouth or by nose, was regarded by militants as a form of state torture.

VIII 'The Bugler Girl': designed by Caroline Watts and published by the Artists' Suffrage League, originally to advertise the NUWSS procession of 13 June 1908. *The* Common Cause *glossed this image through Elizabeth* *Barrett Browning ('Now press the clarion to thy woman's* *lip'), and stressed the symbolism of the Bugler Girl's* spiritual *armoury.*

This is "THE HOUSE" that man built,
And this is the Flag of the Woman's Franchise,
Which is making our Ministers open their eyes:
Fighting with grit, to the front bit by bit;
Determined in Parliament one day to sit,
The bold Suffragette who is sure to get yet
Into "THE HOUSE" that man built.

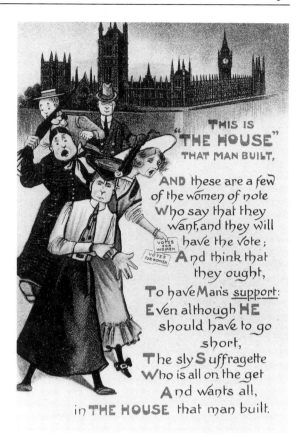

THIS IS "THE HOUSE" THAT MAN BUILT,

AND these are a few
of the women of note
Who say that they
want, and they will
have the vote;
And think that
they ought,
To have Man's support:
Even although HE
should have to go
short,
The sly Suffragette
Who is all on the get
And wants all,
in THE HOUSE that man built.

27 & 28 'Pro' and 'anti' cards from the BB series of twelve, 'The House that Man Built'. The more flattering (if scarcely inspiring) version features Laurence Housman's 'From Prison to Citizenship' banner.

market in 1899 after a protest campaign organised by the publishers Raphael Tuck & Sons. By the Edwardian period one publisher alone (Evelyn Wrench) was talking in terms of a monthly output of 3 million cards. New designs were produced and collected in sets, displayed in albums, exhibited in competitive circumstances where medals were awarded and circulated among collectors and connoisseurs. Any subject was a possible theme, and any theme a collector's speciality: views, sporting pictures, theatrical and music-hall personalities, inventions, crazes, official pageantry, varieties of transport including the new cars, aeroplanes and the twopenny tube, the clothes and customs of other nations, important politicians, writers or sportsmen, members of the Royal Family in Britain or abroad. It was inevitable that in all this the postcard manufacturers would document the personalities and activities of the suffrage campaign, parody it, and find the postcard itself diverted by suffragists to their own political ends.

Commercial cards treat suffrage material under the headings of topical views (such as the Photo Chrom Co. Ltd's card of Mrs Pankhurst's arrest in 1908) or comedy (as in William Ritchie & Sons Ltd's set on 'The Humours of Women's Suffrage').[150] Commercial publishers had, osten-

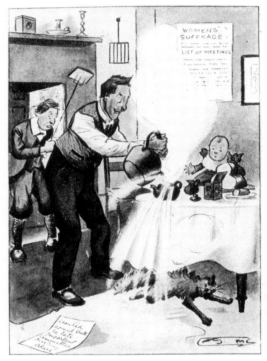

The Suffragette not at home.

29 'The Suffragette Not at Home', C. W. Faulkner and Co.
There are no popular cards that make fun of the antis (antis in this respect swam with the tide). But the humour in role-reversals is at the expense of both parties. If there was nothing wickeder than a woman deserting her family, there was little funnier than a husband attempting to cope.

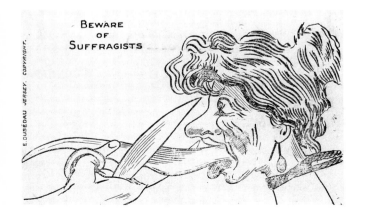

sibly, no political axe to grind. They were neither employed nor encouraged by the anti-suffrage organisations. But their notion of what was sensational or funny (and hence likely to sell) depended on a music-hall tradition of humour about women that was deeply misogynist and long rooted in Victorian and Edwardian culture. Postcards parodying other political themes – Home Rule, free trade, the Insurance Act – did not have the same kind of existing seam on which to draw. There are even instances of 'humorous' cards devoted to fat, thin, gossiping, ugly, aggressive or socially embarrassing women that have been overprinted with an anti-suffrage slogan to give them a more topical and political gloss.[151]

This extensive and residual anti-feminism provided the anti-suffragists with an asset that enabled them to orchestrate their own campaign in a different way. They had neither to organise nor to pay for it. They could even affect to disdain its vulgarity but it was there for them to use, and there were moments at which they were happy to drop their more high-minded tone and exploit its derogatory depictions of women. There were two ways in which the suffragists sought to counter this. The first was in the production of their own representations, including photographic portraits of their leaders, documentary records of demonstrations, and cartoon postcards, to combat the unthinking misogyny of much contemporary postcard 'humour'. The second was by, as it were, producing themselves: by taking to the streets in public spectacles that were intended to demonstrate not only the strength of support for their cause, but also the look and the manner of the women who stood for it.

30 'Beware of Suffragists', E. Dusédau, Jersey: a card postmarked 1909, well before the onset of militant violence.
The urge to render women speechless – gagged, mutilated or in scold's bridles – was insistent. There are two particularly vicious examples among the suffrage memorabilia in the People's Palace Museum, Glasgow.

3 · SPECTACLE

31 WSPU procession, 18 June 1910; looking down on the WSPU Drum and Fife Band, bandleader Mary Richardson.

In these modern times women who have a great cause to advocate come out into the open. Petitions go into parliamentary waste-paper baskets. They cannot put a procession of fifteen thousand women into waste-paper baskets. They cannot ignore them and pretend that they are not there. All London comes out to see them, and those that see the amazing spectacle of two miles of women – women of every class, of every profession and calling – realise perfectly well that they represent a very great and widespread and irresistible demand.[1]

In the House of Commons debate on women's suffrage in 1892, Asquith had expressed the view that 'as to the great mass of the sex, the only thing that can be asserted with truth is that they are watching with languid and imperturbable indifference the struggle for their own emancipation.'[2] As prime minister from 1908, he continued to demand proof that a substantial majority of women wanted the vote before he was prepared seriously to entertain the possibility of giving it to them.

It was not clear, however, what form this proof might take, or by what means public opinion could be established. It was often suggested that a constitutional change must be 'put before the country' at a general election before it could be effected, but none of the political parties had ever adopted women's suffrage as an election issue, and suffragists themselves were loath to accept the verdict of a franchise which excluded them. As the electorate expanded in the nineteenth century and political influence was partially dispersed, so it became more necessary, but also more difficult, to establish the extent of support for particular causes and their likely effect upon party interests. Political parties were not yet clearly identified with particular legislative programmes on which they might be voted in or out of office, the systematic opinion poll did not exist and pressure groups that claimed to

speak in the public interest might, or might not, be justified in doing so.[3]

Suffragists and anti-suffragists alike were assiduous collectors of petitions, but neither group could make a serious impact on the 10.5 million women in the country. Each disputed the findings of the other, and there was no agreement on methods of canvassing and petitioning or on how the results should be interpreted. Organising a demonstration was in many respects the logical next step from organising a petition. Embodying their political commitment in this way helped women to underline it. Spectators could see that suffragists were not the shrews and harridans of popular imagery and the yellow press, and women's physical presence did away with the frequent objection to petitions: that they were fraudulent or signed in ignorance and haste. The public demonstration was founded on a politics of 'seeing as believing' which, if carefully attuned to the sensibilities of the watching crowds, could be a powerful instrument in winning their sympathy to the cause.

But in 'taking to the streets' as men had to redress their political grievances, women were subject to the domestic and social constraints peculiar to their sex. Either they were free to demonstrate but hemmed in by practical difficulties, or they were untrammelled by domestic cares but bound by the social conventions of their class. The Women's Freedom League complained in 1908 that Asquith's demand could not be met, even by ardent suffragists, because their duties kept them at home on Saturday afternoons and Sundays when men were free, because their husbands and employers forbade them to go, because society frowned on it. 'Everybody must know that women cannot demonstrate publicly in the way men can,' and yet they were called upon to support their claim with an overwhelming majority in circumstances where that majority could not be mobilised. 'Women must not be freed till they show that they want to be free; but they cannot show they want to be free, because they are not free; and so the vicious circle ever goes round.'[4]

First to break were not the bonds of practical constraint but those of social convention. If Mrs Fawcett and Lady Frances Balfour, together with other women of social standing and unimpeachable respectability, could survive the experience of marching from Hyde Park to the Exeter Hall with 3000 members of the NUWSS, then there was no need just to endure the experience; it might even become possible to enjoy it. In the organisation of an impressive and unprecedented sequence of public demonstrations between 1907 and 1913, the suffragists developed a new kind of political spectacle in which they dramatised the cause by means of costume, narrative, embroidery, performance, and all the developing skills of public entertainment at their disposal.[5]

A sense of this spectacle, necessarily ephemeral, has to be reconstructed from contemporary sources. The account which follows is drawn chiefly from press reports and suffrage commentaries, augmented where possible from photographs, fragments of newsreel footage, letters and reminiscences. These sources are not always in agreement with one another.[6] The participant saw a different march from the spectator, the sympathiser from the opponent, and sometimes the reporter from the leader-writer. Personal sympathy, political allegiance and vested interests of one kind and another inflect the press accounts as they informed the experience of those present at the time. There is nevertheless a fair measure of agreement, particularly in matters of description rather than interpretation, and in many cases the suffragists were able to win admiration for their organisation and pageantry even where they failed to gain converts to their cause. In contradictory

accounts, too, an unintended and covert agreement can sometimes be found at those points where the text stumbles, is silent, or obsessively rehearses a phrase, a metaphor or an incident from the procession it describes. Such moments are often the focal point for contemporary anxieties, pleasures and assumptions as they were aroused or challenged by the novel spectacle of women on the streets.

Three kinds of precedent provided a context for suffrage spectacle, and its organisers were conscious of drawing on at least two of them: state ritual, which refined and developed the public image of the British monarchy in the heyday of 'invented traditions' between 1877 and 1914;[7] labour-movement activities from May Day celebrations to the ritual welcome of released prisoners (emulated by the WSPU); and a more diffuse Edwardian fascination with pageantry which the suffragists fused with the political demonstration in the production of their own, and as it was remarked at the time particularly 'feminine', kind of spectacle.

On the occasion of the Coronation of George V in 1911, the *Labour Leader* remarked on 'the curious fact that parallel with the development of democracy has proceeded the rehabilitation of the monarchy'.[8] What has been called the 'enhanced and ritualised public face'[9] of the British monarchy in this period, and the general proliferation of civic ritual that accompanied it, used pageantry to secure the ideological domination of the ruling elite. The 'official traditions' of the late Victorian and Edwardian period were intended to ensure the continuity of liberal institutions and liberal ideology by popular means, to appeal to a mass electorate at a time of unprecedented social and industrial development, to win consent where consent had previously been presumed.

The suffrage relation to 'invented traditions' was complicated. They were in the business of inventing some of their own, but they occupied an oppositional position and their spectacle, like their campaign, was essentially counter-hegemonic. They might have been, and mostly were, opposed to the legitimising effects of state ritual as they were opposed to that 'despotism of custom' which would keep women in their allotted sphere. On the other hand it provided certain precedents for them, though these were not unique: the ordered progression of separate contingents, the national symbolism, the appeal to an eye educated by an accompanying programme in the identification of key participants and the order of march.[10] And more profoundly, at the same time as suffragists argued their right to reform society, their first demand was simply to be allowed to join in. They were meshed uncomfortably with the status quo and the strains of their position with regard to the state – which varied according to their political beliefs and class allegiances – surfaced at particular moments. The 'Women's Coronation Procession' of 1911 was one such moment when the emphasis on imperial pomp, *plus royaliste que le roi*, sat uneasily with the participation of more radical and international elements. These equivocations arose directly from the double nature of the women's struggle: against a presumed consensus, and at the same time for the right to be more fully represented within it.

The labour movement offered the example of a clearly oppositional group engaged in the invention of its own symbolic tradition, and some of its activities were adapted by the Pankhursts in the early years of the WSPU. Through socialism, the Pankhurst family was well versed in the strategies of the large public meeting, in a range of by-election work, and in the politics of tactical imprisonment. They worked with the labour movement during the period in which it acquired its cultural forms and built the rituals that gave cohesion to its rapidly expanding membership: an annual May Day celebration, fund-raising activities such as bazaars and jumble sales, demonstrations with banners and bands, outdoor meetings, picnics and social occasions. (Seventeen bands took part in the Edinburgh 'Labour Day' of 1894, thirty-seven organisations, 10,000 marchers and an estimated 120,000 spectators.)[11]

Working-class women who took part on these occasions, and whose parents had marched together in Chartist processions, were not unfamiliar with demonstrations. Although there is some evidence that they took a less public part in the labour movement from about the middle of the nineteenth century they were not politically inactive, and the codes of bourgeois decorum that kept respectable middle-class women in the home did not apply in quite the same way to them. Working women from the East End of London formed the backbone of the WSPU procession that marched to Trafalgar Square in 1906 to accompany a deputation of suffragists from all societies which Campbell-Bannerman, as prime minister, had reluctantly agreed to receive.[12]

Despite the links between the WSPU and the Independent Labour Party in its early years, however, and despite the Pankhursts' adoption of certain socialist tactics to the suffrage cause, Christabel decided soon after her arrival in London that the Union was 'too exclusively dependent for its demonstrations upon the women of the East End'. They turned out because they were used to doing so for labour demonstrations, but in her view this made them too predictable and less influential. She claimed that the WSPU was being accused of fielding a 'stage army', and that evidently 'the House of Commons, and even its Labour members, were more impressed by the demonstrations of the feminine bourgeoisie than of the feminine proletariat'.[13] Whether or not this was the case, it formed the basis of her successful attempt to mobilise influential and middle-class women in the WSPU campaign, and eventually to sever its ties with the labour movement to Sylvia's abiding regret.

Suffrage connections with Edwardian pageantry, a late and rather feeble diffusion of the nineteenth-century flirtation with medieval chivalry, are important but elusive.[14] Accounts of monks, princesses, knights and burghers, played by local dignitaries in historical narratives of places and events, surface regularly in the pre-war press, their attraction remote to us in an age of mass entertainment, their impact blurred in smudgy photographs that reek of fancy dress.[15] They seem to have answered to a sense of the meanness of contemporary life, and a longing, absurd perhaps but real, for the lost rituals that in imagination brought order and beauty to it. Women had a special place in this idea, as the muses of medieval chivalry, as the weavers and stitchers and fixers of most of the bits and bobs required for the local pageant and as possessors of that 'instinct for seemliness and refinement'[16] which would be their contribution to a world transformed and dignified by order and beauty. The fusion of elements from the contemporary pageant with those from the political demonstration seems to have been initiated by Mary Lowndes for the NUWSS in 1908, and it is possible to find the roots of her desire to bring 'the feminine trooping into public life'[17] in her arts and crafts background, and in a particular reading of courtly chivalry compounded of Victorian medievalism and nineteenth-century feminism.

Such a project was not without its risks. Even in 1907 the association between women and the streets in the public mind was an almost entirely degrading one. There was a danger that suffragists would jeopardise their cause rather than further it, and those who participated in the first important procession in that year endured the public gaze; they did not court it. But in a very short space of time (just over a year in fact), this changed. Confidence grew as modes of organisation and presentation were developed; the public proved largely sympathetic – or at least, productively astonished – and even the newly founded Women's National Anti-Suffrage League acknowledged the impact of the NUWSS demonstration of 13 June 1908.

The suffrage spectacles of the pre-war years served a number of different constituencies as they developed and addressed themselves, not always consciously at first, to particular points in the political system. They had to impress Asquith as prime minister, and Parliament in general, that they had a credible claim to speak on behalf of a majority of women. Their opponents continued to argue that most women did not want the vote, and that the suffragists were not authorised to speak for them. A large-scale suffrage demonstration was intended literally to embody that demand, and by so doing to make those who witnessed it see something of its importance and the scope of its support. Anti-suffragists could quibble that very large numbers were not the same as a majority and that the biggest procession could not mobilise as many names as a petition or referendum, but then its impact was of a different and more complex kind. 'More and more it became difficult to belittle a Movement,' Laurence Housman remembered, 'which could hold up the traffic of London with processions two or three miles long, and decked from end to end with hundreds of banners, some of them of vast size; while in the ranks the most unexpected people were to be seen testifying their support . . .'[18]

Huge crowds watched these demonstrations and assembled at the public meetings with which they ended, but larger numbers still read about them in the daily press. What justified the suffragists' use of spectacle as a political strategy was the hold it gave them on the newspapers (hitherto aloof or apathetic) and, through the newspapers, on public attention in general. And what gave them this hold was the existence of the new popular, national, halfpenny dailies with their half-tone photographic facilities and appetite for sensational events. The circulation of *The Times*, 11,000 in 1830, 38,000 in 1850, 70,000 in 1870, was overtaken by the *Daily Telegraph*, 100,000 in the 1860s, 200,000 in the 1870s; but neither could compete with Lord Northcliffe's *Daily Mail*, founded in

1896, which rapidly achieved a daily circulation of 1,000,000. The *Daily News, Daily Sketch, Daily Mirror* and *Daily Mail* all built up tremendous circulations in the late Victorian and Edwardian period, and enhanced their appeal with photographic reproductions popularised by the *Daily Mirror* in 1904 and the *Daily Sketch* in 1909. In a few years hardly a newspaper office of importance was without its photo-engraving department, which is to say that the development of photographic reproduction in the daily press and the development of suffrage spectacle go hand in hand.[19]

Traditional pressure-group activity with the press went on (in 1912 the London Society for Women's Suffrage had thirty-three press secretaries working in sixty-one constituencies):[20] patient and unspectacular effort devoted to the insertion of news items, the writing of letters, the soliciting of special articles with predigested information, the courting of editors. But meetings made dull copy, and the appeal of militant activity to the more sensationalist press impelled the constitutionalists to find a peaceful way of making a comparable impact with their own campaign. One woman breaking a window could make all England ring. This was the militant discovery, and they did not mind if the publicity was unfavourable so long as there was *noise*. The constitutionalists were more discriminating, but both groups learned to exploit an appetite for something topical, sensational and amenable to vivid illustration. They extended their audience, through the press, to many more than those who lined the route, and through the copy they provided coached their readers in the political symbolism of the procession and the tactical refinements of their campaign. The *Referee* in 1908 was acute, if unsympathetic, in the observation that it was 'only by means of the wide publicity given by the press to the intentions and actions of the suffragettes that mighty mobs of people are brought together. The newspapers at present advertise the movements of the militant

maids and matrons before a demonstration, during a demonstration, and after a demonstration. Publicity is the life-blood of the campaign.'[21] The relations between Parliament, the press and a mass electorate, each of them subject to shifts in constitution and identity in the second half of the nineteenth century, were still unclear. Asquith wanted to know the 'feeling of the country' on matters that did not appear before it at a general election. The suffragists were required to show proof that they represented a genuine and overwhelming demand without the terms of that proof being clear or agreed.[22] The role that mass-circulation newspapers could play in the moulding of public opinion or the presentation of an opinion as publicly held was not yet known, but it was emerging as a very powerful one, in lieu of more systematic means either for revealing a national consensus or producing one. Suffragists knew they had to court the press, and they also knew, given the limited opportunities for women journalists, that that meant courting an overwhelmingly masculine and conservative profession.[23]

Two further points are important in the choice of spectacle as a means to do this. In so literally embodying their demand they were able to demonstrate not only the scale of its support but two related propositions: that all sorts and conditions of women wanted the vote, and that women who wanted the vote were not as they were popularly conceived to be in the public mind or caricatured in the illustrated press.

No doubt some spectators still saw what they wished to see. Mrs Fawcett recalled on 13 June 1908 one 'stern-looking and very long-legged man' walking 'rapidly down our lines facing us and saying from time to time, "Yes, yes, all one type, all alike, all old maids," '[24] but it was widely acknowledged that the stereotype would not hold, and there was much press comment on this point. The probity of Mrs Fawcett or of Lady Frances Balfour, the glamour of the actresses, the charisma of Christabel Pankhurst, the fading prettiness and elegant clothing of her mother, the respect held for women active in social service such as Charlotte Despard; none of this fitted the popular image of the 'suffragette', when paraded in all its diversity and with accompanying pageantry through the London streets.

Secondly, we might consider the impact of suffrage spectacle, as of the campaign generally, on the participants themselves. 'It meant to women the discovery of their own identity, that source within of purpose, power and will . . . While working for the idea of political liberty, we were individually achieving liberty of a far more real and vital nature.'[25] Suffragists themselves, directly and through their own rapidly expanding press (the circulation of *Votes for Women* alone was over 30,000 in 1909), were also part of the audience for suffrage spectacle. They were organised and educated and entertained by it, as the grim endurance of 1907 gave way to reports of excited and triumphant contingents arriving flushed and victorious in Hyde Park or at the Albert Hall. Women experienced their collectivity in the act of presenting it to the public gaze. The 'Suffrage Campaign was our Eton and Oxford, our regiment, our ship, our cricket match,' as Rachel Ferguson observed. 'For thirty years I made jokes about the feminine ballot, to please the men. And one fine day, I found myself at the head of a section surrounded by banners bearing many a strange device, marching down Whitehall, and revelling in every minute of it! By my side marched a dowager duchess and a laundry maid. Commonly, I detest these sentimental contrasts, but there it was.'[26] As Emmeline Pethick-Lawrence added more prosaically, it was 'our education in that living identification of the self with the corporate whole'.[27]

Banners and Banner-Making

Suffrage spectacle was heavily dependent on 'the long array of pennons, banners, trophies, garlands and badges, most resplendent in their gorgeous

execution and workmanship'.[28] Banners celebrated a 'women's history' in their iconography, their inscriptions and their collective workmanship; they focused a sense of shared identity and imbued it with political significance. In so far as they made reference to the past it was as part of a political strategy for the present; and in so far as they mobilised women's traditional needlework skills – so much a part of the contemporary feminine stereotype as to be almost a secondary sexual characteristic – it was to challenge the terms of that femininity in a collective political enterprise.

Banners served both as rallying points for the march and as commentary on it. Women formed up around them in predetermined sequence, so that a procession several miles long could be ordered according to its programme and move off smoothly. At the same time, for the onlookers (and for readers of the next day's newspapers perusing their half-tone photographs), they acted as a gloss on the procession itself, developing its meanings, identifying and grouping its participants and clarifying its themes. Together with the programme of the march, the banners emphasised the broad base of suffrage support, the diversity of women's achievements and the benefits the women's vote would bring to society at large. In this sense they were an essential part not just of the spectacle of suffrage demonstrations but of their argument. They went some way to informing the casual onlooker as to the 'what' and 'why' of women's presence on the streets.

32 Page from the *Illustrated London News*, 20 June 1908, reporting the NUWSS demonstration of 13 June and illustrating twenty-three of the 'heroine' banners designed by the Artists' Suffrage League.
This shows several banners that are now missing. Angelica Kauffman's with palette and brushes would have been a pair to that of the flower painter Mary Moser (both women were founder-members of the Royal Academy in 1768). Elizabeth Cady Stanton's belonged with Susan B. Anthony's and Lucy Stone's in a trio of American pioneers. Lydia Becker was an important British pioneer of women's suffrage from its organised beginnings in the 1860s until her death in 1887.

THE WOMAN MILITANT: LEADERS OF THE SUFFRAGIST PROCESSION
AND THEIR SYMBOLIC BANNERS COMMEMORATING GREAT WOMEN OF ALL AGES.

1. MRS. DESPARD,
Leader of the Women's Freedom League.

2. LADY HENRY SOMERSET,
Who delivered the first speech at the Albert Hall.

3. THE REV. DR. ANNA SHAW,
American Divine, Leader of the American Suffragists.

4. MRS. ISRAEL ZANGWILL,
Among the Women Writers.

5. LADY FRANCES BALFOUR,
President of the London Union for Women's Suffrage.

6. MISS BEATRICE HARRADEN,
Among the Women Writers.

7. MISS CICELY HAMILTON,
Among the Women Dramatists.

8. DR. GARRETT ANDERSON,
The first Woman Physician.

9. MRS. AYRTON,
Electrical Engineer.

10. MRS. ALFRED LYTTELTON,
Among the Women Dramatists.

Seventy banners were carried in the procession commemorating the great women of all ages. All the pursuits and professions to which women have been admitted in groups of processionists, and also the various branches of the suffragist movement.

They did, however, have other uses. They were portable, decorative, and in their own way informative,[29] so that they made good window-dressing for suffrage committee rooms and convenient backdrops to the public platform. They decked out the Albert Hall for larger meetings and took the place of honour like battle trophies, evoking the associations of the regimental colours rather than of the church banners of Mothers' Unions, stitched in Marian humility. Banner-makers themselves straddled the interests of arts and crafts and ecclesiastical embroidery, of women's domestic needlework and of the suffrage campaign. The banners they made could speak to each of these constituencies, and thereby bring within the parameters of the campaign women who had never before expressed an interest in it. As cultural artefacts the banners could be admired for their design and workmanship, but it was neither possible nor desirable wholly to sever their political connections. An exhibition of banners, such as the Caxton Hall display preceding the NUWSS demonstration of 1908, made a rather convenient and unthreatening focus for attendant events – speeches, music, local newspaper publicity, competitions and school visits – altogether instructive and politically stimulating. A pilot exhibition in Yorkshire left in its wake the nucleus for a local suffrage society, and no doubt the broad audience attracted to the banners that 'looked gorgeous as the afternoon sun fell softly upon them'[30] swelled campaign funds with their sixpenny entrance fees. Banners produced a useful confusion of disparate categories: they were tributes to women of spiritual, moral or intellectual attainment and evidence of the 'feminine' capacities of the 'shrieking sisterhood'. In 1908 and 1909 they were relative novelties,[31] as yet uncomplicated by the associations of militant violence: conveniently ambivalent objects that were simultaneously soothing and subversive, celebratory and political, 'art' and propaganda, feminine and feminist.

There were various kinds of precedent for the suffrage banners and one significant point of comparison – with trade-union banners of the 1890s and early 1900s – was constantly returned to in the press and by the women themselves. John Gorman dates the earliest trade-union banner to 1821, but the 1890s was the true decade of 'banner mania', when ambitious examples were produced as part of an 'explosion of new union pageantry' for an expanding and increasingly powerful membership.[32] Women had designed and embroidered many of the most striking Chartist emblems, and it was not uncommon in unions to hear that 'Mother made the first banner the branch had.' But from 1837 more than three quarters of all the banners produced were manufactured by George Tutill, who built up a world-wide near-monopoly that lasted for more than fifty years.[33]

Tutill's banners were mostly expensive, allegorical, very large-scale and painted, with woven surrounds.[34] Most of the suffrage banners, on the other hand, were embroidered or appliquéd. This was significant for several reasons. Although presumably the forerunners of the union banners were the embroidered insignia of the incorporated livery companies, and although men *and* women professionals had produced the work that was the great glory of English embroidery, such needlework had become identified in the course of a series of social and economic shifts as craft rather than art, the product of amateurs rather than professionals, the product – indeed the guarantee – of a chaste and domestic femininity. The Victorians, who revived an interest in medieval embroidery, misconstrued its history according to the ideals of their own time. In their account the medieval embroiderer was not a skilled artisan of either sex but, as they imagined her, the gentlewoman of courtly love or the convent workshop. What such accounts crystallised was the assumption that the embroiderer was a woman who worked out of love and dedication in the service of others. What they masked was the process by which needlework as a middle-class accomplishment kept women chastely at home, producing the adornments which helped to guarantee the social standing of the bourgeois household.[35]

But for women like Mary Lowndes looking for a history and a justification for women's political needlework, the Victorian association of women with embroidery had its uses, in the production of banners that dignified womanly skills while making unwomanly demands. She borrowed from nineteenth-century medievalism the claim that in 'all the ages it has been woman's part to make the banners, if not to carry them,' and mourned the loss of that tradition. 'Woman has been out of work a long time in the matter of adventurous colours'; only women's church banners continued 'to be seen and loved'. But for the first time women were in a position to exploit an ancient, honoured, and particularly female service to their own ends: 'And now into public life comes trooping the feminine; and with the feminine creature come the banners of past times, as well as many other things which people had almost forgotten they were without.'[36]

By conventional criteria, of course, the feminine could *not* by definition come trooping into public life. That was not the arena for women, and straying there would sully them. In Mary Lowndes's account, however, the times were changing. Fighting heroes now came tailor-fitted 'and any flags they want can be ordered from the big manufacturers'. In streets, in camps, on ships, 'a tame uniformity of enormous size and intense vulgarity flaunt the taste of the present day for the shop article'. But with the new century a new phenomenon had come to fruition: 'Political societies started by women, managed by women and sustained by women. In their dire necessity they have been started; with their household wit they manage them; in their poverty, with ingenuity and many labours they sustain them.' The conventional association of embroidery with love (as women's amateur and domestic production it could not be called work), is reversed here to disparage the fighting heroes tailor-fitted (by Tutill's, presumably), and to celebrate by contrast women's su-

perior taste, skills and collective endeavour. She does not use the word but it haunts her text: the associations of chivalry, banners, romance, and common commitment in the pursuit of just ends are those of the crusade. She uses the historical romance of the Middle Ages that was the Victorians' 'dream of order' implicitly to elevate the values of spirituality, femininity and justice above the claims of the tawdry, the commercial and the everyday.[37]

Certainly money came into it. Most trade-union banners were, by suffrage standards, very expensive. In 1890 a 128-by-11-foot woven and painted banner with poles, carrying harness and box cost about £55[38] (more than a year's wages for the highest-paid women industrial workers). The seven great silk banners donated for the 1908 WSPU procession cost 14 guineas each, and the organisers supplied the fabric for 500 others at eight shillings and sixpence each, or sixteen shillings ready-made with appliquéd lettering.[39] The silk and velvet materials for the more ambitious, emblematic banners of the Artists' Suffrage League, produced for the NUWSS procession eight days earlier, cost between fifteen shillings and £2.[40]

Trade-union banners were also much larger. Gwyn Williams remarks an increasing tendency towards banners 'as big as mainsails' that would embody in one enormous and cumulative statement the 'pictorial representation of the craft . . . its Samaritan functions, its history and traditions and its aspirations, all wreathed in scrolls and laurels and figurative females . . . a *cathedral*'.[41] The cumulative effect of women's banners, on the other hand, derived from the honeycomb of their distribution across a particular procession. Some were bigger, but Mary Lowndes suggested that something 4 feet 6 inches by 6 feet 6 inches was 'as large as women . . . can carry should there be any wind'.[42] (The Men's League helped on occasion, but there was a certain pride and significance for the women in carrying their banners themselves.)

33 Electrical trades union banner: woman as angel.

34 National Union of Vehicle Workers (Aldgate
Branch) banner: woman as widow.

Because they are appliquéd, stencilled and embroidered rather than painted, and because of their smaller scale, the women's banners are emblematic rather than pictorial. They conceived of a banner as less of a painting and more of a flag, which sorted better with the methods of the needlewoman than those of George Tutill's teams of portraitist, sign-writer and 'corner-man'. As Mary Lowndes put it, a banner was not a literary affair, or a placard, but 'a thing to float in the wind, to flicker in the breeze, to flirt its colours for your pleasure, to half show and half conceal a device you long to unravel: you do not want to read it, you want to worship it.' Her training as a stained-glass designer encouraged the use of bold appliquéd shapes and a love of full, rich colours (striking combinations of green and blue, magenta and orange) combined with the free use of a heraldic vocabulary. 'You may think over *nebulée*, *ragulée*, *indented*, *engrailed*, as a method for bringing two edges together; your field may be *barred*, *fretty*, or *billetée*, the *chevron*, the *bend*, or the *saltire* may break its surface. There are a score of ways such as I speak of, some simple and easy, as the fesse; some only to be attempted by the most skilled workers, as the blue and white of vair and counter-vair.'[43]

In their designs the labour movement borrowed armorial bearings associated – in fantasy at least – with the craft guilds, and embellished them with all kinds of devices symbolic of the unions' aspirations and fraternal aids: rising suns, clasped hands, the all-seeing masonic eye, the bundle of fasces (united we stand), the serpent of capitalism, the muscular hero, the allegorical feminine virtue. Women had no such half-world of shadowy symbolism on which to draw, and the problems that confronted them in the depiction of women, as heroines or in a variety of female occupations, were difficult to resolve. They did not use 'figurative females' much, nor were their banners 'all wreathed in scrolls and laurels',[44] since they were rooted in arts and crafts embroidery and not in fairground or other vernacular motifs. Only in their cumulative effect did they emphasise a sorority equivalent to the iconography of fraternity packed into a single trade-union image. And it was a sisterhood based on diversity, not on what, for example, workers in a particular occupation held in common: obviously, the power of union organisation depended on a unity of class, whereas the women sought to identify and organise against an oppression shared across the different class positions that inflected it. Between and within the suffrage organisations there were a great many conflicts over questions of class, but the collective rhetoric of the banners, as of the accounts of processions in which they were carried, emphasises above all the image of the milliner or shopgirl shoulder to shoulder with the duchess. As *Votes for Women* described the constituents of the 'Coronation' procession in 1911, they were 'toilers from factory, workshop, field and garret; wave after wave, rank after rank ... Endless it seemed – Science, Art, Medicine, Culture, Ethics, Music, Drama, Poverty, Slumdom, Youth, Age, Sorrow, Labour, Motherhood – all there represented.'[45]

Distinctions between union and suffrage imagery which the suffragists had themselves promoted were in the end taken over by the press and used to divide them. Suffrage banners were praised for their picturesque elegance at the expense of labour images ('tawdry and muscular'),[46] but the femininity that was admired in them came close to repressing their politics and inhibiting their effect. A contributor to the *Vote* in 1910 remarked the crowds at a demonstration in Hyde Park in which a cabinet minister's wife was recognised, but asked whether a single member of the government had looked on. 'This is the sixth great Procession since "the great mud march". The danger is that London may get to regard us as a pageant of music and colour, a mere Roman holiday, and forget our march is the outward and visible sign of an inward and spiritual longing for Freedom and Justice.'[47]

The Iconography of the Banners

Banners can be grouped under three main headings: the regional, the occupational and the historical (celebrating what the *Sunday Times* called 'a Valhalla of Womanhood'). A fourth category emerged as suffrage groups proliferated, which includes the designs for various church bodies and the women's sections of political parties, the Fabian Women's Group, the Women's Tax Resistance League, the Actresses' Franchise League, the Writers' Suffrage League, the Suffrage Atelier and the Artists' Suffrage League themselves.[48]

Regional banners mobilised existing emblems for convenience and legibility. Mary Lowndes specifically recommended the use of 'the old symbols always when they will serve', but with a new twist for the 'new thing we are doing'.[49] Her own East Anglian banner, emblazoned at Mrs Fawcett's request with the wolf's head, crowns and arrows of St Edmund, set them against a regional motto piquantly transposed: Pope Gregory's comment on the English in a Roman slave market – 'Non Angli sed Angeli' – became 'Non Angeli sed Angli', in approximation to 'Not Angels but Citizens'.

Occupational banners ranged from the Home-Makers' ('Remember their Homeless Sisters') to new professions for women like medicine and shorthand ('Speed! Fight On'). Struggles to expand the limited field of middle-class women's employment had been a crucial impetus in the Victorian women's movement and one of its dominant themes. Occupational banners were intended to consolidate women's achievements thus far and spur them to further goals including that full citizenship which their ambitions and attainments merited. Against the fragile but still dominant assertion that women's place was in the home, such banners demonstrated that women could, and did, and had to, operate successfully in the public sphere. And if they looked sufficiently 'womanly' on their processions, beneath insignia embroid-

35 Banner of the Oxfordshire, Buckinghamshire and Berkshire Federation of the NUWSS, probably designed and executed by the Artists' Suffrage League.

ered with feminine taste and skill, then perhaps the anxieties aroused by their as yet limited invasion of public life might be expediently contained. (It is not unusual to discover the subjects of contemporary interviews with successful women insisting, in covert apology or compensation, on their particular love of needlework.)[50]

Most of the occupational banners celebrate middle-class careers. No Victorian or Edwardian working woman had to struggle to be accepted as a rag-picker, a Cradley Heath chainmaker, a textile operative or any of the other occupations that did not register in the public mind as 'unfeminine' because they did not much register in it at all. Many working-class women's occupations, much sweated labour and home-working for example, were invisible, and made no real dent on the image of idealised femininity which in fact required the economic security of the bourgeois family to support it.

In the labour movement, where we might have expected to find representations of working women, they are rare. On trade-union banners women are chiefly angels or widows: they are allegorical and they inspire, or they are concrete and they are bereft. In these roles they share between them the function of indicating the aspirations of the movement on the one hand and the material benefits of union organisation on the other. Only in exceptional instances (on some of the textile-union banners for example) do women appear as workers themselves.

Most of the regional banners are now lost or dispersed. There were probably few professional banners – the NUWSS pamphlet lists ten and there is evidence of a handful more – of which about seven remain. But the 'heroine' banners commemorating famous women for the procession of 13 June 1908 are preserved as a set in the collections of the Fawcett Library and the Museum of London. Most of these were designed by Mary Lowndes and all of them were made by members of the Artists' Suffrage League. The collection as a

36 'Caroline Herschel' banner: designed and worked by the Artists' Suffrage League, 1908.
Caroline Herschel (1750–1848) was the sister of William Herschel and an astronomer in her own right.

whole evoked a pantheon of virtues, in Cicely Hamilton's phrase, 'a pageant of great women': a scattered pedigree for the 'relative creatures' of the second sex.[51]

It was not uncommon for union banners to be embellished with portraits of MPs (notably Keir Hardie), labour-movement leaders or celebrated luminaries like Marx or Lenin, sometimes all together in the same image. There are few equivalents to this in women's banners. (Significantly, the portrait head of Mrs Pankhurst on one of the WSPU banners in 1908 was the work of a commercial manufacturer, probably Tutill or Toye.) It is historic women that the commemorative banners celebrate, with the exception of Florence Nightingale who died in 1910 at the age of ninety, and the model they remind us of is Boccaccio's *De Claris Mulieribus* and other instances of the 'famous women' genre. This was a favourite theme in sixteenth-century embroidery, but as Rozsika Parker indicates, an ambivalent one on which to draw.[52] It commemorated selected individuals for their unique qualities while ensuring that the capacities attributed to the sex as a whole remained unchanged.

What the suffrage artists attempted in resurrecting this tradition was the celebration of a large number of women, most of them from the eighteenth and nineteenth centuries, whose attributes could be held to be present but repressed in the sex as a whole.[53] Many of them were women active in fields far removed from the province of domestic virtue (Mary Somerville, Marie Curie, Caroline Herschel); others were exemplary in a traditionally pious and nurturing role (Elizabeth Fry, Florence Nightingale); still others were militant heroines of national sentiment (Boadicea). The effect was to emphasise their diversity, their status as part of a 'women's history' and ultimately to stress their distinction as part of a political argument for reconsidering the social roles of women and their potential as full citizens. The purpose of the 'heroine' banners was to be celebratory, com-

memorative, inspirational, educational and political all at once. In Lady Frances Balfour's rolling cadences, on 13 June 1908 'Many a legend, many a history, many a consecrated life in the roll-call of our "rough island story", went down the long lane which for us women has come to the turning. If to some the march was a trial to mind and body, faith and courage were renewed, and those of little faith were rebuked as they ranged themselves under the names of the strong hearts, now at rest, who had so bravely fought in their day and for their generation.'[54] Lest these points should be lost, they were set out and circulated in accompanying commentaries of one kind and another: in the suffragist press, in those submitted to editors looking for copy to go with their topical photographs and in pamphlets distributed where the banners were later exhibited. Together, the historical, regional and occupational banners outlined in 'womanly' stitchery the range and relevance claimed for the movement, in contrast with the narrow privilege of the anti societies organised in 1908, and also with the labour movement's emphasis on unity and the image of the manual (and masculine) worker. Suffrage imagery stresses diversity, against a single notion of what 'femininity' was and against a widespread fear that women would vote 'all one way'.

Banner Makers and Designers

A cautious estimate would assume that at least 150 banners were produced between 1908 and the NUWSS Pilgrimage of 1913.[55] Those responsible for their design and execution were, principally, the Artists' Suffrage League, the Suffrage Atelier,[56] and their friends. Behind these lay the names of several other artists (Laurence and Clemence Housman, May Morris, Mary Sargant Florence and Sylvia Pankhurst); large numbers of anonymous women responsible for the execution of their work; local branches that devised and carried out their own designs; and quite complex and obscure questions to do with the interests of

37 WSPU banner-making for the procession of 23 July
1910 (the structures resting against the wall are visible
in press photographs of the demonstration).

the designer, the skills of the executant, the
demands and expectations of the client and the
relations between all three.

Most of the banners that survive were designed
by the Artists' Suffrage League (which means in
effect by Mary Lowndes) for the National Union,
its constituent societies or professional groups that
were loosely allied with it. Mary Lowndes's album
in the Fawcett Collection contains many of the
designs for the 'famous women' series of 1908 with
fabric samples attached and many regional devices
for provincial societies, others of which may have
failed to heed the inscription to 'please return'.
Some of these were executed by members of the
League themselves. Referring to the exhibition of
banners in Caxton Hall which preceded the

NUWSS procession of 1908, the *Daily News* remarked that 'eighty ladies have accomplished the task since Christmas,' and another, unidentified, press cutting refers to 200 members of the League carrying out designs.[57] Their 1910 *Report* records the completion of banners for Manchester, Woking, Weybridge, Epsom and the Hants and Sussex Federation at their King's Road premises. Others were presumably carried out by the local societies that had commissioned the design, as the students of Girton and Newnham embroidered the 'Cambridge Alumnae' banner that Mary Lowndes drew up for them in 1908.

At this same moment in the late spring of 1908 the WSPU was also commissioning a series of banners, partly to their own designs and chiefly from a commercial manufacturer. In preparation for their march on 21 June they planned a ceremonial 'unfurling' on 17 June in the Queen's Hall. The *Evening News and Evening Mail* announced on 15 May that 'excitement at present centres chiefly in eight large silk banners which are being prepared in strict secrecy.' Six would have green backgrounds, one would be white, and the last purple (i.e. they would all be in the newly established WSPU colours). Mrs Pethick-Lawrence was presenting the purple banner and promised that its motto would be 'almost as startling as the final shout of the combined hosts' at the culminating meeting in Hyde Park: it turned out to be a portrait head of Mrs Pankhurst with the motto 'Deeds Not Words', the date of the WSPU's founding – 1903 – and the inscription (from George Eliot): 'Famed far for deeds of daring rectitude'. Four of the other banners were designed by Sylvia Pankhurst. That for the Bradford Union had the city arms with the motto 'Grant to Womanhood the Justice England should be proud to give'. A second, entwined with wreaths of flowers, proclaimed that 'Human Emancipation must Precede Social Regeneration'. A third, depicting a pelican feeding its young from its breast (a traditional emblem of religious sacrifice), carried the motto 'Strong Souls Live, Like

Fire-Hearted Suns, to Spend their Strength'. The last, just visible in contemporary photographs with Christabel and Mrs Pethick-Lawrence posed in front of it, had 'Rebellion to Tyrants is Obedience to God' worked in gold lettering on a violet ground with roses, thistles and shamrocks. All of these were large (eight by nine feet), and relatively expensive at 14 guineas each.[58] Only Laurence Housman's 'From Prison to Citizenship' design for the Kensington branch was worked by local members, who may have become in the process the nucleus for the Suffrage Atelier the following year.[59]

Atelier banners are hard to identify and few have survived. Nor is it quite clear (because the few references in her letters confuse the issue) whether Clemence Housman worked *for* the Atelier or as a member of it. Laurence referred to her as 'chief banner-maker to the Suffrage between the years 1908 and 1914'. She probably worked on the 'From Prison to Citizenship' design; she certainly executed her brother's banner for the Church League for Women's Suffrage which is now in the Museum of London; and she worked another of his designs for the United Suffragists, a group formed in 1914.[60] She made up a Conservative banner that is now lost, she may have worked the Oxford Graduates' banner designed by E. H. New, she probably made the Actresses' banner, and there is much to suggest this was only a part of her output.[61]

At moments of pressure before the really large demonstrations, hundreds of anonymous women, 'nimble fingered ladies of all classes'[62] as the press described them, were busy stitching banners for processional use. In Elizabeth Robins's account of the preparations for the 'Women's Coronation Procession' of 1911, women were active in centres all over London, cutting, sewing, stencilling, gilding. 'The hours are long in these places where the preparations go forward, but the women who work longest are the women who have the privilege (as some think it) to play all the time, if they prefer.

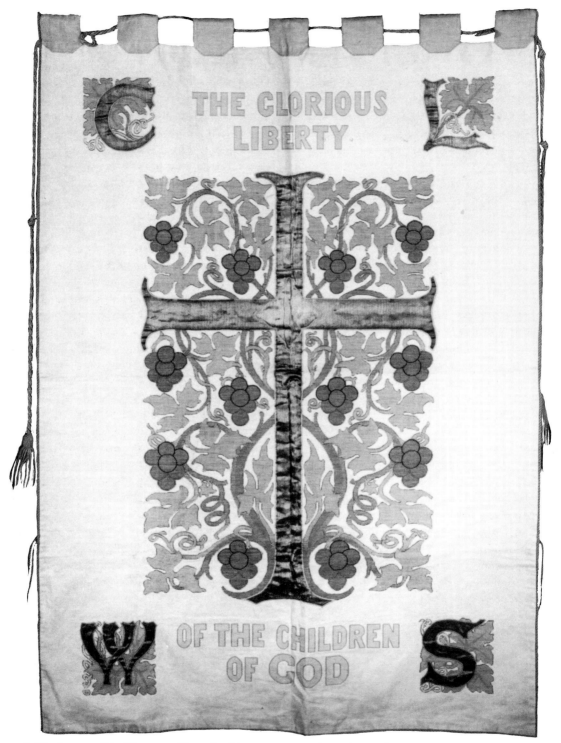

38 The banner of the Hampstead branch of the
'Church League for Women's Suffrage' (founded
1909), worked by Clemence Housman to a design by
Laurence Housman.

Women who have never worked hard before have been working for the Pageant these hot June days, from eight in the morning till ten at night.' At the other end of the social scale 'dressmakers in a small way of business have been among the best and most generous helpers.'[63]

Professional needlewomen were no doubt in particular demand, but most women of the middle classes were in this period sufficiently competent to lend a hand where it was required. It was almost unthinkable that a respectably brought up Victorian or Edwardian woman should be unable to sew. Banner work could draw on a common fund of female skills (Mary Lowndes insisted that if you could make your curtains you could make a banner) and in consequence a mixed but willing and unpaid workforce, in a way that was not available to men. Three kinds of needlework activity had contributed to the comfortable familiarity of the Victorian woman with her sewing materials, and all in different ways had enhanced the standing of the 'Angel in the House'. The first was a tradition of domestic embroidery that had filled the bourgeois home with anti-macassar covers, mantelpiece drapes, smoking caps and slippers, often in Berlin woolwork. The second was a revived tradition of ecclesiastical embroidery, often from medieval models, instigated by the architects and theorists of the Gothic Revival who frowned on domestic 'trumpery'. And the third was made up of 'art needlework' promoted by the practitioners of the arts and crafts movement. A generation of needlewomen in this last tradition worked coverlets, portières, religious items and finally suffrage banners in appliqué and crewel stitch, with silks and velvets that might have been used in the drawing room and lettering that might have been embroidered on altar cloths, but now with an unexpectedly radical intent.

Traditional embroidery had enabled women to sit companionably together and not feel that they were neglecting their families or their household tasks. Organisations such as the Ladies' Ecclesi-astical Embroidery Society flourished because women wished to work together on projects that were both communal and creative. These pleasures were drawn into the collective banner-making of the suffrage movement too. ('Clearly remembered still are the humours and the work in the little white studio in a Kensington garden, lent for the making of 252 great caps and banners and the hundreds of smaller flags.')[64] For partisan women the campaign offered all the satisfaction of collective and creative work directed, in Mary Lowndes's expression, 'for the first time in history to illumine woman's own adventure'. One banner embodies this best: the WSPU Holloway banner which bears the signatures of eighty prisoners imprisoned and forcibly fed in the suffrage cause. Some of the signatures are beautifully, and some clumsily stitched. The needlework is as personal as the handwriting within its art-nouveau frame. But the tradition of women's needlework, of embroidered mementos and 'friendship quilts' is put here to a new and more militant purpose.

The Major Processions in the Suffrage Campaign

By the autumn of 1906 the WSPU was established in London, growing in strength and engaged in the development of a policy of militant activity which owed something to the tactics of the Independent Labour Party: heckling meetings, organising deputations and courting imprisonment. Although the traditional societies had not been idle they had not been visible, and in avoiding controversy they had, in the eyes of the general public, prevented their cause from seeming either topical or urgent. The WSPU led the way in demonstrating that the press was there to be used: the established press with its penchant for moral and political deliberation, but more particularly the popular press, with its appetite for sensational copy and striking photographs, and eventually a developed suffrage press ready with analysis and detailed commentary on suffrage activities.

In making their cause more newsworthy and more vital (albeit at the same time more controversial), the WSPU spurred the older societies to do the same. The NUWSS 'Mud March' of February 1907 – so-called because of the mud, slush and fog through which 3000 women trudged from Hyde Park Corner to the Exeter Hall – was the first public open-air demonstration the non-militants had ever held. In the years between 1906 and 1909, inspired or provoked by the WSPU, the NUWSS threw itself into processions, election activity and other forms of agitation new to it, in an attempt to vindicate the constitutional movement while emulating the dedication and commitment of the militants. Having borrowed the concept of the demonstration from the WSPU they were also prepared to surpass them at this moment in carrying it out.[65] Although modest by subsequent standards, the 1907 procession was the largest and most significant ever held – a bid for the kind of publicity the militants had attained, but by more peaceful methods which would advertise the cause without alienating its potential support.

The NUWSS was encouraged in this strategy by its assessment of the political climate. With a Liberal government returned to power, a rapidly increasing membership and a revived campaign, they believed they would be able to persuade Parliament to effect a measure of women's suffrage. They had only to prove that women themselves wanted the vote and that there was sufficient popular support behind them. They were probably wrong in this belief, which underestimated the opposition to women's suffrage in the government and overestimated Liberal commitment to a principle which the party was unlikely to consider separately from its consequences, or from other measures of electoral reform. But it was the NUWSS reading of the situation nonetheless, and it raised their hopes and encouraged the adoption of unusual tactics which were to include for the first time the large-scale public demonstration.

The Mud March, 9 February 1907

What became known as the Mud March had its origins in a meeting of the Central Society for Women's Suffrage, one of the constituent bodies of the NUWSS, in November 1906.[66] A large open-air demonstration was proposed which would coincide with the opening of the next session of Parliament, and in which all the women's organisations would participate. The proposal was adopted, but it quickly ran into difficulties. It appeared that the Women's Liberal Federation (a crucial lever on the Liberal government) and the British Women's Temperance Association were unlikely to participate if the WSPU was invited; and the Women's Co-operative Guild was only prepared to come if the resolution at the final meeting was drawn up on terms which did not refer to the conditions on which the franchise should be granted. All sensibilities and political disagreements had to be soothed in order to ensure that the demonstration was as representative as possible. The terms of the resolution were decided, and after some discussion it was finally agreed on 16 January 1907 'that as the WLF and the BWTA were unable to join in procession with the Social and Political Union, no official invitation should be sent to S & P Union to cooperate in the Procession'. (Despite many subsequent attempts to achieve a united constitutional and militant demonstration, this was to happen only once, in 1911.)

On 29 January the Executive Committee held a special meeting to consider final arrangements for the march. A diagram for the formation of the procession in Hyde Park was submitted, reports were received as to the value of tickets and donations, advertisements for the *Morning Post* and the front page of the *Tribune* were agreed for February, and an organist was hired for the Exeter Hall. Everything was in hand. Only the outcome was uncertain, and even in the emotionally uncommunicative framework of a committee minutebook the apprehension is almost palpable.

Shortly after 2 pm on the wet and dreary afternoon of 9 February, 3000 women led by Lady Frances Balfour, Lady Strachey, Mrs Fawcett and Dr Edith Pechey-Phipson[67] marched with banners and massed bands from Hyde Park Corner to the Exeter Hall: 'long skirts trailing on the ground, and hearts in which enthusiasm struggled successfully with propriety'.[68] It was a gay enough procession by most accounts, despite the weather. Little touches of red and white splashed its length in rosettes and favours,[69] posies bound with red and white ribbons, cars and carriages decorated with scarlet and white shields, street vendors selling red and white handkerchief programmes and, above the line, white banners with vivid scarlet lettering. The Northern Franchise Demonstration Committee, which had arranged to halt and hold its own meeting in Trafalgar Square, was accompanied by the brilliant silk banners of the women's trade unions represented in it. Behind them followed the white banner of the NUWSS with its scarlet motto: 'The Franchise is the Keystone of our Liberty'. The branches of the Central Society, headed by a band, carried more banners: 'Gentle but Resolute' (South Kensington); 'Failure is Impossible' (Fulham); 'For Hearth and Home'; 'Be Right and Persist'; 'Representation our Goal'; and 'Justice not Privilege'.

More than forty organisations took part (though not, officially, the WSPU), and even *The Times* acknowledged that the demonstration was remarkable 'as much for its representative character as for its size'. There were 'plenty of well-dressed ladies and a few persons of distinction' to head it and 'a long line of carriages and motor-cars to wind it up, – altogether an imposing and representative array'. The *Tribune* remarked particularly on the social mix in the procession over all. This was to become a leitmotif of many a subsequent account; one of the aspects of a suffrage procession which struck the press most forcibly was the sight of women of different classes marching side by side. (Or perhaps, one suspects, that of a collectivity of different women at all, as opposed to that unified

and abstract 'Womanhood' which dominated the imaginations and the arguments of the masculine bourgeoisie.) The *Tribune* discovered that, 'Not one class of women alone was represented in this great procession of voteless citizens who had come to plead at the bar of public opinion for the right to representation in the counsels of the State ... There were the brilliant women of the London world, high-born dames with their Girton and Newnham daughters, there were literary and professional women by the hundred – the woman doctor, the high school mistress, the woman artist – and there were the women of the great industrial north – women who had left their factories in far-away Lancashire to take part in the march.' (There was also a small and unofficial contingent from the WSPU, led by Charlotte Despard who exchanged rueful glances with Inspector Jarvis, an old acquaintance from Cannon Row police station.)

Despite the rain the route was thronged with onlookers attracted, apparently, by the novel spectacle of women marching in the London streets. The impact the procession made on them is hard to gauge. Their reactions were ambivalent, and press reports are inflected by the sympathy or otherwise of particular newspapers for the suffrage cause. A paper which stressed that nothing was more marked than 'the altered demeanour of crowds of spectators' went on to publish a quite contrary account by one of the participants called 'How it Felt: Reflections on Men's Chivalry', which remarked on 'the insults the women had to endure'.[70] 'There can be nothing worse to the average woman,' she continued, 'than the sensation of being ruthlessly planted in full view of all the people she knows and does not know.' Or as the *Manchester Guardian* put it: 'Nobody can suppose that most of the women who took part ... can have done so for sport or for the pleasure of the thing ... It requires some courage for a woman to step out of her drawing room into the street to take her place in a mixed throng for a cause probably distasteful to

SNAPSHOTS OF INCIDENTS OF SUFFRAGETTES' MARCH FROM HYDE PARK TO THE STRAND.

Suffragettes marching gaily through the mud on Saturday from Hyde Park Corner to the Strand. Mrs. Despard (marked with a cross) is one of the leaders of the movement.—(*Daily Mirror* photograph.)

Red and white were the colours worn by the suffragettes on their march. (1) A policeman being offered a badge. (2) Lady Carlisle's daughter carrying a banner in the procession.—(*Daily Mirror* photographs.)

Titled demonstrators formed part of the striking procession of suffragettes— (1) Lady Frances Balfour, (2) Mrs. Fawcett, (3) Lady Strachey.—(*Daily Mirror* photograph.)

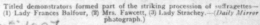

The procession starting from Hyde Park, showing the deputations from the Midlands and the North of England. (*Daily Mirror* photograph.)

Lady Carlisle and her daughter in the ranks of the suffragettes.—(*Daily Mirror* photograph.)

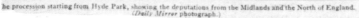

39 Incidents from the Mud March, 9 February 1907 (*Daily Mirror*, 13 February 1907).

SUPPLEMENT TO THE GRAPHIC, February 16, 1907. 3

ATTENDING TO THE INNER WOMAN

DISTRIBUTING BADGES

THE CHILD IS MOTHER OF THE WOMAN

WELL MANNERED AND WELL BANNERED

"OH, MAUDE, BE CAREFUL AND DO HOLD IT UP"

PARK RAILINGS HAVE NO TERRORS FOR THE SUFFRAGETTE

THE MILITARY TYPE

GENERAL AND HER AIDE

THE MASCULINE TYPE

SWEET GIRL GRADUATES

WON'T YOU JOIN US SISTER!

PEACEFUL PERSUASION

AN EXCEPTION TO THE GENERALLY RESPECTFUL DEMEANOUR

"How dare those opposed to woman's suffrage," asked Mr. Zangwill at Exeter Hall, whither the army of suffragists marched in the mud and rain the other day, "defend their monstrous proposition that one-half of the human race shall have no votes?" "Let the House of Lords," he added, "be replaced by a House of Ladies." He certainly struck the note of the afternoon. The army stormed Trafalgar Square, and bombarded the crowd with speeches. Many women's interests were represented—cigar-makers, power-loom weavers, pipe-finishers, shirt-makers, textile workers, hank and bobbin winders, gassers, doublers, reelers—as was shown by the banners. Among the demonstrators were the grey-haired Lady Strachey, Lady Carlisle and her two daughters, Lady Frances Balfour, Mrs. Fawcett, Lady Cecilia Roberts, and Lady Dorothy Howard.

The Suffragists' Progress: Incidents of the Latest London Demonstration

DRAWN BY RALPH CLEAVER

40 The Mud March (*The Graphic*, 16 February 1907).

many or most of her acquaintance, and to see herself pilloried in the newspapers next morning by name as one of the "Suffragettes". That old ladies and delicate ones, and timid ones to boot, should have done this quite simply and bravely argues at least a good deal of quiet conviction and a resolution not likely to be easily broken.'

In this light, women's distaste for public display became, like the weather, an obstacle that proved the strength of their conviction. No one was quoted in the press as having enjoyed the experience, although the working women portrayed on the cover of *Black and White* look cheerful enough.[71] The *Daily Graphic* insisted that women 'as well as men, have a perfect right to march in orderly procession through the streets,' and claimed that 'such a means of demonstrating political convictions is both convenient and valuable.' There are hints that the working-class women, for whom respectability was a very important issue but one measured by slightly different criteria, had a more enjoyable experience than their middle-class sisters who grimly endured it; and also that the mood of all the participants lightened into a spontaneous camaraderie as they began to feel that the 'exceedingly unpleasant task'[72] they had set themselves might have some effect. According to one of the demonstrators writing in the *Manchester Guardian*, it was not the status implied by the cars and carriages alone, or the banners, or the mix of working women, artists, doctors, nurses, teachers and writers, but the whole spectacle of thousands of women 'who would not naturally court the public gaze, tramping through muddy streets for the sake of an ideal' that 'bettered all our old arguments and all our faultless logic'. They poured into the Exeter Hall with their furled banners, changed by the experience. 'We had done what had seemed to so many the ridiculous thing, and the crowd, by taking us seriously, had robbed it of its absurdity.'

The Mud March, modest and uncertain as it was by subsequent standards, established the

precedent of large-scale processions, carefully ordered and publicised, accompanied by banners, bands and the colours of participant societies. 'In that year,' Ray Strachey argued, 'the vast majority of women still felt that there was something very dreadful in walking in procession through the streets; to do it was to be something of a martyr, and many of the demonstrators felt that they were risking their employments and endangering their reputations, besides facing a dreadful ordeal of ridicule and public shame. They walked, and nothing happened. The small boys in the streets and the gentlemen at the club windows laughed, but that was all. Crowds watched and wondered; and it was not so dreadful after all . . . the idea of a public demonstration of faith in the Cause took root.'[73] And with it the constitutionalists joined the militants as part of a movement emerging from the 'region of the debating society into that of what is called "practical politics" '.[74]

The *Tribune* was premature, however, in concluding that the 'woman's battle is practically won'. A new strategy was triumphantly established, a large amount of publicity was acquired, and even their opponents conceded that the suffragists had made an impressive and dignified display. But for the battle to be won Parliament had to be convinced, or more precisely – given that a majority of Liberal MPs had supposedly pledged their support – conviction had to be translated into the successful passage of a bill for women's enfranchisement.

Four days after the procession the NUWSS executive committee met with the Parliamentary Committee for Women's Suffrage to discuss the introduction of such a bill. At the same time the WSPU 'Women's Parliament' passed a resolution condemning the omission of women's suffrage from the King's Speech, and sent a deputation of about 400 women who tried to deliver it to the Prime Minister. Refusing to halt outside Westminster Abbey, they were ridden down by mounted policemen and for several hours embroiled in a mêlée from which fifty-one women were eventually arrested. On 8 March Willoughby Dickinson, the Liberal MP for St Pancras North, introduced a Women's Enfranchisement Bill for its second reading.[75] The NUWSS went to considerable lengths to organise support for it, hoping that the momentum of their march would augment a campaign of letters and deputations to MPs. Several speakers noted the large attendance for the second reading and the serious demeanour of the debate. Despite this, however, Dickinson's bill was talked out on 9 March like many of its predecessors. Their efforts come to nothing, the NUWSS turned to the by-election work already initiated by the WSPU.

In the months following the defeat of Dickinson's bill, MPs were lobbied, new branches founded, speaking tours organised, caravan tours despatched, by-elections contested, all kinds of church, women's and political associations addressed, marches held in regional centres and thousands of meetings arranged.[76] In all this, parliamentary leaders continued to demand 'proof' that large numbers of women wanted the vote; without it, they were not inclined to take the question seriously.

The Conservative leader Arthur Balfour, in private correspondence with Christabel Pankhurst in the autumn of 1907, refused the invitation to make a public statement on the possibility of a government measure should the Conservatives be returned to office at the next election. But he was prepared to accept that 'if it can be shown either that women as a class seriously desire the franchise, or that serious legislative injustices are being done them . . . the change should be made.' (Christabel's response voiced the exasperation of all active suffragists: 'If only you would say what you would regard as proof that a demand exists! I know that we can fulfil any condition that you may lay down, but at present we are working in the dark.'[77]) Herbert Asquith, Chancellor of the Exchequer and already rumoured to be the next prime minister, echoed Balfour's views in December. 'I am prepared to withdraw my opposition, which is a very unimportant factor in the case . . . the moment I am satisfied of two things, but not before, namely, first that the majority of women desire to have a parliamentary vote, and next, that the conferring of a vote upon them would be advantageous to their sex and the community at large.'[78]

Christabel's response lay in the formulation of a 'comprehensive plan of campaign', announced in the January 1908 issue of *Votes for Women*, which would culminate in a mass meeting in Hyde Park on 21 June. The NUWSS, apparently independently of the WSPU, was also planning a spring demonstration; and such plans could only have been confirmed by the contribution of Herbert Gladstone, the Home Secretary, to the debate on the second reading of Henry York Stanger's bill to enfranchise women on 28 February. 'On the question of women's suffrage, experience shows that predominance of argument alone, and I believe that this has been attained, is not enough to win the political day . . . There comes the time when political dynamics are far more important than political argument . . . Men have learned this lesson, and know the necessity for demonstrating the greatness of their movements, and for establishing that *force majeure* which actuates and arms a government for effective work. That is the task before the supporters of this great movement . . . Looking back at the great political crises in the thirties, the sixties and the eighties it will be found that people . . . assembled in their tens of thousands all over the country . . . Of course it cannot be expected that women can assemble in such masses, but power belongs to the masses, and through this power a government can be influenced into more effective action than a government will be likely to take under present conditions.'[79]

Stanger's bill passed its second reading by 179 votes, but was referred to a committee of the whole House and hence effectively blocked. Nevertheless Gladstone's statement was taken by many to indicate, as Sylvia Pankhurst put it, that 'the government was not hostile, and waited only a larger manifestation of demand.' The NUWSS in particular was encouraged to believe that propaganda was effective in influencing MPs and, given the predominance of Liberals supporting them in the division lobby, that their faith in the Liberal Party was not misplaced. The constitutionalists, committed by definition to non-militant activity, were coming to believe that only the mass demonstration could provide evidence – through its scale that large numbers of women wanted the vote, and through its administration and design that the community at large would gain by it. These were the two things of which Asquith claimed he needed to be convinced. The moment he was satisfied on them he had promised to withdraw his objections. And in April Asquith became prime minister.

The NUWSS Demonstration of 13 June 1908[80]

Asquith's public pronouncement was treated as an undertaking by the suffrage movement, a call which it set out to meet. Accounts of preparations for the 13 June procession, in both the national and the suffrage press, stressed the importance of 'women of all shades of opinions on Suffrage methods and of all religious and political parties'[81] sinking their differences and speaking with one voice in the demonstration and at its culmination in the Albert Hall. Once they had proved the case 'that their movement is really all that is claimed for it, and that behind it there is the powerful fulcrum of public opinion', the battle would be won.[82]

A special NUWSS Procession Committee was set up, an appeal for funds inaugurated, and negotiations entered into with the various railway companies (whose cooperation was essential for a truly large-scale and national representation).[83] Caroline Watts designed the Bugler Girl poster for the Artists' Suffrage League – 'a woman trumpeter, standing on ramparts, flag in hand, and blowing an inspiriting call to the women of Great Britain to come out and stand by their sisters in this

fight'[84] – and it was displayed on hoardings all over the country in the weeks leading up to the day of the demonstration. Shops were taken, meetings held and posters, leaflets and procession maps distributed: publicity material that enhanced the promise of a stirring spectacle and whetted the appetite of the national and local newspapers. The richly embroidered banners worked by the Artists' League, and exhibited in Caxton Hall, attracted considerable attention as what even the hostile *Times* referred to as the art exhibition of the year. ('London will have a new experience; and if it be true that who wins the eye wins all, the Artists' Suffrage League will not have laboured in vain.')[85]

Advance publicity like this was crucial, especially when the suffrage press was in its infancy. Only with its aid could the artists, organisers and participants feel confident in their enterprise, the Albert Hall be sold out in advance and the public, schooled in the politics of the campaign and attentive to the symbolism of the march, be encouraged to line its route. Publicity bred further publicity, since if the crowds were persuaded to turn it into a national event, the procession would secure the attention of reporters and leader-writers for days, perhaps weeks, to come.

On the morning of 13 June *The Times* published Mrs Fawcett's lengthy account of the preparations for the afternoon's procession and its plan of march. She stressed the scale of the demonstration, with thousands of women arriving by special trains from Liverpool, Manchester, Sheffield, Nottingham, Leeds, Leicester, Hull, Birmingham, Bristol and assorted towns along the route. There would even be representatives from America, Europe and India. She promised a glorious spectacle enhanced by the gowns of doctors and graduates and 'nearly a thousand beautiful banners and bannerettes, each different, each wrought in gorgeous colour and rich materials'. She listed the well-known women participating in the demonstration and speaking at the Albert Hall (Lady Henry Somerset, 'most eloquent of Englishwomen', the Reverend Anna Shaw, 'the most distinguished woman speaker of the United States') or contributing their musical and artistic talents to the occasion. She acknowledged the special participation of working women, some at the risk of forfeited wages or even dismissal, but 'feeling themselves bound in duty to take up Mr Asquith's challenge'. She argued that women, precisely because their life experience was different from men's, needed the vote if Parliament were to be truly representative of 'the whole rather than only one half of the nation'; and she asked, mischievously, what other political reform could unite in its support the late Marquess of Salisbury and Keir Hardie, George Meredith and the Right Hon. Richard Seddon, Archbishop Temple and George Bernard Shaw. In short she pleaded the women's cause, while at the same time promising London 'the opportunity of seeing a street procession unique in character, not only in this country, but in any part of the world'.

The impact of the Mud March had been enhanced by the dignity and determination of its participants, the gaiety of their red and white favours, the appeal of the mottoes on their banners and the organisational skills evident in the whole enterprise. But above all else it derived from the novelty of the spectacle, which rested on the impropriety, by conventional standards, of women demonstrating on the public streets at all.

That card was a risky one, and it could not be played twice. The 1908 procession had to be made to surpass the Mud March by means other than the courting of notoriety. The solution was to 'embroider' the precedent of 1907: symbolically, by elaborating its political arguments and orchestrating their presence as spectacle, and literally, through the production of an unprecedented series of art-needlework banners that would embellish and articulate the procession at the same time as they guaranteed the 'womanliness' of its participants. The traditional associations of the political demonstration were by these means transformed

in what the press subsequently referred to as 'a masterpiece of stage management'.[86] With elegant sleight of hand, women responded to the accusation that they were 'making a spectacle of themselves' by doing precisely that, in full self-consciousness and with great skill and ingenuity.[87] They were indeed part of the spectacle, but they also produced and controlled it; as active agents they need not passively endure the gaze of onlookers who were curious or perhaps indifferent. They could invite it, respond to it, work with it and then move on. Their bodies were organised collectively and invested politically and therefore resistant to any simply voyeuristic appropriation.

Perhaps this is why they seem also to have enjoyed themselves, no longer facing 'a dreadful ordeal of ridicule and public shame'[88] as in 1907, but arriving at the Albert Hall flushed with pleasure and triumph. 'A new force is making its mark upon the history of the race,' Cicely Hamilton wrote as a participant in the *Daily Mail*, 'the force of a womanhood conscious of its own individuality, conscious of latent capacities and eager, fiercely eager, to develop them – a womanhood that declines to see life henceforth only through the eyes of men, and will take upon its own soul the responsibility for its own actions.'[89] In struggling to change their political circumstances, women were also changing themselves.

From eleven o'clock on the morning of 13 June, suffragists poured into the London termini on special trains from all over England. They were met by station stewards wearing red and white scarves, whisked off to Strand restaurants for quick lunches where necessary and escorted to the Embankment by tube. Robing rooms were provided in Buckingham Street for the medical and university women, and their hats and coats were taken in boxes to await them at the Albert Hall.

By two o'clock the Embankment presented a scene 'of extraordinary animation and brilliance'[90] as the skeleton of the procession, sketched out with banners and placards held by messenger boys, began to fill in six abreast. By 2.30 pm crowds thronged the adjacent streets and tram traffic to and from Westminster had to be stopped, but the procession continued to form up smoothly and without confusion as stewards marshalled participants to their appointed blocks. From the bottom of Northumberland Avenue it stretched for two miles along the Embankment to Westminster Bridge, up Bridge Street, round the corner into Parliament Street and down Whitehall in a peaceful embrace of the government offices.

As three o'clock approached the river side of the Embankment flooded with thousands of dark-suited home-bound city commuters – the *Daily Telegraph* remarked that by their timing the women 'secured an audience at once important and sympathetic' – while on the other thousands of curious onlookers spilled on to the street, milling around the long phalanx of women in summer dresses, watching the stewards in red and white sashes marshal the last participants, waiting expectantly for something to happen as the processionists were told: 'What you are doing today will be in the history books.'[91]

Punctually at three, with a drum roll as signal, the procession led off to the music of the Walthamstow silver band: 'a bright river flowing between the banks of the jostling crowd', 'in faultless array', and 'under a display of banners the like of which, for artistic effect and "flaunted argument", has never before been seen in London'.[92]

At its head was the banner of the National Union with the motto 'The Franchise is the Keystone of Our Liberties'. Beneath its folds walked Mrs Fawcett, president of the NUWSS, in the blue and scarlet robes of an honorary LL.D. of St Andrew's University; Lady Frances Balfour, president of the London Society for Women's Suffrage; Dr Sophie Bryant of the Education Committee of the LCC; and Miss Emily Davies, whose appearance at the start of the procession had sent up a cheer along the column and from the crowd. She had handed in the first women's suffrage petition to John Stuart

Mill in 1866, and now in her late seventies she walked the two miles to the Albert Hall because 'I should never have forgiven myself if I had missed such a magnificent tribute to our work.'[93]

The first of the eight major blocks of the demonstration was made up of the provincial societies of the NUWSS, arranged alphabetically under their banners from Bristol to Worcester. Each of them represented a device, a local dignitary or events of some celebrity and an appropriate motto. Women from East Anglia walked under the flag of St Edmund ('Non Angeli sed Angli'), and from Portsmouth under the anchor from Nelson's *Victory* ('Engage the Enemy More Closely'). Warwick had 'Might is Right', Stratford 'To Be Or Not To Be', Manchester 'Now or Never', Cheltenham 'Be Just and Fear Not', Brighton 'In Deo Fidemus', Hazlemere 'Weaving Fair and Weaving Free England's Web of Destiny', Leeds 'Leeds for Liberty' and North Hertfordshire 'North Herts Undaunted'.

The local societies were accompanied by the banner of the International Delegates, and with it a contingent of colonial and foreign representatives with their national flags. Indian women wore saris, French women carried the banner of Marie Curie, Australian women the banner (now in the Fawcett collection) with the motto 'Trust the Women, Mother, as I have done', and there were representatives from Irish and Scottish societies, together with a strong American contingent which included a deputation from the League of Self-Supporting Women of New York. This section was much commented on in the press, which noted the presence of the Reverend Anna Shaw, the 'silver-tongued orator' from Philadelphia, Miss Anthony (Susan B. Anthony's niece) and Mrs McCulloch, the only woman Justice of the Peace in the United States. (Banners representing the American pioneers Susan B. Anthony, Lucy Stone and Elizabeth Cady Stanton had been specially ordered from the Artists' Suffrage League.) Representatives from Russia, Hungary and South

41 NUWSS members with Artists' Suffrage League
banners, 13 June 1908.
*The missing Elizabeth I banner is just visible between 'Joan
of Arc' and 'Lucy Stone'.*

Africa were also present, many of them on their
way to the International Woman Suffrage Congress in Amsterdam.

Almost 140 women doctors headed block two in
a blaze of scarlet – 'quite the most picturesque
section' according to the *Evening Standard* –
followed by dons and graduates with the mauve
hoods of Durham, the bright red and green of
Dublin, the brown of London, the pale blue of
Birmingham, and splashes of pink, yellow, orange
and crimson from the other colleges that admitted
women. There was a strong contingent from the
Royal Holloway College and another of about
400 women from Newnham and Girton. The
Cambridge women carried the 'gorgeous banner
of light blue silk'[94] designed for them by Mary
Lowndes ('Better is Wisdom than Weapons of
War'), and wore favours of light blue ribbon on
the shoulders of their gay summer costumes. (The

Oxford and Cambridge universities did not entitle them to wear gowns, a fact which *The Times* suggested was probably lost on the spectators, although some wore the hoods extended to them by courtesy of Trinity College, Dublin.) Behind them came the teachers and graduates of Somerville College and Lady Margaret Hall in Oxford, and of Edinburgh and Manchester universities.

They were followed in turn by the business women and clerical workers of block three, including those from the National Union with their banner 'The Office', and the Shorthand Writers with theirs and the motto 'Speed! Fight On' (from Browning). They were disappointingly few in number according to the *Sunday Times*, but the professions in block four were out in force. The Writers' Suffrage League ('a very merry lot'), all wearing scarlet and white badges transfixed with quills, walked beneath the dramatic black and white folds of the banner designed for them by Mary Lowndes and worked by Mrs Herringham of the Artists' Suffrage League. It was carried in turn by Cicely Hamilton, Evelyn Sharp, Sarah Grand, Beatrice Harradon and Elizabeth Robins. Behind them the banners commemorating the Brontës, Jane Austen, Elizabeth Barrett Browning and Josephine Butler were held aloft by other members of the contingent. The Artists carried their own banner ('Alliance Not Defiance') embroidered in silver and light blue silks in the colours of the League. Then came the actresses, musicians and nurses (with the Florence Nightingale banner) – nurses were held to demonstrate above all other professions that a keen desire for the vote was not incompatible with womanliness – gymnasts with the Physical Training banner, gardeners with theirs wreathed in flowers and fruit, farmers, and the Home-Makers ('Remembering their Homeless Sisters'): a walking argument for home-making as the justification for the women's vote rather than their disqualification from it.

Block five contained substantial detachments of working women including a thousand from the Co-operative Guilds, and representatives from the National Union of Women Workers, the Ethical Societies with their banner and motto from Emerson ('Hitch your Wagon to a Star') and the Women's Employment Defence League. The political societies followed in block six: Liberals, Conservatives, and the Fabian Women's Group with their new banner designed by May Morris, sinking their party differences in the larger cause.[95]

They were followed by the Women's Freedom League (the only militant society invited), headed by the banner of 'Vashti', an Old Testament heroine, and led by the venerable figure of Charlotte Despard: a tall, ascetic woman with white hair, wearing her own eccentric variant on a Spanish mantilla in place of a hat, her lips pursed in grim determination, greatly cheered by an enthusiastic crowd. The Women's Freedom League 'Holloway' banner in black and yellow, with broad arrows and the ironic inscription 'Stone Walls Do Not a Prison Make', was much commented on in the press.

The London Society brought up the rear of block eight by alphabetical order of its constituencies, but these were followed in turn by 'a long line of brakes and wagonettes, private carriages and motor-cars, all lavishly decorated with red and white favours, union jacks and in some cases magnificent bouquets of red and white flowers'.[96] Among these were two carriages with placards hung on either side denoting the LCC Women Teachers' Union; a 'gorgeously decorated wagonette'[97] conveying prominent members of the uninvited WSPU and an advertisement for their own demonstration march to Hyde Park the following week; and the four-in-hand of Countess Markievicz, who was to become the first woman elected to a seat in Parliament in 1918.

All along the route the banners made a great impression through their numbers and in their spectacular effect. As the *Sunday Times* reported, 'there seemed to be thousands of them, every

42 Cicely Hamilton and members of the Women Writers' Suffrage League with the Writers' banner in 1910.

43 Mary Lowndes's 'Scriveners'' design, made up by the Artists' Suffrage League in 1908 as the Writers' banner, perhaps because the Scriveners' Company wrote to *The Times* to complain.

fourth or fifth woman carrying something in the shape of an ensign.' Each contingent carried its own device, and embroidered tributes to queens, scientists, artists, writers, musicians, saints and suffrage pioneers were distributed the length and breadth of the march. But what impressed the onlookers and the newspapers more was the fact that the women carried them themselves. 'Nothing could have been more admirable,' *The Times* remarked a trifle pompously, 'than the endurance of the ladies who had undertaken this burden, and who went through with it so gallantly.' The Artists' League recommended webbing shoulder straps with stitched pockets to steady the pole ends – they even provided diagrams for making them up[98] – but not all the bearers seem to have had them. It was harder than it looked to keep a banner taut and in line. Sudden gusts from Northumberland Avenue sent one flag flapping wildly in the faces of the ranks behind and almost threw its bearers off balance, but gradually women acquired the knack of this, as of so many other unfamiliar tasks. There was no logical connection between their right to vote and the ability to carry a cumbersome object in a stiff head wind, but the crowd could not resist a jibe, or the press a reference to women struggling 'manfully' to master their burden. In return they seemed prepared, at least, to recognise the symbolic significance of what Cicely Hamilton called 'doing this for ourselves'.[99]

Between ten and fifteen thousand women[100] walked the route that Mrs Fawcett had covered in forty minutes the day before, but it took the procession an hour and a half to reach the Albert Hall, where it ended 'in triumph and enthusiasm',[101] the massed flags crowding the narrow streets around the entrances reminding one reporter of 'ages when pageantry of colour naturally adorned all ceremonies'.[102] The last detachment filed into the Albert Hall some time after five o'clock. Inside the banners were 'piled in terraced ranks of raw and flaming colour' below the organ, where they 'glowed like a beautiful piece of vivid coloured

tapestry', framing the platform and its distinguished speakers.[103] Even *The Times* acknowledged the scene as one 'of an imposing character'. There were some men present (including George Bernard Shaw) – about one in ten according to the *Daily News* – but what struck the commentators forcibly was the look of a large gathering of women, brilliant with summer dresses and the glowing accents of silk banners and university robes, the heavy mass of banked red and white flowers that edged the platform; altogether a scene 'as remarkable as any that have been witnessed in that great building. From floor to topmost corner and furthest angle of the huge galleries, the interior was alive with women and bright with colour.'[104]

Mrs Fawcett rose to speak amid scenes of such enthusiasm from her audience that it was some minutes before she could begin her speech. The meeting, described in *The Times* as 'harmonious, dignified and business-like', was interrupted by the announcement that some flowers would be presented to Mrs Fawcett in token of the love and esteem in which she was held, and in commemoration of her fortieth year in the service of the cause. Thirty or forty women then filed past, each bearing a bouquet, until the National Union president was buried breast-high in flowers, the audience rose to its feet, handkerchiefs fluttered from stalls and balconies, and the great hall rang with cheers and broke into 'For she's a jolly good fellow' as the organ struck up again. Mrs Fawcett, overwhelmed, thanked the audience with a tear-stained face. The work of hundreds of women and the participation of thousands reached a temporary culmination in this personal tribute which, because it was made to a woman active for forty years in the suffrage campaign and widely respected by all its supporters, symbolised in turn the maturity of that cause itself.

For the procession to be judged effective, certain criteria had to be met: large numbers of people had to turn up to watch it, the crowds needed to be sympathetic and responsive, and – which was more

difficult to prove – the spectacle had to make a *political* impact on its onlookers. Certainly the numbers were impressive, and the crowd's attention was engaged. They lined Northumberland Avenue four deep, packed Trafalgar Square, clustered on refuges and around the statue of Charles I, thinned out in Lower Regent Street (although customers, waiters and waitresses thronged the doors and windows of clubs, hotels and restaurants, and flowers were thrown from their balconies), turned into a large throng again around Piccadilly Circus, and a congested mass at Hyde Park Corner. Laurence Housman wrote to Janet Ashbee that 'people had turned out in quite as big numbers all about Trafalgar Square and Regent Street as they do to see Royalty on semi-state occasions. So that shows that the thing has got into the popular mind and is being paid attention to,' but he also admitted that the crowd, though good-humoured, was politically quite apathetic.[105]

The suffrage press and its national sympathisers naturally stressed the crowd's support. The *Daily News* leader claimed that the women's 'bravery, their admirable organisation and their skilful use

44 View of the Albert Hall decorated with banners at the end of the NUWSS procession.

of beautiful and decorative banners, impressed a crowd which obviously came prepared to laugh'. On its inside pages it reminded its readers that it was still something of an ordeal for women, requiring moral courage as well as physical strength, to join a demonstration for two miles through the streets of London, when, as it claimed, riots had been threatened, sackings promised to working women and ridicule and abuse attempted.

Here and there a ribald jest or the snatch of a music-hall refrain was heard – 'Put me amongst the girls' was always a favourite at suffrage processions, especially if a bandsman or male banner-bearer came into view – but these 'altogether missed fire in presence of the dignified attitude of the women'.[106] Maud Arncliffe-Sennett, carrying the banner of Queen Victoria, encountered a man in Knightsbridge who 'kept on ejaculating softly, "I'm ashamed of you, I'm ashamed of you and you all belong to the Street!"' – this was precisely what women were fighting for, she claimed, 'to purge from these minds the connection of Women and the Street' – but incidents like this were rarer now. The changed demeanour of the crowds in general made a great impression for, as she acknowledged, 'whereas in the March of February 1907 it was often coarse and brutal, on this occasion it was mostly kind and seldom coarse.'[107] Or as Cicely Hamilton put it, the expression of the average onlooker had changed from one of amused tolerance: 'The Londoner may not like us yet, but unless his face belies him, he is beginning to respect us.'[108]

In securing press coverage for the campaign the procession could scarcely have been more successful, particularly as compared with the meagre coverage accorded the Mud March of the year before. Virtually every national daily, all the important periodicals and most of the provincial and local London newspapers published accounts of it. With the demonstration the suffrage issue could be said to have invaded the press – the editor of the *Daily Chronicle* rejected another article from Maud Arncliffe-Sennett on the grounds that his paper 'like other journals has latterly contained little else than Suffragist information' – and leading articles were compelled by the procession to discuss the politics of the campaign which had produced it, a situation the suffragists were quick to exploit.[109]

Three aspects struck the press (and presumably the crowds) most forcefully, and surface in almost all accounts of the afternoon: the impact of its pageantry, that is, its effect as spectacle; the dignity and social diversity of its participants; and its organisation as a public event. James Douglas reached the highest flights of rhetoric in the *Morning Leader*,[110] but his report was not untypical, and more sober accounts circled the twin reference points of femininity and medievalism in the same way. 'I have seen many processions. But they were all processions of men. On Saturday I saw a procession of women. It was more stately and more splendid and more beautiful than any procession I ever saw. When men march through the streets of London they carry huge banners with ugly paintings on their glazed surface. The colours are violently crude. The portraits are hideous. A banner is a lovely thing, but the banners borne by men are grotesque. The Twelfth of July procession in Belfast is tawdry because the Orange banners are harsh and hideous in their colouring, and the portraits painted upon them are daubs. The women have done what the men have failed to do. They have revived the pomp and glory of the procession. They have recreated the beauty of blown silk and tossing embroidery. The procession that wound like a gigantic serpent of a thousand hues from the Embankment to the Albert Hall was a living miracle of gracious pageantry. It was like a medieval festival, vivid with simple grandeur, alive with an ancient dignity ... The gay banners, emblazoned with wisdom and tolerance, were not the gonfalons of a Joan of Arc, sworded and in arms. They were the symbols of something stronger than physical strength and mightfuller than weapons of war, the conquering thought and the triumphing ideal. The names wrought upon the delicate silk were the names of women whose power was the power of the intellect and whose strength was the strength of the soul. As the wind wrestled with the frail banners borne by frail hands, I began to feel the might of weakness and the strength of simplicity.'

This is quite a complicated piece of rhetoric which employs the tropes of an idealised femininity in a manner too equivocal to be entirely comfortable. In quoting from it the suffragists prudently excluded its references to feminine frailty. While they were prepared to draw on evangelical arguments that endowed women with moral superiority in compensation for their subordinate social role, talk of weakness and simplicity was at odds with the impression of achievement, intellect and organisational competence they were at pains to convey.

It was for this reason that the contingent of medical and university women in academic robes was such an essential and influential part of the procession. They made a deep impression on the public and the press, and their contribution to the day's effect was enhanced by marshalling them into a single contingent. The appearance of this section set the tone of the crowd's response and startled it out of its preconceptions. 'The ordinary business man and the stay-at-home woman know indeed, in a vague way, that women now attend universities and receive degrees "the same as the men". But they still figure to themselves such women as half-human monsters, devoid of natural feminine instincts and attractiveness. This opinion they found it hard to reconcile with the appearance and bearing of the graduates on Saturday, and their bewilderment was visibly reflected in their faces.'[111] The nurses were widely cheered, and the spectators who looked on from the service clubs bared their heads at the sight of the Florence Nightingale banner with which they marched. Her name and reputation were powerful implements in the suffrage cause – she was 'already an immortal' as one of the suffragists explained[112] – and even the

Cockney wags were moved to respect. From this point every major demonstration had its group of nurses.

The *Daily Chronicle* went on to describe the procession as 'a microcosm of the womanhood of the nation', and to comment, perhaps ingenuously, that distinctions of rank and class were obliterated in it. Perhaps it would be better to suggest that they were temporarily held in suspension. (Only by remaining visibly differentiated, after all, could the political point of their unity-in-diversity be maintained.) The medical women made an impact because the 'spectacle of ladies entitled to wear the doctor's robe, and yet not entitled to exercise the vote,' was bound to be dramatic.[113] But most impressive was the social mix itself, described in this instance from the *Daily News*: 'on Saturday, one could see fair dames of Mayfair in costly lace and silk fraternising with working girls in shawls and feathers, while famous novelists and actresses walked side by side with workers from the factory or the farm. It was something more than a demonstration of women. It was a demonstration of all classes of women. Men only demonstrate in sections. There have been great demonstrations of temperance men, of Labour men, of Church men, but never men of all classes and of all creeds and of all callings. It has been left to women to unite in a single cause.'

One other theme asserted itself – almost obsessively as though the reporters' own astonishment spurred their repeated observation of it – that of the image of woman which was *absent* from the procession: nowhere the 'shrieking sisterhood' of popular imagery. 'No man need have apologised for having a sister or an aunt in that procession' (the *Weekly Dispatch*); this was 'no haphazard mob, no gathering of fanatics, no outbreak of feminine hysteria' (the *Kensington News*); 'no rambling excursion of the "shrieking sisterhood"' (the *Morning Post*); 'no hysterical Hebe clanged the discord of dinner-bells or tea-trays into the scene. It was not a pantomime, nor a comedy, nor a farce' (the

Morning Leader). What surfaces here is not just a generalised fear of the 'mob', but something more particular, a deep anxiety of 'hysterical' female militancy infused with scorn and spite.[114]

It was the constitutionalists' triumph to have allayed these fears, to have established with this procession that the commitment and intensity of the campaign was not exclusive to the militants, described by the *Daily Graphic* as 'a small crowd of neurotic and shrieking sisters, incapable of anything but twisting door-knockers, embarrassing policemen, and achieving the cheap martyrdom of a few weeks in Holloway'. It was not yet evident that in allaying them they might also have weakened their own position and further isolated the militants (with, it must be said, the WSPU's tacit collusion) as a band of fanatical extremists in the public eye. In the short term it was essential to the constitutionalists that they achieve the recognition they did, but the very womanliness that courted praise invited patronage: 'a feminine charm and daintiness about these accessories ... might perhaps have suggested agitation in an *édition de luxe*, but for other circumstances.'[115]

The suffragists' last card went some way towards countering this dainty femininity to which *The Times* might otherwise have reduced them. Their organisational flair astounded a public for which domestic efficiency represented the limit, as well as the proper end, of feminine capacity. 'Their organisation was perfect,' as others acknowledged, besides the *Morning Leader*. 'It displayed military (apart from militant) genius to a degree that was quite astonishing.'[116] They had evidenced against all expectations 'a faculty for organised, orderly, and picturesque demonstration on popular lines' such that even 'the most unprogressive critic feels constrained to admit that the foundations of a new political development have been laid.'[117] For the pro-suffrage press at least, 'the revelation of the power of woman as organiser' was itself evidence of the justice of their demand and its necessary outcome. 'These Women Suffragists can do anything,

can accomplish all that they have set out with the purpose of accomplishing. In their vocabulary there is no such word as fail, and they will get the vote just as sure as the morrow will dawn, and, what is more to the purpose, they will deserve it.'[118]

There had been a time, as Lady Frances Balfour recalled in reviewing the procession she had led, when she believed with others that women could not demonstrate in public. But it had become evident that all the precedents for constitutional change pointed to the public procession as a political lever and accordingly, at whatever cost in money, time and energy, it had proved necessary for the cause to 'proceed'. Furthermore a cabinet minister 'had asked that women should show themselves in masses before he and his Government can really believe they need and desire the Franchise. If these things are demanded of women they must be done.'[119]

They had been done, and done successfully. The Liberal press agreed with the *Daily Graphic* that Asquith's challenge had been met 'with a promptitude and an impressiveness for which the great bulk of the British public were little prepared'. Millicent Fawcett claimed at the Albert Hall that 'the day of our final triumph is now within measurable distance'; and Cicely Hamilton in the *Daily Mail* that it was (perhaps for the first time in history) 'good to be a woman, since we live at the beginning of things and our feet are on the threshold of a world that is new'. But this optimism, centred on the belief that women's suffrage would dominate other issues at the next general election and that the electorate would give it their consent, was premature.

The anti-suffrage press, led by *The Times*, distinguished between the success of the procession as a popular spectacle on the one hand, and its validity as a political demonstration on the other. *The Times* was the most grudging in its assessment of the crowd's response, it queried the number of participants and it gave the lowest estimate of the time taken by the demonstration to pass a given point. It acknowledged the impact of the event, the demeanour of the spectators, the creativity of the suffragists and the skills of their organisation; but it was not prepared to concede the political argument. 'If the object . . . was to prove that the great masses of the people are deeply moved on this suffrage question, it cannot be regarded as an unqualified success,' although in 'every other respect, its success is beyond challenge'. Similarly, the *Pall Mall Gazette* insisted that what had been proved was that *many* women wanted the vote, not necessarily that a *majority* did, and still less 'that it would be to the advantage of the country and the Empire that they should have it'.[120] And Asquith, as we shall see, following this cue, declined the opportunity to declare himself convinced.

WSPU 'Woman's Sunday', 21 June 1908

Within days a second and much larger demonstration was organised by the WSPU. This had been promised in *Votes for Women* in January, and in the *Annual Report* published by the WSPU in February. 'We have been challenged by the Government to show numbers. We accept the challenge. We will bring hundreds of thousands of women from all over the country to demonstrate on that (midsummer) day in Hyde Park . . . We will silence once and for all those who deny the strength of women's demand for the vote.' A monster demonstration would 'make History for the Women's Movement'. It would be the final answer to those still wanting 'proof'.[121]

Preparations were intensified in April and May. New offices were opened and additional clerical help engaged. Large sums of money were raised for the processions and their nationwide advertisement. Frederick Pethick-Lawrence took charge of the plans and persuaded the authorities to take up a quarter of a mile of park railings. Thirty special trains were organised to run from seventy towns, and demonstrators were advised to save a little each week towards the cost of their excursion tickets. Seven processions would absorb arrivals at

all the London termini and converge on Hyde Park in the afternoon, 'marching as to certain victory with bands playing, colours flying, and trumpets sounding,' where they would assemble with the waiting crowds around twenty temporary platforms accommodating eighty women speakers. In May an enormous wall poster was produced and despatched to hoardings around the country. It was 13 by 10 feet, and it featured life-sized photographic portraits of the women who would chair the platforms in Hyde Park, together with a map showing the routes of the seven processions. (Multiple platforms were necessary to address an audience on the scale the suffragettes were aiming for, since megaphones were primitive and loudspeakers not yet in use.) An advertising drive 'like an immense open-air by-election campaign' culminated in a 'crusade fortnight' in early June. London was divided into districts with shops and committee rooms in each. Handbills were distributed and pavements chalked with notices. WSPU canvassers toured factories, shops, hospitals and restaurants publicising the demonstration and calling on women to join them. Cyclists went out into the suburbs every evening on decorated or illuminated bicycles to distribute handbills and programmes. The Chelsea Palace featured lantern slides from the campaign and persuaded Sylvia Pankhurst to provide speakers before each performance of the 'cinematograph'.[122]

The processional banners were unfurled with pomp and circumstance in the Queen's Hall on 17 June: ten silk banners, seven of them to head the various processions, each specially donated for the occasion. Shop windows were filled with displays, buses were covered with posters, and three days before the procession Mrs Drummond took a steam launch to the terrace of the House of Commons while the Members took their tea and, surrounded by suffragettes and bunting, with a brass band playing, addressed them through a megaphone from the cabin roof until she was chased off by the river police.[123] Escapades like

MRS. DRUMMOND OPPOSITE THE TERRACE OF THE HOUSE OF COMMONS ADDRESSING M.P.'S,

this attracted press attention by their novelty and, appearing in the papers next morning, gathered further publicity for the cause. The unveiling of wax portraits of Christabel and Mrs Pankhurst, Annie Kenney and Mrs Pethick-Lawrence at Madame Tussaud's the day before can only have added to their celebrity and heightened the general sense of expectation. As Sylvia Pankhurst concluded: 'London had probably never before been flooded with such intensive propaganda for any cause.'[124]

In a stroke of genius Emmeline Pethick-Lawrence had decided that the Union should have its own colours – purple, white and green – no doubt stimulated by the red and white of the NUWSS, which advertised its processions and added greatly to their decorative effect. Broadly speaking the colours were intended to stand for purity (white), hope (green) and dignity (purple), but there was some uncertainty about them in the press and Mrs Pethick-Lawrence, who was liable to sentimentalise them in later years, allowed a broader and sometimes contradictory symbolism to accrue to them. They were not selected until the middle of May, but according to Sylvia Pankhurst had 'achieved a nation-wide familiarity before the month was out'. By the 21st they were marked indelibly and politically on the public mind: to see them was to be reminded of the WSPU and its campaign; they were its tricolour, its regimental colours, 'a new language of which the words are so simple that their meaning can be understood by the most uninstructed and most idle of passers-by in the street'.[125]

45 WSPU wall poster showing the platforms in Hyde Park, with portraits of the twenty women chairing them on 21 June 1908.

46 Mrs Drummond addressing MPs on the terrace of the House of Commons, a few days before the WSPU demonstration of 21 June 1908.

The usefulness of 'colours' lay in their universal application. Anything in any combination of purple, white and green could become a symbol and reminder of the cause: a button, a pamphlet, a dress, a procession, a decorated hall. Anything could be 'got in the colours' and soon everything was: playing cards, motoring scarves, flags, bicycles, flower arrangements, hatpins, ties, purses, buttons and brooches. Commercial manufacturers and retailers from dressmakers to florists were quick to advertise their wares in the purple, white and green. They may have been politically sympathetic, but they were also commercially astute. If anything between 40,000 and 250,000 women needed white dresses for Hyde Park in 1908, they represented a very sizeable market. 'Suffrage modes have become the topic of the moment,' the *Daily Chronicle* announced on the 19th, 'and the suggestion that all should wear white has been eagerly taken up. To expedite shopping several drapers have arranged to make displays of the suffrage colours ... White frocks will be prominent in the windows, with a plentiful supply of dress accessories in violet and green.' White or cream with purple and green accents would complement the 700 banners in the procession and give it a summery and unified effect; with the support of suffragettes the WSPU colours could become the reigning fashion, and Emmeline Pethick-Lawrence suggested that 'strange as it may seem, nothing would so help to popularise the Women's Social and Political Union.'[126]

From noon until half past one on 21 June the West End streets 'resounded to the beat of the drum, the call of the bugle, and the tramp of marching feet, as detachment after detachment hurried to its appointed rendezvous'.[127] Stewards met the train arrivals and escorted participants to their places. Each of the seven processions was organised by a chief marshal, with group marshals, captains and banner marshals under her, and crowds gathered to watch their mustering as little knots of women in summer dresses and suffragette sashes began to fill out into processions that blocked the London traffic for more than an hour. A stranger might have been forgiven, the *Standard* suggested, 'if he thought that some royal pageant was in the making'. Each procession was preceded by the WSPU tricolour and by one of the great silk banners unfurled on the 17th. Women from Wales, the Midlands and the west of England formed up behind Annie Kenney at Paddington. The Chelsea contingent assembled in Cheyne Walk, where they were joined by women who marched over the Albert Bridge to the music of the Battersea Borough Prize Band.[128] The Kensington procession of local members, together with writers, artists, nurses and teachers, assembled 5000 strong behind Laurence Housman's 'From Prison to Citizenship' banner and led off to the accompaniment of five brass bands.[129] In Trafalgar Square spectators lined the square itself and the surrounding parapets to watch the women arrive. Behind the mounted police the band of the Amalgamated Musicians' Union struck up a lively march as Mary Gawthorpe led the way beneath Sylvia Pankhurst's Phoenix banner ('Great Souls Live Like Fire-Hearted Suns to Spend their Strength'). The scarlet banner of the Fabians was carried this time by Maud Pember Reeves, wife of the Agent-General of New South Wales, accompanied by a group to which George Bernard Shaw tipped his hat in passing since it included both his colleagues and his wife. Keir Hardie and Mrs Philip Snowden walked with the ILP banner ('The World for the Worker'), and hospital nurses carried a Red Cross banner with the words 'Faithful Doing Day by Day'. Women from the Midlands and the eastern counties made up a Marylebone contingent with groups of teachers and more women workers. Mrs Pethick-Lawrence and Christabel (in the robes of a Bachelor of Law) headed the procession from the Victoria Embankment. Photographs show them standing in front of Sylvia Pankhurst's banner with roses, thistles and shamrocks worked in gold on a violet ground

('Rebellion to Tyrants is Obedience to God'). The Euston Road procession was led by Mrs Pankhurst herself, dressed in purple, and accompanied by the octogenarian Mrs Wolstenholme Elmy, another living link to the women's suffrage petition of 1866. There were six bands, a splendid array of standards, the banner with Mrs Pankhurst's portrait donated by Mrs Pethick-Lawrence ('Famed Far for Deeds of Daring Rectitude'), and a cheerful contingent of Lancashire mill women that attracted a good deal of friendly attention from the crowds.

There were altogether about 30,000 women in the seven processions, most of them wearing white with here and there some academic robes. Sprays of violet or gardenia, with favours in purple, white and green, were pinned to breasts and shoulders or worn as hat trimmings, belt ribbons or shoulder sashes. Mrs Drummond – henceforth known as the General – wore the quasi-military uniform donated for the occasion by a firm of regalia manufacturers.[130] Most of the women wore scarves (more than 10,000 were sold on the Friday and Saturday preceding the march at two shillings and elevenpence each), and the men wore ties in the colours. The WSPU offices in Clement's Inn completely sold out of 'women's tricolour' ribbon at ninepence a yard.

Sympathetic newspapers repeated the phrases of 13 June while remarking the larger numbers involved and a more assertive demeanour in the participants.[131] 'One missed, indeed, the exquisitely designed banners and the dignified ranks of the Lady graduates in cap and gown,' as *The Times* put it, but there was in compensation 'a dash and "go", a high spirited energy . . . not to be found on the earlier occasion'.[132] Others described the crowds as motivated chiefly by curiosity and the diversion of a sunny Sunday afternoon. For whatever reason – and Mrs Pankhurst and Christabel were now celebrities whom even the unconverted strained to glimpse – crowds assembled around the formation points and along the routes, packing the

47 Mrs Pankhurst with Mrs Wolstenholme Elmy, in front of the WSPU banner donated by Emmeline Pethick-Lawrence and dedicated to Mrs Pankhurst ('Famed Far for Deeds of Daring Rectitude'), 21 June 1908.

48 Christabel Pankhurst, in the robes of a Bachelor of Law, with Emmeline Pethick-Lawrence in front of a new WSPU banner ('Rebellion to Tyrants is Obedience to God'), on the militant demonstration of 21 June 1908.

windows and balconies of Trafalgar Square and accompanying the various processions with parallel rivulets of sightseers, as they moved towards their destination in Hyde Park. Their arrival shortly after 2.30 pm was awaited by 'an innumerable swarm of humanity', and it was with some difficulty that the processions wound their way to the twenty platforms, 'each like a wounded snake, dragging its slow length along'.

To read an account of the scene now, such as that in *The Times*, is to thrill to the description of an event without precedent and such as we have never seen, and at the same time to admire the cadences of a quality of writing that is lost to journalism now. 'All London seemed to have mustered in that stretch of green between the Serpentine and Marble-arch. No doubt the great majority were there simply from curiosity and love of diversion. Every circumstance conspired to make the occasion attractive. The weather was beautifully fine; and the park was in the height of its summer glory; but if there had not been in addition a powerful human interest to make an appeal to the public, such a spectacle as that of yesterday would have been impossible.' The crowd was 'a flood with its slow but steady currents, setting hither and thither,' in which the platforms emerged like white islets shimmering with cream and white dresses: 'the multitude yesterday was not in its total effect black, as is usually the case, but as variegated as an illimitable flower-bed. Straw hats, parasols, and the millinery of thousands and thousands of ladies in gayest summer attire, combined to banish any suggestion of drab monotony.' Or in the *Daily Express*'s more prosaic summary: the 'Women Suffragists provided London yesterday with one of the most wonderful and astonishing sights that has ever been seen.'

Crowds on that scale could scarcely be counted. The suffragettes had set themselves a target of a quarter of a million and it was probably surpassed. *Votes for Women* claimed that it was 'no exaggeration to say that the number of people present was

the largest ever gathered together on one spot at one time in the history of the world';[133] and *The Times* was scarcely more sober: 'it is impossible to recall anything at all comparable in mere magnitude . . . That expectation [of 250,000] was certainly fulfilled. Probably it was doubled; and it would be difficult to contradict anyone who asserted confidently that it was trebled. Like the distances and numbers of the stars, the facts were beyond the threshold of perception.'

The twenty platforms were set about 100 yards apart in a great circle, the wagons emerging above the seething mass of the crowds 'like an ant heap suddenly opened'.[134] In the centre was a large pantechnicon, hired as a 'conning tower' from which proceedings could be directed. Around it the crowds were chiefly orderly and good-humoured, and cordial relations were maintained with the 6000 constables drafted in for the occasion; but little eddies of disruption surfaced around the platforms of Mrs Pankhurst, Christabel and Mrs Martel as missiles were thrown, suffragists jostled and heckled, and women fainted in the crush.[135]

At three o'clock a bugle from the 'conning tower' signalled for the speeches to begin. What was actually said, *The Times* suggested, was of less moment than the saying of it. 'The staple of the speeches seemed to be pungent criticism of the Government in general and Mr Asquith in particular. But it was impossible not to be struck by the skill and resource with which the speakers held the attention of this restive, heterogeneous, crowd or the remarkable manner in which without apparent effort, they made their voices heard. Most of them were quite young women, and the ordeal of facing that crowd must have been tremendous; but not one of them was in the least dismayed.' Across the park, between the circles within which the speakers could be heard, only their image remained: the curiously novel and invigorating spectacle of young women in white dresses, gesticulating now in this direction and now that, rising to the occasion,

taking courage from the scale of the gathering, the interest of the crowds and the passion of the moment – a picture with all the flickering poignancy of a silent film.

At a bugle call from the pantechnicon at five o'clock the resolution was put simultaneously from every platform: 'That this meeting calls upon the Government to give the vote to women without delay.' Immediately 'thousands of hands and hats were raised in enthusiastic salutation, and from thousands of voices rose a great cheer. To the eye the effect was as if the level of the great tide that flooded the Park had suddenly risen by a foot.'[136] With a thrice-repeated shout of 'Votes for Women!', the meeting closed.

Publicly, the demonstration was counted as a great success: 'daringly conceived, splendidly stage-managed, and successfully carried out'.[137] Privately, participants acknowledged that the feelings of the crowd were mixed; that inevitably it included opponents as well as those who were ignorant or indifferent. As Helen Fraser, a WSPU organiser in Scotland, described it to a colleague,

49 A section of the crowds in Hyde Park, 21 June 1908.
The Times *estimated that between a quarter and half a million people were present, and the* WSPU *claimed it as the largest political meeting ever held in England.*

'the 21st was very wonderful ... and yet not entirely satisfactory ... the vast mass of people were simply curious – not sympathetic – not opposed.'[138] But despite the caveats it was hard to see how Asquith's challenge had not been met. Twice in eight days women had taken to the streets: first in a procession of predominantly professional women, elaborately ordered and embellished; second, in an unprecedented demonstration of tens of thousands which had filled a hot June afternoon with massed bands, streaming banners, a crowd of confetti-like brilliance and a sense of imminent victory. 'We were buoyed by delighted triumph in this success ... Self was forgotten; personality seemed minute, the movement so big, so splendid.'[139]

Christabel hurried from Hyde Park to Clement's Inn and despatched to Asquith by special messenger the resolution which had been put, together with a note asking what action the government now intended to take. Two weeks earlier in *Votes for Women* she had written that the critical question for the demonstration would be the effect it would have on the government, rather than on the public. 'If the Government still refuse to act, then we shall know that great meetings, though they are indispensable for rousing public interest, fail as a means of directly influencing the action of the Government. We shall then be obliged to rely more than ever on militant methods.'[140]

If a threat was implied here, Asquith was not sensible to it. His answer was curt. Christabel received a reply from his private secretary on the 23rd, informing her that the Prime Minister had nothing to add to his statement of 20 May. On that day he had stated the government's intention to introduce a reform bill capable of private amendment to include the women 'on democratic lines'. This promising-sounding suggestion in fact gave him room to object to any amendment narrow enough to have a chance of passing a free vote, and Christabel had rejected it as a vague and negative

proposal. That she was justified was borne out by Asquith's response to a question in the House on 26 May: asked if a women's suffrage amendment, once carried, would become part of government-sponsored legislation, he replied, 'My honourable friend asks me a contingent question in regard to a remote and speculative future.'[141]

Commenting on both processions in its leader of 22 June, *The Times* remarked that certainly 'Mr Asquith's advice is bearing fruit.' But the limits of the public meeting had now been reached, and it was not clear that the women's cause was, after all, nearer to fruition. Ironically these two impressive and apparently successful demonstrations came at a time when Asquith had succeeded Campbell-Bannerman as prime minister, and he was both powerfully intransigent and a clever, evasive opponent. His 'challenge' would not easily be met in terms that he would be prepared to recognise. It has been argued that his fastidious legal mind recoiled from the fervour of mass demonstrations; in which case, called upon to prove their numbers, the women were damned if they succeeded as well as if they failed. And he did not need *The Times* to prompt him (though it did) that 30,000 demonstrators and a crowd of a quarter or half a million was still not proof such as he had demanded that an overwhelming majority of Englishwomen wanted the vote.

Emmeline Pethick-Lawrence announced in *Votes for Women* on 25 June that, 'We have touched the limit of public demonstration ... Nothing but militant action is left to us now,' and Christabel added immediately that militancy would be resumed. The journalist Henry Nevinson, who visited the Pethick-Lawrences on the evening of the 23rd, 'found them obdurate in every way and determined to renew violence'.[142]

Meanwhile, and apart from the success of its claims on public attention, the intensified suffrage campaign of the summer of 1908 achieved one further thing: it helped to mobilise the opposition. On 12 June *The Times* informed its readers that 'a counter movement of considerable force is being organised' and that 'the fiery appeals of the suffragists and their friends, of which we are likely to hear more than enough during the coming week, will not be allowed to hold the field unchallenged.'

In the eyes of the anti-suffragists the matter was urgent: 'judgement may go by default, and our country drift towards a momentous revolution, both social and political, before it has realised the dangers involved.' Mrs Humphry Ward, a principal figure in the Women's National Anti-Suffrage League, outlined the omens at its inaugural meeting. 'When a Women's Enfranchisement Bill has passed its second reading in the House of Commons by a large majority; when we have a militant Society, amply supplied with money, and served by women who seem to give their whole time to its promotion; when we have before us the spectacle of marchings and counter-marchings, alarums and excursions, on behalf of the Suffrage cause, in all parts of England; when Ministers' houses are attacked and political meetings broken up; when besides the pennyworth of argument, added to an intolerable deal of noise, with which the Women's Social and Political Union provide us, we have the serious and impressive sight of Mrs Fawcett's procession of a month ago – then, indeed, it seems to be time that those women who, with no less seriousness . . . hold the view that Woman Suffrage would be a disaster for England, and first and foremost for women themselves – that they should bestir themselves, that they should take counsel, that they should organise opposition, and prepare to see it through.'[143]

The National Women's Anti-Suffrage League, founded in July 1908, amalgamated with the Men's League for opposing Female Suffrage (formed in December 1908) as the National League for Opposing Women's Suffrage (NLOWS) at the end of 1910. As a body the anti-suffragists were not to be underestimated, since they were both wealthy and influential.[144] They had no organised working-class support but through their membership of the

Edwardian establishment on the one hand, and their appeal to popular prejudice on the other, they occupied a position of influence which the comparative feebleness of their propaganda did little to compromise. There were contradictions in their position, however, and the suffragists worked to expose them.

First, it was possible that the anti position was more powerful when unarticulated; that as a set of a priori assumptions passed off as common sense it was hard to contest. Shrewder suffragists welcomed the advance of their opponents as 'the best thing that has yet happened in England'.[145] Once anti-suffrage opinion was organised publicly it was obliged to mobilise residual prejudice into rational argument, and in doing so it helped to clear away apathy and indifference, which in the suffragists' view was the most serious obstacle to their own campaign. Second, the wealth and influence of the antis could be turned against them. As a member of the NUWSS observed (apropos of a published list of their early supporters), with a title and several thousand a year you could get anything you wanted *without* the parliamentary vote.[146] Third, and as Brian Harrison has indicated, the accusation that the anti-suffrage movement was run by a wealthy elite was probably less damaging than the claim that it was run by men. (This claim was explored in detail by Lady Chance in a pamphlet which argued that 'the bulk of the financial support of the League' came from men whose interests were disguised behind 'a carefully arranged screen of women'.)[147] Fourth, the antis' position, which was essentially conservative and defensive, was almost impossible to produce in any dynamic or progressive language. And most important of all, it was founded on the disabling paradox that the mobilisation of women opposed to women's suffrage was itself a political act, which led them to write pamphlets, address meetings, administer branches, and thereby undermine the credibility of their own case. As Arnold Ward praised his mother and her colleagues in the House of Commons, these 'noble women' had 'emerged only to retire, are agitating against the cause of female agitation, and by the garrulity of the moment are purchasing the silence of a lifetime'.[148]

Mrs Humphry Ward had promised the Women's League that they would be 'meeting the tactics and arguments of the Suffragists with counter-tactics and counter-arguments', organising throughout the country to break down the 426 pledges given to women's suffrage in the current parliament.[149] It was not clear, however, what these tactics could legitimately be. To a greater extent even than the constitutionalists, the antis needed to make themselves heard from within the bounds of womanly decorum. Asquith offered a very convoluted piece of advice to an anti-suffrage deputation in 1911: if they would pursue 'effective militant operations of a constitutional kind', he entertained very strong hopes that 'some of the jubilations heard from the supporters of woman suffrage would prove to have been premature'.[150]

What were 'militant operations of a constitutional kind'? The suffrage processions of the years between 1907 and 1913 effectively set the pace for the antis, but in a direction where their own convictions did not permit them to follow. They imitated in a rather diluted fashion the suffrage use of posters and public meetings, but they could not follow their opponents on to the streets, and the claim that they spoke for the silent majority was thereby diminished. The burden of proof, the *New Age* remarked facetiously at the end of July 1908, was returned to Asquith: 'let him produce the anti-Suffragist League; let it find a hundred respectable women, whose names are known beyond their parish boundaries, who will walk – not to the Albert Hall or Hyde Park, but once round Trafalgar Square, as a declaration that they have not sufficient intelligence to vote at a parliamentary election. And for every one, the Suffragists will produce a hundred on the other side. Surely that is fair? If the anti-Suffragists desire to walk with their faces covered, that will be considered quite reason-

able; they may even send dressmaker's dummies, if a magistrate will certify that the duplicates exist. But make a show of some kind, otherwise the world must proceed on its way; we cannot always loiter about with the social habits of the veiled East.'[151]

The Pageant of Women's Trades and Professions, 27 April 1909

At the end of April 1909 the International Woman Suffrage Alliance held its Quinquennial Congress in London, and local organisations went out of their way to entertain the foreign delegates. The NUWSS, as a society affiliated to the Alliance,[152] was its official host, and responsible for a meeting at the Albert Hall for which the Artists' Suffrage League and the London Society produced the Pageant of Women's Trades and Professions.

The Pageant of Women's Trades and Professions developed the self-presentation of women as workers, in determinate social and historical conditions, rather than as members of a conglomerate and domestic 'womanliness'. In its structure, its symbolism, and through the written commentary accompanying its programme, it was intended to make a number of points pertinent to women, work and female enfranchisement. First, it was meant to demonstrate (again) that the suffrage movement was not constituted solely of middle-class women with their own interests at heart. Second, that the matter of the vote weighed heavily on the employment opportunities and working conditions of women struggling to enter the professions, or engaged in industrial labour or sweated homeworking. Third, to emphasise the number of middle-class women who wanted to work and the much greater numbers of working-class women who were simply obliged to. Above all, it was intended to show 'that the demand for the vote is not limited to any class, but that all wage-earning women are equally interested in securing the franchise,' and to provide picturesque illustration and support for the resolution put to the Congress on 30 April: 'That women who are dependent on their own earnings for a livelihood have political as well as economic interests and therefore especially need the vote to safeguard their position in the industrial world.'[153]

The programme offered specific suggestions as to why each particular group of workers needed to vote. Women farmers were instanced as women who paid heavy rates and taxes, who were employers of labour and who had interests in questions such as tariff reform, railway rates, adulteration acts and the inspection of smallholdings, dairies and cowsheds. Housewives – included here with the professions and trades – suffered unlimited hours, often poor or insanitary conditions and great responsibility, yet because they received no direct wages their contribution to the nation's wealth was overlooked. (Nearly half the female population over fifteen was married, the programme noted: 'Marriage is the most extensively followed occupation, and one of the hardest.') Shop assistants were subject to arbitrary regulations and fines, waitresses to the objectionable 'tip' system and impertinence, artists were excluded from the Royal Academy, and house decorators from qualifying as architects. A number of female trades were injurious to health (lead-poisoning affected pottery painters and tuberculosis rates were high in cotton mills). Others that were safe and hospitable to women, such as typing and shorthand, offered little advancement or responsibility. Some of the most heartfelt entries were clearly written by participants, or by unionists or philanthropists directly engaged with them: journalism, a difficult profession owing to the conservatism of editors and proprietors, was one of these. On the other hand several occupations were recommended as having been opened to women relatively recently. Embroidery was noted as a craft for which England had been celebrated throughout Europe in the Middle Ages, and photography was recommended as a 'wide field for artistic skill'. Mary Lowndes must have written the entry on stained glass which noted the new impetus whereby 'women are taking

their part with men in the front ranks . . . though it is probable that twenty years ago there was not among artists a single woman glass painter.'

In all this the commentary argued two related propositions. First (a point addressed to the labour movement), that even on a limited franchise the better-paid working woman and not just her middle-class sister would qualify for a vote; and second (a point for philanthropists as well as socialists), that the women's vote was expedient. It would help to end the particular forms of exploitation that workers suffered from as women: sweated labour, low pay, taxation without representation, restrictive practices, unhealthy working conditions – and at the same time those forms of state legislation that restricted their earning capacity by interfering in the hours and conditions of their employment.

The pageant began at dusk on the afternoon of 27 April (the anniversary of Mary Wollstonecraft's birthday), as 1000 women from ninety different occupations gathered under the trees in Eaton Square. They made a 'charming spectacle', according to the *Daily Telegraph*, with their emblems and lanterns under the white gaslights beneath a lavender-grey sky. In the gathering dark they moved up Sloane Street, a 'long column of stars of orange light' and skirted Hyde Park 'gemmed and ablaze'.[154] Night fell quickly and the gusty weather kept the number of spectators low, but the procession served its purpose of attracting attention to the Albert Hall meeting, the press proved responsive and favourable reports appeared in the morning's newspapers.

There was great excitement as the five divisions of the procession paused in each of the hall's main entrances, and then filed into the brilliant interior from the stormy darkness outside. The detail of the emblems and bannerets now clearly visible, a small army of working women moved down the arena to the music of the organ and the cheers of the assembled delegates. As the applause faded away they were greeted by the president of the

International Suffrage Alliance, Carrie Chapman Catt, with the memorable phrase: 'You are an argument.'

The first block consisted of the farmers, beekeepers, market and flower gardeners, jam and sweet makers, waitresses, cigar and cigarette makers, housewives and housekeepers. The second was made up of artists and craftswomen: painters and sculptors, house decorators (we would now call them interior designers), glass workers, woodcarvers, jewellers, embroiderers, photographers, pottery painters, florists, fashion designers, dressmakers and milliners. Block three contained the industrial women: chainmakers and pit-brow women (who were roundly cheered), cotton operatives, silk workers, tailoresses, machinists, boot and shoe workers, felt and straw hat makers, hosiery workers, artificial flower makers, furriers, machine and hand lacemakers, laundresses and shop assistants. Block four consisted of writers, journalists, secretaries, typists and shorthand writers, indexers, printers and bookbinders, bookfolders, public speakers, actresses, singers and musicians. The last group contained doctors and surgeons,[155] nurses, midwives, pharmacists, sanitary inspectors, women in physical training and teachers in higher education, elementary education and kindergarten schools.

Each group contained ten or twelve women from one trade or profession, headed with emblems designed by Mary Lowndes.[156] The nurses and midwives were in uniform, the graduates in academic dress, the pottery workers in aprons or smocks, and the pit-brow women wore shawls over their heads. The chainmakers carried miniature hammers and anvils and their plight being topical, received 'specially hearty cheers'.[157] The pit-brow women carried an emblem of the winding machine from the pit head, or the pick, shovel and sieve with a copper model of the Davy lamp.[158] The weavers' emblem was a golden spider and web for Arachne, the first weaver, with shuttles, spools and threads of various colours. An old Buckinghamshire lacemaker carried her bobbins and pillow, supported on either side by younger suffragists, and took a scarlet and white rosette back home to wear like a veteran. The midwives' emblem contained a lotus flower as the ancient symbol of life, with infants' heads wreathed in flowers and the motto 'Vita donum Dei'. The housewives had the cresset of 'Hearth and Home', the cooks golden gridirons with copper pans and bundles of herbs, the housemaids a shield with caps and aprons and feather dusters. The florists carried baskets of flowers, the poultry farmers a row of eggs, the journalists a carrier pigeon and quill pen, and the photographers shields in black and silver, with devices for the camera and the sun. The woodcarvers' banneret was inscribed 'Pray devoutly, hammer stoutly'; the jam makers' shield had Adam and Eve, the old emblem of fruiterers; the charwomen's motto across their buckets was 'Cleanliness is next to godliness'. The glass workers bore shields 'leaded up of stained glass' with the rose of England below and the tools of the glazier and painter surmounting it. The secretaries had secretary birds in red and silver with red tape and sealed documents; and the fashion designers two poles, contrasting a crinoline with a contemporary sheath gown, and a motto evoking the premise of the procession as a whole: 'The old order changeth, yielding place to new.'

Reports were brief but not unflattering. The *Morning Leader* described it as a superbly stage-managed spectacle which 'had the best Lord Mayor's Show that anyone can remember worn to the weariest frazzle'. The *Common Cause* compared it to a medieval trades-guild pageant, and commended its emblems (with some exaggeration) as artistically and historically correct. The National

50 & 51 Painters, Nurses and Midwives from the Pageant of Women's Trades and Professions, 27 April 1909. The emblems were designed by Mary Lowndes and executed by members and associates of the Artists' Suffrage League.

Union was confident that the procession had made a successful impact on the spectators who lined the route, on the delegates assembled in the Albert Hall and on the participants themselves (who were gratified both by the experience of the march and by the reception they were given). The Americans were particularly impressed, and Carrie Chapman Catt extended the ultimate compliment by planning to reproduce the pageant in New York.[159]

On 29 April it was the militants' turn to entertain the visitors, and characteristically they did so with a demonstration not of workers but of martyrs. Long lines of ex-prisoners filed on to the platform to be presented with commemorative badges, and Mrs Pethick-Lawrence opened the proceedings with a call for three cries of 'Shame!' on the government for imprisoning women. The *Common Cause* reported the events rather waspishly, commenting on the 'glorification and justification of their own deeds' by which the foreign delegates were treated to an exposition of militant methods.[160] In the temporary spotlight of the International Suffrage Congress, rivalry between the competing strategies of the NUWSS and the WSPU was particularly intense. Subsequent developments in the course of 1909, notably the adoption of the hunger strike and the introduction of forcible feeding, added to the growing estrangement between the constitutional and militant wings of the campaign.

*

In publicising their thirteenth march to Parliament on 19 June 1909, the WSPU issued leaflets quoting the 1689 Bill of Rights: 'It is the right of subjects to petition the King, and all commitments and prosecutions for such petitioning are illegal.' In their view this obliged Asquith to receive their deputation as the King's representative, and rendered any attempt by the police to obstruct their passage illegal.[161]

On 24 June, after an earlier and unsuccessful attempt, the painter Marion Wallace Dunlop –

described by Christabel as 'an artist of very resourceful mind' – stencilled this extract on the wall of St Stephen's Hall in the House of Commons as an 'aide-memoire to the Government and Members of Parliament'. She refused a fine, and was sentenced to one month's imprisonment for wilful damage. Her request that she be placed in the First Division as a political prisoner was denied. Three days later she began a hunger strike, and after refusing food for ninety-one hours she was released.[162]

The unsuccessful deputation of 19 June had ended in confusion with 122 arrests, which were followed by an evening of window-breaking in which the Privy Council, Treasury and Home Offices were slightly damaged. Thirteen stone-throwers were arrested, convicted, and sent to Holloway, where they went on hunger strike and were released after six days. By August hunger-striking was normal practice, and thirty-seven women had terminated their sentences in this way by the time that Mary Leigh and Charlotte Marsh were imprisoned in Winson Green, Birmingham, for interrupting one of Asquith's meetings by raining slates down on the roof of the Bingley Hall from an adjacent building.

Mary Leigh and Charlotte Marsh began fasting on 18 September. In August Herbert Gladstone, the Home Secretary, had received a missive from Marienbad informing him that 'His Majesty would be glad to know why the existing methods which must obviously exist for dealing with prisoners who refuse nourishment, should not be adopted.'[163] The King was not alone in expressing unease at the situation and the pressure to do something about it was mounting. Gladstone ordered that the women be forcibly fed by means of a rubber tube passed through the mouth or nose and into the stomach.

In the controversy that followed, rival representations of the law, of women and the process of force-feeding itself struggled for dominance. In that struggle a series of related but covert assumptions stood revealed, unconstrained by the normal conventions of sexual decorum.

News of forcible feeding appeared in the press on 24 September, and Keir Hardie tabled a parliamentary question. C. Masterman replied for the Home Office, describing forcible feeding as 'hospital treatment' (it was used in insane asylums and occasionally in prisons for 'ordinary' criminals). Hardie called it a horrible, beastly outrage, and in a letter to the press denounced both the action itself and the House's response to it. 'Women, worn and weak by hunger, are seized upon, held down by brute force, gagged, a tube inserted down the throat, and food poured or pumped into the stomach. Let British men think over the spectacle . . . I was horrified at the levity displayed by a large section of Members of the House when the question was being answered. Had I not heard it, I could not have believed that a body of gentlemen could have found reason for mirth and applause in a scene which I venture to say has no parallel in the recent history of our country.'[164]

Forcible feeding was a torturous procedure likely to produce pain in various organs, vomiting and lacerations to the resisting patient. First-person accounts of it, such as Mary Leigh's, written in Winson Green, are horrifying to read: 'on Saturday afternoon, the Wardresses forced me on to the bed and the two doctors came in with them, and while I was held down a nasal tube was inserted. It is two yards long with a funnel at the end – there is a glass junction in the middle to see if the liquid is passing. The end is put up the nostril, one one day, and the other nostril, the other. Great pain is experienced during the process . . . the drums of the ear seem to be bursting, a horrible pain in the throat and the breast. The tube is pushed down 20 inches. I have to lie on the bed, pinned down by Wardresses, one doctor stands up on a chair holding the funnel at arm's length, so as to have the funnel end above the level, and then the other doctor, who is behind, forces the other end up the nostrils. The one holding the funnel end pours the liquid down;

about a pint of milk, sometimes egg and milk are used. . . . Before and after use, they test my heart and make a lot of examination. The after-effects are a feeling of faintness, a sense of great pain in the diaphragm or breast bone, in the nose and the ears . . . I was very sick on the first occasion after the tube was withdrawn.'[165]

The WSPU called on sympathetic medical opinion to support their representation of forcible feeding not as 'hospital treatment', but as a physical outrage that aggravated bronchial conditions and risked injury, especially to the heart, lungs and digestive organs of the prisoner. It was, in Dr Forbes Ross's phrase, 'an act of brutality beyond common endurance',[166] and 116 surgeons and physicians signed a memorial against it that was presented to the Prime Minister. Keir Hardie and others protested in Parliament (where Gladstone sheltered behind the prison commissioners and medical officers). H. N. Brailsford and Henry Nevinson, suffrage sympathisers and distinguished journalists, resigned their positions on the *Daily News*, explaining in a letter to *The Times*: 'We cannot denounce torture in Russia and support it in England, nor can we advocate democratic principles in the name of a Party which confines them to a single sex.'[167] The WSPU took legal proceedings on behalf of Mary Leigh against the Home Secretary and the governor and doctor of Birmingham prison. Distinguished surgeons and doctors testified on her behalf, but on 9 December the Lord Chief Justice ruled that it was the duty of the prison medical officer to prevent a prisoner from committing suicide.

Clinically, morally, legally and politically the question was a complex one. The government felt that in effectively allowing women to end their own prison sentences they made a mockery of the law. It was, as a subsequent Home Secretary described it, 'a phenomenon absolutely without precedent' in British history.[168] On the other hand, in preventing suicide either for humanitarian reasons, or in an attempt to avoid making martyrs to the cause, they

used inhumane means and made martyr-victims nonetheless. Militancy and martyrdom went hand in hand.[169]

Women, with a range of provocations that justified them in militant eyes, were committing criminal damage for political ends. In doing so they sacrificed their respectability and their 'femininity', but it was nevertheless clear that they did not belong to the criminal classes. With great courage and resolution, if sometimes questionable political strategy, they could be said to have brought their suffering upon themselves. They did not *have* to hunger-strike. But the government was unable to secure its own representation of the women as so declassed and unsexed by their actions that the nature of their treatment was justified. The sexually charged levity that had shocked Keir Hardie in the House, and that runs through contemporary postcard illustrations (as through most violence against women), seemed to justify the WSPU's outrage at the assault on 'innocent' victims. It is not hard to understand how the instrumental invasion of their bodies by force, in a process accompanied by great pain and personal indignity, was felt as a kind of rape by the women who suffered it (though the word is not used directly), and that the sexual analogies present in their descriptions cannot be dismissed as the turn of a phrase, but were present to both parties in the experience.[170]

The controversy inside and outside the suffrage movement on forcible feeding was fuelled by the sexual and sadistic element attributed to the overcoming of women's resistance, and by the case of Lady Constance Lytton which pointed to discrepancies in the treatment of prisoners from different social classes. Constance Lytton had been arrested in October 1909 with Mrs Jane Brailsford and other members of the WSPU. On their conviction

52 'English Inquisitors': anon., Suffrage Atelier, *c.* 1912.
Forcible feeding, introduced to deal with hunger-striking suffragette prisoners in 1909, was regarded by suffragists as a form of torture.

the other women were placed in the Third Division, reserved for the commonest criminals, and forcibly fed. Lady Constance Lytton and Mrs Brailsford were placed in the Second Division, not subjected to forcible feeding and released on 13 October on medical grounds. Believing with the WSPU that as the daughter of a peer accompanied by the wife of a prominent journalist she had received preferential treatment that had little to do with her defective heart, Constance Lytton contrived to get herself rearrested, disguised this time as a working-class seamstress 'Jane Warton'. She was given a fourteen-day sentence and on the fourth day of her hunger strike forcibly fed without medical examination. She was fed in all eight times before her collapse in a state of exhaustion, and subsequently released, her identity discovered. She suffered a stroke in 1912 that left her partly paralysed, and died in 1923. The treatment accorded to a plain, ill-dressed, working-class seamstress in January 1910 was clearly distinct from that accorded to Lady Constance Lytton as a peeress with a heart murmur in October 1909.[171]

The NUWSS blamed the government for provoking acts of militancy through its own delays and evasions, for refusing the suffragettes the status of political prisoners, for hypocrisy in the matter of Ireland where much graver acts were committed in the agitation for Home Rule and for lack of political insight: the 'suffrage problem' would be solved by the vote and not by violence on either side. But the constitutionalists had also become increasingly critical of militant tactics which they disliked on principle, and which they believed to be counterproductive. (On its part the WSPU was sceptical of the National Union's Liberal sympathies, and impatient of the niceties of social convention.)

By the end of 1909 the NUWSS and the WSPU were scarcely on speaking terms, and the suffrage question seemed to have reached a political impasse. The optimism that had attached to mild and early militancy and the favourable publicity accorded the demonstrations of June 1908 had

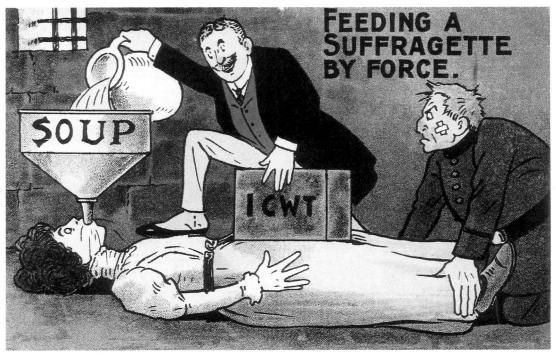

faded. The Prime Minister was intransigent, MPs were infuriated by militant attacks on the government,[172] and the Liberal and Labour parties had separately indicated a preference for adult suffrage over any limited measure. Women's suffrage was only one of the political issues pressing on the government in the second half of 1909, and not the most urgent. Lloyd George's 'People's Budget' of April 1909, proposing an increase in taxes on wealth and property, had been debated for seven months and eventually thrown out by the House of Lords. This in turn precipitated a constitutional crisis which obliged the Liberals to 'go back to the country', and a general election was called for January 1910.

This prospect raised hopes that the parliamentary stalemate on women's suffrage might be resolved – 245 candidates mentioned in their election address that they supported the extension of the franchise to women – and these hopes were enhanced by statements made early in the campaign by Churchill, Asquith and Grey.[173] The NUWSS interpreted this as meaning that the women's cause was a significant electoral issue for the Liberals, and went vigorously about their political activities, publishing their 'election manifesto' in *The Times* on 18 December, organising a voters' petition which gained 280,000 signatures on polling day, and circulating enormous quantities of propaganda by the beginning of 1910. New posters and postcards were produced by the WSPU (concentrating on forcible feeding and on the implications for women of the constitutional struggle with the House of Lords) and by the Artists' Suffrage League, principally for the NUWSS. The *Vote* informed the members of the Women's Freedom League that this was the moment when every effort must be increased. 'Sleeping hours must be curtailed, recreation found in slogging away at some aspect or other of "Votes for Women". Husbands must be informed that for the time being they must either take on the housekeeping for themselves or get an "anti" to do it for them . . .

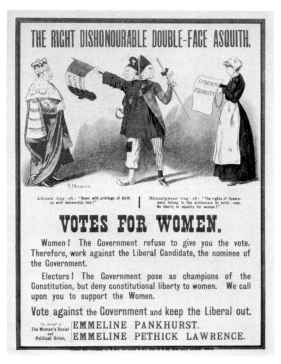

55 'The Right Dishonourable Double-Face Asquith': designed by A. Patriot (Alfred Pearse) at the end of 1909, on behalf of the WSPU for use in the General Election of January 1910.
In the context of the government's struggle with the House of Lords (the principal election issue of 1910), Asquith is shown appealing to the peers as a democrat while refusing women's claims to representative government.

opposite page
53 'The Prevention of Hunger Strikes', R. F. Ruttley, Suffragette Series.

54 'Feeding a Suffragette by Force', National Series.
As Maud Arncliffe-Sennett remarked of the comic postcard: 'must be a – woman – must be old and must be ugly and there you have it. Real solid British Humour catered for.'

56 'Who's Afraid? Not I!': postcard and poster, anon.,
Suffrage Atelier, *c.* 1911–12.
*Supporters had calculated that the terms of the Conciliation
Bill would enfranchise one woman for every seven male
voters, and that fears of 'petticoat government' were therefore
ungrounded. In 1909 the Artists' Suffrage League had
published a postcard with the slogan 'Seven to Two!', based
on a more liberal interpretation of a limited female franchise.*

This must be the last General Election in this
country at which women do not vote.'[174]

Suffrage propaganda was extensive, resourceful
and dedicated, but many MPs believed that theirs
was a cause on which votes were neither lost nor
won, and the January election remained focused on
the questions that had precipitated it: that is, on the
budget and the power of the House of Lords.[175]
The Liberals were returned to power with a drasti-
cally reduced majority. (In 1906 they had gained
400 seats out of a total of 670; now they held only
275, two more than the Conservatives, and the
balance of power lay with the Irish Nationalists,
who had two, and the Labour Party, which had
forty.) The result made it even less likely that a
private member's bill framed in the Liberal interest
would pass the House of Commons, and in the
light of this, and of Asquith's pre-election promise
to look sympathetically at the question, an all-party
Conciliation Committee of fifty-four MPs was
formed.[176] In February 1910 they drew up a bill
based on the household franchise, which would
enfranchise single women householders and a
number of married women occupiers (about 1
million women altogether). From this point the
suffrage campaign entered a new phase, centred on
the struggle to get the Conciliation Bill through its
parliamentary readings and into law.

The bill produced a possible solution, but not
one on which everyone was agreed.[177] Suffragists
nevertheless saw their only chance in supporting it,
and in June 1910 Mrs Fawcett sent a circular letter
to all the National Union's branches urging meetings and demonstrations in support of what she
believed to be the most promising opportunity for
women's suffrage since 1884.[178] The militants
announced a truce and suffragists and suffragettes
drew closer together in bringing pressure to bear in
support of the bill. On 14 June 1910 it passed its
first reading, and on the 18th both the WSPU and
the Women's Freedom League organised another
major demonstration in its support.

'From Prison to Citizenship', 18 June 1910

As early as 24 September 1909 Maud Arncliffe-Sennett had written to Philippa Strachey urging the organisation of a massive and united demonstration before the general election of January 1910. 'I want a Procession – 20 times as large as the last one of June 1908 – & please don't laugh at the "I want" – and then for the women either to turn into Hyde Park or else be drafted off to fill *every* Hall in London. I want! The National Union with Mrs Fawcett to lead off . . . and *all* other women to be invited to co-operate . . . We have, for fifty years appealed to their sense of Justice, reason, logic – all to no avail. We must *appeal to their emotions* . . . Asquith *won't* after what has happened climb down – we *must* go to the people & before the Election.'

Philippa Strachey's response was cool and brief: the National Union societies had debated the matter at their quarterly meeting and come 'to the serious conclusion that it was essential that the constitutional suffragists should separate themselves completely from those who employ different methods . . . there are now questions of principle at stake which cannot be overlooked.' Undeterred, Maud Arncliffe-Sennett wrote to Lady Frances Balfour, but at the end of the year received a similar reply. 'Processions were good enough to show our demand, but I think we have marched past the days when they were useful.'[179]

What made processions possible again in 1910 was the introduction and subsequent progress of the Conciliation Bill, together with the WSPU's temporary truce and their commitment to a major demonstration in its support. The militants planned a procession in May (postponed until 18 June because of the King's death), and on 5 April Emmeline Pethick-Lawrence offered the NUWSS the use of a box at the Albert Hall, adding that the WSPU would be 'very glad to welcome your members if they will walk in the Procession'.[180]

On 18 April Edith Dimmock, Honorary Secretary of the NUWSS, returned the tickets with a carefully worded note which stressed that this should not be considered an 'unfriendly act'. 'We are all working for the same object and for this reason have a strong fellow feeling for one another: but our methods differ, as we consider fundamentally, and we have therefore most reluctantly come to the conclusion that it is in the best interests of our common cause that we should keep entirely apart as far as our work is concerned, and that the National Union of Women's Suffrage Societies should not be officially represented at your demonstration.'[181]

It appears that many members of the NUWSS regretted this decision, and that there was a groundswell of popular opinion against it. Numerous letters were sent to the London Society and to the *Common Cause* urging that the constitutionalists should participate. Correspondents believed the Conciliation Bill to be 'trembling in the balance; its fate depends partly on the size and the importance of the demonstration.'[182] Absence would scarcely register with the public, and whatever the official policy of the NUWSS committee, constitutional suffragists would participate anyway: 'we have therefore only to choose whether a large number of our members should be forced to walk under WSPU colours or whether a very large number should walk under our own colours.' The NUWSS, however, remained unmoved, and without it the WSPU and the Women's Freedom League pressed ahead with their preparations for 18 June, the first large-scale public procession since the suffrage demonstrations of 1908.

In this the position of the WFL was equivocal. It urged its members to 'show the public that we are stronger and more energetic than ever before. The eyes of the whole of Great Britain will be on the militants on this occasion, and we must show that militancy has proved a success, and has drawn to the cause a great army of women from all ranks of life.' At the same time its relations with the WSPU were sensitive and competitive. An imposing scheme in the League's colours (green, white and gold) was now quite as important as sheer numbers in impressing the general public; it would help to unify their separate contingents, and bring home to rival societies the vigorous activity of the WFL. In achieving it they enjoyed the organising and designing skills of Edith Craig and the services of the Suffrage Atelier, which provided banners for almost every section in their procession. (Most of the Artists' Suffrage League banner production had been concentrated in the first half of 1908, and this was the first important opportunity for the Atelier to embark on a burst of urgent banner-making for which volunteers were required to help 'sew, stencil and decorate'.)[183]

The omens were considered favourable, both for the procession on the 18th and for the first reading of the Conciliation Bill four days before. The demonstration was to be 'an object lesson' for Members of Parliament. 'It must be so great that it will fill with enthusiastic determination those MPs who are favourable to Woman Suffrage, and that it will show those who are hostile the futility of further opposition.'[184]

Because of its length, what was subsequently referred to as the 'From Prison to Citizenship' procession formed up along the Embankment in two main sections, facing each other across Northumberland Avenue. Cars and carriages sped back and forth in the brilliant sunshine arranging banners and distributing flowers. Full public mourning for Edward VII had come to an end the day before, and after weeks of black it was in a flurry of white summer dresses, bedecked with flowers and accented in green and purple or gold, that participants slipped through the crowds to their places in the line. Marshals nudged and pulled at the shape of the procession, smoothing out difficulties which caused the contingents to move at the last moment, trying to ensure order as a dense pressure of crowds rendered the whole Embankment impassable.[185]

Punctually at 6.30 pm Mrs Drummond, seated astride 'a huge charger',[186] raised her whip and rode slowly up Northumberland Avenue. An inspector and nine mounted policemen cleared the way in front of her. Behind her a procession of between ten and fifteen thousand women two miles long moved into life, with forty bands and 700 banners and Charlotte Marsh as the WSPU colour-bearer at its head.

Behind Charlotte Marsh came the WSPU Drum and Fife Band with Mary Leigh as bandmistress 'swinging her silver-mounted staff in a manner which would have done credit to the Guards'.[187] The band introduced the Prisoners' Pageant: 617 women in white with their badges and medals like decorations on the left breast and 'a glittering host of steely broad arrows' – the emblems of their imprisonment – glinting in the evening sunshine. They carried Housman's 'From Prison to Citizenship' banner made for the Kensington branch in 1908, and also a new design: the enormous purple, white and green 'Hunger Strikers' Banner' embroidered with the signatures of eighty women who had 'faced death without flinching'. Confronted with their determination, Emmeline Pankhurst asked later in the Albert Hall, what could not the thousands of other women on that march and in that meeting achieve? At the rear of the Prisoners' contingent came the Prisoners' Tableau, arranged by Marion Wallace Dunlop and Edith Downing. Two white horses in trappings of gold and purple with laurel wreaths drew the car, on which sat a suffragette in prison clothes accompanied by 100 young girls in white dresses.[188]

The Women's Freedom League section was headed by the familiar if eccentric figure of Charlotte Despard, erect and purposeful with a bunch of arum lilies in her arms and a black lace mantilla on her white hair. She led a detachment of WFL prisoners and picketers with a new banner representing 'the greatness of woman's patience',[189] a virtue only worth celebrating by a militant society at this moment when it was widely believed that it would finally be rewarded.

57 WSPU procession, 18 June 1910, with Hunger Strikers' banner.

Nurses were as ever essential and all the London hospitals and nursing homes had been circulated to encourage their presence. 'Here, as the eye ran through the lines of women one saw the medals ornamenting the chest of many a tried and trusted nurse, or recognised by the bronzed face that the nurse had seen service out of England in the cause of humanity.'[190] Behind the nurses came the pharmacists, the cyclists with gold, white and green flowers on their bicycles, the athletes with their new banner of Diana, and in a stroke of stage management by Edith Craig, the sweated workers. The physical contrast between this group and the athletes who preceded them silenced the crowd, as boot machinists, box-makers and skirt-makers passed by, hot and toil-worn but unfaltering, 'of any section in that vast procession needing enfranchisement the most'. 'No one told them to "go home and mind the baby" when they passed by many who were wearing the products of their worn hands.'[191]

A series of independent contingents followed the Freedom League. Cicely Hamilton helped to carry Mary Lowndes's big black and white banner for the Writers' Suffrage League (a writer, according to Oscar Wilde, puts 'black upon white, black upon white');[192] and Alice Meynell, Alice Zimmern, Elizabeth Robins and May Sinclair were among those who accompanied her, each with a black and white banneret with the name of a well-known woman writer such as George Eliot, Fanny Burney or Elizabeth Barrett Browning. Eight hundred university graduates, a 'regiment of Portias', included Mrs Fawcett's daughter Philippa and a group of physicians led by her sister Elizabeth Garrett Anderson, 'glorious in Doctor's scarlet'. The Church League included lay members and a number of renegade constitutionalists who had chosen this section to walk in. It was led by a group of clergymen in cap and gown, 'received with rather surprising favour by the multitude',[193] but subject to the cold and impassive gaze of the Archbishop of Canterbury who surveyed the procession from the balcony of the Athenaeum. Perhaps he was better charmed by the actresses, the best dressed contingent according to the *Daily Express*, carrying their banner in rose and pale green, and staves bound with foliage and pink roses. In the absence of the Artists' Suffrage League the artists' section was made up of members of the Suffrage Atelier, their palettes tied with flowers and ribbons in the Atelier colours of orange and blue.

The Irish Women's Franchise League had travelled all night to take part, with a large group of women and a green banner carried by Kathleen Sheely and Mrs Sheehy-Skeffington in academic dress. The Tax Resisters brought the banner of John Hampden. The Men's Leagues walked with Housman's banner in black and gold, 'a sober, grey-coated and . . . grey-haired company in the middle of the army of marching women'.[194] Americans, Canadians and Australians helped counter the argument that the Empire would crumble if British women had the vote by reminding spectators of the quarters in which women already had it. The Fabians, the Ethical Societies, the Younger Suffragists, the New Constitutional Society and hundreds more too numerous to mention brought up the rear, with a stream of motor-cars and carriages garlanded with flowers. Coachmen wore rosettes, horses were caparisoned in purple, white and green, and the shafts and wheels of one landau were picked out in white roses.

Almost all the participants carried flowers – the *Daily Express* remarked that 'the air was fragrant with the scent of iris and lily' – and the garlands, the banners, the light summer dresses with brilliant touches of colour in the academic robes, the festive music and infectious delight of the participants, all under a cloudless June sky after weeks of national mourning, gave the impression of a sudden carnival rather than a political demonstration. (*The Times* compared it to 'a scene to be witnessed in a sunny city of Southern Europe on the high festival of the beneficent patron saint'.)

The crowds assembled to see the procession pass as for a great national occasion, swarming on the pavements, clinging to statues and railings, crowding on doorsteps, filling the windows of adjacent buildings, watching from cabs and the tops of open buses. No less than the suffragists, they were becoming accustomed to their appointed role. 'Not once along the way were the old rudenesses voiced, but the crowd was kind and strangely comprehending.'[195] The prisoners' sections were heartily cheered and the nurses, as ever, applauded all along the route. Hundreds of men leaned from the windows of the Life Guards' barracks in Knightsbridge, 'cheering the colours of ten thousand women' as banner after banner went by.[196] The Men's Leagues endured the 'cold fish-like eyes' of 'dull heavy men' at the windows of West End clubs, but they were cheered by the nurses and patients at St George's Hospital, by the soldiers' wives at Knightsbridge Barracks, and by women in the crowd and on passing omnibuses.

Nobody told them to go home to their golf clubs or assured them that man's place was in the office or the bar parlour, even if the crowds did not always recognise artists, playwrights, poets, magistrates, naval officers or the cricket captains of Oxford and Middlesex in their midst.[197]

Even by the standards the suffragists had set themselves in 1908 it was a massive, impressive, and very festive spectacle without difficulties or hitches – 'perfect in arrangement and temper' – and permeated for the first time with the scent of impending victory. The women were old hands now at something still novel and daring three years before. They had redefined the limits of decorum, and by turning the city streets into a festival they had discovered how to make them comfortably their own. For the duration of the procession at least, the spectators were converted to their presence if not always to their cause.[198]

The Women's Freedom League walked on to their own meeting in the Kensington Town Hall, while the WSPU prisoners' contingent lined up as guard of honour at the Albert Hall. From floor to ceiling the hall was filled with white dresses splashed with the WSPU colours that were echoed in banners hung from the balconies. The thirteen-year-old Esther Knowles gazed down from a balcony to where the heads of the audience swayed 'like a field of summer grasses' in the vast auditorium beneath, and the leaders stood 'like pygmies' on the platform, waiting to speak.[199]

Mrs Pankhurst, a slight and elegant figure, alone in black, rose to open the proceedings. As the cheers subsided she said, 'We have only one word in our thoughts today, and that word is "Victory". If the government should thwart or postpone that victory now, God help them in the times that are coming.' She was followed by Lord Lytton, who outlined the work of the Conciliation Committee and traced the political developments that had brought them to the eve of a hoped-for triumph. Mrs Pankhurst then opened the appeal, and Frederick Pethick-Lawrence set the pace with a

donation of £1000 of his own: within a very short space of time and amid mounting excitement £73,700 had been raised. The strategies of the WSPU were increasingly controversial, but there was no doubt that 'a cause which a few years ago excited ridicule and laughter . . . today stands for systematised agitation, methodical propaganda, for the rights of women.'[200] *Votes for Women* had promised its readers that the public would speak of the procession to their children and grandchildren, as 'the day that consummated the victory of woman suffrage for Great Britain, and so for the whole world'.[201] That victory, however, was still to come.

The Conciliation Bill came before the House for its second reading on 11 and 12 July, and although *The Times* had published articles against it every day for the previous fortnight, it passed its second reading by 110 votes. But because widening amendments were unlikely to be permitted, Lloyd George and Churchill had both voted against it, Lloyd George describing it as 'undemocratic', and Churchill as likely to provide an electoral advantage to the Conservatives. Rosen, the WSPU's historian, concludes that the vote was essentially an affirmation of support for the principle of women's suffrage, rather than for the terms of the Conciliation Bill, since a few minutes later the Commons voted by 320 to 175 to refer it to a committee of the whole House, thereby extinguishing its chances. Nevinson wrote in his diary, 'So another hope is killed'; and on 23 July Asquith informed Lord Lytton that no further time would be granted to the bill that session.[202]

23 July 1910

The day that Asquith communicated the decision that temporarily buried the Conciliation Bill turned out by ironic coincidence to be the day of a second major demonstration in its support. On 25 June a special executive committee of the NUWSS, inspired, perhaps, by the success of the militant procession on the 18th and by a measure of regret that they had not participated, resolved to hold a joint and peaceful demonstration in which all the major societies would collaborate.[203] The tangled history of the July procession rehearsed some of the misunderstandings and injured feelings of the June arrangements, as the National Union and the WSPU tried to agree on the organisation of a united demonstration.

Having argued before 18 June that it would be impossible for them to do so, the National Union decided after all to collaborate with the WSPU. For their part the WSPU refused to suspend militant activity until the second reading was fixed for the Conciliation Bill. The NUWSS promptly withdrew their invitation, and were then astonished to receive a note of regret from Mrs Pethick-Lawrence pressing for a reconsideration. Once the second reading was arranged, difficulties between the societies appeared to be resolved. Mrs Pethick-Lawrence wrote again to the NUWSS inviting them to join a WSPU procession on the 23rd. The National Union decided formally to accept, on the same condition that militant tactics would not be resumed, but the WSPU prevaricated and the on–off demonstration was off again (at least for the constitutionalists, who lost their own initiative in the process).[204] The demonstration proposed by the National Union accordingly passed back into the hands of the WSPU and the opportunity for a united show of strength was lost, no doubt to the regret of individual members of both organisations, as well as that of influential supporters like Brailsford, who had urged a statesmanlike unity for the sake of the cause as a whole.[205]

Once the Conciliation Bill had passed its second reading the preparations took their flavour from that event: the demonstration was to be a means of urging its continued progress in the current parliamentary session and its successful passage into law. Arrangements were made with unprecedented intensity and speed.[206] Handbills were distributed, hundreds of meetings took place, teachers and nurses were canvassed, circulars were sent to the press and groups went out daily who

'chalked London white'. Twenty-two officers were appointed to organise the procession and its constituent sections; forty platforms were planned for Hyde Park (twice as many as in 1908); forty bands were booked including the Drum and Fife Band of the WSPU; and arrangements were made for mounted detachments of police to head the processions. Participants were reminded to avoid trailing gowns and large hats, to keep in line with eyes forward 'like a soldier in the ranks', not to break step, and not to wave handkerchiefs.

At a suggestion from the police it was agreed that there would in fact be *two* processions, with breaks between the contingents for traffic to pass, since the organisers confidently expected 20,000 women to take part. The west procession would form up on the north side of Holland Park, proceeding along the Bayswater Road and into Hyde Park at Marble Arch. The east procession, formed up on the Embankment between Westminster Bridge and Blackfriars, would take what *Votes for Women* called the 'pilgrim-worn track'[207] up Northumberland Avenue via Pall Mall and Piccadilly and enter the park at Hyde Park Corner.

With the procession of 18 June fresh in the public mind, it was particularly important that these processions should seem different and new. If the tempo of propaganda were to be maintained both crowds and participants had to be called out in comparable numbers for the second time in a month. Elaborate schemes were drawn up by Edith Craig and Laurence Housman for the west procession, and by Marion Wallace Dunlop and Edith Downing for the east. Lest its audience should be jaded with demonstrations, *Votes for Women* promised new symbols, massed bannerets and 'an entire change from the scheme carried out on June 18th'. (It is understandable, but perhaps significant, that this kind of talk was beginning to make them sound like a theatrical management.) To this end bands of volunteers were needed for 'nailing, painting, pasting, sewing, machining,' especially those who could spare whole days and bring their own scissors.[208]

Edith Craig and Laurence Housman devised a 'Roman' theme for the west procession which focused on the twin themes of Victory and Justice. The initials of the WSPU were modelled on the 'SPQR' of Roman standards and crowned with wreaths of victory. Housman's 'From Prison to Citizenship' banner was used again, together with a new hunger-strikers' banner devised as a pair to it.[209] Otherwise large banners were eliminated so as not to interfere with the more fluid impression of hundreds of clustered standards and fluttering pennons. Behind the mounted police came three horsewomen with lances, then the colour-bearers and the WSPU Drum and Fife Band, and then Mrs Pankhurst in a long white cloak. It would be tedious to rehearse the list of principal contingents which

58 WSPU procession, 23 July 1910. Artists from the Suffrage Atelier with palettes and ribbons.
This corresponds with press descriptions of 1910 and the inscription 1911 is probably wrong. Dates on Nurse Pine photographs are not always reliable.

followed a well-established pattern, but they included the graduates, the Women Writers' League, the Suffrage Atelier, the Women's Tax Resistance League and the numerous London and suburban branches of the WSPU.

The east procession, designed by Marion Wallace Dunlop and Edith Downing, was intended to demonstrate an 'Oriental' character that would complement the Roman legions of the Bayswater Road. There were few large banners but 'innumerable standards, prison gates, "sails" and pennons' and the tinkling of hundreds of tiny silver wind-bells in the breeze.[210] The prisoners had place of honour as on 18 June, and behind them came the actresses, representatives from the colonies, nurses, the Kensington and Chelsea artists with silver palettes gleaming in the sun, women gardeners with garlands of smilax and heather, chemists, teachers, civil servants, typists, and the green, white and gold pennons of the WFL led by Mrs Despard, with coaches, cars and carriages bringing up the rear.

With flags fluttering, the two processions converged on Hyde Park to the strains of the Marseillaise at half past five. There were 150 speakers at forty platforms and thousands of onlookers crowded between. The resolution was passed almost unanimously at 6.30 pm, there were few dissidents and no rowdyism, and the suffrage press was encouraged to claim the crowd's support although *The Times* insisted that it was merely well-behaved. There is nevertheless an uneasy sense that under its surface pageantry the purpose of the procession had not quite been fulfilled.

If this was so it was not the artists' fault. The spectacle had, as usual, been much admired, and its effect against the massed foliage of the park remarked upon. The resolution had been passed and was widely supported in the press. 'It is all as respectable as a service,' as one observer put it, and therein lay the problem.[211] Estimates of the number of participants (between about 12,000 and 20,000) varied more widely than usual, and the crowds lining the routes were less dense (although many had gathered in the park). The proceedings were picturesque and harmonious, the organisers showed all their familiar skill and sense of pictorial effect, but the impact was limited and numbers reduced by the spectacle coming so soon after the demonstration of 18 June.[212] The novelty was wearing off, and the very pageantry which had been so successfully developed to embody and orchestrate the suffrage demand now threatened its political effect. While they marched the women were unaware that Asquith had refused facilities to further the Conciliation Bill that session. At the end of July, Parliament adjourned until November.

59 Laurence Housman's 'From Prison to Citizenship' banner, carried by the prisoners' contingent on 23 July 1910.
Imprisonment was not a shame to be purged but a martyrdom to be celebrated. Hence the banners and certificates, the Holloway medals, and gold brooches set with flints for the stone-throwers. 'Those who dominate the movement have a sense of the dramatic,' as the Daily News *put it on 22 June 1908. 'They know that whereas the sight of one woman struggling with policemen is either comic or miserably pathetic, the imprisonment of dozens is a splendid advertisement.'*

60 Horsewomen riding astride at the head of the west procession designed by Edith Craig and Laurence Housman, in the WSPU demonstration of 23 July 1910.

*

In the interval before the opening of the autumn session all the suffrage societies worked strenuously to further their cause. Thousands of public meetings and demonstrations were held and resolutions in support of the Conciliation Bill were passed by 182 city, town and urban district councils. It is hard to see what else could have been done.[213] Parliament reconvened on 18 November and was almost immediately dissolved. The conference with the Lords had broken down and the constitutional crisis continued. Asquith

July 17

1910

61 Processionists with emblems of prison gates, 23 July 1910.
'July 17' has been written in error.

announced that for the ten days until dissolution, government business would take precedence. He did not mention the Conciliation Bill, but it was clear that it was shelved.

The WSPU had maintained its truce throughout the summer, but on hearing this news a deputation of 500 women set out for the House of Commons and attempted to rush past the police who held them back. On this occasion they were treated with unexpected and quite exceptional brutality, and after six hours of struggle and confusion 115 women and four men were arrested. Charges against most of them were withdrawn on the following day, on the Home Secretary's decision that 'no public advantage would be gained by proceeding with the prosecution.'[214]

The 18th of November became known in the

suffragette movement as 'Black Friday', and H. N. Brailsford and Dr Jessie Murray began to collect depositions from the women who had suffered in the course of it. Many of them testified to the sexual humiliation of the assaults to which they were subjected. In their summary of the testimony Brailsford and Murray stated: 'The action of which the most frequent complaint is made is variously described as twisting round, pinching, screwing, nipping or wringing the breast. This was often done in the most public way so as to inflict the utmost humiliation. Not only was it an offence against decency; it caused in many cases intense pain . . . The language used by some of the police while performing this action proves that it was consciously sensual.' Of the 139 statements alleging acts of violence, twenty-nine complained of violence with indecency. As one police officer said to a woman whose breast he wrung painfully, 'You have been wanting this for a long time, haven't you,' or in another case, when the woman complained of being manhandled, 'Oh, my old dear, I can grip you wherever I like today.' Women had their clothes and underwear torn, were battered and pushed, dragged by their hair, held upside-down, verbally and physically abused, and flung into the crowd. The WSPU accused Churchill of having given the police specific orders which led to their being knocked about for several hours rather than summarily arrested. Churchill insisted this was not the case and Rosen suggests that the catalyst for the events of Black Friday was a purely administrative decision to draft in police from Whitechapel and other East End districts. Unlike the men of 'A' division who had become accustomed to dealing with militant feminists over a number of years, the East End police had no experience of suffrage demonstrations, nor of disruptions caused by anyone but the poor and ill-educated. In ways that were no doubt spiced by the clash of class as well as gender, a group of physically strong and institutionally powerful men confronted a group of women of whose cause they knew nothing, and who – in the popular expression that makes light of physical and sexual abuse – 'deserved a good hiding'. They had been given leave somehow to believe they had the right to administer it, and they did not hesitate to do so.

The constitutionalists were bitter and disappointed too, but they were also furious at what they perceived as the militants' utter lack of tact and timing. They were convinced that Asquith would not be swayed by violence and they continued to campaign for the Conciliation Bill as the only chance of a women's suffrage measure on the political agenda, precarious as that chance now was.

The second general election of 1910, in December, left the position of the parties virtually unchanged.[215] (Since they had 'appealed to the country' this strengthened the government's hand.) The balance of power lay with the Labour members and the Irish Nationalists as before. Normally they voted with the Liberal Party, and were broadly sympathetic to women's suffrage. However, the Irish were not prepared to jeopardise the attainment of Home Rule through any other commitment whatsoever, and the problem of framing a conciliation measure that would prove acceptable to both sides of the House remained. Home Rule and other matters were pressing, and the constitutional crisis was still not fully resolved. The Liberals would not accept a measure that might upset the delicate balance of power, and although the likely consequences of the different terms of women's enfranchisement were hotly debated, no one could predict for certain what they would be.

The Conciliation Committee redrafted its bill with modifications to meet the criticisms of 1910, and in order to permit of free amendment.[216] Writing in the *Englishwoman* in January 1911, Mrs Fawcett acknowledged that its political prospects were far from clear. It was nevertheless their best opportunity, and there were grounds for optimism: there were more suffragists in the new House, Asquith had pledged facilities, the balance of power favoured a non-party measure, the Parliament Bill should be dealt with in time for it to be debated, and in the not impossible circumstance of Asquith resigning over the Parliament Bill, he might be replaced by Sir Edward Grey or R. B. Haldane, both of whom were more sympathetic to the women's cause.[217]

The redrafted Conciliation Bill passed its second reading with a majority of 167 on 5 May 1911. It was again referred to a committee of the whole House, this time by its sponsors, who challenged Asquith to keep his promise and grant facilities for its further passage. Arguing lack of parliamentary time, the government promised 'to undertake to give a week for its consideration (after a second reading) next session'.[218]

The Conciliation Committee, the NUWSS and the WSPU were infuriated. Three women's suffrage bills – Henry York Stanger's in 1908 and the two conciliation measures in 1910 and 1911 – had now passed their second readings with substantial majorities in the space of little more than three years, and the government's response was further prevarication and delay. Under pressure, Sir Edward Grey promised an 'elastic' week and facilities for a third reading in 1912, and this pledge was endorsed by Asquith in a letter to Lord Lytton reported in *The Times* on 17 June.

The tide seemed to have turned again, and militants and constitutionalists alike found their confidence renewed. Mrs Fawcett declared that they were higher up the ladder of success than they had ever been before.[219] Christabel described the pledge as one 'upon which women can base the expectation of taking part as voters in the election of the next and every future Parliament',[220] and on 7 June she suspended the WSPU by-election policy which had been in force since August 1906. From this point the militants would no longer work 'to keep the Liberal out', but would support or oppose individual candidates according to their position on the Conciliation Bill. The NUWSS again began to cooperate with the WSPU in the summer of 1911, arranging processions, meetings, and by-election activities throughout the country on an unprecedented scale. On 17 June, after several false starts in the preceding years, all the suffrage societies, including the NUWSS and the WSPU, joined for the first (and last) time in a procession of 40,000 women that reflected a new spirit of unity in the movement, and a new confidence in its success.

The Women's Coronation Procession, 17 June 1911

The suffrage procession of 17 June was the most spectacular, the largest and most triumphant, the most harmonious and representative of all the demonstrations in the campaign. It was the culmination, not only of months of work and negotiation, but also of the organisational and artistic skills which had transformed the propaganda campaign since that cold and muddy day in February 1907 when 3000 constitutionalists had braved the weather and the occasion and trudged from Hyde Park to the Exeter Hall. Forty thousand women from at least twenty-eight women's suffrage organisations marched five abreast in a gala procession with floats, banners, music and historical costumes that was seven miles long. Inspired by the occasion, by a sense of impending victory and by the spirit of harmony prevailing temporarily between the constitutionalists and the WSPU, the suffragists produced a pageant to rival the official Coronation procession, to question their exclusion from it and also the values on which it was based. With it, they reached the limit of public spectacle not just as a political device, but as a practical possibility, and they never attempted to organise in this way or on this scale again.

On 20 March 1911 Mabel Tuke, joint Honorary Secretary of the WSPU, wrote to the London Society of the NUWSS to invite their cooperation in 'a great procession which will march with banners flying, through the streets of London on June 17th (that is the Saturday before Coronation Day) to culminate in a mass meeting in the Albert Hall'. Because of the Coronation and the Imperial Conference, London would be thronged with visitors from overseas; it would be a golden opportunity to bring the women's suffrage movement 'before the eyes of all our fellow subjects from the Colonies' in a 'most striking and impressive object lesson' that would persuade this audience of the scope and strength of British women's demands for the same right that was now enjoyed by women in several of the colonies. The WSPU would organise the procession, but it invited all other suffrage societies 'to augment the ranks and to bring variety and beauty into the procession by the introduction of your own scheme of decoration'.[221]

This proposal split the constitutionalists. The executive committee of the NUWSS was divided, but on 6 April it voted with two dissentients to cooperate, thus effectively reversing its position in 1910. The executive committee of the London Society, the National Union's powerful London affiliate which had organised processions for it in the past, voted against it.[222] The NUWSS executive, including Mrs Fawcett, now believed that they needed to show the constitutionalists' strength and hoped to make their presence felt while dissociating themselves from militant sentiment and the WSPU resolutions in the Albert Hall. They were no doubt encouraged in this decision by the peaceful nature of the processions of 1910, and by the pressure of renegade constitutionalists who had joined in them.

The decision of the NUWSS executive provoked a flood of protest from its membership, including such distinguished individuals as Clementina Black and the veteran Emily Davies, and in particular from the London Society which sent a deputation to protest as 'a matter of principle and in the best interests of the cause' the decision to cooperate with the militants.[223] Only at the end of April, and under pressure from the NUWSS executive, did the London Society give way. Despite a conciliatory letter from Mrs Fawcett in the *Common Cause* on 4 May, another flurry of objections came in now, pointing out that the WSPU might well choose the Coronation period for militant activity, and that members who had wanted to join the processions of 1910 had subsequently changed their minds: those 'who wished it *then* don't wish it *now* because of what happened last November' (Black Friday on the 18th and window smashing on the 22nd). Mary Lowndes, piqued at the decision to cooperate with the WSPU but also, on behalf of the artists, at being taken for granted, wrote a detailed letter to the NUWSS and London Society executives setting out the practical difficulties as she saw them.[224]

The first problems were problems of scale. She had watched the drawing up of the WSPU processions in 1910, and as one of the three or four people who had blocked out the NUWSS demonstration of 1908 she was confident there was simply no room for a further 10,000 people. The procession of 23 July had taken two hours to pass a given point – as much as would retain the spectators' attention – so that a procession twice as long 'would be in its latter part quite ineffective and really impossible'. Yet if the constitutionalists *failed* to add substantial numbers there would be little point in 'walking behind Mrs Pankhurst to show our inferiority'. (Since Lady Frances Balfour was unavailable, and Mrs Fawcett due to be in Stockholm for the International Woman Suffrage Alliance Congress, it looked briefly as though the constitutionalists would appear to be led by Mrs Pankhurst, by default.)[225]

The second difficulty concerned the matter of decoration. An immense number of decorative devices had been made by the militants for the two processions of 1910, and it was Mary Lowndes's conclusion that the constitutionalists had nothing as effective for their own use. Many new things would have to be made and a whole scheme of decoration organised, but 'Miss Forbes and I are both absolutely unable to give the time required for organising such a thing at this moment; and I do not know anyone else in the Artists' League who will give up their home and all their work for some weeks.'

Mary Lowndes was a valued member of the London Society and the National Union was well aware how much it owed the Artists' League, but neither would turn back now. In the end it was Emily Ford – a member of the League but apparently on her own initiative – who offered to make shield-shaped banners in the NUWSS colours, inscribed with the names of town councils that had passed resolutions in support of the Conciliation Bill, and 'so made as to show no possible relation to the WSPU'. Her offer was gratefully accepted by Philippa Strachey who promised the costs of eight shillings each: 'The time seems dreadfully short and it will be truly noble if you can manage it.'[226]

By the beginning of May all the chief societies were active in their preparations for 17 June, appointing administrators and procession committees, compiling inventories of their costumes and props, marshalling stewards and out-of-town contingents, planning their meetings and their advertising, and setting up demonstration and finance committees to defray expenses. With all the suffrage societies participating for the first time, the rivalry between them was intensified. Within the new spirit of cooperation each was anxious to outdo the others in splendour of numbers and decorative effect.[227]

Each new spectacle had, for its artistic and political effect (which were no longer quite the same thing), to transcend the last. To this end the tried and trusted formulae were reapplied (the nurses, the graduates, the prisoners' pageant now almost 700 strong), but something different was needed too. Coronation year gave the women not only their audience but their particular theme. June the 17th marked the beginning of a week of holiday and national festivity in which the two royal processions of 22 June and 23 June would take place and London would be thronged with visitors who had come from all over the world to witness them. For the WSPU these two processions would be 'to an overwhelming extent representative of the manhood of the Empire. For women as one half of the people who are the King's loyal subjects there is no place in these two great pageants of national strength and glory.'[228] The Pankhursts, despite their now distant origins in the Independent Labour Party, were quite capable of playing the imperial card when it suited them, and this was the omission they now set out to repair: they would provide the opportunity for women from Britain and overseas to demonstrate in front of the Empire and at its heart 'their sense of patriotism, and their readiness for public service in the interests of their country'.[229] The whole procession, as *Votes for Women* emphasised on 28 April, would be at once national (every suffrage society in Britain was invited to take part); imperial (since a 'Pageant of Empire' was planned, and the imperial section would represent all political parties and sections of the community); and international (with suffragists from every country and flags of every nation). The Women's Coronation Procession would represent the culmination of a series of demonstrations of increasing theatricality, symbolic complexity and decorative effect. Although it was a matter of astute political strategy to insert the procession into a set of dominant and topical representations of sovereignty in this way, it was also indicative of the Pankhursts' increasingly conservative position, which anticipated their 'sense of patriotism, and their readiness for public service' in the First World War.

On the afternoon of 17 June women once again – with practised ease now, but for the last time – assembled along the Embankment on either side of Northumberland Avenue.[230] The pavements were soon almost impassable, and only with difficulty could the stewards and marshals join up the 'bewildering mosaic' and slip participants into the one place in 40,000 that was allotted to them. The long line hummed with excitement, anticipation and a sense of urgency. The crowds milling about it were in celebratory mood. London was on holiday. The weather was brilliant. A week of spectacle and festivity lay in store. In Trafalgar Square, a favourite vantage point, there were people on all the hundreds of seats erected for the Coronation. 'On the big branches of lamp-posts – more people. Up ladders, on signboards, on scaffolding, on the tops of drays, motors, taxi-cabs, on roofs, on other people's toes, on their backs, on the very verge of the fountains, up the long streets which lead to the Square (whether they could see or whether they could not see), anywhere where they could stand, sit, lean, or be pushed, were people – black, buzzing, excited people.'[231]

At 5.30 pm General Drummond led off on horseback with Charlotte Marsh as colour-bearer on foot behind her, and suddenly the miles of pageantry flowed together, and the whole procession gathered itself up and swung along Northumberland Avenue to the strains of Ethel Smyth's *March of the Women*. Behind Charlotte Marsh rode Joan Annan Bryce (daughter of an MP and niece of the British ambassador in Washington), 'in armour, on a white palfrey'[232] as Joan of Arc. The image of female heroism and militant martyrdom glossed in this way, the theme was taken up by a contingent of the recently formed 'New Crusaders'. Each wore a 'royal mantle of purple' and carried the helmet of faith and the lance of courage: 'a group symbolising the militant and idealistic organisation of women in a Holy War, to reassert the rights to possess the Sacred Places'.[233] (The tendency of the WSPU and the WFL to adopt chivalric metaphors for militant righteousness narrowly skirted the bathetic. It was the kind of language that infuriated the women of the National Union.)

The Prisoners' Pageant, the Historical Pageant and the Pageant of Empire were again the work of Marion Wallace Dunlop and Edith Downing. The mobilisation of 700 prisoners (or their proxies) dressed in white, with pennons fluttering from

62 The Women's Coronation Procession, 17 June 1911.
This was the most spectacular of all the pre-war demonstrations, and the only one in which all the suffrage societies participated.

their glittering lances, was, as the *Daily Mail* observed, 'a stroke of genius'. At first the crowd just looked at them as part of the spectacle, 'but in a little while as the 700 went on marching, five abreast, the crowd realised that these women had dared to suffer hardships and humiliations for an idea. There was nothing in their looks to suggest why they in particular should have done it. Some were handsome and some had personality, but taken as a whole they looked just ordinary women.'

The Historical Pageant was intended to illustrate 'the great political power held by women in the past history of these Isles, the last vestige of which was lost with the vote in 1832 when the Reform Bill was passed'.[234] There was some special pleading here, but it was a reasonable attempt to establish that different forms of power had existed before the bourgeois revolutions, and women's gender and social standing had determined their rights and capacities in the feudal and early modern period in complex ways. The important point was to drive a wedge, by whatever means, into that cluster of beliefs which made women's exclusion from political citizenship a *natural* consequence of their feminine gender. To this end the 'gorgeous, changing, scintillating, iridescent colours of the banners flashing in the sun'[235] were followed by a long parade of women in period costume: the Abbess Hilda, peeresses summoned to Parliament in the reign of Edward III, burgesses on the parliamentary register of Lyme Regis in the reign of Elizabeth, women governors and custodians of castles, high sheriffs of counties and Justices of the Peace, freewomen of companies and corporations, voteless women from the period after the Reform Act of 1832 in which the middle-class basis of the modern democratic franchise was first established, representatives from New Zealand, Australia, Norway, Finland and several American states where women had the vote.

The 'Empire Car' was praised by the *Spectator* (not noted for its suffrage sympathies) as 'a thing of beauty . . . far surpassing the crude symbolism of Lord Mayors' shows'.[236] The whole tableau was intended to symbolise the unity of the British Empire, a reinhabiting by women of the allegorical female figures by which such sentiments were conventionally expressed (as in the Victoria Memorial, unveiled the same year in 1911). 'High on the car two figures representing East and West were seated; at their feet rested the islands of the East and the West, symbolised by children sheltered under the Emperor King's roof tree; below were the women who symbolised the dominions over the seas, and linked with the colonies was India. The four corners of the earth were bound in unity to the Crown.'[237] The symbolism is a trifle garbled, if not in intention then in its reinterpretation in the local press. There is an uneasy edge to these descriptions now, which reveal how suffrage imagery at this moment sought to exploit the 'invented traditions' of a resurgent state ritual, and was perhaps not always successful in bending them to its own ends.

In order to give substance to their claim for international representation the suffragists were obliged to draw on the rhetoric of national identity. All the national costumes, tokens, music and assorted cultural signifiers that could be mobilised (some of them of fairly recent origin) were pressed into service. Scottish pipers, Welsh choirs, Irish harps, joined the fern tree (New Zealand), the kangaroo (Australia), the maple leaf (Canada), the springbok (South Africa) and the elephant (India) among the colonial and international contingents. In lieu of a history of their own, women turned to an accumulated language of symbolic identities, much of it claiming ancient authority but in fact a fairly recent development along with the nation-state. Boadicea was for them not the embodiment of 'an ancient past beyond effective historical continuity' as she was for British nationalism, but like Joan of Arc a type of militant femininity. If all invented traditions attempt to use history as the cement for group cohesion as Eric Hobsbawm has argued,[238] then the women's use of historical

63 The Pageant of Empire from the Women's
Coronation Procession, 17 June 1911.

components was no more and no less selective than those of the discourses to which they were opposed.

The Welsh contingent in the Women's Coronation Procession provides in microcosm a very good example of the way in which even radical movements, raiding the past for their own purposes, built their own symbolic syntax out of the heterogeneous ingredients of other, sometimes hegemonic and often recently established traditions. Wishing to contribute to the picturesque effect and uphold their own identity in the Pageant of Empire, the Welsh organisers went to a great deal of trouble in 1911 to track down 'authentic' costumes to be borrowed or copied by their participants.[239] In doing so they drew on a spurious folk revivalism, on the basis of which elements of seventeenth-century English lowland dress such as tall hats and cloaks, which had lingered on in Welsh mountain areas to the 1790s and even after, were turned into a national costume in the 1830s as a result of the efforts of several different figures in the Romantic nineteenth-century Welsh revival. The costume was soon adopted to serve as a representation or caricature of 'Wales', reproduced on thousands of Victorian postcards and pottery figurines, and worn by schoolchildren all over the country on St David's Day in celebration of their national identity. Meanwhile 'the old native costumes in all their local varieties (even including here and there a tall beaver hat and a large cloak) died away as Wales became one of the most industrialised countries in the world.'[240]

Thus one 'invented tradition' piggy-backed on another. Symbols must be recognisable if they are to be used in public discourse or they will not carry meaning. What matters is their legibility and not, for the purposes of communication, their 'truth'. Once Welshness was associated with a certain costume, so that association was consolidated by its use in a new construction of 'women-of-Britain'. The consequence was a polyglot symbolism in which one discourse drew its elements, and with

them its legitimacy, from another. In the process both were further secured: 'Welshness' and its meanings on the one hand, 'Votes for Women' and the spread of support for it on the other.

The Prisoners' Pageant, the Historical Pageant, and the Pageant of Empire were the most striking, because they were the newest features of the procession of 1911. There is space here only to indicate a few of the hundreds of other sections and subsections that made up its cumulative effect.

The International contingents were followed by the pale blue, white and gold of the Conservative and Unionist Women's Franchise Association, and then by a pageant of queens: Bertha, Boadicea, Ethelflaed, Eleanor, Anne Boleyn, Jane Seymour, Lady Jane Grey, Mary Queen of Scots and Henrietta Maria in the royal robes of their period. Charlotte Despard, as always, headed the green, white and gold contingents of the Women's Freedom League – so formidable a figure on these occasions that she reminded Henry Nevinson of 'The Fighting Temeraire'[241] – preceded by a banner with the League's motto: 'Dare to be Free'. Representatives from each of the forty-four WFL branches carried gilt staves topped with laurel wreaths. Special contingents commemorated the militant activities of the previous five years, an emphasis tactfully modulated by the presence of twenty-one members with white flags and a 'Truce Banner', reminding the onlookers that militancy had been suspended during the passage of the Conciliation Bill. The *Vote* had promised that 'the industrial slaves of Britain, the sweated women workers of today' would march under banners 'blazoning forth their bitter state' to emphasise the 'widespread appeal that the democratic constitution of the League makes to women of all classes'.[242] Their banner, inscribed 'Six Million

64 The Welsh contingent in 'national dress', 17 June 1911.

65 Mrs Despard in front of the Women's Freedom League banner, 17 June 1911.

Women Workers Need the Vote', was greeted with tremendous applause along the route, and helped to secure the WFL as an organisation with the compassion of the constitutionalists as well as the courage of the WSPU.

The Church Leagues followed the WFL, and then it was the turn of the National Union, headed by Mrs Fawcett and the new NUWSS banner, making 'a vivid line of colour as their ten thousand went past in white and red'.[243] The constitutionalist section was rich with banners. There were the eighty new ones designed by Emily Ford, banners from the Irish, Scottish, and five English federations, and many of those made by the Artists' Suffrage League in 1908 which were brought out again. Further groups of industrial women, women from Oxford and Cambridge, and the independent 'Graduates' Union' marched under their own devices, and finally the red, white (and now green) of the NUWSS gave way to the colours of other contingents: the Women Writers' Suffrage League with a new banner based on the painting of Justice by W. H. Margetson; the Artists' Suffrage League and the Suffrage Atelier in their blue overalls;[244] Yvette Guilbert and Lillah McCarthy among the Actresses; Annie Besant bare-headed in yellow silk at the head of the Order of Universal Co-Freemasonry; the Women's Tax Resistance League, the Fabian Women's Group, the Ethical Societies, sanitary inspectors, gardeners, gymnasts, the Kensington and Chelsea artists and the Men's Leagues including the Men's Political Union led by a nervously mounted Henry Nevinson (his mare did nothing worse than eat the daisies from a little girl's hat);[245] 40,000 women and the Men's Leagues in seven miles of 'gold and glitter and sparkling pageantry'.

Press coverage for the procession was the most extensive and the most flattering that the suffragists had ever received. Suffrage and anti-suffrage papers alike were virtually unanimous in their enthusiasm for the demonstration as a public spectacle, and its salient points were stressed across the whole spectrum of political positions: the richness of its pageantry, the brilliance of its organisation, the courage and diversity of the participants (with special reference to the cooperation of the National Union), the size and response of the crowds 'agape for pageantry'.[246]

Philip Snowden in the *Christian Commonwealth* invoked for his readers the 'tens of thousands of cultured and refined women to whom it must have been a struggle . . . to face, possibly, the jeers and jests of an ignorant crowd of sight-seeing men'.[247] But strictly speaking this was no longer true. A participant who remembered the Mud March of 1907 remarked on the change that had taken place since then: 'the Suffragist was an untried curiosity. Now she and her leaders are recognised public characters . . . women who, in a wonderfully short time, have fortified for themselves an inexpugnable place in the life of the nation.'[248] The *Vote* described the call of camaraderie that spread from processionists to the waiting crowd, and how all along the line came the sounds of applause and encouragement. Even the *Anti-Suffrage Review* described the pageant as a 'charming spectacle, and well stage-managed';[249] though it argued that 'the absence of the vote never yet prevented women from doing noble work' (as the Historical Pageant inadvertently demonstrated), and it was wisely silent on the half-dozen sandwich men hired by the Anti-Suffrage League to parade with boards proclaiming 'Women Do Not Want the Vote' in the face of 40,000 marching women who clearly did.[250] Suffragists were confident their day had come: the 'mass of people are convinced, and, that being so, Mr Asquith may ply his mop, but the tide will swamp him – and that quickly'.[251]

There was, however, another way of looking at their success. As one processionist wrote in the *Daily Sketch* (in contrast with Philip Snowden's arguments in the *Christian Commonwealth*): 'There were no objections, no taunts; the thing required no more temerity than if it had been a bridal procession to a village church. In the greatness and

beauty of the pageant one felt that London had forgotten the protest by which it was inspired.' The suffragists had won universal acclaim for the beauty and skill of a strategy whose political effectiveness had still to be proved.[252]

66 The Actresses' Franchise League, assembled for the Women's Coronation Procession, 17 June 1911.

*

The spirit of optimism and cooperation in the suffrage campaign continued into the autumn. With the passage of the Parliament Act in August 1911, two months later, the constitutional crisis was resolved and the government was able to turn to other parts of its programme, including the matter of electoral reform. Meanwhile the militant truce and the suspension of the WSPU's anti-government by-election policy were maintained.

Christabel seems to have got wind in October of 'a conspiracy of wreckers and reactionaries'[253] bent on destroying the Conciliation Bill. But no one was prepared for Asquith's surprise announce-

67 'Political Conjuring': postcard designed by Hope
Joseph for the Suffrage Atelier, 1912.
*The reference is to the introduction of the Reform Bill in
1912, which displaced the Conciliation Bill and threatened
to give no votes to women and more votes to men. Asquith
had a reputation as a wily, sophisticated and slippery
politician. He had already been portrayed as a political
conjurer by Alfred Pearse in* Votes for Women, *17
December 1909.*

ment on 7 November, in which he disclosed the
government's intention to introduce a Reform
Bill which would not include women, but which
would be open to amendment in the interests
of women's suffrage. Such a move inevitably
undermined the prospects of the Conciliation
Bill, and indeed appeared to the suffragists precisely calculated to do so. 'If it had been his object
to enrage every women's suffragist to the point of
frenzy,' wrote Mrs Fawcett, 'he could not have
acted with greater perspicacity. Years of unexam-
pled effort and self-sacrifice had been expended
by women to force upon the Government the
enfranchisement of women, and when the Prime
Minister spoke the only promise he made was to
give more votes to men.'[254] Nevinson found the
Pankhursts, convinced that the House would never
attach a women's amendment to the new Reform
Bill, 'livid with rage and deaf to reason'.[255] Militancy was immediately resumed, and with it the old
conflicts over strategy that divided the campaign.

A temporary and fragile sense of unity was
broken, and at the end of November the National
Union issued a statement denouncing the militants
and distancing itself from any implication in militant activity.[256] Through the winter of 1911–12 the
NUWSS persevered with the Conciliation Bill,
liaising with the Conciliation Committee, struggling with the government's evasions, and attempting to distance itself from the effects of WSPU
militancy. On 23 February 1912 it held a large
meeting with the London Society in the Albert
Hall, specially decorated by the Artists' Suffrage
League for the purpose, and launched an appeal
for £40,000. Its object, as expressed briefly in the
main resolution, was to call upon Parliament to
enfranchise women in 1912.[257]

On 16 February, at a welcome dinner for re-
leased prisoners, Mrs Pankhurst declared that,
'The argument of the broken pane is the most
valuable argument in modern politics.'[258] In the
West End on 1 March and in Knightsbridge and
Kensington three days later, well-dressed women

produced hammers from innocent-looking bags and parcels and fell to smashing the shop windows. The WSPU was jubilant at thrusting itself into the limelight again, but for the supporters of the Conciliation Bill its timing was disastrous. MPs complained to the NUWSS that even sympathetic members had been led to withdraw their support and that inevitably, despite the differences between the National Union and the WSPU, 'the odium of association attaches to the whole of those who hold the principle of their views.'[259] *The Times* announced that 'the window-smashing outrages have given such a setback to the cause of women's suffrage as none of its opponents could have hoped for under normal conditions,' and Austen Chamberlain predicted that 'if a few more windows were smashed the Bill would be smashed at the same time.'[260]

Nothing could now stem the tide of desertions in the House, and on 28 March the bill was defeated by a vote of 222 to 208. Mrs Fawcett later wrote that she felt as though what she had been working for for forty years was destroyed at a blow (although she added with characteristic tenacity that she also felt like beavers feel when their dam is destroyed, that there is nothing to be done but build it up again from the beginning).[261]

The 'argument of the broken pane' was only one factor in the bill's defeat, although one conveniently to hand as a justification for members who had reversed their votes (forty-three Conservatives voted against it in 1911, and 114 in 1912). The more radical government Reform Bill had indeed 'torpedoed' the conciliation measure by turning the Liberals against the comparative narrowness of its terms. The Irish Nationalists defected because they feared its successful passage would provoke Asquith's resignation and jeopardise Home Rule. The Labour vote was critical since the party had committed itself to the principle of women's suffrage at the January conference, but when the bill came before the House thirteen Labour MPs were visiting their constituencies because of the coal strike. Any one of these factors was enough to turn the balance, but there is also evidence that militancy itself lost sufficient votes – perhaps as many as 132 – to ensure defeat.[262]

Lobbying for the Conciliation Bill had become a Sisyphean task.[263] But it was the nearest the suffragists had ever come to victory, and its defeat brought serious consequences to the campaign as a whole. The last semblance of cooperation between the constitutional and militant wings was sundered, the psychological impetus derived from working for a government measure with a chance of success drained away, and with the Conciliation Committee broken up the sense of a parliamentary focus and the chance of a non-party solution were lost.

The defeat of the bill also completed the National Union's disillusion with the Liberal Party, and prompted a revaluation of its political strategies and party commitments. It had always been a non-party organisation with strong Liberal sympathies in practice. The Liberal vote on the Conciliation Bill persuaded its executive to form an alliance with the Labour Party – the only party, as Mrs Fawcett pointed out, to have adopted an official resolution in favour of women's suffrage.[264] In May 1912 the NUWSS formed a special committee, the Election Fighting Fund, that would raise 'a sum of money for the specific object of supporting individual candidates standing in the interests of Labour in a constituency where the NU thinks it advisable to oppose a Liberal Antisuffragist'.[265]

The new by-election policy was distinct from the WSPU's in that it proposed actively to campaign for (Labour) candidates, and only to challenge *anti*-suffrage Liberals. It rewarded Labour support (all the Labour members present had voted for the Conciliation Bill) and it acted as a spur to the Liberals. Writing on 'The Election Policy of the National Union' in the *Englishwoman* for June 1912, Mrs Fawcett insisted that the new tactics did not necessarily involve supporting the whole of the

Labour programme. The NUWSS remained 'neutral' in so far as it was quite prepared to support Conservative or Liberal candidates as soon as their parties took a similarly positive stand on the suffrage issue. Brailsford (a Liberal himself) had persuaded Mrs Fawcett of the need to prove to the government in by-election work 'that the suffragists could transfer seats from one side of the House of Commons to the other'.[266] (This was a different order of threat from WSPU militancy, which increasing numbers of MPs felt morally bound to resist.) Given the delicate balance of power in the House, the Liberals could not afford to have the NUWSS supporting – with energy and cash – Labour candidates who might split the progressive vote in three-cornered elections and put the Conservatives back in power.

At the same time as the National Union opened its campaign for the women's amendments to the Reform Bill in July, the WSPU embarked on a campaign of violence that stopped short only at the risk to human life. Against the background of industrial unrest and the threat of civil war in Ireland, they appear to have believed that only serious criminal damage would 'maintain Votes for Women in the centre of the political stage'.[267] They pointed to what they saw as provocation from anti-suffrage ministers including C. E. Hobhouse, whose speech at Bristol in February 1912 was described by Sylvia Pankhurst as 'like a match to a fuse'.[268] Taunted that the pinpricks of militant activity had scarcely grazed the government's flank, the WSPU embarked on the last phase of its campaign, in which, between 1912 and 1914, property was destroyed on an extensive scale. In doing so they were deaf to Mrs Fawcett's pleas that they maintain a truce, at least during the passage of the Reform Bill, in order that the women's amendments might not be jeopardised. What the NUWSS was trying to effect by parliamentary means, the WSPU believed they could achieve through violence, which many of their members seem to have perceived as the only argument that men would

68 'Now Ain't That a Shame', Donald McGill. *Several paintings in Manchester Art Gallery were damaged by militants on 2 April 1913, but the most serious outbreak took place in the spring and summer of 1914, beginning with the best known instance: Mary Richardson's attack on Velazquez' 'Rokeby Venus' in the National Gallery on 10 March. The fullest – though not the most coherent – account is to be found in Mary Richardson's statement on arrest, in reports of her speech from the dock and in the relevant pages of her autobiography,* Laugh a Defiance *(Weidenfeld & Nicolson, London, 1953). 'I have tried to destroy the picture of the most beautiful woman in mythological history as a protest against the Government destroying Mrs Pankhurst, who is the most beautiful character in modern history' (the* Suffragette, *13 March 1914).*

finally understand. No longer interested in converting the public, they set out to astound and appal it: pillar boxes were set on fire, paintings slashed (including the Rokeby Venus, in the best known of several similar incidents), golf courses treated with acid, telegraph wires cut, empty country houses, churches, a school, a railway station and cricket and tea pavilions burned. The WSPU became focused on daring deeds of furtive guerrilla activity performed by a small number of individuals tasting what Christabel (safely secluded in Paris) referred to as 'the exultation, the rapture of battle'.[269]

By this stage militancy carried its own momentum: as it increased in intensity so the WSPU fell from the headlines in periods of truce but alienated the public, the constitutionalists and the politicians to no productive end when violence was resumed. The major difficulty with militant tactics, in these final years of the campaign, lay in the fact that serious militancy would not work if the government was not threatened, and women were never in a position to ensure that it was. As a correspondent put it in the *Manchester Guardian* in 1912: 'obdurately reactionary Governments are never inspired to reforms by a violence which they can crush, and they can crush all violence except that which the great mass of people applaud and are prepared to participate in. Had the violence of the WSPU possessed the essential virtue of popularity it would by now have won women the vote.'[270]

The Reform Bill and the proposed Home Rule Bill were the two major pieces of legislation for the session of 1912–13. The Franchise (i.e. Reform) Bill passed its first reading on 17 June, and its second on 12 July, by which point four alternative women's suffrage amendments had been formulated for consideration at the third reading. Each offered a different degree of enfranchisement, and they were to be taken in descending order, so that supporters of earlier and broader amendments, if defeated, could transfer their votes to the later and narrower ones. This was a promising opportunity

to include women within the terms of a government-sponsored Reform Bill, and the NUWSS campaigned all through the summer of 1912 and on into January 1913 in its support.

How the increasing restlessness of Irish Nationalists over Home Rule, or militant activity by the WSPU, would have affected voting on the amendments remains a matter for speculation. A totally unexpected ruling by the Speaker resulted in a Cabinet decision to withdraw the whole bill, a move which led to uproar both inside and outside Parliament. It seemed as though the government had found a way of duping the suffragists yet again. The evidence suggests that Asquith was himself genuinely surprised by the ruling – which remains controversial to this day – but not displeased with it. (He wrote to a friend on the evening of 27 January 1913, the day the Cabinet decided to withdraw the whole bill: 'The Speaker's *coup d'état* has bowled over the Women for this session – a great relief.'[271]

It has been suggested that the loss of the Reform Bill secured the decline of the Liberal Party in the long term, but this was no consolation to the women. It closed a chapter in the history of the suffrage movement, and guaranteed that in parliamentary terms the women's cause would remain a dead issue at least until after the next general election, scheduled for 1915. After a brief truce on the eve of the bill, the WSPU resumed violent activity. They had turned their back on peaceful demonstrations and their last important public spectacle was to be a martyr's funeral. For the National Union, too, the time for processions was past. It was not clear what direction the peaceful propaganda campaign could take next, or by what means it might salvage something from one of the gloomiest moments in the history of the cause.

The WSPU's reaction to the withdrawal of the Franchise Bill was the inauguration of an arson campaign in February 1913. In the last days of January Mrs Pankhurst described the militants as 'guerrillists' who 'were going to do as much damage to property as they could'.[272] In the following weeks an orchid house at Kew and the refreshment pavilion in Regent's Park were burned down, windows at London clubs were broken, slogans burned with acid into golf courses, a jewel case was smashed at the Tower, and Lloyd George's half-completed house in Surrey was bombed. On 24 February Mrs Pankhurst was arrested for incitement to violence.

The Pankhursts were indifferent to public opinion. ('If the general public were pleased with what we are doing, that would be a proof that our warfare is ineffective. We don't intend that you should be pleased.')[273] But the public was not indifferent to them, and on occasion the militants met violent retaliation from men who broke their windows, disrupted meetings, threw missiles and tore clothing, where before they had listened with curiosity if not always respect.

As the crimes for which they were jailed became more serious, the government's exasperation that suffragettes were effectively terminating their own sentences – despite the introduction of forcible feeding – increased. On 6 March 1913 the police raided the Notting Hill studio of the artist Olive Hocken and found there licence plates, hammers, firelighters, wirecutters, corrosive fluid and strips of ribbon with the slogans 'No votes – no telegraphic connection' and 'No security by post or wire until justice be done to women'.[274] On the same day the Cabinet decided to introduce a bill that would authorise the rearrest of prisoners released through self-induced ill health. The Prisoners' Temporary Discharge for Ill-Health Act, soon popularly known as the Cat and Mouse Act, received Royal Assent on 25 April.[275] Under its terms the Home Secretary, Reginald McKenna, was empowered to permit the release of weakened prisoners on licence and return them to prison on recovery with no remission of sentence. Women could be weakened by hunger strike, obliged to suffer the brutalities and indignities of forcible feeding if they persisted in it, released temporarily

and taken back into custody for the whole process to begin all over again. By such means, as the *Daily Mail* remarked, a month's imprisonment could be converted 'into a sentence of unbearable torment';[276] and Christabel commented acidly on the speed of the Act's passage and implementation that 'a Liberal Government preferred this unprecedented measure of repression to giving women the vote.'[277]

For his part McKenna argued that he could neither allow the women to end their own sentences nor let them die. That would be inhumane, and also very bad tactics. 'For every woman who died there would be scores who would come forward for the honour, as they would deem it, of the crown of martyrdom ... We should have woman after woman, whose only offence may have been obstructing the police, breaking a window, or even burning down an empty house, dying because she was obstinate ... I could never take a hand in carrying that policy out.'[278]

The cause was to have its martyr nonetheless. On 4 June 1913, having apparently set out to wave the WSPU colours in front of the horses at Tattenham Corner, Emily Wilding Davison ran on to the Derby course instead, colliding with the King's horse Anmer and fracturing her skull. She died five days later without regaining consciousness.

The evidence as to her intentions is mixed. She had not told anyone that she meant to run on to the course, it cannot have been evident that if she did so she would be killed, and she had two folded WSPU flags and a return railway ticket from Victoria in her coat. But she felt herself infused with the spirit of martyrdom (she had tried to commit suicide in 1912 by jumping from a balcony in Holloway prison) and believed by open analogy with the Christian Calvary that the cause needed

69 'McKenna's Cat "Bill"': anon., Suffrage Atelier, *c.* 1913.
The image and title pun on the 'Cat and Mouse' Bill: see colour plate 6.

this 'last consummate sacrifice of the Militant!'[279] The WSPU had neither predicted her death nor desired it. But once she had died the palm of martyrdom was hers, and the hero's funeral they accorded her became a last, tragic occasion for public spectacle in the WSPU campaign.

Emily Wilding Davison's Funeral, 14 June 1913

As militant violence increased in scope and intensity the time for large public processions passed for the WSPU, as Emmeline Pethick-Lawrence had predicted it would. Joan of Arc no longer paraded on horseback at the head of 40,000 women. But for the suffragettes who had prepared so many processions, a solemn funeral cortège was the natural expression of their grief, and a way of assimilating the associations of Joan of Arc into the imagery of a guerrilla campaign.

At about 12.30 pm on Saturday 14 June, a train with funeral car attached drew into Victoria Station from Epsom, bringing the body of Emily Wilding Davison, accompanied by her half-brother Captain Davison and his family. Access to the platform was restricted as the coffin was lifted on to an open carriage, attended by suffragettes with black sashes and a black-draped WSPU flag, who stood to salute it. A purple velvet pall embroidered with silver arrows was draped over the elm casket, and laurel wreaths, emblems of commemoration and victory, placed on top. Floral tributes from all over the world were arranged in waiting carriages and two taxi-cabs as the cortège began to form up in Buckingham Palace Road.

Shortly after 2 pm the procession set off, headed by the tall, fair-haired figure of Charlotte Marsh in white, carrying a gold processional cross. (The *Illustrated Chronicle* described her leading off 'as Joan of Arc', which shows how tightly drawn the associations of her public presence had now become.)[280] She made her way with difficulty at times through the waiting crowds which parted silently, and clumsily, to let her pass. The procession which followed was organised in wedges of

colour at once solemn and picturesque, which struck the press forcibly: white and green, black and purple, purple and red, relieved by splashes of colour here and there in the uniforms of bandsmen or in academic robes. Young women in white carrying laurel wreaths and a purple banner ('Fight On, and God will Give the Victory', from Joan of Arc), were followed by women in white with madonna lilies, and then in violent contrast by the scarlet and yellow of a military band. Hundreds of women in black with purple irises were succeeded by another band in scarlet, and then by women in purple with crimson peonies, then by the London members in white, with more madonna lilies. (Crimson for sacrifice, purple for loyalty, white for purity, according to the gloss in the *Daily News*.) Each section carried banners with inscriptions worked in white on a purple ground: 'She hath Done what she Could', 'Give me Liberty or Give me Death', 'Victory, Victory'.

Captain Davison accompanied the horse-drawn bier, followed by intimate friends of the deceased and Sylvia Pankhurst – the only member of the family present – looking pale and ill. Christabel was in exile in France and Mrs Pankhurst, wearing deep mourning, had been rearrested under the terms of the Cat and Mouse Act as she left to join the cortège. Her empty carriage, surrounded by hunger-strikers, wound round London with the procession while she was escorted back to Holloway.

The women graduates in scarlet and blue robes, with hoods of gold and silver, purple and blue, rivalled the carriages of flowers in a sudden burst of quite unfunerary brilliance. Behind them followed representatives of a range of suffrage societies and labour organisations, each with their banners: the

70 The funeral cortège of Emily Wilding Davison passing through Piccadilly Circus, 14 June 1913.

71 A WSPU guard of honour salutes its martyr as Emily Wilding Davison's coffin is carried into St George's Church, Bloomsbury.

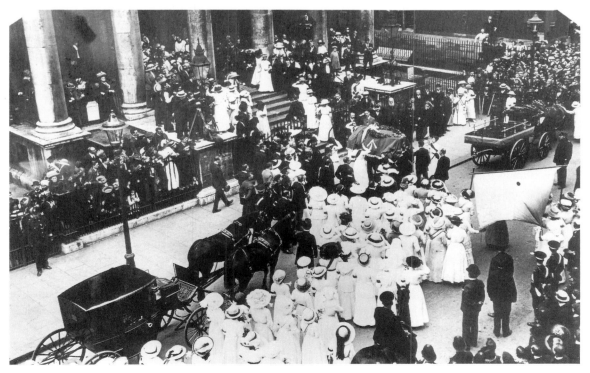

actresses, the writers, the Women's Freedom League, the men's groups and the church leagues, together with the Central Labour College, the Tea Operatives, the General Labourers' Union, the Gas Workers and the Dockers' Union led by Ben Tillet. There was, as the *Daily Herald* remarked, 'no class warfare here'.

A guard of honour formed on the steps of St George's, Bloomsbury, and the coffin was given a military salute as it entered the church. The Reverend Baumgarten conducted the service, which commemorated Emily Wilding Davison as having 'offered up her life for her faith' with hymns that included 'Nearer My God To Thee', 'Lead, Kindly Light', 'Onward Christian Soldiers' and 'Fight The Good Fight'.[281] After the service the cortège proceeded to King's Cross, where tens of thousands of spectators crowded into St Pancras approach and out into the roadway. The coffin was removed from the bier on to the 5.30 train to Morpeth in Northumberland, and seen off on its final journey to the village that Emily Wilding Davison came from, and where she was to be buried next day.

Through all this the onlookers were chiefly silent and respectful, the scene was 'both mournful and picturesque',[282] and even those unpersuaded by the nature of the 'final sacrifice' treated it with the reverence due to an English funeral. There were some minor incidents. A murmur of booing had greeted the coffin as it was first brought out of Victoria Station and manoeuvred into place in the procession. In Shaftesbury Avenue a man had shouted wildly about him, 'Don't take your hats off,' as the bier passed by. Outside St George's church there was some hustling, and an attempt to throw pepper on the coffin. And a woman was arrested for breach of the peace when she rushed at one of the banners as the procession formed up, shouting 'Down with votes for women' and attempting to drag it away.[283] But these were isolated incidents which threw into relief the re-spect of Londoners who 'might have been saluting

the corpse of some great conqueror, instead of the dead body of a rebel heroine who had laid down her life as a protest at the insane cruelty of the present order of things'.[284] Laurence Housman was speaking to a large crowd in Hyde Park when the news of her death came through, and remembering the hats removed, and the low murmur of sympathy that ran across it, he suggested that in some strange way her act was popular: 'It caught the public imagination.'[285] Perhaps it did so in ways that confused that public, as well as touched it. 'They knew this cause to which they were growing friendly, and they knew militants, at whom they were accustomed to jeer; and now they were faced with a martyr, at once reckless and tragic, and they were moved and distressed.'[286] As Winifred Mayo wrote to Maud Arncliffe-Sennett: 'I should think all criticism must be hushed in the face of such devotion.'[287] Until the memory of the funeral faded, displaced in the reader's mind by detailed accounts of 'suffragette outrage' of different kinds elsewhere,[288] it converted irritation into awed respect, and secured for the WSPU its unlooked-for martyr-saint.

*

In the summer of 1913 the parliamentary outlook for women's suffrage was gloomy, as the *Common Cause* observed.[289] With the Franchise Bill withdrawn and the Dickinson Bill defeated there was for the first time in several years no urgent incentive, no single measure for which to organise and fight. The Women's Coronation Procession of 1911 had apparently reached the limits of public spectacle. The momentum that had built steadily from the first tentative steps of the Mud March in 1907 was briefly stilled, and a growing suspicion apparently confirmed: the public had come to take suffrage pageantry as a natural part of its outdoor entertainment. Without some effective lever on the government its political effectiveness was dulled. The principal NUWSS demonstration of 1913, planned long before Emily Wilding Davison's dash on to the Derby racecourse, provides a striking contrast with her quasi-military funeral. But it was a different response to an identical problem: the problem of re-establishing the tactics of suffrage spectacle.

The National Union Women's Pilgrimage, June and July 1913

What was to become known as the Women's Pilgrimage was proposed to the NUWSS Executive Committee by a Mrs Harley on 17 April, and discussed by its Organisation Committee the following day. The scheme entailed a constitutional campaign throughout the country in July, with marches starting from seventeen large cities (one in each federation), which would culminate in London.[290] The aim was both to 'provide striking evidence of the growth among the law-abiding men and women of the country of the insistent demand that some measure for the enfranchisement of women be granted without delay', and to raise 'a Fund so large that it shall at once place the National Union of Women's Suffrage Societies in a position to increase the efficiency of its work a hundredfold during the coming Autumn'.[291]

There were to be eight main routes across the country: along the Great North Road, Watling Street, the Portsmouth Road and the Brighton Road, from the east coast, the West Country, the Fen Country, and along the Kentish Pilgrim's Way. Some members would follow their route from start to finish over several weeks, but most would join for a few days at a time. Since it was important to secure an effect of numbers and to identify the pilgrims to casual onlookers, a uniform was devised: coats and skirts or dresses in white, grey, black or navy, with blouses the same colour as the skirt or white, and hats in the same colours but with a raffia cockade dyed to the red, white and green. The point was to eliminate colour except on the hat-badge and haversack, and to enable participants to wear anything white, grey, navy or black

they already possessed.[292] (Manufacturers were quick to advertise 'Serviceable Attire at Moderate Prices', 'Holeproof Hose' and Burberry coats as 'The Ideal Coat for the Pilgrimage'.)[293]

An elaborate advertising programme was drawn up (a scheme of this kind which required sustained public interest would flop if it was ignored); and £35 was allocated to place posters on sixty motor-buses, and on the Hampstead and City of London, Bakerloo, Piccadilly, Central and Metropolitan tube lines.[294] The crucial point, however, was that once started the Pilgrimage was to be its own advertisement, as well as drawing attention more generally to the campaign and to the NUWSS and its constitutional methods. Its structure, which involved a fluctuating membership spread across several different routes, gradually converging on London in the course of more than a month, was quite distinct from that of a massed procession taking place over several hours in the city streets. Large numbers of women would be involved, but not all at the same time or in the same place. They would have ample opportunity for holding meetings, collecting funds and distributing literature along the way. They would make contact with people in towns and villages all over the country, not just those who could travel to London (or Manchester, or Edinburgh) for a major demonstration, and they would reach them in smaller groups and on a more intimate basis. 'We have been urged to "advertise" ourselves, our objects, and our methods. Here is a giant advertisement, which all the country will hear of and will see . . . It would cost hundreds of pounds adequately to post the hoardings and newspapers of this country with the appeal we want to make and the grounds on which we make it. Here is a chance to make it heard by those who have never listened before.'[295]

The second aim of the Pilgrimage was to oblige a public, daily regaled with stories of militant arson in the popular press, to recognise that there *was* a constitutional wing to the movement commanding greater support than the WSPU, by whose notoriety

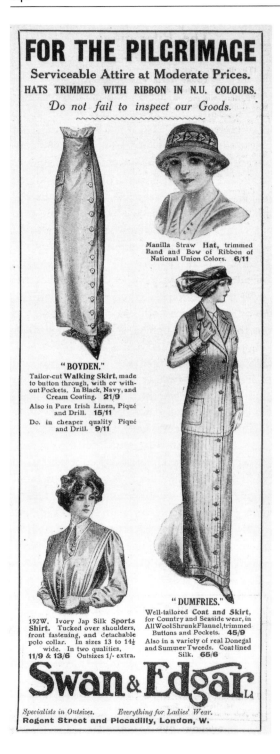

FOR THE PILGRIMAGE

Serviceable Attire at Moderate Prices.

HATS TRIMMED WITH RIBBON IN N.U. COLOURS.

Do not fail to inspect our Goods.

Manilla Straw Hat, trimmed Band and Bow of Ribbon of National Union Colors. 6/11

"BOYDEN."
Tailor-cut **Walking Skirt**, made to button through, with or without Pockets. In Black, Navy, and Cream Coating. 21/9
Also in Pure Irish Linen, Piqué and Drill. 15/11
Do. in cheaper quality Piqué and Drill. 9/11

"DUMFRIES."
Well-tailored **Coat and Skirt**, for Country and Seaside wear, in All Wool Shrunk Flannel, trimmed Buttons and Pockets. 45/9
Also in a variety of real Donegal and Summer Tweeds. Coat lined Silk. 65/6

192W. Ivory Jap Silk **Sports Shirt.** Tucked over shoulders, front fastening, and detachable polo collar. In sizes 13 to 14½ wide. In two qualities, 11/9 & 13/6 Outsizes 1/- extra.

Swan & Edgar Ld

Specialists in Outsizes.   Everything for Ladies' Wear.
Regent Street and Piccadilly, London, W.

it was regularly eclipsed. The public needed to be convinced, in Mrs Fawcett's words, that 'the great majority of women who are asking for the vote are opposed to violence, and . . . firmly believe that women's suffrage can only be won by peaceful and orderly methods of propaganda *by appeals to reason*, not to force.' The Pilgrimage was intended as an 'act of devotion': to the cause, and to the men and women who had started it fifty years before. 'Coming from the ends of the country to its capital, without either bombs or paraffin oil, with no other appeal than that of reason and order, risking whatever there may be of violence against us, but using none ourselves, we shall have the opportunity of a life-time of stating our case.'[296]

The appeal to reason and order was in effect an appeal to language rather than spectacle, to the ear rather than the eye. ('And, after all, there is no appeal like that of the living voice.')[297] A pilgrimage refused the thrill attendant on women's militancy, no matter how strongly that militancy was denounced, but it also refused the glamour of an orchestrated spectacle. If, from 1908, the suffragists had learned to put themselves on show, the Pilgrimage suggested that they were deliberately divesting themselves of their status as processionists. It was a return – marked by much that had been learned in the intervening years as to the production of political meanings on the streets – to the earnest simplicity of 1907. The narratives woven around the Pilgrimage are in their medieval references ascetic rather than courtly, and if there is talk of spirit and dedication, there is none of pageantry, of silken banners and pennons flying. A proposal for 'symbolical cars' was, significantly, dropped.[298]

The first pilgrims began their journey on 18 June, and from that date groups began to set out all over the country, discreetly in some places, with

72 Advertisement from the *Common Cause*, 20 June 1913; one of a number advertising goods and services in connection with the Pilgrimage.

73 Cyclists at Clayton on the Brighton Road, on the NUWSS Pilgrimage in the summer of 1913.

bands and banners and a civic send-off in others. Most travelled on foot, though some rode horses or bicycles, and wealthy sympathisers lent cars, carriages, or pony traps for the luggage. The intention was not that each individual should cover the whole route but that the federations would do so collectively. This led to some taunts that they were not a 'proper' pilgrimage, but the sharper suffragists turned these round in claiming that even feminists had homes, and that contrary to popular belief, virtuous suffragists did not neglect them.[299] They held innumerable meetings, gathered petitions, sold the *Common Cause*, literature and accessories, and enlisted sympathisers as members or 'friends'. They found accommodation from fellow suffragists and in small hostels and boarding houses along the route, paying their own expenses. And on Sundays they went to services at which sympathetic Anglican vicars preached from ingeniously selected texts.[300]

It is difficult now to reconstruct that summer of 1913, and a sense of their purpose and experience as they walked through the towns and villages of a pre-war England, an England without motorways (or motor-cars, to speak of), where a sophisticated railway system was the chief means of inter-city transport, and in which newspapers and political meetings were not only the basis of an education in public affairs but a major source of diversion. Sometimes the villages they passed through *demanded* a meeting, so as not to be cheated of their entertainment. The suffragists were treated sometimes roughly and sometimes with sympathy – the recipients, literally, of brickbats and bouquets – but accorded audiences and newspaper attention on a scale that would startle us now. For its participants the Pilgrimage was an adventure as they mounted makeshift platforms and spoke in marketplaces and town halls, rested in fields and orchards, endured the ribaldry and jostling of unsympathetic crowds, or were rewarded with attentive audiences and an enhanced sense of their own spirit and camaraderie.

The *Common Cause* published detailed accounts of its 'pilgrims' progress' every week, and correspondents were quick to draw a suffrage lesson from the social, geographic and historical diversity of the routes. Some areas were noted for traditions of suffrage or trade-union activity, some for the exploitation of women in local industries, others for the fame of women aristocrats, saints or heroines.[301]

The pilgrims on the southwest route were not untypical. They set out from Land's End on 19 June, cheered on by a group of working men and the *Daily Mirror* photographer. They met up with members from the Penzance branch and held their first meeting in the market place at Trereife in the pouring rain, with an attentive crowd of about 1200. By the time they reached Cambourne they had been joined by the contingent from St Ives, and 'dusty but with swinging stride' they marched together to their hotel. That evening they found their pitch in Commercial Square already packed with 10,000 people, some filling adjacent windows

and climbing on to the roofs of nearby houses. At Falmouth their meeting was presided over by the deputy mayor, and they had an audience of about 2000 and some minor disorder. At Looe they suffered an 'ill-mannered reception' by the children which prefigured later difficulties with 'a group of about forty objectionable persons whose conduct was deeply resented by the majority of the crowd'. On 27 June they crossed into Devon, satisfied with 'admirable, full and accurate Press reports' and with the work they had done in Cornwall, an area 'hitherto almost untouched'.

At Newton Abbot, notorious for turbulent meetings, they addressed a crowd of 3000 people without disturbance. At Exeter they were welcomed by 300 suffragists from the local society, and marched with them through the streets in 'a most picturesque spectacle'. Large crowds gathered to watch them pass, and 6–7000 people assembled for the meeting at the bottom of Paris Street. The whole town turned out for an open-air meeting in Wellington, and from there the pilgrims journeyed to Taunton, Bridgwater, and on to Street. From Street the local supporters marched out with banners and a band to meet them, and led them back into town accompanied by a decorated donkey carriage, from which the two great-grandsons of John Bright collected twelve shillings for the Pilgrimage Fund. They had a good send-off from Bristol, but just as things seemed to be going smoothly, they were mobbed by hooligans in Bath.

Wiltshire was also rough, and the pilgrims discovered themselves preceded by their opponents, who whipped up feeling against them by insinuating that they were not truly 'anti-militant'. At Calne Miss Sterling, protected from the crowd's 'rushes' in the local police station, left disguised in a uniform. The same gang broke up a meeting in Marlborough and pushed the luggage van into the river. Meanwhile the group from Swindon, which joined them in Marlborough, had been pelted with rotten eggs and cabbages in Cheltenham, their hats torn off and their cyclists mobbed, so that the

Gloucestershire banner had 'narrowly escaped destruction'.

Most of the other routes had comparable stories, locally flavoured, of triumphs mingled with adversity. The Watling Street pilgrims set out from the Market Cross in Carlisle on 18 June, and left Manchester on 5 July, headed by Lady Rochester (president of the Manchester and District Federation) and representatives from the ILP, the Women's Co-operative Guild, and the local trades councils. The squalid poverty and deprivation they witnessed in the manufacturing towns of the Midlands, as they marched through the Stoke potteries and on to Stafford, confirmed their belief that these were conditions which only the women's vote could change.

The route of the Great North Road pilgrims passed through some of the principal manufacturing towns and mining communities of the north, and at every town and village along the route crowds would gather to watch them pass. In Darlington they were heckled by a drunk in the crowd, but on the 'suggestion that he should come to the platform and be exhibited as a sample of the men who have votes, order was restored'. In July Mrs Fawcett walked with them (a notable coup), and from the small villages around Sheffield and Mansfield children were sent out by their mothers to bring them flowers.

There were enough hostile incidents to demand of the suffragists on all routes the courage of their convictions, if not so many as to detract from the conclusion that the Pilgrimage was generally a success. Their reception was better in the northern counties, owing to the prominence of working women in the industrial centres and the relative friendliness of the trade unions. No doubt there were cross-class, cross-sex antagonisms (men disliked being lectured to by women, especially women of a different class), but there were also cross-class alliances. The Durham University students who came to disrupt the women's meeting in the hope of a 'rag' were frustrated by the working-class men who encircled the platform and afterwards ducked their ringleaders in the river.

The worst problems arose in parts of Yorkshire and the Midlands. Despite being warned by the local suffrage society, the Wakefield police were quite unprepared for the size of the meeting or the roughness of the crowd. One of the speakers received a black eye from a stone, one returned home with an injured spine, a third damaged her foot, and in the general scrimmage all of them were more or less bruised. In Mansfield Mrs Fawcett's voice was drowned in the tumult and 'all manner of objectionable missiles' were hurled at the platform. At Newark a drunken man 'was especially interested in our respective ages and knowledge of laundry work' and stones, mud, vegetables and eggs were thrown at the speakers. Three unarmed women stood alone on a lorry assailed by the rushes of 3000 men, a storm of missiles hailing round them, while a trembling magistrate pleaded for calm by assuring the crowd that 'these women will not hurt you.' At Stamford a feeble and unsuccessful attempt was made to hustle the pilgrims into the river, but they were consoled by police who told them that the inhabitants seldom listened quietly at meetings, and were in 'specially playful mood' on Saturday nights.

They had expected hostility, ridicule and even abuse, and had not been entirely disappointed: each band, as the *Common Cause* concluded, had met with some success and some calamity, 'but the result was nothing less than a revelation, to those who doubted it, of the almost universal sympathy given to the Non-militant Suffrage Cause once it is understood'. They had reached new constituencies, not in the ways opened up by the popular press, but by walking across the country and speaking with its inhabitants in all the town and village and market halls and open spaces available to them. Hundreds of meetings had been held, tens of thousands of people had come to them, half a million leaflets had been distributed, 39,540 'Friends of Women's Suffrage' had been enrolled and they had collected over £8000.[302]

Around 24 and 25 July the pilgrims converged on London, and during those days the London Society organised a series of thirty meetings at which there were no dissidents and no rowdiness. There is some suggestion that the pilgrims gratefully caught their breath in these last days, and regained a cheerfulness that had been sorely tried at moments along the route. On the morning of the 26th, under a leaden sky and against trees greyish in the haze, separate contingents formed up in Kensington, Maida Vale, Bloomsbury and Trafalgar Square to march to the final meeting in Hyde Park. There were bands and banners at the head of each section and a special souvenir programme in the *Common Cause* (as well as a pirated twopenny version on sale in the streets). The crowds, which were not dense until they neared the park, seem to have been cordial rather than enthused. They raised their hats and waved handkerchiefs from windows, cheered at some moments and threw roses across the road at others. Two well-known aviators made flights over northwest London and dropped suffrage literature from their aeroplanes. Carriages and motor-cars adorned in the National Union colours accompanied the pilgrims, who sold the *Common Cause* and rattled collection boxes along the route. The crimson London banner, in the *Manchester Guardian*'s otherwise sober account, 'went through the grey streets like a flame'. The battered Pilgrimage banners contrasted proudly with the gay silks and velvets carried by the various societies and federations in the long line behind them.[303] *The Times* and the *Daily News* commented on the women's brown skins and high spirits. It had been a great adventure, all was brightness and good humour, 'never was so peaceful, so pleasant a raid of London – and rarely one more picturesque or more inspiring.'[304]

Yet something is missing here. The pageantry, the spectacle, the size and intensity of the crowds, the feeling that something *matters* and is about to

happen, the spice even of controversy, of flouting the rules of political argument and feminine etiquette, have drained away. This is reflected in the reasoned, friendly, but almost apologetic and fragmentary tone of the newspaper reports. It was something the women seem to have wanted for themselves. Mrs Harley (its originator) wrote 'A London Impression' of the Pilgrimage for the *Englishwoman* in which she suggested that 'there was a subtle difference between the applause and admiration accorded to the suffrage processionists of 1911 and the serious, quiet welcome which greeted the entry of the pilgrimage last month. No great crowds were seen on the streets, for there was no spectacular display to attract the sightseer . . .'[305]

The constitutionalists had decided that spectacle entertains a crowd, and that what they needed to do was to convert a mass of individuals. If they ever had been, by 1913 these two things were no longer compatible in a context shaped by militant violence. Some papers had decided that the average Londoner would not be stirred. He was 'notoriously the most apathetic and unpatriotic of citizens' who could only be whipped out of his Saturday afternoon sloth by 'a football final or Mafeking night';[306] or, as there was now evidence to suggest, by a spectacle rich in pageantry, novel in content and massive in scale. The Pilgrimage, by design, was none of these things, but it needed its final meeting to impress or its passage would go for little in the capital, and its arguments be lost.

But if the four processions that marched to the park entrances at Alexandra Gate, Victoria Gate, Marble Arch and Hyde Park Corner were short on pomp and circumstance, the meeting itself was substantial enough to irritate the militants and impress the morning papers. The pilgrims broke into open ground with a tumultuous clash, the throb of their drums no longer muffled by the trees, and wound their way through 50,000 spectators to the nineteen platforms. There were between eighty and ninety speakers, including Mrs Fawcett on the

74 Mrs Fawcett addressing the crowds in Hyde Park at the culmination of the Pilgrimage, 26 July 1913.

London Society platform; Mrs Chapman Catt of the International Suffrage Alliance; Mrs Philip Snowden, wife of the Labour MP; Lady Strachey and her daughter-in-law Ray Strachey; Miss Stephen, the Principal of Newnham College; and Ebenezer Howard, founder of the garden city. The speeches were good and the crowd enthusiastic and attentive, with a high proportion of foreign visitors, and what the *Daily Telegraph* called the 'loafing element' conspicuous by its absence.[307]

In moving the resolution Mrs Fawcett outlined the three objects of the Pilgrimage as they were now perceived. It had 'provided an opportunity for the great mass of suffragists to dedicate themselves anew to the service of their cause'; it had demonstrated the mass and power of the constitutional movement; and by visiting people in their own streets and homes it had made thousands recognise for the first time *why* women wanted the vote, their resentment at being governed as if they were pol-

itical serfs rather than intelligent beings playing their part in industrial and social life, and their determination to gain the weapon with which to bring about social reform. It was to this end (she mentioned particularly 'that most terrible of all evils, the white slave traffic') that the pilgrims had come to demand a government measure on women's suffrage.[308] The resolution was passed with scarcely a dissentient voice when the bugle rang out at six o'clock, and it was followed by cheers for Mrs Fawcett, and cheers for the constitutional movement.[309]

*

On 29 July Mrs Fawcett wrote to Asquith 'on behalf of the immense meetings which assembled in Hyde Park on Saturday and voted with practical unanimity in favour of a Government measure', begging him to receive a deputation of law-abiding suffragists. Replying on the 31st, Asquith acknowledged that the demonstration had 'a special claim' on his consideration and stood 'upon another footing from similar demands proceeding from other quarters where a different method and spirit is predominant'. But he felt bound to warn her that he had nothing to add to recent statements in the House on government policy.[310]

Despite this caveat, the National Union regarded his agreement to receive them as proof of their success. They hoped to build up such a pressure of public support that even an anti-suffragist as powerful and entrenched in his views as Asquith would be forced to concede to them. They regarded their task as one of neutralising the effects of militancy and converting the public to their cause. They believed that they had accomplished it, and in doing so provided the government with a mandate on which to act. But the government was reluctant to act, and therefore unwilling to acknowledge that the case was made. To the constitutionalists' intense aggravation the same old arguments were raised against them by the suffrage ministers who received their deputation on 8 August. After the meeting they sent an exasperated reply.

We came to you with fresh evidence of the demand for Women's Suffrage in the Country . . . In reply you all assured us that in your opinion [it] is unpopular . . . As we said at the time, it is not the experience of our speakers and workers that Women's Suffrage is unpopular in the country, nor in our opinion is it a cause which needs to be 'rehabilitated'. You suggested that we may be misled by the success of meetings which consist of our supporters. But our experience is not of meetings only; besides our meetings are always open to the public, they are frequently held out of doors, and during the past six weeks we have spoken at many hundreds of these in all parts of the country. On the other hand the meetings which you address are party meetings accustomed to applaud only those subjects which have been adopted by the party, and the Liberal party machine has done its best to put Women's Suffrage in the class of unapproved subjects. You will never get applause for Women's Suffrage at a party meeting till you speak of it not as a personal idiosyncrasy to be apologised for, but as a fundamental part of your political creed . . . It is Militancy, not Women's Suffrage, which is unpopular, and Militancy is due to the failure of the Government to deal adequately with this question, or to fulfil the promises made to Suffragists . . . It is hardly generous or fair to allege the unpopularity for which you individually are indirectly responsible as a reason for doing nothing, whilst you urge *us* to 'rehabilitate' the movement, with no prospect that when we have done so Militancy will not be provoked afresh by yet further evasion and delay on the part of the Government. We have done, we are doing, and shall continue to do, everything within our power to promote the enfranchisement of women. We have brought every evidence that has been asked for, we have undertaken tasks that have been laid upon the supporters of no other cause. We came to you to ask what you, on your side, were prepared to do, and whilst thanking you for receiving us, we can only regard the result of the deputation as profoundly disappointing.[311]

The suffragists had organised, demonstrated, suffered and even died for their cause; they had given every rational and sensational proof of their determination and commitment, including marching for six weeks from the ends of England in its support. They might have been forgiven for lapsing into pessimism and despair. But the militants – impervious to criticism and riven with internal dissension – were not dissuaded from guerrilla activities; and the constitutionalists continued their work of planning, organising and consolidating through the winter of 1913 and on into the summer of 1914. In Ray Strachey's words, 'they looked forward to another winter of hard work, and then to an election which might open the door to their triumph, when suddenly upon them, as upon the rest of Europe, there fell the calamity of war.'[312]

4 · REPRESENTATION

75 'John Bull: Excuse Me If I Laugh': designed by Harold Bird for the National League for Opposing Woman Suffrage, 1912.

The NLOWS commissioned a number of posters to promote their most important demonstration on 28 February 1912. The theme of the painter who sees through rose-coloured spectacles was used by Catherine Courtauld in 'The ASS as Portrait Painter.'

Society is a battlefield of representations, on which the limits and coherence of any given set are constantly being fought for and regularly spoilt. T. J. CLARK[1]

The purpose of suffrage propaganda was to build up an irresistible pressure of public opinion and at the same time to convert MPs to active support of the cause in parliamentary debates. In order to mobilise public opinion – beyond that of a handful of radicals – suffragists had to persuade the working as well as the middle classes, men as well as women, the unions and the labour movement as well as Tories, Free Traders, Home Rulers, Anglicans and Non-Conformists (there being in the end no such homogenous entity as 'public opinion'), that women's suffrage was a good and desirable thing by which the family and the whole social fabric might be strengthened, not destroyed. It had somehow to be understood as a very serious question that could also be treated light-heartedly if that was the way to open people's minds, and as a very large question that was in some respects a small and unimportant one. The vote had to be seen as the key to sweeping and entirely beneficial kinds of social reform, and at the same time as the simple correction of a historical and anomalous injustice drawing no unwanted consequences in its wake. A lazy audience needed to be persuaded that giving women the vote would bring the least struggle, and a principled one that they could not justly be denied it. Conservatives needed to believe that the educated women's vote would offset in their party's interest the working-class enfranchisement of 1867 and 1884 and any reduction in the plural vote that Liberals were able to secure. The labour movement wanted to hear that even on a limited measure, working women would qualify for the franchise, would benefit from the reforms it would

bring, and through their improved conditions cease to undercut the industrial wages of men. All this could be argued and was; and understandably suffrage propagandists cut their cloth according to the context in which they found themselves.

Demonstrations and the suffrage press performed an integrative function by welding supporters into a shared *esprit de corps*. In this sense the movement as a whole can be seen not only as the source of propaganda but as one of its most important audiences. Suffrage imagery, especially when it was centred on some icon of womanliness, held up a mirror that invited identification and offered reassurance, both to potential converts and to suffragists themselves. This was of necessity one of its principal tasks, and for two reasons. First, because the assumption that the 'public' woman was an unsexed harridan ran deep in contemporary thought, and even those who scoffed at it were vulnerable to its barbs; and second, because the Victorian and Edwardian public expected to see the virtues and vices of femininity *written on the body*, and were coached by moralists, novelists, journalists, illustrators and the writers of etiquette manuals in the detailed interpretation of physiognomy, gesture and pose. Since this was a visual matter it was of particular concern to suffrage artists. The depiction of a recognisably 'womanly' woman – that is, recognisable by the traits through which she was conventionally defined – pursuing her legitimate feminine interests unscathed into the arena of public affairs, carried an impact that written description could never convey. The image, striking and condensed like a slogan, could cut through the fine detail of political argument and impress itself directly on even the illiterate, the uneducated or the casual passer-by.

Suffrage propaganda made a selection and an

arrangement of its evidence and drew its con-
clusions on that basis, no more and no less than did
the arguments it was ranged against. Its essential
purpose was to demythologise the dominant
ideology of Edwardian femininity,[2] to fill out its
absences and exploit its contradictions. (Ideology
is often as much a matter of silence as of speech,
or as Foucault once put it, what is never said is
easier said than done.)[3] The disparity between an
idealised bourgeois femininity and the plight of
the sweated woman worker is one such theme in
suffrage imagery, echoing Harriet Martineau's
observation that a 'social organisation framed for a
community of which half stayed at home, while the
other half went out to work, cannot answer the
purposes of a society, of which a quarter remain at
home, while three-quarters go out to work.'[4] Suffrage artists – helped by the fact that they were the
beneficiaries of all the social changes in the position of women which had taken place since the
1850s – used all the rhetorical devices at their
disposal (analogy, parody, hyperbole, reversal)[5] to
impugn the motives and puncture the arguments of
their opponents.

We might say that the iconography of the campaign was produced out of two sorts of ingredients:
pro- and anti-suffrage arguments developed primarily in written or spoken form; and a repertoire
of pictorial resources that included illustrative
styles, reproductive techniques, existing codes of
representation, and something approaching a tax-
onomy of recognisable feminine types. The difficulty with this formulation is that it seems to point
to two independent categories of material, which
provided the suffragists first with their content (or
argument), and only secondly with the means to
give it form.

But pro and anti arguments were alike the
product of representations, and subject in turn
to the impress of the pictorial resources at their
disposal: the use in suffrage imagery of an allegorical female figure derived from Pre-Raphaelite and
art nouveau painting, for example, may have

absolved them from the sin of 'unwomanliness' at
the cost of blunting the analysis of the ideological
construct of 'womanliness' itself.[6] But it would be
wrong to see these resources solely as constraints
on the construction of suffrage propaganda, when
they represented at the same time its conditions of
existence.[7] There was no alternative tradition of
repressed but 'feminine' meanings to bring into
play, no ultimate or essential femininity to be
unveiled behind the layers of (mis)representation.[8]
Representations of the 'feminine', together with
overt and covert arguments regarding the appropriate moral, social and political functions of
women, were constantly produced in such contemporary institutions and discourses as those of
education, law, medicine, journalism, fine art and
popular illustration. If they were not always coherent, they managed to be mutually determining
in certain essential respects. Suffrage propaganda
is sited within (and cites) this *intertextuality*, which
provided its major themes and the context in which
it sought to make its effects.

The sections that follow are intended to do three
things. First, to outline the principal arguments in
the suffrage debate; second, to indicate the circumstances in which suffrage artists intervened in
the representation of women and of feminism in
Edwardian illustration; and third, to identify a
series of representational 'types' around which
particular skirmishes took place. In all this it is
necessary to keep in mind the *interdependence* of
suffrage imagery and suffrage argument – they are
finally inextricable – in pictorial resources already
imbued with political significance and political
arguments framed in terms of an appeal to the
'mind's eye'. ('Like a tide coming up on a wide
beach, it may find the gradients steeper in one part
than in another, the breakwaters more obstructive,
the cliffs more stubborn in their resistance; but
sooner or later, both here and there, it must reach
its mark, for the flood is behind it.')[9]

Pro- and Anti-Suffrage Arguments

The real question is, whether it is right or expedient that
one-half of the human race should pass through life in a
state of forced subordination to the other half . . . [when]
the only reason which can be given is, that men like it.
HARRIET TAYLOR MILL[10]

The relations between pro- and anti-suffrage
arguments were complex, developing and interdependent. Under what John Stuart Mill had
called the 'despotism of custom'[11] the consensual
position scarcely needed focusing. As women's
suffrage became an issue, however, so both sides
developed positions in relation to each other. It
was the renewed vigour and militancy of early
twentieth-century feminism that provoked the
formation of the anti-suffrage leagues in 1908.

By this point the standard arguments had long
trajectories. Some could be traced back to the
Enlightenment feminism of Mary Wollstonecraft
and the radical politics of Owenite socialism.
Others were consolidated in the writings of Harriet
Taylor (particularly the anonymously published
'Enfranchisement of Women', 1851) and her husband John Stuart Mill ('On the Subjection of
Women' was drafted in 1860 but did not appear in
print until 1869). Mill introduced the question to
serious parliamentary debate in his speech in the
House of Commons in May 1867 'On the Admission of Women to the Electoral Franchise'. Most
of the central arguments had been repeated *ad
nauseam* by the Edwardian period, but this did not
prevent their zestful elaboration on both sides,
together with the incorporation of new evidence
drawn from developments abroad, from the consequence of women's admission to the municipal
franchise and their enhanced educational and professional opportunities, from social Darwinism
and the developing human sciences, and from
public and philanthropic inquiries into the condition of industrial women workers.[12]

There was not one feminism but several, as a
number of contradictory streams fed into the decidedly heterogeneous flow of suffrage argument.
Differences of opinion existed not simply between
pro- and anti-suffrage positions but within each of
them. (Some suffragists were not feminists in the
sense that they made no larger claim than for the
vote, and some of their opponents were dedicated
to the emancipation of women in other fields,
particularly education.) Different concepts of
femininity and of politics informed the position of
those suffragists who were anxious to demolish the
notion of 'woman's sphere', and of others who
founded their arguments on its consolidation and
potential for social transformation. For some the
vote was an end in itself, the removal of an anomalous injustice, and for others a means to the end
of moral or political regeneration. For some, what
women needed were equal rights with men, and for
others (as egalitarian arguments were fused with
elements of Evangelicalism), what the state needed
was women's virtuous influence: if politics was too
dirty for women then women must clean it up.
There was no single feminist ideology, and suffragists who fought for the vote did so for different
reasons and were often divided on questions of
principle as well as strategy.[13]

By the Edwardian period we are dealing with a
palimpsest of earlier debates, and although they
can be summarised schematically this does scant
justice to the richness of their history, and to the
variety of contexts in which they were expressed.
They are to be traced in an enormous mass of
material of varying degrees of sophistication: in
suffrage and anti-suffrage literature where the
arguments are most committed and entrenched; in
public opinion, where that is refracted in the press
and in letters and memoirs of the period; and in
Hansard, where popular misconception and political sophistry collided at the cutting edge of political debate – the point at which, according to
liberal democratic theory, the rational argument of
well-organised pressure groups could effect legislative change.

The arguments were not always consistent, but they did not have to be to take effect. (Antis insisted that the natural distinction between the sexes was so great that women could not participate in government, and so fragile that to remain womanly women *must* not participate in government; that Parliament already met women's legislative needs and that women would vote selfishly to redress their grievances; that women did not *want* the vote, but would use it to combine against men.) What mattered was not the contradiction in these ideas but their *embeddedness*: their influence in institutions and social practices and the interests they were made to serve. Anti-suffrage propaganda worked to resolve the problems posed by feminism; impugning motives, refuting premises, and organising old arguments into new narratives legitimated by the developing social, medical and psychiatric sciences. For their part suffragists tried to evade or resist the efforts of their opponents in order to secure the rights of citizenship (and the definition of femininity) in their own interest and on their own behalf.[14]

*

Suffragists argued primarily from two positions, 'rights' and 'expediency', already explicit in Harriet Taylor Mill's essay of 1851: 'As a question of justice, the case seems to us too clear for dispute. As one of expediency, the more thoroughly it is examined the stronger it will appear.'[15] From the first they argued women's right, in essence and particularly in a democracy, to full human citizenship. From the second they argued for the benefits that women's enfranchisement would bring to society at large. The legal subjection of women was in their view wrong in itself, and at the same time one of the chief obstacles to human improvement and social reform.

Anti-suffragists (by nature conservative) were either opposed to the concept of 'natural rights';[16] or claimed that women's enfranchisement had to

be related to the public interest (no one could be accorded a 'right' that would damage the state); or argued that women were a special instance deprived by nature of such 'natural rights'. As Asquith put it in the House of Commons in 1892: 'the inequalities which democracy requires we should fight against and remove are the unearned privileges and the artificial distinction which man has made, and which man can unmake ... not those indelible differences of faculty and function by which Nature herself has given diversity and richness to human society.'[17] In sum, the antis argued that women were not a *case* for the vote (they did not want it, did not need it, and would not gain by it); they were not *fit* for it (by reason of their inferior capacities, lack of education, physiological frailty and economic dependence); and society would not benefit from it (women would be diverted from their domestic duties, and the home and family would be destroyed). In the elaboration of this account women were subject to flattery and abuse of varied kinds. What underlay them both was the assumption that women were excluded from the franchise by virtue of the very things that *made* them 'womanly', however these were valued or defined.

Anti-suffragists drew heavily on the Victorian ideology of 'separate spheres': 'Man for the field and woman for the hearth; / Man for the sword, and for the needle she; / Man with the head, and woman with the heart; / Man to command, and woman to obey; / All else confusion.'[18] Their use of it led to the claim that female enfranchisement would sexualise politics and unsex women, confusing the proper boundaries of masculine and feminine, public and private, domestic and political, by which the natural complementarity of a harmonious social order was maintained. In some arguments there is a hint that the austere and rational preserve of political inquiry and disinterested legislation (a notion difficult to square with the daily realities of party conflict) risked pollution from an influx of something dangerously, hysterically feminine. In more complimentary versions it is not women who are unfit for politics, but politics that is unfit for women: 'a woman could not touch that pitch without being defiled,'[19] or as Gladstone put it in 1892, to burden women with a political role was to 'trespass upon their delicacy, their purity, their refinement, the elevation of their whole nature'.[20]

Antis also argued that women themselves did not *want* the vote – no group of men had ever actively opposed their own enfranchisement and it was indeed unfortunate that some women organised against it – and in addition, that they did not need it.[21] First, because the 'natural' division of function between the sexes accorded them men's support and protection (with the vote woman would forfeit, according to Lord Curzon, 'much of that respect which the chivalry of man has voluntarily conceded to her').[22] Second, or perhaps as an extension of the same point, because a series of legislative developments had indicated that women's interests could be attended to without their direct participation. Third, because women were popularly supposed to enjoy an *indirect* political influence.[23]

The effect of the vote on women and on the family would, in the anti view, prove a disaster. Violet Markham called it a 'gamble with the future of womanhood', and Lord Curzon claimed that women would be distracted from their 'proper sphere and highest duty, which is maternity'. The 'womanly woman' would be unsexed, the children neglected and the home destroyed, either through the wife's neglect of her domestic duties or through the 'introduction of political differences into domestic life'.[24] (Perhaps significantly there is a division of labour on this point in anti-imagery: it is the middle-class woman who is unsexed and the working-class home we see destroyed.)

With varying degrees of tact the antis proposed that women were intellectually men's inferiors and emotionally unstable. The expanded electorate that had resulted from the Reform Bills of 1867

and 1884 was considered quite inexperienced and unpredictable enough, without the addition of those elements of inconstant and emotional behaviour with which women were popularly associated.[25] The fourth of Lord Curzon's 'Fifteen Good Reasons against the Grant of Female Suffrage' insisted that: 'Women have not, as a sex, or a class, the calmness of temperament or the balance of mind, nor have they the training, necessary to qualify them to exercise a weighty judgement in political affairs.' The anti-suffrage manifesto was more discreet, placing the emphasis on experience rather than capacity. 'The admission to full political power of a number of voters debarred by nature and circumstances from the average political knowledge and experience open to men, would weaken the central governing forces of the State, and be fraught with peril to the country.'[26]

The antis' trump card, or as Brian Harrison calls it, 'the jewel in their apologia',[27] was the 'Physical Force' argument, according to which the vote had to be backed by physical force in the last resort. The imperialists who were extremely prominent in the anti-suffrage leagues clung tenaciously to the view that 'those persons ought not to make laws who cannot join in enforcing them'. Since women were excluded from the police service and the armed forces they were 'incapacitated from discharging the ultimate obligations of citizenship'.[28] The discourses of imperialism and militarism left their imprint on the values of civil society, encouraged a form of social Darwinism in which international conflict was inevitable and necessary to the 'survival of the fittest', provoked anxiety as to the precarious survival of the Empire and the state of British defences and recruits, and 'increased the complexity of the governmental process and elevated its mystique'.[29] In the opinion of Lord Curzon the enfranchisement of women would 'weaken Great Britain in the estimation of foreign Powers' and prove 'a source of weakness in India' where it would be 'gravely misunderstood'.[30]

A further anti-suffrage argument was founded

on the premise that women were not breadwinners, but what Almroth Wright called 'insolvent citizens'. (He granted few exceptions since he claimed that women with independent incomes had come to them through men, and he appears to have overlooked the category of working-class women wage-earners altogether.) Even those anti-suffragists who failed to agree with him were anxious to rebut the suffrage argument that the women's vote would improve the condition of industrial workers. In so far as this was possible or desirable, anti-suffrage literature recommended that it be achieved by cooperative organisation, the fixing of a minimum wage, or 'a more even distribution of the female population throughout the territory of the Empire, by means of emigration'. But they took it for granted that 'Laws cannot alter the facts of Nature. Women, as producers of wealth, are not equal to men. If the legislature attempted to compel employers to pay women the same wages as they paid to men, the business of the country would be deranged, financial disaster would ensue, and women, as well as men, would be worse off then than they are now.'[31]

Two further arguments, or anxieties, blocked the path to the women's vote. The first derived from the assumption that women would vote 'all one way', and in the case of adult suffrage constitute a majority which might 'force upon the country a law or a policy opposed to the deliberate will and judgement of the majority of Englishmen'.[32] The second might be termed the gradualist or 'slippery slope' argument, according to which the real danger of women's suffrage lay in the changes that would follow in its wake. This might be universal suffrage – Curzon claimed there was 'no permanent or practicable halting-stage before' – or the emancipation of women in other and self-evidently inappropriate spheres. Almroth Wright warned his readers that the women's movement would demand 'that women shall be included in every advisory committee, every governing board, every jury, every judicial bench, every electorate, every

parliament, and every ministerial cabinet: further, that every masculine foundation, university, school of learning, academy, trade union, professional corporation, and scientific society shall be converted into an epicene institution – until we shall have everywhere one vast cock-and-hen show'.[33]

*

Suffragists did not, as their opponents claimed, deny the fact of sexual difference. They argued that 'femininity' was a matter of artifice, as Wollstonecraft and the Mills had done; or they based their position on a traditionally domestic femininity and argued for the benefits of its emancipation into public life. If the different natures and responsibilities of the sexes were part of the rich diversity of social life, as Asquith had claimed in 1892, it was surely reasonable to make the political system more representative by encompassing them both. The separate spheres argument was easily turned back by suffragists on their opponents: 'the more they prove it the more difficult it is to deny women the only adequate means of protecting their own sphere against the competing interests of those who are at present supposed to look after both.'[34] Either women were the same as men, and could not be denied men's rights, or they were different from men, and men could not then speak to their needs and interests.

The separate spheres argument polarised the debate between the terms of similarity and difference, in a way that more analytically minded suffragists tried to avoid. They recognised that women's social, political, legal and economic position was inflected by their social class, but they constructed arguments that identified a common subordination of women *as* women, symbolised by their shared exclusion from the vote, and with the vote as the key to the various forms of emancipation that would revise their place in law, under Parliament, in industry and in the professions from which they were chiefly barred. They insisted that sexual difference, founded in human nature or the social and domestic division of labour, did not in itself exclude women from the concept of 'natural rights', and that democratic principles and democratic practice must be made to converge. They argued that women, in far greater numbers than was recognised, *did* want the vote, and that mass demonstrations proved this to be the case. The fact that some women did not want to vote was no reason for denying it to those who did. They would not after all be obliged to use it, whereas a blanket exclusion bound all women by the prejudices of some women and some men. There was no historical precedent according to which the franchise was extended only to those sectors of the population that had unanimously proved their desire for it. On the contrary, the men enfranchised by the acts of 1867 and 1884 had never 'proved' their demand, or not by any means different from those by which the women supported theirs. ('Habits of submission make men as well as women servile-minded,' as Harriet Taylor Mill had written, and the case of women was peculiar in that 'no other inferior caste . . . have been taught to regard their degradation as their honour'.)[35]

Most passionately, suffragists argued that women *needed* the vote – where was this chivalry? – as the sweated worker, the prostitute and the wronged wife, to some degree *all* women as economic and political subjects, whatever their individual circumstances, were subject to exploitation by individual men or subordination to a legislature framed to meet the interests of the other sex. *The Times* was outraged by Lady MacLaren's suggestion that old, ugly, working-class and feminist women were excluded from the gracious parameters of men's reverence, protection and service, but it is hard to see how she was wrong. The *Common Cause* ran a regular column listing the various abuses women suffered, under the heading 'Men's Chivalry', and the *Vote* a list of cases of neglect, abandonment, battering and sexual assault with the title 'The "Protected" Sex'. Eunice

76 'How the Law Protects the Widow': designed by 'MaC' for the Suffrage Atelier, 1909.
The pair to 'How the Law Protects the Widower', and part of a set on legal discrimination against women. Others include 'How the Law Protects the Wife', 'The Husband' and 'The Daughters', and 'The Law and the Mother'.

77 'How the Law Protects the Widower': designed by 'MaC' for the Suffrage Atelier, 1909.

Murray remarked that whereas everyone was familiar with the cry, 'That is not women's work' when women knocked on the door of well-paid trades, no one objected if the work was familiar. 'Does the charwoman raise feelings of compassion in the heart of man as she moves heavy furniture or washes down the long flight of stairs, or stands at the washtub from morn till night? . . . Does the heavy load the servant carries arouse his sense of chivalry? No, the sanctity of *his* home falls upon her work, and no matter how heavy or hard the day's work may be she is working in his home, so all is well.'[36] 'Chivalry' was briskly dismissed by Cicely Hamilton as 'a code of deferential behaviour affecting such matters and contingencies as the opening of doors, the lifting of hats, and the handling of teacups; but not touching or affecting the pre-eminence and predominance of man in the more important interests of life'.[37]

Almroth Wright had argued that the compact of chivalry was infringed 'when woman breaks out into violence; when she jettisons her personal refinement; when she is ungrateful; and, possibly, when she places a quite extravagantly high estimate upon her intellectual powers'.[38] From this it is evident that the concept of chivalry, borrowed by the Victorians to grace the relations of nineteenth-century industrial capitalism, far from 'protecting' women served on the whole to regulate a preferred form of sexual behaviour. It had ideological work to do, and as a principle governing relations between individuals it was conveniently ineffectual in the larger case. Where it was not useful to the existing order – for example in ameliorating the conditions within which working-class women were particularly vulnerable to sexual and economic exploitation – it was not applied. Any infringement of the decorum proper to middle-class women (ingratitude, intellectual ambition, lack of refinement or aggressive behaviour) excluded them from its benefits. The threadbare nature of the protection of chivalry was usefully tested and advertised by suffragette prisoners who were forc-

ibly fed. Even their opponents, who disliked their principles and abhorred militancy, were appalled by the brutality with which it was applied. 'Women do not want chivalry,' Keir Hardie concluded in the House of Commons in 1910, 'they ask to be allowed to defend themselves . . . by the strength of their own vote.'[39]

The 'indirect influence' which was the other side of chivalry was vigorously despatched by Lady MacLaren's letter to *The Times* in June 1908. 'Indirect influence in politics is not only a weak influence but it is a bad influence. What women want is not power over men, but over themselves and the conditions of their own lives. Women are weary of conjugating the verb "to wheedle" . . . Men pay attentions to young and pretty and well-dressed women because it pleases men to pay them, and not because it does any particular good to the women who receive them . . . And yet even you, Sir, talk actually of this deference as a reason why women should live in political subjugation for ever. A heavy price to pay for nothing.'[40]

The very title of the *Common Cause* was intended to refute the notion 'that women's suffrage means the breaking up of the home, the causing of domestic strife, the setting of woman against man',[41] and suffragists were keen to argue the compatibility of motherhood and the vote. First of all, not all women were mothers, and not all mothers spent their whole lives mothering. (If the vote meant a five-yearly visit to the polling booth, 'the interests of the home and children need not be wholly despaired of.')[42] Second, and mothers or not, women occupied a variety of other roles on which their legal and political subordination produced particular kinds of constraints. And third, they had political needs as mothers too. Suffragists refused the distinction between the private (maternal and domestic) and the public (political) spheres, on the grounds that it was already blurred by the exigencies of modern life. The concerns of municipal and parliamentary politics were no longer distinct in the Edwardian period, and suffragists argued that when women entered the factories and the state invaded the home the last excuse for refusing them the vote had disappeared. What Jane Addams called 'city housekeeping' failed when women, the traditional housekeepers, were excluded from it. 'Politics governs even the purity of the milk supply,' as one American postcard quoted Charlotte Perkins Gilman. 'It is not outside the home but inside the baby.'[43] Or, as a British pamphlet argued citing the Registration of Midwives Act, the Children's Charter, temperance legislation, tariff reform and free trade, women needed the vote to safeguard their interests *as* mothers and *in* the home.[44]

Suffragists naturally refuted the suggestion that women were intellectually incapable or emotionally unstable. They presented themselves as various, reasonable and educated – graduate gowns featured prominently in processions – and as possessed of womanly qualities such as compassion and moral integrity that were as necessary to the state as to the family. A favourite theme in suffrage imagery pictured woman with her 'political peers': the voteless immigrant, criminal or lunatic.[45] They distinguished 'fitness to govern' from 'fitness to vote for those who govern', as Mill had done in *Representative Government* (1861); but unlike Mill they spoke not of 'the unspeakable gain in private happiness' to women offered 'a life of rational freedom' but of responsibilities shouldered, and women's duties to the community.[46]

The 'physical force' argument was rejected on the grounds that men enjoyed the vote whether or not they were likely to fight in person, and that women also paid through their taxes into the defence budget. As Balfour had put it in a speech to the House of Commons in 1892: 'The *posse comitatus* does not go out and fight the enemy; the enemy is fought by the disciplined forces of the country, and the chief duty of the ordinary citizen consists not in shouldering a rifle and going off to the frontier; it consists in paying the bill.'[47] Commenting on the NUWSS procession of June 1908 *The Times* reverted to the argument that a voter had to

78 'What a Woman May Be . . .': poster and postcard, anon. Suffrage Atelier., *c.* 1912.
George Bernard Shaw (writing on the Womanly Woman in The Quintessence of Ibsenism*) suggested that 'if we have come to think that the nursery and the kitchen are the natural sphere of a woman, we have done so exactly as English children have come to think that a cage is the natural sphere of a parrot: because they have never seen one anywhere else.' 'What a Woman May Be' reminds its audience of women's non-domestic (but womanly) duties, and contrasts each of them with 'what a man may be, and yet not lose the vote': against the mayor, the convict; against the nurse, the lunatic; against the mother, the proprietor of white slaves; against the doctor or teacher, the man who is unfit for active service; against the factory hand, the drunkard.*

79 'Twentieth Century Robbery!': postcard and poster designed by Gladys Letcher for the Suffrage Atelier, 1912.
Asquith is the highwayman and Lloyd George (Chancellor of the Exchequer) his accomplice. Suffragists frequently adapted to their campaign the classic liberal-democratic tenet of 'No Taxation without Representation'.

argue out his views for the country's good and, in the last resort, knock his opponent down. The response of the *Westminster Gazette* that such an assumption had 'in recent years been somewhat frowned upon by the police'[48] was deliberately flippant, but it echoed a serious suffrage assertion that force was a regressive element in civilised politics, and as such not to be appealed to but deplored. As for the imperialist argument that the women's vote would undermine British prestige abroad – one of the 'Old Fogeys and Old Bogeys' addressed by Israel Zangwill in 1909 – if 'this is the price of Empire – to be slaves to our own subjects, to be dragged down to *their* ethical level – well may we ask ourselves the great question: What shall it profit a nation to gain the whole world and lose its own soul?'[49]

Arguments from women's economic dependence were countered by pointing out that enormous numbers of working-class women *were* breadwinners, at unequal wages and in appalling conditions.[50] The vote was not just a matter of middle-class 'rights'. It was necessary for the protection of working-class women, both from the exploitative relations within which they worked, and the well-meaning discrimination of protective legislation on which they were never consulted. Talk of politics as an intrusion into feminine refinement could only be maintained by those resolutely blind to the spectacle of millions of women earning their own livelihoods in conditions of extreme hardship.

Suffragists insisted that women who already belonged to a range of party political organisations were hardly likely to vote 'all one way'. (They did not add, as Mill had done, that an exception would arise when their interests as women were directly engaged, and that in such cases they needed the vote as their guarantee of just and equal consideration.) According to the context, and their lights, they either denied that the vote was intended to have any further consequences, or they insisted on the justice and expedience of any further changes

that it might bring. Both sides pointed to women's participation in local government as a result of the acts of 1869, 1888 and 1894, and to the founding of women's auxiliaries to the major political parties: suffragists to stress their beneficial consequences (and the fact that men were only too glad to have their support), and antis to argue that this had granted women all the political power it was necessary for them to wield. But if it was appropriate to use women as canvassers to educate, persuade or cajole the male voter, it was hard to claim that their political judgement was inferior, and even harder to prove they had been 'sullied' by municipal politics (or would be by the parliamentary vote).[51] In a public refutation of the arguments of Lord Curzon in Edinburgh in 1912, Lord Lytton reminded his audience that 'women are already in politics and have been so for years.' He invoked Asquith's statement to the House in 1892, that democracy was opposed to artificial distinctions and not to natural ones, in order to point out that it was precisely with artificial distinctions that suffragists were concerned. 'It is not a law of Nature which says that a woman may be a County Councillor or a Mayor, but that she may not vote for a Member of Parliament. It is not a natural law that allows a woman to vote in New Zealand, Australia, and the Isle of Man, but forbids her to vote in Great Britain. That is not a law of Nature; it is a law of man, and Mr Asquith knows well enough how to change it.'[52]

Women and Suffragists in Edwardian Illustration and Caricature

They cannot represent themselves; they must be represented. KARL MARX[53]

. . . a gaunt, unprepossessing female of uncertain age, with a raucous voice, and truculent demeanour, who invariably seems to wear elastic-sided boots, and to carry a big 'gampy' umbrella, which she uses as occasion demands either to brandish ferociously by way of emphasizing her arguments, or to belabour any unfortunate member of the opposite sex who happens to displease her. ('A Typical Suffragist', *Votes for Women*, 1907)[54]

Suffrage propaganda, particularly as it concerned the representation of women, was obliged to place itself in relation to a long-standing tradition of political caricature and the popular illustration of social 'types'. Contemporary formulations of the shrew, the embittered spinster or the strong-minded woman – some of which had ancient histories – shaped 'the imagination of the newspaper artists and the uninitiated public'[55] and hence their perception of the suffragists, in advance of any particular programme or activity. The image of the shrew, and increasingly of that locus of medical and popular attention in the nineteenth century, the hysteric, were there waiting for the militant before she had thrown her first stone.

Stereotypes of femininity and ideals of womanliness were naturalised in 'common knowledge' and legitimated by scientific discourses (like medicine) which scorned the sloppiness of popular thought while bearing the imprint of its prejudice. (The middle-class illustrated press of the period, for example, fascinated as it was with class, manners and social mobility, produced a whole typology of femininities which also surface in the anti-suffrage literature of medical authorities like Sir Almroth Wright.) This being the case, the suffragists and their artists were inevitably concerned not just with the position of women in the economic and political spheres, but also with a struggle for meaning in all those representational – that is, ideological – practices where definitions of femininity were produced and contested.

Cardinal Newman once lamented that the Englishman 'gets his opinions anyhow, some from the nursery, some at school, some from the world, and has a zeal for them, because they are his own . . . he takes them as he finds them, whether they fit together or not, and makes light of the incongruity, and thinks it a proof of common-sense, good sense, strong, shrewd sense, to do so.'[56] This is a loose but evocative account of how ideology operates, which illuminates at the same time the tenacity of ideological processes and their fragmentary and contradictory nature. More analytically, we might suggest that ideology is compounded of the mental categories and systems of representation through which we make sense of our conditions of existence in the world. Ideology is a practice of representation although it does not present itself as such, but as a set of common-sense propositions which are self-evidently 'true'. This 'naturalisation' of a constructed reality serves the interests of particular social groups. 'Hegemony' is Gramsci's term for the process by which a set of organising principles, a world view, seeks to secure a consensus in the interests of an established order (or of an alliance of class interests and social groups which are becoming established). Such an order is structured not only around inequalities of class, but also around a series of other relations of domination and subordination including those of gender and race. As Virginia Woolf argued, men and women do not always hold to the same values but where she differs it is the woman who will appear the deviant, 'perpetually wishing to alter the established values – to make serious what appears insignificant to a man, and trivial what is to him important. And for that, of course, she will be criticised; for the critic of the opposite sex will be genuinely puzzled and surprised by an attempt to alter the current scale of values, and will see in it not merely a difference of view, but a view that is weak, or trivial, or sentimental, because it differs from his own.'[57]

The League and the Atelier were made up of artists, and their specific purpose was to produce representations – which would contest this hegemonic order – in the sense of actual images and pictures. But images in this sense cannot be separated from images in the sense of mental representations, and concepts that may be put into words rather than pictures. All images are traversed by language, and images are also 'texts' in

which codes are operative and meanings are produced. The visual image may make a special kind
of impact – Freud believed that thinking in images
was older, in the individual and in the race, than
thinking in words, and more closely approximate to
unconscious processes – but no image is purely
'visual'. Images are not ideologically pure because
they are images (or because they are 'art'); nor can
their ideological content be precipitated out to
leave a distinct and neutral perceptual sensation.
Meaning gets into and out of the image through the
social processes of its production and consumption. Barthes suggested that we have in our heads a
'lexicon', or dictionary of social meanings, or more
precisely an individual combination of dictionaries
which he termed an 'ideolect'. These lexicons and
ideolects are activated in communication. They are
held in common, broadly speaking, by residents in
a common culture, and oppositional meanings
must still be produced out of a negotiation of their
elements if those meanings are not to appear
deviant, hallucinatory or simply unintelligible.[58]

Representations of femininity received currency
(and detail, and inflection) in all the rich variety of
graphic material of the late Victorian and Edwardian period, and these were the great decades of
printed ephemera and popular illustrated journalism of all kinds. Much of it was produced from
such informal sources as those of commercial
lithographers, advertisers and postcard manufacturers, who contributed almost incidentally to a
public imagery of the female form, and for whom
suffragettes and feminists were simply topical or
humorous types. These were not consciously
propagandist (nor were they always unsympathetic), but taken as a whole with the illustrated press
they produced a rich sediment of anti-feminist and
even explicitly misogynist material that obviously
informed the 'higher' levels of political debate and
was certainly cited in them.

It made no difference that the bulk of this
material was not intentionally anti-suffrage; it was
so in effect, through its mobilisation of the princi-

pal definitions and prescriptions of Edwardian
womanhood (of stereotypes of femininity and the
feminine ideal). All else flowed from the fact that
it was ideologically congruent with the dominant
discourses of the day on questions of sexuality and
sexual difference. It represented an enormous
mass of material, and some very deep-seated
prejudice, against which the suffrage artists stood
as David to Goliath. They were organised and
committed but they were very small against the
accumulated weight of individual and institutional
misogyny. They were formed precisely to intervene
in these representations of femininity, which were
heterogeneous but mutually determining in important respects: and chiefly in placing women in
the sphere of the private and domestic, as distinct
from the public realm in which men governed,
administered and legislated (or if they were of a
class to do none of these things, had at least the
opportunity of electing those who did).

Hilaire Belloc assured the House, in the
women's suffrage debate of July 1910, 'that the
great weight of popular opinion is utterly against
the proposal. Members must know it. In the songs
of the populace, in their caricatures, in their jokes,
in their whole attitude towards the movement, the
populace dislike it.'[59] In doing so he pointed not
only to a widespread if intangible resistance to the
suffrage cause (the visual record is perhaps the
only relic of a strongly verbal and anecdotal culture
of misogyny), but also to the particularly close
relation between women and humour in the music
hall, in illustrated journalism and in comic postcards. (Seaside humour is rooted in the Edwardian
period and overlaps so conveniently with anti-
suffrage sentiment that it is not altogether surprising to find Donald McGill turning his hand to that
as well.) But what was so *funny* about feminism
(and about women); and what were the implications of this for suffragists, who like all women
objecting to the ways in which they are portrayed
were accused of having no sense of humour?

It is at least arguable that the relation between

women and jokes is both ancient and intimate. George Orwell, who thought comic postcards 'something as traditional as Greek tragedy', concluded in a famous essay that between half and three-quarters of those produced in forty years had been devoted to sex jokes, closely followed by hen-pecked husbands and a cast of stock characters, among which the suffragette was 'too valuable to be relinquished'.[60] (After 1918 she was transformed into the feminist lecturer or the temperance fanatic and survived unchanged in physical appearance.) In *Jokes and their Relation to the Unconscious*, published in 1905, Freud drew a distinction between the innocent joke which is merely amusing, and the tendentious joke which is an outlet for repressions. 'Since we have been obliged to renounce the expression of hostility by deeds – we have . . . developed a new technique of invective. By making our enemy small, inferior, despicable or comic, we achieve in a roundabout way the enjoyment of overcoming [her] – to which the third person, who has made no efforts, bears witness by his laugh.' The tendentious joke is either hostile ('serving the purpose of aggressiveness, satire, or defence') or it is obscene ('serving the purpose of exposure').[61]

In another context Freud discussed the tendency, innate in the structure of masculinity, either to idealise or to denigrate the female sex,[62] a tendency that was common in Victorian and Edwardian culture and was enhanced by the single-sex institutions of the period. Both kinds of tendentious joke made possible the satisfaction of a lustful or hostile instinct in the face of an obstacle which they circumvented. This obstacle 'is in reality nothing other than women's incapacity to tolerate undisguised sexuality, an incapacity correspondingly increased with a rise in the educational and social level'.[63] Hostile and obscene jokes serve the purpose of exorcising men's dislike and fear of women – the hatred, anxiety and disgust packed into some of the vulgar examples of anti-suffragism are unmistakable – but they are simultaneously impelled by an idealisation of feminine purity which was at its most intense in the Victorian and Edwardian period.[64] Most jokes involving women *were* tendentious, because those in public circulation had been drawn up by men ('No woman has ever yet been a caricaturist,' wrote M. H. Spielmann in *The History of Punch* in 1895),[65] and because feminism touched a raw social, sexual and political nerve. Nothing was more absurd for some audiences than the spectacle of a woman trying to become like a man, or more defective than a suffragist 'unsexed' by her political activities: nothing was more fundamentally unnerving, and therefore more productive of the laughter by which tension is released and anxiety transformed momentarily into pleasure.

Ridicule is a potent weapon in the maintenance of hegemony, and the ideological import of tendentious jokes is enhanced by their capacity 'to turn the hearer into a co-hater or co-disposer'[66] and offer the comforts of collusion. The joke upsets critical judgement, according to Freud: it operates as a kind of short-circuit to argument in the interests of preserving the status quo. The listener is bribed with the promise of pleasure into taking sides; and the tendentious joke in a single movement sweeps its audience into ridicule of its object and constructs that object – the militant suffragist as hysterical virago, for instance – as a reference point or warning buoy which those thus stigmatised must negotiate. Labelled and libelled in this way, suffragists had to divest themselves of the powerful characterisations which clung to their public presence and were manifest in painful and daily skirmishes with their families and at the dinner tables of their friends. Humour in this respect was on the side of the antis, and feminists had to work hard and against the grain to harness it to their own campaign.

Two particular categories of women already current in nineteenth-century illustration offered themselves for appropriation against the suffrage cause. The first was that of the domineering and nagging wife. The second, and more influential, was that of the embittered spinster, already current in *Punch* by the 1870s (when a women's suffrage bill was brought in and debated every year except for 1874). The distinction is embodied in Mrs Witherington Mildeu, the famous Advocate for Women's Rights, who is accompanied by her husband ('a most Lady-Like Person, and considered rather Pretty') in *Punch* in 1871; and Miss Gander Bellwether, the famous Champion of Women's Rights, who appears in 1874.[67]

Mrs Witherington Mildeu towers over her cowed mate (that other traditional figure of fun, the hen-pecked husband). Miss Gander Bellwether is tall and gaunt with cropped black hair, a sharp-featured 'masculine' profile with pronounced black eyebrows and a severe 'dress reform' silhouette which is thrown into relief by the oval-faced, blond-haired and softly dressed young woman who looks on. Very particular signifiers in the draughtsmanship of popular illustration, from *Punch* cartoons to seaside postcards, were devised to convey the character and associations of the embittered spinster and the suffragist as she was constructed on that foundation. Their authenticity was loosely guaranteed by the continuing popularity of physiognomy and phrenology (the belief that temperament could be read off from the disposition of facial features or the cranial formation), and by the practical need of the artists who were influenced by it to deal in a repertoire of easily available types.

The spinster is almost always thin, lacking the curves appropriate to pleasurable femininity, motherhood and charm. The angles of her body are echoed in the sharpness of her features and the lines that mark her face (for she is by definition beyond the stage at which she might still expect to find a mate). Her expression is excitable, bewildered or vindictive. The lines of disappointment are etched deep by the illustrator's pen. She wears pretentiously 'arty', shabby or masculine clothes and probably spectacles. Her appearance is pre-

sumed to derive from her indifference to her femininity, her desire to ape men's place in the world, and the hardening effects of public speaking on a woman's countenance and sensibility. She is devoid of feminine attributes, in fact, which explains both her looks and her political sympathies in a way which allows each to reflect the other. She is probably a fanatic but she is unlikely to be effective. The seriousness of her purpose is farcical because it is undermined by her ludicrous appearance. She is a figure of pity and ridicule, and we are invited to consider that those are also the appropriate responses to her cause. The vinegary spinster who was sexually or emotionally embittered was a popular figure of fun in the music hall, the novel and in illustrated journalism (through to Gilbert and Sullivan), long before Almroth Wright blamed the suffrage movement on the frustrations of 'surplus' women better accommodated by emigration and motherhood in the service of the Empire.[68] No new 'type' was needed for the militant in representation: she simply filled out an old one in a new way.

This wedge that popular illustration drove between the normal and contented mother and the frustrated spinster was unfortunately only too easily mapped on to the earlier women's franchise proposals which extended only to unmarried women.[69] On the other hand, it was difficult to maintain in practice as the suffrage movement became more public, when a number of late-Victorian and Edwardian feminists were remarkably dignified and good-looking women. Mrs Pankhurst and Christabel were not portrayed as ugly when they were not. But the general idea that 'one never sees any pretty women among those who clamour for their "rights" '[70] or as *Punch* put it, 'The women who want Women's rights / Want, mostly, Woman's charms' – had its own momentum. (An MP in the 1871 debate thought the House should demand photographs of the women who wanted the bill;[71] this had scarcely been a requirement of the working-class men and agricultural

AT MRS. LYONS CHACER'S 'SMALL AND EARLY'

Fair Enthusiast: 'Look! Look! There stands Miss Gander Bellwether, the Famous Champion of Women's Rights, the Future Founder of a New Philosophy! Isn't it a Pretty Sight to See the Rising Young Geniuses of the Day all flocking to her Side, and hanging on her Lips, and feasting on the Sad and Earnest Utterances wrung from her indignant Heart by the Wrongs of her Wretched Sex? O, isn't she *Divine*, Captain Dandelion?'

Captain Dandelion (of the 17th Waltzers): 'Haw! Affair of Taste, you know! Wather pwefer *she*-Women myself—wather pwefer the wetched Sex with all its Wongs—Haw!'

Mr. Millefleurs (of the 'Ess Bouquet' Club): 'Haw! Wather a gwubby, skwubby Lot, the wising young Geniuses! Haw-aw-aw!'

80 Miss Gander Bellwether ('At Mrs Lyon Chacer's "Small and Early"'), *Punch*, 14 March 1874.

labourers enfranchised in 1867 and 1884.) *Appearance*, therefore, and ludicrously since it had nothing to do with either justice or expedience (it was used to impugn motive), was a crucial term in the imagery of the suffrage campaign.[72]

Well might the suffragists complain that the popular image of the Women's Rightist did not exist 'outside the imagination of newspaper artists and the uninitiated public'. The power of that imaginative prototype was considerable, and constitutionalists and militants alike were touchy on the question of personal appearance because of its damaging effects. They eschewed the fashionable extremes of feather and furbelow, which it suited them to associate with a representation of their opponents as wealthy, ignorant and careless of matters more serious than the choice of a hat. But they went to some lengths to distinguish themselves not only from the image of the dowdy spinster with large feet and shabby clothes, but also from the dress reform movement with which they might have been expected to share some generally emancipatory goals.[73] The militants, who threw caution to the winds in the matter of public sympathy after 1912, were perhaps surprisingly elegant and conventional in matters of dress. Ethel Smyth complained that Mrs Pankhurst adored shopping for clothes, and that there could be 'no severer trial to people who loathe gazing into shop windows than to walk down Regent Street with her any day'.[74] Sylvia complained that her family sneered at the shabby clothing she wore, first as an impoverished art student and then as an East End activist. Early photographs show her in variants of aesthetic dress that might have come from Liberty's or might have been home-made.[75]

Emmeline Pethick-Lawrence recalled that at public meetings, instead 'of the large, aggressive, ill-clad agitators depicted in caricature, people were surprised to see slight girls of small stature (Mary Gawthorpe was tiny and the Pankhursts and Annie Kenney not much taller) dressed quite simply and attractively, and able at the first sen-

tence to rivet the attention of their hearers'.[76] There is some evidence that the growth of the suffrage movement and its increasingly public presence, together with the suffragists' own objections to the ways in which they were portrayed, weakened the popular stereotype of the flat-footed and angular spinster in the Edwardian period. Pictorial journalism was giving way to photographs, which in so far as they appeared to be a more truthful record were more likely to challenge received accounts of what the suffragists were like. Newspaper reports described picturesque processions in which political determination was offset by the youthful gaiety of white dresses, embroidered banners and massed bouquets. Where the stereotype survived intact, it did so as part of the more overtly misogynist tradition that surfaced in picture postcards and the cheap weekly press. Women's advances in other areas had by this point modified their presentation in the serious papers, and even where the editorial policy was anti-suffrage such images could not but help their cause. Women doctors, 'new' women and 'sweet girl graduates' weakened the force of the argument that only the home-bound mother was 'womanly', and with it the force of the deviant images that made up her antithesis.

Against the stereotypes suffragists stressed 'the infinite variety of texture, so to speak, of the class lumped together under the term "woman"'.[77] The suffrage campaign was not the only arena in which the redefinition of 'womanliness' was taking place, and for this reason the analogy of the suffrage artists defiant and unaided in the face of the Goliath of popular opinion will not quite do. If women were not as a category 'emancipated' by the turn of the century, their political, legislative, social and economic positions had been to some extent transformed. Shifts in the representation of women did not, of course, take place as a direct consequence of social changes or tidily in step with them. Both kinds of change were limited, complex, and to an extent mutually determining. Representation takes place within hegemony. Within hegemony the hold of ideology, of what Gramsci termed 'common sense', is tenacious but also contradictory and provisional. The signification of events is part of what has to be struggled over, and within hegemony negotiation is possible and alliances may be broken and remade. The strains and abrasions between social representations and individual experience (however predisposed), between broader industrial, economic and social upheaval and the aspirations and struggles of organised groups: all this had exhausted the languages in which Victorian femininity was conventionally expressed. The old types would no longer serve. As Bernard Shaw wrote in 1911, there were no 'women' in his plays: 'Don't think that I mean that they are untrue to life. I mean exactly the contrary . . . There are no women in the real world . . . woman, of whom we hear so much, is a stage invention, and . . . a very tiresome one.'[78]

For suffrage imagery to be effective it had to connect with changes and organised struggles elsewhere. It almost certainly had to eschew the minor acts of disobedience which characterised the contemporary avant-garde, in order to stay intelligible. And ironically but inevitably it had to stay within the social discourses from which the 'lexicons' and 'ideolects' of its audiences were composed. Suffrage propaganda is neither autonomous nor utopian. It is a discourse of opposition, but it is subject to the same historical determinations, and it contests and manipulates the same ingredients, as that to which it is opposed. It was a real task to produce work that was intelligible, persuasive (neither deviant nor hallucinatory) and vital (undepleted by argument). By definition these problems were not posed to those image-makers whose project lay along the grain of ideology rather than against it: artists working for the anti-suffrage organisations, or the much larger group of illustrators who produced, sometimes unthinkingly, a body of misogynist material out of the elements, and serving the interests, of the sexual status quo.

Why Types?

The stereotype is truly an instrument of subjection; its function is to produce ideological subjects that can be smoothly inserted into existing institutions of government, economy, and perhaps most crucially, sexual identity . . . The stereotype inscribes the body into the register of discourse; in it, the body is apprehended by language, taken into joint custody by politics and ideology. CRAIG OWENS[79]

There is no longer any need for the militants to wear their colours or their badges. Fanaticism has set its seal upon their faces and left a peculiar expression which cannot be mistaken. Nowadays, indeed, any observant person can pick out a suffragette in a crowd of other women. They have nursed a grievance for so long that they seem resentful of anyone who is happy and contented and appear to be exceptionally bitter against the members of their own sex who do not support their policy of outrage. ('The Suffragette Face: New Type Evolved by Militancy', *Daily Mirror*, 25 May 1914)

Truth to Appearances

Suffragists were engaged in skirmishes (which could prove decisive), around ideal, normative, and deviant types of femininity. Their artists were obliged to negotiate a set of inherited and interdependent categories: the womanly woman, the fallen woman, the shrew, the slut, the strong-minded woman, the hysteric, the 'girl of the period', the 'shrieking sisterhood'. These were produced as distinct moral and physical entities and journalists lingered lovingly over the detail of their classification and pathology.[80] But they entered political argument and imagery as fragments, so that any signifying detail of clothing, profile, expression or stance (spectacles, pinched features or an umbrella) could be summoned up to haunt the debate about women and women's rights. Suffragists went out of their way to reject some ('Mrs How-Martyn making jam' is a silent riposte to the 'shrieking sisterhood'), and to lay claim to others (such as the definition of the 'womanly woman' which both sides fought for); but either way the terms had already been laid down, and the argu-

The Bystander, December 31, 1913   705

Present Day Types

No. I.—THE SUFFRAGETTE

BY ARTHUR WATTS

ment was less *about* those terms than about the values and possibilities ascribed to them.

The immanent truth of appearances, for those attuned to read them, was a constant theme in nineteenth-century medicine, phrenology, physiognomy, and eugenics;[81] in the developing social sciences (established in mid-century through a unified system of scientific societies); in the detective novel (where Sherlock Holmes admonishes Dr Watson for failing to recognise 'the importance of sleeves, the suggestiveness of thumbnails, or the great issues that may hang from a boot-lace';[82] in what the artist W. P. Frith called 'hat and trouser pictures' (paintings of modern life and manners);[83] and most popularly in the reportorial style of illustrated journalism.[84] These were practices of varying degrees of sophistication and scientific pretension, but what linked them was a common impulse to explore, to observe, to bring under classificatory systems of different kinds the bewildering and threatening diversity of the social 'flux'. The specific significance attached in physiognomy to thin, restrained, unfeeling mouths, strong-willed or feeble chins, retroussé noses or low foreheads ('feminine' in women but weak and deficient in men), is evident alike in *Punch*, in novelists' descriptions of their female characters,[85] and in Thomas Laycock's 'Clinical Lectures on the Physiognomical Diagnosis of Disease', which stresses the revelatory nature of the patient's appearance and reproduces four heads from *Punch* along with medical photographs of imbeciles and cretins.[86]

Types were evoked in a kind of iconographic shorthand that was indispensable to the comic draughtsman, and in the process their visual symptomatology was developed and confirmed. Individuals were subjected to a more or less affectionate or abusive manipulation of their features in the service of social or political comment.[87] Subordinate and marginal groups such as the Irish, the Jews, women or the working class, were reduced to a generalised physiognomy of the type, or to a

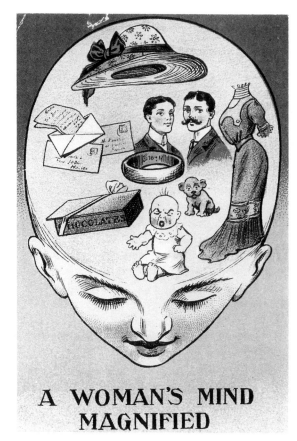

82 'A Woman's Mind Magnified'.

opposite page
81 'The Suffragette, Number 1 in a series on Present Day Types', the *Bystander*, 31 December 1913.

proliferation of sub-types. As the influence of physiognomy and phrenology declined the illustrated press, and subsequently the mass-circulation newspapers with their half-tone photographs, continued to rehearse their readers in the emergence of new types and the detailed decoding of others. This fascination with types, and particularly with the typology of modern femininity, had important implications for suffrage politics and suffrage imagery. A self-perpetuating circuit was easily built up – between the assertion that this was what spinsters looked like, for example, and the depiction of spinsters like this – and readers were encouraged to believe that there was such a thing as 'The Suffragette Face: New Type Evolved by Militancy'.[88] The point was not so much that this was unflattering or untrue, but that in a system which condemned behavioural or aesthetic deviance it served to undercut their claim. They were not real women; or alternatively, they were real examples of unwomanliness.

By the 1880s physiognomy and phrenology had been displaced by more 'scientific' concerns, but the fascination with types and appearances was developed in the arguments of social Darwinism and eugenics (the study and management of inheritance in the interests of improving the race).[89] Evolutionary theories were taken up in such a way as to suggest the inevitable determination of individual capacities and social structures by biological laws. Natural selection appeared to encourage the idea that morphological discrepancies were linked to inherited and racial characteristics, and that primitive, feeble, or degenerate nations stood little chance in a global 'survival of the fittest'. The work of Herbert Spencer provided a precedent for sociological and anthropological theorists of the 1880s to adapt the principles of natural selection as a justification for national, class and racial privilege. For eugenicists (and imperialists) the scientific scrutiny of the body was supposed to offer evidence of the natural stratification of social and racial hierarchies. At the heart of the new eugenic enterprise, as David Green points out, lay the old physiognomic assumption that 'physiological and anatomical differences between individuals could be regarded as the indices of relative intellectual ability, moral qualities and psychological disposition.'

This influential and apparently scientific nexus of imperial, eugenic and diagnostic concerns had important implications for the position and representation of women in the decade before the First World War. Anxieties provoked by industrialisation and the threat of social instability in the late nineteenth century were enhanced by unrest and militancy among women in the early years of the twentieth. It was widely asserted that 'masculine' women and 'feminine' men were among the indices of social degeneration,[90] that women pursuing emancipated activities in higher education or the professions impaired their fertility and maternal capacities, that the birth rate was falling among the middle classes who would be swamped by the eugenically inferior inheritance of the lower orders, and that enfranchising women would compromise the virility of the state and promote unrest in the colonies. Woman, or rather 'womanliness', was the linchpin in bourgeois ideology and a structuring category in the principal discourses of civil society (medicine, law, politics, education, the family). If woman was out of place everything was out of place. For those concerned with social stability it was the actual or potential change in the social place of women (limited though this was) which seemed the major threat to the security of the family, state and empire. Because of its ideology of social progress, eugenics crossed the party spectrum and appealed to socialists and radical conservatives alike. But as Philip Abrams has pointed out, it 'culminated in demands not for a new social order but for the reconstitution of the old order at a higher level of efficiency'.[91] The

83 'The Suffragette Face: New Type Evolved by Militancy', *Daily Mirror*, 25 May 1914.

May 25. 1914   THE DAILY MIRROR   Page 5

THE SUFFRAGETTE FACE: NEW TYPE EVOLVED BY MILITANCY.

Mrs. "General" Drummond.

When attacking the police.

She is defiant

Ecstasy on arrest.

Screaming with impotent rage.

Mrs. Pankhurst, the chief leader of the militant movement.

Youth looks like old age.

Dishevelled after fighting

She uses supplication.

Rather emotional.

Addressing a crowd.

A male suffragist has to be protected from the crowd.

"Cads!" hisses a woman because the crowd jeered.

There is no longer any need for the militants to wear their colours or their badges. Fanaticism has set its seal upon their faces and left a peculiar expression which cannot be mistaken. Nowadays, indeed, any observant person can pick out a suffragette in a crowd of other women. They have nursed a grievance for so long that they seem resentful of anyone who is happy and contented and appear to be exceptionally bitter against the members of their own sex who do not support their policy of outrage. The public are becoming enraged at their tactics, and open hostility was shown to them at a meeting in Hyde Park yesterday.

basis of any measure of eugenic reform was that it should reduce the rate of reproduction among the lower orders and encourage it among those classes whose superior social position was supposed to rest on their 'naturally selected' capacities. This tended to have the effect of reinforcing a conservative definition of femininity (particularly for middle-class women who threatened to escape their 'separate sphere'), and obliged women to counter with evolutionary arguments of their own to the effect that modern womanhood was neither mutant nor perverse.

Stereotypes and Social Types

Richard Dyer defines a type as 'any simple, vivid, memorable, easily grasped and widely recognised characterisation in which a few traits are fore-grounded and change or "development" is kept to a minimum'.[92] We could say of the particularly fixed and regulatory form of the stereotype what T. J. Clark says of ideology in general: that it is an order of knowing 'most often imposed on quite disparate bits and pieces of representation'; that its sign 'is a kind of inertness in discourse: a fixed pattern of imagery and belief, a syntax which seems obligatory'.[93] Stereotypes are deceptively simple, easily communicated and apparently consensual. (For technical reasons the stereotypes in visual propaganda are particularly exaggerated and de-fined.) They are to be understood as evaluative concepts held by groups about other groups, most frequently and effectively by dominant groups about marginal groups.[94] Like jokes (according to Freud), they short-circuit critical judgement by cliché. They are related to the socialisation of major structural groups and to disruptions in the relations between dominant and subordinate groups; and they produce subjects not by persua-sion but through deterrence: 'the stereotype works primarily through intimidation; it poses a threat.'[95]

This brings us back to the question of rep-resentations of women. Types, like other elements of signification, have their own level of effect, their own 'reality' in so far as our perception of reality is ordered by the categories which they invoke. Vic-torian and Edwardian representations of women (like our own) were not neutral, but hegemonic: the sexualities on offer served the interests, broadly speaking, of those in power (men of the ruling-class faction). T. E. Perkins has argued that be-cause women's socialisation is problematic, they give rise to very powerful stereotypes, and because they are not cohesive as a group but strung out in institutionalised intimacy with men, to a great number of often contradictory ones. She suggests that a group undergoing shifts in its structural position will throw up new stereotypes, and that if its challenge is threatening these will be pejorative.[96] All this helps to make sense of the range of visual stereotypes invoked in anti-suffrage propaganda, as well as of the peculiar viciousness of the more monstrous parodies of women. Sander Gilman, for whom stereotypes are fabricated solutions to social and psychic conflict, suggests something similar. He uses the example of the Jew who became the 'white Negro' in nineteenth-century Germany 'because the demands of the Jew for political and social equality created in the privileged group, the Germans, the need to see the Jews as politically subservient and immutably different'.[97] The suffragette became the hysterical virago on very much the same pattern.

At the same time 'a group which is presenting a problem also has a problem'[98] (it struggles with self-definition and evaluation, as well as with the definitions and evaluations imposed on it by others). Suffragettes refused hysteria and pro-duced the counter-type of the allegorical warrior maiden. Constitutionalists and militants alike affected to dodge the designations of their oppo-nents. Because their exclusion from the franchise was justified primarily on grounds of sex, their counter-meanings had to be mobilised around the redefinition of femininity, or the use of conven-tional designations (like 'womanliness') in new ways. The *raison d'être* of the suffrage movement was the campaign for the vote but one of the aims that motivated its supporters, that was necessary for the production of propaganda, that developed their own sense of identity and capacity to counter their opponents, was the legitimising of new representations of women. Or, more precisely, the contesting, modifying and restructuring of representations of women already in circulation or in the process of emerging (owing to shifts in the socio-economic positions of women, or in signifying practice, or in both).

Sociologists often distinguish stereotypes (which are deviant) from social types (which are normative).[99] One of the chief strategies of both organised and informal anti-suffrage imagery was to characterise the suffragists not as individuals or according to their membership of social groups, but by pathological stereotypes: the masculine woman, the unsexed woman, the hysteric and the shrew. (In the more vicious instances sexual, criminal and psychological pathology are conflated.) Suffragists tried to evade the mantle of deviance by developing the variants of *social type*, placing particular emphasis on the combination of women's familial duties with new roles in education and employment. Already typified within the dominant culture *as* women (that is, biologically and domestically), the social type performed for them a differentiating, individuating function that placed them in the public world as doctors, workers, graduates, teachers, or any of the other roles embodied in their processions and represented on posters such as the Atelier's 'Polling Station'. An alternative strategy adopted by the WSPU invoked a different register of imagery altogether (neither social nor stereotype), in the use of personifications and allegorical figures like Justice, Liberty, or Joan of Arc as the spirit of militant womanhood.

The stereotype characteristically disguises its origins and the interests it serves (Norman Bryson likens it to an alibi, or to a prerecorded message which indicates the speaker is 'elsewhere').[100] In addition to contesting the 'truth' of representations of women, suffrage propagandists had the further option of unmasking the antis as the source of the message. Within the limits of their own sense of strategy and decorum, they produced a typology of their own, characterising their opponents as wilful, ignorant, selfish and out-of-date, and pointing discreetly to masculine investments in prostitution, the liquor trade and the maintenance of professional monopolies of one kind and another. At the very least, women could deal the same cards differently. Even the fixity of a stereotype is threatened by its insertion in different discourses. There was no single answer to the question of how to depict women – as domestic, heroic or oppressed. Suffrage artists shared these functions out in a range of representations addressed to different arguments in the campaign. Four types or personifications recurrent in suffrage imagery are the Working Woman, the Modern Woman, the Militant Woman (which gains its resonance from the principal anti-type, the Hysteric) and the Womanly Woman. The working woman offered a class reproach to 'anti' privilege. The modern woman, defined as a progressive social type in language borrowed from social Darwinism, was used to characterise traditional femininity as full of artifice and out-of-date. The womanly woman, a more idealised and nebulous accretion of feminine virtues, was too valuable an identification to concede to the antis, so that it was not 'womanliness' which suffragists attacked but the power to define it.

These social types, stereotypes and allegorical personifications were neither definitive nor exclusive. They were invocations. They invited identification and summoned up the outline of suffrage arguments: the powerlessness of working women with no say in the legislation of factory acts in Emily Ford's 'They've a Cheek', for example. Unlike those in the labour movement, the suffrage artists did not gravitate towards the consolidation of an ideal type. They had too much invested in the idea of heterogeneity. No single representation could have served a movement compounded of such different political, religious, social and professional affiliations divided between a militant and a constitutional campaign. What linked the range of representations they produced was not a common content, but their strategic use: not a relation to women in the 'real' world, but a deployment within and against the femininities 'on offer' in the Edwardian period.

Bryson has argued that through its constitution 'as repetition and typicality' the stereotype is the form of representation most subject to fatigue.[101] If the stereotype aims at fixity but is intrinsically precarious, then it is arguable that such fatigue in the representation of women in the Edwardian period was not the consequence of repetition alone, but of the contradictions arising from industrialisation and modernisation, and of the concerted efforts of particular groups to fracture the consensus as to how they should be seen. It may be finally the experience of the *stereotyped* (in this case women) that unsticks the claim of the type to represent a fully evident, if generalised 'truth'. The struggle is then to make it come unstuck in the minds of those for whom it is part of the habit of thinking 'woman', and who keep it in currency from positions of power. Almost any suffrage account of a House of Commons debate on women's suffrage is evidence of how they saw this task, and of how difficult it was to do. Generalisations about women were resilient beyond the point of evidence or consensus. How to put back the fullness of women's perception, and personal and political aspiration and experience: that was their problem. And it could not be done literally, since *all* images are flat and empty.

The Working Woman

> The number of women who are engaged at this time in producing the wealth of this country is double the population of Ireland ... These women are all labouring under the gross disability and industrial disadvantage of an absolute want of political power. Every day we live this becomes a more grave dis-

advantage, because industrial questions are becoming political questions which are being fought out in Parliament. EVA GORE BOOTH[102]

The representation of working women in suffrage imagery made several important connections. It suggested an alliance between suffragists and the working classes against the anti-suffragists (whose leaders did indeed come from a wealthy and conservative elite, and whose ideology contained a strong element of anti-democratic feeling). It reminded a middle-class audience that many women were breadwinners, often at low rates of pay and in conditions completely at odds with the traditional conception of femininity. It marked an important point on the spectrum of women's social and economic activity, which the suffragists were anxious to demonstrate in all its diversity. Above all, it provided poignant instances of unequal pay, infant mortality and the sexual and economic oppression which they argued would only be solved by the women's vote.

Working women in general, as they are ranged across 'The Polling Booth', were an important group through which to invoke women's resourcefulness, competence and capacity for social and economic independence. They were a reminder of the dramatic increases in the numbers of women teachers, nurses, shop assistants, clerical workers and civil servants which had taken place since the foundation of the Society for Promoting the Employment of Women in 1859. Working-*class* women, especially those at the bottom of the heap like the sweated seamstress in 'Votes for Workers', offered a special instance of economic and sexual oppression. Because they claimed the vote would lift or ameliorate this oppression, suffragists were able to produce in the context of the campaign an imagery of the working-class woman which had as one of its referents the cause itself ('for these we fight').[103] The gist of the argument was that neither philanthropy nor socialism could be expected to touch the nub of the problem, in which the class and gender oppressions of working-class women combined to determine their economic and sexual exploitation.

Between 1890 and 1914 when the suffrage campaign was at its height, a whole series of philanthropic and investigative works on poverty and unemployment appeared, which reflected and influenced the formulation of social and industrial policy. The effect of such studies 'was to make poverty in England actual, a matter of facts and figures that demanded public attention'.[104] At the same time a number of other titles were published, some of them produced out of the women's or labour movements, which addressed specifically the question of women's work and its associated difficulties. Ramsay MacDonald edited the Women's Industrial Council Inquiry published as *Women in the Printing Trades* in 1904; the influential *Handbook of the Daily News Sweated Industries' Exhibition*, edited by Richard Mudie-Smith, outlived the exhibition with which it was published in 1906; *Women's Work and Wages*, edited by Edward Cadbury, Cecile Matheson and George Shann, appeared in 1909; *The Married Working Woman* by Anna Martin in 1911; two reports from the Women's Co-operative Guild, *Working Women and Divorce* and *Maternity*, in 1911 and 1915; Maud Pember Reeves's *Round About a Pound a Week* in 1913; and Clementina Black's *Married Women's Work* in 1915.

From this it is evident that the suffragists had at their disposal a range of research material to which they had themselves contributed, and from which it was possible to draw a series of related propositions concerning the position of women in the labour force, the right to certain conditions of employment, and the parliamentary vote. They were chiefly concerned to establish, against popular assumption and the arguments of their opponents, that large numbers of women *did* work, that an honourable independence was greatly desired by many women who had otherwise no need to work, that there was no natural or equitable distinction between most kinds of male and female labour

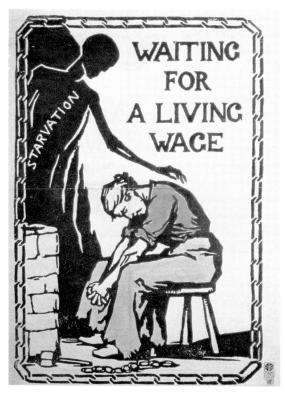

84 'Waiting for a Living Wage': postcard and poster designed by Catherine Courtauld for the Suffrage Atelier, *c.* 1913.
Starvation hangs over the figure of a Cradley Heath chainmaker in a motif that is bordered with chains. For suffragists this was an image in which the oppression of women's industrial labour was neatly condensed.

(that which obtained had emerged out of industrialisation and the transformation of the economically productive household), and that the conditions of their work would be improved by even *some* women's possession of the vote.

Between 1861 and 1911 the proportion of women in the total paid labour force had actually declined, from 34.1 per cent to 29.7 per cent. But there was a tremendous increase (307 per cent) in the numbers of women employed in teaching and nursing, and as shop assistants, clerks and civil servants. During this period the number of women teachers rose from 79,980 to 183,298, of nurses from 24,821 to 77,060, of shop assistants from 87,276 to 366,268 (by far the largest group of middle-class women workers in the country), of clerks from 279 to 124,843, and of civil servants from 2082 to 39,773. There are inconsistencies in these figures but the overall picture is clear.[105] Women's own efforts to improve their employment prospects had interacted with a number of other factors: industrialisation and the restructuring of the retail trades, shifts in the division of skilled and unskilled labour, the invention of the typewriter and the emergence by 1900 of the 'shorthand-typist', a radical change in the function and structure of the civil service, and the expansion of the Post Office into the largest business organisation in England (in 1911 it employed 92 per cent of all women working for central government). In all these sectors women were a welcome supply of cheap and efficient labour. (Sydney Webb estimated from the Board of Trade Report on Earnings and Hours for 1906 that the average weekly wage was 25s. 9d. for men and 10s. 10½d. for women.)[106] Unskilled working-class women in sweated and homeworking trades earned far less than this in appalling and sometimes dangerous conditions.[107] The lowest-paid workers cited in *Women's Work and Wages* (Cadbury *et al.*, 1904) included charwomen at 1s. 6d. to 2s. a week, chainmakers at 3s. to 15s. a week, and pin makers at 3s. 10d. to 10s. 6d. a week. The total average wage of the out-working trades at the Sweated Industries Exhibition in 1906 was a penny an hour.

Middle-class women were excluded by law or custom from the principal professions of Edwardian life: the Church, the armed services, the law, the higher reaches of the civil service. Only with great difficulty had they won the right to study and practise as doctors. A broader range of opportunities had opened up to them by the early years of the twentieth century, but in most instances they were arbitrarily confined to less skilled and more poorly paid employment than men, whether as secretaries, shop assistants, factory inspectors or elementary-school teachers.

Working-class women were subject to the conditions of industrial legislation enacted in their interest (but framed without their participation or consent) and to the restrictive practices of male trade unions. Two questions in particular brought the suffragists into open conflict with the trade unions: protective legislation and the 'family wage'. From the mid-1870s union leaders had used the TUC's Parliamentary Committee to influence industrial legislation, but for women this influence – which they greatly envied and hoped to emulate – encouraged attempts to 'save' them from degrading work, and facilitated the passage of bills that limited their working hours. The difficulty for women thus protected, or offered protection (such as pit-brow workers and chainmakers), was that these were often the only conditions in which they could make a living.[108] Protective legislation was founded, supposedly, on a concern for women's special needs but, as Maud Royden pointed out, in practice 'men keep on deciding that the best-paid and most honourable work is beyond the powers of women, or in some mysterious way "unwomanly".' This seemed to have a great deal to do with whether the work in question brought women directly into competition with men. Almost any work was 'proper' to women that was private and domestic: 'the heaviest kinds of laundry work . . . the sorting of refuse, cleaning fish, picking fur, and other hard or disgusting forms of labour, are freely permitted them; while efforts are repeatedly made to forbid them work which used to be regarded as essentially "womanly" . . . brewing and baking, spinning, weaving, knitting and dyeing, the making of garments, the making of soap and candles, of medicines, and salves . . . have been removed to the factory, and when women, impelled by necessity, seek to follow them there, they are met with indignant protests by the men, and by an appeal to legislation to keep them out.'[109]

The arguments for and against protective legislation were controversial. The *Anti-Suffrage Review*, for example, pointed to 'that great fabric of legislation for protecting and befriending women and children which has been steadily built up during the last eighty years by a Parliament of men, voted for by men' as evidence that women could rely on men's chivalry, and did not need the vote for themselves.[110] Suffragists resented the exclusion of women from the processes of a legislature that affected their livelihoods, however benevolent. But they also tended to argue against any interference with women's right to compete freely in the labour market, on the grounds that protective legislation was arbitrary and discriminatory in practice, that it lessened the competition for men while providing no alternatives for women, and that it confirmed a questionable assumption about what could be considered 'womanly' or 'degrading' activities. In their view the regulation of work was in effect bound up with the regulation of femininity, through the maintenance of women's economic dependence and a particular industrial division of labour. But this brought them into bitter conflict with socialists like Mary MacArthur of the Women's Trade Union League, who intended to make it clear that the League had toiled for a generation for protective legislation in the interests of women, and was not prepared to have its efforts undermined by a middle-class appeal to the freedom of contract in a market economy. (As Robert Gray has pointed out, the debate about fac-

tory legislation focused a contradiction within bourgeois ideology, between the ideal integrity of the family and the individual freedom to buy or sell labour power including that of women and children.)[111] The case was crisply argued by Beatrice Webb, who blamed feminists for misconstruing the issues and influencing the rejection of several important clauses in the Factory Act of 1895: 'When we are concerned with the propertied classes – when, for instance, it is sought to open up to women higher education or the learned professions – it is easy to see that freedom is secured by abolishing restrictions, but when we come to the relations between capital and labour an entirely new set of considerations comes into play. In the life of the wage-earning class, absence of regulation does not mean personal freedom . . . It is the law, in fact, which is the mother of freedom.'[112]

The struggle of male trade unionists for a 'family wage' was a similar source of contradiction for feminism. Was the working-class wife under the relations of industrial capitalism more vulnerable because of her economic dependence or because of the exploitative conditions in which she sought to earn a wage and augment the family income? The fight for the family wage took place against the interests of capital in the sense that it claimed a higher return for the worker's labour, but in the interests of capital in that it confirmed the economic subordination of the wife that capitalism had itself taken over and developed from the productive household of the manufacturing period.[113] The transfer of the sexual division of labour within the family into social production ensured women's subordinate position and produced a reservoir of cheap female labour. From the 1830s philanthropists discussed the 'social problem' of women's industrial labour almost exclusively in terms of its effects on the family; and by the 1870s trade unionists like Henry Broadhurst were drawing on the essentially bourgeois ideal of a domestic 'womanliness' to promote the elimination of female competition as a first step toward the realisation of a 'family wage'.[114]

Few women were unionised, outside the textile industries of the north of England, since women worked chiefly in casual, low-paid and sweated work where union organisation was impossible. For many years relations between women's associations such as the Women's Protection and Provident League and the male trade-union movement were hostile and patronising.[115] In such a context suffragists were partly justified, if also tactless, in identifying conflicts between the interests of men and women as workers: between the need to ameliorate women's vulnerable and exploited position in the labour force and the efforts of the unions to suppress female competition in the pursuit of wages and conditions adequate to the maintenance of family life.[116] Suffragists who addressed themselves to these conflicts had no developed theory of the articulation of masculine interests with those of capital – they drew as Mill had drawn on the liberal tenet of individual competition in a market economy – nor were they necessarily concerned completely to displace the notion of 'separate spheres' and its concomitant femininity. But they believed that working women were subject to a double oppression, and that in viewing them as the wives and relatives of working *men* whose best hope lay with the family wage, the unions colluded in keeping them unskilled, underpaid and economically dependent on the husbands that one in five or six of them would never have.[117] 'Many men have no families to support, or refuse to support them; they are not paid the less. Many women have families to support: they are not paid the more.'[118] Hence the emphasis in suffrage imagery on unsupported female breadwinners: 'Votes for Mother who works for us now Father's dead'. How this point was taken depended on how it was made and by whom – working-class men were justly sensitive to political lectures from middle-class women – and on the sympathies of those to whom it was addressed. Some trade unionists were not prepared to entertain it at all.[119]

The point is that conflicts between the economic interests of men and women of the industrial working class were not a natural consequence of sexual antagonism, but the product of the mobilisation by capital of an existing division of labour within the family. Women's social and economic dependence, and men's fear of being undercut by a reserve army of female labour, were both buttressed by the ideology of the family, and both were important structural elements in the foundation of the capitalist mode of production.

In all this suffragists, if they were to make the plight of working women a plank in their own campaign, had to argue that the vote would raise their wages or improve their positions. This was vehemently denied by the antis (who could not afford to seem uncaring), who argued that women were numerous, unskilled and unorganised, and the vote was not a remedy for that. One of Lord Curzon's 'fifteen sound, valid and incontrovertible arguments' against the extension of the franchise was that the vote was not required for the removal of hardships and disabilities, which might 'be equally well removed or alleviated by a legislature enacted by men'. For their part the suffragists drew a direct parallel between women's disadvantaged and exploited industrial position and their exclusion from trade unions and from the vote. Low wages might not be caused by the lack of a vote, but they were maintained by it. The history of trade unionism was held by suffragists to demonstrate the axiom that 'economic power follows political power'. This might seem to have been putting the cart before the horse, but they believed that women were infamously sweated in government employment, where men were protected by the 'Fair Wages Clause' their votes had won for them. (Since there was no 'fair' or union rate in women's sweated trades they were unprotected, which led the suffragists to claim a direct relation between sweated labour and the lack of a parliamentary vote.) They expected the franchise to help women's industrial organisation by providing it

"SHE WORKS FOR US NOW FATHER'S DEAD"

with political muscle. They argued that with its leverage they would be able to open some of the apprenticeships, trades and professions that were arbitrarily closed to women, and to acquire technical and vocational training that would turn women into skilled workers who were better organised.[120]

Anti-suffragists were never quite satisfied with invoking the womanly woman who did not want the vote, but were prepared to play quite unscrupulously on the anxieties of working-class men concerning 'petticoat government' in the home or the state. At such moments the high-minded rhetoric of 'separate spheres' is betrayed by the effort to put women in all senses 'in their place'. John Hassall's poster 'A Suffragette's Home' needs to be understood not only in relation to a general iconography of the deserting wife in comic illustration, but specifically in the light of a tract such as *Power and Responsibility* (published by the Men's League for Opposing Woman Suffrage, no. 53): '*Resent* this attempted *tyranny* and let the Suffragists know that you simply will not have *petticoat government . . . the subjection of man to woman*, turning the order of nature upside down.' The 'just claims of men' were in this argument based on their exclusive responsibility for all the material work and worth of the world. 'Look round you as you read this leaflet. On every side you see THE RESULT OF MASCULINE LABOUR. At every moment you are using some item of a great organisation, every material portion

WOMEN UNDERPAID -- MEN OUT OF WORK

Jones "Our Guvnor don't want women to get the vote because their wages would go up; I'm often out of work but my missis and the girls can always get a job but the pay don't keep one let alone a family! LET'S HELP TO GET THEM THE VOTE AND A LIVING WAGE."

85 'Votes for Mother': postcard (and four-colour poster) produced by the Artists' Suffrage League, 1910. Probably by Joan Harvey Drew.

86 'Women Underpaid, Men Out of Work': postcard, anon., Suffrage Atelier, *c.* 1913.
As trade unionists argued increasingly that women's place was in the home and that men should be paid a 'family wage', so suffragists argued that women undercut men's wages because they did not have the strength of the vote to improve their industrial position. It was therefore in the interests of working-class men to support women's claims to political enfranchisement.

of which is made by MAN . . . The whole material fabric of civilised life has to be brought into existence, and to be maintained by men. That is to say, before a woman can perform the simplest action of her life, before she can eat a mouthful of food, or put on a stitch of clothing, she is wholly dependent on mechanisms supplied and worked by men.'[121]

So much for complementarity. The image of the Angel in the House had come to obscure the fact that a majority of women had always done hard physical work inside and outside the home, including washing, cleaning, cooking, sewing, serving, childcare and laundry work, in their own households and as paid domestic servants. These and related forms of women's work passed unnoticed because they were compatible with conventional definitions of femininity, and incompatible with the concept of work as *waged* labour that now prevailed. Other kinds of work remained invisible, either because they were carried out in private like the worst forms of sweated labour, or because they were in full view, but somehow remained unseen by those without eyes to see.[122] Lady MacLaren's response to the speeches opposing the Women's Suffrage bill in 1908 was addressed to the MP who had declared in the Commons 'by a strange hallucination, that women had no physical force at all'. It could be said to sum up the argument for the *necessary* invisibility of women's work to the maintenance of the status quo. 'And yet this Member had that morning ordered a number of women in his household to get out of bed at dawn while he was comfortably sleeping. He was then roused from his slumbers by the knock of a woman; his hot water was heated and brought to him by a woman; he donned a shirt that a woman had made and that a woman had newly washed, and he put on a collar she had ironed; he dressed himself in clothes which a woman had brushed and which another woman had probably done much to make; he went down to eat the breakfast which a woman had prepared, and walked out to go to the House of Commons over steps which a woman had knelt to

scrub. From the cradle to the grave, that man depended for his comforts on the physical force of women. They had nursed him in infancy, washed all the plates and dishes he had used, tidied away all the disorder he had created, and prepared at least nine-tenths of the food he had consumed. And yet he was not aware that the greater part of all the dirty, disagreeable, monotonous and ill-paid work of the whole of this country is performed by women, and proclaimed to an applauding House that women have no physical force at all!'[123]

One of the principal tasks of suffrage propaganda lay in the vigorous assertion of women's contribution to the productive work of the world – it was one of the arguments on which their claim rested – and in this their iconography diverged not only from conventional representations of women but also from those in the labour movement. The heroic, muscular, half-clad manual worker was in one sense an inappropriate identification for a union membership made up of skilled workmen and labour aristocrats, but it was an image that answered the needs of a labourism for which the trade-union movement, the working class, the labour process and the class struggle itself were essentially 'masculine'.[124] Working women emerge only fitfully through the filter of Victorian and Edwardian representation, cast in roles that accord with the prevailing tendency to view them primarily as the wives and dependents of working-class men. This was as true of labour imagery as it was in a different way of their depiction in the earlier and more radical traditions of *Punch*, in the socially conscious illustration pioneered by journals like the *Graphic* in the 1870s, and in the embryonic social realism of artists such as Luke Fildes, Hubert von Herkomer and Frank Holl (none of whom was politically radical, and all of whom became Royal Academicians).

The image of the working woman, derived from or enhanced by the investigative activities of philanthropists, journalists, documentary photographers and social reformers, was a potent icon of exploitation and one that usefully cut across other tendencies towards generalisation, idealisation or burlesque in the representation of women. But it was a 'type' nonetheless, and a convenient one, and it might be argued that in their concentration on the extremes of economic and sexual exploitation in sweated labour and casual prostitution, the suffragists enforced the representation of working-class women as victims, rather than as women organised in their own interest.[125] The imagery of the working woman, sometimes contrasted with the womanly woman who stoops to save her sister, or the comfortable woman who like the bad Samaritan turns away, was intended to be effective in winning supporters to the campaign. These might be fellow workers who would identify with the argument that it was in their own economic and industrial interest that women should gain the vote, or they might be socialists or philanthropists of either sex who were sympathetic to women's needs. It was not the purpose of the suffragists to produce representations adequate to what might be perceived as the social reality of working-class women, or to further their interests in other respects. In this sense the suffrage artists, who were predominantly middle-class, were engaged in their own particular and well-meaning form of exploitation: that of the image of the oppressed and sweated worker to further the progress of their own campaign.

This image and its associated arguments were fraught with difficulty. They glossed the structure of class relations within the campaign, and between the campaign and institutions outside it, in ways that were only partly justified. They were useful because they were highly politicised, but they had to be mobilised in such a way as not to offend against party interest. The link between sexual and economic exploitation, which was a very important one to the suffragists, had to be made discreetly if they were not to imply that working-class women were unchaste.[126] An iconography borrowed from the Madonna of Mercy, in which the enfeebled,

87 'The Comfortable Women': anon. (but obviously by the same hand as 'Bogies'), Suffrage Atelier.
Glossed in the Vote, *10 August 1912: 'The women here are seen shutting their eyes to the sight of their sisters' burdens and closing their ears to those who plead their cause'.*

WHITE SLAVE TRAFFIC

SWEATED LABOUR

-M HUGHES-

THE SCYLLA AND CHARYBDIS OF THE WORKING WOMAN.

88 'The Scylla and Charybdis of the Working
Woman': postcard designed by M. Hughes for the
Suffrage Atelier, probably *c.* 1912.
*Suffrage interest in enforced prostitution (the White Slave
Trade) reached a climax in 1912. Suffragists regularly
argued that sweated labour – the greed of men as well as their
lust – drove women to prostitution. Only the vote would save
women from economic and sexual exploitation by men. But
suffragists themselves had to steer a careful course if they were
not to imply that working-class women were unchaste. Maud
Royden, editor of the* Vote, *was typically discreet in her
pamphlet on 'Votes and Wages': '[Homeworkers] are getting
6s. and 5s. and less. They are supported, for the rest, on the
rates, on charitable doles, and on the price for which they
may sell themselves in the street. Those who keep straight –
and there are many – are heroines. Those who do not – and
they are not few – which of us shall blame?'*

the impoverished and the bereft huddle together
under the protection of womanly charity, was also
risky. It put the 'womanly woman', albeit on an
allegorical level, back into the same frame as the
working woman, but in such a way as to suggest –
even with the best of intentions – that it was
somehow not possible to be both. One, desired,
meaning (the sweated woman worker as emblematic of that sexual and economic oppression the
vote would cure) produces through this division of
labour in the image another, unwelcome, reading
that shadows it uncomfortably. The image of
woman as victim is waiting to take its place as the
return of the repressed. Sylvia Pankhurst's
working-class militants are unique in suffrage
propaganda. Suffrage imagery served its purpose,
but it is haunted now by a sense of distance
between that purpose and the representations of
working-class women it produced; a distance that
has as much to do with the pictorial resources and
principal tropes of the period as with the political
allegiances of the campaign or the class position of
the artists themselves.

The Modern Woman

The Eternal Feminine is in process of change, and the
woman of political and social activity will be different
from the domestic woman, no doubt, just as palaeolithic
man differs from his neolithic brother, but she will not be
any the less Woman ... Let us watch the modern
woman; no longer doll-like, she is now energetic and
assured; not less beautiful, only differently beautiful ...
This evolution of woman is inevitable. When everything
in the modern world is changing, can woman remain
unchanged? JEAN FINOT, quoted in *Votes for Women,*
1911[127]

Modernity, femininity, evolution – the principal
terms in Jean Finot's article on 'The Passing of the
"Eternal Feminine"' cited approvingly in *Votes for
Women* – were brought together in suffrage argument to defend the natural and inevitable development of a new type of modern femininity. (The
antis they characterised as social dinosaurs, a rem-

nant of the *ancien régime* beached on the shores of industrial, urban, bourgeois society.) But for these arguments to be secure, they had to negotiate two particular kinds of obstacle: the literary heritage of the 'New Woman', a type the suffragists were anxious to repudiate, and the claims of their opponents that the so-called 'modern' woman was a perverse and degenerate form of femininity, an index of social decline and a threat not only to the family but to the security of the Empire and the future of the race.

Holbrook Jackson looked back on the 1890s from the vantage point of 1913 as a decade obsessed with the 'new': the New Age, the New Spirit, the New Humour, the New Fiction, the New Hedonism, the New Drama, the New Realism – and the New Woman.[128] At once a sociological phenomenon and a literary type, the New Woman focused a number of contemporary debates concerning the emancipation of women, and joined them to a movement to modernise contemporary fiction through the exploration of the social constraints on feminine sexuality. Feminist heroines were fashionable in England after the first performance of *Hedda Gabler* in 1891. The sexual and economic exploitation of women was one of the principal themes in the plays of Arthur Pinero and Oscar Wilde in the 1890s, and in the social drama of Henrik Ibsen as it was developed by George Bernard Shaw and Harley Granville Barker. (When the Men's League prepared 'A Declaration of Representative Men in Favour of Women's Suffrage' its signatories included Pinero, Shaw, Granville Barker, Hardy and Meredith as well as J. M. Barrie, E. M. Forster, John Galsworthy and H. G. Wells.) Many of the popular New Woman novelists of the 1890s were women – Mona Caird, 'George Edgerton', May Sinclair and Sarah Grand – who wrote passionately about women's right to lead fulfilled and independent lives for an avid readership (Grand's *The Heavenly Twins* sold 20,000 copies in its first week), and who helped to make the public discussion of

femininity and female sexuality possible. Thomas Hardy, George Gissing, George Moore and George Meredith (who produced in successive years *Tess*, *The Odd Women*, *Esther Waters* and *The Amazing Marriage*) were known for their controversial New Woman heroines: fulfilments in part of their own dreams of sexual freedom.[129]

Two factors which made the New Woman irresistible to novelists, and which novelists particularly explored, were her association with explicit sexuality – in 1896 the *Saturday Review* equated New Woman fiction with 'works dealing intimately and unrestrainedly with sexual affairs' – and the purely personal nature of her rebellion.[130] These were both characteristics which, in their embrace of modernity, the suffragists sought to avoid. The minor New Woman novelists drew on feminist debates about marriage, divorce, sexuality and bachelor motherhood which the suffragists, for strategic reasons, had largely succeeded in pushing to the margins of their campaign. Authors who explored such topics, and who sold in enormous quantities to an apparently insatiable audience, were criticised for encouraging women to do what they read about. They opened up the topic of feminine sexuality for serious exploration by novelists of the calibre of Hardy, Meredith and Gissing; but at the same time they did the suffragists an unwitting disservice by associating women's emancipation with sexual emancipation, and with heroines whose principled independence leads them back into domesticity, or to a stickier end.[131] The challenge to sexual taboos was for literary reasons an important ingredient in New Woman drama and fiction, but the hint of promiscuity which hung around the popular image of the advanced woman of the 1890s was something the Edwardian suffragist was at pains to avoid. Mrs Fawcett emphasised that free love was not a feminist concept, and in her review of Grant Allen's bestselling *The Woman Who Did* (1895) described him as 'not a friend, but an enemy, and it is as an enemy that he endeavours to link together the claim of women to citizenship and social and industrial independence with attacks upon marriage and the family'.[132]

The second identifying characteristic of the New Woman in fiction was her integrity; her conflict with convention was a matter of principle, but one expressed in a personal rebellion that was outside any organisation and allied to no political or reforming ends. This made her a suitable subject for the nineteenth-century novel, which in England had always been interested in psychological motive and the clash between individual aspiration and social convention. In this sense the unconventional heroine was perfectly congruent with the drama of love, marriage and the family which characterised the English novel. But in her idealistic, frequently neurotic and explicitly sexual nonconformity she was a very bad model for the respectable, responsible and *collective* politics of the suffrage campaign.

The period between the defeat of a women's amendment to the Reform Bill of 1884 and the beginning of militancy in 1905 – the 'doldrum years' of the suffrage campaign – is therefore crucial to the understanding of Edwardian feminism. In those years major changes took place or were consolidated in women's social, legal and political position, new representations of femininity were generated, and 'women writers played a central role in the formulation and popularisation of feminist ideology'.[133] The New Woman was fading as a literary phenomenon by 1905. By that point her principal characteristics had been absorbed into a more generalised notion of modern femininity and the reading public was bored with the label. The New Woman existed only in the flickering and composite image that emerged from the various identifications of journalists,[134] moralists, politicians, novelists, dramatists and illustrators, from Ibsen to *Punch* (though 'real' women chose to perceive themselves, or were perceived, in terms of it). But even as a cliché she remained a spectral presence to haunt the arguments of feminists and inflect their public reception.

The New Woman of the 1890s and the campaigning, organised suffragists of five to ten years later shared the same heritage of social and political change, and the same aspirations towards a wider range of identities and activities for middle-class women. (As the American journalist and suffragist Rheta Childe Dorr described her, the New Woman wanted 'to belong to the human race, not to the ladies' aid society to the human race'.)[135] They were in favour of the development of women's capacities and opposed to the doctrinaire definition of what these might be; they were against submissiveness, frivolity and fashion insofar as it perpetuated a passive and narcissistic femininity; and they were in favour of health, activity, and social and economic independence. But the suffragists were committed to political change and to organisations that worked to bring it about. Their strategies required them to avoid the taint of sexual laxity and any public association with that impropriety of manner, costume or speech which was part of the allure of the fictional New Woman, but which could not be allowed to threaten an already controversial and political campaign. In emphasising their own modernity they played down the New Woman's idiosyncratic and libertarian attributes, and appealed over her head, as it were, to such elements of 'womanliness' as they could renovate and deploy.[136]

Modernisation was an uneven process in Victorian and Edwardian Britain. (Paul Thompson has pointed out that Rutherford was already working on the atom in Cambridge when tenant farmers on St Kilda were burning lamps of sea-bird oil and bartering hand-woven wool to pay their rent.)[137] The social consequences of industrialisation and mechanisation were different for urban and rural populations, for the property-owning and the working classes, for men and women. The Victorian middle-class woman has been called the first modern woman,[138] because the impact of modernisation was greater for her than it was for her upper-class or working-class sisters. Modernisation brought new patterns of work, including those kinds of retailing and clerical work responsible for the expansion of middle-class women's paid employment before the First World War. It was middle-class women who benefited from new educational and professional opportunities, who engaged in new patterns of consumption (their acceptance of innovative technologies made them a significant force in the development of a modern consumer economy) and who exhibited what are now thought of as more modern sets of social values. They were the women who became graduates, doctors and public officials (all recognised sub-types of the genus New Woman); who took up sports such as tennis, cricket, golf or bicycling; who read French novels or political tracts like Ann Veronica's chocolate-and-yellow-covered pamphlet; who wore tailor-made costumes, shirt-blouses and Petersham belts; who aspired to independence and the enlargement of their social round; who went to matinées, or met each other in tea shops or in the new and inexpensive restaurants set up in department stores especially to cater for female customers.[139]

And as Patricia Branca emphasises, modernisation 'brings about not only changes in work and style of living, but also a new attitude of mind, which in the long run is probably its more significant feature'.[140] Feminists were encouraged to believe in the identification of emancipation with social progress, in the importance of innovation and new technology, and in the possibility of social intervention as a means to improve the quality of human life. On one level the struggle for women's emancipation can be read as a struggle for women's rights to the fruits of modernisation: social mobility, urbanisation, the growth of education and of new forms of industrial organisation and negotiation, the development of social services and the extension of the franchise. On another, as the right to be seen as modern themselves, as educated, capable citizens. Thus the virtues of an earlier

Victorian 'womanliness' could be strengthened, educated, and exercised for the public good in a way that was perfectly congruent with the desire for greater personal autonomy. These arguments were brought together in posters like the Atelier's 'Polling Station', which emphasise the diversity of modern women's social roles to prove their equal rights to the franchise and to demonstrate the trained capacities they can now contribute to the modern state.

The impact of modernisation on women's lives and opportunities was, however, complicated by the role which ideologies of femininity played in the various discourses on social progress or decline. The tendency in Western thought to imagine women as aligned with nature and men with culture placed women on the side of biology and tradition against the forces of technology and change. One way of perceiving the Enlightenment project of a humane, civilised and rational society with its concomitant ideology of social progress was therefore as 'a struggle between the sexes, with men imposing their value systems on women' in order to facilitate social change.[141] The paradox here lay in the proposition that modernisation did not apply to women, that social progress could only be achieved by women keeping their 'womanliness' safe and unimpaired. Certainly the medical and social sciences, as they consolidated their professional status and claims to scientific authority, set themselves against the modernisation of women's lives and argued that evolution favoured a high degree of specialisation between the sexes – that women's special role was motherhood, and that intellectual or physical activity impaired their reproductive powers. From this perspective the partial measure of female emancipation that had taken place by the Edwardian period was evidence only of degeneration and decline: a view expressed by Almroth Wright (among many others) with a characteristically racist inflection. 'If to move about more freely, to read more freely, to speak out her mind more freely, and to have emancipated herself from traditionary beliefs – and, I would add, traditionary ethics – is to have advanced, woman has indubitably advanced. But the educated native too has advanced in all these respects; and he tells us that he is pulling up level with the white man.' Clearly the idea was preposterous, and Wright quotes Nietzsche to the effect that 'Progress is writ large on all woman's banners and bannerets; but one can actually see her going back.'[142] For society to modernise, women had to stay where they were.

Expressed in more sober terms than Almroth Wright's, the idea that women's struggle for emancipation was a symptom and cause of social decline was quite widespread. It gained currency from contemporary anxieties as to the 'condition of England' and the stability of the Empire, and from the language of social Darwinism in which these were expressed. The humiliations of the Boer War, the *Report of the Inter-Departmental Committee on Physical Deterioration* of 1904 (though it refuted rumours that 60 per cent of Englishmen were unfit for active service), an apparent increase in the number of mentally defective persons discussed in the *Report of the Royal Commission on the Care and Control of the Feeble-Minded* of 1908, an uneasy sense of German economic strength and military preparedness: all this helped to make the public receptive to talk of physical, moral or intellectual decline and prescriptions for dealing with it.

The language of social Darwinism encouraged the idea that 'God's unalterable law concerning the survival of the fittest is just as applicable to the life of the Nation as it is to the briefer existence of an animal or a human being.'[143] Nations could progress or decline; indeed the full title of Charles Darwin's 1859 publication was *On the Origin of the Species by Natural Selection, or the Preservation of the Favoured Races in the Struggle for Life*. The emphasis on natural selection as a random and unwilled process was augmented by the concept of sexual selection in *The Descent of Man* which appeared in 1871. This helped to focus attention on the role of social values and individual will in shaping a

nation's racial destiny, and it sharpened discussion of the role of women as mothers – as progenitors of the race – at just that moment when the processes of modernisation were helping to open up extra-domestic educational and employment prospects for middle-class women. Eugenics was one of the principal strands in social Darwinism, and late-Victorian and Edwardian debates on racial vigour and 'national efficiency' drew constantly on medical and eugenic theory to press the message that women were abandoning motherhood or rendering themselves unfit for it.[144] Between the mid-1870s and 1910 the birthrate dropped by almost 30 per cent, and few paused to notice that with increased longevity and lower infant mortality the population as a whole was not in decline.[145] Lawson Tait argued in the mid-1880s that 'to leave only the inferior women to perpetuate the species will do more to deteriorate the human race than all the individual victories at Girton will do to benefit it.'[146] Throughout the 1880s and 1890s doctors, eugenicists and moralists accused emancipated middle-class women of shirking their racial duty. 'Unwomanly' women, including those who squandered the energies that should have been devoted to reproduction and nurturing on intellectual or physical activities, were thought to be sterile or to produce sickly or defective offspring. Together with the feckless and unstable, but fecund, poor, they became the principal focus of eugenic anxieties over an apparently declining and degenerate population. Within these debates there was an inevitable conflict of interest between women's demands for greater autonomy and self-fulfilment, and the progress of the race. 'If child-bearing women be intellectually handicapped, then the penalty to be paid for race-predominance is the subjection of women.'[147]

In the tussle over the modern women, suffragists, as well as their opponents, drew from evolutionary theory – or at least from evolutionary concepts loosely understood. Social Darwinism was not a coherent creed but a loose assemblage of

90 'The ASS as Scientist': card by Catherine Courtauld for the Suffrage Atelier.

89 'Polling Station': anon., printed and published by the Suffrage Atelier. Undated, c. 1912.
Eliza Lynn Linton summed up the anti-suffrage position when she claimed that a woman's raison d'être was maternity: 'the cradle lies across the door of the polling-booth and bars the way to the senate.' But the women here are barred from the polling station by a uniformed policeman. Behind him a queue of men, led by an agricultural labourer (enfranchised 1884), a figure from the industrial working classes (enfranchised 1867) and a top-hatted member of the bourgeoisie (enfranchised 1832) enter to register their votes. Suffragists were particularly indignant at women's exclusion from the 1884 act (part of a Liberal strike against the political power of the landed aristocracy) since large numbers of illiterate farmworkers were granted the vote. The situation was particularly poignant for the 30,000 women tenant farmers, whose labourers could now vote while they

themselves remained excluded. (See Charles Seymour, Electoral Reform in England and Wales, Yale, 1915, pp. 476–77).
In the foreground a mother stoops to embrace her child, flanked by seven professional women. On the right, a graduate is followed by a nurse, a mayor (Millicent Fawcett's sister Dr Elizabeth Garrett Anderson became the first woman mayor, of Aldeburgh, in 1908) and a woman in legal robes (women like Christabel Pankhurst could take law degrees but not practise as barristers or solicitors until 1919). On the left an artist with palette and brushes accompanies a woman who may be a writer or journalist, and a factory inspector (by 1914 there were about 200 women factory inspectors in government employment, and their example was significant far beyond their modest numbers).

beliefs with sufficient elasticity to become for a generation or more all things to all people.[148] References to the antis as dinosaurs or the suffragists as mutants, to the life struggle and the future of the race, did not need Darwin to sustain them, but such terms gave the arguments a spurious scientific authority. In the process of permeating most aspects of cultural life beyond the confines of natural history, evolutionism underwent some revision and mutation of its own, settling into the general vocabulary as an essentially *purposeful* concept in a way that was quite at odds with Darwin's account of it.

The Descent of Man gave credence to the ideology of separate spheres (drawn on by anti-suffragists) with the suggestion that sexual divergence was part of the evolutionary process: the more refined and distinct the sexes and their social attributes, the higher the order of civilisation to which they belonged. Darwin believed that the male brain was more highly evolved than the female, and that the biological characteristics of femininity – in which he included intuition, rapid perception, irritability and imitation – were those of the 'lower' races and belonged to an earlier stage of development. The combination of Darwinian theory with anthropometry – the systematic measurement of cranial capacity and brain weight – appeared to confirm the popular view that women were more emotional and less intellectual than men (their brains were smaller, though not in relation to their body weight), and added the quasi-scientific gloss that women occupied a lower place on the evolutionary scale.[149] In the writings of Darwin and Herbert Spencer (the enormously influential Victorian philosopher), women were biologically speaking arrested or undeveloped men, as a consequence and condition of their role as the mothers of the race. It is not difficult to see how Darwinism could be used in defence of the status quo and against any invasion by women of the masculine sphere. Either women were biologically unsuited to intellectual and public activities (education, professional employment and the parliamentary vote), or the modern woman, extending her activities beyond the limits fixed by her reproductive capacities, became 'thoroughly masculine in nature, or hermaphrodite in mind' and 'lost her feminine attractions, and probably also her chief feminine functions'.[150] As Patrick Geddes put it: 'What was decided among the prehistoric *Protozoa* cannot be annulled by act of parliament.'[151]

For their part suffragists drew on evolutionary concepts either to argue that uniquely feminine characteristics should be represented in social life; or that femininity itself evolved and found its appropriate expression according to the circumstances of the age. After the work of Darwin and Spencer it was probably easier to argue from sexual difference in the language of evolutionism, than it was to argue from equality in the liberal-political discourse of 'natural rights'. The profound anxieties stirred up by the thought of a 'masculinisation' of women (and the degeneracy of men they would mate with and breed) could be countered with the claim that modern woman was a naturally evolved, socially desirable and perfectly womanly type, and that educated, healthy and active mothers could only benefit the racial stock.[152] To the traditionalists the ideal of womanliness was fixed in nature, and any deviation from it was a perversion that imperilled the future of the state: there was no room for talk of modernity, maturity or progress. For suffragists, Darwin provided a platform from which to argue that 'nothing is more certain than that human material is plastic and that the human race is in a constant state of transition in obedience to the pressure of outside circumstance or perhaps to some innate impulse still unrecognised by science.' Under conditions of social and industrial modernisation a natural femininity might be rediscovered beneath the alienated surface of feminine artifice; or (which was not quite the same thing) a newly evolved femininity retaining some of the characteristics of the old 'womanliness' might emerge naturally from

STUDIES IN NATURAL HISTORY.
The Antysuffragyst or Prejudicidon.

The Antysuffragyst or Prejudicidon. This curious animal has the smallest brain capacity of any living creature. Its sight is so imperfect that it cannot see further than the end of its nose; but it has a wonderful capacity for discovering the stupefying plant called "Humbugwort," on which it feeds voraciously. It is closely allied to the Lunaticodon, and it is a fierce enemy of the Justiceidon.

the unfolding of the evolutionary narrative in its interaction with the conditions of the time. The slide into teleology here is characteristic of the way Darwin's ideas were popularly taken up, in the 'hope at least that evolution is leading us towards an ultimate unfolding of faculty and a high degree of morality as remote from our present conditions as they are from the brutality and instinctive unreason of primitive man'.[153] It was also one of the ways in which they were available for adaptation to the suffrage cause.

The Descent of Man had stressed that the development of moral and altruistic faculties was central to human evolution, and that these habits would probably become fixed by inheritance with the passage of time. The older traditions of Evangelicalism had accorded women a special moral and spiritual responsibility, and the unlikely fusion of Evangelical and evolutionary concepts enabled women to shift their place on the evolutionary scale and urge their active participation in the regeneration of the race. Social progress in this perspective depended on altruistic women gaining the political power necessary to balance the com-

91 'The Antysuffragyst', the *Vote*, 26 September 1913.

petitive individualism of men.[154] At their most extreme, feminist arguments from women's 'moral mission' made men's sexual appetites the cause of social degeneration, and in *The Cosmic Procession, or the Feminine Principle in Evolution* (1906) the feminist theosophist Frances Swiney drew on a mélange of anthropological and evolutionary theory to turn Darwin on his head and claim that 'man, on a lower plane, is undeveloped woman'.[155] More generally, women used the ideas of social Darwinism that were often turned against them to refute the notion that women's emancipation flew in the face of social progress and argue that women's 'abject economic and political dependence on man, must inevitably, by crushing the intellect and initiative of the mothers of the race, render futile and vain the progress, advancement and development of man'.[156] Or as Amy Bulley had put it in 1890: 'As a social factor, as an engine of evolution, of human development, the entry of women into full life is a change so vast and so pregnant, that to those who take in its significance the idea is overwhelming. Its final outcome cannot be foreseen; it is only clear that with the development of society is bound up henceforward the more complete and perfect evolution of women.'[157]

To women like Harriot Stanton Blatch the anti-suffragist was an isolated fugitive from the eighteenth century, lost to the democratic ideals of modern society. British suffragists often echo the American commentator Thorstein Veblen, apparently unwittingly, in drawing a parallel between the bourgeois wife as vicarious consumer and exemplar of her husband's wealth, and the decadent luxury of the aristocracy in the *ancien régime*.[158] They demanded in effect a modernising of femininity that would grant women a stake in the rights of the nineteenth-century bourgeois man: citizenship, education, employment without patronage and a voice in the state. They pleaded for something sober, respectable and responsible at the expense of frivolity and display, usefully signified in representations of anti-suffragists en-

cumbered by the bonnets and crinolines of a less enlightened period. In this the suffragists were undoubtedly helped by the department stores and advertisers of the Edwardian period, which had their own investments in the image of woman as a new kind of consumer.[159] What has been called the 'new commerce' opened up employment opportunities to women but more significantly it addressed women as consumers, inviting them to identify with specifically *modern* (active, sporting) images of themselves. Together with public transport, public lavatories for women, the growth of tearooms and the gradual decline of the chaperone, department stores helped to open up to middle-class women the hitherto masculine domain of modern, public, urban life. 'The needs of the modern woman are carefully studied at Selfridges,' runs the slogan along the bottom of pages in the *Suffrage Annual and Woman's Who's Who*, and copious advertisements (in the suffrage press as elsewhere) offer new goods and services specifically to women in the years before 1914.

It was possible to argue on the one hand that nineteenth-century developments had been aberrations in a longer historical continuity of women's activities which, after a disruption caused by the effects of the industrial revolution, the modern woman simply resumed;[160] and on the other, that it was now simply too *late* for a return to womanliness in the traditional sense: that social, industrial and economic developments had under-

92 'A Little Behind the Times': postcard designed by Joan Harvey Drew, published by the Artists' Suffrage League, *c.* 1909.
The figure of John Bull addresses a quaintly garbed Times *and* Spectator *(prominent anti-suffrage papers), and accuses them, as suffragists regularly accused their opponents, of being outmoded. John Bull was easily legible as the most popular contemporary embodiment of the British people, but confusingly (for the meaning of this image) he has to be depicted in eighteenth-century dress.*

93 'Time to shut up shop', *Votes for Women,* 4 July 1913.

John Bull: "Very charming, I'm sure; but aren't you a little behind the times."

Printed and Published by the Artists' Suffrage League, 259, King's Road, Chelsea.

TIME TO SHUT UP SHOP

WOMAN OF TO-DAY: "Surely you don't expect me to put up with any of these!"
MRS. HUMPHRY WARD: "I am sorry we have nothing newer. This style of thing gave every satisfaction—fifty years ago."

(According to the "Times," Mrs. Humphry Ward said at the Annual Meeting of the National League for Opposing Woman Suffrage, last week, that "she wished some one would provide them with some new arguments.')

mined for ever the structural determinants of the Angel in the House. Israel Zangwill was one of many suffrage speakers to make the point that the anti-suffrage ideal was built on an 'idyll of domesticity' that had lost its base in fact. Industrial developments that destroyed the productive household and took women out of the family had shaped the evolution of modern society so that women's suffrage was 'not the begetter and forerunner of an impending revolution, but the seal and consecration of a revolution that has already succeeded'. In one great crescendo Zangwill advised 'Old Fogeys' who wanted to go back to the old ideal to make a counter-revolution like the Old Turks. 'Take women away from the coal-pit and the factory; dissolve their trade unions; send them back to their little ones; dismiss them from the post-offices and the shops; banish them from their municipal positions, from your county councils and borough councils and parish councils and Royal Commissions, from your school boards, your boards of guardians, and your education committees; drive them out of Girton and Newnham; forbid them to work in your hospitals and exhibit in your picture galleries; expel them from your Navy Leagues and your Primrose Leagues, your National Service Leagues and your Liberal Federations and your Tariff Reform Leagues; stop them from canvassing at your elections; put back the movement of evolution and the march of civilisation, and then you may begin to talk of women's place being in the home. But if you will not, or cannot, do this, then neither can you deny our noble professional women the dignity of a vote, nor our sweated factory women its protections.'[161]

Suffragists argued at different moments that they represented a rich diversity of social types, that they were the heirs to a pre-industrial womanliness only temporarily obscured by the advent of a simpering, Victorian femininity, and on occasion that they were themselves the very type of modern womanhood. Perhaps they were. An American writer on 'The Evolution of a New

Woman' watched the suffragists 'swing with easy step from one end of Fifth avenue to the other' and reflected on the new vigour of young women of whom any nation would be proud.[162] Laurence Housman, writing to Janet Ashbee on the day after the NUWSS demonstration on 13 June 1908, described the 'large number of beautiful and noble types' among the graduates and concluded that 'the twentieth-century type is something quite new: – hatched in the nineteenth century of course, but not yet registered down in portraiture as I suppose it will be before long.'[163] To her critics the modern woman was a symptom of the social decline she helped to precipitate (and after 1906 the militants were often written about in this way); to her champions she was not unwomanly, but womanly in a new and developing way.

The Hysterical Woman and the Shrieking Sisterhood

One does not need to be against woman suffrage to see that some of the more violent partisans of that cause are suffering from hysteria. We use the word not with any scientific precision, but because it is the name most commonly given to a kind of enthusiasm that has degenerated into habitual nervous excitement. (*The Times*, 11 December 1908)

No doctor can ever lose sight of the fact that the mind of woman is always threatened with danger from the reverberations of her physiological emergencies. It is with such thoughts that the doctor lets his eyes rest upon the militant suffragist. He cannot shut them to the fact that there is mixed up with the woman's movement much mental disorder; and he cannot conceal from himself the physiological emergencies which lie behind. (Sir Almroth Wright, 'On Militant Hysteria', *The Times*, 28 March 1912)

94 'No Votes Thank You': designed by Harold Bird for the NLOWS, published probably in the early part of 1912 as part of the intensified NLOWS campaign. *In Bird's poster the Womanly Woman is the anti-suffragist; curvaceous, draped and garlanded. The suffragist behind her is the Hysteric, the 'shrieking sister', angular and awkward. Louise Jacobs's Suffrage Atelier poster 'The Appeal of Womanhood' (ill. 108) is a direct response to this image. Her Womanly Woman appeals for the vote 'to stop the white slave traffic, sweated labour, and to save the children.'*

Horace Walpole had called Mary Wollstonecraft 'a hyena in petticoats' (scavenging, hybrid and sexually ambivalent);[164] a phrase echoed in Eliza Lynn Linton's 'shrieking sisterhood', first coined for 'Modern Women and What is Said of Them' in 1870, but still in common currency in the Edwardian period. (One suffragist complained in 1907 that after 'all these years we still cannot escape her well-known epithet . . . it stares at us from letters to the newspapers almost daily'.)[165] What it evokes is hysteria: a renewed focus for medical debate but also, as Stephen Heath remarks, 'coming increasingly readily to hand as an all-purpose term to characterize any "female" behaviour'.[166]

Developments in nineteenth-century medicine located the woman's body as a site of special disturbance and difficulty, and Foucault has suggested a contemporary 'hysterisation of woman' which involved 'a thorough medicalisation of their bodies and their sex . . . carried out in the name of the responsibility they owed to the health of their children, the solidity of the family institution, and the safeguarding of society':[167] that is, in the name of those very institutions which, according to their opponents, suffragists set out to destroy. For half a century and more, feminism and hysteria were readily mapped on to each other as forms of irregularity, disorder and excess, and the claim that the women's movement was made up of hysterical females was one of the principal means by which it was popularly discredited. Charles Kingsley warned John Stuart Mill in 1868 that 'we must steer clear of the hysteric element,'[168] and the older and constitutional societies had done everything in their power to do so, but militancy gave a new lease of life to the view expressed in Almroth Wright's letter 'On Militant Hysteria': 'that there is mixed up with the woman's movement much mental disorder'.[169]

What made the whole nexus femininity/sexuality/hysteria so powerful was its spread across common parlance as well as its increasingly specialised articulation within the developing disciplines of medicine and psychiatry. In the light of it feminism became a species of sexual disorder. (Almroth Wright's five categories of militant suffragist included the intellectually and sexually embittered and the sexually atrophied, for all of whom he prescribed emigration and motherhood in the service of the Empire.) The ideological impact of the term in the regulation of femininity both inside and outside of medical discourse means that we cannot speak of 'hysteria' in any purely clinical sense. Its lay usage, however imprecise, was guaranteed by its 'scientific' authority, which was itself informed by popular misconceptions of both feminism and the psychic and social consequences of female biology.

Officially the anti-suffragists based their case on complementarity: on the idea that men and women had different roles and temperaments, and that for either to trespass on the duties and activities of the other was an offence against God, nature, or 'national efficiency'. This argument developed in practice through an idealisation of 'womanliness' on the one hand and the categorisation of deviant femininities (which refused to be complementary) on the other. Ideal and aberrant femininities were then assigned to either side of the suffrage debate. There is thus a division of labour in anti-suffrage imagery between the representation of woman *on* the pedestal, the type of ideal femininity who neither needs nor wants the vote; and the woman *off* the pedestal, whose deviant or compromised femininity does not deserve it. In this tidy formulation 'womanliness' was at risk from the vote, and the state from unwomanliness. It remained in the interests of all concerned – men and women, voters and non-voters – to preserve the status quo. 'For the happy wife and mother is never passionately concerned about the suffrage. It is always the woman who is galled whether by physiological hardships, or by the fact that she has not the same amount of money as a man, or by the fact that man does not desire her as a co-partner in work, and withholds the homage which she thinks he ought to pay to her intellect.'[170]

There is a rich variety of galled and blighted womanhood in popular anti-suffrage imagery, but it is the hysteric – as *The Times* said, we use the term 'not with any scientific precision' – which was the very type of aberrant femininity, and for several reasons the most useful to the antis' cause. Polemicists traditionally engage each other's arguments while at the same time impugning the character and motives of the opposition. Hysteria offered the advantages of a term that was generously elastic in everyday use, where it bore the marks of earlier tropes of female deviance (such as maenads, viragos and shrews), but as a clinical concept it sharpened the diagnosis of feminist reformers as simply 'faddists' or 'fanatics'.

The idea of hysteria is a very ancient one, which dates back at least to Hippocrates, since when 'its demarcation has followed the meanderings of the history of medicine.'[171] (The term remains in general use but the diagnosis is rarely made, and it has dropped out of the *Standard Nomenclature of Diseases and Operations*.) Hysteria was ascribed in antiquity to the malfunctioning of the wandering or unsatisfied womb (*hysteron*), for which marriage and motherhood were the appropriate remedies. The representation of hysteria as the product of sexual dissatisfaction was modified by the Christian emphasis on chastity, and the hysteric gradually ceased to appear as the subject of individual deprivation, becoming instead the type of the social outcast or possessed. Hysteria moved out of the field of medicine and into that of the Church and its executors. An important development took place in the seventeenth century with the notion of hysteria as a disorder of the mind (which weakened the uterine link), but its subsequent history was, as Heath puts it, 'messy and contradictory'.[172] Aspects of all these representations are mingled in nineteenth-century usage, in both common parlance and in the language of an increasingly powerful medical establishment, which set out to reclaim or consolidate its jurisdiction over the pathology of the human body. Doctors and psychiatrists in the

"HER MOTHER'S VOICE."

95 'Her Mother's Voice', Harold Bird, *Anti-Suffrage Review*, January 1912.
A family tragedy: the father comforts the child who looks out of the window to see framed there her mother: a militant virago with banner and hammer.

Victorian period addressed themselves to the question of a socially reproductive heterosexuality, and to the designation and investigation of other forms of sexual activity as excessive or deviant. The sexual norm became the pattern of health, and deviant sexualities were defined as at once antisocial, immoral, illegal and pathological. In Foucault's formulation four major categories of sexual behaviour were identified – or rather produced – and in that process subjected to clinical inquiry and therapeutic attention. The discursive creations of the reproductive couple, the masturbating child, the perverse adult and the hysterical woman focused the techniques of production of knowledge and power around the socialisation of procreative behaviour, a pedagogisation of children's sex, a psychiatrisation of perverse pleasures, and a hysterisation of women's bodies.[173]

The womanly woman is part of the ideal Malthusian couple. Her sexuality is equivocal, discreet and reproductive. Hysteria was both inside and outside of womanliness: its obverse, but also its unravelling. The hysteric was not the womanly woman, but hysteria was a condition that all women were heir to: as a feminine condition it was a condition of femininity ('the mind of woman is always threatened with danger from the reverberations of her physiological emergencies'). Femininity was itself unstable and destabilising in its effects, and whether the claim was made openly or by implication it was a powerful recommendation for keeping women out of politics. At the same time the 'physiological case', as it was caused, was one from which women anti-suffragists were obliged to dissociate themselves for the sake of their own self-respect, and once it was out in the open it was a powerful source of dissension in the anti-suffragist camp.[174]

Hysteria was increasingly a focus for medical debate in the closing decades of the nineteenth century: the years – it cannot be coincidence – in which the Victorian ideology of a domestic and maternal femininity was disrupted by the effects of the women's movement and the organised suffrage campaign, by a series of developments in women's legal, educational, professional and industrial positions, and by the increasing instability of contemporary sex roles to which these gave rise. That many of these changes concerned a statistically small and relatively privileged number of women does not detract from the seriousness with which they were discussed or the anxiety which they provoked. It is perhaps not implausible to suggest that the 'hysterisation' of women's bodies that Foucault refers to, their becoming more completely gynaecological as Heath has it (a process that went hand in hand with a remarkable ignorance of the female reproductive system),[175] had as one of its regulatory effects the reassertion of women's essentially *biological* destiny in the face of their increasingly mobile and transgressive social roles. Over and over again in the course of the suffrage campaign – as of movements for the reform of women's educational and employment prospects – distinguished scientists and lay authors alike affirmed that women were dominated physically, intellectually and morally by their reproductive systems. Biology and psychology, as Rosalind Rosenberg puts it, came to the service of those seeking scientific authority for the border patrols on women's proper sphere: a process which was enhanced by the professionalisation of medicine, and the dominance of a pathological model in the analysis of social phenomena.[176] As the terms of criminality, sexual deviance and disease drew closer together, so the hysterical woman (especially the hysteric as she was conflated with the militant suffragist) became the focus and symptom of social degeneration and moral decay.

In the same period research into the causes and treatment of hysterical symptoms was conducted in European institutes and consulting rooms with increasing sophistication, most notably by Jean-Martin Charcot, Pierre Janet, and subsequently Josef Breuer and Sigmund Freud. Freud had studied with Charcot in Paris in 1885, and together with Breuer published *Studies in Hysteria* in 1895, which first appeared in an English translation in 1909. Like Charcot, Freud looked upon hysteria as a well-defined psychical disorder requiring explanation in terms of a particular aetiology; like Breuer, he believed this aetiology to be sexual in nature; and with Janet he saw hysteria as a 'malady through representation', which for Freud meant that the bodily symptoms of the hysteric were the displaced physical expression of mental ideas and memories that had been repressed.[177]

Psychoanalysis made its principal discoveries – of the unconscious, phantasy, repression, identification and transference – in the investigation of hysteria. The uterine theory was abandoned, but the links between hysteria, femininity and sexuality were reworked in a new formulation. Both Charcot and Freud recognised the existence of male hysteria (Freud presented a male hysteric to the Viennese medical society in 1886), but Freud believed that hysteria was essentially a 'feminine' neurosis, as obsessional neurosis was a 'masculine' one, within the context of the innate bisexuality of the drives. Hysteria was sexual in the sense that the energies of the sexual drive and those originally used to repress it were condensed into the hysterical symptom. Neither of these things amounted to the proposition that women were hysterical because of the biology of their sexual and reproductive systems, though this was both the popular, and probably the most widespread medical view in England in this period.[178]

If Almroth Wright was an extreme case of medical anti-suffragism founded on the assertion that women are innately, or potentially, hysterical, he was by no means an isolated one. Medicine remained the privileged discourse in the definition and regulation of sexualities – 'a science subordinated in the main to the imperatives of a morality whose divisions it reiterated under the guise of the medical norm'[179] – and as Harrison observes, doctors made a major contribution to British anti-suffragism by contributing to its organisations and elaborating its largely spurious theoretical foundation.[180]

Feminist distrust of the medical profession was exacerbated by the engagement of women in the campaign to repeal the Contagious Diseases Acts, and their suspicion that male doctors disparaged prostitutes while condoning the double standard and promiscuity in men; by their own struggle for entry to the medical profession and by the ways in which men sought to dominate women's paramedical activities as nurses and midwives, and finally by the collusion of prison doctors in the sometimes brutal administration of forcible feeding. Women were well acquainted with the conservative force of a medical establishment ranged, as they saw it, against them, and they were anxious to insist that 'Votes for women is no more a question to be settled by physiologists than by lawyers or political intriguers.'[181] There was nothing to be gained in this struggle by an attempt to separate a scientific from a more general sense of the term 'hysteria', since both had a shared basis in the contemporary definition of femininity, and perhaps also in unconscious fantasies and anxieties about female sexuality and the social role of women.

Hysteria itself may have been a form of resistance to that role. Juliet Mitchell has described it as by the nineteenth century 'the battleground on which women and men fought in an unconscious, pre-political manner'. That is, men used it as a weapon to define women's place, and women used it as a mode of resistance. In this sense hysteria was functional – a failure of order, a refusal to take the place assigned. 'To put it somewhat glibly, at a simple *social* level, hysteria, with its malingering invalidism, tantrums and wilfulness was the nineteenth-century woman's protest against confinement in the home-sweet-home of bourgeois industrial capitalism.'[182]

If this was the case, then certainly by the Edwardian period the battle was both fully conscious and highly political. Persons subject to swoons and vapours, as Cicely Hamilton drily remarked, stood 'a very poor chance of regular and well-paid employment as teachers, sanitary inspectors, journalists and typists' (i.e. as 'modern' women), so that in these classes 'an actual uncertainty prevails as to the nature of vapours, and swooning is practically a lost art.'[183] The suffrage movement offered a collective alternative to hysteria as a private (and costly) solution to the social and emotional conflict experienced by middle-class women. At the same time suffragists sought to free themselves from the taint of hysteria and to unfix its exclusive connection with femininity: the militants pointed out that men were also 'hysterical', and that women had their own rights to 'stridency' as part of their struggle to be heard. Both suffragists and anti-suffragists acknowledged that the central feature of hysteria was conflict. Anti-feminists located conflict in the woman's body, in her 'physiological emergencies' as they were exacerbated by unsuitable (political) activities. Feminists argued that psychic conflict was caused by the exclusion of women from active participation in the social and political spheres, and social conflict by the resistance of men at all levels to women's emancipation. Even constitutional suffragists objected that at election times political wire-pullers and sections of the press would 'use the worst and most degraded methods of working upon men's nerves, till you find whole audiences interrupting a speaker with a sort of blood chaunt and intoxicating themselves with it'. And they recommended that men 'who are so ready to theorise about the nature of woman and who confidently assert that women "as women" are hysterical, should gravely study the faces and utterances of these groups of male electors and consider whether it is likely that women will exceed them'.[184] Mrs Pethick-Lawrence was ready to meet the charge head on. 'Now you know we have been called "The Shrieking Sisterhood", but you see how much need there is for our "shrieking". It is the duty of every woman here to come and help us shriek. Perhaps you say, you don't know how to

THE SHRIEKING SISTER
THE SENSIBLE WOMAN. 'YOU HELP OUR CAUSE? WHY, YOU'RE ITS WORST ENEMY!'

96 'The Shrieking Sister', Bernard Partridge, *Punch*, 17 January 1906.

opposite page
97 'Votes for Women' ('Always make room for a lady'), published by Archibald English and Edward Wise, postmarked 1910.
The masculine woman (like the effeminate man) was a popular theme in Edwardian imagery and in the calculated transvestism of the music hall. The suffragist emancipated (as one card put it) was a theme on which antis were happy to draw. 'No man cares to be libellously caricatured,' wrote Marie Corelli in Woman, or – Suffragette?, *'and a masculine woman is nothing more than a libellous caricature of an effeminate man.'*

98 'Even Strong-Minded Suffragists have their Weak Moments'. Suffragette Series.
Punch *had used the theme of women agitators frightened by mice in 1848 ('How to Treat the Female Chartists', 15 July). It was still enormously popular in the Edwardian period.*

shriek. Come and join the Women's Social and Political Union. We will teach you.'[185]

But it was hard to duck the charge so easily. It was relatively straightforward for anti-suffragists to activate the tendencies in the political establishment and popular opinion to equate militant activity with hysteria, to elide the question of the constitutionalists or describe them as 'tarred with the same brush', and thereby to account all suffragists hysterical and discredit the whole campaign. The pathological picture of hysteria was one in which the essential characteristics of 'womanliness' were perverted or suppressed. (Janet described the hysteric as 'egocentric in the extreme, her involvement with others consistently superficial and tangential' and as 'asexual and not uncommonly frigid'.)[186] This made it possible to transfer the term – which Freud had by this point established as entailing the translation of repressed anxieties into physical symptoms – into a description of general motivation and behaviour held to be unwomanly. 'Hysteria' became a catch-all for any kind of neurotic behaviour, and beyond that, for any kind of behaviour which could be made susceptible to a psychological interpretation. (In 1892 Eliza Lynn Linton had described the 'Wild Women' and their advocates as 'hysterically susceptible' and likened them to 'an angry bee-hive which a rough hand has disturbed. They care nothing for home; quietness is abhorrent to them . . . They will not hear of differences in virtues, in functions, in duties, in spheres.')[187] For suffragists the snag here lay in the fact that those commentators who appealed to the notion of hysteria as an explanation for irrational feminine behaviour were prone to see as irrational (and therefore hysterical) more or less any kind of behaviour by women they disapproved of. This left political activists with the choice of staying ladylike and being ignored, or gaining attention by means that would get their cause dismissed. (Arnold Ward argued in the course of the parliamentary debate of 1910 that 'the hysterical action which has characterised their agitation for the vote will remain inherent in their political activities after they have secured it,' and warned that on those grounds to enfranchise women would be 'to incorporate that hysterical activity permanently in the life of the nation'.)[188]

'Hysteria', however loosely understood, was one of the few available categories through which to comprehend the unprecedented phenomenon of militant agitation by women in British political life. Men and women outside the militant societies were genuinely astonished, angered and confused by their activities. As Sylvia Pankhurst said of the members of the House of Commons: 'The long inequality of the sexes had bitten deeply into them; they had grown up with it in every relation of life. What from men might have been received as a commonplace of political controversy, from women was an intolerable impertinence, an unpardonable offence.'[189] There was some comfort to be gained in ascribing these offences to the 'physiological emergencies' of embittered or frustrated women, since that explained them in more familiar terms. It relocated the political conflict in the dangerous equilibrium of women's reproductive systems, and reminded the public how perilous would be the incorporation of these instabilities into the structures of political life. We can say of women what Heath says of the sexual (given the identification of women *as* the sexual): that there is no conception of it (them) outside of reproduction, 'other than as trouble, disorder, an ever-threatening disturbance of the regulation of the economy of the body – and of society with it'.[190]

The effectiveness of militant propaganda had at some point to be determined by the extent to which it could retain its status as *political* representation and activity, and not be reduced – the cause and its adherents along with it – to the category of feminine hysteria. If the suffrage movement posed, not a demand to be met but a symptom of social and sexual pathology to be attended to, then its cause was lost, and there is no doubt that the final phase of militant activity encouraged such a view.

The difficulty for the suffragettes was not that they were violent, but that they were not violent enough. (Or perhaps to put it another way, violent to insufficient effect, since as the arson campaign erupted in 1913 they managed to antagonise public opinion without having the power directly to threaten the government.) Harrison has argued that tactical violence was no more than a nuisance, unsupported by a mass violence which the Pankhursts were unable to attain.[191] Teresa Billington-Greig, earlier an advocate of the new militancy, opposed its final phase as weakening to the movement's popular base. 'Now violence is openly advocated – but only the small violences which can be effectively contrasted with the greater ones committed by the Government. This is not advance; it is the search for a new thrill for the public and a new chain for the women who pay the price.'[192] The best that women could hope for was that they would force the state to display its own coercive power (which was out of all proportion to their demand) and hence puncture the notion of consensus on which that power was partly based. In a contest with the law-enforcing agencies of the state, victory 'was bound to go to the gaoler, the policeman, the doctor'.[193] Tactical violence (unlike mass violence) could be contained and denounced. Violence by women (which was doubly unnerving) could be contained and denounced as hysterical fanaticism. This was itself still threatening – as Home Secretary an awed McKenna likened the militants to the natives of the Sudan, fearless of death in the cause of the Mahdi[194] – and WSPU artists sought to maintain the image of the militant woman as heroine and martyr. Their opponents domesticated and diminished it in representations of the 'shrieking sisterhood', of the little girl in a tantrum or of suffragettes in the rough embrace of the law (a motif full of sexual innuendo on which innumerable variations were worked). Such images worked to isolate women politically and to ridicule the campaign with 'a knowing pseudo-scientific condemnation of the female sex'.[195]

99 Arrest of Miss Helen Tolson, 8 August 1909.

*Slow march, constable, I'm having the
time of my life!*

"COME OVER HERE"

100 'Are We Down-Hearted?', Donald McGill.
The theme of 'suffragettes and policemen' was an obsessive one in commercial anti-suffrage imagery. Its sexual innuendoes were heightened by what was construed as increasingly provocative behaviour by the militants, and by a class distinction between the protagonists (evident in the photograph of Helen Tolson's arrest). The light-hearted humour of some of the cards falls into perspective when read through participants' accounts of the six-hour struggle with police on 'Black Friday' (18 November 1911). The sexual component in such conflicts was clear. (Fenner Brockway recalls another occasion on which the police held women upside down so that their skirts fell over their faces.) The more the militants took to violence, the more delighted was the Edwardian judiciary, its police force and prison officers to deliver the hiding they believed was deserved. But they could not do so without invoking the spectre of female martyrdom. Humorous postcards defused the issue by domesticating it. The militant became the little girl in a tantrum; the middle-class woman encountered the rough embrace of the law; and the harridan got – or sought – her just deserts.

In 1908 – long before the development of the arson campaign – the *Daily Chronicle* justified its use of the term 'suffragist hysteria' on the grounds that: 'no other name adequately describes the recent tactics of the aggressive suffragists. No sense of reverence prevents them from disturbing meetings in churches; no sense of honour deters them from gaining access to meetings under false pretences . . . If the movement degrades itself into hysterical exhibitions of hooliganism of this kind, it will alienate public sympathy at a far greater rate than it is doing.'[196] The reference to hysterical hooliganism is significant, since it pulls together the terms of clinical disorder and criminal deviance and helps to explain why, in visual representations, the clinical term shades off into descriptions of any kind of especially working-class, strident female behaviour. (At this point it meets up with figures familiar in the vernacular and music-hall traditions such as those of the termagant, virago or shrew.)[197]

101 'Slow March Constable', postmarked 1916.
Even The Times *(13 October 1908) suggested that 'the opportunity of a brush with the long-suffering police in Parliament-Square is embraced by a certain proportion of the women suffragists as a more stimulating alternative for the characteristic delights of mixed hockey.'*

102 'The Scarem Skirt' ('Not in these trousers').
The reference to Paul Poiret's 'harem pants' (1911) exploits at the same time (through clumpy shoes and graceless features) an older notion of women 'who want to wear the trousers'. Like the bloomer of sixty years before (which was briefly adopted by feminists in America), Poiret's trousers were ambiguously masculine and feminine. Their orientalism was scarcely progressive – it conjured up the luxuriant passivity of the harem – but as bifurcated garments in the West they reeked of masculinity, and hence of subversion as well as decadence. They were part of the sexual confusion that was itself part of the promise and threat of feminism in the fantasy scenario of popular imagery. But they were far too controversial for suffragists, who avoided them. (Viscountess Harberton was a member of the WSPU, but by the Edwardian period her presidency of the Rational Dress Society and advocacy of the divided skirt in the 1880s was largely forgotten.)

103 'Come Over Here'.

Perhaps only hysteria explained why middle-class women became hooligans; and perhaps hooligan-women could only be represented, in all their raucous, unsexed quality, with the older signifiers of the low-life fishwife or crone. Perhaps women's violence needed to be sexually differentiated (as hysterical) and classed (as belonging with the other disruptions of the urban proletariat which was in fact remarkably free of hysteria).

Feminists in anti-suffrage imagery are a de-generate type because they are unwomanly, and in nineteenth-century popular illustration, physiog-nomic and eugenic theory, degeneracy is a charac-teristic of the residuum and a product of inferior breeding and an unnatural environment. It is evi-dent in a poorly developed moral faculty and sense of restraint, and within its rather elastic sense of the 'hysterical' anti-suffrage imagery produces the signs of feminine deviance in flushed expressions, wild gestures, and cognate lapses from womanly decorum. In direct contrast with the suffrage mobilisation of the deserving but exploited poor ('Votes for Workers'), popular anti-suffrage rep-resentations play around an imagery of the unsexed lower-middle-class spinster and the working-class crone.[198] The extraordinary *excess* in these images seems to derive partly from the place of women in the vernacular traditions to which they relate (seaside postcards and the music hall); partly from fantasies and anxieties brought to the surface by the question of women's emancipation; and partly (by an odd confusion, since the suffrage movement was also characterised as exclusively middle-class), from an identification with what the *Lancet* in 1869 had called the 'natural predominance of the animal life in the illiterate [which] renders the control of the animal lusts difficult or impossible'.[199]

The Times, it should be emphasised, along with the rest of the press, was talking about 'maenads' and 'hysterical hooliganism' before the first win-dow was broken and five years before the arson campaign of 1913. That final phase of the militant campaign provoked some extraordinarily revealing

passages in which profound political and psychic anxieties are fused with fantasies of domination by the sexual or racial 'other'. 'Vanoc', writing on 'Frenzied Femininity' in the *Referee* in July 1914, argued that to give women the franchise would be to 'pay blackmail to a felon', which would be none the less wrong because 'the felon is a female, and the female is hysterical, ungovernable, and impossible'. The government could not afford 'to surrender to the demands of viragos'. It was necessary to find 'a manly method of meeting epidemic crime'. Personally, the author confides, he 'would very much rather be shot or poisoned than surrender to epilepsy and hysteria, even in the form of a beautiful but unblushing maiden'. The return of the repressed within a white, male, bourgeois order is more naked in the troubled dreams of 'Vanoc' than in the urbane prose of a *Times* leader. Two kinds of reversal provoke his diatribe against 'frenzied femininity': that of women victorious over men, and the black races over the white. The unmanliness of men in dealing with women's hysteria 'is closely connected with the happiness or misery of innumerable lives for the next ten generations. Deep in their hearts men reverence women because they are potential mothers. Epileptics are tainted for motherhood.' And worse is to come, since 'the progeny of un-manly men mated to unwomanly women is unlikely to last out and to make good for many decades in the coming struggle for life between Asiatics, Afri-cans and white men.'[200]

Perhaps it is partly their own inner conflict that men project on to the feminine sphere as the repository of inner life, as the emotional and per-sonal world. It is at least arguable that men have a narcissistic investment in initiating change, and that at times when women attempt to do so there is a resurgence of envy and fear of femininity. But mixed with this are sadistic and masochistic fantasies (or an oscillation between the two) of punishing women, or of taking an eroticised pleasure in an imaginary identification with the 'feminine' role of passive experience. Images of forcible feeding as kinds of penetration and rape, the thinly veiled castration allusions in drawings like that of scissors cutting a woman's tongue, 'Vanoc's' preference (?) for death over surrender to the hysterical but 'beautiful and unblushing maiden', seem explicable only in the register of psychoanalysis. It is surely significant that (as Heath puts it) what psychoanalysis hears in hysteria is a problem of sexual identity: that for centuries hysteria had indicated 'a failure of the order, a refusal to take the place assigned, to be the difference, the woman – to support the position of "the man", so powerful and oppressive for both sexes'. The problem is a problem of law and order: 'how to get women properly in position, deal with the problem they *are* – and that men will be too if the fixed terms of difference and identity should slip'.[201] On one level there is little connection between hysteria as a clinical diagnosis and the generalised use of the term to refer to any kind of strident or emotional female behaviour. On another, they are closely related. What anti-suffrage imagery does to great effect is to give feminism a sexual pathology which makes it a 'law and order problem', not only for the interests of the Empire and the state, but at the deepest levels of sexual identity.[202]

'Hysteria' in the hands of the anti-suffragists was thus a powerful weapon to negotiate. Broadly speaking, the suffragists adopted two courses of action, each of which used as its talisman another and particular representation of femininity. The constitutionalists divested themselves of its taint by every means at their disposal, believing that hysteria, and militancy, damaged their cause, and they did battle with their opponents for the definition of the 'womanly' woman. The WSPU and its allies developed the representation of the allegorical and 'militant' woman, which countered the image of the hysteric as victim and deviant with the image of an active (and phallic) if unearthly agent of moral, social and political reform.

The Militant Woman

More Allegories!! They label Woman – Liberty, Justice, Humanity & rob her of every power or share in these abstract names. MAUD ARNCLIFFE-SENNETT[203]

Liberty's torch can stand for Victory. Or Fidelity. Or Truth . . . the monumental monument tends to be, in this way, an open emblem. It tends to be FOR RENT. WILLIAM GASS[204]

The iconography of the Militant Woman was strongest, predictably, in the WSPU and during the final years of the militant campaign. In 1910 Emmeline Pethick-Lawrence had predicted that in their turn processions, demonstrations and mass meetings would become played out (as petitions were played out), and had promised that when that time came 'we shall find new and more advanced methods of agitation.'[205] Once the 1912 Conciliation Bill had been defeated, and in the absence of a general election that might have focused a campaign directed at the electorate, militant violence began to take over from more orthodox forms of propaganda activity. After the Women's Coronation Procession of 1911 the WSPU held no more large-scale demonstrations except on the occasion of Emily Wilding Davison's funeral in 1913.

For the Pankhursts, militant activity was itself a form of representation. It involved the public embodiment of a new femininity, or what Christabel called 'the putting off of the slave spirit'.[206] The difficulty lay in securing this representation of a just crusade, when outside the WSPU's own interpretive community the associations pulled in another direction, towards deviance and hysteria.

In the summer of 1913 *Punch* gently satirised the militants as domestic incompetents in a series of cartoons devoted to the arsonist who has mislaid her matches, or whose kitchen fire refuses to 'catch'. But in general the press and the public were simply outraged by women's political violence (even in a context of open drilling and gun-running by Ulster Unionists), and at a loss for an explanation other than that the militants had lost 'all sense

"Votes for Women," May 24, 1912.   Registered at the G.P.O. as a Newspaper.

VOTES FOR WOMEN

VOL. V. (New Series), No. 220.   FRIDAY, MAY 24, 1912.   Price 1d. Weekly (Post Free, 1½d.)

AT THE OLD BAILEY, MAY 22, 1912.

The Jury: "We desire unanimously to express the hope that, taking into consideration the undoubtedly pure motives that underlie the agitation which has led to this trial, you would be pleased to exercise the utmost leniency in dealing with the case."

The Judge: "Nine months in the Second Division with the costs of the prosecution."

PRISONERS OF WAR

WSPU

-Poyntz Wright-

"We wage war, O disciples; therefore are we called warriors.
Wherefore, Lord, do we wage war?
For lofty virtue, for high endeavour, for sublime wisdom;
Therefore are we called warriors."

— Sayings of Buddha —

of proportion and become absolutely reckless through the intoxication produced by their delusions . . . [in] a kind of delirium'.[207] Following a WSPU demonstration on 21 May 1914, when 200 women had tried to break through a cordon of 1500 police surrounding Buckingham Palace, the press carried large photographs of dishevelled women locked in combat with the police, and captions such as 'Screaming with Impotent Rage', 'Rather Emotional' and 'Ecstasy on Arrest'.[208] Mrs Pankhurst, much weakened by her prison experiences, was arrested early in the proceedings and lifted into a waiting cab in the arms of Chief Inspector Rolfe. The reproduction of this now famous photograph could only endorse the view that 'Women never show up their real weakness so much as when they attempt force.'[209]

It was against these images of violent activity as hysterical and futile, as the work of bungling incompetents or screaming viragos, that the iconography of the Militant Woman was intended to serve. It was an iconography that drew on a long tradition of winged Victories, mythical heroines (Athena, Boadicea) and personified Virtues (Justice, Fortitude), and it was close at hand in the sculptural monuments of Edwardian London. (The demonstration of 21 May had regrouped in the shadow of the Wellington quadriga at Hyde Park Corner, and been repulsed before Thomas Brock's Victoria Memorial at the palace gates.)[210]

The Militant Woman remained exclusively an allegorical type (Emily Wilding Davison came closest to impersonating her in life, or rather in death). She had, arguably, little to do with women and the daily experiences of their lives, but the suffragists wrenched her meanings round to serve their cause, making of abstract female signifiers the signifiers of a new femininity. She was not domesticated. She claimed her 'womanliness' from another source, that of female heroism in history, allegory and myth. She functioned as an idealised representation of the militant movement and the embodiment of its motto: 'Deeds Not

105 Mrs Pankhurst arrested by Inspector Rolfe outside Buckingham Palace, 21 May 1914.
Mrs Pankhurst wrote to Ethel Smyth on 29 May 1914: 'I was released on Wednesday . . . On Sunday it was reported that I was dead and I don't think McKenna would have been sorry if that had been the result of the horrible bear's hug that huge policeman gave me when he seized me. Fortunately for me I have "young bones" or my ribs would all have been fractured. After it I suffered from a form of nausea just like very bad sea-sickness . . .'

opposite page
104 *Votes for Women*, 24 May 1912: 'Prisoners of War'.

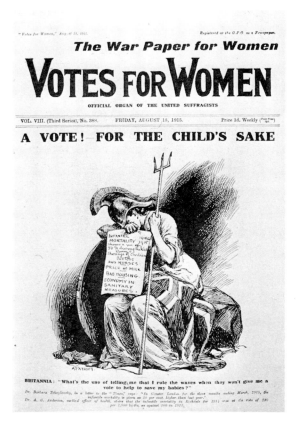

106 *Votes for Women*, 13 August 1915: Britannia: 'A
Vote! For the Child's Sake'.
Militant woman and civic motherhood combined.

Words'. She represented the chivalry that Justice
or Liberty offers the oppressed when the much-
vaunted chivalry of men has long evaporated. Her
role in suffrage imagery was to throw over individual acts of violence the mantle of Boadicea or
Joan of Arc; in the face of accusations of hysteria,
criminality and incompetence (not all of which
were without foundation) to assert the possibility of
a collective political struggle by women, for their
own emancipation and against all that was venal
and bumbling in the world. In various guises she
embodied the spiritual aspirations to which the
cause laid claim, and the desire and demand of
women to be allowed to fight for them. (In 1913
Mrs Pankhurst told the men in her audience at
Madison Square Garden 'that amongst the other
good things that you, consciously or unconsciously,
have kept from women, you have kept the joy of
battle'.)[211] Through the invocation of Joan of Arc,
militant women considered themselves blessed; on
her behalf they embarked on their 'new crusade'.
She was the type of female heroism, the reforming
spirit of Evangelicalism in a newly militant and
feminist guise. On the wings of Victory she urged
their efforts on, with the flaming torch she lit their
darkness, and with trumpet and banner she was the
herald of the new day. In her gentler capacities she
crossed over into constitutional imagery – the
military accoutrements of the NUWSS 'Bugler Girl'
are purely spiritual – and the iconography of the
labour movement: in Crane's Souvenir for May
Day 1909 she is Socialism, in a breastplate and
Phrygian cap, who strangles the serpent of capitalism with one hand while holding the torch of
enlightenment aloft with the other.[212]

As women, the suffragists were subject to the
alienating effects of serving as the raw material for
allegory and myth; but as artists, perhaps for the
first time, they were peculiarly placed to exploit it.
Like the labour movement they were faced with the
antique language of personification and a continuing tradition of humanist allegory that had
existed since the Renaissance and was also rooted

in classical antiquity.[213] Like the labour movement they had the choice of rejecting it as inappropriate and outmoded or of appropriating it to their own ends.

Anthropologists have identified the processes whereby the secondary status of women in society, together with their procreative physique and activities, has contributed to cross-cultural representations that accord them a half-way place between 'nature' and 'culture'.[214] Within a given society this mediating position may offer representations of women greater symbolic ambiguity than representations of men. As they are marginal in the culture they may carry any of the meanings that accrue to the 'other' (whether utterly exalted or utterly debased); and for the same reason they can come to symbolise in the abstract that from which they are excluded in the concrete (Justice is a woman, though women may not practise law). The 'traffic in women' is not a matter of kinship systems alone, but of the exchange of cultural meanings (through representations of 'femininity') by men. There is no necessarily direct (and there is sometimes an inverse) relation between the status of women in a given society and its principal ideologies, and the reverence accorded to social values that are personified in female form.

The task for suffrage art and rhetoric in this context was to reinhabit the empty body of female allegory, to reclaim its meanings on behalf of the female sex. Generalised symbols are often iconographically female because that is the way to encompass the mundane variety to which they allude. 'Woman' can stand for abstractions, or represent a diversity of men: 'Liberty Guiding the People' in Delacroix's painting is not identified with any of the different classes and occupations whose concentrated force as 'the people' she represents. For this very reason, and contrary to what we might at first expect, the allegorical female is *not* an altogether suitable representation of the generality of women. She has too much in common with them, although features such as drapery, sandals, military accoutrements, wings, gestures and assorted allegorical paraphernalia will help to maintain her symbolic distance, and hence her efficacy. But some sort of oscillation will still go on between sign and referent (Womanhood and women, as it were), producing a confusion not present in the use of female symbols (Liberty, Justice, Truth), exchanged between men. The more women placed themselves under the image of the inspiring angel (as in the imagery of Sylvia Pankhurst or Walter Crane), the more they emphasised the associations of femininity and virtue, but the more they lost the sense of women as living beings of heterogeneous occupational and social groups that they were otherwise so keen to stress. Sometimes the solution was to put the allegorical figure and the 'real' women together (as in 'Justice Demands the Vote'); but there is a tendency in suffrage (as in labour) iconography, for the competing demands of realism and symbolism to pull apart. Only in suffrage imagery the feminine virtue has a longer-lasting and more militant role: in the labour movement she is largely displaced by the turn of the century by gentler goddesses – radiantly fair women with sandals, garlands and white drapery – and by a complementary iconography of idealised proletarian labour.[215]

The archetypal militant, continually evoked in the final years of the WSPU campaign, was Joan of Arc: 'not only perfect patriot but perfect woman'.[216] To her virginity, vigilance, martyrdom and beatification (in 1909) other associations were easily attached. Those of Boadicea or Athena for instance (whose emblems of wisdom and war were the symbols of the Suffrage Atelier); or that argument for the moral superiority of women in the face of male sexual corruption that Christabel wields in *The Great Scourge* (1913): 'Votes for Women and Chastity for Men'.

Joan of Arc symbolised the women's 'holy crusade', and women impersonating her in armour and riding astride white horses ('palfreys') led WSPU processions. Christabel referred to her as

107 Miss Annan Bryce as Joan of Arc, 17 June 1911.

'our patron saint', for which purpose she was borrowed from the French and made the central emblem of feminist rebellion against the state. She had been 'thrust into prison with the rest, as an unsexed, shrieking sister'.[217] She was the paradigm both for female militancy and for its persecution. 'The day of visions and celestial voices is not yet past, and there are women in England at this moment who are ready, as Joan was, to pay the extreme penalty for the faith that is in them.'[218] The English government was '500 years behind the times. Their predecessors burned Joan of Arc,

and they themselves are now persecuting her spiritual descendants.' Joan served the millennial zeal of the WSPU, and also its increasing antipathy to men (neither of which the National Union could understand).[219]

Evelyn Sharp wrote in *Votes for Women* in 1909 that there could scarcely be another character in history that needed such little explanation: the 'girl in armour on the great white horse stood for a battle against prejudice that is as ancient as it is modern.'[220] But Joan was a more equivocal resource than this, as Marina Warner's biography points out.[221] She was a universal female figure who eluded the categories in which women gained status – neither a queen, courtesan, mother, artist

ix **a.** 'Spiritual Militancy', **b**. 'Joan of Arc', **c**. 'Florence
Nightingale' and **d**. 'North Berwick': four designs for
banners from Mary Lowndes's album. The Joan of Arc
banner (designed by Barbara Forbes) and the Florence

Nightingale banner (now in very poor condition), are
also in the Fawcett Collection. Both date from 1908;
the others may be later.

x Banner in appliquéd velvets designed by Mary
Lowndes for the Women Writers' Suffrage League,
executed by Mrs Herringham of the Artists' Suffrage
League for the NUWSS procession of 13 June 1908.

xi **a**. 'Deeds Not Words': the banner of the Hammersmith branch of the WSPU.
The banner is reversible, like a triptych, with crewel stitch embroidery, velvet appliqué and painted motifs.

b. Design for a banner for the Conservative and Unionist Women's Franchise Association, by the Fabian suffragist and stained-glass designer Caroline Townshend.

XII **a**. 'Cambridge Alumnae': banner designed by Mary Lowndes and worked by the students of Girton and Newnham for the Cambridge contingent in the NUWSS procession of 13 June 1908.
The borders are stencilled in silver with the daisies of Newnham and the irises of Girton.

b. Newnham and Girton College staff and students with the Cambridge banner.
The Girton Review *and the* Newnham College Letter *contain information on Cambridge students' and graduates' contributions to suffrage activity. In the popular mind New Woman and Suffragist alike were Newnham and Girton girls. Philip Bagenal complained to Violet Markham that his own daughter, 'a very sensible girl indeed' had turned suffragist at Newnham and that 'there is a regular manufactory of very advanced women going on at Cambridge.'*

XIII The Artists' Suffrage League banner, designed
presumably by Mary Lowndes, *c.* 1908.

XIV a. 'Physical Education', b. 'The Office', c. 'Mary Moser', d. 'Boadicea'.
Banners executed by the Artists' Suffrage League for the NUWSS procession of 1908. Probably designed by Mary Lowndes.

xv 'A Suffragette's Home': designed by John Hassall, published by the National League for Opposing Woman Suffrage, 1912.
Hassall's poster needs to be understood not only in relation to a body of popular imagery on the theme of the neglectful wife, but also in relation to anti-suffrage literature directed at working men, such as the Men's League Tract no. 53, 'Power and Responsibility': 'Resent this attempted tyranny and let the Suffragists know that you simply will not have petticoat government . . . It is the subjection of man to woman, turning the order of nature upside down . . . Don't
make yourselves and your country the laughing stock of the world . . . Look round you as you read this leaflet. On every side you see THE RESULT OF MASCULINE LABOUR. At every moment you are using some item of a great organization, every material portion of which is made by MAN . . . The whole material fabric of civilised life has to be brought into existence, and to be maintained by men. That is to say, before a woman can perform the simplest action of her life, before she can eat a mouthful of food, or put on a stitch of clothing, she is wholly dependent on mechanism supplied and worked by men.'

XVI a. 'A Perfect Woman': designed by John Hassall for the National League for Opposing Woman Suffrage, 1912. John Hassall's Day Books in Essex University archives indicate that 'A Perfect Woman' and its companions, 'Sermons in Stones' and 'Going Shopping', were designed as posters, although they have survived only as postcards.
b. 'Votes for Women': anon.

c. 'We Want the Vote'.
d. 'Hear Some Plain Things': anon.
Anti-suffrage propaganda characteristically identifies suffragists as excessively feminine (hysterical) or masculine (lesbian), but in either case as plain and unmated. Women's enfranchisement becomes a political threat fused with a sexual threat.

nor even saint until her canonisation in 1920 – and the significance of her life was never stable, but gained its impact from the various cultural and political contexts in which she was used. She defied order, division and convention in all the aspects of her marginality and strange, militant sanctity. In her virginity, transvestism and military vigilance she subverted the order of femininity, but she was something other than a masquerade. She was and was not a woman. She transcended the limitations of her sex and yet it was from the position of femininity – however unorthodox – that she posed a challenge to the English and to men. This was precisely what made her so useful to the suffragettes and gave her such prominence in their iconography. She offered an identification which was neither that of the domestic feminine ideal nor of its obverse, the hysterical fanatic. By the 1880s and 1890s when her cult intensified, she was claimed by all shades of political opinion in France, by socialists and sceptics, and with increasing enthusiasm by right-wing monarchist Catholics. Yet at the same time her female gender made possible her passage from the role of patron saint of a nation to that of patron saint of a sex. 'She has taught us the loveliness of simplicity, purity, courage and militancy. Joan of Arc belongs to France, but she belongs also to the womanhood of the whole world, and the women of our country are one with the men and women of France in adoring her memory.'[222]

Eric Hobsbawm has claimed that she was an icon of female militancy that could never become a model for real women: there was only room for a few Joans.[223] But this is to underestimate the power of her representation and its fluidity. It was conflated with all the associations of Justice and Liberty, and was all the more fruitful a resource for remaining both vague and historically remote. Her political and ideological instability made her more, not less, adaptable to the different factions of the suffrage campaign. She was the touchstone that spiritualised militancy and linked it with that to which it was in all other respects utterly opposed:

an Evangelical ideal of femininity that accorded women moral pre-eminence. She was 'Sans Peur et Sans Reproche', as the constitutionalists inscribed her banner. 'Fight on,' she had promised, 'and God will give the victory,' as the militants put on theirs at Emily Wilding Davison's funeral. She was the paradigm for militant virtue compounded with feminine audacity. Everyone could have their own Joan.[224]

On the whole the NUWSS and its artists avoided the iconography of the Militant Woman, but with the 'Bugler Girl' designed by Caroline Watts of the Artists' Suffrage League for the procession of 1908 they claimed a stake in the allegorical image, and in something more rousing than had marked the posters published before. The Artists' Suffrage League primed the *Manchester Guardian* to explain to its readers how 'the Amazon who stands on the battlements of the fort may be said to be heralding the new day of which the sun is just seen rising.'[225] By 1913, however, when the NUWSS executive was exercised on the topic of a new cover for the *Common Cause*, increased WSPU militancy and an urgent need to distinguish the NUWSS from the militant campaign had made her a controversial image.[226] But just when the editor, Maud Royden, had concluded that the 'Bugler Girl' could not be used, the Council decided at their Newcastle meeting to adopt her after all. In November 1913 they provided a revealing gloss in the *Common Cause* beginning with the inspiration provided by Elizabeth Barrett Browning's 'Now press the clarion to thy woman's lip.' It is the definitive account of what we might call 'constitutional militancy'; the National Union's response to the stakes as they had been raised by the WSPU, and its use of the same crusading rhetoric divorced from the political strategy of criminal damage and the increasing separatism of the WSPU. '"Does she represent Joan of Arc?" one critic asks. No – except as far as Joan of Arc herself embodies for women the spirit of courage and love . . . Our Bugler Girl carries her bugle and her banner; her sword is sheathed by her side; it is there, but not drawn, and if it were drawn, it would not be the sword of the flesh, but of the spirit. For ours is not a warfare against men, but against evil; a war in which women and men fight together . . . We are militant in the sense that the Christian Church is militant . . . We are in arms against wrong, but we inflict none. The great adventure to which we are called is . . . not to overcome evil with evil, however heroically undertaken, but to overcome evil with good. It is the supreme adventure, and to it we summon all who care for the things of the spirit, all who welcome hardship and suffering in the great hope that by suffering themselves, they may shorten and lighten the sufferings of others, all who refuse to be sheltered and protected and happy while their sisters are exploited and enslaved.'[227]

Joan of Arc, as the *Common Cause* reminded its readers, carried her standard into battle in her right hand, her sword in her left so that she should not kill anyone. Heroism and sanctified suffering were not to be conceded as the exclusive province of the WSPU. The NUWSS had a greater stake in 'womanliness' than the militants, but they could not afford to seem feeble or servile as they struggled to maintain their identification with the campaign in the face of WSPU notoriety. The 'Bugler Girl' gave them an image of female heroism, constrained by its allegorical register and by the illustrative style that Caroline Watts had already contributed to a series of contemporary Arthurian romances. It was rousing in a not unfamiliar convention, and distinct from the campaign's most militant imagery, which was not that of the warrior maiden at all but of WSPU lithographs such as 'Modern Torture' and Atelier block-prints like 'English Inquisitors'. These are images of women as victims (which are always equivocal), but their force and modernity derive from the anger infused with their cutting and draughtsmanship. They depict what made the Militant Woman militant.

The Militant Woman was an allegorical figure whose exact significance was not precise. She

brought to the campaign, and specifically to its claims for social regeneration, all the associations of armoured maidens (Justice, Britannia, Joan of Arc) and their struggle for good against the forces of evil. The armoured maid, as Marina Warner points out, was a long-surviving protagonist of that ancient duel. Her armour masculinises her, defines her role as the personification of a concept, 'renders her a watertight, strong container . . . [and] inverts the sign of the woman's body so that it can properly represent virtues or ideals; it emphasises that a leaky vessel . . . has turned into a sound vessel.'[228]

Perhaps a deeper and unconscious struggle between the militant and the hysteric goes on here too. All the representations of a debased and deviant femininity, with which 'hysteria' had a special relation, had to be contested by women and could in no way serve their cause. The idealisation of femininity in the guise of the maiden warrior was, however, a trope available 'for rent'. But powerful impulses linked these apparently opposite tendencies in representation. In his paper 'On the Universal Tendency to Debasement in the Sphere of Love' (1912), Freud suggests a propensity in men (the consequence of the masculine passage through the Oedipus Complex) to split the debased and sexual object from the idealised, maternal woman: 'where they love they do not desire and where they desire they cannot love.'[229] It is at root the pre-Oedipal, phallic mother that they love, and the damaged, 'castrated' but non-incestuous object they both fear and possess. The Militant Woman in her idealisation no less than in her phallic armoury (swords, banners and trumpets are conspicuous) is joined in underground battle with the woman who is sexually debased, available but despised. The Militant Woman is a type wielded (by women) against the sexual denigration of women, in ways historically useful to the suffragettes in their alliance with the social purity campaigns of the years before 1914. But she is a type made from the same psychic mechanism as her opposite, and women laid claim to the phallic mother as the image of female heroism, only at the cost of perpetuating the dichotomy between idealisation and debasement with which she is bound up.[230]

The Womanly Woman

We call it womanliness when a lady of refinement and culture overcomes the natural shrinking of sense, and voluntarily enters into the circumstances of sickness and poverty, that she may help the suffering in their hour of need; when she can bravely go through some of the most shocking experiences of humanity for the sake of the higher law of charity; and we call it womanliness when she removes from herself every suspicion of grossness, coarseness, or ugliness, and makes her life as dainty as a picture, as lovely as a poem. She is womanly when she asserts her own dignity; womanly when her highest pride is the sweetest humility, the tenderest self-suppression; womanly when she protects the weaker; womanly when she submits to the stronger.
ELIZA LYNN LINTON[231]

Amid the quiet conditions of country life, and especially in the narrow society of small provincial towns, one finds no argument so persistently raised against the movement for Woman's Enfranchisement, and more particularly against the 'militant' methods, as the assertion that they are 'unwomanly'; and by 'unwomanly' one soon finds that the objectors mean 'unladylike', for they immediately go on to apply such adjectives as 'screaming', 'hysterical', 'unreasonable' – attributes which we know very well are, in this particular school of thought, regarded as essentially and almost exclusively feminine. Suffragists, therefore, are accused, almost in the same breath, both of deserting and of accentuating the characteristics of their sex. LAURENCE HOUSMAN[232]

Suffragists did not argue for the right to be unwomanly (they had constantly to struggle against the assertion that they were) but rather the right to define its terms. 'Who,' as Louisa Thomson-Price demanded in the *Vote*, 'is to be the ultimate authority as to what constitutes a "womanly woman"?'[233] In arguing that some women were unwomanly, nineteenth-century critiques such as Eliza Lynn Linton's *The Girl of the Period* (1883) were obliged to recognise the gap between a biological category and a preferred form of social behaviour. Unwomanly women (strong-minded, 'platform' or new women, 'girls of the period', reluctant mothers, constitutional or militant suffragists) were in the eyes of their opponents pathological symptoms of the 'abnormal physiological ambience'[234] produced by industrialisation and a surplus of marriageable females. For suffragists, on the other hand, the space between 'women' and 'womanliness' was the space in which new definitions of femininity could be negotiated and produced.

The roots of 'womanliness' as an ideology were cultural and historical rather than biological, although developments in the natural sciences were used to lend it credibility. It was an influential idea, not only because it permeated all the principal institutions and social arrangements of the period but because it was embraced by women themselves, who found in it a source of identity and, paradoxically, a position from which to speak with moral authority in the public sphere from which, supposedly, they were excluded.

The evolution of the 'woman's sphere' accompanied the emergence of the industrial middle classes at the turn of the eighteenth and nineteenth centuries. It was consolidated in the break-up of the economically productive household, the centralisation of factory production and the transformation of domestic work into an activity that was perceived as having no commercial value. Masculinity and femininity became associated with a division between the rational, competitive and public world of production on the one hand, and the affective, nurturing and private sphere of the suburban home on the other.[235]

This process of differentiation did not go uncontested. Mary Wollstonecraft's *Vindication* argues against Rousseau's invocation of a pious, submissive and dependent femininity (in *Emile*), that women 'may have different duties to fulfil, but they are *human* duties'. She claimed that women had been 'decked with artificial graces that enable

them to exercise a short-lived tyranny', and demanded their right to a stake in the Enlightenment concept of the virtuous and self-determining individual: 'I extend it to women, and confidently assert that they have been drawn out of their sphere by false refinement, and not by an endeavour to acquire masculine qualities.'[236]

The Evangelicals, as conservative reformers vehemently opposed to the godlessness and political radicalism of the French Revolution, shared Mary Wollstonecraft's distaste for feminine artifice, but not her solution. They were utterly resistant to any notion of women's 'equality' with bourgeois men, and through their influence helped to secure that fundamental division between the attributes, duties and activities of men and women which became so distinctive a feature of the class hegemony of the bourgeoisie and its allies by the mid-Victorian period.[237] Civil society was centred on the concept of the self-determining bourgeois citizen in the field of public life: but that citizen was male. The concept and practice of liberal individualism was secured with the support of self-effacing women ('The profession of Ladies,' as Hannah More described it, 'is that of daughters, wives, mothers and mistresses of families'),[238] and through the opposing characteristics of 'womanliness' as those were excluded from it. ('She must be enduringly, incorruptibly good; instinctively, infallibly wise – wise, not for self-development, but for self-renunciation: wise, not that she may set herself above her husband, but that she may never fail from his side: wise, not with the narrowness of insolent and loveless pride, but with the passionate gentleness of an infinitely variable because infinitely applicable, modesty of service.')[239] In an increasingly complex world it suited the (male) bourgeoisie to remove women from professional competition, to be serviced by them domestically, to enjoy the private sanctuary of the haven-home, to have women personify all Christian and moral values while expressing vicariously the wealth and social standing of their husbands, and to

109 'The Prehistoric Argument': designed by Catherine Courtauld of the Suffrage Atelier, 1912.

opposite page
108 'The Appeal of Womanhood': designed by Louise Jacobs of the Suffrage Atelier, 1912.
See the anti-suffrage poster 'No Votes Thank You' by Harold Bird (ill. 94): this is a parody of it, and at the same time a response. Suffragists claimed equal rights with male citizens while also pressing a claim from difference. It was because they were women that men could not speak for them, that Parliament needed their womanly virtues, that they had the interests of their exploited sisters at heart. A mother, a laundress, a prostitute and a chainmaker are visible in the little catalogue of misery and exploitation set against the towers of Westminster behind.

define womanliness itself on their own terms. As Elsie Clews Parsons commented drily in 1916: 'Womanliness must never be out of mind, if masculine rule is to be kept intact.'[240]

By the end of the eighteenth century both religious and secular literature had begun to associate femininity with piety, reversing an ancient belief in women's libidinal appetites in favour of womanly 'passionlessness'.[241] Middle-class women were seen as a collective agency of moral reform, and in a burst of philanthropic and reforming activity in the early decades of the nineteenth century, 'Woman's Mission' was extended outside the home to such charitable and educational activities as could be seen to derive from women's nurturing roles in the service of their families.[242] Specialist magazines for women (which had existed since the seventeenth century) shifted their emphasis from public affairs to questions of etiquette and household management, in order to cater for their expanding middle-class readership.[243] 'Womanliness' was disseminated in a vast and varied literature: in newspapers, pamphlets, sermons, novels, domestic manuals and what Ray Strachey called 'poisonous little books of moral maxims'[244] which coached women in the proper exercise of their moral influence. They did so with such insistence, and towards the end of the century and on occasion with such desperation, that it begins to seem as though the concept of womanliness was most fully articulated as it came under attack. In a climate of moral panic over social degeneration and 'race suicide', as the home ceased to define the limits of female activity it was that much more vigorously prescribed.

In all this 'womanliness' was a complex construct, full of contradictions and capable of being exploited to surprisingly diverse ends. It is easily seen as a restrictive concept that constrained women's opportunities and regulated their spheres of action; but at the same time it provided them with a strong sense of identity, restored to them socially valued responsibilities, and gave them the

moral authority to pursue an actively regenerative role. ('Let men enjoy in peace and triumph the intellectual kingdom which is theirs . . . The moral world is ours – ours by position; ours by qualification; ours by the very indication of God himself.')[245] This is the reason why the vote was so often presented in suffrage rhetoric as the key to social reform: not only because philanthropically minded suffragists genuinely believed it to be the case, but because such a formulation could be produced from the valued position of womanliness. In the struggle for definitions of femininity that was one part of the suffragists' campaign against their opponents, it was a relatively straightforward matter to turn back accusations of 'unwomanliness' on the grounds that it was the antis who were unwilling or unable to pursue the civic consequences of women's capacity for social reform.

'Womanliness' did not go uncontested. Jane Harrison echoed Mary Wollstonecraft in pointing out that 'womanly' virtues were the virtues of the underdog (the conquered, the slave, the governess, the private secretary and the tutor): 'they are virtues not specially characteristic of the average duchess. In a word they are the outcome not of sex but of status.'[246] Cicely Hamilton complained that if women were going to be valued primarily for their reproductive capacities then society might just as well reverence the rabbit.[247] But women had their own investments in an ideology which formed in most instances an integral part of their sexed identity, and they were reluctant to remake that identity in every particular. There were positive incentives for women in embracing the ideals of womanliness as well as in resisting them. Feminine attributes such as sensibility and compassion, if apparently lower down the Darwinian scale of things, were socially sanctioned as Christian and humanitarian values of which the state stood in need. The heritage of Evangelicalism invoked in the white dresses of processions, on banners and in the language of Christabel Pankhurst's *The Great Scourge* could be welded (if uncomfortably) with more 'masculine' virtues in the development of 'a new type of woman, active in every sphere of life: a new worker out in the world, a new ruler of the home'. As Miss Barfoot puts it in George Gissing's *The Odd Women*: 'Of the old ideal virtues we can retain many, but we have to add to them those which have been thought appropriate only in men. Let a woman be gentle, but at the same time let her be strong; let her be pure of heart, but none the less wise and instructed.'[248]

The new womanliness was held by suffragists to compare favourably with the old, which they described in a familiar Victorian metaphor as the 'shrinking, clinging, "ivy-round-the-oak"' type of woman.[249] Women who were womanly in the conventional sense were well provided for, well protected, and ignorant or indifferent to 'a great, crowded world of oppressed and over-driven womanhood'. It is the comfortable women who are unwomanly, 'hugging to their hearts a domestic peace which they have not earned'.[250] 'To be declassified,' as Elsie Clews Parsons remarked, 'is very painful to most persons and so the charge of unwomanliness has ever been a kind of whip against the would-be woman rebel.'[251] In reality the class basis of the womanly ideal denied it to the majority of women who worked to keep their homes together, whose refinement could scarcely survive the circumstances of sweated labour, and whose chastity might be abandoned as the price of keeping body and soul together. Appealing to such cases the unwomanly suffragists claimed to embody true womanly compassion in fighting for the conditions of womanliness for all women degraded by their social and economic circumstances. By whatever means, they had to refuse the Hobson's choice laid out by their opponents, the choice between a domestic femininity and an unsexed unwomanliness. Women would humanise public life. If it was sordid, they would clean it up. To do so it might be necessary to lay aside 'the garments of old-time respectable conventions' and adopt 'an attitude of revolt', but paradoxically these would be the means of earning for the word 'womanly' 'a finer and a grander meaning than it has hitherto borne'.[252]

For both pro- and anti-suffragists motherhood was the touchstone of womanliness, and the definition of specifically feminine virtues as domestic ones resulted in arguments from both sides on the proper relations between women, the family and the state. The picture painted by Eliza Lynn Linton in 'The Rights and Wrongs of Women' was one of 'Homes deserted, children – the most solemn responsibility of all – given to a stranger's hand; modesty, unselfishness, patience, obedience, endurance, all that has made angels of humanity ... trampled underfoot, while the Emancipated Woman walks proudly forward to the goal of the glittering honours of public life, her true honours lying crushed beneath her, unnoticed.'[253]

Modern notions of the family and of mothering were first established in the late eighteenth century. Child-rearing became more exclusively the province of the mother, and natural maternity the guarantee of health in the social body. (As Rousseau put it: 'Where mothers resume nursing their children, morals will be reformed; natural feelings will revive in every heart; the state will be repopulated; this first step alone will reunite everyone.')[254] A century later eugenic concern with a falling birth rate licensed official and therapeutic interventions into the supposedly private circumstances of reproduction in the national interest.

The sentimentalising of motherhood that accompanied these changes was often the last straw in women's economic subordination as well as their most celebrated attribute. 'Motherhood' was a site of contradiction for women. It was the principal element in the definition and regulation of female sexuality and at the same time a source of feminine power. It was precisely the sharpness of the distinction between maternal attributes and the attributes of the successful, bourgeois man in the public world, that gave motherhood its cutting edge as a critique of masculine power. The partici-

Modern Culture

110 'Modern Culture' by 'Cynicus'.
Socialists were also accused of threatening home life.
Unionist pamphlets claimed that 'Socialism would destroy
family life and take away those sweet things that make the
English idea of home the best thing in the world. For
"home", socialism would substitute giant barracks where you
would be compelled to live and have your meals divided out to
you . . .' (quoted in Donald Read, Documents from
Edwardian England 1901–1915, *Harrap, London, 1973,*
pp. 125–6).

I·PRAY·FOR·ALL·THE·GROWN-UPS·WHEREVER·THEY·MAY·BE· ·
WHO·DONE·ONE·TEENY·WEENY·THING·TO·GET·A·VOTE·FOR·ME·
WHEN·I·AM·OLD·I'LL·USE·IT· I'M·NEITHER·RICH·NOR·CLEVER·
BUT·I·CAN·GIVE·THEM·LOTS·OF·LOVE· FOREVER·AND·FOREVER·

pation of women in a range of reforming movements in the nineteenth century was made to derive
its legitimacy from motherhood. Josephine Butler
went into rescue work as a mother to save
daughters.[255] Mrs Pankhurst was introduced to a
Presbyterian congregation in Chicago on Mother's
Day as 'one of the great Mothers of the World':
'today the deepest instincts of *Motherhood* and the
loftiest ideals of *Womanhood* are one as Mrs Pankhurst leads us into the atmosphere and defines the
obligations and duties of *World-Mothering*.'[256] Mrs
Fawcett argued that women's suffrage was needed
'because we want the home and the domestic side
of things to be more fully represented in
politics';[257] and the WSPU claimed to fight for
'conditions which will not block the mainsprings of
good motherhood and crush the life out of it'.[258]

In response to their opponents suffragists insisted on the absolute compatibility of motherhood
and the vote – indeed the absolute necessity, in the
interests of their families, of mothers *having* the
vote.[259] Reversing once more the expected terms
of 'womanliness', they aligned themselves with
mothers who believed in votes and babies, against
idle, feckless, gossiping, fashionable women, who
were anti-suffragists because they thought their
men preferred them to be. They argued that
women were not so much claiming a stake in the
public sphere as a voice in the state that had
invaded their homes. Standards of health, infant
mortality, pregnancy and work, inadequate housing and hygiene, the purity of the milk supply, had
all become parliamentary issues as well as women's
intimate concerns. The choice was thus not 'votes
or babies' because 'every Suffragist worth her salt
. . . *wants the vote for the sake of the baby*.'[260] The
special qualities of women and mothers were held
to represent the strongest possible reason for their
enfranchisement, and politics was too important
and inclusive a thing ('no part of the life of any
single individual in the nation can remain
untouched by it')[261] to be left to the men.

Since most women continued to live as wives

112 'Mummy's a Suffragette': commercial anti-suffrage postcard.

opposite page
111 'I Pray for All the Grown-Ups' ('The Votes for Women Prayer'): postcard designed by C. Hedley Charlton, a professional illustrator associated with the Artists' Suffrage League.

and mothers or retained the aspiration to do so, suffrage propagandists were wise to concentrate on the uses to which womanliness could be put, rather than on the fruitless task of displacing the idea altogether.[262] Despite its difficulties it was a powerful trope with which to stitch together the 'we' articulated in propaganda with the 'you' to whom it was addressed.[263] Whether as the allegorical harbinger of a new age, or in humbler guise as Mrs How-Martyn making jam, the identification of womanliness with the campaign offered the assurance that suffragists were not unfeminine, and invited womanly women to join them. More specifically, the cause was structured to offer a point of identification from which the social problems it evoked – exploitation and injustice of one kind and another – might be resolved. But to do this the suffragists had to maintain a grasp on 'womanliness' in the face of their opponents' efforts to dislodge them. The choice posed to the electorate by anti-suffragists was that between the home and the street corner for women (graphically depicted in an American poster);[264] between the harmony of complementarity and a 'world all at war' in which women competed with men for 'power, wealth, honour, franchises and votes'.[265] Womanliness was too valuable a ground to concede, but there were moments particularly during the militant campaign when anti-suffragists had the force of public opinion behind them, and it was an uphill struggle for the suffragists to retain their stake in it. It sometimes seems as though all the principal themes of the campaign are articulated in the contest for 'womanliness', in the attempt to develop its power while remaking the terms of sexual difference and the sexual division of labour on which it was based.[266]

In novels, religious tracts and etiquette books, 'womanliness' was a matter of plot, motivation and behaviour. Looks were important, and coded by physiognomical references to suggest feminine or unfeminine attributes, but the ways in which 'womanliness' might be conjured up pictorially were limited. Suffrage artists drew on two kinds of resource: on an allegorical imagery of angels, virtues and goddesses of spring and regeneration (at this point the Militant and the Womanly Woman come together by way of a common reference point in moral reform), and on the depiction of contemporary feminine types and everyday activities, which extend beyond the domestic realm to embrace such figures of modern womanhood as the doctor, graduate, writer and nurse.

The allegorical women are womanly by virtue of their history in representation. (There was a particular point at which angels became feminine, and particular reasons why even militant virtues like Justice and Fortitude were depicted as female in classical tradition.)[267] The imagery of seed-time and harvest was developed by artists like Sylvia Pankhurst from the example of Walter Crane. Agricultural and feminine metaphors for plenty were dominant in socialist iconography until after 1917 – they signified *through* the female figure by invoking her reproductive capacities – but they have a different inflection in suffrage posters such as 'Woman Offering Her Gifts at Her Country's Door'. This suggests a harvest festival of neglected female attributes, a counter to the antis' argument that even womanly traits could endanger the state, if they were operative outside the private sphere.

The images in this category are unspecific in so far as they are allegorical. They answered the need to identify a common category of womanliness across all other social differences, and to find a means of giving it visual form. Their strength and their weakness lay in this. They provided a rallying point, as the muscular hero of proletarian imagery did for the labour movement, but it was a rallying point that depended on the image of idealised womanhood developed from the pictorial vocabulary of Pre-Raphaelitism and art nouveau. A certain *frisson* arises from the contrast between Raphael's Sistine Madonna, reproduced on the cover of the *Suffragette* in 1913,[268] and the awesome record of arson and destruction laid out inside; but in her

allegorical register the Womanly Woman was by definition not adapted to the radical critique of a femininity from which she had been partly forged.

Womanliness in everyday life was evoked through the depiction of maternal and domestic tasks with a political twist ('Political Help', or 'Won't You Let Me Help You John?'); and through illustrations of mothers or children, often in a style derived from contemporary children's books ('Votes for Mammies').[269] But if the boundaries of womanly decorum were to be extended in this process and not just confirmed, other figures had also to be deployed, in less familiar roles but with feminine grace and dignified mien. The woman graduate was a tremendously important figure here. (*Punch*'s lady doctors and sweet girl graduates have noble brows, large eyes, clear expressions and Roman profiles.) Women's successes in higher education, to which they had been so recently and so grudgingly admitted, had proved spectacular; and attractive young students in white dresses with embroidered banners were among the most popular features of any suffrage demonstration. They were widely respected (a number of prominent anti-suffragists were in favour of the extension of university facilities to women), and collectively they embodied a serious challenge to the notion that intelligent women were ugly, as well as to the 'scientific' arguments that women had lower intellects or that their intellectual development was paid for by the atrophy of their feminine attributes and reproductive capacities. The figure of the woman graduate or doctor – one of the arguments for women doctors was based on womanliness, and on the impropriety of women being intimately examined by men – forced a recognition of women's capacities beyond the purely domestic, and encouraged the idea that in their development new types of womanliness would emerge.

At their most explicit, suffragists responded to the accusation of unwomanliness by depicting themselves engaged in household tasks. The *Vote* offered a prize for the best example in 1910, which

"Won't you let me help you John?"

113 'Won't You Let Me Help You John?': designed by Joan Harvey Drew of the Artists' Suffrage League, *c.* 1909.
Against a lightly sketched country-house garden, John Bull is beset by a series of political and legislative problems ranging from old-age pensions through the Deceased Wife's Sister's Bill to infant mortality rates and free school dinners. The antis' theme of the neglected home is reversed (as in the companion poster, 'Why Won't they Let the Women Help?') and an alternative proposition advanced: without women's help the needs of the state *are neglected and its burdens — even where they impinge most closely on women and the family — remain unshared.*

114 'Mrs How-Martyn Makes Jam', published by the Women's Freedom League.

THE WOMEN'S FREEDOM LEAGUE, 1, Robert Street, Adelphi.

SUFFRAGETTES AT HOME.—(3.) Mrs. How Martyn Makes Jam.

was won by a picture of 'Mrs John Russell Tending Her Invalid Mother'. (Among the other contenders, later published as postcards, were 'Mrs Snow Makes Pastry', 'Mrs Despard Knits a Comforter', 'Alison Neilans Cleans the Stove', 'Miss Agnes Leonard Cooking a Vegetarian Dinner', 'Mrs and Miss Hicks Spring Cleaning', 'Miss Gill Home Dressmaking', 'Mrs G. Ballam's Washing Day' and 'Mrs How-Martyn Makes Jam'.)[270] This helped to invite identification with the political campaign; but in an age of industrial production, the transcendant embodiment of womanliness – of fecundity and social harmony – was finally still allegorical and agricultural, a secular Ceres or Flora.

Womanliness signified in representation by virtue of what it was not. For the anti-suffragists this was hysteria; for suffrage propagandists it was prostitution. Both were deviations from the middle-class feminine ideal and both were treated as pathological conditions, in the woman's or in the social body. (In his work on *Prostitution* Dr William Acton talked of ending a spurious modesty 'which lets fearful forms of vice swell to rank luxuriousness' in order to locate and remedy the 'wounds and putrefying sores' of the body politic.)[271]

The womanly woman and the prostitute (the madonna and the whore) formed a familiar couplet in Victorian sexual ideology and its reformulation in later histories of the period. They are elements in a model that assumes a unitary Victorian culture and sexual code, and within it a sexual drive controlled or expressed in men, absent or repressed in (womanly) women, unspoken in polite society, but leaking out into large-scale prostitution and an undergrowth of pornographic representation. The crisp duality of this model is in most respects inadequate to the complexity of nineteenth-century beliefs and practices, and to a proliferation of discourses on the sexual and of sexual identities and the means for their identification and control. A new 'science of sexuality' identified sex as a public issue, incorporated perversions such as

homosexual acts into individual sexual identities, drew a rigid distinction between the economics of male and female sexuality, and identified extra-marital sexual activity as a source of danger and disease. The sexual/political field was reconstituted around a preoccupation with perversion, reproduction and degeneration, which focused underlying anxieties about racial purity and descent.[272]

The place of women in this was complicated. Suffrage attempts to mobilise sexual issues in their propaganda were made possible, but also constrained, by the debates they inherited from nineteenth-century campaigns, which shaped their perceptions and representations of the problem. They drew on a rhetoric of women's purity and moral authority and made it the basis of an argument for the vote that would further women's participation in social reform. They argued that the vote would raise the social and economic status of the industrial woman worker and hence save her from sexual exploitation. They claimed (in the case of the militants, with increasing vehemence) that men's vested interests would always prevent them from stamping out political and sexual corruption. In all this they forged a feminist critique of the patriarchal control of women's sexuality in the family and by the state. But they did so largely by mobilising the ideology of womanliness with all its associated difficulties. Their licence to provide a critique of the double standard derived from it, but as 'womanliness' was invoked on the one hand, and on the other the prostitute as victim of male sexual and economic exploitation, both were confirmed. That which enabled them to speak tied them to the position from which they spoke. They were automatically obliged to see the prostitute as victim (and therefore had difficulty recognising the woman who had freely and probably temporarily chosen her vocation), and womanliness as essentially chaste. Suffrage propaganda – because of its inheritance from earlier campaigns, its critique of private and institutional male power, and the needs of the cause to which it was addressed – reaffirmed a particular representation of illicit sexuality as subject to the cleansing crusade of the womanly woman. This in turn confirmed the divide at the very heart of Victorian bourgeois sexual ideology between the chaste and the 'fallen' woman.

Many nineteenth-century debates on prostitution tacitly assumed that male vice was elusive, inevitable or invisible. (The Contagious Diseases Acts enshrined the double standard in assuming the need for controlled heterosexual outlets for a bachelor army and navy, while identifying working-class prostitutes as the source of venereal disease and subjecting them to forced identification and restraint.)[273] Against this feminists struggled to relocate the figure of the accommodated male, and to substitute for the figure of the polluting prostitute the whole complex of social relations she served to disguise. For them the image of sexual depravity could be made to stand for a whole structure of social inequality in need of the women's vote (an argument sometimes turned against them by men who warned that women would meddle like prudes in the social and sexual status quo). Suffragists attacked the patterns of class and gender domination through the social and legal controls on sexuality which rendered them peculiarly transparent, and the heritage of the Contagious Diseases campaign made them especially sensitive to the ways in which the double standard was enshrined in the representations and practices of the law.[274]

There was no agreement on the nature and rights of female sexuality in the Edwardian period, but suffragists were chiefly successful in pushing to the margins of their campaign a dissident tradition that argued for 'free unions' and women's right to equal sexual expression with men. Male sexual radicals like Havelock Ellis and Edward Carpenter, and advocates of birth control and free unions including Annie Besant, Stella Browne and the libertarian Dora Marsden, offered a challenge to the social purity position which continued to dominate the Edwardian women's movement. But this challenge, which represented in some respects the most 'modern' position on female sexuality, was seriously weakened by the fact that its definitions of sexual activity were drawn from heterosexual male models, that it joined a misogynist tradition in discrediting the spinster's life as one of 'sterility and a slow atrophy of bodily and mental power', that it overlooked the material conditions which made 'free unions' impractical for most women, and most of all that it lost the cutting edge which the purity stance gave to women's critiques of male sexuality and the double standard.[275] Whatever its restrictions in private life (and it enabled certain forms of control over their own bodies to be retained by women there too), 'passionlessness' was a powerful tool in a campaign that increasingly based its strategies on women's moral authority, and furthered its demands through the fight for a single standard of sexual control: 'Votes for Women and Chastity for Men'.

This pithy slogan appeared in *The Great Scourge and How to End It* by Christabel Pankhurst, which first appeared as a series of articles in the *Suffragette*[276] on the effects of venereal disease as 'the great cause of physical, mental, and moral degeneracy and of race suicide', and was published in book form in December 1913. It argued that venereal disease (the 'Great Scourge') spread by prostitution (the 'Social Evil') was the fruit of 'woman slavery' and the chief of society's ills. For these ills Christabel prescribed militancy as the 'moral purge' that would effect finally 'sweetness and cleanness, respect and trust, perfect equality and justice' and reconciliation between men and women. The WSPU made the issues of male immorality and white slavery (enforced prostitution, particularly of minors) central to its militant campaign in 1913, and to the 'Moral Crusade' that accompanied it. In a speech in New York in October, Mrs Pankhurst described prostitution as 'a slavery more awful than Negro slavery in its worst form ever was', and promised that, 'We will not

115 Advertising *The Great Scourge*, 1913.

have the health of one-half of the community, their pretended health, maintained at the expense of the degradation and sorrow and misery of the other half.'[277]

This kind of argument infuriated Teresa Billington-Greig, who accused the Pankhursts of setting middle-class women on the rampage against something they knew little about, 'feeding and flattering a sexual ideology which juxtaposed the perfection of women against the bestiality of men'.[278] Mrs Pankhurst and Christabel considered themselves justified by the mutilation of the 1912 White Slave Traffic Bill[279] (which had been before Parliament since 1909 and for which a wide range of women's groups had lobbied along with purity campaigners), by violence against women and children that was scantily punished in the courts, and by discrepancies in the treatment of prostitutes and madams compared with their male clients and pimps. At the same time the heightened language of the 'Moral Crusade' was useful to them in masking the inequalities of class by its insistence on those of sex. As the NUWSS consolidated its links with the labour movement, the WSPU turned its back on its industrial roots and emphasised the injuries of women in the *sexual* relationship as the chief justification for militancy. Their propaganda 'encouraged fevered emotions', as Sylvia remarked bitterly, it cut across party division and 'did not offend the sensitive class-consciousness of those frail hot-house blooms, the Conservative supporters of women's suffrage, whom the WSPU was eager to encourage'.[280]

Certainly the obsession among sections of the Edwardian women's movement with white slavery, and their engagement with criminal law as the focal point of feminist politics, distracted them both from the economic basis of prostitution and from its frequently casual nature. In adopting some of the goals of the social purity movement (with which they shared an overlapping membership), feminists risked replacing the struggle against sexual exploitation with the repression of deviant sexualities, at the cost of the further coercion of vulnerable working-class women, and the rejection of any exploration – outside a small minority – of the possibility of *women's* sexual rights and pleasures.

The rhetoric of moral outrage required men to be venal and prostitutes to be victims. As articulated by the WSPU it sharpened sexual antagonism and disguised the circumstances in which prostitution in fact took place. It enabled them to cut their way out of the tangle of social and sexual oppression which feminism attempted to unravel, by the expedient of identifying a main cause that would serve as the focus for an all-out attack.

Women's entry into prostitution was apparently voluntary, gradual and not necessarily permanent. The social profile of the prostitute, as Judith Walkowitz has reconstructed it, was unskilled, poor working-class, with local origins but displaced family relations. Prostitution offered a temporary refuge from difficult circumstances; it gave limited access to social and economic independence, but at the risk of alcoholism, venereal disease, physical danger and constant harassment by the police.[281] This is not a story that fits the contemporary narrative of seduction and betrayal (and therefore the image of the rake), nor the picture of the prostitute as primarily a social outcast: 'ill-fed, ill-clothed, uncared for, from whose misery the eye recoils, cowering under dark arches and among bye-lanes'.[282]

That was, however, the construction deployed in the suffrage campaign, not only because cultural representations were perhaps more influential on its members than personal knowledge, but because of the needs of their own arguments in support of the vote. The prostitute as victim, which was not so much a false representation as a partial one and one that deprived the women concerned of any active part in their own lives, was the only image to fit the arguments of the WSPU's 'Moral Crusade', or the emphasis placed by other groups on the links between economic and sexual exploitation. The sisterhood invoked in a recognition that (middle-class) womanly women and exploited (working-class) women could struggle together against male sexual licence and oppression had about it a distinctly philanthropic sense of condescension. But it was at the same time the only means by which suffragists could exercise their moral authority to contest the undoubted fact of male sexual power. In doing so they simplified the complexity of contemporary sexual ideologies and practices, which were themselves in the course of codification and change, and made the prostitute a passive victim in their representations as they claimed she was in life a passive victim of economic circumstance and men's lust. In that simplification, however, lay the strategic power of their arguments, which could then be fitted to an increasingly influential concern with the relation between moral behaviour and social stability. If they could speak in the terms of moral and social regeneration, they would be using a language familiar to everyone in support of a wider cause to which, in theory, a number of different and powerful interests within the community were committed.

*

The Womanly Woman was both an empty category (a mere doubling of terms) and a point of constant reference; a blurred and shifting constellation of attributes, underpinned on the one hand by an appeal to female biology and domestic responsibility, and on the other by their exclusion from the virtues of an ideal masculinity. 'The man's power is active, progressive, defensive. He is eminently the doer, the creator, the discoverer, the defender. His intellect is for speculation and invention; his energy for adventure, for war, and for conquest . . . the woman's power is for rule, not for battle – and her intellect is not for invention and creation, but for sweet ordering, arrangement and decision.'[283] These were Ruskin's words in 1865, and *Sesame and Lilies* was still an influential text in the Edwardian period. His appeal to the complementarity of separate spheres permeates the anti-suffrage conviction that the first step towards 'a nobler ideal of womanhood' must be 'the destruction of the false ideal of the suffragists, which would make woman man's rival instead of man's loving helpmate'.[284]

Womanliness – that 'characteristically Victorian word, idea and article of faith'[285] – was in some respects a less coherent category in the twentieth century than it had been in the 1860s. The impact of industrialisation and modernisation on women's lives, together with the various campaigns for female emancipation, had combined to disturb it.[286] But change produced conflicts and uncertainties which made the impetus to define and secure the place of women more urgent. The eclectic but influential ideas of social Darwinism and eugenics were used to lend scientific credibility to a conservative view of women's primarily domestic role. Womanliness (middle-class and reproductive) became a 'racial duty'; a necessary bulwark against physical and moral deterioration and the enfeeblement of a virile and imperial nation by unfit mothers and unmanly men.

Womanliness had an imaginative centrality in Victorian and Edwardian culture that like all normative and stereotyped categories was often at odds with 'the messiness and pragmatic complexity'[287] of lived experience. Its cultural significance did not derive from the actual political, legal or economic positions of women (which it did not reflect, but helped to maintain), but from the enormous symbolic significance accorded to femininity as the repository of natural feeling and spirituality on the one hand, and of fears for the social order as they were displaced on to the regulation of sexuality on the other. In reality, women were participants in the social and industrial life of the nation in ways that the Working Woman and the Modern Woman were intended to emphasise. But in the symbolic register the mean-

ings accruing to femininity were the embodiment of women's physical possibilities alone – motherhood, nurture, sexual pleasure and comfort (or conversely the instinctual, the excessive, the disordered, the hysteric). The Working Woman (the sweated female labourer) and the Modern Woman (the emancipated middle-class working woman) were social types. They played the part of fragmentary icons of the 'real' deployed against the sentimentalising of maternal womanhood that was one of the most conservative elements in anti-suffrage propaganda. The Hysterical Woman was a deviant or pathological type, and the Militant Woman its allegorical antidote. The Womanly Woman was a rich conglomerate of partly contested qualities which neither the suffragists nor their opponents could afford to relinquish. In this sense she was open ground, less a type (although she could be encoded as one through details of physique, expression, costume and accessory) than a field in which consensual definitions of femininity were renegotiated. 'The problem of ideology,' as Burton and Carlen put it, 'is a problem concerning rights – a quarrel about rights of possession, a quarrel, initially, between those who claimed a right to occupy a particular place.' The contenders for this space are 'locked in constant litigation with each other', even over 'the existence of the court where their claims [are] to be represented'.[288] This was certainly the case with 'womanliness'. The antis identified themselves with the interests of the womanly woman against the image of the unsexed, hysterical virago with whom they identified their rivals. Suffragists presented themselves as the true, the *evolved* embodiment of a womanliness to which they gave a new, expanded and public frame of reference. In doing so they modernised the concept and contributed to its longevity. Through their representations as well as their activities this modern womanliness was vindicated – an unlooked-for irony – in women's work and in the imagery of munitions recruitment posters during the First World War.

5 · EPILOGUE

116 Signing up for munitions work on 17 July 1915.

On 4 August 1914 England declared war on Germany, and the women's suffrage movement as it had hitherto existed came abruptly to an end. The war changed the course of suffrage politics, divided its principal organisations and threw up strange alliances, most notably that between the Pankhursts and Lloyd George. Paradoxically it put an end to organised suffrage agitation while providing the catalyst that finally released the issue of women's suffrage from the parliamentary stalemate in which it had been caught since the withdrawal of the Reform Bill in January 1913.[1]

After two days of meetings, the executive committee of the NUWSS suspended all political activity on 6 August 1914 and declared itself diverted to 'help those who will be the sufferers from the economic and industrial dislocation caused by the war'. Mrs Fawcett urged members to shelve their grievances against the government and show themselves 'worthy of citizenship whether our claim to it be recognised or not'.[2] Members of the National Union set up Red Cross centres, registered Belgian refugees, donated ambulances, organised canteens, formed a Women's Service Bureau to provide advice for women who lost their jobs in the national upheaval, campaigned against the inadequate representation of women on government Relief Committees, and by the end of 1914 had set up a Women's Interests Committee to enable women to take on work, including 'men's' work, while protecting them from exploitation as cheap or voluntary labour. The Actresses' Franchise League turned to providing women's entertainments at troop camps, producing six to eight concerts a week in 1916. Mary Lowndes of the Artists' Suffrage League established a welding workshop that trained women for skilled work in engineering.[3]

On the evening of 4 August Mrs Fawcett had addressed a women's peace meeting protesting against England's involvement in the war. She did not pursue this line, but pacifist feeling ran high in the NUWSS and led eventually to a split in its ranks. In the spring of 1915 all the national officers apart from the treasurer and Mrs Fawcett resigned to form the Women's International League for Peace and Freedom, an organisation that included Quakers, socialists, and constitutional and ex-militant suffragists (Emmeline Pethick-Lawrence among them), and which set up the Women's Peace Conference at the Hague in 1915.[4] All the women who had been 'radical suffragists' were pacifists (the labour movement, like the suffrage movement, was divided by the war), as were Sylvia Pankhurst and the members of the East London Federation.

The East London Federation of Suffragettes became the Workers' Federation, and its paper, the *Women's Dreadnought*, became the *Workers' Dreadnought*. Prices had risen, factories closed, reservists were called up and hunger, unemployment and fear were rampant in East London. The Federation opened five Mother and Infant Welfare centres, a toy and garment factory for unemployed women, cost-price restaurants, and a League of Rights for Soldiers' and Sailors' Wives and Relatives. They turned the Gunmakers' Arms (a disused public house) into the Mothers' Arms (a clinic, day nursery and Montessori school). They fought for equal pay for women, for wages that kept pace with inflation, for the vote and for peace, all of which made the split between the ELF and the WSPU more bitter and provoked Mrs Pankhurst to cable from the United States: 'Regret I cannot prevent use of name.'[5]

Eleven suffragettes were still in prison when war

broke out, and others were liable to re-arrest under the provisions of the Cat and Mouse Act. On 10 August the Home Secretary offered them an amnesty, and with it the militant suffragette movement came to an end. On the 13th Mrs Pankhurst issued a statement to the effect that with the release of its prisoners, it had become possible to consider the appropriate course of action for the WSPU in a context of national crisis.[6] Even 'the most vigorous militancy' would count for nothing in wartime, and peaceful argument, which the suffragettes had never believed effective, would be even less so. The WSPU announced its intention to economise on its energies and financial resources by a temporary suspension of activities. Militant rhetoric and the image of the just crusade remained, but their object shifted, and the Pankhursts remade their allegiances in the face of a new 'Great Scourge': that of German hostility.[7] Militants could not be pacifists, and the larger conflict was permitted to take temporary precedence over the lesser. But at the same time as the question of the vote was suspended, the concept of militant feminism was actively pursued in the context of 'women's right to serve'.

Mrs Pankhurst and Christabel seized the opportunity to become in effect political leaders for the government they had opposed, committing the WSPU to mobilise the women of Britain in national service, supporting internment, making recruitment speeches, calling for conscription, organising what Annie Kenney called an 'anti-Bolshevist' campaign in the trade unions and handing white feathers to men not in uniform. All this was very distasteful to feminist pacifists, who believed with Sylvia Pankhurst that the adoption of militancy to recruitment drives was 'a tragic betrayal' of women's stand for peace.[8] But they granted that it was at least consistent with the WSPU's pre-war glorification of 'the power of the primitive knock on the nose'. Their real anger was reserved for those constitutionalists who, 'though bitterly repudiating militancy for women, are as ardent in

their support of militancy for men'.[9] Strategically, the association of feminism with the patriotic prosecution of the war did much to expunge the more bitter memories of the arson campaign. It offered no radical challenge to the state – at least directly – but it continued to offer a radical challenge to dominant definitions of femininity, in a context that was no longer subversive.[10] However controversially and equivocally, and at whatever cost to a feminist critique of the war, the WSPU succeeded in making women's contribution to the war effort so significant, and so visible, that the possibility of using the old arguments and the memory of militancy against them in any future franchise reform was effectively blocked.

The pattern of work for men and women of different social classes was not at first disrupted by the outbreak of war but, with dramatic losses on the Western Front, women were called on to substitute for men and release recruits for active service. This process was accelerated by the introduction of conscription in April 1916. For the first time women took on such semi-skilled agricultural and industrial tasks as farm work, bus driving, chimney sweeping, train cleaning and work in engineering and munitions factories. Between 1914 and 1918 the total number of employed women rose to 1,345,000, the increase in their industrial activity being largely accounted for by munitions workers: there were 200,000 of them before the war, and 900,000 at its end.[11]

As Minister of Munitions, Lloyd George was urged by the Cabinet Committee on Munitions at the end of 1914 to expand the civilian resources available for such work. On 27 January 1915 the *Daily Sketch* published a photograph of Mrs Pankhurst talking to a woman bus conductor in Paris. According to its caption she was 'anxious to mobilise the women of Britain . . . to take the place of their husbands' in similar activities. In March the Board of Trade issued a circular appealing to women to register at the Labour Exchanges for war service, and began to enrol them on the Special

War Register. (The East London Federation advised women against registering as a protest against the war, and against the conscription they believed it was designed to facilitate.) On 23 March the *Daily Sketch* published Mrs Pankhurst's article on 'Why Women Should be Mobilized',[12] and on 24 June she delivered a rousing speech on the 'right to serve' at the London Polytechnic, reported in detail in *The Times* next day. On 28 June Lloyd George received a letter from George V 'wondering whether it would be possible or advisable for you to make use of Mrs Pankhurst'.[13] Within a few days he had asked her to organise a demonstration 'like those you used to have for the vote', this time in the government interest, and subsidised with a government grant of £2000.[14]

One of the lesser ironies of the First World War found these erstwhile enemies combined in a common cause, or at least finding a use for each other at the same moment. It was convenient to Lloyd George to exploit the Pankhursts' organisational skills and their claim to speak for women, albeit a calculated risk to trust that their newly patriotic fervour had displaced the memory of pre-war arson. But it also suited the WSPU to carve out for itself a place in the limelight, deliberately to court the support of those 'not actively concerned with the question of "women's rights" in ordinary circumstances',[15] and to hold what might *almost* be described as the first major suffrage procession since the NUWSS Pilgrimage of 1913. In that its direct aim was not the vote it was not a suffrage demonstration at all, but the connotations of women's 'right to serve' were unmistakable, especially in the light of pre-war propaganda on the expediency of the women's vote. Women needed no persuading to do munitions work, and Lloyd George knew it. The purpose of the procession, as he outlined it to Mrs Pankhurst, was to 'create an atmosphere',[16] a climate of public opinion in which the opposition of industrialists and trade unions would be forced to melt away.

On 9 July the WSPU issued a circular letter soliciting support for the demonstration,[17] and tactfully recasting it as their own initiative rather than the government's. 'So grave is our national danger, and so terrible is the loss of precious lives at the front due to shortage of munitions, that Mr Lloyd George, as Minister of Munitions, has been asked to receive a deputation and hear women's demand for the right to make munitions and render other War Service.' Not for the first time the WSPU announced 'the biggest demonstration of its kind ever seen', and urged women of all classes to participate. It called for banner-bearers, marshals, paper sellers and 400 young women dressed in white, and promised an 'effective decorative scheme'; not the familiar purple, white and green this time, but the more patriotic red, white and blue. It was all organised in a fortnight, and on 17 July 30,000 women marched in the 'Right to Serve' procession, with all the old suffrage pageantry annexed to this new, and nationalistic cause.

They formed up on the Embankment in driving rain and a squally wind, the white dresses covered with mackintoshes, so that as a women's march it lacked the brilliance of its predecessors.[18] (Even this was turned to account by the *Daily Telegraph*, which announced that, 'No summer gaiety, no prettiness of costume, could have been more in the spirit of the practical purpose of the hour than this pageant of brown and grey and black.') The 125 contingents were marked out by men in the khaki uniforms of the City Territorials; each was organised by marshals in red and blue sashes, and to each a van distributed the requisite flags and banners. By 3.30 pm 100,000 spectators had gathered between Westminster and Blackfriars and the last elements were fitted into place in the mosaic of 30,000 women. All ninety bands struck up the Marseillaise, the first gleam of colour appeared as the flags were raised, and Mrs Pankhurst, 'at last a heroine with the crowd',[19] led the way up Whitehall to Trafalgar Square, along Piccadilly and up Park Lane, along Oxford Street and down Regent Street to Piccadilly Circus, and back via

117 The Women's War Work procession passing through Piccadilly Circus, 17 July 1915.

opposite page

118 'Belgium' from the Pageant of the Allies in the Women's War Work procession of 17 July 1915.

Northumberland Avenue to the Embankment.

Throughout the procession the colours of the Union Jack were sometimes blocked and sometimes mingled in fluttering pennons of red, white and blue; and the lines were punctuated with banners lettered like newspaper headlines: 'For Men Must Fight and Women Must Work', 'Down With Sex Prejudice: Let Women Work', 'Shells Made By a Wife May Save a Husband's Life'. A tall woman in white carried the Union Jack at the head of the foremost section, accompanied by a band, the deputation to Lloyd George and a great wagon of wild flowers with the inscription 'We Demand the Right to Serve'.

The 'Pageant of the Allies' was led by 'Belgium' – 'the spirit of bereaved but unbroken Belgium and

the spirit of British womanhood: the spirit of the March' – a young woman in purple and black who carried the tattered flag of mourning through the driving rain, barefoot in the mud. Behind her came the representatives of the Allies in national dress, or fanciful approximations to it: England in white with crimson roses in her hair surrounded by 'peasant' women from Scotland, Ireland and Wales; a couple dressed in the folk costumes of Serbia; a woman wearing a white stole embroidered with the eagle of Poland; France with the cap of Liberty; Italy with the red shirt of Garibaldi; representatives from Russia and Japan, each with standard-bearers and bands playing an assortment of national airs from the Russian anthem to the Marseillaise.

Spectators packed Trafalgar Square and lined the streets, sometimes six deep, to watch the women pass. Tables were set out at intervals where women could sign up for war work. 'The paper had to be shielded with tarpaulins from the driving rain, the wind lashed fiercely at hat and skirt, but there was no lack of signatures.'[20] In fact this was partly theatre: there was no difficulty getting women to volunteer – only a small proportion of the government register had been called upon – the problem was in persuading the government and the employers to make use of them.

Lloyd George received the deputation at the Ministry of Munitions in Whitehall Gardens, and as the sun came out he mounted a special platform to address a crowd of 60,000 spectators: 'a spread of faces limited only by the grey river beyond'.[21] In his speech he claimed that 50,000 women were already making armaments but that in Germany there were ten times as many, which indicated a great reserve of labour power as yet untouched. He promised a National Register of women willing to do full-time work, he promised equal wages for piecework, and he pledged the government to prohibit 'sweating'. When a woman interrupted with 'We want the vote,' Lloyd George replied amid laughter, 'Yes, but we want you in the shell factory first.'[22] He congratulated the WSPU on the procession, as further proof of the organising capacity of women 'of which I have been a victim in the past', and the meeting ended as all ninety bands 'broke thunderously into the National Anthem'.[23]

The 'spontaneous' response of the women to the national crisis was widely praised in the leading newspapers, many of which devoted their Monday leaders to Saturday's march, and all of which emphasised the characteristics of suffrage pageantry as they had been turned to the new cause: skilled organisation, spectacular effect, the mix of different social classes (peeresses in tailor-mades, typists in mackintoshes, art students in olive-greens) and a spirit that was only enhanced by the driving rain that might have dampened it. *The Times* reminded its readers that at the outbreak of war the vilified militants had 'suspended their demands, dropped their grievances and [thrown] themselves into the work of national education'. What was new and valuable about the procession was 'the determination it shows to help in doing the one thing that matters, the winning of the war'.[24] Only the socialists and pacifists held back, the *Herald* pointing to the contrast with a demonstration organised by Sylvia Pankhurst the same week.[25] The main object of the WSPU procession was to emphasise the willingness of women of all classes to serve the state; that of the East London Federation, to demonstrate that millions of women were already doing so at home, in agriculture or in industry, their services 'recognised' by sweated wages, their labour exploited by monopolists who made their profits out of the war.

Thousands of women answered the call for volunteers, but since there were not yet the facilities or the vacancies for them that call was premature. Mrs Pankhurst blamed the trade unions,[26] which had been able to negotiate the 'dilution' with women of designated war work only, not ordinary production, and as the War Office put it, 'in temporary replacement of men'.

The promotion of Lloyd George to the War Office early in 1916, and the introduction of conscription in April, greatly facilitated the wider employment of women. In July the WSPU organised a second 'Women's War Work' procession in support of government policy, and Lloyd George succeeded Lord Kitchener as Secretary for War on the basis of his 'marvellous efficiency in solving the munitions problem'.[27] For their part women rose magnificently to the challenge, albeit to the disappointment of those who hoped that women's example would 'guide our feet into the way of peace'.[28] It was hardly the case that women had never worked before, although the applause they now received seemed almost to suggest it. But the waged labour of industrial women was often invisible – because they were outworkers or simply because it was overlooked – and regarded as a

regrettable anomaly by trade unionists, socialists, philanthropists and even some feminists. Women's work in the public spotlight, in the national interest and at the government's behest was another matter. It was both important *and* visible. Suddenly there was an unexpected congruence between suffrage representations of an active and capable womanhood and the government's need of it – a novel 'fit' between the graduate, the worker or the militant figure of Joan of Arc in suffrage imagery, and the representation of women on official recruitment posters (though not, it has to be said, on *men's* recruitment posters).[29]

The war turned out to serve the interests of suffragists in unexpected ways. It provided the opportunity for the licensed revaluation of 'womanliness' and for a demonstration of women's crucial contribution to the needs of the state. 'Militancy' had a different currency when the pre-war notoriety of suffragists was refocused through the lens of contemporary patriotism. It had seemed in August 1914 as though 'the great catastrophe of the world war would greatly hamper and retard the movement to which we had dedicated our lives'.[30] Gradually it began to dawn on women that this was not in fact the case. Their cause was furthered by their war work (by the public fervour of the WSPU and the quieter diligence of the NUWSS), and unexpectedly by the need for franchise reform provoked by the delay of the general election due for 1915.

In August 1914 an all-party truce was declared, and in May 1915 the difficulties posed by a general election in wartime were avoided by the formation of a coalition government. In 1915 the Cabinet wished to deal with the electoral registration of troops. Clearly the existing register was now useless, since the residency qualification effectively disenfranchised soldiers who had been fighting at the front. Some politicians were enthusiastic enough to suggest that military service might become a qualification for the vote (which would have enshrined in law the 'physical force' argument and for ever disqualified the women). Mrs Pankhurst herself, in a temporary volte-face, promised not to use the servicemen's vote as a basis on which to agitate for women, and claimed that no woman could face the possibility of the affairs of the country being settled by 'conscientious objectors, passive resisters and shirkers'.[31] Others both inside and outside the suffrage movement pointed to women's war service as the justification for including them in any new electoral reform. Their activities had been so successful and so well publicised that anti-suffragists complained they had cornered the market in public service. 'They sew and knit comforts for the soldiers, but with such a perpetual running accompaniment of suffragist self-laudation that they might as well embroider the sacred name of Mrs Pankhurst or Mrs Fawcett on every sock and every muffler.'[32]

In the face of women's war work some leading opponents and significant sections of the anti-suffrage press recanted their views.[33] A remarkable sympathy of content and tone united suffrage arguments on women's capacities with articles on 'Women in Industry' and 'Women in War Work' in *The Times*, and illustrated publications from the War Office and the Ministry of Munitions. Even Asquith, in an equivocal speech to the House of Commons in August 1916 – in which he reminded his listeners of a record which proved that he had 'no special desire or predisposition to bring women within the pale of the franchise' – suggested that it would not be logical to revise the register in acknowledgement of state service and omit the women. 'It is true they cannot fight, in the gross material sense of going out with rifles and so forth, but they fill our munitions factories, they are doing work which the men who are fighting had to perform before . . . and they have aided, in the most effective way, in the prosecution of the War.'[34]

In May 1916 Mrs Fawcett had written to Asquith pointing to the changed tone of support for women's suffrage, suggesting that the continued exclusion of women from the franchise would prove impossible after the war, and pointing out that amendments designed to deal with the accidental disqualification of servicemen would provide the opportunity of dealing at the same time with the electoral disabilities of women. Asquith denied that there was any move afoot to tamper with the electoral register, but in June a joint Suffrage Conference was established which concluded that if any extension to the male franchise was proposed, agitation for the women's vote would be resumed. The government referred all franchise issues, including the question of plural voting and the possibility of proportional representation, to an all-party committee of thirty-two MPs and peers chaired by the Speaker. The Speaker's Conference met first in October 1916, and reported on 30 January 1917 (by which time Asquith had been replaced as prime minister by Lloyd George).[35] It proposed a revision of the occupational qualification, a simplification of the local government register, the introduction of proportional representation (which was never carried out) and – although not unanimously – 'some measure of woman's suffrage', with an age bar of thirty or thirty-five and an implicit property qualification that would have enfranchised about 7 million women.

It was Asquith himself, in March 1917, who moved the resolution in favour of a bill that would implement the recommendations of the Speaker's Conference. Not altogether plausibly, he maintained that his 'opposition to woman suffrage [had] always been based, and based solely, on considerations of public expediency'. He had years before suggested that women should work out their own salvation, and now they had done so. He stressed their wartime service and the new problems likely to arise, when the war was over, 'in regard to women's labour and women's functions and activities in the new ordering of things – for, do not doubt it, the old order will be changed'.[36] The motion was carried by 341 votes to 62, and the following day (29 March 1917), a deputation from most of the principal suffrage organisations received the assurance from Lloyd George that a women's clause would be inserted before a franchise bill came before the House. The end was finally in sight, albeit on a compromise measure with limited terms.

During these months neither the suffragists nor their opponents engaged in campaigns for popular support.[37] Lord Northcliffe – a late but influential convert to the cause – wrote to Mrs Fawcett to complain about the lack of public demonstrations and to urge some united activity. But the suffragists preferred to leave the reopening of the campaign as a future possibility, relying for the present on the benefits of a favourable conjunction: Asquith replaced by Lloyd George, a coalition government (so that suffrage was not a party issue), the impact of women's war service, enthusiastic support in the press, the suspension of militant activity and the patriotic transformation of the WSPU, the opening up of the franchise issue by the question of the enlisted man's vote, and the recommendations of the Speaker's Conference.

The bill passed through the House of Commons in June and received its third reading in December. The House of Lords did not delay it. Sylvia Pankhurst described the opposition of the anti-suffrage peers as 'dwindled like mist before the sun'.[38] The Representation of the People Act, the last of the great reform bills, became law on 6 February 1918. Mrs Fawcett sat in the Speaker's Gallery to watch its passage, as she had looked down from the Ladies' Gallery on the scene of John Stuart Mill proposing a women's amendment to the Reform Act of 1867 more than half a century before.[39] All adult males received the vote, and all women over thirty who were householders, the wives of householders, university graduates or occupiers of property worth £5 per year. (Not until 1928 when the voting age was lowered to twenty-one did women gain the franchise on the same terms 'as it is or may be' granted to men.) Universal adult suffrage was

still a decade away, but the old concept of household suffrage, like that of 'fitness' for the rights of citizenship, had finally been supplanted by the individual vote.[40]

The victory was not without its ironies. Women gained the vote after a long period in which propaganda activities had been suspended, and not through the separate statute they had long campaigned for but through a clause tacked on to a comprehensive measure for adult male suffrage. A further bill which had never been sought or struggled for enabled them to sit as Members of Parliament. The first women to be elected MPs were not those who had been associated with the agitation that secured their right to do so. And lastly but most significantly for the subject of this book, the 'pageantry and rejoicing, the flaming ardour, which in pre-war days would have greeted the victory, were absent when it came'.[41] The National Union held a meeting in the Queen's Hall, with the banners of the earlier campaign and decorations by the Artists' Suffrage League which emerged from retirement for the purpose, but England was still at war and victory celebrations were subdued.[42] Neither the constitutionalists nor the militants, the pacifists nor the government's supporters, judged the moment right for what might otherwise have been the suffrage demonstration to surpass them all.

This is not the place to discuss the consequences of the women's vote.[43] Neither its supporters nor its opponents found their prophecies fulfilled. In the post-war period of reconstruction, male workers and politicians alike stressed the importance of women's role in the home, the necessity of the 'family wage' and of 'jobs for heroes'. Women were easy scapegoats for the high unemployment levels of the 1920s and 1930s. Suffrage organisations continued to struggle for equal citizenship, but the women's vote did not of itself open up the political structure to organised feminist pressure groups. The WSPU 'Women's Party' had ceased to exist by 1919 (when the NUWSS became the National Union of Societies for Equal Citizenship), Christabel became a travelling evangelist, and although she and her mother stood unsuccessfully as Coalition and Conservative candidates respectively neither was active in British feminism in the inter-war period. 'Gone was the mirage of a society regenerated by enfranchised womanhood as by a magic wand,' as Sylvia Pankhurst regretted.[44] Women voted across the spectrum, as suffragists had often argued they would. They entered Parliament in very small numbers and never comprised a block vote. Seventeen women stood at the 'Coupon Election' of November 1918, including Edith How-Martyn (with an election poster designed by Edith Craig),[45] Christabel Pankhurst and other old campaigners. The one success was Countess Markievicz in Dublin who triumphed for Sinn Fein, but since she did not take her seat the first woman MP was Nancy, Lady Astor, who stepped into her husband's constituency when he was elevated to the peerage in 1919.[46]

Women were enfranchised but they were not emancipated, nor was the vote the key to that emancipation or to the social regeneration for which so many feminists had hoped. As Teresa Billington-Greig had prophesied, the clamour for change was stilled as soon as the personal indignity was removed. And yet a programme of legislation related to the needs of women was passed in the 1920s, beginning with the Sex Disqualification Removal Act of 1919 and including measures on equal divorce, child legitimacy and guardianship; and after the Second World War the provisions of the welfare state incorporated many of the policies first advocated by women's organisations as a feminist programme for women and the family during the First World War.

The broader aims of the Edwardian suffrage campaign, and of Victorian and Edwardian feminists in general, remained to be taken up in a new phase of the women's movement which began at the end of the 1960s, often in ignorance of the work of our grandmothers, consigned as that now was to a very reduced footnote in the political history of the twentieth century. In the context of this movement many questions have been raised about the definition of femininity and the social experience of women, about the forms of domination that place women in specific ways (ways that are implicated in the hegemonies of class and race), and about the role of cultural practices in perpetuating the relations of power to which we are subject. Many of these debates had taken place before, couched in different terms, in the particular circumstances of utopian socialism, or in the labour movement and the suffrage campaigns of the late nineteenth and early twentieth centuries. The strategies to which they gave rise required the revision or displacement of dominant representations of femininity in social circulation, and the production of a politically effective imagery and spectacle. One of our last discoveries has been how far down that road the suffrage artists travelled before us.

APPENDICES
SELECTED BIBLIOGRAPHY
NOTES
LIST OF ILLUSTRATIONS
INDEX

The Suffrage Atelier: Constitution and Addresses

Constitution

The Society shall be called The Suffrage Atelier.

The object of the Society is to encourage Artists to forward the Woman's Movement, and particularly the Enfranchisement of Women, by means of pictorial publications.

Each Member of the Society shall undertake to give the Society the first refusal of any pictorial work intended for publication, dealing with the Woman's Movement. In return the Artist shall receive a certain percentage of the profits arising from the sale of her or his work.

A Committee to consist until further notice of 8 Members and the Officials of the Society shall be elected annually by the Members. The Committee to transact the business of the Society and report at each General Meeting.

Rules

1. The minimum subscription shall be 1/6 per annum.

2. The Society shall be entirely non-party and work as far as possible for all the Women's Suffrage Societies impartially.

3. The Society shall be at liberty to elect Honorary Members.

4. The percentage due to the artist on post cards and other cheap publications shall be 50% on the first 2000 sold, and 25% on subsequent editions. The percentage due to the artist on Pictures, Statuary and Cartoons not published by the Society shall be 75%. The designs for posters published by the Society and not intended for sale shall be paid for by the Society at a rate agreed upon between the Artist and the Society.

5. Notice of any alteration in the Constitution or any important suggestion, must be given at least a week before it is brought up for decision, and if possible at the previous General Meeting.

6. Such notice shall be posted to Country Members, who shall be allowed to vote by post.

7. One quarter of the Members shall form a Quorum for General Meetings.

The Suffrage Atelier

As it is essential that the Committee should realize what support is likely to be given to the various schemes by which the Society could forward the Woman's Movement, each Member is asked to communicate with the Hon. Secretary stating in what way she or he will volunteer to assist the Society. The following suggestions for assistance which can be rendered by the artists are submitted. It is hoped that each member will undertake to do as much as she or he can to make the Society a success. Members can forward the object of the Suffrage Atelier:

1. By sending in designs for Cartoons, suitable for the general press, or for those papers especially devoted to the Woman's Movement, also by submitting designs for Post Cards, Posters etc. for publication by the Suffrage Atelier.

2. By undertaking to send Pictures, Statuary, Black & White work & Craft work to any Exhibition held by the Suffrage Atelier.

3. By volunteering to be responsible for a certain amount of secretarial work. This may be carried on at home and will be quite acceptable even if only of temporary assistance, such as the secretarial work in connection with any Exhibition to be undertaken by the Society.

4. By helping to place our post cards and other publications by (a) selling them privately, (b) introducing them to some shop or local branch of the Suffrage Society, (c) volunteering to sell them at any Suffrage Meetings. Postcards are supplied to Members at wholesale rates.

5. By taking part in any decorative scheme undertaken by the Suffrage Atelier, such as a Pageant, or the decoration of a Hall.

6. By collecting funds for the Society.

7. By obtaining Members for the Society.

8. By forming Local Branches.

9. By sending suitable suggestions for cartoons, cuttings from the press, quotations from books etc. It would be particularly valuable if Members would undertake to read certain papers and to forward all cuttings from the same of interest to the Woman's Movement.

10. By volunteering to write press notices for the Society.

11. By introducing our cartoons to the notice of Editors, with a view to getting them published in the Press.

12. By sending pictorial political illustrations, photographs, and cartoons appearing in papers or elsewhere, for reference.

13. By lending Drawing-room or Studio for Meetings or Exhibitions & by acting [as] Hostess or volunteering for Musical Entertainment or recitals on these occasions.

14. By sending any artistic work suitable for selling at the Art stall on the occasion of the Exhibition to be held May 13th to 26th by the WSPU. These contributions should be sent to the Hon. Secretary of the Suffrage Atelier at least a week before May 13th.

15. By sending any original written matter suitable for pictorial illustration intended for publication in the form of cartoons, pamphlets, verses, dialogues, magazine articles – only MSS intended for illustration are invited.

16.   By supplying the Society with hand printed publications –
made from wood blocks, etchings, stencil plates etc.

17.   By organising Local Meetings for the encouragement of
Stencilling, Wood Engraving etc., in order that Members may
learn or improve themselves in the art of printing by hand.

*

All communications in connection with the Suffrage Atelier
should be sent to the Hon. Secretary

E. B. Willis,
53 Broadhurst Gardens
Finchley Road N.W.

[Three additional pages announce the next General Meeting on
8 May 1909 at Adelphi Terrace House, where members would
be received by Edith Craig; an exhibition of sketches by Hope
Joseph in the Studio at 53 Broadhurst Gardens; and the retail
and wholesale rates for Suffrage Atelier postcards.]

Source: Suffrage Atelier Papers, Fawcett Archives, Fawcett
Library, Box 154 (undated, *c.* 1909).

Addresses

1.   **1909**: 53 Broadhurst Gardens, Finchley Road, N.W.
See A E H J (Hope Joseph), 'The Intolerable Burden of the
Vote', reproduced in the *Women's Franchise*, 1 April 1909; and
E B W (E. B. Willis) postcard 'The Petition' (Fawcett Collec-
tion), both of which are inscribed 'published by the S.A.' at this
address. See also the Atelier papers cited above.

2.   **1909**: 192 Marylebone Road
This address and the name of the Hon. Sec. as Eva Joseph are
given in the *Common Cause* (24 June 1909, p. 144) and on the
flyer for the Caxton Hall meeting on the 26 June 1909.

3.   **1910**: 1 Pembroke Cottages, Edwardes Square, Kensington
First given for the 'office and workshop' of the Atelier in the
Common Cause, 17 February 1910, p. 634. The Hon. Sec. is
listed as Miss E. B. Willis, later referred to as the 'Hon.
Organiser'. This was the address that Laurence and Clemence
Housman took over from the artist William Rothenstein in
1902. Laurence recalled with affection the early nineteenth-
century cottage at the corner of Edwardes Square and the still
smaller cottage at the end of the garden 'which having been
converted into a studio, gave good extra accommodation' (1937,
p. 194). On 23 July 1909 the Suffrage Atelier placed an advertisement in *Votes for Women*, appealing for a room in a central
location 'to be used for banner-making etc.', at low or no rent.
The Housmans, already associated with the Atelier, seem to
have come to its aid. Laurence (1937, p. 274) notes without any
precise date that his studio became 'the home of the Suffrage
Atelier where banners were made for the movement'. My
thanks to Mr J. A. Gatehouse who has lived at 1 Pembroke
Cottages since 1947.

4.   **1910–11**: 4 Stanlake Villas, Hammersmith
The programme of the Suffrage Fair (October 1910: see Maud
Arncliffe-Sennett Collection, vol. 11, p. 47) gives Miss Willis's
address as 4 Stanlake Villas. The *Vote*, 23 December 1911,
p. 108, refers to a Christmas party and exhibition of work at the
Atelier studio at the same address.

5.   **1912**: 6 Stanlake Villas, Hammersmith
The *Vote*, 20 April 1912, remarked that the 'new quarters into
which the Suffrage Atelier has lately overflowed will give
greater scope for the energies of its talented staff'. This is the
address which appears with the owl motif from Athenian coins
on Atelier posters from 1912. It is also that listed in Kelly's
Directory and the *Suffrage Annual and Women's Who's Who*
(1913). In 1914, Kelly's Directory gave the occupants as the
Atelier, Miss Willis, and Joseph Hope (in error for Hope
Joseph, her longstanding friend). In 1915 it listed them again, as
artists, but made no reference to the Atelier, which had probably ceased to exist on the outbreak of war. Stanlake Villas is
now demolished. The Housmans continued to live at Edwardes
Square, and Clemence to make banners there. It is likely that
the 'new quarters' were used for printing in the poster campaign
initiated by the Atelier early in 1912.

6.   **1913–14**: 2 Robert Street, Adelphi
For a period between 1913 and 1914 the Atelier listed as its
office address in the suffrage press the premises of the Minerva
Publishing Co. (which published the *Vote*). On 20 March 1914
the *Common Cause* noted that Miss Vaughan Jenkins,
proprietress of the Betterment Book Shop, would be 'one of the
Suffrage Atelier's principal selling agents now that the office in
Robert Street has been closed'. *Votes for Women* dropped the
Robert Street listing between its issues of 5 and 12 June 1914.

According to the *Programme and Order of March* for the
Women's Coronation Procession, published by the Women's
Press, 1911 (Museum of London), the mark of the Suffrage
Atelier was an owl; its colours blue, orange and black; its banner
'the figure of Athene with all her symbols, the owl, olive, cock,
serpent, sphinx, the Victory and Medusa head'. (The banner
has not survived.)

There is no comparable body of information for the Artists'
Suffrage League, although two years of Annual Reports survive
(Fawcett Archives, Box 153) and there is a brief account in the
Suffrage Annual and Women's Who's Who (1913). This gives the
Secretary as Miss Barbara Forbes, and the Committee for
1913: Chairman, Miss Mary Lowndes; Vice-Chairman, Miss
Emily Ford; Hon. Treasurer, Miss Sara Anderson; Mrs
Meeson Coates, Miss Violet Garrard, Miss Bertha Newcombe,
Miss Bethia Shore, Miss B. Wigan, Miss M. V. Wheelhouse.
Its offices were at Mary Lowndes's address: Brittany Studio,
259 King's Road, Chelsea. Its colours were blue and silver and
its banner ('Alliance not Defiance') is in the Museum of
London.

A Checklist of Artists

There are difficulties both in tracing the artists who contributed to suffrage propaganda and in generalising about them. Some designs are anonymous, and information on many names is scarce. The more elusive signatories – including Miss E. B. Willis, Honorary Secretary of the Suffrage Atelier – were probably amateurs. Others, like Isobel Pocock, seem to have been minor and otherwise unrecorded members of Victorian artist-families. Most of those who can be traced were women, and women who had trained in the more sympathetic late nineteenth-century artistic environments: in the progressive art schools, particularly the Slade, within the Arts and Crafts movement, or in ateliers abroad.

ASL refers to an affiliation with the Artists' Suffrage League, SA with the Suffrage Atelier. Where dates are not given they are not available. This is not an exhaustive list, and no attempt has been made to identify illustrators who contributed cartoons to the suffrage press. I have drawn on the standard dictionaries of artists and illustrators, on information in the art and suffrage press including *The Year's Art*, on the records of the Slade, Royal College of Art and Royal Academy, on published and unpublished reminiscences and family contacts. I am grateful to all those who answered questions and offered advice.

Adkins, Harriet S.   ASL
Exhib. 1911–14
ASL postcard 'No Representation'.

Andrews, Emily J. Harding, active 1877–1902   ASL
Miniaturist and illustrator of children's books. Born Emily Harding, married the painter Edward Andrews. Exhib. RA and Royal Miniature Society. Illustrated a number of books in the 1890s (see R. E. D. Sketchley, *English Book-Illustration of To-Day*, Kegan Paul, Trench, Trübner & Co, London, 1903), some of which she translated. Author of several ASL posters and postcards.

Barker, May H.   ASL
Exhib. 1884–1909
Figure, black and white, and relief artist. Member of ASL committee until her death in 1912. Exhib. RA and elsewhere.

Bartels, Mary   WSPU
There is no information on this artist.

Billing, Clara (Mrs Jones)   ASL
Exhib. 1910–39
Painter and sculptor. Studied at Manchester School of Art, the Royal College of Art and in Paris. Member of ASL committee before 1913.

Brackenbury, Georgina, 1865–1949
Exhib. 1891–1907
Portrait painter. Exhib. RA and elsewhere. Studied at the Slade 1888–90. Sister of Marie Brackenbury (qv), daughter of General Charles Brackenbury RA, niece of General Sir Henry Brackenbury, Director General of Ordnance at the War Office during the Boer War. With her mother and sister an ardent, militant suffragist, also a Tax Resister and a prominent WSPU speaker. Served brief sentences in Holloway in 1908 and 1912. The Brackenbury home at 2, Campden Hill Square served as a refuge for 'Cat and Mouse' prisoners, and was known as Mouse Castle. Her portrait of Emmeline Pankhurst (1927) is in the National Portrait Gallery.

Brackenbury, Marie, 1866–1946
Exhib. 1899–1907
Landscape painter. Exhib. New Gallery and elsewhere. Studied at the Slade from 1888. Sister of Georgina Brackenbury (qv), and like her a Tax Resister and prominent WSPU speaker. (Both sisters chaired platforms at the Hyde Park meeting of 21 June 1908.) Briefly imprisoned with her sister in 1908 and with her sister and mother in 1912. The Brackenburys joined the WSPU in 1907, and set their artistic careers aside for seven years in order to support it. The *Women's Franchise* (16 January 1908) reproduced Marie's strip cartoon, 'History up to date and more so'. See Marie Brackenbury, 'Some Memories of a Suffragette', *Gateway*, January 1932, pp. 37–38.

Browning, Amy Katherine, 1882–1978
Landscape, still-life and portrait painter. Studied at the Royal College of Art (ARCA in Decorative Painting, 1904) and in Paris. Exhib. RA, the Society of Women Artists, the New English Art Club, the Royal Institute of Oil Painters (of which she was a member) and abroad. Silver medal at the Paris Salon 1912, gold medal 1922. A friend of Sylvia Pankhurst's from the Royal College, she assisted her with the Prince's Skating Rink murals in 1909 (see Pankhurst, 1931, pp. 304–5).

Charlton, C. Hedley   ASL
No information on dates, training or exhibitions. Houfe (1978) notes that he (*sic*) contributed drawings of children in a poster style to *Punch* in 1908. Miss Hedley Charlton's self-consciously cute way with children is reminiscent of Mabel Lucie Atwell. It grates a little now, but it was an important strand in suffrage imagery, disarming and popular. Her 'Good Night Suffrage Prayer' with a little girl and her doll was reproduced in the American campaign. The *Vote* (24 December 1913, p. 152) noted that she was 'organising a Guild of Girl Artists, and deserves notable success, her own work being so full of character and charm'.

Coates, Dora Meeson, d. 1956   ASL
Portrait, landscape, figure and flower painter. Born in Melbourne. Exhib. widely including at the RA, the London Salon, and the Royal Institute of Oil Painters (elected ROI 1919). Studied at the Melbourne National Gallery, at the Slade (1892–93, 1896–98), and at Julian's in Paris. Member of the ASL committee and contributor of designs for postcards and publications including *Beware Suffragists* (c. 1909). For biographical information see Dora Meeson Coates, *George Coates: His Art and His Life*, Dent, London, 1937.

Copsey, Helen Dorothy, b. 1888   SA
Figure and flower painter in watercolour and tempera. Studied at Regent Street Polytechnic 1905–10 and the Royal College of Art 1910–12. Exhib. RA, New English Art Club, Society of Women Artists and elsewhere.

Courtauld, Catherine, 1878–1972   SA
Sister of Samuel Courtauld (1876–1947), head of the Courtauld family firm and art collector, who created and endowed the Courtauld Institute of Art and bequeathed it his collection. It seems that Catherine may have acquired some artistic training while accompanying him on visits to France and Italy at the turn of the century. According to family information she was sent by her father to learn music in Germany but studied sculpture instead. Her monogram is a characteristic 'c' within a larger 'C'. She designed the 'Anti-Suffrage Ostrich', 'Waiting for a Living Wage', the 'Prehistoric Argument' and a number of Suffrage Atelier postcards. I am grateful to her daughter, Mrs Bernard, for answering my queries and for lending me designs.

Craig, Edith (Edy), 1869–1947   SA
Daughter of the actress Ellen Terry and the architect E. W. Godwin, sister of the theatre designer Edward Gordon Craig. Member of the WFL, the Actresses' Franchise League, the Suffrage Atelier and at least seven other suffrage organisations when she was interviewed in 1910. Asked how she received her artistic training, she replied that it came from her early surroundings. (The Godwin–Terry household favoured wooden toys, Japanese prints and Walter Crane. Ellen Terry's autobiography includes a photograph of Edy as a small child in a Japanese kimono.) She was briefly an actress, and became a theatrical costume designer, acquiring skills that were indispensable to suffrage spectacle. She produced Cicely Hamilton's Pageant of Great Women in 1909, and designed the West procession with Laurence Housman for the WSPU demonstration of 23 July 1910. She founded the Pioneer Players in 1911 and staged more than 150 plays in ten years. See interviews in the *Vote*, 12 March 1910, and *Votes for Women*, 15 April 1910; Eleanor Adlard (ed.), *Edy: Recollections of Edith Craig*, with a biographical note by Christopher St John, Frederick Muller, London, 1949; Ellen Terry, *The Story of My Life*, Hutchinson, London [undated]; Julie Holledge, *Innocent Flowers*, Virago, London, 1981.

Dallas, Hilda, 1878–1958   WSPU
Studied at the Slade (1910–11), moving there from the New

Art School in Logan Place. Designed posters advertising *Votes for Women* and the *Suffragette*. The principal of the New Art School was the famous poster artist John Hassall (qv), who produced anti-suffrage designs for the NLOWS.

Downing, Edith E., b. 1857   WSPU
Exhib. 1890–1910
Sculptor, studied at the Slade (from 1892) and under Edward Lanteri. Exhib. RA, Society of Women Artists and elsewhere in London, and in Paris. Member of the committee of the Chelsea branch of the WSPU. Arrested 1910. Designer of a number of WSPU processions including that of 23 July 1910. *Votes for Women* (21 May 1909) advertised copies of statuettes of Christabel Pankhurst and Annie Kenney, available from her Tite Street studio at 5 guineas and 2 guineas respectively.

Drew, Joan Harvey   ASL
Exhib. 1899–1900
Designer and embroiderer. Studied at the Westminster School of Art. See her *Embroidery and Design*, Isaac Pitman, London, 1915, and *A Portfolio of Designs for Embroidery*, Isaac Pitman, London, 1926. The *Studio* (vol. 60, 1914, p. 58) reproduced her 'Panels for a Village Room': hangings executed with the help of a village embroidery class at Chilworth, Surrey, where she lived. Author of a number of ASL posters and postcards. Presumably she also helped with the banners, but there is no information on this.

Dunlop, Marion Wallace, active 1871–1903   WSPU
Portrait and figure painter. Studied at the Slade from 1871. Exhib. RA and elsewhere. Houfe (1978) describes her black and white work as 'extremely competent and heavily art nouveau'. Her work as an illustrator includes *Fairies, Elves and Flower Babies* (1899) and *The Magic Fruit Garden* (1899). She was a member of the Fabian Women's Group and also of the WSPU. In 1909 she was arrested for attempting to stamp an extract from the Bill of Rights on to the wall of St Stephen's Hall. She was sentenced to a month's imprisonment, and because she was refused the status of a political prisoner initiated the hunger-strike, and was released after ninety-one hours without food. Sylvia Pankhurst (1931, p. 359) describes how in 1911 would-be window-breakers 'met Marion Wallace Dunlop, or some other trusted member of the WSPU, at somebody's flat, and were furnished with hammers or black bags filled with flints'.

With Edith Downing she produced the decorative schemes for a number of militant demonstrations.

Florence, Mary Sargant, 1857–1954   ASL
Sister of the sculptor F. W. Sargant. Married an American musician, Henry Smyth Florence, in 1888. Decorative mural painter and fresco artist. (She taught Stanley Spencer fresco painting in preparation for the Burghclere Chapel murals.) Studied at the Slade under Legros and in Paris at the studio of Luc Olivier Merson. Exhib. RA and New English Art Club (member from 1911). Purchased by the Chantrey Bequest (paintings produced in 1913 and 1903), in 1932 and 1949. Lived in Chelsea and at Lord's Wood, Marlow, Bucks, in a house of her own design (see K. Spence, 'A Country Refuge

from Bloomsbury', *Country Life*, 15 November 1973). Walter Crane described her illustrations for *The Crystal Ball* (1895) as full of 'power and decorative feeling'; and the *Studio* (vol. 37, 1906, p. 52) praised the 'confident and virile execution' of her draughtsmanship. In 1912 she won the competition for the 'literature' mural in Chelsea Town Hall, and there are others in the Old School at Oakham and at Lord's Wood. She was a founder member and on the committee of the Women's Tax Resistance League, for which she designed and donated a banner and its badge. In 1914 her goods were distrained and sold for refusal to pay imperial taxes.

She may have had some association with the Suffrage Atelier (the *Vote*, 29 June 1912, p. 177), but produced designs for the Artists' Suffrage League. Jill Craigie's collection contains a drawing and five suffrage prints, including a set of four variants on the theme of 'The Cushion of Advantages'.

Forbes, Barbara, c. 1871–1946   ASL

Barbara Forbes was Mary Lowndes's companion and the paid secretary of the ASL. The design for the Joan of Arc banner has her initials against it. She does not seem to have had a formal artistic training and nothing else by her is signed, but it would be a mistake to underestimate her contribution. She helped to keep the League together, not least by helping with Mary Lowndes's commercial work and releasing her for suffrage activities (Kitty Duff described her as an all-round craftswoman who was indispensable at Lowndes and Drury).

Ford, Emily S., 1851–1930   ASL

Landscape and figure painter. Exhib. RA, London Salon, Society of Women Artists. Studied at the Slade from 1875. Sister of Isabella Ford, a prominent Leeds socialist, suffragist and Quaker, a member of the ILP and active supporter of the Women's Trade Union League. Emily Ford was vice-chairman of the ASL. Dora Meeson Coates (1937, pp. 40–41) described her cottage and studio in Glebe Place as a 'meeting ground for artists, suffragists, people who *did* things' – people as various as Edward Carpenter and the Bishop of Winchester. Her principal suffrage poster is 'They've a Cheek . . .' on the Factory Acts. Her portrait of Josephine Butler is in Leeds City Art Gallery.

Fulleylove, Joan E. A., 1886–1947

Daughter of the architectural draughtsman John Fulleylove. Studied at the Slade 1907–09. Worked as a stained-glass artist (see Cormack, 1985) and jointly with Mabel Esplin carried out the commission for the stained glass in Khartoum Cathedral. (Mabel Esplin assisted with the Pageant of Women's Trades and Professions in 1909.) There is one suffrage postcard by her in the John Johnson Collection, Bodleian Library ('Be just, be generous, give us the key', 1907), published independently.

Garrard, Violet   ASL

Exhib. 1909–25

Exhib. principally at the Walker Gallery, London. Member of the ASL committee. Resident at 43 Glebe Place, Chelsea, a neighbour of Emily Ford's.

Grant, Duncan, 1885–1978   ASL

Painter and decorative artist. Studied at the Westminster School of Art (1902–05), in Italy, in Paris under J. E. Blanche (1906) and at the Slade. His Bloomsbury connections were not only aesthetic: his aunt, Lady Strachey, his cousins Pippa and Pernel, and Ray Costello who married his cousin Oliver Strachey, were all committed and active suffragists. In June 1909 he won first prize with 'Handicapped' (jointly with W. F. Winter's 'Votes for Workers') in the ASL poster competition (apparently not his first submission). He later designed posters for Roger Fry's second Post-Impressionist Exhibition, in support of the scheme to send musical instruments to the front in World War I, and for Shell Mex in the 1930s. See Richard Shone, *Bloomsbury Portraits*, Phaidon, London, 1976.

Herringham, Mrs   ASL

There is no information on Mrs Herringham, who was credited with the needlework on several ASL banners.

Hockin, Olive

Exhib. 1903–15

Figure painter. Studied at the Slade 1901–03 and again 1910–11. Exhib. RA, Society of Women Artists and Walker Art Gallery, Liverpool. Contributed a few designs to the suffrage press, such as the cover for *Votes for Women*, 26 June 1914, with St George and the maiden before an 'Altar of Lust'. Imprisoned for four months in 1913 after Scotland Yard inspectors raided her Notting Hill studio and discovered what the press called a 'Suffragette Arsenal': wire-cutters, hammers, false car licence plates, fire-lighters and bottles of corrosive fluid. In the First World War she became a land-girl, and in 1918 published *Two Girls on the Land: War-time on a Dartmoor farm* (Edward Arnold, London).

Housman, Clemence, 1861–1955   SA

One of the finest wood engravers of the 1890s. Exhib. Baillie Gallery. Sister and lifelong companion of Laurence Housman (qv). Trained with him at the Miller's Lane City and Guilds Art School in Lambeth (a branch of the National Art Training Scheme). Engraved many books after his designs, and as the commercial field diminished, worked for the fine presses of the *fin de siècle*. (Her prints can be seen in the collections of the Victoria and Albert Museum and the British Museum. Rodney Engen, *Laurence Housman*, Catalpa Press, Stroud, Glos, 1983, provides a checklist. Further sources are given in the text.) She was also the author of three remarkable pieces of fiction: *The Werewolf* (1896), *The Unknown Sea* (1898) and *The Life of Sir Aglovale de Galis* (1905). A founder and committee member of the Women's Tax Resistance League, imprisoned for non-payment of taxes in September 1911 (Housman, 1937, tells the story). A skilled needlewoman and according to her brother 'chief banner maker' for the Suffrage Atelier.

Housman, Laurence, 1865–1959   SA

Illustrator, writer, poet and critic. Brother of Clemence (qv) and the poet A. E. Housman. Exhib. Baillie Gallery, Fine Art Society, and New English Art Club. Studied first at the local art school in Bromsgrove, then at the Miller Lane School in South

Lambeth, and afterwards at South Kensington (while Clemence's work for the *Graphic* and the *Illustrated London News* brought in the rent). He became one of the leading book illustrators of the 1890s, contributing to the *Yellow Book*, the *Pageant*, the *Dome* and the *Quarto*, basing his style on the English school of wood engraving of the 1860s which he greatly admired. Engen (1983) gives references, and there is work in the Victoria and Albert Museum. In 1895 Housman succeeded R. A. M. Stevenson as art critic of the *Manchester Guardian*. Failing eyesight caused him to give up illustrative work about 1900. He had already published a book of poems (*The Green Arras*, 1896), and now became a prolific author. The commercial success of *An Englishwoman's Love-Letters* (published anonymously amid much speculation in 1900) brought a measure of financial security on which the Housmans' unpaid labour for the suffrage movement was presumably based.

Laurence was influenced by his sister's outspoken feminism, and both became members of the WSPU. (He left to join the United Suffragists in 1914, sickened by militancy.) He designed the 'From Prison to Citizenship' banner for the Kensington WSPU in 1908 and was a founder member of the Suffrage Atelier, which was based in his studio from 1909. He was also a member of the Men's League for Women's Suffrage, and the writer of a series of biting polemics including *The Bawling Brotherhood* and those collected as *Articles of Faith in the Freedom of Women*. According to Weeks (1981, p. 114) he was a member of the 'Order of Chaeronea', an organisation active from the early 1890s in helping homosexuals in trouble with the law. His homosexual, socialist and feminist politics made him an active member of the British Society for the Study of Sex Psychology, founded in 1914 to campaign for general changes in attitudes to sexuality and for the reform of laws relating to homosexuality.

Jacobs, Louise R. SA
Exhib. 1910–38
Landscape and flower painter. Exhib. RA, Walker Art Gallery (Liverpool), Royal Hibernian Academy, Walker's Gallery. Trained at the Royal College of Art (RCA 1907 in painting). Designer of 'The Appeal of Womanhood' poster and described in the *Suffragette* (8 November 1912) as 'draughtsman of many of the Atelier's publications'. Lived in Chelsea with Mary Wheelhouse (qv) of the Artists' Suffrage League.

Jopling, Louise (Louise Jopling-Rowe), 1843–1933 SA
Portrait, genre and landscape painter. Exhib. extensively including RA, Society of Women Artists, Royal Society of British Artists (first woman to be elected, 1902), Goupil Gallery, Glasgow Institute of the Fine Arts, and Walker Art Gallery (Liverpool). Trained at Heatherley's and in Paris at the studio of Charles Chaplin. Her memoirs (*Twenty Years of My Life: 1867–1887*, John Lane, London, 1925) record that she opened a very popular class for female students on the Paris atelier system in 1886. Founder member of the Women's International Art Club (Paris 1898). Listed in *Some Supporters of the Women's Suffrage Movement* (1897, Fawcett Library). Tax resister. Not,

apparently, a designer, but a supporter of the Suffrage Atelier, lending her studio for meetings (see the *Vote*, 10 August 1912, p. 281).

Joseph, A. E. Hope SA
Exhib. 1907–36
Portrait and landscape painter, woodcut and poster artist, potter. Born in India. Exhib. RA, Society of Women Artists, London Salon. Studied under Stanhope Forbes at Newlyn (Mrs Stanhope Forbes was an artist listed in *Some Supporters of the Women's Suffrage Movement*, 1897, Fawcett Library). Resident in Cornwall 1907 and 1908, but moved to London by 1909 when she exhibited work (and may have been living) at Miss E. B. Willis's address near the Finchley Road. The same address is printed on the earliest Atelier postcards (one by each of them), and both women were later residents at Stanlake Villas, the address of the Suffrage Atelier from 1912. Clearly Hope Joseph had a longstanding relation with the Atelier. Her woodcut style is forceful, witty and accomplished, and it is tempting to speculate that she was responsible for some of the anonymous block-prints such as 'English Inquisitors' and 'McKenna's Cat "Bill"'. (A few postcards are initialled, and together with Cicely Hamilton she produced the Suffrage Atelier's 'A Matter of Sport', Fawcett Collection.)

Lowndes, Mary, 1857–1929 ASL
Pioneer woman stained-glass designer and partner in the firm of Lowndes and Drury. One of eight children of the rector of Sturminster Newton in Dorset (which contains three of her windows). Studied at the Slade from 1883 and privately with the arts and crafts designer Henry Holiday in the late 1880s. Began designing and making windows at the studio of Britten and Gilson in Southwark in the early 1890s. Formed Lowndes and Drury with Alfred Drury, Britten and Gilson's foreman, in 1897. Moved in 1906 to purpose-built studio and workshop accommodation known as 'The Glass House' in Fulham, which provided facilities for independent glass designers, many of them women. For further information on her stained glass see Cormack (1984) to whom I am indebted. (Peter Cormack has a list of about eighty surviving windows by Mary Lowndes, two or three of them designed in collaboration with Emily Ford, qv.) Member of the executive committees of the LSWS and the NUWSS. Chairman of the Artists' Suffrage League. Designer of most of the banners executed for the NUWSS for the demonstration of 13 June 1908 and of the Women's Pageant of Trades and Professions in 1909. Probably (and despite her asthma) the most energetic and influential of all the artists working for the suffrage campaign. She was also a prolific contributor to the *Englishwoman* (1910–20) and active in the organisation of the Women Welders' Union in the First World War (see the *Englishwoman*, vol. 34, 1917, pp. 20–32).

Mills, Ernestine (née Bell), 1871–1959
Metalworker and enameller. Exhib. RA, Arts and Crafts Exhibition Society, Society of Women Artists (member of the council), and Walker Art Gallery (Liverpool). Trained at the Slade, at Finsbury Central Technical School (enamels prize),

and studied enamelling with Alexander Fisher. Her work is reproduced in the *Studio* (vol. 37, 1906, pp. 214–15; vol. 39, 1907, pp. 168–69), and in Callen (1979), p. 158. She edited the *Life and Letters of Frederic Shields* (1912), added a biographical note to *Frederic Shields: The Chapel of the Ascension* (1912) and published a book on *The Domestic Problem, Past, Present and Future* (1925) as well as numerous articles. She won a silver medal at the Paris Salon as late as 1955.

Apparently independently of any of the suffrage societies, published two postcards herself: 'The New Mrs Partington' and 'The Anti Suffragist!' (verse by C. P. Stetson).

Morris, May, 1862–1938
Embroiderer, jeweller, designer of fabrics and wallpaper. Trained by her father, William Morris. Took over the Morris, Marshall, Faulkner and Co. embroidery workshop in 1885. Published *Decorative Needlework* (1893), lectured on embroidery in the USA (1910) and directed the embroidery class at the Central School of Arts and Crafts, London. First president of the Women's Guild of Art, founded 1907. Member of the Fabian Women's Group and designer of the banner they made collectively for the suffrage processions of 1908.

New, Edmund Hort, 1871–1931
Etcher and illustrator specialising in topographical subjects. Exhib. RA, Royal Society of Artists (Birmingham). Studied and taught at Birmingham School of Art. (His meticulous black and white work is considered typical of the 'Birmingham style'.) Illustrated an extensive list of periodicals and books including several on Oxford where he spent much of his working life: *Oxford and its Colleges* (1897), *The Towers of Oxford* (1908), *High Street Oxford* (1912). Designed the banner for the Oxford Women Students' Society for Women's Suffrage, 1912 (known only from its illustration on a published postcard).

Newcombe, Bertha, d. 1947   ASL
Exhib. 1880–1908
Landscape, figure, portrait and flower painter. Member of the New English Art Club from 1888. Exhib. there and at the RA, Society of Women Artists, Royal Society of British Artists, Walker Art Gallery (Liverpool) etc. Studied at the Slade, 1876. Illustrated various books in the 1890s, and contributed scenes of church and village life to the *English Illustrated Magazine*, 1895–97.

Member of the ASL committee. Her painting of Emily Davis and Elizabeth Garrett presenting the first Women's Suffrage petition to J. S. Mill (1910) is reproduced in Kamm (1966, fig. 2).

Pankhurst, (Estelle) Sylvia, 1882–1960   WSPU
Studied at Manchester School of Art. Won the Proctor Travelling Studentship in 1902 and left for Venice and Florence. Returned in 1903 and won a national scholarship to the Royal College of Art. Left in 1906, and scarcely had time to develop as an artist before she was overwhelmed with suffrage commitments. Wavered between the life of a painter and a life of writing and dedicated political commitment, and by 1910 had settled for the second. Her output divides between the Walter Crane-influenced late Pre-Raphaelite symbolism of her work for the WSPU, and a kind of embryonic social realism developed in paintings of women factory and agricultural workers in 1907. She designed the WSPU membership card, the Holloway badge, a few banners which have not survived, and a decorative scheme for the Prince's Skating Rink Exhibition in 1909 which was re-used in 1911. Her trumpeting angel was adapted for a range of suffragette artefacts including teacups and *Votes for Women*. See her autobiographical *The Suffragette Movement* (1931); Richard Pankhurst, *Sylvia Pankhurst: Artist and Crusader*, Paddington Press, London, 1979; and Patricia Romero, *E. Sylvia Pankhurst: Portrait of a Radical*, Yale University Press, New Haven, 1987.

Patriot, A., pseudonym of **Pearse,** Alfred, 1856–1933   WSPU
Black and white artist, portrait miniaturist, wood engraver and illustrator for numerous books and periodicals including the *Illustrated London News*, the *Strand Magazine, Cassell's Family Magazine* and *Punch*. Exhib. 1880–1900. Studied wood engraving 1872–75. Worked as special artist for the *Pictorial World*, 1879–86, and for the *Sphere* on the Royal colonial tour 1901–03. Contributed to the *Boy's Own Paper*, 1878–1923. Apparently known as 'Punctual Pearse'. As A. Patriot, regular cartoonist for *Votes for Women* from the issue of 18 February 1909 (see pp. 346 and 351). Designer of a number of WSPU posters including those on forcible feeding.

Pocock, Isobel   SA
Designer of several Atelier postcards, perhaps an amateur, possibly a member of the extensive Pocock family of artists. An elusive figure, though the *Studio* reproduced an illuminated page by her in its 'Art School Notes' (vol. 60, 1914, p. 166).

Ridley, Ada Paul   WSPU
Exhib. 1908, London Salon. Contributor to *An Anti-Suffrage Alphabet* by Laurence Housman, stencils by Alice B. Woodward (qv), Pamela C. Smith (qv) and Ada P. Ridley, ed. Leonora Tyson, WSPU, 1911 (Laurence Housman collection, item 347, University College London). See also the *East Anglian Daily Times*, 19 June 1911, on the Women's Coronation Procession, which notes that the Ipswich WSPU walked beneath two fine banners designed by Ada Ridley and made by her workers.

Shore, Bethia E. L.   ASL
Exhib. 1891–1914
Landscape painter. Exhib. London Salon, Walker Art Gallery, Liverpool, and the Salon des Indépendants, Paris, from 1906. Member of the ASL committee.

Shute, E. L.   ASL
Exhib. 1883–89
Watercolourist and portrait painter. Exhib. Society of Women Artists, Royal Hibernian Academy. The ASL brought out 'The Widows' Children' by Mrs Shute in 1910.

Smith, Pamela Coleman, b. *c*. 1877   SA
Exhib. 1905–17
American painter and illustrator of children's books. Moved to

England *c.* 1899. Exhib. Baillie Gallery 1905–17. Associated with Walter Crane, Edward Gordon Craig (see the *Page*, 1901), W. B. Yeats and others. Published her own craft magazine the *Green Sheaf* 1903–04 (Callen, 1979, p. 226). Influenced like Beggarstaff and Craig by the stumpy black outlines of the chapbook style. Contributed stencils to *An Anti-Suffrage Alphabet* (see note on Ada Ridley), and poster designs for the Suffrage Atelier (initialled P S).

Thomson-Price, Louisa
Radical member of a Tory family who worked for the Women's Liberal Federation in the 1890s. An admirer of Charles Brad-laugh and a member of the National Secular Society. A journal-ist for twenty-four years who also contributed cartoons to the *Political World*. Left the constitutional suffragists to join the W F L, becoming consulting editor of the *Vote* and one of the directors of the Minerva Publishing Company. Her cartoon of Asquith as 'Little Jack Horner' for the *Vote* was 'by special request transformed into a poster' for the General Election of January 1910; and her 'Anti-Suffragist Types' were repro-duced as postcards. See the *Vote*, 14 May 1910, for further details.

Walters, Jessica Lloyd S A
Exhib. 1905–39
Portrait, figure and landscape painter. Exhib. Cooling and Sons Gallery, London Salon. Resident in Paris (*c.* 1905–08). Played the maid in a Bristol performance of Cicely Hamilton and Christopher St John's *How the Vote was Won*, November 1910. May have been the Miss Walters who was a member of the Women's Tax Resistance League. Author of several striking designs for the Suffrage Atelier ('Eliza Comes to Stay', 'As-quith, Traitor to Liberal Principles').

Watts, Caroline M., b. *c.* 1868 A S L
Studied at the Slade from 1886. Produced medievalist illustra-tions, some with complicated Celtic interlacings, for the Irish Saga Library and the Arthurian Romances Series, 1899–1904 (see British Library catalogue). Designer of the A S L/N U W S S 'Bugler Girl' for the procession of 13 June 1908.

Wheelhouse, Mary V., active 1895–1947 A S L
Painter and illustrator, particularly of children's books. Exhib. Baillie Gallery (one-woman exhibition, December 1912); one or two pictures at R A, New Gallery, Society of Women Artists. Born in Yorkshire and probably a student at Scarborough School of Art, 1895. Studied in Paris for three years. Lived in Chelsea from 1900. Extensive list of books illustrated includes many works by women writers: Louisa M. Alcott (*Little Women*, 1909; *Good Wives*, 1911); Charlotte Brontë (*Jane Eyre*, 1911); George Eliot (*Silas Marner*, 1910); Mrs Gaskell (*Cousin Phyllis*, 1908; *Cranford*, 1909; *Sylvia's Lovers*, 1910; *Wives and Daugh-ters*, 1912). Much of her illustrative work was commissioned by the publisher George Bell. Designed postcards for the A S L and was a member of its committee. Shared an address in Cheyne Walk, Chelsea, with Louise Jacobs (qv) of the Suffrage Atelier. Exhibited toys with her at the Arts and Crafts Exhibition Society in 1916.

Wigan, Bessie (Mrs Charles Marriott) A S L
Exhib. 1894–1939
Watercolour painter. Exhib. Walker Gallery, Goupil Gallery, Royal Hibernian Academy, Society of Women Artists. Listed in *Some Supporters of the Women's Suffrage Movement* (1897, Faw-cett Library). Member of the A S L committee.

Willis, E. B. S A
There is no information on Miss E. B. Willis, Hon. Secretary and then Hon. Organiser of the Suffrage Atelier. There are two S A postcards with the initials E.B.W. in the John Johnson Collection, Bodleian Library. She was almost certainly an amateur.

Wilson, E. Hartley
One postcard in the Museum of London, 'On the Cromer Beach'. Probably an amateur.

Winter, W. F. A S L
Designer of 'Votes for Workers', and joint winner with Duncan Grant (qv) of the A S L/N U W S S poster competition in 1909. Apparently resident in Amsterdam. Clearly a professional artist, but one on whom there is apparently no further information.

Woodward, Alice Bolingbroke, b. 1862 W S P U? A S L?
Watercolourist and illustrator. Contributed to *Cassell's Maga-zine*, the *Daily Graphic*, the *Illustrated London News*, the *Quarto*, and to a long list of books illustrated in the 1890s (including *Alice in Wonderland*) that were greatly admired by the *Studio*. Exhib. R A, the Royal Society of British Artists, the Royal Institute of Painters in Watercolours and elsewhere. Daughter of Dr Henry Woodward, Keeper of Geology at the British Museum. Drew in the Greek and Roman galleries as a child and made drawings and scientific illustrations for her father. Her earnings as a professional illustrator apparently paid for her art education: at the Westminster School of Art, at the Royal College (where she co-founded the student magazine in 1882 and worked in the etching class), and at Julian's in Paris (see the Royal College student magazine, February 1912, vol. 1 no. 3). Contributed stencils to *An Anti-Suffrage Alphabet*, ed. Leonora Tyson and inscribed W S P U (see under Ada Ridley: item 347, Laurence Housman Collection, University College London); but is also mentioned in relation to the A S L Pageant of Women's Trades and Professions in 1909 (as is the black and white artist Ellen C. Woodward). Presumably also related to Kate Woodward, who designed the A S L postcard 'Evolution'.

Wright, Poyntz S A
There is no information on this artist; the name may be a pseudonym.

Anti-Suffrage Artists

Only Bird and Hassall are known to have produced designs commissioned for publication as posters or postcards by the N L O W S; the bulk of anti-suffrage imagery was 'unofficial', in the sense that it was produced for a popular market by commercial postcard publishers and not by the anti-suffrage organisations.

Bird, Harold

There is no information on Bird, who may have been a competent amateur. He produced several drawings for the *Anti-Suffrage Review*, and three posters for the NLOWS. The best known is 'No Votes Thank You', published as part of the run-up to the anti-suffrage meeting in the Albert Hall of 28 February 1912.

Hassall, John, 1868–1948

Hassall was one of the best known and most prolific illustrators and poster artists of the period. (There are more than fifty titles illustrated by him in the British Library, and a substantial collection of posters in the Victoria and Albert Museum, including 'Colman's Mustard' (*c.* 1900), 'Skegness Is So Bracing' (1908) and Conservative and Unionist party posters for the 1906 and 1910 elections.) Exhib. RA, Royal Society of Artists (Birmingham), Walker Art Gallery (Liverpool), Royal Glasgow Institute of the Fine Arts, Royal Institute of Painters in Watercolours, Royal Miniature Society (elected RI and RMS 1901). Educated in England and Germany. Failed to get into Sandhurst. Emigrated to Manitoba to farm with his brother and sent drawings back to the *Graphic.* Returned to study art in Antwerp and at Julian's in Paris (1891–94), where he came into contact with art nouveau designs including the work of Alphonse Mucha. His graphic style is bold and jaunty, with thick outlines and flat colours. Also produced fine watercolour illustrations for boys' adventure stories (such as those by G. A. Henty). One of the first members of the London Sketch Club, and president in 1903. With one of his old teachers, Charles van Havermaet, founded the New Art School (later the Hassall School of Art) and ran it for more than twenty years. His daughter is the distinguished wood engraver Joan Hassall, a past Master of the Art Workers' Guild (1972).

On Hassall see 'The London Sketch Club', *Magazine of Art*, March 1899; 'The Poster Paintings and Illustrations of John Hassall RI', the *Studio*, vol. 36, 1906; the *Studio*, Winter number 1900–01. David Cuppleditch, *The John Hassall Lifestyle*, Dilke Press, London 1979, is not altogether reliable. The artist's day-books and diaries are preserved in the Essex University archives. They have detailed information on his commissions and give some idea of the enormous amount of work he produced. On 16 January 1912 he despatched 'Perfect Woman', 'A Suffragette's Home' (and 'An Allegory', later returned and apparently not used), and on 19 March 'Going Shopping' and 'Sermons in Stones' – all anti-suffrage designs for Captain Creed of the NLOWS. (The NLOWS set up a special campaign committee which drew up plans for agitation at the turn of 1911–12, culminating in the Albert Hall meeting of February 1912.) My thanks to John Sandford for help with John Hassall.

A Checklist of Surviving Posters

All posters are in the Fawcett Collection and/or the Museum of London except where alternative locations are given. Titles and dates are derived from information in the suffrage press, particularly Suffrage Atelier advertisements and broadsheets, and the list of Artists' Suffrage League posters in the *ABC of Politics* (ASL, 1909).

Artists' Suffrage League

Bugler girl
Caroline Watts, 1908
Schlesinger Library, Radcliffe College, USA.
First produced to advertise the NUWSS procession of 13 June 1908.

Coming in with the tide / Mrs Partington
Emily J. Harding Andrews, undated, printed by Carl Hentschel Ltd.
Inevitability of women's suffrage.

The dog in the manger
Anonymous, 1908–09
Anti-suffragists standing in the way of women who want the vote.

Factory Acts / They have a cheek. I've never been asked
Emily Ford (signed), 1908
Women denied a voice in the laws affecting their livelihood.

Handicapped
Duncan Grant, 1909, joint prizewinner of ASL competition with W. F. Winter's VOTES FOR WORKERS.
Library of Congress, Washington, USA.
Women handicapped in all respects by the lack of a parliamentary vote.

It is time I got out of this place / Convicts and lunatics
Emily J. Harding Andrews, 1908–09, reprinted 1910 'in response to urgent demands'. Printed by Weiners of Acton.
Indignity of women being classed with convicts and lunatics as their 'political peers'.

Justice at the door
Mary Lowndes, 1912, in relation to parliamentary debates on the Reform Bill. Published not by the ASL but by the NUWSS directly.
Justice and equal rights.

Justice demands the vote
Anonymous, 1909, published by the Brighton and Hove branch of the NUWSS and distributed through the ASL.
Justice and equal rights.

Political help
Dora Meeson Coates (signed), designed 1907, won the NUWSS/ASL poster competition and was published by the NUWSS in 1908.
Communist Party Archives. Also Library of Congress, Washington, USA.
Women no longer prepared to function as party-political auxiliaries; if they are politically capable they should have the vote on their own account.

Votes for mother / She works for us now father's dead
Joan Drew, 1910. Schlesinger Library, Radcliffe College, USA. Not to be confused with THE WIDOW'S CHILDREN, by Mrs Shute, 1910, an ASL poster which does not appear to have survived.
Women as breadwinners need the vote.

Votes for workers
W. F. Winter (signed), 1909. Joint winner of the ASL poster competition with Duncan Grant's HANDICAPPED.
Votes for working-class women (or in a narrower reading, to protect them from exploitation).

What's sauce for the gander is sauce for the goose
Mary Sargant Florence, 1908, reprinted 1910. Printed by Weiners of Acton.
Communist Party Archives.
Equal rights.

Why won't they let the women help?
Joan Harvey Drew, 1909
Women anxious to contribute to the burden of government (women's votes good for men).

Womanhood offers her gifts at her country's door
Joan Harvey Drew (initialled), 1909. Published as a window bill with a space to advertise meetings.
As above.

Won't you let me help you John?
Joan Harvey Drew, 1909, printed and published by David Allen and Son Ltd.
As above.

Suffrage Atelier

The anti-suffrage ostrich
Catherine Courtauld, undated
Anti-suffrage ignorance.

The appeal of womanhood
Louise R. Jacobs, 1912. Used on the Edinburgh-to-London march of the 'Brown Women' in 1912, and probably a riposte to

Harold Bird's NO VOTES THANK YOU, published for the anti-suffrage meeting at the Albert Hall in February 1912.
The Womanly Woman wants the vote; with special reference to the white slave traffic.

Asquith traitor to liberal principles
J.W. (probably Jessica Walters), *c.* 1913. The Museum of London has both the poster and a related print that may have been a study for it.
No taxation without representation.

Bogies / Votes for women
Anonymous, undated
Irrational fears of women's suffrage: 'petticoat government', the 'unwashed babe', 'woman unsexed'.

180 city and town councils
Anonymous, 1910
180 city and town councils petitioned the government in support of the Conciliation Bill.

The comfortable women
Anonymous, *c.* 1912
Comfortable women (antis) indifferent to burdens of 'unfair legislation', 'starvation wages', 'economic servitude' and 'social evil'.

Crowded out
Catherine Courtauld, undated.
Women's exclusion from parliamentary legislation.

Drink it up daddy
S.R.P., *c.* 1912
Women's suffrage good for the state.

Eliza comes to stay
Jessica Walters, undated.

The English inquisitors
Anonymous, *c.* 1912
Forcible feeding.

Franchise villa
Anonymous, undated.
Determination of suffragists; inevitability of women's suffrage.

The growing movement
Probably E. T. Dana, *c.* 1912
Growing support for women's suffrage. Adapted from Edward Lear.

How the law protects . . .
MaC, 1909
A set of six posters on the legal disabilities of women: the widow, the widower, the husband, the wife, the mother, the daughters.

In the dim and speculative future
Gladys Letcher, 1909
On 26 May 1908 Asquith was asked by a Liberal anti-suffrage MP what would happen if a women's amendment to the proposed Reform Bill were carried. He replied that his honourable friend had asked 'a contingent question with regard to a remote and speculative future'.

In the shadow
Anonymous, *c.* 1912
Women's exclusion from the franchise enhances their economic vulnerability.

John Bull's horse
Anonymous, undated
Equal rights, women's suffrage better for men.

John Bull's umbrella
Anonymous, *c.* 1912
Women not protected by their husbands' votes.

Judy asks a question of the Liberal Party
Anonymous, undated
Women's suffrage and party politics. The majority of Liberals in favour of the women's vote.

Judy drops a hint to the Labour Party
Anonymous, undated
Women's suffrage and party politics. 'To remind it that Men and Women believe that the party can and will demand suffrage for women.'

Judy throws a plank to the Unionist Party
Anonymous, undated
Women's suffrage and party politics. The many supporters of women's suffrage could help the Conservatives back into power.

Lloyd George / Taxation and representation
Anonymous, *c.* 1913. Set of four posters, the other three featuring portraits of Lord Haldane, John Burns and Sir Edward Grey.
Party political principle and practice (no taxation without representation).

McKenna's cat 'Bill'
Anonymous, *c.* 1913
Suffragists will defeat the 'Cat and Mouse' Bill brought in by the Home Secretary, Reginald McKenna, in 1913.

Modern chivalry
Anonymous, *c.* 1913
Addressed to anti-suffrage 'chivalry is women's protection' arguments.

No vote no tax
Anonymous, 1912. Available as a poster, but has survived only as a postcard.
No taxation without representation / payment of MPs (introduced by Lloyd George, 1911).

The paid piper
Anonymous, 1912. Available as a poster, but has survived only as a postcard.
As above.

Political conjuring
Hope Joseph, 1912. Available as a poster, but has survived only as a postcard.
Asquith and the proposed Reform Bill.

Polling station
Anonymous, undated
Fitness for the vote: men with, and women without the franchise.

The prehistoric argument
Catherine Courtauld, 1912
Addressed to anti arguments from 'separate spheres'.

She ain't fit to vote
Anonymous, undated
Fitness for the vote: respectable women and drunken men.

There was an old dame in a huff
Anonymous, 1912. After Edward Lear.
Outdated antis: the Old Dame in a Huff is a thinly veiled reference to Mrs Humphry Ward.

There was an old man who said how
Poyntz Wright, c. 1912–13. Adapted from Edward Lear.
Parliamentary procrastination, probably in relation to the Reform Bill.

Twentieth century robbery!
Gladys Letcher, 1912
No taxation without representation: caricatures of Asquith, and Lloyd George as Chancellor of the Exchequer.

The unionist leaders
Anonymous (comparable with ASQUITH TRAITOR TO LIBERAL PRINCIPLES by Jessica Walters), c. 1913
Disraeli, Salisbury, Balfour, Bonar Law: 'The Unionist Leaders 1868 to 1913 in Favor [sic] of Woman Suffrage.'

Waiting for a living wage
Catherine Courtauld, c. 1913
Sweated labour: voteless women powerless to help.

Welsh poster
Anonymous, c. 1913. Posters were designed in Welsh for the Forward Cymric Suffrage Union.
Fitness for the vote: the Welsh inscription contrasts the woman freeholder without a vote and her hired labourer who has one.

What a woman may be and yet not have the vote
Anonymous, c. 1912
Fitness for the vote: women mayors, teachers, mothers, doctors, nurses, factory hands denied it; male convicts, lunatics, white slave traders, drunkards and those unfit for service able to use or regain it.

What may happen
Anonymous, 1912
Controversy over Lloyd George's Insurance Bill: women excluded from legislation concerning them.

White slave traffic
Anonymous, undated, probably issued around the time of the White Slave Traffic Bill in 1912.
'Woman Suffrage, The Only Solution' to sexual and economic exploitation.

Who's afraid: not I
Anonymous, c. 1911–12. Available as a poster, but has survived only as a postcard.
The Conciliation Bill: which would have enfranchised approximately one woman for every seven men.

Who will be St George?
Anonymous, undated
Asquith as the dragon, six women's suffrage bills having gone down.

Women underpaid – men out of work
Anonymous, c. 1913
Women's wages and the vote: 'Let's help to get them the vote and a living wage.'

WSPU

The cat and mouse act
Anonymous, 1914. Printed by David Allen.
Cat and Mouse Act.

The modern inquisition
A. Patriot (Alfred Pearse), 1910
Forcible feeding: torture of women.

The right dishonourable double-face Asquith
A. Patriot (Alfred Pearse), 1909 (for the General Election of January 1910).
The struggle with the House of Lords: 'The Government pose as champions of the Constitution, but deny constitutional liberty to women.'

The suffragette
M. Bartels, probably 1914 (when a new poster by Miss Bartels was advertised).
Advertisement for the Suffragette, *which replaced* Votes for Women *as the* WSPU *newspaper after the departure of the Pethick-Lawrences in 1912.*

The suffragette
Hilda Dallas, 1912
Advertisement for the Suffragette *featuring Joan of Arc with the* WSPU *banner. Hilda Dallas had designed another poster for* Votes for Women *in 1909.*

Torturing women in prison
A. Patriot (Alfred Pearse), 1914 (by-election poster). Published by the WSPU and David Allen.
Forcible feeding.

Votes for women
Hilda Dallas, 1912
Advertisement for Votes for Women.

Votes for women: the people *not* the commons must decide
A. Patriot (Alfred Pearse), 1910 (for the December General Election).
The struggle with the Lords: Asquith between a woman and a peer (based on a contemporary Ripolin advertisement). Equal constitutional rights.

What is sauce for the goose, is sauce for the gander
A. Patriot (Alfred Pearse), 1910 (for the December General Election). The poster itself has not survived, but the design is reproduced on the cover of *Votes for Women*, 25 November 1910.
The struggle with the Lords; equal constitutional rights.

Official Anti-Suffrage Posters
(NLOWS)

Going shopping *(known only as postcard)*
John Hassall, 1912. According to the Hassall diary and day-books in the University of Essex archives, he sent off 'A Suffragette's Home', 'Perfect Woman' and 'An Allegory' (later returned) on 16 January 1912 (presumably as part of the campaign leading up to the Albert Hall anti-suffrage meeting in February), and 'Sermons in Stones' and 'Going Shopping' (which only survive as postcards) on 19 March. He was paid £10 for each of them. Printed and published by J. Miles and Co. John Johnson Collection, Bodleian Library, and private collections.
Window smashing; the plain spinster.

John Bull: 'You will excuse me if I laugh'
Harold Bird, 1912.
John Johnson Collection, Box 3, Bodleian Library.
WSPU portrait painter misrepresents the plain suffragette as feminine martyr.

No votes thank you / The appeal of womanhood
Harold Bird, 1912. Printed by J. Miles and Co. Produced for the anti-suffrage Albert Hall meeting, February 1912.
John Johnson Collection, Box 3, Bodleian Library.
The Womanly Woman refuses the vote.

A perfect woman, nobly planned *(known only as postcard)*
John Hassall, 1912 (see above).
Fawcett Collection, John Johnson Collection, Bodleian Library, and private collections.
Suffragette as hysterical virago.

Referendum storm
C.H.R., undated.
John Johnson Collection, Box 3, Bodleian Library.
The ship of women's suffrage runs aground on the rocks of a referendum.

Sermons in stones
John Hassall, 1912 (see above). Printed and published by J. Miles and Co.
John Johnson Collection, Bodleian Library, and private collections.
Window smashing; the 'mannish' woman.

A suffragette's home
John Hassall, 1912 (see above).
John Johnson Collection, Box 3, Bodleian Library.
The neglected (working-class) home.

A Checklist of Surviving Banners

Flags and typographical banners are not included. Dates are usually derived from contemporary press reports and photographs. Measurements are given where available (many banners are fragile, and some are not accessible). The Museum of London (and some other collections) have detailed accession cards on which I have drawn. The diverse ways in which the banners were originally fringed, tasselled and suspended from their frames are best seen in the original designs in the Lowndes album.

ML: Museum of London Collection

FAW: Fawcett Collection

Lowndes: Designed by Mary Lowndes, or from her album, or credited in contemporary accounts to the Artists' Suffrage League.

Actresses' Franchise League

Hanging masks of comedy and tragedy framed by wreaths and ribbons stencilled in the AFL colours of pink and green. Used in 1911, may be earlier. (The AFL Musicians' Section had a banner of their own.) ML.

Susan B. Anthony

Lowndes (album p. 56), 1908. Stars above a broad chevron with the name SUSAN B. ANTHONY and vertical stripes below. One of a trio of banners (the others dedicated to Lucy Stone and Elizabeth Cady Stanton), apparently ordered from the ASL by Americans marching in the NUWSS procession of 1908 (*Daily Chronicle*, 11 June 1908). Mrs Stewart, president of the Illinois State Woman's Suffrage Association and one of the leaders of the procession, took the Cady Stanton banner back to the United States for an exhibition in Illinois (NUWSS Exec. Com. minutes, 3 July 1908, Fawcett Archives, Box 83). FAW.

Artists' [Suffrage] League

Lowndes?, 1908. Rectangle with single inverted scallop at bottom edge. 206 cm long, 150 cm wide. Light blue silk with sprigs of flowers (similar fabric was used in the Cambridge banner, qv); pink, turquoise and green. ARTISTS' LEAGUE in metal braid on pink ribbed fabric along the top. Decorative central circular wreath design with motto ALLIANCE NOT DEFIANCE above and below. (A suitably constitutional motto in the tradition of the more conciliatory trade unions: Gorman (1973, p. 74) cites the St Helen's Sheet Glass Flatteners' 'Defence Not Defiance'.) A second Artists' banner with the motto 'Post Laborem Palma' was carried in the NUWSS procession of June 1908. It does not appear to have survived. ML.

Jane Austen

Lowndes, 1908. Rectangle with JANE AUSTEN on riband, dates 1775–1817, above device of quill on open book. Rust and cream. FAW.

Katherine Bar-Lass

Lowndes, 1908. Shield shape with pole-loops above. Device of arm and hand pushed through two latches against a heart. Rust. (Kate Bar-Lass was the popular name for the Scottish heroine Catherine Douglas, whose arm was broken in 1437 when she thrust it through the staple of an unbarred door in an attempt to thwart the would-be murderers of James I.) FAW.

A. Montgomerie Beddoe [*et al.*]

Rectangular, purple velvet, with large central cartouche embroidered with the names of A. Montgomerie Beddoe, Mary Carpenter, Frances Power Cobbe, Lilias Ashworth, Hallett, Adelaide Manning, Harriet Martineau. Appliquéd arts and crafts stylised flowers above. FAW.

Teresa Billington Greig

WFL. Rectangle of cream and green fabrics meeting in a battlemented border. 122 cm long, 86 cm wide. TERESA BILLINGTON GREIG and two stars worked in gold thread outlined in green ribbon, and below HOLLOWAY in green woollen thread outlined in metal braid. There is an otherwise identical banner with the name of Mrs Despard. ML.

Black Agnes of Dunbar

Lowndes (album p. 66 shows axe-head pole), 1908. Rectangle with battlemented design above and below. BLACK AGNES OF DUNBAR, and below in a cartouche: 'Came they early came they late / They found Black Agnes at the Gate.' Black, orange and yellow. (Agnes Douglas, Countess of Dunbar and March, held Dunbar Castle against an English siege in 1339.) National Museum of Antiquities, Scotland.

Elizabeth Blackwell

Lowndes, 1908. Rectangle with V at lower edge. ELIZABETH BLACKWELL MD 1849 above the medical device of a serpent and a lamp. Green. (Elizabeth Blackwell was the first woman to qualify as a doctor in America.) FAW.

Boadicea

Lowndes (album p. 21), 1908. Shield-shaped. 132 cm long, 81 cm wide. BOADICEA in gold paint on cream silk along the top. Wheel motif with scythe-like attachment on diagonal band; mistletoe above, vertical daggers below. Cream, green, orange and blue. *Banners*, the pamphlet drawn up by the Brighton Society of the NUWSS in January 1909, refers to Boadicea standing in her chariot between her two daughters as 'this heroic figure of woman, mother, and ruler' who 'represents a type of the "eternal feminine" – the guardian of the hearth, the avenger of its wrongs upon the defacer and despoiler'. ML.

Britannia

Rectangle of silk satin. 78 cm long. 50 cm wide. Design of

Britannia with trident, shield, and swirling drapery; appliquéd and embroidered in khaki and cream and boldly outlined in black. Main motto NO VOTE NO TAX. Inscription on Britannia's pedestal WOMENS TAX RESISTANCE LEAGUE. The museum has another version in white linen, with black, brown and silver paint. There is also a block-printed poster, possibly by the Suffrage Atelier. ML.

Elizabeth Browning
Lowndes, 1908. Rectangle with five pole-tabs at the top. 100 cm long, 90 cm wide. ELIZABETH B. BROWNING appliquéd across the top, central device of pink silk roses and purple velvet fleur-de-lis, HONOUR US WITH TRUTH along the bottom. Cream, blue, green, brilliant pink and purple; linen, velvets, silks, metal braid. ML.

Fanny Burney
Lowndes, 1908. Shield-shaped. FANNY BURNEY in top third. Fabric with alternating wreaths and fleur-de-lis below. White and dull blue. FAW.

Josephine Butler
Lowndes, 1908. Rectangular with inverted V at bottom edge. JOSEPHINE BUTLER in top third. Gold fleur-de-lis on blue ground below. (*Banners*: 'A worker in a moral field which all shrink from, but which yet belongs most especially to women'.) FAW.

Cambridge Alumnae
Lowndes (album p. 33, initialled), 1908. Worked by the students of Newnham and Girton. Rectangular. Central oval design with boats, bridge and book on sprigged blue silk background (cf. the Artists' League banner); CAMBRIDGE ALUMNAE on riband above and BETTER IS WISDOM THAN WEAPONS OF WAR on riband below. Vertical velvet borders stencilled in silver with the daisies of Newnham and the irises of Girton. (The *Daily Chronicle* thought these were embroidered. Perhaps this had been intended.) The *Women's Franchise* (28 May 1908) had suggested that the banner would bear the motto 'Voteless Women of No Degree'. This was refuted by Dorothy Tarrant on 11 April: 'We are taking part in the Procession as women who claim for our sex the political franchise, and the fact that we in particular are excluded from the degrees of the University of Cambridge is in this connexion irrelevant. That question is to be decided by a particular body, and we feel that nothing would be gained by insisting, on this occasion, upon a point which lies strictly apart from the general question.'

Four hundred women from Newnham and Girton marched in the NUWSS procession of June 1908. There were also representatives and a banner from the Universities of London (qv) and Edinburgh respectively. Newnham College, Cambridge.

Civil Service
Rectangular with pole-tabs. Central wreath motif with CIVIL SERVICE WOMEN'S (above) SUFFRAGE SOCIETY (below). Gold and blue. FAW.

Clitheroe, NUWSS
Rectangular. 152.5 cm long, 99 cm wide. Red, white and green cotton. Appliquéd leaf design with NUWSS above, CLITHEROE SOCIETY below. Small pockets incorporated at lower corners (with red and white roses of Lancashire and Yorkshire), to hold sand to weight the banner. Carried in the Women's Coronation Procession of 17 June 1911, may be earlier. Donated by Mary Cooper, the daughter of Selina Cooper, in whose house the banner was embroidered. Towneley Hall Art Gallery and Museums, Burnley.

Commonwealth of Australia
1908. Rectangular. Dull green ground. Unusual in being painted and not embroidered. Designed and painted by Dora Meeson Coates (see Coates, 1937, p. 63). Carried by the Australian section in the NUWSS procession of 1908. Inscribed COMMONWEALTH OF AUSTRALIA and 'TRUST THE WOMEN MOTHER AS I HAVE DONE' (addressed by the daughter figure of Australia to the maternal figure of Britannia). Purchased by the Commonwealth of Australia for the Parliament Building, Canberra, from the Fawcett Collection, 1987.

Marie Curie
Lowndes (album p. 64), 1908. Rectangular with zigzag bottom edge. 124 cm long, 90 cm wide. Yellow velvet and silk satin. MARIE CURIE in metal braid across brocaded silk panel above. 12 radiating panels of alternate velvet appliqué on pale yellow ground below. RADIUM is appliquéd and outlined in metal braid, one letter in each of the top six panels. ML.

Maria Edgeworth
Lowndes, 1908. Shield-shaped with MARIA EDGEWORTH on diagonal band across sprigged cream background. FAW.

Education
Lowndes, 1908. Given by Philippa Fawcett for the NUWSS procession of 1908 (the *Freelance*, 10 June 1908). Rectangle with scalloped bottom edge. 191 cm long, 128 cm wide. EDUCATION in gold paint with braid edging across top, LEARN AND LIVE lower left. Boy painted on linen and appliquéd, climbing the 'ladder of learning' on right, parallel with a braid snake entwined round a black velvet pole with fleur-de-lis finial. Owl and book painted on linen and outlined with braid, upper left. Red and black velvet, maroon wool, cream linen, gold and cream paint. (The choice of a *boy* climbing the ladder of learning, especially for a banner donated by Millicent Fawcett's daughter who was one of the outstanding successes of women's education in the nineteenth century, is curious, but may have been strategic.) ML.

George Eliot
Lowndes, 1908. Rectangle with deeply scalloped lower edge, diagonally divided between green wool and patterned silk. 136 cm long, 87 cm wide. Striped and patterned cream, yellow and maroon silk, green wool, gold braid, black, white and gold paint. GEORGE ELIOT painted in gold across the top. The names of her books: ADAM BEDE, MILL ON THE FLOSS, SILAS MARNER on cartouche with quill above torch in cloth-of-gold surrounded by an embroidered laurel wreath. ML.

Elizabeth
Lowndes, 1908. Patterned rectangle with vertical velvet borders. Painted portrait in roundel in centre, surmounted by a crown, with ELIZABETH appliquéd beneath. Gold and pink. FAW.

Enfield
From the colours, NUWSS. Rectangular. 154 cm long, 65 cm wide. ENFIELD embroidered in white silk above three red silk roses on green rectangle. Cream border. ML.

Free Churches
Used on a demonstration in 1910, may be earlier. Rectangle with shallow scalloped lower edge and eleven tabs at top. 166 cm long, 118 cm wide. Cream and dull yellow chevron twill cottons, tan cotton, blue and green cotton or linen, yellow sateen, coloured and gold paints. Central device of shield with tree, river and sky, sun and flames radiating from its edges. Painted floral border edged with cord. Mottoes in green: FREE CHURCHES (across the top), IT IS THE DAWN (over sun rising above shield), ARISE, and HEAR WHAT THE SPIRIT SAITH UNTO THE CHURCHES (below). Banner of the Free Church Federation for Women's Suffrage. ML.

Elizabeth Fry
Lowndes (album p. 20, initialled), 1908. Rectangle with battlemented lower edge. 153 cm long, 105 cm wide. Donated by Miss Prothero for the NUWSS procession of 1908. Orange velvet, grey wool, cream and salmon pink cotton sateen, coloured and gold paint. ELIZABETH FRY in black paint across top. Design of prison grille with lamp burning behind it, manacle and spiked ball on chains hanging against stone wall. ML.

Graduates of London University
Lowndes (album p. 68), 1908. Rectangle with scalloped lower edge. 180 cm long, 124 cm wide. Central orange silk and cotton panel (originally scarlet); two striped cream side panels. GRADUATES OF LONDON UNIVERSITY painted across the top with braid edging. University arms on shield centre left, blue velvet, pink silk and cloth-of-gold panels. ML.

John Hampden
Presumably the banner designed by Mary Sargant Florence for the Women's Tax Resistance League (founded 1909), and executed by the Suffrage Atelier for the WSPU procession of 18 June 1910. Canvas rectangle. 189 cm long, 114 cm wide. Figure in monochrome and silver with scroll and sword, labelled JOHN HAMPDEN. Surrounded by laurel wreaths with the mottoes SHIP MONEY 1627, NO VOTE NO TAX 1910. WOMEN'S TAX RESISTANCE LEAGUE across the top. TAXATION WITHOUT REPRESENTATION IS TYRANNY on the reverse. ML.

[Hampstead] Church League for Women's Suffrage
Designed by Laurence Housman (the drawing is in Street Public Library). Executed by the Suffrage Atelier, possibly by Clemence Housman. Rectangle with seven tabs. 183 cm long,

124 cm wide. Yellow cotton sateen, beige silks and cotton, green, purple and yellow embroidery silk. Central rectangle formed by cross entwined with interlacing vine with grapes. A foliate capital in metal thread in each corner: C, L, W, S. THE GLORIOUS LIBERTY (above) OF THE CHILDREN OF GOD (below). Outlining and edging in cord. HAMPSTEAD CHURCH LEAGUE FOR WOMENS SUFFRAGE painted on the reverse.

The CLWS was founded in the summer of 1909 as a result of an initiative by the Reverend Claude Hinscliff. See the *Church League for Women's Suffrage*, May 1913, for an account by Margaret Wynne Nevinson. Other branches had other banners which have not survived. This one was probably made in 1909, or for an important church demonstration in November 1910. ML.

Caroline Herschel
Lowndes, 1908. Rectangle with protruding V-shaped borders framing circle obtruding at bottom edge. Appliquéd stylised floral design in scarlet, cream and green on dark green ground in top border. CAROLINE HERSCHEL on striped cream fabric in centre. Key patterned ribbon framing red hearts in side borders. Blue circle, edged with orange and two rows of cording bottom centre, painted with gold stars in honour of Caroline Herschel's discoveries in astronomy. FAW.

Home-Makers
Lowndes, 1908. Rectangle with seven loops. 138 cm long, 93 cm wide. HOME-MAKERS in yellow silk satin edged with metal braid on dark brown panel above, DEMAND VOTES in satin outlined with braid below. Design of 'the fire of the hearth and the lamp of happy evenings' appliquéd on purple panel in centre with the words REMEMBER THEIR HOMELESS SISTERS on either side. The banner was announced in the *Women's Franchise*, 14 May 1908: 'Under it we hope that any will walk who feel their special sphere is the home. The group should comprise all classes of home-makers, the lady at the head of the house, the housekeeper, the children's nurse, the cook, the parlourmaid etc.' See also 'The Housing Question'. ML.

The Housing Question
1908. Rectangle with battlemented lower edge. 145 cm long, 102 cm wide. Light blue and purple silk satin, cream silk, yellow sateen, cloth of gold, yellow, white and green paint. HOME IS THE WOMAN'S CASTLE in yellow paint on blue silk across the top. Gold star on cream silk on the right, diagonally divided from THE HOUSING QUESTION WILL NOT BE SOLVED TILL WOMEN HAVE VOTES in white paint on purple silk on the left. Variously identified in the press as the banner of the Southwark Working Women and of the National Union of Women Workers. ML.

International Delegates
1908. Rectangle with shallow scallop to lower edge. INTERNATIONAL DELEGATES in cartouche above laurel wreath. Overseas feminists, some on their way to the International Suffrage Congress in Amsterdam, marched with their national

flags behind this banner on the NUWSS procession of June 1908. FAW.

Joan of Arc
Designed by Barbara Forbes, executed by the Artists' Suffrage League (Lowndes album p. 18). Rectangle with shallow scallop to lower edge. JOAN OF ARC (across top) and fleur-de-lis (on vertical borders), blue on cream. Crown above crossed swords and a riband inscribed SANS PEUR ET SANS REPROCHE in central field. FAW.

Mary Kingsley
Lowndes, 1908. Rectangle in yellows with V at lower edge. MARY KINGSLEY across band at top. Curious hooked spade (plough?) on diagonal band across centre dividing a field with three shells on it. (Mary Kingsley was not in favour of the vote for women, which caused some comment in the press.) FAW.

Jenny Lind
Lowndes (album p. 37, initialled), 1908. Rectangle with V-shaped borders framing an inverted V at the lower edge. Orange and grey (the design is red-purple and gold). JENNY LIND across the top of the central field, above a lyre framed in laurel. A swan in a circular device, lower left. The banner was to have been carried in 1908 by Jenny Lind's daughter, Mrs Raymond Maude, but she was indisposed. FAW.

London
Lowndes (album p. 55), probably 1908. Rectangle with inverted scallop. 184 cm long, 139 cm wide. Royal blue velvet, beige striped silk, red and blue cotton, cloth of gold. LONDON in cloth of gold with light blue braid edging at top on blue velvet outer edge. Beige silk inner panel with arms (on shield) and motto (on riband, below) of the City of London: DOMINE DIRIGE NOS.

There was another London banner (Lowndes album p. 52) visible in the *Daily Chronicle* account of the pilgrims converging on Hyde Park (28 July 1913, p. 5): rectangular with extended vertical borders, LONDON above, and on the central field a shield with roses in its upper corners, each side of a cross with five birds above a grille. ML.

Macclesfield
Probably Lowndes, 1908. (See Lowndes album p. 31 for parallel design for Manchester & District Federation.) Rectangular. 114 cm long, 113 cm wide. Silk with white central motif with lettering carried around it above and below. MACCLESFIELD above in green, WOMEN'S SUFFRAGE SOCIETY below in green with initial letters in red. Central motif of golden lion rampant holding sheaf of corn on red shield. Beneath it, a green scroll inscribed NEC VIRTUS, NEC COPIA, DESUNT in gold ('Neither courage nor forces fail'). Manchester Central Library Archives.

The banners of the local branch of the United Suffragists, and of the Men's League for Women's Suffrage, are also in the Central Library Archives. Both are typographical. (My thanks to the archivist, Jean Ayton, for her help.)

Manchester & Salford
Lowndes (album p. 69, but modified in the execution of the banner), probably 1908. Rectangular with castellated top, and inverted scallops on lower edge. Purple velvet with arched inset of diagonally striped red and gold silk. MANCHESTER & SALFORD in gold lettering above the arch. Ship with unfurled sails appliquéd in black on the inset panel, with CONCILIO ET LABORE above and WOMEN'S SUFFRAGE SOCIETY below. Eleven golden bees applied across the velvet borders and silk inset. Manchester Central Library Archives.

Mary Moser
Lowndes, 1908. Rectangular with inverted V at lower edge. Blue and pink on cream silk. MARY MOSER RA above a bouquet of painted flowers. CARNATION LILY LILY ROSE along the bottom edge. The missing banner for Angelica Kauffman, with Mary Moser a founder member of the Royal Academy in 1768, would have been a pair to this one. FAW.

MSPU
Rectangular. 148 cm high, 242 cm wide. White cotton-linen, green and purple cotton. Broad arrow in purple with the letters MSPU in cording, outlined in purple ribbon, on a horizontal white diamond. The whole set on a rectangle of green, with the following addresses outlined in cording: CITY TEMPLE, G. N. R. BRADFORD, 33 ECCLESTON SQUARE, DOWNING STREET. 'MSPU' is confusing; it presumably stands for the Men's Political Union rather than in error for the WSPU. ML.

National Association of Women Civil Servants
Horizontal rectangle with shallow V at lower edge. Purple field with orange signpost (EQUALITY) in roundel in centre. NATIONAL ASSOCIATION OF WOMEN CIVIL SERVANTS in gold lettering above. FAW.

National Union of Women Teachers
Rectangle. Blue green with cream and orange. Rococo ornament in upper corners. Rising sun framed by circular riband with NATIONAL UNION OF WOMEN TEACHERS. Crossed quills below entwined with another scrolling riband: WHO WOULD BE FREE HERSELF MUST STRIKE THE BLOW. FAW.

Newport (NUWSS)
Lowndes (adapted from a design on p. 64), probably 1908. Rectangular with zigzag lower edge and upper tabs. 212 cm long, 130 cm wide. Broad red and gold striped field with NEWPORT across the top in red velvet, a white bull appliquéd in a roundel in the centre, and S. GWINLLIW AND THE RIGHT embroidered beneath. Mary Lowndes's original design has the same format, but the Welsh dragon instead of the bull and the motto 'For Home and Country'. (S. Gwinlliw is the patron saint of the local cathedral, and the banner was once incorporated into an exhibition of church plate.) Newport Museum and Art Gallery.

Newport (WSPU)
Horizontal rectangle with shallow curved lower edge. 120 cm long, 150 cm wide. Green linen with painted lilies and irises in

purple, white and green down the outer edges, and a grille and arrow motif with chains in the centre. NEWPORT WSPU (above); HOW BEGGARLY APPEAR ARGUMENTS BEFORE A DEFIANT DEED (below). (My thanks to Walter Lucas of the Newport Museum and Art Gallery for information on these, and the two typographical suffrage banners in the collection.) Newport Museum and Art Gallery.

Florence Nightingale

Lowndes (album p. 17, initialled), 1908. Rectangular with shallow reverse curve at lower edge. Purple, orange, red and gold velvet and satin. FLORENCE NIGHTINGALE in riband across top. Lighthouse with radiating beams in central field. Curved scroll across base of lighthouse inscribed CRIMEA. FAW.

Northern Men's Federation: Berwick-on-Tweed

Commissioned by Maud Arncliffe-Sennett from the Suffrage Atelier in 1914. Rectangular. 170 cm long, 128 cm wide. Red and white cotton, yellow sateen, red wool, black velvet ribbon. Central shield with three red fleur-de-lis on yellow ground edged with black velvet ribbon. NORTHERN MEN'S FEDERA-TION and BERWICK ON TWEED painted in black on white cotton. On the reverse, DAY DAWNS in black paint on white cotton, and a design of trees and dogs, one chained, one unchained, in white appliqué work. ML.

Northern Men's Federation: Edinburgh

Suffrage Atelier, 1914. Rectangular. Black, red, gold and white (the NMF colours). NORTHERN MEN'S FEDERATION FOR WOMEN'S SUFFRAGE at top; Scottish lion rampant in shield on left; WE'RE BONNIE FECHTERS ILKA ANE centre right; EDINBURGH across the bottom, each section edged in black velvet ribbon. Lion on reverse with motto: YE MAUNA TRAMP ON THE SCOTS THISTLE. Maud Arncliffe-Sennett was the founder and honorary organiser of the NMF (constitutional and non-party): see her albums, vol. 25 (facing) p. 2, and vol. 26 pp. 6 and 8. Similar banners for Glasgow and Berwick-on-Tweed were ordered at the same time. The NMF balance sheet (vol. 26 c. p. 30) gives the cost as £11 15s. 9d. National Museum of Antiquities, Edinburgh.

Northern Men's Federation: Glasgow

1914 (see above). Rectangular. Colours as above. Black wool background with lion rampant and motto NOW'S THE DAY AND NOW'S THE HOUR. The People's Palace Museum, Glasgow.

NUWSS: Let Glasgow Flourish

1911. Horizontal rectangle. White linen, with satin panels. Double-sided. Central shield with the Glasgow coat of arms in green and silver (robin, bell and salmon), with scarlet bars and cerulean green cross-bars. NUWSS above, LET GLASGOW FLOURISH below. The People's Palace Museum, Glasgow.

NUWSS: Partick Branch

c. 1913. Appliqué work with the Partick coat of arms. Vertical borders with a pattern of honesty plants. The People's Palace Museum, Glasgow.

The Office

Lowndes, 1908. Rectangle with single inverted scallop at lower edge. 124 cm long, 88 cm wide. Black velvet, yellow silk and cotton, orange silk and black cotton braid, gold paint. THE OFFICE in gold paint on black velvet across the top. Velvet and silk chequered vertical borders. Three black velvet choughs (crows) bearing quill pens on yellow silk central field. ML.

Oxon, Berks, Bucks

Lowndes? [ASL]. Rectangle with NUWSS in gold braid on five tabs above, and shallow V in centre of lower edge. Richly patterned purple cross-shaped central field, striped dark blue borders, pale blue edging and bands. Rare figurative design of female figure draped in orange with scarlet shield inscribed VESTIGIA NULLA RETROSUM. OXON BERKS BUCKS embroidered in scarlet on gold above, FEDERATION below. FAW.

Edith Pechey Phipson MD

Lowndes, 1908. Shield with EDITH PECHEY PHIPSON MD in upper third, white star on purple fabric below. Edith Phipson was a pioneer woman doctor who had graduated from Berne, before women could obtain medical degrees in England. She was a member of the executive of the NUWSS and died in 1908. FAW.

Physical Education

Lowndes, 1908. Shield shape with four tabs above and rounded lower edges to central point. 115 cm long, 104 cm wide. Purple, black, green and red velvet, green silk satin and metal braid. Shield and helm (described in *Banners* as a fencing mask) with spreading feathers in appliquéd velvet, satin and braid on purple velvet. PHYSICAL EDUCATION on riband across top. ML.

St Catherine of Siena

Lowndes (album p. 19), 1908. Rectangle with zigzag lower edge. Cream, grey and black. ST CATHERINE OF SIENA across top. Stepped central field with shield and lily (to the right) and crown (on the left). *Banners* commends her for her political role as well as for her religious influence in fourteenth-century Italy. FAW.

St George

Shield-shaped. 102 cm long, 84 cm wide. Blue, green, ochre and cream linen, grey and flesh-coloured silk, narrow black silk and green cotton ribbon. Design of St George killing the dragon against a sky of moon and stars. ML.

St Teresa of Spain

Lowndes (album p. 41, initialled), 1908. Rectangular with single stepped indentation at lower edge. 120 cm long, 89 cm wide. Yellow wool, black and rust velvet, cream linen, cream silk-mix fabric, black and brown braid. Yellow ground with rust velvet applied in stripes. Open missal with a flaming heart pierced by an arrow (her symbol) painted on linen and applied in the centre. Hat above and quill in inkpot below in appliquéd black velvet. ST TERESA appliquéd in black velvet across the top and OF SPAIN at the bottom. ML.

Shorthand Writers

Lowndes, 1908. Shield-shaped with shallow inverted ogee curve to lower edge. SHORTHAND WRITERS across the top. Central field of yellow and blue chequers with SPEED! FIGHT ON (from Browning) on a panel diagonally across the centre, secured with spirals (of sealing wax?). FAW.

Sarah Siddons

Lowndes, 1908. Rectangle with inverted ogee bottom edge. 129 cm long, 87 cm wide. Gold-coloured silk-mix, olive green and red silk, green wool, cream silk brocade, rust wool, green knitted ribbon. SARAH SIDDONS across the top in olive green silk outlined in red wool on gold fabric. Green wool inner panel with garland, ribands, and hanging masks in centre. ML.

Mary Somerville

Lowndes, 1908. Shield-shaped. Shades of blue. Decorative floral border. Central motif of astrolabe (Mary Somerville was an astronomer and mathematician 'and excellent mother and wife' according to *Banners*); MARY SOMERVILLE above, 1780–1872 below. FAW.

Lucy Stone

Lowndes, 1908. Rectangle with zigzag lower edge. Red, white and blue. LUCY STONE across diagonal band, six stars in upper right field, stripes on lower left. (Cf. Susan B. Anthony). FAW.

Surrey Sussex & Hants

Lowndes (album p. 40). Executed by the ASL, 1910 (see ASL Annual Report 1910). Rectangular. 159 cm long, 124 cm wide. SURREY SUSSEX & HANTS in applied gold braid filled in with gold paint on olive green velveteen across the top. Three broad vertical stripes of dark and mid-blue sateen on central field. Three applied shields with the arms of Surrey, Hants and Sussex respectively (from left to right: one chequered blue and gold, one with a black ship on a white ground, and one with six gold birds on a blue ground). Beneath them a chevron of applied bands of red, cream and green. Worthing Museum and Art Gallery.

United Suffragists

1914. Rectangle with seven tabs and V in centre third of bottom edge. 168 cm long, 136 cm wide. Purple cotton, yellow cotton sateen, orange silk satin, cream silk, cording. Device of two snakes, entwined around a winged, flaming torch. UNITED SUFFRAGISTS above, USQUE AD FINEM below, JOIN U.S on reverse. Laurence Housman wrote to Sarah Clark on 7 May 1914 (Street Public Library) that he had just done a banner for the United Suffragists and that Clemence was working on it. But it may not have been this one. On the formation of the US see Pethick-Lawrence (1938), p. 303. ML.

Victoria, Queen and Mother

Lowndes, 1908. Shield-shaped. 142 cm long, 103 cm wide. VICTORIA QUEEN AND MOTHER in cloth-of-gold letters, and three lions, edged in gilt braid, on deep pink velvet. The 3000 elegies to the dead queen collected in *The Passing of Victoria* (J. A. Hammerton, London, 1902) were remarkable for the frequency with which they apostrophised her as 'Mother' (Hynes, 1968, p. 15). The suffragists borrowed her popularity, and at the same time used this double invocation to bridge the gulf between private and political life. Maud Arncliffe-Sennett carried this banner in the NUWSS procession of 1908. ML.

West Midlands Federation, NUWSS

Michael Pippet? 1912 (signed and dated at lower edge). Shield-shaped. 223.5 cm long, 151 cm wide. Linen, cotton and braid. Figure of Justice holding scales and sword against a green background. Broad white border with WEST MIDLAND FEDERATION above, and the names and shields of the federation's constituent counties around the sides: Staffordshire, Warwickshire, Herefordshire, Worcestershire and Shropshire. A red border trimmed with gold braid surrounds the whole. Birmingham City Museum and Art Gallery.

Windsor & Eton, NUWSS

Undated. Rectangular. Dull green and red. Double-sided. On one side appliquéd motifs in upper corners, WINDSOR & ETON in art nouveau lettering on patterned ground, NUWSS interlaced in medallion. Arms of Windsor, deer head and castle in lower right corner. On the other side two poplars and a silhouette of Windsor Castle frame a verse from Blake's JERUSALEM. Five small floral motifs below. FAW.

Mary Wollstonecraft Pioneer

Lowndes, 1908. Purple and white, sprigged fabric and velvet. Rectangular with V-shaped lower edge. Diagonally striped border. MARY WOLLSTONECRAFT PIONEER in decorative oval medallion. FAW.

Women's Freedom League (embroidered silk)

Undated. Rectangular. Cream, green and orange embroidered silks. Central device of winged heart in wreath of flowers. DARE TO BE FREE (the WFL motto) across the top. WOMEN'S FREEDOM LEAGUE on riband below. The *Vote* (16 December 1909) refers to a new banner designed by Miss Burton, embroidered by Mrs Gosling, and presented to Mrs Despard for the WFL, which is probably this one. The contrast of religious, sacred heart imagery and traditional embroidery with a militant motto is particularly striking. The Annual Report of the WFL for 1908 (Arncliffe-Sennett, vol. 10, p. 9) refers to two WFL banners admired in the June 1910 procession: the Holloway Banner designed by Mary Lowndes (her only known contribution to a militant society), and another with the motto DARE TO BE FREE made by Mary Sargant Florence, which is probably that listed below. FAW.

Women's Freedom League (votes for women)

Mary Sargant Florence? *c.* 1908. Rectangular. Horizontal stripes of yellow, white, dull green. Across the top, WOMEN'S FREEDOM LEAGUE. Across the bottom, DARE TO BE FREE. In the centre a shield with VOTES FOR WOMEN and motif of two small squares on either side. (The Museum of London and the Fawcett Collections each include another WFL 'Dare to be free' banner with lettering only.) FAW.

Women's Freedom League: Jus Sufragii

Rectangular. Tan, grey, cream, gold thread. Embroidered figure of Justice with scales and sword (very arts and crafts). LUX E TENEBRIS (above), JUS SUFFRAGII (below). On riband at top E.G.M. WFL, 1914. The People's Palace, Glasgow.

Women's Freedom League (Hampstead)

Undated. Shield-shaped. 150 cm long, 106 cm wide. Coarse white linen, green cording, yellow and green paint. Central coat of arms with stag's head. Painted chequered side borders in green and yellow. WOMEN'S FREEDOM LEAGUE in centre top. NON SIBI SED TOTI below, HAMPSTEAD BRANCH at bottom. ML. (The Museum has a second WFL Hampstead banner without the emblems.)

Women's Freedom League (Partick)

Undated. Rectangular. Orange, white, grey-green. WOMEN'S FREEDOM LEAGUE, centre top. Roundel with arms of BURGH OF PARTICK 1852 below, surmounted by crown with WESTERN BRANCH on either side. Vertical borders. National Museum of Antiquities of Scotland, Edinburgh.

Writers' Suffrage League

Lowndes (album p. 10, signed), 1908. Worked by Mrs Herringham. Rectangular with flattened inverted V in bottom edge. Appliquéd black and cream velvet. Perhaps the most striking of all the suffrage banners. The design has SCRIVENERS' across the top, to which the Scriveners' Company objected. The banner has WRITERS' instead, a black crow with a quill above on a stepped central field, and LITERA SCRIPTA MANET below. (Roger Fulford's (1957, p. 158) reference to the Cockney wags calling out 'Here come them Scavengers' is thus pure invention, since 'Scriveners'' was never used.) ML.

WSPU, Hammersmith

Undated. Rectangular central section with vertical side panels machine-stitched together. Reversible. Outer panels 120 cm high, 49 cm wide. Centre panel 96 cm deep, 120 cm wide. Overall width 218 cm. Purple, green and cream satinette, cream cotton damask and purple velvet (the WSPU colours). The central panel has three hammers and horseshoes painted on material over card with HAMMERSMITH and DEEDS NOT WORDS appliquéd on purple and green above and below. The side panels are embroidered with irises in crewel stitch on one side and appliquéd in velvet on the reverse, with hanging tassels. The clash of 'masculine' and 'feminine' components in the imagery, slogan and embroidery techniques is particularly striking. ML.

WSPU Holloway / Policemen

1908. Curious rectangular painted banner 103 cm long, 84 cm wide. Designed for the Chelsea WSPU by Herman Ross (*Votes for Women*, 25 June 1908). Picture of two policemen outside Holloway, from which a woman waves a flag with the motto VOTES FOR WOMEN. Also inscribed WOMEN'S POLITICAL AND SOCIAL UNION [*sic*] CHELSEA. ML.

WSPU Holloway Prisoners'

Carried in the processions of 1910. Rectangular. 248 cm long, 222 cm wide. Purple, green and cream linen. Large rectangle pieced out of smaller rectangles, with the signatures of eighty women hunger-strikers embroidered in purple silk (a politicised version of the traditional 'friendship' quilt). WOMEN'S SOCIAL AND POLITICAL UNION across the top in a style reminiscent of Scottish art nouveau. The signatories include Mrs Pankhurst and Christabel, Mrs Pethick-Lawrence, Annie Kenney and the American suffragist Alice Paul. ML.

WSPU Ilford

Probably 1910. Rectangular. 89 cm long, 80 cm wide. Green, black, silver and white. On one side VOTES FOR WOMEN; WSPU ILFORD; THRICE IS HE ARMED THAT HATH HIS QUARREL JUST in white paint, with Sylvia Pankhurst's trumpeting angel design and two smaller motifs cut out and applied on either side. On the other, FROM PRISON TO CITIZENSHIP with a border of silver arrows pasted on. ML.

WSPU Lewisham

Probably 1910. Rectangular. 191 cm long, 152 cm wide. Large figure of Justice with scales in black and white on a green field. Prison arrows in the corners and the motto DARE NEVER COUNT THE THROE. ML.

WSPU West Ham

Undated. Trumpeting angel design in central medallion adapted from Sylvia Pankhurst by the Misses M. A. and E. Brice; the letters made by Miss Friedlaender and her brother, members of the West Ham WSPU. Rectangular. 105 cm long, 178 cm wide. Grey-green glazed cotton ground, purple and dark green velvet, pale green silk and wool, cream silk. Circular design of trumpeting angel in white silk with banner inscribed FREEDOM. WSPU in cream silk against the bars of a prison cell window in purple on green velvet. WEST HAM on either side at the top and COURAGE CONSTANCY SUCCESS along the bottom, in letters of white silk stretched over a cardboard core. ML.

WSPU Wimbledon

Rectangle with V at lower edge. Purple, white and green windmill design with DEEDS NOT WORDS across the top, WIMBLEDON WSPU beneath, and Sylvia Pankhurst's trumpeting angel applied at the bottom. Compare Mary Lowndes's design (album p. 57) presumably for the Wimbledon branch of the NUWSS. A third banner is visible in contemporary photographs: a horizontal rectangle with WSPU on the four sails of a windmill. FAW.

YWCA Overseas Friends

Undated. Square, 88 cm. Crimson, blue and brown linen or cotton, coloured silks and metallic braid. AFRICA CHINA EGYPT PALESTINE JAPAN INDIA around the circumference of a circular design of a ship outlined in silk threads against a starry sky with YWCA OVERSEAS FRIENDS on its sails. ML.

A Note on the WSPU Silk Banners, Unfurled 17 June 1908

Most of these were made by a commercial manufacturer. It seems that none has survived.

BEHOLD! SPRING COMES, THOUGH WE MUST PASS WHO MADE THE PROMISE OF ITS BIRTH. Gold lettering with initials in white on violet, with a border of fruit trees with fruit and foliage in gold on a green ground. Presented by Miss Allen and Miss Heckles.

EQUAL REWARD FOR EQUAL MERIT, worked on a green ground. Presented by Misses Juliette and Alice Heale.

FAMED FAR FOR DEEDS OF DARING RECTITUDE (adapted from George Eliot). Portrait of Emmeline Pankhurst in roundel with WOMEN'S SOCIAL & POLITICAL UNION on riband across the top, 1903 on each side, MRS PANKHURST FOUNDER CHAMPION OF WOMANHOOD, beneath. Lettering in gold on a purple ground, bordered in white and dark green. Presented by Emmeline Pethick-Lawrence.

FROM PRISON TO CITIZENSHIP. The Kensington WSPU banner designed by Laurence Housman and worked by the members. Symbolic figure of woman in white with broken fetters, on a purple ground trailed with green leaves. Unveiled by Mrs Kerr.

HOPE IS STRONG, with eagles bearing standards with the words AWAKE!, ARISE!, worked in gold on a green ground. Presented by Miss Morden.

HUMAN EMANCIPATION MUST PRECEDE SOCIAL REGENERATION. Gold lettering on a green ground surrounded by entwined wreaths of flowers and a deep border of violet. Presented by Miss Pauline Hull. Made to a design by Sylvia Pankhurst.

STRONG SOULS LIVE, LIKE FIRE-HEARTED SUNS, TO SPEND THEIR STRENGTH. (There are variations, but this is the motto on a photograph showing the actual banner.) Device of pelican piercing its breast to feed its young (a traditional emblem of sacrifice), in gold on green, surrounded by foliage and a violet border. Presented by Mrs Kerwood. Design by Sylvia Pankhurst.

THOUGHTS HAVE GONE FORTH WHOSE POWERS CAN SLEEP NO MORE. VICTORY! VICTORY! City of London WSPU banner unveiled on its behalf by Mrs May and Miss Kerr.

VOTES FOR WOMEN. REBELLION TO TYRANTS IS OBEDIENCE TO GOD, worked in gold on a violet ground with a design of roses, thistles and shamrocks. Presented by Mrs Chibnall. Designed by Sylvia Pankhurst.

Bradford WSPU, with the Bradford city arms and the motto GRANT TO WOMANHOOD THE JUSTICE ENGLAND SHOULD BE PROUD TO GIVE. Made to a design by Sylvia Pankhurst.

APPENDIX 5
Banners & Banner-making

Mary Lowndes's 'On Banners and Banner-Making' originally appeared as an article in the *Englishwoman*, September 1909. It was reprinted as a pamphlet by the Artists' Suffrage League. (A copy is available in the Fawcett Library.)

On Banners and Banner-Making

Great numbers of banners have been seen of late in the streets of London: some beautiful in themselves, many picturesque in effect, and some indifferently ugly and dreary. Banners, however, of one sort and another have evidently become associated with the appearance of women in public life, and it seems likely that they will continue to be so associated, to the great gain of our colourless streets and hitherto sober political gatherings.

In all the ages it has been women's part to make the banners, if not to carry them. How long ago is it that Sigurd, the conqueror of Fafnir's-bane, came to that upper chamber of doom to find Brynhild the Shieldmay at work among her maidens? She whose synonym was the byrny, who had been in battle with the mightiest, whose sword was stained with the red blood of kings, is also spoken of in the saga as one who 'could more skill in handicraft than other women'. Clothed in her coat of mail she yet sat absorbed in the task of embroidering, in gold and colours, the exploits of the hero. When the magnificent red-haired Sigurd rode away from her 'shield-hung tower', the glorious golden-brown dragons of his coat-armour, which so dazzled the sagaman, were doubtless the handiwork of the warrior-maiden.

The divers colours of needlework, handwrought, are coming into play again, and now for the first time in history to illumine woman's own adventure. The oriflammes she made, the silken pennons of the knights, the gorgeous embroidery for the tourneys, the quaintly wrought histories of adventure – such as the Bayeux tapestry – were all in honour and support of her favourite fighting hero. But now the fighting heroes are tailor-fitted, and any flags they want can be ordered from the big manufacturers. Woman has been out of work a long time in the matter of adventurous colours. Her Church-banners alone continued to be seen and loved; in the streets, in camps, on ships, a tame uniformity or enormous size and intense vulgarity flaunt the taste of the present day for the shop article. Individual taste and fantasy, the delicate and the finely wrought, such symbols no longer appeal to the masculine idea of public life.

And now into public life comes trooping the feminine; and with the feminine creature come the banners of past times, as well as many other things which people had almost forgotten they were without.

Political colours were with us all through the Victorian era,

and we were no whit the better for them. Societies have had badges galore, and the dull and ugly streets have not known it: but now with the new century has come to fruition a new thing, and colour has a fresh significance. What is the new thing? Political societies started by women, managed by women and sustained by women. In their dire necessity they have been started; with their household wit they manage them; in their poverty, with ingenuity and many labours, they sustain them.

The men look on. Are their eyes holden, or do they begin to see that in all the stress and strain is a hint of new treasures to be added to the national life?

But to return to banners, of which I must speak in particular, and in the first place draw attention to rather sorry particulars.

We noted that all the banners seen in the streets of late have not been beautiful – indeed some have been ugly enough. Whence come the ugly ones? They arise perhaps in this way.

Imagine to yourself, my reader, Miss Blank, the active Secretary of the newly-formed Branch Society of Troy Town, taking her early tea in bed in the morning. The freshly awakened consciousness brightly seizes upon a forgotten matter. 'Good gracious!' thinks the Secretary, 'we have got no banner, and there's the big demonstration the week after next.' Distracted seconds of consideration! With fatal facility her roving eye travels to the sheet, smoothly spread before her gaze. 'Of course,' she thinks, 'White! What could be better? It will show up so well. Then we can have "Troy Town" on it in red letters. Oh, yes, and of course the name of the Union, and perhaps a motto, and a green edge. That will be delightful!'

Dear lady, it will not, it will be hideous. A banner is not a literary affair, it is not a placard: leave such to boards and sandwichmen. A banner is a thing to float in the wind, to flicker in the breeze, to flirt its colours for your pleasure, to half show and half conceal a device you long to unravel: you do not want to read it, you want to worship it. Choose purple and gold for ambition, red for courage, green for long-cherished hopes. If above these glories of colour you write in great letters 'Troy Town', that is not now a placard, it is a dedication.

Well, then, begin all over again. Dress, and come down to the garden, leaving behind all faintest reminiscences of the bed-clothes.

'If you would have glass,' wrote Theophilus the monk for his neophytes some nine hundred years ago, 'rise early in the morning and gather much beech-wood.' In the same spirit I would urge you to begin betimes if you would have a banner to plan and to consider; and you cannot consider better than by fetching in from the garden the most gorgeous flowers you can gather. Lay these together, trying contrast and harmony, and when you have got those colours you really like, decide upon them for your banner.

But in the matter of the colour, I would make one or two further suggestions.

First of all, no necessity is a hopeless bar to success. Supposing the fates, say for some heraldic reason, ordain you must use red and blue. That sounds bad; but no matter, the whole question is *what* red, and *what* blue, and you have the whole gamut at your choice, as never before in the history of needlework.

Should the time of year permit, fetch in from the garden or from the florist's the deepest blue spike of delphinium you can lay hands on, and beside it place, not a scarlet geranium, but a crimson lobelia. What is wrong now with red and blue?

Now from these lovely flowers learn a further lesson in design. Fetch several crimson lobelias, and make the mass of them equal to the great mass of colour of the blue spike. Why, the thing is spoilt! You begin to think red and blue will not look nice after all. It is not the colours that are wrong, however, it is the proportion in which they are brought together that causes discomfort, as the different proportion before gave delight.

I will illustrate this in another way. You have found a perfectly delightful pansy. Two lovely purples it shows and a golden eye. Well, then, let the banner be of two such purples and golden yellow, and we cannot go wrong. Yes, you can; if you splurge the yellow all about instead of being very reserved with it, and treating it as most precious. If you hunt about the garden you can probably find a pansy gone wrong in just this way; and then it is plain to be seen that the secret of the first pansy was not just two purples and some yellow.

Or take a great red poppy, with its cool green stem and foliage, and wonderful purple black in the inside. You can model a splendid banner on that poppy, but not by spotting red over with purple-black letters. See how Nature has flung out the red, and the reserve of her blacks; notice the subordinate part the greens play. You cannot use too strong or too brilliant colour, only you must use it with cunning.

But to leave the question of colours for the moment, let us consider form. After all what shape is the banner to be? Again, I would say – avoid any tendency to think favourably of the bedclothes; a sheet between two poles is a poor ideal. I know it has its conveniences for street processions, but after all we do not make and carry banners for our convenience – it is indisputably more convenient to walk about without them. 'Who takes the eye takes all,' we are instructed by *Sapolio*. Fling to the winds convenience, and make your banner, whether for two poles or one, in the most beautiful form, namely to my thinking, as a parallelogram depending longways from a cross-bar.

The upper edge must be devised for attachment to the bar, and do not despise the nice adjustment of such devices; in the cutting of the lower edge exhibit your fancy, and give the breezes a chance.

The outward shape being settled, if the banner is to be composed, as suggested, with various colours, on what plan shall they be combined? Here many considerations should be brought forward, and in each individual case there is much, of course, to determine the device that should be displayed. In a

general way I would say, however, be guided by simple rules of heraldry. If you want to have two purples composing the ground, mingle them by adopting some heraldic divisions of the field, as applied usually to a colour and a metal. You may think over *nebulée, ragulée, indented, engrailed*, as a method for bringing two edges together; your field may be *barred, fretty*, or *billetée*, the *chevron*, the *bend*, or the *saltire* may break its surface. There are a score of ways such as I speak of, some simple and easy, as the fesse; some only to be attempted by most skilled workers, as the blue and white of vair and counter-vair. In this fancy heraldry of ours we need not be bound by laws as of Medes and Persians, and the rule may be often, I think, honoured by non-observance which prescribes 'Do not charge metal on metal, or colour on colour, but the contrary.' There will also arise occasions when its strict observance would be most seemly. One thing I would like to lay down as a most important axiom. Make all your charges fill the field as far as they may decoratively. Nothing looks more mean than a large plain surface with, say, three wretched little martlets spotted on to it. If three martlets are to sit upon your fesse crowd them up, head to tail, and make a good show of them.

I have spoken hitherto of dividing up a field for decorative reasons, but it is obvious most banners require as well something more purposeful. Well, use the old symbols always when they will serve, but try and use them in a new way; for it is a new thing we are doing. For instance, in Norfolk and Suffolk the crowns and arrows of St Edmund meet us in every town, so we want them on our East Anglian banner, not forgetting the head of the pious wolf to remind us of many savage things, and the taming of them. But there is no need, in devising such a banner, that we should follow the colours or the precise arrangement of the county arms.

In all decorative matters a little knowledge of heraldry is of value. A certain Society has proclaimed its colours as green, white, and silver. This is a pity, as from time immemorial white and silver have been held to be decorative equivalents, Argent; either to be expressed by white satin, or white calico, or burnished silver, as the fancy takes you.

A little must now be said on the subject of material. Never use anything ugly because it is expensive or because it is cheap. Do not use the wrong colour or the wrong tone because you have a piece of something 'over' which would 'just do'. If it is not exactly right it won't do at all.

Every shade and colour can be got in London in silks, faced cloths, and velvets, but to find exactly what you want may take some time. The quest if weary is worth while, and even if you wander all the way from High Street, Kensington, to Covent Garden, pausing at innumerable shops, call the time well spent if you return at last with the needed yard or two of material exactly the colour you went forth to find.

'Can we make the banner ourselves?' is a question often asked by the inexperienced. I would reply to it with another inquiry. If you want a new pair of winter curtains for your dining-room, can you make them yourself, so that they shall hang straight and true and the linings be not puckered? If you can, I think you can make the banner. If such a task is beyond you, there are many women competent to undertake it, and you must call in the more-experienced worker.

And now for a word as to expense. The silks and velvets you want need not cost very much, as they are not for wear or for handling, but merely to be looked at. How to manage the necessary metals – gold and silver – I cannot enter into here, as the explanations required would be somewhat elaborate; but the cost of them need not be great. Besides these materials, banner-makers must not fail to think of lining and inter-lining, likewise of cords with their tassels, and of fringes, if needed. These fringes, I would remark, may run away with a good deal of money; skilful and ingenious people will make them at home, and they should bear in mind that shining hanks of a material bearing the mysterious name 'mercerised cotton' may be had at low prices in all beautiful colours.

The expense of the whole banner, however, cannot be even roughly indicated, for all depends upon the design, and also upon what is paid for the design, and from first to last remember that is the one thing most worth paying for. If the design is bad, for twenty pounds you will not get a banner worth looking at; if the design is good and practical, you may make a fine thing for three, and make it yourself.

Certain Practical Suggestions

Perhaps the best size for a single-pole banner is 3 feet 2 inches broad by 4 feet 6 inches long. The Artists' Suffrage League has invented a double hook, made on the lines of those used for Church banners, which is fixed to the upright pole at about one foot from the top, and which prevents the banner from swinging round when carried; it may be obtained from the Secretary, price 6d.

A good size for a double-pole banner is 50 inches broad by 6 feet long. This is the size of most of the banners made under the directions of the Artists' League, though some are a little larger. It will be found that banners 4 feet 6 inches wide by 6 feet 6 inches long are as large as women bearers can carry should there be any wind. A very good screw-hook, proved to be the simplest and most secure method of mounting the double-pole banner, is to be had from the Artists' League, price 4d. each. These were invented for Suffrage use, and are forged by a Chelsea smith.

The cross-bars used should be about three inches longer than the width of the banner. Poles should be nine feet long for both single and double-sized banners. For poles and cross-bars nothing is better or cheaper than lengths of rounded wood (like broomstick handles), 1⅛ inch in diameter, which may be obtained at a penny per foot from any wood-yard, and may be painted or gilded as desired. These are better than bamboo poles, they look much better and are safer, since bamboo is liable to split when any strain is put on the plugs necessary for adjusting the screw-hooks.

Arrow-heads to be fixed at the apex of the pole and ends of the cross-bar, made of turned wood, may be obtained from any flag-maker for from 2d. to 6d. each, and are easily painted or gilded by the banner-maker.

M. LOWNDES

APPENDIX 6

Suffrage Colours

The best known suffrage colours are the purple, white and green of the WSPU. These were chosen in May 1908 in preparation for the Hyde Park demonstration on 21 June. They are most extensively glossed in Emmeline Pethick-Lawrence's article, 'The Purple, White and Green' in the *Programme* of the Prince's Skating Rink Exhibition in 1909. White was for purity, green for hope and purple for dignity (see chapter 3, note 125). Purple was sometimes given as 'loyalty' or 'courage' and green as 'youth' or 'regeneration'.

The colours of the NUWSS were red and white on the demonstrations of 1907 and 1908, but in November 1909 the *Common Cause* announced the decision to add green, and urged its readers to make the colours known as part of the struggle to forge a constitutionalist identity in the face of militant notoriety. 'It is more and more imperative in these days that the fact that Constitutional Suffragists are greatest in numbers and most widely spread should be known everywhere . . . Every member can help to ensure that 20,000 red, white, and green badges and ribbons all over the country are being stared at, are being talked of, are bringing in more and more supporters every day . . . Every branch should provide itself with flags and banners in the new colours and decorate every hall in which it holds a meeting . . . At drawing room and afternoon meetings red and white flowers should be got for decoration, and the stewards at our meetings should endeavour to wear one or other of the colours . . . All handbills and posters should be done on red, white, and green paper, or on white in red and green ink. Let us put forth our greatest endeavours to have the colours known everywhere before the general election; not only as Suffrage colours, but as the colours of the greatest society – the law-abiding, non-party society . . .' (The *Common Cause*, 25 November 1909, p. 433).

No symbolic meaning was attached to the NUWSS colours until 1910, when a brief article in the *Common Cause* pointed out that they were also the colours of Garibaldi and Italian nationalism: 'our colours are not . . . as yet unstoried and unhallowed,

merely juxtaposed for the novice to distinguish our Union from another . . . they are already a living unity with a great significa- tion and a glorious history, for they have already served as the symbol of a battle for liberty nobly fought and won.' Their significance in the Italian context is borrowed for the National Union: 'white, the serene faith in ideas which makes the soul divine; green, the perpetual re-florescence of hope and youth into the fruit of well-doing; red, the passion and the blood of martyrs and of heroes' (A. M. Allen, 'The Red, White, and Green', the *Common Cause*, 26 May 1910, p. 99).

The green, white and gold of the Women's Freedom League were chosen by a large majority of the members through a referendum of its branches (WFL *Report* for the year 1908, Maud Arncliffe-Sennett Collection, vol. 10, *c.* p. 9).

As societies proliferated, so they adopted their own colours to satisfy their sense of identity and distinguish themselves on processions. When the Pethick-Lawrences broke away from the WSPU in 1912 and formed the Votes for Women Fel- lowship, they found that 'almost every colour combination has been adopted by the numerous existing societies'. Unable to drop white ('White must enter into every combination wherever large effects are necessary'), and obliged to drop green (which belonged with red to the NUWSS), they settled for purple, white and red, which placed them appropriately half-way between the constitutionalists and the militant WSPU they had just left (*Votes for Women*, 30 May 1913, p. 503).

The colours of the Artists' Suffrage League were blue and silver; of the Suffrage Atelier, blue, orange and black; of the Women's Conservative Union, blue, white and gold; of the Actresses' Franchise League, pink and green; of the Writers' Suffrage League, black, white and gold; of the Church League, white and gold; and of Sylvia Pankhurst's East London Federa- tion, purple, white, green and red. The colours of the National League for Opposing Women's Suffrage were white, pink and black.

The Impact of British Propaganda Techniques in America

The first women's rights convention in the world was held in New York State (at Seneca Falls) in 1848. It marked the beginning of the American women's movement: first, in a series of campaigns concerned with property rights, employment opportunities, the double standard and the custody of children (as in England); and then, increasingly from the 1850s, with the struggle for the vote.[1]

American feminists were prominent in temperance and anti-slavery campaigns, and the American suffrage movement was partly shaped by the conflicts and alliances that these produced. With the North victorious at the end of the Civil War, the Negro vote became an issue, and the cooperation of abolitionists and feminists foundered on the question of racial or sexual priority. In 1870 Congress ratified the Fifteenth Amendment which made it illegal for states to disenfranchise male voters on grounds of race. Suffragists had asked for the category of sex to be included, but were refused.

The National Woman Suffrage Association (led by Elizabeth Cady Stanton and Susan B. Anthony) and the American Woman Suffrage Association (dominated by Lucy Stone and Henry Blackwell), both founded in 1869, merged in the National American Woman Suffrage Association in 1890. Wyoming (1869), Utah (1870), Colorado (1893) and Idaho (1896) had granted women the vote, but there were no more advances between 1896 and 1910. By the early years of the twentieth century the suffrage campaign was dominated by conservative and even racist arguments for the educated, white, middle-class female vote,[2] as an antidote to the enfranchisement of Negroes and immigrants. As in England, but in a way that was sharpened by the cultural and racial tensions of America, the more that poor and ill-educated men were enfranchised, the more keenly middle-class women felt the insult of their exclusion.

An increasingly tired and conservative campaign was revivified by a series of developments that took place between 1910 and 1913. An influx of socialists, social reformers and trade unionists extended its political base; the leadership of two new organisations brought fresh energies which were focused by the decision to concentrate on a federal amendment; and the influence of the British campaign encouraged the adoption of militant propaganda techniques developed initially by the Artists' Suffrage League, the Suffrage Atelier and the WSPU. Washington state was won in 1910, California in 1911, Oregon, Arizona and Kansas in 1912, and the momentum was increased by the growth of the Progressive Party (newly formed under Theodore Roosevelt in 1912), which made women's suffrage an issue in its presidential campaign.

The impact of British techniques on the American suffrage movement was chiefly effected through the influence of key individuals with experience of both. But the ground was prepared by a long tradition of transatlantic relations,[3] by a sense of frustration with orthodox methods, and by detailed accounts of the British campaign in the American press. Hundreds of articles were published by sympathisers and opponents, both British and American. England was seen as 'the storm-centre of the movement'.[4] The visits of suffragists such as Ethel Snowden, Ray Costello [Strachey], Maud Royden, and particularly Sylvia and Emmeline Pankhurst were avidly reported and the accounts were widely syndicated. At the height of American interest in 1910 Sylvia Pankhurst spoke up to three times a day on the militant movement, and papers that failed to gain interviews were not above faking them.[5] In 1913 the United Press Association offered to circulate an article by Mrs Fawcett to 500 American newspapers.[6]

The Reverend Anna Shaw, who succeeded Susan B. Anthony as president of NAWSA, had marched with Mrs Fawcett in the National Union demonstration of 13 June 1908. With other American visitors she had witnessed the Women's Pageant of Trades and Professions at the International Suffrage Congress of 1909. And with Inez Milholland (who played Joan of Arc in American processions) she spoke from a Hyde Park platform after the WSPU demonstration of 23 July 1910.[7]

Harriot Stanton Blatch, the daughter of Elizabeth Cady Stanton, had married an Englishman and settled in England. When she was widowed she returned to New York, and in 1910 set out to revitalise the American campaign by cooperating with labour groups and staging open-air meetings and public parades on the new British model. (The first American women's suffrage procession was held in New York with a plethora of banners in 1911.)[8] Frustrated with the conservatism of the National American Woman Suffrage Association, she founded the rival Women's Political Union, and adopted as its emblem a version of Caroline Watts's NUWSS 'Bugler Girl' but in the purple, white and green of the WSPU.[9]

Alice Paul had even closer connections with the British militant campaign. She had come to England as a university graduate to continue her studies in 1907, joined the WSPU, been arrested six times, received three jail sentences, and been forcibly fed. (Her name appears on the suffragette 'Roll of Honour', and her signature on the WSPU Hunger Strikers' banner paraded in 1910.)[10] She returned to America in 1912 and worked on the organisation of a massive suffrage parade in Washington in 1913. NAWSA officials were chary of her radicalism and her techniques, but she was a brilliant propagandist, and Anna Shaw's experience of constitutional marches in England inclined her to sympathy. Shaw placed Paul at the head of the Congressional Committee of NAWSA in 1912, with authority to use its official letterheads to raise funds for the

Washington demonstration. On 3 March 1913, the day before Woodrow Wilson's inauguration as president, 10,000 women took to the streets with banners and bands. Immediately, they were 'news' as American suffragists had never been news before. Societies were bombarded with demands for information, and Lucy Burns concluded in her report that 'we are not only amusing and sometimes picturesque but we are of real intellectual and political interest.'[11] There is no doubt that the demonstrations inspired by Harriot Stanton Blatch and Alice Paul (such as the parades in Baltimore and New York which followed the Washington march in 1913) – with their floats, heralds, horsewomen, banners and contingents of professional women and graduates in gowns – were modelled on the pageantry of those held in London since 1908.[12]

British posters were available through NAWSA and used in American campaigns.[13] The Artists' Suffrage League claimed to have supplied the Californian campaign in 1911 and the Suffrage Atelier advertised posters printed on yellow paper for American use (yellow was the principal colour of the American societies). There was enough common ground to make this possible – some themes were consciously borrowed and others arose in both places spontaneously – but there were distinguishing factors. Posters were expensive and less frequently issued in America.[14] There seems to have been no group of organised artists equivalent to the Artists' Suffrage League or the Suffrage Atelier.[15] There was no direct parallel in England to the Negro or immigrant vote, nor to the enfranchisement of women in limited states. Nor were the American campaigns focused around general elections and by-elections in the same way. Art nouveau flower and fruit goddesses are more common in America, and images of working women a great deal rarer.[16] There is no equivalent to the illustrative realism of League designs like 'Votes for Workers', or to the graphic style and technique of Atelier block-prints like 'English Inquisitors'.

SELECTED BIBLIOGRAPHY

This is a list of principal sources which does not include all those cited in the footnotes. For further details on archival and printed material relating to the political campaign as a whole, see the bibliographies in Rosen (1974), Harrison (1978) and Hume (1982).

There is a great deal of relevant material in the Fawcett Library, which is housed in the Polytechnic of the City of London. I have distinguished between the Fawcett Library (published material, including pamphlets, on open shelves), the Fawcett Archives (manuscript and printed material, including pamphlets, in numbered boxes), the Fawcett Autograph Collection (separately catalogued letters) and the Fawcett Collection (additional material, including banners, photograph albums, scrapbooks and posters in cupboards or plan-chests).

References to the 30-volume Maud Arncliffe-Sennett Collection are often approximate, since a great deal of material has been tipped in between the numbered pages. The volume and nearest page number are cited thus: 'vol. 8, c. p. 43'.

Press reports, pamphlets, leaflets, annual reports and minute-books are far too numerous to list individually. They are cited in the text or in the footnotes, with a note on their location (see also Hume, 1982).

Primary Sources

Official Papers

Census of England and Wales for the Year 1891, also *1901*, *1911*, HMSO, London

Parliament, Great Britain: *Journals of the House of Lords* (1900–14); *Hansard's Parliamentary Debates*, fourth and fifth series (1892–1919)

Parl. Pap. 1917–18, vol. 25 (Cd 8463), *Conference on Electoral Reform, Letter from Mr Speaker to the Prime Minister*, 27 January 1917, HMSO, London, 1917

Parl. Pap. 1918, vol. 14 (Cd 9164), *Report of the Board of Trade on the Increased Employment of Women During the War in the United Kingdom*, HMSO, London, 1919

Parl. Pap. 1918, vol. 14 (Cd 9239), *Report of the Women's Employment Committee, Ministry of Reconstruction*, HMSO, London, 1919

Parl. Pap. 1919, vol. 31 (Cmd 135), *Report of the War Cabinet Committee on Women in Industry*, HMSO, London, 1919

Women's War Work, issued by the War Office, HMSO, London, September 1916

Home Office Papers, Public Record Office
Metropolitan Police Reports, Public Record Office

Private Papers

Maud Arncliffe-Sennett Collection, British Museum
C. R. Ashbee journals, King's College Library, Cambridge
Collections of Minnie Baldock, Anne Cobden Sanderson, S. Ada Flatman, Caroline Hodgson, Kitty Marion and Nurse C. E. Pine, together with typescript autobiographical notes by Mary Gawthorpe, Kitty Marion, E. Katherine Willoughby Marshall and Hannah Mitchell; Museum of London
Teresa Billington-Greig; Emily Davies; Dame Millicent Garrett Fawcett; and Jane, Lady Strachey papers; Fawcett Library
Violet Markham papers, British Library of Political and Economic Science
Henry Woodd Nevinson journals, Bodleian Library, Oxford
Pethick-Lawrence papers, Trinity College, Cambridge

Fabian Society minute-books, microfiche at BLPES

Newspapers and Periodicals

Dailies and Sundays

Daily Chronicle, Daily Express, Daily Graphic, Daily Herald, Daily Mail, Daily Mirror, Daily News, Daily Sketch, Daily Telegraph, Evening Dispatch, Evening News, Evening Standard, Globe, Kensington News, Manchester Guardian, Morning Advertiser, Morning Leader, Morning Post, Observer, Pall Mall Gazette, Standard, Sunday Times, The Times, Westminster Gazette

Weeklies and Monthlies

Anti-Suffrage Review, Britannia, Christian Commonwealth, Clarion, Common Cause, Conservative and Unionist Women's Franchise Review, Contemporary Review, Englishwoman, Englishwoman's Review, Labour Leader, Nineteenth Century, Punch, Referee, Review of Reviews, Suffragette, Suffragette News Sheet, Vote, Votes for Women, Weekly Dispatch, Women's Franchise, Women's National Liberal Association Quarterly Leaflet, Women's Suffrage

Miscellaneous

Calling All Women (the newsletter of the Suffragette Fellowship), London, February 1947–February 1968

Pamphlets and Articles Published Before 1918

Bodichon, Barbara Leigh Smith, 'Reasons for the Enfranchisement of Women', read at the meeting of the National Association for the Promotion of Social Science, Manchester, 6 October 1866

Davison, Emily Wilding, 'The Price of Liberty', published posthumously in the *Daily Sketch*, 28 May 1914

Gore-Booth, Eva, 'The women's suffrage movement among trade unionists', in Brougham Villiers, 'The Case for Women's Suffrage', T. Fisher Unwin, London, 1907

Grove, Lady A., 'The Human Woman', Smith Elder, London, 1908

Hardie, J. Keir, 'The Citizenship of Women', London, 18 May 1905

Housman, Laurence, 'The Bawling Brotherhood', The Woman's Press, London, undated

Leigh, Mary, 'Fed by Force, a Statement by Mrs Mary Leigh. Who is Still in Birmingham Gaol', 1909

Pankhurst, Christabel, 'The Parliamentary Vote for Women', Manchester, undated [pre-1907]

Pankhurst, Emmeline, 'The Importance of the Vote', London, 1907

– 'Why women should be mobilized', the *Sketch*, 23 March 1915

Pethick-Lawrence, Emmeline, 'The New Crusade', London, 1907

– 'The purple, white and green' in NWSPU, 'The Women's Exhibition 1909, Programme'

Pethick-Lawrence, Frederick, 'The By-Election Policy of the Women's Social & Political Union', The Women's Press, London, undated [c. 1909]

Royden, Maud, 'Votes and Wages: How Women's Suffrage Will Improve the Economic Position of Women', NUWSS, London, 3rd ed, 1912

Saville, A. F., Moullin, C. W. M., and Horsley, Sir V., 'The forcible feeding of suffrage prisoners', the *Lancet*, 24 August 1912

Sinclair, May, 'Feminism: Science and Pseudo-Science', Women Writers' Suffrage League, London, undated [1913]

'The Women's Party', undated

Zangwill, Israel, 'One and One are Two', London, 1907

Contemporary Books, Autobiographies and Letters

Acton, William, *The Functions and Disorders of the Reproductive Organs in Youth, in Adult Age, and in Advanced Life considered in their Physiological, Social and Psychological Relations*, London, 3rd ed, 1862

A. J. R. (ed.), *The Suffrage Annual and Women's Who's Who*, Stanley Paul, London, 1913

Anderson, Louisa Garrett, *Elizabeth Garrett Anderson, 1886–1917*, Faber & Faber, London, 1939

Asquith, Herbert Henry, *Memories and Reflections, 1852–1927*, 2 vols, Cassell, London, 1928

Balfour, Lady Frances, *Ne Obliviscaris; Dinna Forget*, 2 vols, Hodder & Stoughton, London, 1930

Bax, E. Belfort, *The Fraud of Feminism*, Grant Richards, London, 1913

Billington-Greig, Teresa, *The Militant Suffragette Movement*, Frank Palmer, London, 1911

Black, Clementina, *Married Women's Work: Being the Report of an Enquiry Undertaken by the Women's Industrial Council*, G. Bell & Sons, London, 1915

Blackburn, Helen, *Record of Women's Suffrage*, Williams & Norgate, London, 1902

Blease, W. Lyon, *The Emancipation of Englishwomen*, David Nutt, London, 1913

Brockway, A. Fenner, *Inside the Left: Thirty Years of Platform, Press, Prison, and Parliament*, Allen & Unwin, London, 1942

Butler, Josephine, *Personal Reminiscences of a Great Crusade*, Horace Marshall & Son, London, 1911

Coates, Dora Meeson, *George Coates: His Art and His Life*, Dent, London, 1937

Davies, Emily, *Thoughts on Some Questions Relating to Women, 1860–1908*, Bowes & Bowes, Cambridge, 1910

Dicey, A. V., *Letters to a Friend on Votes for Women*, John Murray, London, 1909

Fawcett, Henry, and Fawcett, Millicent Garrett, *Essays and Lectures on Social and Political Subjects*, Macmillan, London, 1872

Fawcett, Millicent Garrett, *Women's Suffrage: A Short History of a Great Movement*. T. C. & E. C. Jack, London, 1912

– *The Women's Victory – and After: Personal Reminiscences, 1911–18*, Sidgwick & Jackson, London, 1920

– *What I Remember*, T. Fisher Unwin, London, 1924

Ferguson, Rachel, *Victorian Bouquet: Lady X looks on*, Ernest Benn, London, 1931

Gollancz, Victor (ed.), *The Making of Women: Oxford Essays in Feminism*, Allen & Unwin, London, 1917

Hamilton, Cicely, *Marriage as a Trade* (1909), The Women's Press, London, 1981

– *Life Errant*, Dent, London, 1935

Housman, Laurence, *The Unexpected Years*, Cape, London, 1937

Kenney, Annie, *Memories of a Militant*, Edward Arnold, London, 1924

Lansbury, George, *My Life*, Constable, London, 1928

Linton, Elizabeth (Eliza) Lynn, *Modern Women and What is Said of Them*, J. S. Redfield, New York, 1870

Lowther, James W., *A Speaker's Commentaries*, 2 vols, Edward Arnold, London, 1925

Lytton, Lady Constance, *Prisons and Prisoners, Some Personal Experiences by Constance Lytton and Jane Warton, Spinster* (1914), E. P. Publications Ltd, Wakefield, 1976

– *Letters of Constance Lytton*, (ed.) Lady Betty Balfour, Heinemann, London, 1925

McKenna, Stephen, *Reginald McKenna, 1863–1943*, Eyre & Spottiswoode, London, 1948

McLaren, Lady, *The Women's Charter of Rights and Liberties*, 4th ed, Grant Richards, London, 1909

Markham, Violet, *Return Passage*, Oxford University Press, Oxford, 1953

Mason, Bertha, *The Story of the Women's Suffrage Movement*, Sherratt & Hughes, London, 1912

Metcalfe, A. E., *Woman's Effort: A Chronicle of British Women's Fifty Years' Struggle for Citizenship 1865–1914*, Blackwell, Oxford, 1917

Mill, Harriet Taylor, *The Enfranchisement of Women*, Trubner &

Co., London 1868 (reprinted from the *Westminster Review*, July 1851)

Mill, John Stuart, *The Subjection of Women* (1869), MIT Press, Cambridge Mass., 1970

Mitchell, Hannah, *The Hard Way Up*, Faber & Faber, London, 1968 (see also her typescript autobiography in the Museum of London)

Montefiore, Dora, *From a Victorian to a Modern*, E. Archer, London, 1927

Nevinson, Henry Woodd, *More Changes, More Chances*, Nisbet & Co., London, 1925

Nevinson, Margaret Wynne, *Fragments of Life*, George Allen & Unwin, London, 1922

– *Life's Fitful Fever: A Volume of Memories*, A. E. Black, London, 1926

Oxford and Asquith, Countess of, *The Autobiography of Margot Asquith*, 2 vols, Thornton Butterworth, London, 1922

Oxford and Asquith, Earl of, *Fifty Years of Parliament*, 2 vols, Cassell, London, 1926

Oxford and Asquith, Earl of, *Memories and Reflections, 1852–1927*, 2 vols, Little Brown & Co., Boston, 1928

Pankhurst, Christabel, *The Great Scourge and How to End It*, E. Pankhurst, London, 1913

– *Unshackled: The Story of How We Won the Vote*, Hutchinson, London, 1959

Pankhurst, Emmeline, *My Own Story* (ghosted by Rheta Childe Dorr), Eveleigh Nash, London, 1914

Pankhurst, E. Sylvia, *The Suffragette*, Gay & Hancock, London, 1911

– *The Suffragette Movement: An Intimate Account of Persons and Ideals* (1931), Virago, London, 1977

– *The Life of Emmeline Pankhurst*, T. Werner Laurie, London, 1935

Pethick-Lawrence, Emmeline, *My Part in a Changing World*, Gollancz, London, 1938

Pethick-Lawrence, Frederick, and Edwards, Joseph (eds), *The Reformers' Year Books*, 1901–1909, London

– *Fate Has Been Kind*, Hutchinson, London, 1943

Rhondda, Viscountess, *This Was My World*, Macmillan, London, 1933

Richardson, Mary, *Laugh a Defiance*, Weidenfeld & Nicolson, London, 1953

Robins, Elizabeth, *The Convert* (1907), The Women's Press, London, 1980

– *Way Stations*, Hodder & Stoughton, London, 1913

Scott, C. P., *The Political Diaries of C. P. Scott 1911–1928* (ed.) Trevor Wilson, Collins, London, 1970

Sharp, Evelyn, *Unfinished Adventures: Selected Reminiscences from an Englishwoman's Life*, John Lane, London, 1933

Smyth, Ethel, *Female Pipings in Eden*, Peter Davies, London, 1933

Snowden, Ethel, *The Feminist Movement*, Collins, London, 1913

Snowden, Philip (Viscount Snowden of Ickornshaw), *An Autobiography*, 2 vols, Nicholson & Watson, London, 1934

Swanwick, Helena, *Women in Industry from Seven Points of View*, Duckworth, London, 1908

– *The Future of the Women's Movement*, Bell & Sons, London, 1913

– *I Have Been Young*, Gollancz, London, 1935

Wollstonecraft, Mary, *Vindication of the Rights of Women*, J. Johnson, London, 1792

Women [anonymous], Martin Secker, London, 1918

Wright, Sir Almroth, *The Unexpurgated Case Against Women's Suffrage*, Constable, London, 1913

Secondary Sources

Books (Other Than Autobiographies) Published After 1918

Adlard, Eleanor, *Edy: Recollections of Edith Craig*, Frederick Muller, London, 1949

Auerbach, Nina, *Woman and the Demon: The Life of a Victorian Myth*, Harvard University Press, Cambridge Mass., 1982

Banks, J. A. and Olive, *Feminism and Family Planning in Victorian England*, Liverpool University Press, Liverpool, 1964

Banks, Olive, *Faces of Feminism*, Martin Robertson, Oxford, 1981

Barrett, Michèle, Corrigan, Philip, Kuhn, Annette and Wolff, Janet (eds), *Ideology and Cultural Production*, Croom Helm, London, 1979

Barrow, Margaret, *Women 1870–1928: A Select Guide to Printed and Archival Sources in the United Kingdom*, Mansell Publishing, New York, 1981

Basch, Françoise, *Relative Creatures: Victorian Women in Society and the Novel: 1837–67*, Allen Lane, London, 1974

Bauer, Carol and Ritt, Lawrence (eds), *Free and Ennobled: Source readings in the development of Victorian feminism*, Pergamon, Oxford, 1979

Beer, Gillian, *Darwin's Plots: Evolutionary narrative in Darwin, George Eliot and nineteenth-century fiction*, Routledge & Kegan Paul, London, 1984

Blewett, Neal, *The Peers, the Parties, and the People: The British General Elections of 1910*, University of Toronto Press, Toronto, 1972

Branca, Patricia, *Silent Sisterhood: Middle-Class Women in the Victorian Home*, Croom Helm, London, 1975

Bridenthal, Renate and Koonz, Claudia (eds), *Becoming Visible: Women in European History*, Houghton Mifflin, Boston, 1977

Bristow, Edward, *Vice and Vigilance: Purity Movements in Britain since 1700*, Gill & Macmillan, Dublin, 1977

Butler, David and Freeman, Jennie, *British Political Facts, 1900–1960*, Macmillan, London, 1964

Callen, Anthea, *Angel in the Studio: Women in the Arts and Crafts Movement 1870–1914*, Astragal, London, 1979

Clegg, H. A., Fox, A., and Thompson, A. F., *A History of British Trade Unions Since 1889*, vol. 1, Clarendon Press, Oxford, 1964

Colebrook, Leonard, *Almroth Wright: Provocative Doctor and Thinker*, Heinemann, London, 1954

Cormack, Peter, *Women Stained Glass Artists of the Arts and Crafts Movement*, William Morris Gallery, London, 1985

Cross, Colin, *The Liberals in Power, 1905–1914*, Barrie & Rockliff, London, 1963

Cunningham, Gail, *The New Woman and the Victorian Novel*, Macmillan, London, 1978

Dangerfield, George, *The Strange Death of Liberal England* (1935), Paladin, London, 1970

Davidoff, Leonore, *The Best Circles: Society, Etiquette and The Season*, Croom Helm, London, 1973

Delamont, S. and Duffin, Lorna (eds), *The Nineteenth-Century Woman: Her Cultural and Physical World*, Croom Helm, London, 1978

Doughan, David and Sanchez, Denise, *Feminist Periodicals 1855–1944: An annotated critical bibliography*, Harvester, Brighton, 1987

Drake, Barbara, *Women in Trade Unions* (1920), Virago, London, 1984

Dreyfus, Hubert and Rabinow, Paul, *Michel Foucault: Beyond Structuralism and Hermeneutics*, University of Chicago Press, Chicago, 2nd ed. with afterword by Michel Foucault, 1983

Ehrenreich, Barbara and English, Deidre, *Complaints and Disorders: The Sexual Politics of Sickness*, Writers & Readers, London, 1973

Emy, H. V., *Liberals, Radicals and Social Politics, 1892–1914*, Cambridge University Press, Cambridge, 1973

Ensor, R. C. K., *England 1870–1914*, Clarendon Press, Oxford, 1936

Evans, Richard, *The Feminists: Women's Emancipation Movements in Europe, America and Australasia*, Croom Helm, London, 1977

Fletcher, Sheila, *Women First: The Female Tradition in English Physical Education 1880–1980*, Athlone Press, London, 1984

Flexner, Eleanor, *Century of Struggle: The Woman's Rights Movement in the United States* (1959), Atheneum, New York, 1974

Foucault, Michel, *The History of Sexuality, Volume 1: An Introduction*, Allen Lane, London, 1979

Freud, Sigmund, *Jokes and their Relation to the Unconscious* (1905), vol. 6 of Pelican Freud Library, Penguin, London, 1976

Fulford, Roger, *Votes for Women: The Story of a Struggle*, Faber & Faber, London, 1957

Gilman, Sander, *Difference and Pathology: Stereotypes of Sexuality, Race, and Madness*, Cornell University Press, Ithaca NY, 1985

Girouard, Mark, *The Return to Camelot: Chivalry and the English Gentleman*, Yale University Press, London, 1981

Giustino, David de, *Conquest of Mind: Phrenology and Victorian Social Thought*, Croom Helm, London, 1975

Gorman, John, *Banner Bright: An illustrated history of the banners of the British trade union movement*, Allen Lane, London, 1973

– *Images of Labour: Selected Memorabilia from the National Museum of Labour History, London*, Scorpion, London, 1985

Grigg, John, *The Young Lloyd George*, Eyre Methuen, London, 1973

Harrison, Brian, *Separate Spheres: The Opposition to Women's Suffrage in Britain*, Croom Helm, London, 1978

Harrison, Charles, *English Art and Modernism 1900–1930*, Allen Lane, London, 1981

Heath, Stephen, *The Sexual Fix*, Macmillan, London, 1982

Hobsbawm, Eric and Ranger, Terence, *The Invention of Tradition*, Cambridge University Press, Cambridge, 1983

Holcombe, Lee, *Victorian Ladies at Work: Middle-class working women in England and Wales 1850–1914*, David & Charles, Newton Abbot, 1973

Holledge, Julie, *Innocent Flowers*, Virago, London, 1981

Hollis, Patricia (ed.), *Pressure from Without in Early Victorian England*, Edward Arnold, London, 1974

Hollis, Patricia (ed.), *Women in Public 1850–1900*, Allen & Unwin, London, 1979

Houghton, Walter, *The Victorian Frame of Mind*, Yale University Press, London, 1957

Hume, Leslie Parker, *The National Union of Women's Suffrage Societies 1897–1914*, Garland, London, 1982

Hynes, Samuel, *The Edwardian Turn of Mind*, Princeton University Press, Princeton, 1968

Jeffreys, Sheila, *The Spinster and Her Enemies: Feminism and Sexuality 1880–1930*, Pandora Press, London, 1985

Jenkins, Roy, *Asquith: Portrait of a Man and an Era*, Collins, London, 1964

Kamm, Josephine, *Rapiers and Battleaxes: The Women's Movement and its Aftermath*, Allen & Unwin, London, 1966

Kraditor, Aileen, *The Ideas of the Woman Suffrage Movement, 1890–1920*, Columbia University Press, New York, 1965

Langan, Mary and Schwarz, Bill, *Crises in the British State 1880–1930*, Hutchinson, London, 1985

Lewis, Jane, *Women in England 1870–1950: Sexual Divisions and Social Change*, Wheatsheaf, Brighton, 1984

– (ed.), *Labour and Love: Women's Experience of Home and Family 1850–1940*, Basil Blackwell, Oxford, 1986

Liddington, Jill, and Norris, Jill, *One Hand Tied Behind Us: The Rise of the Women's Suffrage Movement*, Virago, London, 1978

Liddington, Jill, *The Life and Times of a Respectable Rebel: Selina Cooper 1864–1946*, Virago, London, 1984

Linklater, Andro, *An Unhusbanded Life*, Hutchinson, London, 1980

McGregor, O. R., *Divorce in England*, Heinemann, London, 1957

Mackenzie, Midge, *Shoulder to Shoulder*, Allen Lane, London, 1975

Marwick, Arthur, *The Deluge: British Society and the First World War*, Macmillan, London, 1965

– *Women at War 1914–1918*, Fontana, London, 1977

Mitchell, David, *Women on the Warpath*, Cape, London, 1966

– *The Fighting Pankhursts: A Study in Tenacity*, Cape, London, 1967

– *Queen Christabel: A Biography of Christabel Pankhurst*, Macdonald & Jane's, London, 1977

Mitchell, Juliet and Oakley, Ann, *The Rights and Wrongs of Women*, Penguin, London, 1976

Morgan, David, *Suffragists and Liberals: The Politics of Woman Suffrage in England*, Blackwell, Oxford, 1975

Murray, Janet Horowitz (ed.), *Strong-Minded Women and other lost voices from nineteenth-century England* (1982), Penguin, London, 1984

Newsome, Stella, *Women's Freedom League, 1907–1957*, n.p., London, 1958

Newton, Judith, Ryan, Mary and Walkowitz, Judith (eds), *Sex and Class in Women's History*, Routledge & Kegan Paul, London, 1983

O'Neill, William, *Everyone was Brave: The rise and fall of feminism in America*, Quadrangle, New York, 1969

– *The Woman Movement: Feminism in the United States and England*, Allen & Unwin, London, 1969

Owens, Rosemary Cullen, *Smashing Times: A history of the Irish women's suffrage movement 1889–1922*, Attic Press, Dublin, 1984

Pankhurst, Richard Keir Pethick, *Sylvia Pankhurst: Artist and Crusader*, Paddington Press, London, 1979

Parker, Rozsika and Pollock, Griselda, *Old Mistresses: Women, Art and Ideology*, Routledge & Kegan Paul, London, 1981

Pelling, Henry, *Origins of the Labour Party*, Oxford University Press, Oxford, 1954

Poirier, Philip, *The Advent of the Labour Party*, Allen & Unwin, London, 1958

Prochaska, F. K., *Women and Philanthropy in Nineteenth-Century England*, Clarendon Press, Oxford, 1980

Pugh, Martin, *Electoral Reform in War and Peace, 1906–1918*, Routledge & Kegan Paul, London, 1978

– 'Women's Suffrage in Britain 1867–1928' [pamphlet], The Historical Association, London, 1980

Raeburn, Antonia, *The Militant Suffragettes*, Michael Joseph, London, 1973

Ramelson, Marion, *The Petticoat Rebellion: A Century of Struggle for Women's Rights*, Lawrence & Wishart, London, 1967

Read, Donald, *Edwardian England 1901–15: Society and Politics*, Harrap, London, 1972

– *Documents from Edwardian England 1901–15*, Harrap, London, 1973

Rosen, Andrew, *Rise Up, Women! The Militant Campaign of the Women's Social and Political Union 1903–1914*, Routledge & Kegan Paul, London, 1974

Rosenberg, Rosalind, *Beyond Separate Spheres: The Intellectual Roots of Modern Feminism*, Yale University Press, London, 1982

Rossi, Alice (ed.), *Essays on Sex Equality: John Stuart Mill and Harriet Taylor Mill*, University of Chicago Press, Chicago, 1970

– (ed.), *The Feminist Papers: From Adams to de Beauvoir*, Columbia University Press, New York, 1973

Rover, Constance, *The Punch Book of Women's Rights*, Hutchinson, London, 1967

– *Women's Suffrage and Party Politics in Britain, 1866–1914*, Routledge & Kegan Paul, London, 1967

– *Love, Morals and the Feminists*, Routledge & Kegan Paul, London, 1970

Rowbotham, Sheila, *Hidden from History*, Pluto, London, 1973

Showalter, Elaine, *A Literature of their Own: British Women Novelists from Brontë to Lessing* (1977), revised edition, Virago, London, 1982

Sinclair, Andrew, *The Better Half*, Cape, London, 1966

Strachey, Ray, *The Cause: A Short History of the Women's Movement in Great Britain* (1928), Virago, London, 1978

– *Millicent Garrett Fawcett*, John Murray, London, 1931

Taylor, Barbara, *Eve and the New Jerusalem: Socialism and Feminism in the Nineteenth Century*, Virago, London, 1983

Thompson, Paul, *The Edwardians: The Remaking of British Society* (1975), Weidenfeld & Nicolson, London, 1984

Trevelyan, Janet Penrose, *The Life of Mrs Humphry Ward*, Constable, London, 1923

Trudgill, Eric, *Madonnas and Magdalens: The Origins and Development of Victorian Sexual Attitudes*, Heinemann, London, 1976

Twyman, Michael, *Printing 1770–1970*, Eyre & Spottiswoode, London, 1970

Vicinus, Martha (ed.), *Suffer and Be Still: Women in the Victorian Age*, Indiana University Press, Bloomington, 1972

– (ed.), *A Widening Sphere: Changing Roles of Victorian Women*, Indiana University Press, Bloomington, 1977

Walkowitz, Judith, *Prostitution and Victorian Society: Women, Class and the State*, Cambridge University Press, Cambridge, 1980

Warner, Marina, *Monuments & Maidens: The Allegory of the Female Form*, Weidenfeld & Nicolson, London, 1985

Weeks, Jeffrey, *Sex, Politics and Society: The regulation of sexuality since 1800*, Longman, London, 1981

Yeldham, Charlotte, *Women Artists in Nineteenth-Century England and France*, Garland, London, 1984

Articles

Alexander, Sally, Davin, Anna and Hostettler, Eve, 'Labouring Women: A reply to Eric Hobsbawm', *History Workshop Journal*, no. 8, Autumn 1979

Christ, Carol (1977), 'Victorian Masculinity and the Angel in the House' in Vicinus (ed.), 1977

Cominos, Peter, 'Late-Victorian sexual respectability and the social system', *International Review of Social History*, vol. 8, 1962

Cott, Nancy, 'Passionlessness: An Interpretation of Victorian Sexual Ideology, 1790–1850', *Signs*, vol. 4 no. 2, Winter 1978

Cowling, Mary, 'The Artist as Anthropologist in Mid-Victorian England: Frith's *Derby Day*, the *Railway Station*, and the new Science of Mankind', *Art History*, vol. 6 no. 4, December 1983

Davidoff, Leonore, L'Esperance, Jean and Newby, Howard (1976), 'Landscape with Figures: Home and Community in English Society', in Mitchell and Oakley (eds), 1976

Dubois, Ellen Carol and Gordon, Linda, 'Seeking Ecstasy on the Battlefield: Danger and Pleasure in Nineteenth-Century

Feminist Sexual Thought', *Feminist Studies*, vol. 9 no. 1, Spring 1983

Dyer, Richard, 'Stereotyping' in Dyer (ed.), *Gays in Film*, British Film Institute, London, 1977

Fahnestock, Jeanne, 'The Heroine of Irregular Features: Physiognomy and Conventions of Heroine Description', *Victorian Studies*, vol. 24 no. 3, Spring 1981

Fraser, John, 'Propaganda on the Picture Postcard', *Oxford Art Journal*, vol. 3 no. 2, October 1980

Gray, Robert, 'Bourgeois Hegemony in Victorian Britain', in Jon Bloomfield (ed.), *Papers on Class, Hegemony and Party*, The Communist University of London, 1977

Green, David, 'Veins of Resemblance: Photography and Eugenics', *Oxford Art Journal*, vol. 7 no. 2, 1984

Green, Nicholas and Mort, Frank, 'Visual Representation and Cultural Politics', *Block* 7, 1982

Hall, Catherine, 'The Early Formation of Victorian Domestic Ideology', in S. Burman (ed.), *Fit Work for Women*, Croom Helm, London, 1979

Hall, Catherine, 'The Butcher, The Baker, The Candlestick-Maker: The shop and the family in the Industrial Revolution', in E. Whitelegge *et al.* (eds), *The Changing Experience of Women*, Martin Robertson/Open University, Oxford, 1982

Harper, Paula, 'Suffrage Posters', *Spare Rib*, no. 41, November 1975

– 'A Graphic Episode in the Battle of the Sexes', in Henry Millon and Linda Nochlin (eds), *Art and Architecture in the Service of Politics*, MIT Press, Boston, 1978

Hobsbawm, Eric, 'Man and Woman in Socialist Iconography', *History Workshop Journal*, no. 6, Autumn 1978

Jordanova, Ludmilla, 'Natural Facts: A Historical Perspective on Science and Sexuality', in Carol MacCormack and Marilyn Strathern (eds), *Nature, Culture and Gender*, Cambridge University Press, Cambridge, 1980

Kanner, S. Barbara, 'The Women of England in a Century of Social Change, 1815–1914: A Select Bibliography' in Vicunus (ed.), 1972

L'Esperance, Jean, 'Doctors and Women in Nineteenth-Century Society: Sexuality and Role', in J. Woodward and D. Richards (eds), *Health Care and Popular Medicine in Nineteenth Century England*, Croom Helm, London, 1977

Liddington, Jill, 'Rediscovering Suffrage History', *History Workshop Journal* 4, Autumn 1977

McGregor, O. R., 'The Social Position of Women in England, 1850–1914: A Bibliography', *British Journal of Sociology*, March 1955

McLaren, Angus, 'Phrenology: Medium and Message' in the *Journal of Modern History*, vol. 46 no. 1, March 1974

Millett, Kate (1973), 'The Debate Over Women: Ruskin vs Mill' in Vicunus (ed.), 1973

Mitchell, Juliet, 'Feminism and Femininity at the Turn of the Century' in Mitchell (ed.), *Women: The Longest Revolution: Essays on Feminism, Literature and Psychoanalysis*, Virago, London, 1984

Mulford, Wendy, 'Socialist–Feminist Criticism: A case study, women's suffrage and literature, 1906–14', in Peter Widdowson (ed.), *Re-Reading English*, Methuen, London, 1982

Neale, R. S., 'Working-Class Women and Women's Suffrage' in R. S. Neale (ed.), *Class and Ideology in the Nineteenth Century*, Routledge & Kegan Paul, London, 1972

Neale, Steve, 'Propaganda', *Screen*, vol. 18 no. 3, Autumn 1977

Newberry, Jo Vellacott, 'Anti-war Suffragists', *History*, vol. 62, October 1977

Orwell, George, 'The Art of Donald McGill', *Horizon*, vol. IV no. 21, 1941

Perkins, T. E., 'Rethinking Stereotypes' in Barrett *et al.*, *Ideology and Cultural Production*, 1979

Pugh, Martin, 'The Politicians and the Women's Vote, 1914–1918', *History* 59, October 1974

Rolfe, David, 'Origins of Mr Speaker's Conference during the First World War', *History*, vol. 64, February 1979

Summers, Anne, 'A Home from Home – Women's Philanthropic Work in the Nineteenth Century' in S. Burman (ed.), *Fit Work for Women*, Croom Helm, London, 1979

Thomas, Keith, 'The Double Standard', *Journal of the History of Ideas*, vol. 20, April 1959

Wilson, Alexander, 'The Suffrage Movement', in Hollis (ed.), 1974

Yeo, Stephen, 'A New Life: The Religion of Socialism in Britain, 1883–1896', *History Workshop Journal*, no. 4, Autumn 1977

NOTES

EPIGRAPH

1 – Adapted from *The Eighteenth Brumaire of Louis Bonaparte* (1852), Progress Publishers edition 1977, p. 10. Marx, of course, has 'Men make history . . .'

INTRODUCTION

1 – *Votes for Women*, 14 May 1908, p. 164.
2 – 'Discourse' in the sense of an ensemble of beliefs, concepts and specialised terms through which disciplines organise and understand – indeed produce – their objects of study. See the work of Michel Foucault, in particular *The Archaeology of Knowledge* (1972) and *Discipline and Punish* (1979).
3 – The *Common Cause*, 15 July 1909, p. 173.
4 – John Gorman, *Banner Bright: an illustrated history of the banners of the British trade union movement*, Allen Lane, London, 1973, p. 22. There are important exceptions. In his book *Marianne into Battle: Republican Imagery and Symbolism in France 1789–1880* (Cambridge University Press, 1981), the French historian Maurice Agulhon remarks that political imagery may be considered a marginal subject though it is better described as 'a frontier zone, a kind of "no man's land"', which is worth exploration (p. 3). Adrian Rifkin has written a number of important articles on French political prints (see for example *Block*, no. 8, 1983, the *Oxford Art Journal*, vol. 8 no. 1, 1985, and his review of Agulhon in *Art History*, vol. 6 no. 3, September 1983).
5 – There are two exceptions. Paula Harper's article 'A Graphic Episode in the Battle of the Sexes' in H. Millon and L. Nochlin (eds), *Art and Architecture in the Service of Politics*, MIT Press, Boston, 1978, and the brief discussion of suffrage banners in Rozsika Parker's useful study *The Subversive Stitch*, Women's Press, London, 1984.
6 – 'Writing the history of the present' is an expression Foucault uses in *Discipline and Punish* (1979) and elsewhere. It refers to a project which neither reads the present back into the past, nor sees the present as the final and inevitable outcome of past developments, but traces the processes by which particular contemporary manifestations took shape and gained influence.
7 – Both quotations from *The Suffrage Annual and Women's Who's Who*, A. J. K. (ed), Stanley Paul, London, 1913.
8 – See *Selections from the Prison Notebooks of Antonio Gramsci*, ed. Quintin Hoare and Geoffrey Nowell-Smith (1971). Raymond Williams provides a useful précis in *Keywords* (1976) and an account in *Marxism and Literature* (1977) which stresses the essentially mobile, consensual, negotiated and fluid processes of hegemonic power as opposed to those of direct coercion. It is impossible to understand the social positions of women without understanding the ways in which the hege-monies of class (and race) are articulated with those of gender. As Sheila Rowbotham remarks in *Hidden from History* (1973), under the new social relations of capitalism, men continued to 'own and control female creative capacity in the family and to assume that the subordination of women in society was just and natural – though the consequences of this for women from different classes were not the same' (p. ix).
9 – Jane Marcus, introduction to the Women's Press reprint of Elizabeth Robins's *The Convert* (1980, first published 1907), p. x.
10 – For a detailed discussion of the concept see Steve Neale, 'Propaganda', *Screen*, vol. 18 no. 3, Autumn 1977. Neale points out that the liberal humanist definition which dominates the discussion of propaganda is tangled in its own unacknowledged ideologies of subjectivity, politics and art.
11 – All of which, operating together in uneven ways, participate in the regulation of female sexualities through the definition of norms and deviance.
12 – Sylvia Pankhurst, *The Suffragette Movement* (1931), p. 284.
13 – There are two dictionary definitions for propaganda: the first describing the act or method of spreading specified doctrines, the second concerned with false or distorted information. In common usage we have come to conflate the two.
14 – Mona Caird, 'A Defence of the so-called "Wild Women"', the *Nineteenth Century*, vol. 31, 1892, p. 829.
15 – Osbert Sitwell, *Great Morning*, Little Brown and Co., Boston, 1947, pp. xiv–xv: 'who, today, would not wish to have been eighteen in England in 1911, even though the years before him might be brief? The air of our ancient civilisation had then a lightness about it . . . The fruit was ripe, and we were eating it! . . . The world was prospering and progressing; the poor were plainly, and without struggle, obtaining, at any rate in Great Britain, a fairer proportion of the products of the earth.' Donald Reed, in the introduction to his *Documents from Edwardian England 1901–1915* (Harrap, London, 1973), remarks two dominant narratives in the histories of pre-war England: the golden age of Sitwell's autobiography is one, the other is that of 'an epoch lurching inevitably towards Armageddon'.
16 – *The Strange Death of Liberal England*, in George Dangerfield's memorable title: a period in which the Liberal government and liberalism alike were 'dying with extreme reluctance and considerable skill' (p. 205).
17 – Cicely Hamilton, *A Pageant of Great Women* (1909). Foreword to the 1948 reprint for The Suffragette Fellowship.

I PROLOGUE

1 – Sheila Rowbotham, *Resistance and Revolution* (1972), Vintage Books, New York, 1974, p. 16.

2 – As Barbara Taylor points out (*Eve and the New Jerusalem*, Virago, London, 1983, p. x), the term 'feminism' was not used in England until 1895, but the ideology it described existed for at least a century before that as 'a distinct and identifiable body of ideas and aspirations commonly known as "the rights of women", the "condition of women" question, the "emancipation of women" and so on'.

3 – For a useful and concise account of the different strands of nineteenth-century feminism see Olive Banks, *Faces of Feminism*, Martin Robertson, Oxford, 1981. Dorothy Thompson discusses women's contribution to Chartism in 'Women and Nineteenth-Century Radical Politics: A Lost Dimension' in Juliet Mitchell and Ann Oakley (eds), *The Rights and Wrongs of Women*, Penguin Books, Harmondsworth, 1976; and more generally in her book *The Chartists*, Temple Smith, Hounslow, 1984. For a fascinating and detailed study of feminism and utopian socialism see Taylor (1983). Alice Rossi (ed.), *Essays on Sex Equality by John Stuart Mill and Harriet Taylor Mill*, University of Chicago Press, 1970, gives an account of their relationship and the intellectual circles in which they moved. This is summarised in her introduction to excerpts from *The Subjection of Women* in Rossi (1973), *The Feminist Papers* pp. 183–96. See also William Thomas, 'The Philosophic Radicals' in Patricia Hollis (ed.), *Pressure from Without*, Edward Arnold, London, 1974; and Raymond V. Holt, *The Unitarian Contribution to Social Progress in England*, The Lindsay Press, London, 1938, for information on the dissident intellectual circles in which feminist and egalitarian ideals were promoted in the first half of the nineteenth century.

4 – Ray Strachey, *The Cause* (1928), Virago, London, 1978, p. 12.

5 – Juliet Mitchell remarks that 'The theme is present in the seventeenth century, but a hundred years of confirmation has made its mark.' See the essays by Juliet Mitchell ('Women and Equality') and Margaret Walters ('The Rights and Wrongs of Women: Mary Wollstonecraft, Harriet Martineau, Simone de Beauvoir') in Juliet Mitchell and Ann Oakley (eds) (1976). (Mitchell is cited from p. 392.) Walters adds a helpful note on the best sources for Wollstonecraft, p. 434. Rowbotham (1972, p. 45) refers to the *Vindication* as 'the important theoretical summation of bourgeois radical feminism still in the phase of moral exhortation', preceding the feminist component in utopian socialism and the mid-nineteenth-century women's movement.

6 – Taylor (1983, p. 280) points out that in her introduction to the 1891 edition of the *Vindication*, Millicent Fawcett presented Wollstonecraft as a paragon of domestic virtue.

7 – See Banks (1981), pp. 13–27, 85–102; Taylor (1983), pp. 12–15, 123–30; Margaret George, 'From Goodwife to Mistress: The Transformation of the Female in Bourgeois Culture', *Science and Society* 37, 1973, pp. 152–77; and Catherine Hall, 'The Early Formation of Victorian Domestic Ideology' in Sandra Burman (ed.), *Fit Work for Women*, Croom Helm, London, 1979. On the pervasive influence of Evangelical morality Hall cites Noel Annan's assessment in *Leslie Stephen*, MacGibbon and Kee, London, 1951.

8 – Banks (1981) provides a judicious summary of the relations between feminism and Evangelicalism, and argues that the Enlightenment tradition was more significant in the emergence of the British women's movement than in that of the United States. (Cf. Nancy Cott, *The Bonds of Womanhood: 'Woman's Sphere' in New England 1780–1835*, Yale University Press, New Haven, 1977.)

9 – Quoted in Taylor (1983), p. 279. In Taylor's judicious summary: 'The movement which they built was bold in its political demands; militant in its opposition to masculine privilege; charitably philanthropic in its attitude towards working-class women (who were generally viewed as objects of sisterly compassion and concern rather than active agents in their own liberation); highly respectable and decorous in its day-to-day proceedings . . . and very cautious in its approach to all sexual matters . . .' (p. 280).

Strachey (1928) is still useful as an overview of these reforming activities although there are now more specialised studies of particular campaigns. See for example Judith Walkowitz, *Prostitution and Victorian Society: Women, Class and the State*, Cambridge University Press, Cambridge, 1980, on the Contagious Diseases Acts and the movement for their repeal; Lee Holcombe, *Wives and Property: Reform of the Married Women's Property Law in Nineteenth-Century England*, Martin Robertson, Oxford, 1984; Rita McWilliams Tullborg, *Women at Cambridge: A Men's University – though of a Mixed Type*, Gollancz, London, 1975.

10 – Wollstonecraft (1792) quoted in Rossi (1973), p. 68.

11 – Barbara Leigh Smith (later Bodichon) and Bessie Rayner Parkes, two women from unorthodox radical Unitarian backgrounds, operated with their associates from three small rooms in Langham Place 'in which there was a constant coming and going of crinolines' (Strachey, 1928, p. 95). They collected petitions in support of the Married Women's Property Bill (1856), founded the *Englishwoman's Journal* (1856), the Society for the Promotion of the Employment of Women (1859) and the Victoria Press (1860). Emily Davies, a pioneer of higher education for women, Elizabeth Garrett Anderson, the first British woman doctor, and other like-minded figures were drawn into their circle, from which an expanding network of feminist activity stretched into the fields of medicine, education, property rights, employment and eventually 'the vote'.

12 – Strachey (1928), p. 279. I am indebted here and in subsequent paragraphs to Martin Pugh, *Electoral Reform in War and Peace 1906–1918*, Routledge & Kegan Paul, London, 1978.

13 – *The Times* Woman's Supplement, 19 November 1910, 'How to Help your Party'.

14 – From notes on the 'Public Speakers' section in the programme of *The Pageant of Women's Trades and Professions*, 27 April 1909.

15 – Millicent Fawcett, *Women's Suffrage*, T. C. & E. C. Jack, London, 1912, p. 33.

16 – In what follows I am indebted to Pugh (1978 and also his outline account of *Women's Suffrage in Britain 1867–1928*, The Historical Association, London, 1980), and to the principal historians of the suffrage movement as a political campaign:

Leslie Parker Hume, *The National Union of Women's Suffrage Societies 1897–1914*, Garland, New York, 1982; Jill Liddington and Jill Norris, *One Hand Tied Behind Us: The Rise of the Women's Suffrage Movement*, Virago, London, 1978; David Morgan, *Suffragists and Liberals: The Politics of Woman Suffrage in England*, Blackwell, Oxford, 1975; Andrew Rosen, *Rise Up Women! The Militant Campaign of the Women's Social and Political Union 1903–1914*, Routledge & Kegan Paul, London, 1974; and Constance Rover, *Women's Suffrage and Party Politics in Britain 1866–1914*, Routledge & Kegan Paul, London, 1967.

17 – Quoted in Walter L. Arnstein, 'Votes for Women: Myths and Reality', *History Today*, 8, 1968, p. 539. Pugh (1980, pp. 17, 26) points to the Liberal cabinet as divided between Lloyd George, Haldane, Runciman and Birrell, all ostensibly in favour, and Asquith, Harcourt, Pease, McKenna, Crewe and Samuel, opposed to women's suffrage. Lords Robert Cecil, Selborne and Lytton were prominent supporters among the Tory peers; Lord Curzon, Walter Long and Austen Chamberlain were antis. Neither Balfour nor Bonar Law, who succeeded him as leader of the Conservatives in 1911, were in a position to impose the principle of women's suffrage on a reluctant party.

18 – Statistics were produced at various points in an attempt to prove that this was not the case: see Rover (1967), pp. 114, 182–4 and Hume (1982), p. 37.

19 – The Lancashire textile workers were unionised and comparatively well paid, the only women workers with organisational, political and economic power, the only ones with a substantial stake in trade-union membership. (Pugh, 1980, p. 20, points out that 126,000 women had joined trade unions by 1904, of whom 110,000 were in the textile industry.) They were particularly sensitive to the question of the proposed trade-union levy to fund the salaries of Labour MPs, since as women they would not be able to vote for them. See Liddington and Norris (1978), especially chapter XIII, 'The Debate with the Labour Party'. The North of England Society (which was affiliated to the NUWSS) worked with the Labour churches, the ILP and the Women's Co-operative Guild.

20 – Belfort Bax published *The Legal Subjection of Men* (1908) and the *Fraud of Feminism* (1913); and Sylvia Pankhurst recalled Hyndman telling her that 'Women should learn to have influence as they have in France instead of trying to get votes' (Sylvia Pankhurst, *The Suffragette Movement* (1931), Virago, London, 1977, p. 111). Unlike the SDF, the ILP had feminist sympathies from its inception. The Women's Co-operative Guild supported suffrage within the labour movement, and the Fabians adopted a pro-suffrage policy in 1906 (Banks, 1981, pp. 123–24).

21 – The People's Suffrage Federation was formed in 1904 to uphold the concept of adult suffrage. No doubt its members were men and women of probity but their position was also shared by those whose democratic principles were simply a cover for anti-feminism. Those who supported a more pragmatic measure were exasperated by the fact that the adult suffragists spent more energy blocking that cause than advancing their own. As Keir Hardie remarked, the Adult Suffrage Society 'holds no meetings, issues no literature . . . [and] is never heard of, save when it emerges to oppose the Women's Enfranchisement Bill. Its policy is that of the dog in the manger' (quoted in Liddington and Norris (1978), p. 232, see also p. 126 and pp. 180–83). The Adult Suffrage Society was formed under Margaret Bondfield, a trade unionist who had publicly deprecated votes for women 'as the hobby of disappointed old maids whom no one had wanted to marry' (p. 231).

Suffrage societies regularly arranged debates with adult suffragists as well as with anti-suffragists: see for example the *Vote*, 12 March 1910.

22 – See *The Times*, 25 June 1910, 'The Present Strength of the Woman Suffrage Movement' ('there are 21 suffrage organisations working for the woman's vote to-day, where there were three in 1905') or the programme of march for the Women's Coronation Procession in 1911 for a more extensive list.

23 – For pressure groups see Patricia Hollis (ed.), *Pressure from Without in Early Victorian England*, Edward Arnold, London, 1974. Alexander Wilson contributes a chapter on the men's suffrage movement which comments on the impact of mass demonstrations on the passage of the 1867 Reform Act. Strachey (1928, pp. 40–43) and Rover (1967, pp. 61–62) among others remark on the connections between the first generation of suffragists and the anti-slavery and anti-Corn Law campaigns.

24 – Quoted in Ray Strachey, *Millicent Garrett Fawcett*, John Murray, London, 1931, p. 154. Hollis (1974) suggests that it was always easier to get a law repealed by pressure-group activity than to get a new one passed, and that women's suffrage, at least until the First World War, did not benefit from the kind of 'precipitating factor' that carried other pressure-group causes to victory (p. 23).

25 – Hume's detailed and painstaking account of the NUWSS (1982) is an essential corrective to a historical picture dominated by the more sensational activities of the WSPU.

26 – Hume (1982, p. 13) describes them as 'a sort of feminist cousinhood'.

27 – In 1903 the constituent societies of the NUWSS were organised into a more cohesive national pressure group, 133 new committees were founded and an election fund of £2520 raised (Hume, 1982, pp. 21–23).

28 – The Annual Reports of the WSPU do not give membership figures. Pugh (1980, p. 25) argues that at its peak it had eighty-eight branches, chiefly in London and the Southeast. Rosen (1974, pp. 211–12) suggests that there was a marked decline in the rate of new memberships between 1909 and 1913. The NUWSS developed from a small organisation of seventeen societies in 1897 into a national union of 500 branches with more than 50,000 members by 1914 (Hume, 1982, p. 226).

29 – Sylvia Pankhurst (1931), p. 189. See also Christabel Pankhurst, *Unshackled*, Hutchinson, London, 1959, p. 49. Even the constitutionalist Ray Strachey acknowledged the impact of the Free Trade Hall incident on the press (Strachey, 1928, pp. 294–95): 'Here was NEWS, thrilling NEWS, involving a future Cabinet Minister and a cause about which ridicule and

cheap joking were easy . . . by this one act hundreds of people who had never thought about Women's Suffrage before, began to consider it, and though the vast majority of them deplored what had been done, this did not make the result any the less important.' See also Rosen (1974, p. 53) re press reports, large audiences at WSPU meetings and increased membership figures in the weeks following October 1905.

30 – According to Emmeline Pethick-Lawrence, *My Part in a Changing World*, London, Gollancz, 1938, p. 180.

31 – 'There was a spring in it, a spring that we liked,' Christabel recalled, and in October 1912 she called her new paper the *Suffragette*: a name originating in the popular press that had subsequently 'by use and association, been purified of any opprobrium or distasteful significance' (foreword to the first issue, 18 October 1912). See also her autobiography (1959), p. 63: 'Suffragists, we had called ourselves till then, but that name lacked the positive note implied by "Suffragette". Just "want the vote" was the notion conveyed by the older appellation and, as a famous anecdote had it, "the Suffragettes (hardening the 'g') they mean to get it." '

32 – Sylvia Pankhurst (1931), p. 182: 'different indeed from the rousing Socialist meetings of the North, to which I was accustomed'.

33 – Emmeline Pethick-Lawrence (1938), second page of un-numbered preface.

34 – Emmeline Pankhurst, *My Own Story*, Eveleigh Nash, London, 1914, p. 116.

35 – Emmeline Pankhurst (1914), p. 58. Hollis (1974) argues that the period between the Reform Acts of 1832 and 1867 was far from being the golden age of the independent MP ('even before, and certainly after, 1832 MPs were party men'); but the influence of the individual MP declined as parties began to offer a political platform in the second half of the nineteenth century and not just to represent an interest (p. 24).

36 – Emmeline Pankhurst (1914), p. 58.

37 – Sylvia Pankhurst (1931), p. 223.

38 – On 19 May 1906 a massive deputation of 400 women went to plead the cause of women's suffrage with Campbell-Bannerman, the Prime Minister. They included representatives from the WSPU, the Liberal and Temperance women's organisations, and fifty 'radical suffragists' down from Lancashire with their banners to represent a quarter of a million working women. It was the last occasion on which the WSPU and the radical suffragists collaborated (Liddington and Norris, 1978, pp. 203–07). Eva Gore-Booth wrote to Millicent Fawcett on 25 October 1906 that the class respectability of working women was at stake: 'It is not the fact of demonstrations or even violence that is offensive to them, it is being mixed up with and held accountable as a class for educated and upper-class women who kick, shriek, bite, and spit' (Manchester Public Library Archives M/50 Box 10, quoted Hume (1982), pp. 29–30). See also Liddington and Norris (1978), p. 205.

39 – Rosen (1974, pp. 86–94) gives an account of the split that led to the formation of the Women's Freedom League in 1907.

40 – Emmeline Pethick-Lawrence (1938), pp. 175–76, quoted Rosen (1974), p. 90.

41 – The WSPU became officially the NWSPU (the National Women's Social and Political Union), and for a brief period the splinter group claimed rights to the title WSPU before settling for 'The Women's Freedom League' (announced in the *Women's Franchise*, 28 November 1907). I have kept the initials WSPU throughout for the parent body, to avoid confusion: they were in any case the ones in common use. Rosen (1974, p. 94) points out that it was the more politically experienced women who left, often from the labour movement, and that their loss proved decisive for the development of militancy in 1913–14. The WFL had twenty branches in 1908. It expanded to a membership of about 7000 in 1913 but was probably only about an eighth of the size of the WSPU (see Linklater, 1980, p. 167).

42 – Emmeline Pankhurst (1914), p. 59. Many did indeed leave. The severing of relations with the radical suffragists (1906) and with the members who became the Women's Freedom League (1907) was followed by the departure of the Pethick-Lawrences (in 1912), of Sylvia's East London Federation of Suffragettes (in 1914, though they had been effectively independent for some time), and a group including Henry Nevinson, Evelyn Sharp, George Lansbury, Laurence Housman and Louisa Garrett Anderson, who formed the United Suffragists in 1914. On the question of democracy, Frederick Pethick-Lawrence remarked that there were arguments on both sides: 'The analogy of the constitution of a democratic country pointed one way, the analogy of a military campaign the other' (*Fate has been Kind*, Hutchinson, London, 1943, p. 75).

43 – The *Common Cause*, 15 July 1909, p. 173.

2 PRODUCTION

1 – For a detailed account of women's educational and exhibiting opportunities see Charlotte Yeldham, *Women Artists in Nineteenth-Century England and France*, Garland, New York and London, 1984: and more generally Ann Sutherland Harris and Linda Nochlin, *Women Artists 1550–1950*, Knopf, New York, 1976; Germaine Greer, *The Obstacle Race: The Fortunes of Women Painters and their Work*, Secker & Warburg, London, 1979; and Rozsika Parker and Griselda Pollock, *Old Mistresses: Women, Art and Ideology*, Routledge & Kegan Paul, London, 1981. On the opportunities for women's training and employment in the arts and crafts movement see Anthea Callen, *Angel in the Studio: Women in the Arts and Crafts Movement 1870–1914*, Astragal Books, London, 1979. (Margaret Bartels, Joan Drew, Emily Ford, Joan Fulleylove, Caroline Townshend, Mary Sargant Florence, Ernestine Mills, Pamela Coleman Smith, Louise Jacobs and Mary Wheelhouse – all suffrage artists – exhibited with the Arts and Crafts Exhibition Society.) Michael Holroyd, in *Augustus John* (Heinemann, London, 1974), chapter 2, 'Slade School Ingenious', gives an account of the formation of the Slade School of Fine Art and its role in the 1890s when a number of talented women were students there. (John famously remarked that they outshone the men, but with the exception of his sister Gwen they were chiefly swallowed up by domesticity as he predicted: Augustus John, *Chiaroscuro*, Cape, London, 1952, p. 48.)

Women came from all over the world to study at European and especially Parisian studios like the Académie Julian. See Cecilia Beaux, *Background with Figures*, Houghton Mifflin, Boston and Newport, 1930; Marian Hepworth Dixon, 'A Personal Reminiscence' in the *Fortnightly Review*, February 1890; *The Journal of Marie Bashkirtseff* (1890), Virago, London, 1985, pp. 304 ff.; William Rothenstein, *Men and Memories*, Faber & Faber, London, 1931, vol. I, pp. 36–43; A. S. Hartrick, *A Painter's Pilgrimage through Fifty Years*, Cambridge University Press, London, 1939, pp. 13–27. In 1904 Clive Holland published his account of 'Lady Art Students' Life in Paris' in the *Studio* (no. 21, pp. 225–31). He noted the increasing numbers of women choosing to study in Paris, provided a slightly piquant account of their semi-bohemian lifestyle and recommended the available facilities: quaint surroundings, untrammelled friendships, a sound training and hard but rewarding work, at a modest cost of about £94 per annum in furnished accommodation. Mary Sargant Florence, Dora Meeson Coates, Jessica Walters and several other suffrage artists trained in Paris.

2 – The *Census of England and Wales* for 1901 (HMSO, London, 1902) gives comparable figures for male and female artists in 1881, 1891 and 1901 (Appendix A, Table 33). Given the fluidity of the profession and the fact that presumably anyone could claim to be an artist on their census return, the figures can only be approximate, but they are not without interest. 9099 men and 1960 women registered as artists in 1881; 9250 men and 3032 women in 1891; 10,250 men and 3699 women in 1901. (In 1901 there were 10,775 male and six female architects, and 9026 male and two women accountants.)

3 – Octave Uzanne, *The Modern Parisienne*, Heinemann, London, 1907, pp. 129–30.

4 – Within the bosom of the family women might practise those musical and artistic accomplishments – George Eliot's 'small tinkling and smearing' – which had filtered down from the gentry and into leisured, middle-class households. Harris and Nochlin (1976, p. 41) quote *Middlemarch* (1871) (Penguin, London, 1965, p. 89). As Sarah Stickney Ellis described the art of drawing, it was of all genteel occupations 'the one most calculated to keep the mind from brooding upon self, and to maintain that general cheerfulness which is a part of social and domestic duty' (*The Daughters of England*, P. Jackson, London, 1842, p. 141).

5 – See Thomas Purnell, 'Woman and Art', *Art Journal*, 1861, p. 108; and 'Art Work for Women', parts I, II and III, *Art Journal*, 1872, pp. 66, 102 and 130. These articles assure the reader that women's activities as artists need not encroach on their 'separate sphere': 'there is here no question of the introduction of women to new employments, or of the danger of tempting them from their homes' (quoted in Callen, 1979, p. 25). The *Art Journal*, 1858, p. 143, a review of the exhibition of the Society of Female Artists, and 'Women Artists' in the *Westminster Review* of July 1858 are also relevant.

6 – Uzanne (1907), pp. 129–30.

7 – That is, incompatible both with the feminine ideal and with the material reality of middle-class women's daily lives, in which there was no space, no money and no time (not two minutes

together, as Florence Nightingale complained). Anna Lea Merritt concluded that the 'chief obstacle to a woman's success is that she can never have a wife'. Wives were indispensable to a successful artistic career ('A Letter to Artists: Especially Women Artists', *Lippincott's Monthly Magazine*, 1900, vol. 65, pp. 467–68). The woman artist was a popular character in New Woman fiction, where the heroine's 'happy ending' usually required the abandonment of her career for marriage and motherhood.

8 – Mrs Elizabeth Ellet, *Women Artists in All Ages and Countries*, Richard Bentley, London, 1859, p. v. See also Ellen C. Clayton, *English Female Artists*, Tinsley, London, 1876, and Clara Erskine Clement, *Women in the Fine Arts from the Seventh Century BC to the Twentieth Century AD*, Houghton Mifflin, Boston, 1904. The most ambitious women's exhibition was that in the Woman's Building (designed by Sophia Hayden) in the Columbian Exposition, Chicago, 1893, for which Mary Cassatt designed her mural 'The Modern Woman'. See the frontispiece illustration (and assertion) of the 'creative woman' to Maud Howe Elliott (ed.), *Art and Handicraft in the Woman's Building of the World's Columbian Exposition*, 1893.

9 – Virginia Woolf, *Three Guineas* (1938), Penguin, London, 1977, pp. 73–74.

10 – The prestige of the Royal Academy, already challenged in the 1880s, was seriously undermined by the report of a Select Committee set up in 1904 to investigate its administration of the Chantrey Bequest and by criticism in the press of its selection procedures and its hostility to anything progressive in style or subject matter. The New English Art Club, a breath of *plein air* in the English art world of the 1880s and 1890s, had become a conservative force in British art by 1907.

11 – Quoted in Frances Spalding, *Vanessa Bell*, Macmillan, London, 1983, p. 37.

12 – Giles Edgerton, 'Is there a Sex Distinction in Art?', *The Craftsman*, June 1908, vol. xiv no. 3, pp. 239–51. See also Laurence Housman, 'Women Exhibitors at the Royal Academy' in *Votes for Women*, 9 May 1913.

13 – For a characteristic formulation see Walter Shaw Sparrow, *Women Painters of the World*, Hodder & Stoughton, London, 1905, where he turns from the 'alpine heights' of masculine genius to a consideration of 'woman's garden in the art of painting'. Vigée Lebrun is praised for the 'complete womanliness' in her maternal self-portraits: 'Such pictures may not be the highest form of painting, but highest they are in their own realm of human emotion' (p. 11). This kind of writing keeps women's work marginal and identifies it with the characteristics of a reproductive and domestic femininity, which are understood *not* to be the characteristics of great art. In this sense Sparrow's text must be seen as a response to the implicit or explicit feminism of Ellet, Clayton, Clement and other contemporary writers who claimed that institutional discrimination alone had held women artists back. As Giles Edgerton commented (1908, p. 242): 'The minute that you label any sort of exhibit as exclusively "women's" you have let loose the flood gates of masculine sentimentality.'

14 – See Parker and Pollock (1981, pp. 82–83 and 99) for an

outline discussion of the processes by which bourgeois definitions of the artist, and of respectable femininity, diverged in
the nineteenth century. The artist developed as the type of the
outsider, creature of inspiration and disorder, as 'womanliness'
was defined in terms of domesticity and reproduction. By the
early twentieth century, if not before, feminists were coming to
recognise the contradiction and to refuse it. Women like Cicely
Hamilton (militant spinsters, one might call them) attempted to
focus the identity of the independent working woman on her
productive labour and economic independence (like that of the
bourgeois man) and not on her reproductive sexuality. In
Marriage as a Trade (1909), The Women's Press, London, 1981,
p. 130, Hamilton speaks of the class she knows intimately and
respects: that of 'journalists, artists, typists, dressmakers, clerks;
practically all of them dependent on their work and practically
all of them poor'. The suffrage movement was a cross-class
movement, but this type of woman played an important part in
it. 'The sense of a common interest, the realisation of common
disabilities, have forced her into class-consciousness and parti-
sanship of her class ... I know hardly one whose life is not
affected, to an appreciable extent, by the sense of fellowship
with her sisters.'

15 – Some of these images are discussed, illuminatingly, in
Lynda Nead, *Representation and Regulation: Women and Sexuality
in English Art c. 1840–1870*, unpublished PhD thesis, University of London, 1985. The obsession with feminine sexuality is
quite as marked, if differently produced, in the early twentieth-
century avant-garde. See Carol Duncan, 'Virility and Domination in Early Twentieth-Century Vanguard Painting' in Norma
Broude and Mary D. Garrard, *Feminism and Art History: Questioning the Litany*, Harper & Row, New York, 1982. Renoir's
'Portrait de M. Ambrose Vollard' (1908) offers a poignant
instance of the cross-currents between feminism and the high
art idealisation of naked femininity as a touchstone of aesthetic
appreciation among men. The famous dealer, collector and
connoisseur gazes appreciatively at the Maillol statuette he
turns in his hands. Woman in art and woman as art are
momentarily the same. Renoir's obsession with femininity and
hatred of feminism is well known. The portrait was painted in
the year of two major suffrage demonstrations in London. It
belonged to Samuel Courtauld and is now in the Courtauld
Institute galleries. Samuel Courtauld's sister Catherine was a
member of the Suffrage Atelier and the author of designs such
as 'Waiting for a Living Wage'. The haggard chainmaker which
that depicts is a symbol of the economic exploitation of industrial working women and the antithesis of Renoir's dream of the
eternal feminine, the pastoral nude.

16 – They also discussed the institutional restrictions on
women's careers, and the notions of creativity to which women
were subject. See for example Laurence Housman, 'Women
and the Royal Academy', *Votes for Women*, 10 May 1912; *Votes
for Women*, 5 and 26 May 1911 and 15 May 1914; and Mary
Lowndes, 'Genius, and Women Painters', the *Common Cause*,
17 April 1914. Cicely Hamilton's lecture on 'Women and Art',
partially reworked from *Marriage as a Trade* (1909), was reported in the *Vote*, 4 June 1910.

17 – 'Genius, and Women Painters', the *Common Cause*, 17
April 1914.

18 – *Votes for Women*, 26 May 1911, p. 563. Others made the
connection too, intending it as either an insult or a compliment.
The *Bystander* (13 March 1912) paralleled militant suffrage
'hysteria' with Futurism ('The Hysteria Wave Spreads to Art');
Frank Rutter, art critic and honorary treasurer of the Men's
Political Union for Women's Enfranchisement, dedicated
Revolution in Art (Art News Press, London, 1910) to 'Rebels of
either sex all the World over who in any way are fighting for
freedom of any kind'. A certain redefinition of the artist took
place in avant-garde circles from 1910–14, as the rising Turks
differentiated themselves from those they characterised as
dilettante or effete. The notorious Round Robin signed by
Wyndham Lewis and others who broke with the Omega Workshops in 1913 dismissed Roger Fry and his associates as a
'family party of strayed and dissenting Aesthetes ... compelled
to call in as much modern talent as they could find to do the
rough masculine work'. *Vital English Art*, the Futurist Manifesto
written by Marinetti and C. R. W. Nevinson (son of the
journalist and suffragist Henry Woodd Nevinson), castigated
the 'effeminacy' of English art and called for an art that was
'strong, virile and anti-sentimental', characterised by 'a worship
of strength and a physical and moral courage'. But the militants
were exempt from this damning effeminacy: *Blast* blessed the
suffragettes ('We make you a present of our votes, so long as you
leave works of art alone'); and in his address to the Lyceum
Club in 1910 Marinetti extolled the suffragette and exonerated
her from a general raillery against the pernicious influence of
woman that was apparently an essential part of the Futurist
programme. (Her 'snake-like coils' had ever 'choked the
noblest ideals of manhood'.) This play of sexual differentiation
across the rhetoric of British modernism suggests that the
piling-up of characteristics unfavourably designated 'feminine'
helped to secure the hegemony of a masculine avant-garde at a
time when women were gaining ground in institutional terms.
See Sarah Shalgosky, Rod Brookes and Jane Beckett, 'Henri
Gaudier: Art History and the "Savage Messiah"' in Jeremy
Lewison (ed.), *Henri Gaudier-Brzeska, sculptor 1891–1915*,
Kettle's Yard Gallery, Cambridge, 1983; C. R. W. Nevinson,
Paint and Prejudice, Methuen, London, 1937; and 'Futurism
and Woman', the *Vote*, 31 December 1910, p. 112.

19 – Elizabeth Robins, *The Convert* (1907), The Women's
Press, London, 1980, pp. 265–66. This edition has an
informative introduction by Jane Marcus, which sketches
Robins's biography as actress, Ibsenist, novelist and playwright,
and member of the executive committee of the WSPU. *The
Convert* was based on her own play, *Votes for Women*.

20 – Mary Lowndes, 'Genius, and Women Painters', the
Common Cause, 17 April 1914, p. 31. See also Laurence Housman's address on 'Art and National Movements', delivered at
an early public meeting of the Suffrage Atelier, for the argument that art needed feminism; that 'art had long suffered from
a want of connection with life' which the women's movement
could rectify (the *Common Cause*, 1 July 1909, pp. 158–59).

21 – 'The Spirit of the Movement', speech by Cicely Hamilton,

3 January 1911, reported in the *Vote*, 14 January 1911, pp. 140–41.

22 – Edith M. Mason-Hinchley, 'Why We Want the Vote: The Woman Artist' (one of a series), the *Vote*, 12 August 1911.

23 – 'Some Supporters of the Women's Suffrage Movement' published by the Central Committee of the National Society for Women's Suffrage and the Central National Society for Women's Suffrage, 1897 (Fawcett Archives). On Barbara Bodichon's work as an artist see Hester Burton, *Barbara Bodichon 1827–1891*, John Murray, London, 1949; and John Crabbe, 'An Artist Divided', *Apollo*, vol. 113, May 1981, pp. 311–17. Mrs Swynnerton headed the Chelsea artists' section together with Mrs Stilman (Marie Spartali, a member of the Rossetti circle) in the Women's Coronation Procession of 1911 (*Votes for Women*, 23 June 1911, p. 633).

24 – Sylvia Pankhurst (1931), 1977, p. 359.

25 – *Votes for Women*, 14 March 1913, p. 345: 'Propaganda on the Pavement'. Paintings with suffrage subject-matter were also exhibited: see *Votes for Women*, 5 July 1912, p. 651 (Mme Arsène Darmesteter, a member of the WSPU, had exhibited a portrait of Mrs Barbara Ayrton Gould, another WSPU member, at the Salon of 1911); and *Votes for Women*, 18 July 1913, p. 621, which notes Mary Robinson's painting of 'the Most Sensational Derby on Record: Suffragette and the King's horse, Anmer', and Mrs L. Delissa Joseph's study of 'The Woman's March' at the sixth London exhibition of the Allied Artists' Association.

26 – There are three sources for the formation of the Artists' Suffrage League: *The Suffrage Annual and Women's Who's Who*, A. J. K., ed., Stanley Paul, London, 1913 (this quotation is from p. 12); the 'order of march and descriptive programme', *Memento of the Women's Coronation Procession Saturday June 17th 1911* (Museum of London); and the NUWSS *Annual Report 1907* (Fawcett Archives, Box 145).

27 – See *The Suffrage Annual and Women's Who's Who*, 1913, p. 12: 'The posters of the Artists' Suffrage League have also been constantly supplied to America for the use of the National Association, whose headquarters are in New York. They also played a part in the successful campaign in California.' There are many League and Atelier posters in American collections, particularly in those of the Library of Congress in Washington, and the Schlesinger Library, Radcliffe College, Cambridge, Massachusetts.

28 – *The Suffrage Annual and Women's Who's Who*, 1913, p. 12.

29 – The terms of the competition had been set out in the *Women's Franchise* on 27 June 1907 (p. 4): 'The Union, through the generosity of one of its members, has been enabled to offer a prize of six guineas for the best poster in favour of Women's Suffrage, for use at Parliamentary Elections. To make the competition still more interesting, the first prize (open to men as well as women) will be supplemented by a second prize of £5 for the best design sent in by a woman, offered by another benefactor. Designs must measure 30 in. by 40 in. or 20 in. by 30 in., must be suitable for reproduction, and must not contain more than two colours, besides black and white . . . A nom-de-plume should be written on the back of each drawing (*not* the real name of the artist).' The prize was not awarded as the judges decided

that none of the designs had 'reached a sufficiently high standard both as to artistic merit, suitability for reproduction, and excellence of idea' (The *Women's Franchise*, 17 October 1907, p. 176). The competition was thrown open again, and artists invited to submit thumbnail sketches for approval. Results were announced in the *Women's Franchise*, 30 January 1908, p. 352. The second prize was awarded jointly to Emily Harding Andrews and Miss Williams.

30 – See for example the *Common Cause*, 30 September 1909, p. 315 and *Votes for Women*, 8 October 1909, p. 30 for details of a postcard competition. There were twenty-five entries (Artists' Suffrage League *Report*, January 1909–January 1910, Fawcett Archives, Box 153).

31 – *Votes for Women*, 18 February 1909, p. 365.

32 – See Artists' Suffrage League *Report*, January 1909–January 1910, Fawcett Archives, Box 153.

33 – *Common Cause*, 4 November 1909, p. 389.

34 – Information from Richard Shone, letter to the author, 4 February 1983. Shone owns Duncan Grant's sketchbook for this period which includes preliminary drawings for 'Handicapped', the letter from Barbara Forbes (which also suggests an alternative possibility where both figures are awash in the sea of labour but the man has the lifebelt of the vote and Justice holds another on the bank), and a second letter from Barbara Forbes dated 17 February 1909 on ASL paper inviting Grant's contribution: 'I send you a notice of the poster competition as you sent such an excellent drawing to the National Union one 2 years ago.' I am very grateful to Richard Shone for this information.

35 – That which follows is culled from the sources listed above, together with the list of posters and postcards printed in *The ABC of Politics*, published by the Artists' Suffrage League (undated but probably 1909); the *Common Cause*, 28 October 1909, p. 374 and 18 November 1909, p. 422; and the ASL *Report* for the year ending 1910 (Fawcett Archives, Box 153 – only these two *Reports*, for 1909 and 1910, survive).

36 – Emily Ford, 'Factory Girl', 1908; Emily J. Harding Andrews, 'It's Time I Got Out of this Place', 1908/9 reprinted 1910; Mary Sargant Florence, 'What's Sauce for the Gander' probably 1908, reprinted 1910; W. F. Winter, 'Votes for Workers' (joint winner with 'Handicapped'), 1909; Duncan Grant, 'Handicapped', 1909; Joan Drew, 'Why Won't They Let the Women Help?', 1909, 'Won't You Let Me Help You John?', probably 1909, and 'Votes for Mother now Father's Dead', 1910; Mrs Shute, 'The Widow's Children', 1910; anonymous, 'The Dog in the Manger', 1908/9. The eleventh design was probably the 'Bugler Girl', designed by Caroline Watts on behalf of the ASL for the NUWSS procession of 13 June 1908. Dora Meeson Coates's 'Political Help' was published by the NUWSS in 1908 although she was a member of the League; Mary Lowndes's 'Justice at the Door' was also published by the NUWSS, in 1913; Emily J. Harding Andrews's 'Mrs Partington' was published by the League, but presumably after the end of 1910. The League also produced a new picture leaflet, 'The Householder' by Joan Drew, for the general elections, two Christmas cards, and a new rose badge for the

National Union designed by Miss Woodward. Individual members published drawings in the *Common Cause*, designed two posters and a calendar for the London Society and decorated the Queen's Hall for the National Union meeting in June (ASL *Report* 1910, Fawcett Archives, Box 153).

37 – Information contained in Mary Lowndes's letter to the *Common Cause* published 22 December 1910 in which she begs 'anyone who has a good idea for a poster or leaflet to be sure and send it to us without delay . . . [it] should be capable of illustration by not more than three figures.'

38 – The ASL accounts (in the two ASL *Reports*) list income from subscriptions and donations as £8 9s. 7d. in 1909, £4 10s. 1d. plus £6 donations in 1910. If their subscription was the same as the Suffrage Atelier (1s. 6d.) a figure of £4 10s. 1d. would suggest that there were about sixty members (although it does not account for the penny).

39 – I have kept the term 'chairman' as I have used 'Miss' and 'Mrs' where Christian names are not known, or where titles were in common use. Emmeline was conventionally known as 'Mrs Pankhurst', her daughters familiarly as 'Sylvia' and 'Christabel' in order to distinguish them from each other and from her. Millicent Fawcett was virtually always referred to as Mrs Fawcett.

Mary Lowndes was a member of the Executive Committee of the London Society for Women's Suffrage, and of the Magazine Committee of the NUWSS which preceded the founding of the *Common Cause* in 1909. The Artists' Suffrage League was constitutionalist and closely tied to the NUWSS, although there seem to have been links with the Women's Freedom League in its early years. Dora Meeson Coates belonged to both the ASL and the WFL. The WFL 'Holloway Badge' was designed by the ASL and presented to WFL prisoners through the generosity of one of its banner-makers, Mrs Herringham. And the 'Holloway' banner carried by the WFL in the NUWSS procession of 1908 was apparently designed by Mary Lowndes (WFL *Report*, 1908, p. 11, Museum of London).

40 – Fred Miller, 'Women Workers in the Art Crafts', *Art Journal*, 1896, pp. 116–18.

41 – See Cormack (1984). I am grateful to Miss Kitty Duff for sharing her reminiscences of Barbara Forbes, and for showing me letters between Barbara Forbes and Mary Lowndes. One, undated but presumably from 1896–97, reads: 'You will soon head a large firm – just design and superintend . . . And you'll have lots of real apprentices who will be fined 1/– for every broken piece of glass poor things.' Drury was in charge of the daily running of the workshops leaving Mary Lowndes, who put up most of the money, to pursue her activities as designer, writer and suffragist.

42 – Membership of the ASL committee appears to have remained constant between 1907 and 1913, except for the loss of Mary Barker, who died in 1912 (*Common Cause*, 1 August 1912, p. 294), and Clara Billing. Barbara Forbes appears from the accounts to have been a paid secretary. The King's Road address of Brittany Studios is now occupied by Green & Stone, who sell artists' materials. The proprietor, Jass Cameron, discovered a cache of ASL papers in the 1970s and passed them

on to Amy Katherine Browning, a suffrage artist who had worked with Sylvia Pankhurst on mural designs for the WSPU, and a local resident. Unfortunately they seem to have been destroyed, since there were no such papers in her possession when she died in 1978 at the age of ninety-six. I am grateful to her sister Barbara Day Jenkinson for information and advice. On the connection between Spencer and Mary Sargant Florence see *Stanley Spencer R. A.*, Royal Academy of Arts and Weidenfeld & Nicolson, London, 1980, p. 97.

43 – See Yeldham (1984), chapter 2 part 3, 'Societies of Women Artists'. Yeldham suggests (p. 97) that such societies tended to become less defensive and more vocal in their support for the woman artist as a capable professional in the late Victorian and Edwardian period. The Women's International Art Club, open to all women who had studied in Paris and did 'strong work', had more than 100 members from seventeen different countries by 1900, when its first London exhibition was held in the Grafton Galleries. In 1910 the exhibition included work by women artists of the past (Yeldham, p. 96). There is a real sense of women exploring their capacities and their heritage at this moment, in the face of those critical discourses that secured their work as 'feminine' and hence inferior. By the late nineteenth century women artists had begun to perceive themselves as a group with a particular identity, one that suffered from certain difficulties but to which new possibilities were opening. Greer (1980, pp. 321–23) also lists women's exhibitions at this period.

44 – D. M. Coates, *George Coates: His Art and His Life*, Dent, London, 1937, pp. 32–43. The Artists' Suffrage League held three general meetings in 1909 and two in 1910, one of which took place in Bessie Wigan's studio, and others at Emily Ford's address in Glebe Place (see *Reports*, Fawcett Archives, Box 153).

45 – Mary Lowndes to Philippa Strachey, 25 July 1908, Fawcett Autograph Collection. In the same letter she recommends Ruth Cross, 'a first rate person' and a needleworker with workrooms and apprentices. 'I really want her for my committee – but I would give her to you.'

46 – Note appended by Barbara Forbes to a letter from Mary Lowndes to Philippa Strachey, October 1909 (Fawcett Archives, Box 146, LSWS general correspondence).

47 – The *Common Cause*, 24 June 1909, p. 144. See also Fawcett Archives, Box 154, circular letter from Gertrude Cullen, 28 February 1909, addressed to the LSWS: 'A new Society has been formed to support the Women's Suffrage Movement by means of pictorial advertisement (cartoons postcards posters etc). I have been requested to write and ask you if you can give me the names and addresses of any members of the various branches of the LSWS of which you are secretary, who might possibly be interested in the new Society. We shall be glad of any kind of help (artistic, literary, clerical, pecuniary etc).'

48 – The *Vote*, 15 June 1912, p. 145: 'The value of pictorial art in Suffrage propaganda has not hitherto been sufficiently recognised, and until . . . [the Atelier] began its valuable work of educating the public by its pictorial displays, poli-

tical pictures had scarcely been thought of in the suffrage world.'

49 – See the *Common Cause*, 1 July 1909, pp. 158–59, and *The Suffrage Annual and Women's Who's Who*, 1913: 'An Arts and Crafts Society composed of suffragists, whose object it is to help any and every Suffrage Society through their arts'.

50 – See the 'Suffrage Fair' programme bound into the Maud Arncliffe-Sennett cuttings albums in the British Museum (vol. 11, *c.* p. 47) in which the Atelier advertises not only its banner-making services but its members' skills in embroidery and stencilling for curtains, dresses and 'other Fancy Articles'. The *Suffragette*, 22 August 1913, p. 791, mentions an exhibition of needlework by members of the Atelier at the Westminster Tea Shop, to be followed by others on the first Saturday of the month. The October exhibition was devoted to lithography, engraving, etching and other printing methods. There are numerous other references to Atelier exhibitions and 'At Homes' in the suffrage press.

51 – Fawcett Archives, Box 154.

52 – The *Common Cause*, 1 July 1909, pp. 158–59. Laurence Housman had spoken on 'Art and National Movements' and Muriel Matters on 'The Usefulness of Pictorial Representations as Propaganda'. John Russell, headmaster of King Alfred's co-educational school in Hampstead, had also spoken. There was a generous response to the appeal for funds and a number of new members had joined. The badge of the society was a red rose (which must have conflicted with that of the NUWSS, and was later dropped). The first members' meeting of the Atelier had been held on 8 May and been reported in the *Women's Franchise* (20 May 1909). Members had been received by Edith Craig and had discussed plans for future work and exhibitions including the Women's Freedom League Green and Gold Fair.

53 – The *Common Cause*, 27 October 1910, p. 467, noted that the Atelier had now 'added a printing press to their other industries' (and produced calendars for 1911). The *Women's Franchise* (8 July 1909, p. 670) noted that the Atelier's 'Cartoon Club' specifically included instruction in hand colour printing and in process-block (i.e. photo-mechanical) reproduction.

54 – There is a copy in the Museum of London collection.

55 – The *Vote*, 23 December 1911, p. 108, address by Mrs Vulliamy of the WFL on the Atelier's usefulness both to the suffrage movement and to women artists.

56 – *Votes for Women*, 18 February 1910, p. 329, and the *Common Cause*, 17 February 1910, p. 634. The *Common Cause*, 30 December 1909, had noted that the Atelier was discontinuing general meetings and demonstrations and concentrating on its pictorial work until after the general election.

57 – Fawcett Archives, Box 154.

58 – The *Vote*, 15 June 1912, p. 145. Like the Artists' Suffrage League, the Atelier organised poster and postcard competitions. See *Votes for Women*, 1 April 1910, p. 430, and the *Common Cause*, 13 January 1910, welcoming suggestions for cartoons and posters.

59 – The *Vote*, 5 October 1912, p. 401.

60 – The painter William Rothenstein had leased 1 Pembroke Cottages in 1898, and Augustus and Gwen John stayed there during his absence in 1899. Alice Rothenstein insisted that the floor be scrubbed and the walls whitewashed to make the place habitable again after their departure (William Rothenstein, *Men and Memories 1872–1938*, abridged edition Mary Lago (ed.), London, Chatto & Windus, 1978, p. 214).

61 – See *Votes for Women*, 11 June 1908, pp. 229–30: 'The stitching of the banners in the studio has drawn many new friends to help in working out Mr Housman's beautiful design, and we hope to have some fine things ready for the ceremony on the 17th.' Everyone who could do so was invited to lend a hand in the preparations, and the address for the secretary of the Kensington branch of the WSPU was given as The Studio at 1, Pembroke Cottages, Edwardes Square; that is, the studio at the bottom of the Housmans' garden.

62 – See Laurence Housman, *The Unexpected Years*, London, Cape, 1937; Rodney Engen, *Laurence Houseman*, Catalpa Press, Stroud, 1983; the catalogue of an exhibition of the Housmans' work at the National Book League (5–19 February 1975) organised by I. G. Kenyur Hodgkins; Katherine Lyon Mix, 'Laurence, Clemence and Votes for Women' in *The Housman Society Journal*, vol. 2, 1975, pp. 42–52; Ann Born, 'Collecting Laurence and Clemence Housman', the *Antiquarian Book Monthly Review*, vol. 5 no. 10, October 1978; James Guthrie, 'The Wood Engravings of Clemence Housman' in *The Print Collector's Quarterly*, vol. 2 no. 2, April 1924; and Reginald Reynolds, 'The Third Housman' in *English*, vol. x no. 60, Autumn 1955. Laurence's and Clemence's enthusiasm for women's suffrage was not shared by their brother Alfred, who declined to sign a petition in its favour, partly because he did not consider that 'writers as a class are particularly qualified to give advice on the question', and partly because it was 'signed by Galsworthy and Hewlett and everyone that I can't abide' (Laurence Housman, *My Brother, A. E. Housman*, Cape, London, 1937).

63 – In Laurence's account, 'Clemence was released from the Victorian bonds of home, for the sole reason that it was considered too risky for me to go alone without someone of more stable character to look after me' (Housman, 1937, pp. 104–05).

64 – Ricketts and Shannon were studying engraving, as was Clemence, but the men's and women's classes were separated and the intercommunicating doors between them remained decorously closed (Housman, 1937, p. 107). Laurence established himself as an influential illustrator in the *fin de siècle* manner (see John Russell Taylor, *The Art Nouveau Book in Britain*, Methuen, London, 1966) and published a book of poems, *The Green Arras*, in 1896. But his brother brought out *A Shropshire Lad* in the same year, and Laurence was condemned for the next five years to labour 'under the shadow of that bright cloud'.

65 – See Laurence Housman's pamphlet on 'National Art Training', an address delivered at the Municipal School of Art, Manchester, 18 September 1911, in Street public library, Somerset: 'We have killed out from our midst one of the most beautiful schools of popular art that ever existed, the school of

the illustrators of the sixties.' Clemence's engravings can be seen in the print rooms of the British Museum and the Victoria and Albert Museum. See Engen (1983) appendices for Housmaniana.

66 – All these quotations are from Housman (1937), p. 263; see also p. 277: 'I was forced, against my inclination, into a higher standard of moral courage than I had ever practised before.'

67 – Housman (1937), p. 274.

68 – Clemence was too retiring to speak for the suffrage cause except on rare occasions and with great reluctance. She was sent to Holloway for refusal to pay four shillings twopence inhabited house duty. She and Laurence were delighted to note that the cost to the government of the taxi that took her there was precisely four shillings and twopence (see Housman, 1937, pp. 284–85). Her commitment to the Women's Tax Resistance League had its personal ironies, since as a schoolgirl assisting her solicitor father she had been 'the expert who worked out all the Income Tax calculations for half the County of Worcestershire' (Housman, 1937, p. 94). Clemence was also the author of three remarkable novels: *The Were-Wolf* (John Lane, London, 1896), *The Unknown Sea* (Duckworth, London, 1898), and *The Life of Sir Aglovale de Galis* (Methuen, London, 1905).

69 – Housman (1937), p. 141. Velazquez' 'Rokeby Venus' was slashed by the WSPU militant, Mary Richardson, in the National Gallery, in 1914. He renewed his subscription as a matter of principle when the public prosecutor threatened supporters of the WSPU with imprisonment, but no action was taken against him. In 1914 he became a founder member of the United Suffragists, co-author (with Henry Nevinson) of their manifesto and designer of the banner that Clemence made for them.

70 – The *Vote*, 12 March 1910, pp. 232–33; *Votes for Women*, 15 April 1910, p. 455 ('I certainly grew up quite firmly certain that no self-respecting woman could be other than a Suffragist'). See also Eleanor Acland (ed.), *Edy: Recollections of Edith Craig*, with a biographical note by Christoper St John, Frederick Muller, London, 1949. According to St John (p. 10) she played a number of bit parts in Irving's productions and toured in the 1890s, and went into business as a stage dressmaker after making the costumes for Irving's *Robespierre* in 1899. Between 1911 and 1921 she produced 150 plays for the Pioneer Players, a Sunday theatre she founded, and which according to George Bernard Shaw 'by singleness of artistic direction, and un-flagging activity, did more for the theatrical vanguard than any of the other coterie theatres' (p. 24). For more on the Pioneer Players (and the Actresses' Franchise League) see Julie Holledge, *Innocent Flowers*, Virago, London, 1981. Presumably through Edith Craig, the Suffrage Atelier organised theatrical performances, putting on two of Housman's plays, for example, at the Court Theatre in May 1910 (see the *Common Cause*, 19 May 1910, p. 93).

71 – Other contributors to the Suffrage Atelier included Isabel Pocock, Jessica Walters, Louise Jacobs, Gladys Letcher, Poyntz Wright (a pseudonym?), Catherine Courtauld and Hope Joseph. Eva Joseph was succeeded early on by Miss E. B. Willis as Honorary Secretary, and afterwards Honorary Organiser.

Late in 1912 Mrs Gatty was recommended as the Honorary Secretary in *Votes for Women* (13 December 1912, p. 174) as one 'who has won her spurs by repeated imprisonments and has been seventeen times subjected to forcible feeding'.

72 – Entry in *The Suffrage Annual and Women's Who's Who*, 1913. See also a letter (2 November 1910) from Catherine Courtauld on behalf of the Atelier to the secretary of the LSWS, enclosing two hand-printed posters 'thinking you may be able to use them during the Election', and offering to supply more at threepence each (Fawcett Archives, Box 154).

73 – The *Vote*, 9 November 1912, p. 35.

74 – See the *Vote*, 23 December 1911, p. 108: 'In the New Year the Suffrage Atelier will inaugurate a special poster propaganda [sic] in the country.' This may have been associated with a shift in the Atelier's headquarters from the Pembroke Cottages address of the Housmans to the Stanlake Villas address of Hope Joseph, and a concomitant shift in emphasis – no doubt encour-aged by parliamentary developments and the fact that there were no further suffrage processions in the offing – from banner to poster work.

75 – 'The Suffrage Atelier and the *Vote*', 13 April 1912, p. 294 (see also the *Vote*, 20 April 1912). The idea seems to have come from Miss Willis of the Atelier, and to have reached the National Executive Committee of the WFL in January 1912, already endorsed by the Minerva Publishing Company which published the *Vote*. Difficulties and misunderstandings as to the political and economic relations between the Atelier, the WFL and the Minerva Publishing Company had to be ironed out before the scheme could proceed. See the National Executive Committee Minute Book of the WFL 1912, 29 January 1912, pp. 46–48, Fawcett Archives, Box 54.

There is information on the founding of the *Vote* and its development in the WFL National Executive Committee Minutes from May 1909: see Fawcett Archives, Box 54, pp. 76, 79, 80, 102, 141 and 147–48. A special effort had been made to build up sales in 1910. In 1912 the monthly sales figures varied between 11,000 and 15,000.

76 – Woodcuts are made with a knife on the long grain of a plank of soft wood, cut so as to leave areas that will print in relief. Wood engraving involves the use of an engraver's burin to carve fine lines across the end grain of a very hard wood, traditionally box. The conventional effect of a woodcut is that of black masses on a white ground. That of a wood engraving is usually that of a series of fine white lines on a dark ground. See Michael Twyman, *Printing 1770–1970* (Eyre & Spottiswoode, London, 1970), for a detailed account of the development of nineteenth-century printing processes. Wood engraving stood up well to the pressures of mechanised printing and large-scale editions. Its development and mechanisation formed the basis for a revolution in mass-produced imagery. With the subdivision and subsequent reassembly of large blocks, worked on by teams of artists, it was possible to meet the deadlines of the weekly press and satisfy an apparently insatiable public appetite for illus-trated periodicals as well as books. The *Illustrated London News* (founded 1842) trained a whole generation of draughtsmen and engravers, and was unrivalled until the appearance of the

Graphic in 1869. Callen (1979, pp. 32–33) notes that wood engraving was thought to be a suitably feminine occupation since it required the patient transcription of an original design, repetitive labour and manual dexterity, and it could be carried on at home (a view insulting equally to women and to skilled engravers). From the mid-1880s photographic techniques began to be incorporated into the printing processes themselves, nearly all of which were fully mechanised by the end of the nineteenth century. 'Process' was the collective term for the various photo-mechanical methods for producing the print surface, all of them cheaper than hand engraving, which they had virtually superseded by the 1890s. By that point Clemence Housman was 'one of a small band of workers involved in a desperate struggle – not only for their own livelihood, but for the survival in the commercial world of a noble craft, which – with the coming of "process" – was being slowly strangled to death' (Housman, 1937, p. 110). Campbell Dodgson noted that after Tenniel's retirement in January 1901 the cartoons in *Punch* were wood engravings no more, and that Clemence Housman remained as 'the last representative of a great tradition' (introduction to Bernard Sleigh, *Wood Engraving*, Isaac Pitman, London, 1932, pp. 43–44). The 'noble craft' of fine hand-printing was revived in the private presses of the arts and crafts movement at the same time as it died out in the commercial sector. And 'process' began to attract artists of the calibre of Aubrey Beardsley in the 1890s, whose drawing styles exploited its particular characteristics. Articles on 'Drawing for Reproduction' such as that in the *Studio* (1893, vol. 1, p. 69) and handbooks, notably C. G. Harper's *A Practical Handbook of Drawing for Modern Methods of Reproduction*, London, 1894, advised students on the preparation of illustrative material. Suffrage Atelier classes in drawing for photo-mechanical techniques (which were not used in their own block-printed posters and postcards) have therefore to be seen as part of an attempt to improve the opportunities for women in this rapidly expanding area of commercial illustration. It is worth noting that appeals had already been made 'for the further development of remunerative work for women' in the arts, and for 'utilising the talents now being frittered away, on the painting of fourth and fifth rate pictures'. See Alice Gordon, 'Woman as Students in Design', the *Fortnightly Review*, vol. LV, 1894, pp. 521 ff.

77 – The first cartoon by 'A Patriot' appeared in *Votes for Women* on 18 February 1909, and Pearse was identified as its author and thanked for his contribution (pp. 346 and 351). On 26 February *Votes for Women* introduced 'another complimentary cartoon by Mr Alfred Pearse', and announced that 'a friendly firm of engravers has kindly consented to reproduce these each week for us free of charge.'

78 – If it is by Pearse, and it has affinities with his designs on forcible feeding, then his reputation as a competent but unimaginative artist deserves to be revised. Alternatively – and granted that the image has affinities with a whole nineteenth-century theatrical tradition of the 'monstrous' – it may have been produced by a designer working for David Allen's, the commercial lithographers who printed it.

79 – Richard Pankhurst, *Sylvia Pankhurst: Artist and Crusader*,

Paddington Press, New York and London, 1979, pp. 103–04. For Sylvia Pankhurst's artistic career see *The Suffragette Movement* (Pankhurst, 1931); Sylvia Pankhurst in the Countess of Oxford and Asquith (ed.), *Myself When Young by Famous Women of Today*, Frederick Muller, London, 1938; and Richard Pankhurst, 1979 (chiefly a reprint, with valuable illustrations, of the first two sources).

80 – Her autobiographical account (1931) describes the family residence in Russell Square, a centre for gatherings of socialists, Fabians, anarchists, suffragists, free thinkers, radicals and humanitarians of all schools, amid a decor (fit for *Punch*'s Cimabue Browns) of Morris cretonnes, Turkish rugs, old Persian plates, Indian brass and Japanese embroideries (p. 83). Mrs Pankhurst had long tried to augment the family income with a series of shops – one of them was Emerson's in the Hampstead Road – aimed at purveying artistic furniture and decorations in the style of a miniature Liberty's (p. 89).

81 – Sylvia Pankhurst in the Countess of Oxford and Asquith (ed.) (1938), p. 267.

82 – Sylvia Pankhurst (1931), p. 170.

83 – According to her own account, she left the Royal College despite her tutor's advice that she apply for a free studentship to complete her five years' study, because she could not see how to support herself.

84 – Sylvia Pankhurst (1931), p. 271. See also *Votes for Women*, 26 August 1910, which published an article and illustration on 'Women Farm Labourers in the Border Counties' from a 'forthcoming book on women's trades' by Sylvia Pankhurst.

85 – Sylvia Pankhurst (1931), p. 252. By this point she had produced the WSPU membership card and a series of sketches from Holloway Prison published in the *Pall Mall Magazine* between January and June 1907.

86 – Sylvia Pankhurst (1931), p. 128.

87 – Countess of Oxford and Asquith (ed.) (1938), p. 285.

88 – Countess of Oxford and Asquith (ed.) (1938), p. 284.

89 – Countess of Oxford and Asquith (ed.) (1938), pp. 311–12; this despite the fact that the *Daily Mirror* had previously announced that Sylvia Pankhurst 'is retiring from the suffrage movement, because of ill-health [and] will follow the calling of an artist' (12 February 1908).

90 – The term is Nicos Hadjinicolaou's, from *Art History and Class Struggle* (1973), Pluto Press, London, 1978. See chapters 7, 'Style', 8, 'Style as Visual Ideology' and 9, 'Visual Ideology and Social Classes'. These raise important questions about how the concept of 'style' can be reformulated in an analysis of the processes by which social meanings are produced in pictorial form. But there seems to be a residual tendency to identify particular 'visual ideologies' over-tidily with those social classes whose interests they are presumed to serve. Suffrage artists were adept at turning inherited styles to new ideological ends (propaganda is often a matter of putting new wine in old bottles), although it is also true that these ends were sometimes compromised by the terms in which they were expressed.

91 – The self-descriptions of the Artists' Suffrage League and Suffrage Atelier; see notes 57 and 87.

92 – The development of the broadsheet style is discussed by

Simon Houfe, *The Dictionary of British Book Illustrators and Caricaturists 1800–1914*, Antique Collectors' Club, London, 1978 (pp. 175–78).

93 – Sylvia Pankhurst (1931, p. 104) remembered her father buying Walter Crane's Toy Books for the nursery. Edith Craig, who lived as a child among the rush matting and Japanese prints of her parents' house, claimed to have been 'brought up on Walter Crane' (the *Vote*, 12 March 1910, pp. 232–33).

94 – He was part-time Director of Design at Manchester Art School from 1893, Art Director at Reading College in 1898 and Director at the Royal College of Art from 1898–99.

95 – Sylvia Pankhurst (1931), p. 104. Crane's influence seems to lie behind her account of how she and Christabel would lie in bed in the dark, telling each other how: 'Wonderful processions and pageants passed by, lovelier than one could tell' (p. 105).

96 – See Sylvia Pankhurst (1931), pp. 304–05; the gloss in Emmeline Pethick-Lawrence, 'The Purple, White, and Green', in *Votes for Women*, 27 May 1909, pp. 626 ff.; and *The Women's Exhibition 1909*, WSPU programme (Museum of London). The traditional, rather literary imagery and Crane-like style of these designs is in marked contrast with Mary Cassatt's mural of 'The Modern Woman' for the Women's Building at the Columbian Exposition in Chicago in 1893.

97 – Her travels around England painting working-class women while living with them and writing about their lives are described in Pankhurst (1931), pp. 261 ff.

98 – See the *Vote*, 27 April 1912, p. 30.

99 – The *Freewoman*, 7 December 1911, p. 47, quoted in Brian Harrison, *Separate Spheres: The Opposition to Women's Suffrage in Britain*, Croom Helm, London, 1978, p. 19.

100 – Sir Almroth Wright, *The Unexpurgated Case against Woman Suffrage*, Constable, London, 1913, pp. 2–6.

101 – The *Common Cause*, 10 December 1910, p. 606. The editor claimed that election helpers confirmed the truth of Price's characterisations, and that *as* caricatures her drawings were therefore not to be compared with the falsehoods of the gutter press.

102 – Antis claimed that no stigma attached to the fact that women did not vote. In the United States middle-class women's resentment at their exclusion was fuelled by the enfranchisement of Negroes (the fifteenth amendment) and immigrants. The betrayal of the abolitionist–feminist alliance by leaders of the Negro cause led to some instances of racist arguments and imagery being mobilised in the suffrage campaign. There is only one British suffrage postcard – '*this* is allowed to vote' – that comes anywhere near to 'American Woman and her Political Peers' (1893) in this respect (reproduced in Paula Harper, 1975, fig. 11).

103 – The *Women's Franchise*, 17 October 1907, p. 176.

104 – The *Common Cause*, 22 December 1910. See for example Bernard Partridge's cartoon in *Punch*, 10 May 1905, reproduced in Constance Rover, *The Punch Book of Women's Rights*, Hutchinson, London, 1967, p. 103.

105 – This is not really the 'missing theme' that Paula Harper suggests.

106 – Stephen Yeo, 'A New Life: the Religion of Socialism in

Britain, 1883–1896', *History Workshop*, no. 4, Autumn 1977 (quotations here from p. 17 and p. 6).

107 – See Pearse's cartoon for the cover of *Votes for Women*, 25 November 1910.

108 – See Atelier posters such as 'There was an Old Dame in a Huff' or 'There was an Old Man who said How'; and 'Alice' cartoons by 'A. J. S.' in the *Common Cause*, 11 and 25 August and 8 December 1910, 9 March, 25 May and 1 June 1911. There are many other examples. Laurence Housman wrote a suffrage play called 'Alice in Ganderland'.

109 – Or Mrs Partington, already invoked at the time of the Reform Bill of 1832, who had supposedly tried to sweep back the Atlantic after the great storm of 1824. The *Suffragette*, 3 July 1914, reproduced a drawing of her on its cover, together with a quotation from Sydney Smith: 'She was excellent at a slop or a puddle, but she should not have meddled with a tempest.'

110 – Quoted on the cover of *Votes for Women*, 1 July 1910.

111 – Almroth Wright (1913), p. 7.

112 – *Votes for Women*, 4 June 1909, p. 757 (accounts); and the *Programme* of the WSPU exhibition, 1909, p. 12 (Museum of London). The WSPU demonstration of 1908 had cost almost £4800 to stage, towards which £900 had been raised from the sale of railway tickets.

113 – See the WSPU *Annual Reports*. Sylvia Pankhurst (1931) provides rounded-up figures on p. 222.

114 – Sylvia Pankhurst (1931), p. 222; Frederick Pethick-Lawrence (1943), p. 77.

115 – WFL Cash Statement published in the *Vote*, 5 February 1910, p. 175.

116 – See *Votes for Women*, 14 May 1908, p. 164: 'Five hundred people can each give a banner. We can supply all the materials for a banner 8 ft long by 3 ft wide, with poles 6 ft 6 ins in height, with carrying straps and everything complete except the lettering for 8s. 6d., or the whole banner complete, with lettering and all, for 16s.' This implies collective organisation of the design (however basic the lettering), and bulk purchase of the materials (or a special arrangement with commercial suppliers).

117 – Sylvia Pankhurst (1931), pp. 304–05, 514–15. She wrote later that she was always 'torn between the economic necessities of the immediate moment . . . and the urging of conscience to assist in the movement' (p. 218).

118 – Sylvia Pankhurst (1931), pp. 222–23.

119 – Fawcett Archives, Box 153.

120 – The *Common Cause*, 22 December 1910, pp. 617–18.

121 – The *Common Cause*, 21 March 1912, p. 852.

122 – Mrs Louis Fagan, widow of the assistant keeper of prints and drawings at the British Museum, reported in the *Common Cause*, 26 October 1912, p. 450.

123 – See price list in the *Vote*, 10 August 1912, p. 27.

124 – Accounts appeared in the *Vote*, 29 October 1910, and *Votes for Women*, 28 October 1910. The Housmans' garden was turned into a 'continental market place' with peasant-costumed suffragists for the occasion. In 1911 the Atelier held a Christmas party to which guests brought donations (a mangle and a file were particularly appreciated); see the *Vote*, 23 December 1911, p. 108.

125 – Unsigned letter from 6 Stanlake Villas to Maud Arncliffe-Sennett, 26 January 1914, bound into volume 26 of the Maud Arncliffe-Sennett albums in the British Library following p. 8. I have put in minimal punctuation for the sake of clarity. Maud Arncliffe-Sennett owned a small business, had been an actress and was a dedicated suffragist and founder of the Northern Men's League for Women's Suffrage.

126 – With little money they were obliged to be ingenious. See the *Vote*, 15 June 1912, p. 145, on the activities of the Suffrage Atelier: 'the various processes form a most interesting object-lesson as to what can be done on small means. Necessity knowing no law, the visitors would often be startled at the various novelties so successfully introduced by these capable women.'

127 – The *Vote*, 27 January 1912, p. 159.

128 – The *Vote*, 15 June 1912, p. 145.

129 – Sylvia Pankhurst (1931), p. 224. Posters were also available from the International Suffrage Shop in Adam Street, the Minerva Publishing Company in Robert Street, the Women's Press, Betterment Books, and from the WSPU, the League and the Atelier directly. Photographs in the suffrage press show shop windows filled with posters, particularly at by-elections.

130 – *Women's Franchise*, 4 June 1908, p. 579 and 11 June 1908, p. 591 and cutting in Mrs Spencer Graves's Women's Suffrage Album for 1906–18 (Fawcett Archives). The premises were at 100 Westbourne Grove.

131 – See WFL Minute Books, 19 October 1912 (Fawcett Archives, Box 54) re posting Atelier designs on public hoardings; *Votes for Women*, 15 March 1913, p. 629, the *Suffragette*, 18 April 1913, p. 447 and 5 September 1913 re poster sites and the holiday campaign.

132 – WFL report on the Annual Conference 1908 (Museum of London). See also the *Women's Franchise*, 28 November 1907, p. 251: 'Though not so "womanly" as flattening noses on the millinery shop windows, it is still to be highly recommended from the health point of view. The amount of wood borne about by our brothers in the trade was voted unnecessary, and the boards were made of light cardboard. This method of advertisement is cheap and effective.' Twyman (1970, p. 12) notes that sandwich-men had been a familiar part of the London scene since 200 of them paraded the streets to announce the first number of the *Illustrated London News* in May 1842.

133 – Housman (1937), p. 278.

134 – Elizabeth Banks, *The Remaking of an American*, Double-day, New York, 1928, p. 10. See the *Vote*, 13 February 1914, p. 259: 'The opening of Parliament found us as usual in Parliament-square, carrying posters with pictures and mottoes designed to touch the conscience of erring Members.' A poster 30 by 20 inches was described as 'sandwich-board size'. Posters were also pasted on to carts, carriages, hansom cabs, and on one occasion an elephant.

135 – Three verses by Jessie Pope in the *Pall Mall Magazine*, reprinted in *Votes for Women*, 21 April 1911, p. 472, together with a response by Frank Witty, the last stanza of which reads: 'Oh, you who voice the little moan / Of out of date society – /

Your vapid little creeds make known / With sentimental piety – / What right have YOU to carp and groan / At gutter notoriety?' The inspiration seems to have come from a socialist lament for sandwich-men by Langdon Everard, published in the *Labour Leader*, 17 June 1910, p. 371 ('With downcast eyes, and dragging feet, / They pass – a wretched crew / Against the boards their weak knees beat / The Devil's own tattoo').

136 – See W. E. D. Allen, *David Allen's: The History of a Family Firm 1857–1957*, John Murray, London, 1957. Carl Hentschel, a suffrage sympathiser (and the original of 'Harris' in Jerome K. Jerome's *Three Men in a Boat*, 1899), was another of their printers: a popular and respected figure, a photo-engraver since 1887 and head of the largest process firm in London. See Geoffrey Wakeman, *Victorian Book Illustration: The Technical Revolution*, David & Charles, Newton Abbot, 1973.

137 – Cited by Luigi Salerno in McGraw Hill's *Encyclopedia of World Art*, pp. 787–88. The first English poster exhibitions were held at the Royal Aquarium in 1894 and 1896. They included work by Cheret, Grasset, Toulouse-Lautrec, Bonnard, Steinlen, Beardsley, Beggarstaff, Brangwyn and Crane.

138 – 'The Collecting of Posters – a New Field for Connoisseurs, *Studio*, vol. 1, 1893.

139 – See D. A. Hamer, *The Politics of Electoral Pressure: A Study in the History of Victorian Reform Agitations*, Harvester, Brighton, 1977.

140 – Cited in Neal Blewett, *The Peers, the Parties and the People: The British General Elections of 1910*, University of Toronto Press, Toronto, 1972, p. 312.

141 – The *Common Cause*, 3 February 1910, p. 599.

142 – Blewett (1972), p. 312.

143 – The *Common Cause*, 3 February 1910, p. 599. According to their *Annual Report* for 1910, the Artists' Suffrage League had by the end of the year printed 7000 postcards, 25,000 picture leaflets, 6000 Christmas cards and 4000 posters.

144 – My comments on the party political, tariff reform and free trade posters are based on an examination of those in the collections of the Victoria and Albert Museum, the British Museum, and the British Library of Political and Economic Science at the London School of Economics, and a photograph album of posters on hoardings during the 1910 general elections at Conservative Party headquarters in Smith Square. I am grateful to the staff at all these institutions for access to their collections.

145 – Blewett (1972), p. 312.

146 – Cited in Blewett (1972), p. 312.

147 – 'The Woman's Reply' by Janet Robertson, reproduced on the cover of the *Common Cause*, 27 January 1910. *Votes for Women* (15 July 1910, p. 698) noted that a 'lively but silent battle' had been waged the previous week, when anti posters announcing that women did not want votes had been pasted up in the tube stations and paraded by sandwich-men. Some had had the 'not' pasted out overnight, others were embellished with slips saying 'Don't they, come to Trafalgar Square and see', and counter-images with the slogan 'Sane people do want votes' were speedily produced.

148 – There are many sources on the picture postcard, notably Anthony Byatt, *Picture Postcards and their Publishers*, Golden Age Postcard Books, Worcester, 1978; William Duval and Valerie Monahan, *Collecting Postcards*, Blandford Press, Poole, 1978; Frank Staff, *The Picture Postcard and its Origins*, Lutterworth Press, London, 1966; and Richard Carline, *Pictures in the Post: The Story of the Picture Postcard*, Gordon Fraser, London, 1971. I am indebted in this paragraph to John Fraser's elegantly concise account of propaganda postcards in the *Oxford Art Journal*, vol. 3 no. 2, October 1980 ('Propaganda on the Picture Postcard').

149 – See Norman Alliston, 'Picture Postcards' in *Chambers Journal*, 21 October 1899; *The Picture Postcard and Collectors' Chronicle* (1900–07); W. J. Scott's *All About Picture Postcards* (Leeds, 1903); the *Picture Postcard Budget and Collectors' Magazine* (1904); *The Postcard Connoisseur for Postcard Collectors* (1904); and *The Picture Postcard Annual and Directory* (Rotherham, 1906, 1907).

150 – Reproduced in Byatt (1978), pp. 202 and 234. Topical views seem sometimes to have been taken 'on spec' and sent to suffrage societies with the suggestion that they be reproduced for sale. See letter from the Rotary Photographic Co. Ltd to the NUWSS (19 June 1911) offering to reproduce pictures of the previous day's demonstration 'in our REAL PHOTOGRAPHIC POSTCARDS . . . and put you upon our very best terms for these' (Fawcett Archives, Box 298).

151 – And also of commercial publishers producing both pro and anti designs, if rarely so symmetrically as in the 'This is the House that Man Built' B. B. Series, which published six of each in an identical format.

3   SPECTACLE

1 – Emmeline Pethick-Lawrence, 'An Army with Banners', *Votes for Women*, 15 July 1910, p. 689.

2 – See *The Debate, 1892, in the House of Commons on Women's Suffrage*. Special Report published by the Central National Society for Women's Suffrage, p. 45 (Fawcett Library).

3 – The problems are discussed in Brian Harrison, *Separate Spheres: The Opposition to Women's Suffrage in Britain*, Croom Helm, London, 1978, pp. 54–55.

4 – The *Women's Franchise*, 4 June 1908, p. 582.

5 – In making politics a spectacle, the suffragists were furthering a tendency described by Guy Debord as characteristic of modern life. 'The entire life of societies in which modern conditions of production reign announces itself as an immense accumulation of *spectacles*. Everything that was directly lived has moved away into a representation.' On the other hand, the demonstration could be seen as a *way* of living the abstract relations and demands of politics (Guy Debord, *The Society of the Spectacle*, Black and Red, Detroit, 1970, p. 1).

6 – In addition to press reports, published memoirs, documentary footage in the National Film Archive and an interview with Lord (Fenner) Brockway, I have drawn on cuttings albums in the Fawcett Library (SvL 1907–29 Suffrage 3, and Mrs Spencer Graves, Women's Suffrage 1906–18), the

Fawcett Archives, Box 385 (How-Martyn, press cuttings of marches), the Fawcett Photographic Collection, the Nurse Pine Collection and related photographs in the Museum of London, and the Maud Arncliffe-Sennett albums in the British Library.

7 – And more broadly, a cluster of other new or revamped traditions: the Lord Mayor's Show, the Olympic Games, the Cup Final, an enhanced sense of civic dignity in the new baroque town halls of provincial cities. See Eric Hobsbawm and Terence Ranger (eds), *The Invention of Tradition*, Cambridge University Press, Cambridge, 1983, particularly David Cannadine, 'The Context, Performance and Meaning of Ritual: The British Monarchy and the "Invention of Tradition" *c.* 1820–1977'. Hobsbawm (p. 1) defines 'invented tradition' as 'a set of practices, normally governed by overtly or tacitly accepted rules and of a ritual or symbolic nature, which seek to inculcate certain values and norms of behaviour by repetition, which automatically implies continuity with the past'. 'All invented traditions, so far as possible, use history as a legitimator of action and cement of group cohesion' (p. 12).

8 – The *Labour Leader*, 23 June 1911, p. 392 (editorial).

9 – Cannadine in Hobsbawm and Ranger (eds) (1983), p. 138.

10 – Laurence Housman wrote to Janet Ashbee on 14 June 1908, apropos the NUWSS demonstration the day before: 'the main fact to note was that people had turned out in quite as big numbers as they do to see Royalty on semi-state occasions. So that shows the thing has got into the popular mind and is being paid attention to.'

11 – Yeo (1977), p. 40. See also John Gorman, *Banner Bright*, pp. 21–22.

12 – Sylvia Pankhurst (1931), p. 208. This was the famous occasion on which Campbell-Bannerman preached the virtue of patience to Emily Davies and Elizabeth Wolstenholme-Elmy, who had each been working for the suffrage cause for more than forty years.

13 – Christabel Pankhurst (1959), pp. 66–67.

14 – See Alice Chandler, *A Dream of Order: The Medieval Ideal in Nineteenth-Century Literature* (1970), Routledge & Kegan Paul, London, 1971; Mark Girouard, *The Return to Camelot: Chivalry and the English Gentleman*, Yale University Press, New Haven, 1981.

15 – Roger Fulford (*Votes for Women*, Faber & Faber, London, 1957, p. 157) refers to 'a remarkable spate of pageants organised by Mr Louis N. Parker', who passed 'from St Albans to Coventry, from Bury St Edmunds to the Isle of Wight, from Chelsea to Cheltenham and from Winchester to Pevensey: at a wave of the Parker wand county ladies strolled among ruins as medieval princesses, mayors thundered across wet meadows disguised as crusaders, the rotund figures of Edwardian gentry did not look amiss as dignatories of monastic life while burgesses tried to feel comfortable masquerading as Hengist and Horsa'. Fulford dates his spate of pageants to the summers of 1907 and 1908 (that is, contemporary with the first suffrage spectacles), but their fascination survived until the outbreak of war. On 16 June 1913, on the same page as it reported the funeral of Emily Wilding Davison, the *Daily Telegraph* described a pageant held before 700 people in the vicarage garden

at Child's Hill, in aid of the work of the Church abroad. A series of tableaux enacted scenes from early Church history and the participants, drawn from the local branch of the Society for the Propagation of the Gospel, had been coached in their parts by the director of the pageant, Mr Kenneth Richmond, assisted by the Rector of Spetisbury and Mr Louis N. Parker. Feminists were prepared to contest these masques and pageants when they disagreed with the representations they produced. See for example Helen Normanton's critique of Patrick Geddes's 'Masque of Learning' at London University in the *Vote*, 11 April 1913, p. 397. They were also prepared to adapt them to their own ends; the best example being Cicely Hamilton's influential and widely produced 'Pageant of Great Women', 1909.

16 – Emmeline Pethick-Lawrence, 'The Purple, White, and Green', *Programme* of the WSPU Exhibition 1909, p. 14 (Museum of London): 'Hers, generally speaking, has been the instinct for seemliness and refinement . . . What the woman has effected in the world of the home she will effect in those spheres which are now opening to her. She will bring her artistic sense, her ritual of order and beauty to dignify and enrich the man-made schemes of things . . . not only in the political but in the professional and the commercial world.'

17 – Mary Lowndes, 'On Banners and Banner-Making', re-printed from the *Englishwoman*, September 1909, by the Artists' Suffrage League, p. 2. See Appendix 5.

18 – Housman (1937), p. 275. Millicent Fawcett (*Women's Suffrage*, T. C. & E. C. Jack, London, 1912, pp. 35–36) complained that the anti-suffrage press reported only those events which it calculated would damage the suffrage cause (i.e. militancy), 'and say nothing about those facts which indicate its growing force and volume'. As a newsworthy event, a procession of women two miles long made it impossible for the press to maintain that silence.

19 – Twyman (1970), pp. 51 and 96–97; A. J. Lee, *The Origins of the Popular Press in England: 1855–1914*, Croom Helm, London, 1976; Curran in James Curran, Michael Gurevitch and Janet Wollacott (eds), *Mass Communication and Society*, Edward Arnold, London, 1977. The spectacular expansion of the British popular press in the late nineteenth century was based on the exploitation of new technology (cheaper paper and faster printing), advertising revenues, a high adult literacy rate due to the Education Act of 1870 and a well-developed railway and distribution network. The suffrage press was itself a rapidly expanding resource for the dissemination of information and illustrations of suffrage spectacle. Between October 1907 and July 1909 the circulation of *Votes for Women* rose from 2000 per month to more than 30,000 per *week* ('The Story of Votes for Women', Supplement to *Votes for Women*, 1 October 1909).

20 – LSWS *Report of Press Work*, October 1912–January 1913 (Fawcett Archives, Box 320). See the *Common Cause*, 4 January 1912, p. 677, for a breakdown of the press into pro, anti and neutral categories.

21 – The *Referee*, 18 October 1908 (in Maud Arncliffe-Sennett's albums, vol. 5, p. 63). The expanding cinematograph business also had important implications for suffrage publicity. Emily Wilding Davison's dash on to the Derby racecourse took

place in front of the newsreel cameras. Large-scale suffrage demonstrations attracted film companies who sold prints to the suffrage societies. (See Fawcett Archives, Box 52: the NUWSS Executive Committee minutes for 1 February 1912 record its decision to buy a print of the Richmond demonstration from the Castle Cine Syndicate, and for 1 June 1911 'to get good cinematographic views' of the Women's Coronation Procession 'with a view to using them at meetings afterwards'.) In 1912 Inez Bensusan of the Actresses' Franchise League persuaded Mr Barker of Barker's Motion Photography to film her script *True Womanhood*, with herself in the central role of a sweated woman worker (Holledge, 1981, p. 81). Short commercial dramas with suffrage subjects were often scurrilous. There are several in the National Film Archive.

22 – The question of a referendum was mooted at particular moments but suffragists were wary of it. Lady Strachey believed that 'the result of such an experiment would be the ruin of our cause for an incalculable period of time' (Lady Strachey to the Countess of Selborne, 23 January 1912, Fawcett Autograph Collection, quoted Hume, 1982, p. 129). See Hume, pp. 129–30, for the NUWSS's opposition to Churchill's referendum proposal in 1911–12, and pp. 212–13 for its reluctant consideration of a referendum in 1913–14.

23 – See the programme of the *Pageant of Women's Trades and Professions*, 1909: 'Journalism is one of the least progressive professions for women. Editors and proprietors are conservative where the employment of women is concerned, and at the present moment, with perhaps two exceptions, no woman on the inside staff of a London daily has secured a good and remunerative position . . . There are many women who earn a good livelihood by writing on dress, doing shop notices, and supplying society news, but these are outside the true sphere of journalism . . . Woman's real fight to secure a foothold in the genuine ranks of journalism has not commenced, yet the fact that some have succeeded will encourage others to go on.'

24 – See Millicent Fawcett, *What I Remember*, T. Fisher Unwin, London, 1924, pp. 191–92; and unidentified cutting, June 1908 (Fawcett Suffrage Album, SvL 3): 'Early satirists of the feminist movement led us to believe that this class of agitator invariably conformed to one type, and that a somewhat soured, uncomely, and unwomanly type. A glance at the rank and file of the Suffragette battalions yesterday afternoon would have convinced the ancient satirist that such shafts fall very wide of the mark today. The possession of youth and good looks is evidently no insuperable bar to the existence of suffragette fervour.'

25 – Emmeline Pethick-Lawrence (1938), p. 215.

26 – Rachel Ferguson, *Victorian Bouquet*, Ernest Benn, London, 1931.

27 – Emmeline Pethick-Lawrence (1938), p. 215.

28 – *Votes for Women*, 30 June 1911, p. 640.

29 – They were easily rolled up and driven round London in vans, or sent by rail to provincial demonstrations. Hannah Mitchell recalled the WFL 'Holloway' banner in black and grey velvet going missing en route to a large procession in Manchester. It had been sent as a practical joke to a builders' yard.

30 – NUWSS Executive Committee minutes, 3 July 1908 (Fawcett Archives, Box 83). See the *Women's Franchise*, 9 July 1908, p. 16, for the decision to keep the banners together and tour them: 'Undoubtedly we have here an opportunity of presenting an artistic feast of the first order under circumstances that make it in itself, and in all the attendant conditions that may be grouped round it, a unique act of propaganda.' And see also NUWSS Executive Committee minutes, 23 July 1908: 'Decided that the National Union lend out the banners to societies and make a fixed charge of £3 10 0d for the whole number 76 and £2 0 0d for the half, the calculation being 1/- per banner, all expenses to be borne by the local Society with the exception of the carriage one way. Decided that the banners cannot be loaned for outdoor work.' The *Women's Franchise* (6 August and 17 December 1908) and the *Kensington News* (19 March 1909) refer to exhibitions in Manchester, Cambridge, Birmingham, Liverpool, Fulham and Camberwell. The NUWSS was so gratified with the response that it compiled a page of extracts from 'Press Reports of the Banners' (see Mary Lowndes's album in the Fawcett Archives, p. 60). *Reynolds's Weekly News* referred to it as 'almost another field of the cloth of gold'.

31 – Probably there were a few suffrage banners in existence before 1908. The *Common Cause* (1910, p. 385) refers to 'a large white-and-gold banner made twenty-five years ago by the Bristol Suffrage Society, under the late Miss Helen Blackburn's direction' which was brought out on a Bristol demonstration in support of the Conciliation Bill. But these would not have been for outdoor use, and the banners made for the Mud March seem to have been chiefly lettered in red and white. It was Mary Lowndes and her colleagues of the Artists' Suffrage League who were responsible for the women's 'explosion of pageantry' in 1908. Only the 'ten great silk banners' of the WSPU were pictorial, and most of those were made by a commercial manufacturers (which might even have been Tutill's).

32 – Gwyn A. Williams, introduction to John Gorman, *Banner Bright: An illustrated history of the banners of the British trade union movement*, Allen Lane, London, 1973, p. 7. The emergence of the unions as substantial working-class organisations with radical middle-class support and a national leadership in the 1860s (the first TUC Congress took place in 1868), and their development in the late Victorian and Edwardian period, exactly parallels the organisation, development and increasing militancy of the suffrage campaign.

33 – Tutill's also produced banners and regalia for temperance societies, Sunday schools, Masons, Orange lodges, Friendly societies and even 'robes and false beards for the United Ancient Order of Druids'. John Gorman estimates that the firm produced about 10,000 banners between 1832 and 1939 (pp. 52 and 18).

34 – Gorman (1973), p. 50. In 1861 Tutill took out a patent for his process of coating the silk with india-rubber to improve its durability. He used an elastic paint to prevent cracking, which Gorman observes is often bright and pliant 100 years later. The painting itself was highly specialised, with artists working solely

on portraits, architecture, lettering, or as 'corner-men' on the baroque scrolls of the surrounds.

35 – This history has been explored by Rozsika Parker, *The Subversive Stitch: Embroidery and the Making of the Feminine*, The Women's Press, London, 1984 (see particularly chapter 2, 'Eternalising the Feminine: Embroidery and Victorian Medievalism 1840–1905'). Callen (1979, p. 98) notes that the revival of embroidery in the later nineteenth century was partly an effect of the religious revivals and partly a reaction against machine production.

36 – All quotations from Mary Lowndes, 'On Banners and Banner-Making', reprinted from the *Englishwoman*, September 1909 (there is a copy inserted in Mary Lowndes's album in the Fawcett Archives). The celebration of women's needlework skills in a *political* context was profoundly subversive of the conventional identification of femininity with embroidery which had developed from the Restoration onwards, and subversive in a manner that recognised the possibilities for creative pleasure which needlework allowed, as distinct from the direct refusal of them by some earlier feminists. Parker (1984, p. 105) quotes Ann Finch, Countess of Winchelsea: 'Nor will in fading silks compose/Faintly the inimitable rose'.

37 – See also the *Common Cause*, 16 February 1911, p. 727: 'The Suffrage Societies have many such beautiful banners worked by Suffragists FOR LOVE, and into them have been stitched many hopes and aspirations, pretty fancies and steadfast resolves, memories and beliefs. It comes natural to women to use their clever fingers in decorating the outwards and visible signs of their heart-felt faith, and when we find the civic consciousness of women expressing itself through needlework, we may be sure that this consciousness has become part of the "WOMANLY WOMAN", and that its force is overwhelming.'

At the same time Mary Lowndes shifts the standing of femininity in courtly chivalry, taking her noble embroiderer back from the hearth and into the lists: her Brynhild (the warrior-maiden who 'could more skill in handicraft than other women') had a sword stained red with the blood of kings. No inimitable roses in fading silks in her castle. As Alice Chandler points out in *A Dream of Order* (1970, see note 14), the Victorians used their myth of the middle ages to justify and reconcile the unequal dependencies of social life in the concept of 'chivalry'. Suffragists like Mary Lowndes (and militant suffragettes particularly) drew on the same language to opposite ends. (One might almost say that in so far as they were liberals they dreamed of a society in which each individual was free to compete equally, and that in so far as they were socialists they dreamed of a society in which inequalities and competition were dissolved.) In the order they dreamed of, exploitation was avenged by warrior virtues; and through the classical tradition of personification as it was conflated with the evangelical view of woman's 'mission', those virtues were *feminine*.

38 – Gorman (1973), p. 54.

39 – *Votes for Women*, 14 May 1908 and the WSPU *Annual Report* for the year ending 28 February 1909 (Museum of London).

40 – See unidentified cuttings in Fawcett Archives Suffrage Album 3, SvL 1907–29: one (*c.* February 1908) notes the

donation of fine silks and velvets for the Artists' Suffrage League banners (one exquisite piece of silk had been sent from India); the other (*Daily Chronicle*, June 1908) appeals to anyone who will give a banner – 'it costs something between 15s and £2' – or help make one. Mary Lowndes insisted that nothing should be used because it was a scrap of something left over that would 'just do', and the design was 'the one thing most worth paying for. If the design is bad, for twenty pounds you will not get a banner worth looking at; if the design is good and practical, you may make a fine thing for three, and make it yourself.'

41 – Williams in Gorman (1973), p. 11.

42 – Trade-union banners could be anything up to 16 by 12 feet, or even 20 feet.

43 – The firm of Lowndes and Drury advertised that it specialised in heraldic windows, and the heraldic associations of the banners were picked up and commented on in the press: 'As the procession moved away … it reminded one somehow of a picturesquely clad mediaeval army, marching out with waving gonfalons to certain victory' (*Sunday Times*, 14 June 1908).

44 – Gorman (1973), p. 49.

45 – *Votes for Women*, 30 June 1911, p. 640.

46 – This is a leitmotif of press comment in 1908, which reasserts the connection between embroidery and a middle-class, drawing-room femininity, at the expense of the popular and 'muscular' imagery of working-class men. See the NUWSS 'Press Reports of the Banners' particularly the *Daily News*, *Daily Chronicle*, *Manchester Guardian*, *Sunday Times* and *Daily Telegraph*.

47 – *The Vote*, 30 July 1910, p. 168.

48 – Gorman (1973, pp. 26–27) discusses the categories into which trade-union banners appeared to fall most readily for the purposes of his book.

49 – Mary Lowndes devised heraldic shields for fifty National Union branches for an Albert Hall meeting in 1910, and in the same year the Artists' Suffrage League produced large banners for Manchester, Woking, Weybridge, Epsom and the Hampshire and Sussex Federation. Her album contains a large number of additional designs for regional towns and for the Oxon/Berks/Bucks and West Midland Federations. None of the other societies could compete with the national spread and organisational structure of the National Union.

50 – See the *Daily Chronicle*, quoted in the NUWSS circular 'Press Reports of the Banners': 'The beauty of the needlework on many of them should convince the most sceptical that it is possible for a woman to use a needle even when she is also wanting a vote'; and conversely (the *Women's Franchise*): 'The excellence of the needlework … disposes for ever of the taunt that Suffragists do not care for womanly occupations.'

51 – See 'Banners: Designed by the Artists' Suffrage League for the Procession of June 13th, 1909, organised by the National Union of Women's Suffrage Societies', a pamphlet prepared by the Brighton Society in January 1909 (Fawcett Library). Out of a total of thirty-three, five are now missing: those for Emily and Charlotte Brontë; for Vashti (an Old Testament heroine); Angelica Kauffmann (who would have been paired with Mary Moser as a founder-member of the Royal

Academy); Elizabeth Cady Stanton (who would have completed a trio of American suffrage pioneers with the banners of Susan B. Anthony and Lucy Stone); and Lydia Becker (the Manchester pioneer whose banner was inscribed with a line from Walt Whitman. Even celebrities were included for the work they performed: 'Victoria Queen and Mother', for example, as 'a signal instance of a woman's capacity for public affairs' (tactfully echoing Tennyson: 'A thousand claims to reverence closed / In her as Mother, Wife and Queen' – 'To the Queen', 1851).

52 – Parker (1984), pp. 66, 97, 103.

53 – This led to controversy with relatives and opponents, who cavilled at some of the names adduced in the suffrage cause. Most people were aware that Queen Victoria disapproved of it, even if they could not then know that she thought one of the ladies of the court should be horsewhipped for her feminist sympathies. Charles Kingsley wrote indignantly to the *Morning Post* about his sister Mary (17 June 1908), and Lady Gordon to *The Times* with regard to her great-aunt Caroline Herschel, repudiating the 'mis-use' of their names. Mrs Fawcett replied to Lady Gordon and to other objections (15 June 1908) that 'the names of "distinguished women who did noble work in their sphere" are in themselves an argument against relegating the whole sex to a lower political *status* than felons and idiots … whether the particular distinguished women named on the banners were suffragists or not. The names of Joan of Arc and Queen Elizabeth are found on the banners. The inference is surely clear.'

54 – *Women's Franchise*, 25 June 1908.

55 – Excluding the purely typographical examples and the many hundreds of less spectacular shields and pennons used in demonstrations or to decorate public meetings.

56 – The Suffrage Atelier advertised its banner-making services in the *Vote* (15 June 1912, p. 145), offering work 'in both cheap and costly materials, to suit all purposes', the most expensive not necessarily being the most beautiful, 'design and colouring being the chief aim of the Atelier'.

57 – The *Daily News*, 12 June 1908 and unidentified cutting, c. February 1908 (Fawcett Archives, Suffrage Album 3, SvL 1907–29). Another cutting in the same album emphasises that the 'whole of the work entailed by this gigantic scheme is a voluntary effort on the part of lady artists, all subscriptions received being expended on the necessary materials, and any surplus money will be devoted to the propaganda work of the League'.

58 – See *Votes for Women*, 25 June 1908, 'Unfurling the Banners' and Sylvia Pankhurst (1931), pp. 284–85.

59 – See letter from Laurence Housman to Janet Ashbee, undated but evidently 14 June 1908: 'My Banner for Kensington WSPU is now practically finished. Everyone says it is the most beautiful that has been done. It is very simple – just a figure standing against a grill holding broken chains with the motto "From Prison to Citizenship" – but it has taken a lot of time' (Ashbee Journals, King's College, Cambridge).

60 – This seems to have involved a complicated design with a boat and shields, and is not the United Suffragists banner in the Museum of London.

61 – For the Conservative banner see Laurence Housman to
Sarah Clark, 6 August 1913; and re Oxford (if such it is), 22
March 1913 (Street Public Library collection): 'The banner is
blooming into form. I hope New is designing one for you.' Re
the Actresses' banner, see Clemence to Laurence Housman,
undated (Street Public Library collection). Laurence refers to
his sister wearing herself out with banner work, and describes
her with leg trouble, sitting 'on a floor cushion most of the day
doing needlework' (Laurence Housman to Sarah Clark, 6
December, undated but possibly 1912, Street Public Library
collection). Clemence seems to have supervised other work,
perhaps for the Atelier. In another letter to Laurence (undated,
Street Public Library collection), she complained of 'a stupid
mistake of Mrs Watson's too late to remedy – she has done 3
letters wrong A.M.N. thick and thin strokes wrong . . . now I
think everyone who looks will be uneasy they know not why.'
Some insight into the processes by which a small suffrage body
came to the decision that it needed a banner and went about
acquiring one can be gained from the minute-books of the
Women's Tax Resistance League (Fawcett Archives, Box 59).
62 – *Reynolds's Weekly Newspaper*, quoted in the NUWSS circular
'Press Reports of the Banners'.
63 – Elizabeth Robins, *Way Stations*, Hodder & Stoughton,
London, 1913, p. 248. See NUWSS annual, half-yearly and
quarterly meetings, 1908–18 (Fawcett Archives, Box 301); on
14 July 1908 Mary Lowndes (who was on the executive)
reported that 'the Women of the League . . . gave their time
ungrudgingly' in making the banners for 13 June. The *Freelance*
(10 June 1908) noted that 'Education' was given by Philippa
Fawcett and worked by artists belonging to the League; 'Music'
was given by Mrs Davies and worked by her and her daughters;
and 'Scriveners' (writers) was worked by Mrs Herringham.
64 – Sylvia Pankhurst (1931), p. 395; probably her own studio at
42 Linden Gardens, now part of the complex that houses the
Mansell Collection from which I have borrowed illustrations for
this book.
65 – There is some spite in Sylvia Pankhurst's account of the
NUWSS (1931, p. 252). She describes the National Union
'waking from a long inertia' in consequence of the WSPU activity
of which they disapproved, so far emulating it as to organise a
procession, and then discovering themselves so proud of it that
'they forgot such efforts were already habitual in the WSPU'.
This is not entirely fair. The most important precedent was the
demonstration and deputation of 300 women representing
the WSPU, the NUWSS, the Women's Liberal Federation, the
British Women's Temperance Association and the Labour and
Co-operative Women, to the Prime Minister in 1906 (Strachey,
1928, p. 301); but this was much smaller and less structured
than the Mud March, which seems in 1907 to have established
all the principal elements of suffrage spectacle as they
developed up to 1913.
66 – The following information is drawn from the Central
Society for Women's Suffrage, Executive Committee minutes,
May 1906 to October 1907 (Fawcett Archives, Box 136) (Miss
Sterling had proposed 'a big open air Demonstration to be held
at the opening of the next session' on 21 November 1906).

67 – Lady Frances Balfour, daughter of the eighth Duke of
Argyll, was president of the London Society for Women's
Suffrage; Jane, Lady Strachey, was a long-standing suffragist,
president of the Women's Local Government Society and
mother of ten (including Lytton and Philippa, the secretary of
the London Society); Mrs Fawcett was president of the
NUWSS; and Edith Pechey Phipson was one of the first English
women to qualify in the medical profession.
68 – Strachey (1928), p. 306. The accounts which follow draw
on a range of press reports and other sources listed in the
bibliography. Newspapers are not individually cited at every
point. Unless otherwise stated, the issue in question is that
immediately following the demonstration to which it refers. In
the case of a Saturday demonstration this will be the next day's
Sunday paper or the Monday's daily paper. Unless otherwise
noted therefore, newspaper references to the Mud March are to
11 February 1907.
69 – Apparently through the generosity of Maud Arncliffe-
Sennett, whose company (which made Christmas crackers
and other novelties) supplied the rosettes (see Central Society
for Women's Suffrage, Executive Committee minutes, 21
February 1907, Fawcett Archives, Box 136).
70 – Unidentified cutting (Fawcett Archives, Suffrage Album 3,
SvL 1907–29): 'There seemed to be two main points of view:
that shared by the poorer class of men, namely, bitter resentment at the possibility of women getting any civic privilege they
had not got; the other, that of amusement at the fact of women
wanting any serious thing, and wanting it badly enough to face
the ordeal of a public demonstration.'
71 – *Black and White*, 16 February 1907.
72 – *Manchester Guardian*, 'By One of the Demonstrators'. This
is a long and fascinatingly equivocal account by a participant
struggling to come to terms with the experience and assess its
political validity. See also the *Morning Post*, 13 February 1907:
'By the time they reached the Strand many of the women on foot
presented a decidedly bedraggled appearance but . . . they
marched bravely on with a stout heart and a perfect indifference
to the scoffs and jeers of enfranchised male persons who had
posted themselves along the line of the route, and appeared to
regard the occasion as suitable for the display of crude and
vulgar jests.'
73 – Strachey (1928), p. 306. See also the NUWSS *Annual
Report* for 1907 (Fawcett Archives, Box 145), in which the
National Union concluded that the 'procession had an excellent
effect in drawing public attention to the question, and . . . was
widely and sympathetically reported by the Press'. The National
Union had voted £200 towards the expenses, but funds were
subscribed and the money was not required. The Report of the
Demonstration Sub-Committee (Central Society for Women's
Suffrage, Executive Committee minutes, 21 February 1907,
Fawcett Archives, Box 136) indicates a profit of about £17 on
expenses of about £233. Banners and shields cost less than £22,
all of which indicates a modest enterprise by subsequent standards: the WSPU demonstration and Hyde Park meeting of
1908 cost about £4800.
74 – *Manchester Guardian*, 11 February 1907.

75 – Bill stages in the House of Commons were: first reading (presentation), second reading (vote on principle), committee and report (individual clauses and amendments), third reading (vote on amended bill).

76 – Mrs Fawcett became the first woman to address the Oxford Union when she debated the issue of women's suffrage there (see *The Times*, 21 November 1908).

77 – Balfour papers, 23 and 28 October 1907, quoted Rosen (1974), pp. 95–96.

78 – Reported in *Votes for Women*, January 1908; quoted Rosen (1974), p. 98.

79 – Quoted in Sylvia Pankhurst (1931), p. 278. See also the WSPU's *Third Annual Report* 1908–09, p. 7: 'In the last Annual Report attention was drawn to Mr Gladstone's challenge to Women Suffragists to show, by outdoor demonstrations, in support of their cause, numbers approximating to those which men exhibited when they demanded the franchise. This challenge it was said would be taken up by the Women's Social and Political Union, and previous demonstrations would be not only equalled but surpassed. This promise has been amply fulfilled during the year.'

80 – Sylvia Pankhurst (1931, p. 283) claimed that the 'constitutional suffragists, not to be out-done, though starting later, cut in before'; but this is unfair, since their decision is recorded in the minutes of the quarterly Council Meeting for 29 January 1908 (Fawcett Archives, Box 301). The NUWSS later claimed that they had invited the WSPU, but that unlike the WFL, the National Union of Women Workers, the Women's Co-operative Guild, the ILP and the Fabians, they had refused to participate (LSWS circular, 19 May 1910, Fawcett Archives, Box 147).

81 – *Women's Franchise*, 25 May 1908, p. 564.

82 – *Morning Post*, 15 June 1908.

83 – See NUWSS Executive Committee minutes during April and May 1908 (Fawcett Archives, Box 83) and the *Report* of Quarterly Council Meeting, 1 May 1908 (Box 301). The Procession Committee consisted of two members from the National Union, two from the London Society (one of them Philippa Strachey, the organiser) and two from the Artists' Suffrage League: Mrs Herringham and Mary Lowndes. Expenses were estimated at £350 excluding rail fares. In the event the whole demonstration cost rather more (about £650, with the artists and needlewomen donating their services) but turned unexpectedly into a financial, as well as a propaganda, triumph. By 23 July the profits stood at almost £350 and donations were still coming in. The Executive Committee decided not to deter further contributors by publishing the profits, but to continue with the appeal. All money, after all, was money for the cause (see NUWSS Executive Committee minutes, 23 July 1908, Box 83; LSWS Correspondence, letter from Mrs Stanton Coit to Philippa Strachey, 5 November 1908, Box 146; and NUWSS Annual, Half-Yearly and Quarterly Council Meetings, 14 July and 9 October 1908, Box 301).

84 – *Women's Franchise*, 25 May 1908, p. 564.

85 – *The Times*, 12 June 1908.

86 – See 'The Press and the Procession', the *Women's Franchise*, 25 June 1908, p. 617.

87 – It seems to have been Mary Lowndes's idea to turn a demonstration into a pageant, and the work of the Artists' Suffrage League that accomplished it. See letter from Philippa Strachey in reply to Mrs Fawcett's letter of congratulation to her, 22 June 1908 (Fawcett Autograph Collection, Part C, 1908): 'Please don't think that I personally deserve so very much credit for the procession. I stared at it as it went by and wondered at the amount of work it must represent. Hundreds of people must have worked very hard but I don't think any of them did anything difficult or talented except the Artists – which means to say Miss Lowndes. She really is splendid. Besides being responsible for the plan of making the procession into a pageant, she actually designed nearly all of the banners herself which I think is a wonderful achievement. Her organising capacities are just as remarkable. She got the banners made and she worked out every detail in connection with them without letting us have the smallest trouble about them from first to last. On the Committee she was most helpful about everything and was delightful to work with because she was entirely free from any sort of nonsense; she only cared about the success of the Procession as a whole and she was perfectly willing to subordinate her decorations and give up all her cherished ideas when difficulties cropped up. She really did an immense amount of work for us and I shudder to think of what was happening to her own trade meantime.'

88 – Strachey (1928), p. 306; contrast the *Observer*, 14 July 1908: 'They marched with spirit. They greeted all the jokes with merry laughter; they carried themselves with the air of people who meant to win.'

89 – Cicely Hamilton in the *Daily Mail*; daily newspaper references are to 15 June 1908 unless otherwise noted.

90 – *Daily News*.

91 – *Daily Mail*.

92 – *Morning Leader*.

93 – *Daily News*.

94 – *The Times*.

95 – The Fabian Women's Group was formed at a meeting in March 1908. It decided immediately to march with the NUWSS on the 13th and the WSPU on 21 June, 'and to provide itself with a banner for such occasions'. By 9 May a Banner Committee had been formed, and May Morris had produced a design together with some of the material for its execution. The design was transferred to the fabric by the stained-glass designer Caroline Townshend, and the work was carried out by nineteen needlewomen who included Marion Wallace Dunlop of the WSPU. I have been quite unable to trace the banner, which is either lost or destroyed, and there is unfortunately no surviving description of it (minutes of the Fabian Women's Group, 14 March 1908–2 February 1914, card 107, C/8/A/1, British Library of Political and Economic Science).

96 – *The Times*. There were 200 vehicles according to the *Sunday Times* (14 June 1908). The colours of the National Union were still red and white, as in 1907. Green was added in 1909.

97 – *Westminster Gazette*, undated (Fawcett Archives, Suffrage Album SvL 1907–29).

98 – See the *Women's Franchise*, 4 June 1908, p. 581.

99 – *Daily Mail*. See also the comments of 'The Lady Demonstrator' in the *Daily News* ('nothing seemed easier than to carry aloft a banner you were proud of, until you actually attempted to do so'); and *The Times*: 'Nothing could have been more admirable than the endurance of the ladies who had undertaken this burden, and who went through with it so gallantly. At one point the guiding cords of a banner broke away, and seeing the distress of the bearer, someone in the crowd called out, "You want a man's help." "No, I don't," replied the banner-bearer emphatically, as she wrestled with the intractable folds of the flapping silk; and she showed that she did not speak in vain.'

100 – Estimates of the numbers varied: *The Times*, as always, was the most grudging, with 6–7000; Sylvia Pankhurst estimated 13,000 and Ray Strachey 15,000.

101 – *Morning Leader*.

102 – *Daily News*.

103 – *The Times*.

104 – *Morning Leader*. It was, wrote Cicely Hamilton in the *Daily Mail*, 'something to remember and be glad of, the thronged assembly of women, rising tier above tier,' gaiety and enthusiasm rippling through the crowd 'without any of the drab uniformity that would inevitably characterise a similar assemblage of men'.

105 – Laurence Housman to Janet Ashbee, undated but clearly 14 June 1908 (Ashbee Journals, King's College, Cambridge).

106 – *Daily News*.

107 – 'The Great March and Meeting 13 June 1908: Impressions of a Banner Bearer' (Maud Arncliffe-Sennett papers, vol. 3, *c*. p. 79).

108 – Cicely Hamilton in the *Daily Mail*. The *Daily News* identified hostility from two different sections of the crowd: the cockney girls in 'tawdry finery' along Northumberland Avenue, who greeted the suffragists with cries of 'Go 'ome and mind the biby'; and further west some carriages 'filled with a detachment of the "smart set"' who regarded the participants as 'specimens of some strange animal'. The anti-suffrage *Times* insisted that the crowd's keen interest 'was purely the detached interest of curiosity that never at any moment kindled into enthusiasm'. It was not unsympathetic, and it was strikingly respectful, but it was in *The Times*'s view reserved. 'Certainly the demonstrators may congratulate themselves, first, on having attracted so much public attention, and, secondly, on having been received with such extreme politeness; but they cannot pretend they moved the public heart.'

109 – See letter from the *Daily Chronicle*, 15 June 1908 (Maud Arncliffe-Sennett Papers, vol. 3 *c*. p. 79). The extent and the importance of the publicity attracted to the cause by the NUWSS demonstration can scarcely be exaggerated. The account which follows is based on reports in the *Daily Chronicle*, *Daily Express*, *Daily Graphic*, *Daily Mirror*, *Daily News*, *Daily Mail*, *Daily Sketch*, *Daily Telegraph*, *Evening Standard* and *St James' Gazette*, the *Globe*, *Manchester Guardian*, the *People*, the *Morning Post*, the *Morning Leader*, the *Observer*, the *Referee*, the *Pall Mall Gazette*, *The Times*, the *Sunday Times*, the *Westminster Gazette*, the *Free-Lance*, the *Illustrated London News*, the *Kensington News*, the *Bristol Mercury*, *East Anglian Daily Times*, *Glasgow Evening Times*, *Leicester Post*, *Liverpool Daily Courier*, *Liverpool Daily Post and Mercury*, *Manchester Courier*, *Newcastle Chronicle*, *North Mail*, *Western Daily Press* and the *Scotsman* (also the weekly issues of the *Women's Franchise* during May and June). The list is not exhaustive, and many daily papers devoted several reports and their leaders to the occasion. Publications throughout the country and of all shades of political opinion were virtually invaded by the question, and the NUWSS exploited this attention with halfpenny leaflets of extracts circulated to MPs and other interested parties: 'The importance and variety of the papers quoted from will greatly add to the value of their testimony; they will also be useful in controverting the argument often advanced that Processions do no good, as no one is convinced by them' (*Women's Franchise*, 25 June 1908, p. 615).

110 – 14 June 1908.

111 – *Daily News*. See also the *Morning Leader*: 'the sweet girl graduates in their flowing robes made the prettiest picture of any'; although the *Observer* (14 June) added the caveat that 'from the picturesque point of view, too many of them wore spectacles'.

112 – See the *Daily News*.

113 – *Bristol Mercury*, quoted in 'The Press and the Procession', the *Women's Franchise*, 25 June 1908, p. 615.

114 – The *Weekly Dispatch*, 20 June 1908; the *Kensington News*, 19 June 1908.

115 – *The Times*. On the other hand the *New Age* (27 June 1908) remarked that there was 'a vision of Revolution as one looked at these marching women; which was not dulled by their prim propriety, by their dainty dress, or by the note of gentleness'.

116 – *Glasgow Evening Times*, quoted in 'The Press and the Procession', the *Women's Franchise*, 25 June 1908, pp. 617–18.

117 – *Western Daily Press*, as above.

118 – *Reynolds's Weekly Newspaper*, as above.

119 – The *Women's Franchise*, 25 June 1908, p. 615.

120 – The report acknowledged that the demonstration was orderly, representative and impressive, but insisted that it was typical of 'our modern tendency towards hysteria in politics' that it should be taken like a referendum as evidence of an 'overwhelming demand'.

121 – See the (N)WSPU *Report* for the year ending 29 February 1908 (Museum of London), and Emmeline Pethick-Lawrence (1938), p. 182. In the preceding twelve months 5000 meetings had been held, thirteen by-elections contested, 130 women arrested and imprisoned, and 100,000 publications sold. The premises at Clement's Inn had been extended from three to thirteen rooms, the staff doubled, the annual income considerably more than doubled, and the number of subscribers trebled. 'It was with a very good heart,' Emmeline Pethick-Lawrence recalled, 'that we entered upon the third year of our national existence.'

122 – Sylvia Pankhurst (1931), pp. 283–84 and *Votes for Women*, chiefly 14 May and 4 June 1908. Copies of the poster were available at five shillings, copies of the women's portraits at threepence each, and maps at sixpence.

123 – Reported in the press on 19 June 1908: see the *Daily Chronicle*, the *Daily Mirror*, etc.

124 – Sylvia Pankhurst (1931), p. 284. For Tussaud's see *The Times*, 22 June 1908.

125 – On the colours see the (N)WSPU third annual *Report 1908–09* ('They have proved a very attractive means of stimulating the "esprit" of members and of propagating the movement'), and *Votes for Women*, 30 July 1908; but for their most extensive elaboration, Emmeline Pethick-Lawrence in the programme of the WSPU exhibition at the Prince's Skating Rink, 1909 (Museum of London), from which this quotation is taken. White stood for purity 'in public as well as private life'. Green stood for hope, signifying 'that the "green fire" of a new spring tide has kindled life in a movement apparently dead'. Purple stood for dignity, 'for the growing sense on the part of the womanhood of the world, of that self-reverence and self-respect which renders acquiescence to political subjection impossible and gives determination to women's claim for freedom'. Purple was sometimes glossed as 'loyalty' or 'courage' in the press, and green as 'youth' or 'regeneration'. So long as the concepts were positive the exact niceties of the symbolism were less important than the decorative impact of the colours and their effect in unifying the march and evoking the cause. They may have helped to subdue its class distinctions (particularly since ostentatious dress was frowned on in processions), although as Anna Davin has pointed out, few working women could afford the white dress recommended for younger participants. (*The Times*, 22 June 1908, noted that white was recommended as appropriate to the season, 'effective from the spectacular point of view, and as inexpensive materials are to be had in white, a ready means of enabling the procession to present a uniform appearance symbolical of their united demand'.) Lord Brockway (in conversation with the author, 21 November 1984) recalled how conscious he was of the colours, in Hyde Park on 21 June and afterwards, how widespread they were, and how it was impossible to see them without being reminded of the cause.

126 – *Votes for Women*, 18 June 1908, p. 248, and 2 July 1909, p. 890. See also 26 March 1909, p. 483: there is 'no lack of choice; indeed so many of the best dressmakers and milliners are laying themselves out to supply dresses and hats in the colours that there is almost an *embarras de richesses*'.

127 – *The Times*, 22 June 1908. All daily papers quoted are from the 22nd unless otherwise noted. Press sources drawn upon are given in the bibliography. Sunday was chosen as the day on which most working women could be free, and on which there would be least traffic to impede the passage of the seven processions converging on Hyde Park.

128 – See *Votes for Women*, 14 May 1908, p. 165: 'Twenty or even thirty people can each provide a band for the day by paying £12 for one of the leading bands, or for a lesser band £5.'

129 – See Laurence Housman letter to Janet Ashbee, 24 June 1908 (Ashbee Journals, King's College, Cambridge): 'My banner had the honour of being the only one that was kept unfurled throughout the whole demonstration: it travelled on a wagon being too big to be borne by hand, and it really did arouse

enthusiasm. Perhaps I am destined to end as a poster-artist! Anyway this was good training.' The WSPU produced Christmas cards based on Housman's design in 1908 and the banner was used on numerous subsequent occasions (*Votes for Women*, October 1908, p. 18). According to Housman the Kensington contingent was 5000 strong. It included an artists' section, with a banner presented by Louise Jopling Rowe, which has not survived (*Votes for Women*, 18 June 1908, p. 256).

130 – See the *Daily News* article, 12 June 1908, by a reporter who had called at Clement's Inn and inspected the 'wonderful dress novelties' laid by for the procession, including General Drummond's 'glorious regalia, with its golden epaulettes and peaked cap of purple, white and green'.

131 – See G. R. S. Taylor in the *New Age*, 27 June 1908, p. 168: 'It may not be a strictly fair description, but the Saturday March was of the people who wanted the vote if it did not inconvenience anyone to grant it. On Sunday, they were determined to have it whether it inconvenienced anyone or not.'

132 – The ten large silk banners made in haste by a commercial manufacturer were augmented by 500 smaller banners: horizontal strips of fabric between two poles, lettered in the colours according to the inclination of the branch that made them. Kits had been available from Clement's Inn, or they could be had ready-sewn for sixteen shillings if the motto was not too long. Mottoes noted in the press included 'Who would be free, themselves must strike the blow', 'Not chivalry but justice', 'The only hope for the unemployed', '237 women imprisoned for the vote. 540 weeks in Holloway', 'Righteousness exalteth a nation' and 'The Women of England hope this tonic will open the eyes of the mind'. Onlookers sometimes refused to be persuaded. See for example 'An Unbeliever's View' by Arnold White in the *Daily Chronicle*, 22 June 1908: 'But will the women's vote increase employment, give us an efficient Army, an irresistible Navy, lower taxes and cheaper justice?'

133 – *Votes for Women*, 25 June 1908. Lord (Fenner) Brockway was there, and described the scene as without precedent and absolutely unforgettable. (His first girlfriend was the 'baby suffragette', the eighteen-year-old Jessie Spinks, who changed her name to Vera Wentworth and became a popular speaker.) See Laurence Housman letter to Janet Ashbee, 24 June 1908 (Ashbee Journals, King's College, Cambridge): 'The crowd was something marvellous to look upon. I have never seen anything approaching it even at the two Jubilees – not all gathered together within a single point of view, I mean.'

134 – *The Times*.

135 – Laurence Housman gave an account of the disruptions in a letter to Janet Ashbee, 24 June 1908 (see note 147).

136 – See *The Times*, *Votes for Women*, 25 June 1908, and unidentified cutting in Fawcett Archives, Suffrage Album 3, SvL.

137 – The *Standard*.

138 – H. Fraser to I. Seymour, 6 July 1908 (Museum of London folder 'Constitution–Organisation', quoted Rosen (1974), p. 105).

139 – Sylvia Pankhurst (1931), p. 285.

140 – *Votes for Women*, 4 June 1908, quoted Rosen (1974), p. 105.

141 – House of Commons Debate, 4s, vol. 189 col. 962, quoted Rosen (1974), p. 106. See also Sylvia Pankhurst (1931), p. 282. *The Times* considered it 'a lamentable weakness in the Prime Minister to state that he would allow to be incorporated in a Government measure a principle of which he disapproved, and that, too, without previously taking the sense of the country on the matter. He appears to have earnt little gratitude by the concession, perhaps because it is recognized by the advocates of the measure that his condition was somewhat difficult of proof.'

142 – Nevinson Journals, 23 June 1908 (Bodleian Library Dep.e 71/1, quoted Rosen, 1974, p. 106).

143 – The Women's National Anti-Suffrage League leaflet no. 3 (Museum of London) printed Mrs Humphry Ward's speech and the manifesto from its inaugural meeting of 21 July 1908. The objects of the WNASL were summarised in the *Anti-Suffrage Review*, first issued in December 1908. They were: 'To resist the proposal to admit women to the Parliamentary Franchise and to Parliament'; and 'To maintain the principle of the representation of women on municipal and other bodies concerned with the domestic and social affairs of the community'. Mrs Humphry Ward (the novelist Mary Ward) had been a leading figure in drafting the 'Appeal' against woman suffrage published in the *Nineteenth Century* in June 1889, and the WNASL manifesto gave the same five reasons for opposing women's suffrage in 1908. *The Times*'s account drew directly from a circular letter put out by the WNASL, for which see Fawcett Archives, Box 298, LSWS correspondence relating to anti-suffrage opinion and activities. On anti-suffragism see Brian Harrison's detailed and informative study, *Separate Spheres: The Opposition to Women's Suffrage in Britain*, Croom Helm, London, 1978.

144 – Harrison (1978, p. 94) maps out in a useful diagram the ties of kinship, friendship and career advancement by which the anti-suffrage leadership was bound together under three principal headings: the Oxford–academic, the legal–political and the imperialist–political. Lord Curzon was an expert fundraiser with influential contacts. He told Lord Cromer that 'the real people to go at are the rich business men in every big industrial or manufacturing or shipping city' (7 February 1912, Curzon papers MSS. Eur. F. 112/33, quoted by Harrison, p. 126).

145 – Mrs Chapman Catt: see Fawcett Library, suffrage pamphlets, personal authors A–C. See also the *Common Cause* editorial of 15 April 1909: 'Perhaps no one piece of agitation has done us quite so much good as the anti-suffrage agitation . . . Most of them frankly admit that they do not hope to make converts: their aim is merely to organise the existing opposition. But in the process of being organised a good deal of this opposition becomes converted into support. Many people are drawn into an anti-suffrage meeting who are afraid to come to our meetings; but, when they have come, and found the bareness of the argument and antediluvian nature of the prejudice which it covers, they begin to think – and thinking is a process which is even more difficult to stop than to initiate.'

146 – Quoted in the *Daily Chronicle*, 10 June 1908. Harrison (1974, p. 127) cites Maud Arncliffe-Sennett's letter to Curzon (21 July 1910, Curzon papers MSS. Eur. F. 112/33) in which she pointed out that of the 103 names of antis published in *The Times* that day, thirty-six were peers and peeresses, not to mention the baronets.

147 – Lady Chance, 'The Predominance of Men in Anti-Suffrage Finance and Organisation', NUWSS leaflet 37, published by the Conservative and Unionist Women's Franchise Association, July 1913 (Fawcett Library). Harrison does not cite Chance, but she proves his point. She argued that since the anti-suffrage women were unsupported by any organised body of women in the country, they needed to avail themselves of the men's funds and organisational expertise. For their part the men needed the women to shield them from criticism invoked by 'the spectacle of a powerful body of rich and titled men financing and controlling a concern whose purpose is to delay [reform]'.

148 – Arnold Ward's speech on the second reading of the Conciliation Bill, July 1910, quoted in Henry Nevinson, *More Changes More Chances*, Nisbet, London, 1925, p. 307.

149 – WNASL leaflet no. 3, see note 143. As Robert Cholmeley remarked sarcastically in his pamphlet on 'The Women's Anti-Suffrage Movement', of 'one thing at least the peccant four hundred and twenty may rest assured: there will be no violence used towards them; no one will even ring their doorbells without previous introduction.'

150 – Asquith quoted in Christabel Pankhurst (1959), p. 194.

151 – G. R. S. Taylor, 'The Franchise for Walkers', *New Age*, 27 June 1908. Harrison (1978, p. 148) observes that the antis, and in particular the Girls' Anti-Suffrage League, preferred to operate through balls, garden parties and receptions rather than through processions and demonstrations.

152 – The president of the International Woman Suffrage Alliance was Carrie Chapman Catt, and its second vice-president, Millicent Fawcett. There were affiliated societies in Australia, Bulgaria, Canada, Denmark, Finland, Germany, Great Britain, Hungary, Italy, the Netherlands, Norway, Russia, South Africa, Sweden, Switzerland and the United States. The Reverend Anna Shaw was president of the National American Woman Suffrage Association.

153 – Fawcett Archives, Box 296, LSWS correspondence relating to meetings. See also the *Common Cause*, 6 May 1909, pp. 59–61, and the *Suffrage Annual and Women's Who's Who*, 1913. The official programme of the Pageant of Women's Trades and Professions is in the Fawcett Library.

154 – *Morning Leader*, 28 April 1909. See also the *Common Cause*, 6 May 1909, pp. 59–61. Press coverage was slight compared with that accorded the two demonstrations of 1908.

155 – The programme claimed that 538 of the 553 registered medical women in Great Britain had declared themselves in favour of women's suffrage. It placed great store by the presence of doctors (who could sign a certificate of insanity that would deprive a man of his vote, whilst having none of their own) and nurses (who experienced daily the need for the woman's vote as they came into contact with the consequences

of poverty, inadequate housing, unemployment, infant mortality and sweated labour).

156 – Before the emblems could be made the trades had to be settled on and representatives found for them, since bona fide practitioners were required, not just people with emblems or banners prepared to stand in for them. Fawcett Archives, Box 296 (LSWS correspondence in relation to meetings) contains complicated lists of participants, with names of contacts or institutions against them. ('Sweet makers – Could we get Cadbury to send a contingent? Are they suffrage?') Some trades were not in the end represented (upholsterers, frame gilders, brick-makers). Mary Lowndes (whose idea this may have been) designed all the emblems herself and they were made up by members of the Artists' Suffrage League.

157 – *Daily Chronicle.*

158 – Their expenses were paid by the LSWS: see Fawcett Archives, Box 296 (LSWS correspondence in relation to meetings), letter to Philippa Strachey from Bertha Johnson, 2 May 1909. Pit-brow women continued to work at the pit-head, shifting and grading coal and loading trucks, after the exclusion of women from the coalface in 1842. They were noted for their independence, robust physique and 'unfeminine' dress (i.e. trousers), and various attempts were made to close this occupation to women by law. The Cradley Heath nail and chain-makers, 'probably the most sweated skilled workers in the world', were also subject to legislative interference that would have improved their conditions at the cost of limiting them to the lighter and worse-paid work. The cases of the pit-brow and Cradley Heath women respectively had come to symbolise the interference of men and the state in the control of women's employment, and that hard labour which underlay the concept of 'womanliness' peddled with no less vigour by those whose business depended on the exploitation of female labour.

159 – The *Common Cause*, 6 May 1909, p. 60, and letter from Mrs Chapman Catt to Mary Lowndes, 17 May 1909 (Fawcett Autograph Collection, vol. 1 part E, 1909). The *Morning Leader* commented particularly on the banked masses of red and white flowers on the platform, with delegates, speakers and representatives from the press of twenty-seven countries ranged behind them.

160 – The *Common Cause*, 6 May 1909, p. 59. The badge was presumably the 'Holloway' badge designed by Sylvia Pankhurst.

161 – See *Votes for Women*, 25 June 1909. Rosen (1974, p. 118) points out that their right to petition was never in question, but only their manner of doing so.

162 – See *Votes for Women*, 16 July 1909. Rosen (1974, p. 120) quotes Frederick Pethick-Lawrence's letter to Marion Wallace Dunlop in which he says that, 'Nothing has moved me so much – stirred me to the depths of my being – as your heroic action.'

163 – Ponsonby to Gladstone, 13 August 1909, quoted Rosen (1974), p. 123 (Gladstone papers, British Museum Add. MSS 45985).

164 – Quoted in Sylvia Pankhurst (1931), chapter v, 'Forcible Feeding', p. 317. Rosen (1974, pp. 126–27) points out that Gladstone was in a contradictory position. He was broadly pro-suffrage, and he had suggested in 1908 that women would only gain their ends by violence as men had done; but as Home Secretary he was responsible for the safety of the Prime Minister and Cabinet, which he now believed to be at risk.

165 – From 'Fed by Force, a Statement by Mrs Mary Leigh, Who is Still in Birmingham Gaol' (leaflet), 1909; also quoted in Rosen (1974), p. 124. Sylvia Pankhurst's account of her own forcible feeding is in Pankhurst (1931), pp. 443–44.

166 – Sylvia Pankhurst (1931), p. 318.

167 – *The Times*, 5 October 1909, quoted Rosen (1974), p. 125.

168 – Reginald McKenna, quoted in Sylvia Pankhurst (1931), p. 568.

169 – Teresa Billington-Greig condemned in militant tactics 'the crooked course, the double shuffle between revolution and injured innocence'; and even Sylvia Pankhurst believed that what the movement really needed was 'not more serious militancy by the few, but a stronger appeal to the great masses to join the struggle'. See Liddington and Norris (1978), p. 219, and Sylvia Pankhurst (1931), p. 316.

170 – See the letter published in *The Times*, 29 September 1909, from Mrs Pankhurst, Christabel, Emmeline Pethick-Lawrence and Mabel Tuke, which described the victims as having 'violated bodies'.

171 – Most suffrage histories give an account of the case of Constance Lytton. See the signed typescript statement of her experiences as 'Jane Warton' (31 January 1910) in the Museum of London collection, and her book *On Prisons and Prisoners*, Heinemann, London, 1914.

172 – Rosen (1974, pp. 127–28) quotes an exasperated Herbert Gladstone (Gladstone papers, British Museum Add. MSS 46067), Gladstone to Emily Hobhouse, 9 November 1909: 'If the spirit of any movement is exemplified by actions of incredible folly which exasperate reasonable and friendly opinion, it can only be the worse for the movement. On different occasions in recent years I have spoken as strongly as I could for enfranchisement. But for three years I have been pursued by the militant section with venom and falsehood simply because I have been discharging a public duty . . .'

173 – Hume (1982), p. 61.

174 – *The Vote*, 16 December 1909, p. 92.

175 – See Neal Blewett, *The Peers, the Parties, and the People: The British General Elections of 1910*, University of Toronto Press, Toronto, 1972, pp. 330–33. According to the NUWSS *Annual Report* for 1910, the National Union spent £1460 on election expenses for questioning, canvassing and petitioning, in addition to the funds spent by local societies.

176 – Rosen (1974, pp. 134–35) gives details of the committee's membership and of the bill. See also Pugh (1980), p. 15.

177 – Lloyd George declared the bill would 'on balance add hundreds of thousands of votes throughout the country to the strength of the Tory Party' (Pugh, 1980, p. 15).

178 – See Hume (1982), pp. 72–73.

179 – Maud Arncliffe-Sennett to Philippa Strachey, 24 September 1909 ('wheedle Mrs Fawcett to agree to it . . . the Demonstration being so immense it will give incoming Governments an excuse to put us officially on their programme');

Philippa Strachey's response, 8 October 1909 (both in Fawcett Archives, Box 146, LSWS general correspondence); letter from Lady Frances Balfour to Maud Arncliffe-Sennett, 31 December 1909 (between pp. 38 and 39 in vol. 9 of the Arncliffe-Sennett papers, British Library).

180 – The account of the disagreements and misunderstandings between the constitutionalists and the WSPU which follows is drawn from the papers in Fawcett Archives, Box 147, LSWS correspondence.

181 – See note above. On 19 April Edith Dimmock of the NUWSS wrote to the LSWS forwarding the correspondence with the WSPU and urging them to present a united front. She outlined the three main considerations that had led the executive to refuse to cooperate with the WSPU: it was their policy to keep distinct from militant societies, there was no guarantee that it would be a constitutional demonstration, and there was in fact every reason to believe that it would be an anti-government one (see also NUWSS executive meeting, 5 May 1910, and LSWS circular letter, 19 May 1910, Box 147).

182 – Clara Morden to the LSWS, 18 June 1910. It would appear that the NUWSS membership was more inclined than its executive to risk a further demonstration and cooperation with the militants.

183 – The Vote, 21 and 28 May 1910.

184 – The Vote, 3 June 1910, p. 581.

185 – Votes for Women on 11 June listed more than thirty separate divisions and organisations, with the WFL (and its own distinct contingents) listed only as one. The WSPU had provided the chief impetus for the procession, and more than half the contingents.

186 – The Sunday Times, 19 June 1910, which noted that onlookers were 'somewhat staggered' at the sight of General Drummond cantering along the ranks in her long green riding coat 'giving a skilful display of horsemanship'. She was accompanied by Miss Vera Holme and the Hon. Mrs Haverfield in close dark riding habits and silk top hats. They appear in archive newsreel footage, among spectators clearly astonished by the procession, the stewards and the camera that records the scene. Daily newspaper accounts are from 20 June 1910 unless otherwise noted. Press sources are listed in the bibliography. See also Nevinson's account in Votes for Women, 24 June 1910, and the Vote, 25 June 1910. A number of press reports estimated the procession at about 10,000; the Vote at 12,000, and Votes for Women at 15,000.

187 – The Sunday Times. The press had commented before on the lack of a women's band. The WSPU Drum and Fife Band was formed probably in 1909, and advertised the WSPU exhibition at the Prince's Skating Rink.

188 – All quotations from Nevinson's account in Votes for Women, 24 June 1910.

189 – The Vote, 28 May 1910.

190 – The Planet, 25 June 1910. The nurses marched with a new Florence Nightingale banner (not the one designed by Mary Lowndes in 1908).

191 – The Vote, 25 June 1910.

192 – The Vote, 25 June 1910.

193 – Votes for Women, 24 June 1910.

194 – Men's League for Women's Suffrage Monthly Paper, July 1910. Laurence Housman had also designed them a new black and gold badge.

195 – The Vote, 25 June 1910.

196 – Daily Mail.

197 – Men's League for Women's Suffrage Monthly Paper, July 1910.

198 – On the tube to Charing Cross a hardened processionist was heard coaching novices in the responses to stock injunctions such as 'Go 'ome and mind the baby / do the washing / cook the old man's supper'; but they were redundant on the march. 'The temper of the crowd has changed; there is sympathy in it, there is welcome.' See the Vote, 30 May and 21 July 1910.

199 – Quoted (from direct communication) by Antonia Raeburn, Militant Suffragettes, Michael Joseph, London, 1973, pp. 161–62.

200 – The Planet, 25 June 1910.

201 – Votes for Women, 3 June 1910. See also the Daily Telegraph, 20 June 1910: 'The countless spectators witnessed an event probably unique in their lifetime.'

202 – Nevinson Journals, 12 July 1910, quoted Rosen (1974), p. 137 (Bodleian Library Dep.e 72/1). Rosen gives details of the vote on the bill; see also Hume (1982), pp. 81–83.

203 – Reported in LSWS circular, 29 June 1910, from Mrs Fawcett (Fawcett Archives, Box 151). Subsequent accounts of the preparations for the July procession are vague or misleading: see Christabel Pankhurst (1959), p. 155; Sylvia Pankhurst (1931), p. 339; and Emmeline Pethick-Lawrence (1938), p. 253, where she mistakes it for the June procession and misdates that to the 17th.

204 – LSWS circular, 29 June 1910 (Fawcett Archives, Box 151); NUWSS report of the proceedings at the Council Meeting in Bristol, 1 July 1910 (Fawcett Archives, Box 301); letter from Mrs Pankhurst to Philippa Strachey, 29 June 1910 (Fawcett Archives, Box 147).

205 – Brailsford to Mrs Fawcett, 30 June [1910] (Archives of Manchester Public Library, M/50 Box 10) quoted Hume (1982), pp. 77–78. 'We can succeed only by unity now and in the future. Ought we not to set the personal factors aside and as statesmen consider solely what use we can make of all our forces?'

206 – See Votes for Women, 15, 22 and 29 July 1910 ('chalked London white' is from 22 July); and handbill 'To Hyde Park' on Votes for Women notepaper (Fawcett Archives, Box 147).

207 – Votes for Women, 29 July 1910.

208 – Votes for Women, 15 and 22 July 1910.

209 – The Vote, 30 July 1910: 'For device it bore a prison gate, surmounted by an olive branch, and a dove, with a sprig of olive, flew against the bars; below were the words, "The light shineth in the darkness and the darkness comprehendeth it not".' Press sources are cited in the bibliography. Unless otherwise noted, reports in the daily papers are from 25 July 1910.

210 – Votes for Women, 22 July 1910. Many women wore badges inscribed 'Where there's a Bill there's a way' (The Times). There

was a simultaneous demonstration in Edinburgh, to which all the principal societies contributed, and in which each participant carried a flag, banneret or 'Roman Standard'.

211 – Quoted in the *Manchester Guardian*.

212 – See the *Daily Graphic*: 'There were signs of declining public interest, the spectators being fewer, probably on account of the frequency of these spectacles'; and the *Daily Telegraph*: 'many people appeared to regard the occasion as a spectacle rather than a political demonstration.'

213 – See Millicent Fawcett, *Women's Suffrage* (1912), p. 76; Sylvia Pankhurst (1931), p. 339; NUWSS leaflet 'A Brief Review of the Women's Suffrage Movement since its beginning in 1832', April 1911 (Museum of London). See Fawcett Archives, Box 296, LSWS circular letters (25 October and 8 November 1910 and 23 February 1911, together with the Statement of Accounts 1910), re the NUWSS demonstrations in support of the Conciliation Bill, which culminated in a joint mass meeting in the Albert Hall on 12 November 1910. The Hall was decorated for the occasion by the Artists' Suffrage League.

214 – *Votes for Women*, 25 November 1910, quoted Rosen (1974), p. 139. See also Hume (1982), p. 66. The following account is based on Rosen, pp. 139–141. The quotations are from H. N. Brailsford and Dr J. Murray, 'The Treatment of the Women's Deputations by the Metropolitan Police' (forwarded to the Home Office by the Conciliation Committee), London, 1911.

215 – Conservatives 272, Liberals 272, Irish Nationalists 84, Labour 42.

216 Hume (1982, p. 101) gives details of the modifications made to the 1910 Conciliation Bill.

217 – Millicent Fawcett, 'The Political Outlook for Women's Suffrage', the *Englishwoman*, January 1911.

218 – Quoted Hume (1982), p. 107 (CAB 41/33/16, 24 May 1911).

219 – In the *Englishwoman*, January 1911, quoted Hume (1982), p. 109.

220 – In *Votes for Women*, 23 June 1911, quoted Hume (1982, p. 109) and Rosen (1974, p. 150). Pugh (1978, p. 34) claims that the Conciliation Bill would never have passed since virtually the whole Cabinet was opposed to its terms.

221 – Fawcett Archives, Box 147.

222 – NUWSS Executive Committee minutes, 6 and 13 April 1911 (Fawcett Archives, Box 152). The NUWSS Receptions and Public Meetings Committee recommended that it should not go ahead if Hyde Park was not available for their meeting, or alternatively that the NUWSS procession might start at a different hour and go by a different route.

223 – Letter from Clementina Black to Edith Palliser, 26 April 1911 (Fawcett Archives, Box 298, Processions); and NUWSS Executive Committee minutes, 13 April 1911 (Box 152).

224 – Mary Lowndes, letter to Philippa Strachey at the LSWS (undated) (Fawcett Archives, Box 298, Processions).

225 – See NUWSS Executive Committee minutes, 4 May 1911 (Fawcett Archives, Box 152). Mrs Fawcett had been engaged to go to the International Woman's Suffrage Alliance Congress in Stockholm, but she agreed to cancel her trip if Helena Swanwick would go in her place.

226 – Emily Ford, 7 June 1911, and Philippa Strachey's reply, 9 June 1911 (Fawcett Archives, Box 298, Processions). See also NUWSS Executive Committee minutes (Box 152) for information on the preparations. Geraldine Cooke became procession organiser, and was appointed an assistant at a salary of thirty shillings per week.

227 – The Suffrage Atelier produced a model of its proposed scheme of decoration which WFL members were urged to inspect for themselves at the WFL offices. WSPU preparations were announced weekly in *Votes for Women*, and WFL arrangements in the *Vote*. See also WFL Executive Committee minutes, 22 and 23 May 1911 (Fawcett Archives, Box 54).

228 – *Votes for Women*, 2 June 1911.

229 – As above. Decorations were again in the hands of Marion Wallace Dunlop and Edith Downing. Local unions and provincial contingents were urged to communicate with them to ensure a unified scheme (*Votes for Women*, 28 April 1911). Processionists were encouraged to wear white or cream, and William Owen and Peter Robinson advertised 'Smart White Robes' and walking skirts for the 17th. On 5 May *Votes for Women* was already promising 'The Greatest Procession of Women Ever Witnessed' and recalling with rather faulty memory the Hyde Park demonstration of 1907 (they meant their own of 1908, not the Mud March), which 'gave the first indication of the forces which were behind the Votes for Women Movement'. Students at the Slade, the Royal Academy and the Royal College, together with students of music, drama and education, were encouraged to recruit their colleagues for the various pageants. The historical pageant was rehearsed in the Gardenia Restaurant on 16 July (*Votes for Women*, 9 June 1911).

230 – The principal suffrage accounts are in *Votes for Women*, 23 and 30 June 1911, the *Vote*, 17 and 24 June 1911, the *Common Cause*, 22 June 1911, and the *Official Programme of the Women's Coronation Procession* (WSPU) (Fawcett Library). Press sources are cited in the bibliography; daily paper reports are from 19 June 1911 unless otherwise noted.

231 – Frederic Lawrence in *Votes for Women*, 30 June 1911.

232 – The *Vote*, 24 June 1911. The WSPU sections stepped out to Ethel Smyth's 'The March of the Women' which they had been urged to learn by heart. The words were printed in the *Vote*, in *Votes for Women* and on postcards: 'Dawn is breaking / Hope is Waking / March on ... Shoulder to shoulder, and friend to friend.'

233 – The *Vote*, 24 June 1911.

234 – WSPU *Official Programme of the Women's Coronation Procession*.

235 – The *Vote*, 24 June 1911.

236 – Quoted in *Votes for Women*, 30 June 1911.

237 – The *Kensington News and West London Times*, 23 June 1911.

238 – Hobsbawm, in Hobsbawm and Ranger (eds) (1983), pp. 6, 12.

239 – See contributions to *Votes for Women* in the weeks

immediately preceding 17 June, when advice was offered on how to make tall hats out of buckram covered with black plush, and a full skirt, apron and shawl adapted to the purple, white and green. Newspapers such as the *Daily Telegraph* and *Morning Leader* commented on 'the ancient costume dominated by the familiar sugar-loaf hats'.

240 – Prys Morgan (whose account this is), in Hobsbawm and Ranger (eds) (1983), p. 81.

241 – Nevinson (1925), pp. 309–10. The *Vote*, 24 June 1911, noted among the new banners those of the nurses (a red cross on a gold ground); the graduates (with a design of mortarboard, book, pen and inkpot); the civil servants (with the figure of a government official); the athletes (with dumb-bells and clubs); the agriculturalists (with sheaves of golden corn); the business and professional women (with scale, weights and office paraphernalia); and the women factory workers (with the design of a factory town). It appears that these were chiefly painted, in the WFL colours of gold and green. None has survived, to my knowledge.

242 – The *Vote*, 10 June 1911.

243 – *East Anglian Daily Times*, 19 June 1911. See also the *Common Cause*, 22 June 1911. The NUWSS had been concerned about their place in the procession, not wishing to appear subordinate to the WSPU, but this difficulty must have been resolved. They had a new banner for the occasion, probably one based on Mary Lowndes's heraldic design with a unicorn (Lowndes Album, Fawcett Collection).

244 – Despite the reservations of Mary Lowndes, the Artists' Suffrage League marched after all, followed by the Suffrage Atelier. The *Manchester Guardian* noted 'a bevy of suffrage artists in their blue overalls' in the Albert Hall.

245 – Nevinson (1925), p. 328. The entire procession was reviewed by Elizabeth Wolstenholme-Elmy, the oldest militant suffragist, and the ranks of the WSPU dipped their pennants in salute as they passed her on the balcony of 67a St James's Street.

246 – *Daily Sketch*. See also the *Spectator*, the *Star*, *The Times*.

247 – 'The March of the Women' by Philip Snowden, 21 June 1911.

248 – *Men's League for Women's Suffrage Monthly Paper*, July 1911.

249 – *Anti-Suffrage Review*, July 1911.

250 – See the *Vote*, 24 June 1911.

251 – *Men's League for Women's Suffrage Monthly Paper*, July 1911 (the reference is to 'Mrs Partington' who appears in suffrage posters and postcards).

252 – The WSPU meeting in the Albert Hall began as the last contingents were leaving the Embankment. The WSPU target of £100,000 was reached, and a new set of £250,000. Mrs Pankhurst's speech proclaimed: 'We have proved we can combine, we have proved we can put aside all personal beliefs and all personal objects for a common end; we have proved that women have great powers of organisation; we have proved that women have great artistic capacity.' The resolution was moved and passed: 'That this meeting rejoices in the coming triumph of the Votes for Women cause, and pledges itself to use any and every

means to turn to account the Prime Minister's pledge of full and effective facilities for the Women's Enfranchisement Bill' (*Votes for Women*, 23 June 1911). Socialists made pointed comparisons between the Women's Coronation Procession and that of George V five days later (for which see Dangerfield, 1970, pp. 53–54). Philip Snowden in the *Christian Commonwealth* argued that 'the women's march typifies the promise of the future; the Coronation Procession . . . with its barbaric pomp and pride, is a survival from the childhood of a people.' Henry Holiday published a long letter on 'Pageants and National Life' in the *Daily News* (28 June 1911) contrasting the suffragists' 'delightful and elevating pageant' with 'the poverty-stricken attempts of the men' as evidence of 'the enormous value of women's influence in public life'. (For men's pageants not to be funereal their participants had to be tricked out in masquerade, or drawn heavily from the ranks of the army and navy, which permitted their members gay colours, lace and gold buttons to disguise what Holiday termed the horrors of their calling.)

253 – *Votes for Women*, 6 October 1911, quoted Rosen (1974), p. 151.

254 – Millicent Fawcett, *Women's Suffrage* (1912), p. 79.

255 – Nevinson Journals, 8 November 1911 (Bodleian Library, Dep.e 73/1), quoted Rosen (1974), p. 152. Lloyd George only confirmed suffragist suspicions by boasting at a meeting of the National Liberal Federation on the 23rd that the Conciliation Bill was once and for all 'torpedoed' (reported in *The Times*, 25 November 1911).

256 – See NUWSS Executive Committee minutes, 30 November 1911 (Fawcett Archives, Box 152); also Hume, pp. 121–23.

257 – See Fawcett Archives, Box 296. The Hall was decorated with banners and shields with heraldic devices devised for the federations and branches of the National Union. The designs are in Mary Lowndes's album in the Fawcett Collection, and there are accounts in the daily press (including *The Times* and the *Daily Telegraph*) from 24 February 1912.

258 – Sylvia Pankhurst (1931), p. 372. See also p. 373: 'that time-honoured weapon'; and Laurence Housman (1937, p. 267): 'plate-glass windows are a symbol of the consent of the governed'.

259 – Alan Burgoyne, Conservative MP for Kensington North, to Helen Chadwick, 15 March 1912, quoted Hume (1982), pp. 132–33.

260 – See *The Times*, 2, 7, 11, 18, 22 and 25 March 1912, quoted Hume (1982), p. 133; and Rosen (1974, pp. 159–61) for similar press reports, and for comment by suffrage supporters alienated by militancy. Lloyd George had written to Mrs Fawcett on 30 November 1911, warning her that the antis were delighted to find constitutional propaganda neutralised by the militants, and that if something was not done about militant activity there would be no hope of a women's clause in the next year's bill. On 5 April 1912 Sir Edward Grey wrote that in his view the Conciliation Bill was lost due to the window smashing (Fawcett Archives, Box 89 vol. II, Millicent Fawcett correspondence). Harrison (1978, p. 176) points out that by 1912 expressions of disgust at militant activity formed the staple diet

of the *Anti-Suffrage Review*; and he argues that militancy made the antis' task a great deal easier.

261 – Millicent Fawcett, *What I Remember* (1924), quoted Hume (1982), pp. 205–06.

262 – Hume (1982, pp. 135–36) and Rosen (1974, pp. 162–63) discuss the fate of the Conciliation Bill. Hume (p. 137) calculates that had all the Labour members been present and voted for the Bill, it would have passed by one vote.

263 – The phrase is Hume's (1982), p. 140.

264 – Arthur Henderson had pushed through a resolution at the 1912 Labour Party Conference, which obliged the Parliamentary Labour Party, though supporting the principle of adult suffrage, to oppose any franchise bill that did not include women.

265 – NUWSS Executive Committee minutes, 18 April 1912 (Fawcett Archives, Box 152); Millicent Fawcett, 'The Election Policy of the National Union', the *Englishwoman*, June 1912; NUWSS leaflets 'The Best Friends of Women's Suffrage' and 'The New Development in the Policy of the NUWSS', 1912 (Fawcett Library). See also Hume (1982, pp. 143–45) and Pugh (1978, pp. 22–25). The WSPU changed its by-election policy in the same year, deciding to fight the Labour Party too unless it agreed to vote against the government on every issue. This was scarcely feasible, given the Lib–Lab pact, and it increased the Parliamentary Labour Party's suspicion of women's suffrage.

266 – Millicent Fawcett, *The Women's Victory and After* (1920), p. 37, quoted Hume (1982), p. 148. Hume (p. 155) indicates that the Election Fighting Fund and the 'Friends' scheme in combination drew the NUWSS closer to working-class organisations and sympathies, and helped to undermine its middle-class image. The NUWSS believed that the 'Friends' would provide the nuclei for party political organisation in the constituencies. By linking the women's suffrage issue with labour interests and politics in this way they avoided, as Pugh points out, the Pankhursts' tactical error of seeming to preach as middle-class women to working-class men.

267 – Sylvia Pankhurst (1931), p. 370. Among others the seamen, dockers, and railwaymen had struck in 1911, and the miners in February 1912. Sylvia Pankhurst (pp. 366–67) claimed that suffragette militancy encouraged militant tendencies in the labour movement; but also that the WSPU's labour sympathies were long abandoned. They believed that as many working men had votes they could ameliorate their conditions without resort to strikes.

268 – Sylvia Pankhurst (1931), p. 373. Hobhouse was addressing an anti-suffrage meeting on 16 February, in which he argued that in the case of the suffrage demand 'there has not been the kind of popular sentimental uprising which accounted for Nottingham Castle in 1832, or the Hyde Park railings in 1867. There has been no great ebullition of popular feeling, but skilfully directed noise' (Sylvia Pankhurst, 1931, p. 373 and the *Anti-Suffrage Review*, November 1912).

269 – Christabel Pankhurst quoted in Dangerfield (1970, p. 340).

270 – H. M. Richardson, 20 August 1912, quoted Harrison

(1978), p. 192. The Pankhursts, however, refused 'to be deflected one hair's breadth from the course which they had determined to pursue' (Frederick Pethick-Lawrence, 1943 p. 100). The Pethick-Lawrences left the WSPU in October 1912 over the new militant policy, believing that mass demonstrations were not yet exhausted and that it was still possible to 'outdo anything achieved before'. (Emmeline Pethick-Lawrence, 1938, p. 277; Rosen (1974) discusses the split in chapter 14. See also the Pethick-Lawrence papers at Trinity College, Cambridge, particularly P-L 9 31 (1), 32.) Sylvia Pankhurst deplored the 'life of furtive destruction . . . and punishment' that militancy brought to the new suffragette guerrillas (Pankhurst, 1931, p. 401).

271 – Quoted in Roy Jenkins, *Asquith*, Collins, London, 1964, p. 250, Constance Rover, *Women's Suffrage and Party Politics in Britain 1866–1914*, Routledge & Kegan Paul, London, 1967, p. 196. See also Pugh (1978), pp. 41–42, Hume (1982), pp. 186–87, Rosen (1974), pp. 186–87.

272 – Mrs Pankhurst in the *Globe*, 28 January 1913, quoted Rosen (1974), p. 188. Rosen (tables 16.1–16.5) gives details of the escalating damage to property each month.

273 – Police report on her speech at the Pavilion Theatre, 10 February 1913 (Public Record Office, HO 45.231366) quoted Rosen (1974), p. 189.

274 – *Morning Post*, 21 March 1913.

275 – Rosen (1974, p. 193) quotes Lord Robert Cecil who had referred to it in debate on 2 April as a 'cat and mouse' proposal; Frederick Pethick-Lawrence (1943, p. 83) believed he first christened it the 'Cat and Mouse Act' in the pages of *Votes for Women*.

276 – Quoted by Sylvia Pankhurst (1931), p. 453.

277 – Christabel Pankhurst (1959), p. 242.

278 – Quoted in Sylvia Pankhurst (1931), p. 568.

279 – *Daily Sketch*, 28 May 1914. See also Rosen (1974), pp. 198–200, and for her previous WSPU career Sylvia Pankhurst (1931), pp. 362, 372–78, 476–78.

280 – The *Illustrated Chronicle* was a Newcastle paper. Press reports are from 16 June 1913 unless otherwise stated. Sources cited in bibliography.

281 – The Memorial Service leaflet can be found in the Maud Arncliffe-Sennett papers, vol. 23, following p. 22.

282 – *Daily Chronicle*.

283 – Reported in the *Daily Telegraph* and the *Daily Chronicle*. When police stopped a section of members of the Dockers' Union to let a mail van pass towards the rear of the procession, the act was so resented that one of the dockers flung himself at the horses' heads and attempted to force them back.

284 – *Daily Herald*.

285 – Housman (1937), pp. 295–96. Housman did not see much of the procession he walked at the rear of until he 'saw later at the cinema, what a wonderful and beautiful sight it was'.

286 – Strachey (1928), p. 332.

287 – Maud Arncliffe-Sennett papers, vol. 23, before p. 21.

288 – On the same page as its account of the funeral, the *Daily Chronicle* carried reports of WSPU speakers 'ignominiously rushed' out of Hyde Park, Kitty Marion and a second woman

charged with setting fire to the Hurst Park grandstand and other buildings, and a 'pillar box outrage' on Sunday night in Lewisham.

289 – The *Common Cause*, 1 August 1913: 'It is to be borne in mind that the Pilgrimage was organised when there might have been expected to be a set-back in Suffrage enthusiasm. The Franchise Bill had been withdrawn, the Dickinson Bill defeated. For the first time for several years, Suffragists had no Bill in being to work for; no immediate and urgent incentive; no feeling that *one* ounce of energy might win the day . . . [the NUWSS] had to appeal generally for support, and general appeals are not usually interesting.' The *Common Cause* (25 July 1913) acknowledged the precedent of Mrs de Fonblanque's 'Women's March' from Edinburgh to London in 1912, and credited her with inventing 'the march of propaganda' for women's suffrage. For the Women's March (which involved only very small numbers) see Fawcett Archives, Box 296, Edinburgh–London 1912; *The Suffrage Annual and Women's Who's Who*, 1913, pp. 145–49; Maud Arncliffe-Sennett papers, vol. 19, pp. 68–89 (Mrs de Fonblanque was Maud Arncliffe-Sennett's sister); and the suffrage press, October and November 1912.

290 – NUWSS Executive Committee minutes, 17 April 1913 (Fawcett Archives, Box 301), and minutes of the special meeting of the Organisation Committee, 18 April 1913 (Box 85). For the organisation of the Pilgrimage see: Box 298 (Pilgrimage); Box 301 (NUWSS Executive Committee minutes, *passim*); Box 85 (bound as NUWSS Women's Interests Committee, March 1913–April 1915, includes Demonstration Committee and March Demonstration Committee 1913–14); Box 137 (LSWS Executive Committee minutes); the *Common Cause passim*, particularly 1 August 1913; and 'The Pilgrimage: Its Effect in the North' by Ida S. Beaver and 'A London Impression' by K. M. Harley, the *Englishwoman*, September 1913.

Mrs Harley was chairman of the West Midlands Federation of the NUWSS, and according to Millicent Fawcett a woman 'of great originality and imagination' (*The Women's Victory – and After*, 1920, pp. 58–59). In December 1914 she joined the first unit of the Scottish Women's Hospitals under Dr Elsie Inglis. She worked in France as a hospital administrator and moved with the unit to Salonica, where she was awarded the Croix de Guerre. She was killed by shell-fire at Monastir in 1917.

291 – Philippa Strachey, LSWS circular letter, June 1913.

292 – Pilgrimage Committee meetings 8 May and 6, 13 and 23 June 1913 (Fawcett Archives, Box 85). Not everyone agreed that these were the best alternatives ('There is nothing that looks as dusty, as badly groomed, shows mud-stains as much as black does . . . White, too, is an extraordinary suggestion for the actual march') but objections were countered in the *Common Cause* (30 May and 13 June 1913).

293 – The *Common Cause*, 13 and 20 June 1913. The advertisers of 'Serviceable Attire' included Swan and Edgar, who with other West End firms had just won their action for damages against the WSPU.

294 – Pilgrimage Committee, 8 May 1913 (Fawcett Archives, Box 85). The Demonstration and Decorations Sub-Committee

undertook to advise on the poster, and Mary Lowndes pointed out that at a printing of 2000 they would cost about fourpence each. E. H. New produced a design which was printed by Carl Hentschel.

295 – The *Common Cause*, 13 June 1913. The Pilgrimage was only possible because of the organisational skills and burgeoning membership of the NUWSS. By 1913 it had more than 400 constituent societies and it was still growing. The list of new WSPU members was shrinking, and it was plagued by schism in the years between 1910 and 1914.

296 – LSWS leaflet 'The Pilgrimage: What does it Mean?', 1913.

297 – The *Common Cause*, 13 June 1913.

298 – See Fawcett Archives, Box 85: 23 June 1913.

299 – Descriptions of the purpose and development of the Pilgrimage – its very name, in this context – exploit a confusion of political and religious rhetoric that was also common in the labour movement. Stephen Yeo (1977) quotes Katherine Conway from the *Workman's Times*, 25 March 1893: 'In the birth of the [labour] movement there is a great need of lives absolutely consecrated to the work . . . It is a new band of pilgrims who are needed today to go through the length and breadth of Great Britain.' 'Who are these Women?' the *Common Cause* inquired, rhetorically, on 25 July 1913; and answered that they were women 'coming from every county, from every district, voicing the needs, the sufferings, the hopes of the women whose very poverty and misery keep them silent,' but who were deprived of political power and hence helpless to effect political change.

300 – Mrs Fawcett chose the text from Leviticus xxv 10 to preface her chapter on the Pilgrimage in *The Women's Victory – and After* (1920): 'Proclaim liberty throughout the land unto all the inhabitants thereof.' The account which follows draws from the sources cited in note 290, contemporary press reports, and the weekly progress reports in the *Common Cause*.

301 – See the *Common Cause*, 4 July 1913, which references the Countess of Northumberland, who defended Alnwick Castle for three months; Philippa, wife of Edward III who led an army against the invading Scots; Ebba and Hilda as local saints; Margaret of Anjou, Queen Matilda, and Grace Darling 'whose name will be a household word'; while sparing a thought for the nineteenth-century feminist Caroline Norton in passing Kettlethorpe Hall.

302 – NUWSS Executive Committee minutes, 31 July 1913 (Fawcett Archives, Box 301); *Manchester Guardian*, 28 July 1913; and Strachey (1928), p. 334.

303 – Daily newspaper accounts of the procession to Hyde Park are from 28 July unless otherwise noted. The *Common Cause* noted the factory chimneys on the Huddersfield banner and the spires of Oxford on the new design by E. H. New; the *Daily Chronicle* commented in addition on the phoenix of the East Midlands, the lion of Dundee and the scarlet dragon of Wales; the *Daily Telegraph* on the blue and silver of Cambridge and the gold and violet of Bolton; and *The Times* on Nottingham's castle and Eastbourne's lighthouse. Some of the 1908 banners (Joan of Arc, Queen Victoria, Boadicea and Jane Austen) were used again, and several reports stress the now familiar comparison

with trade-union banners 'whose solidarity is as a rule more pronounced than their artistic taste' (*The Times*).

304 – *Daily News and Leader*. According to *The Times* almost half the women carried red bannerets with the words 'law abiding suffragists'. Some confusion remained, however, and a writer to the *Daily Graphic* chided its editor for captioning a photograph of the Pilgrimage with the term 'suffragettes' (28 July 1913).

305 – The *Englishwoman*, September 1913.

306 – *Daily News and Leader*.

307 – The park was sprinkled with WSPU sashes and flags, and relations between militants and constitutionalists were strained. Sylvia Pankhurst's account was particularly condescending. She described the NUWSS as 'so staid, so willing to wait, so incorrigibly leisurely'; while for its part the *Common Cause* described militancy as 'a policy of feverish impatience and despair' (Sylvia Pankhurst, 1931, p. 485; Wilma Meikle in the *Common Cause*, 1 August 1913).

308 – *Manchester Guardian*; the *Common Cause*, 1 August 1913.

309 – The next day more than 1000 pilgrims attended an afternoon service at St Paul's Cathedral. Mrs Fawcett (1920, p. 57) noted with satisfaction the text of the first psalm for evening service on the 27th day of the month: 'They that sow in tears shall reap in joy.' The *Common Cause* (1 August 1913) developed the idea of a continuing pilgrimage: 'With high hopes, with unconquerable spirit, with that knight-errantry which will not be denied, we "go on to the end".' In the following morning's papers the accounts of the meeting in Hyde Park appeared on the same pages as reports of the WSPU's Sunday raid on Downing Street. The *Westminster Review* concluded that: 'Fairly weighed, the two things are not in the least comparable, but none the less, taken together, the effect is to show how militancy undoes the effect of agitation conducted on constitutional and law-abiding lines. It would almost seem as if the militants were jealous of the success of the Pilgrimage, and were anxious, at all cost, to do something to assert their own particular claims to notice.'

310 – The NUWSS Executive Committee minutes, 3 July 1913 (Fawcett Archives, Box 83), had already suggested five ways to make 'political use of the Pilgrimage': by a deputation to party leaders, to suffragist Cabinet ministers, or to as many MPs as possible from their constituents; by petitions presented in the House; and by sending copies of the resolutions carried in Hyde Park to the party leaders, Chief Whips and chairmen of the various suffrage committees in the House of Commons. The letters exchanged between Mrs Fawcett and Asquith are in the Fawcett Archives, Box 89.

311 – Copy of a letter directed 'To the Suffragist Ministers who received the deputation from the National Union of Women's Suffrage Societies, on August 8th, 1913' (Fawcett Archives, Box 89).

312 – Strachey (1928), p. 336.

4 REPRESENTATION

1 – T. J. Clark, *The Painting of Modern Life: Paris in the Art of*
Manet and his Followers, Thames & Hudson, London, 1985, p. 6.

2 – I have used the expression 'dominant ideology' in relation to Edwardian femininity since I believe that there was – broadly speaking – such a singular, distinct and influential cohesion of precepts around the concept of 'womanliness'. I take the point from Abercrombie *et al.*, who dismiss what they call the 'dominant ideology thesis', that a dominant ideology can have as a principal function the incorporation of the group whose interests it serves. But marginal and oppositional groups also construct their identities in the process of contesting those representations to which they are still, I believe, in some sense 'subject'. And although the effect of a dominant ideology may be to 'inhibit and confuse the development of the counter-ideology of a subordinate class' (or gender), insofar as that inhibition is overcome, not ideas only but the powerful hold of social practice is strained and weakened (Nicholas Abercrombie, Stephen Hill, Bryan S. Turner, *The Dominant Ideology Thesis*, Allen & Unwin, London, 1980, foreword by Tom Bottomore, p. ix).

3 – Cited in Frank Burton, *Official Discourse*, Routledge & Kegan Paul, London, 1979, p. 17.

4 – Harriet Martineau, *Edinburgh Review*, CIX, 1859, p. 298.

5 – For a discussion of pictorial 'rhetoric' see Roland Barthes, 'The Rhetoric of the Image' in Stephen Heath (ed.), *Image–Music–Text*, Fontana, London, 1977; Jean-Louis Swiners, 'Problèmes de photo-journalisme contemporain', *Techniques graphiques*, nos. 57–59, 1965; and Jacques Durand, 'Rhétorique et image publicitaire', *Communications*, vol. 15, 1970, as discussed and developed in Victor Burgin (ed.), *Thinking Photography*, Macmillan, London, 1982, pp. 70–82. Durand is taken up by Gillian Dyer in *Advertising as Communication*, Methuen, London, 1982.

6 – This is Paula Harper's argument in 'A Graphic Episode in the Battle of the Sexes', in H. Millon and L. Nochlin (eds), *Art and Architecture in the Service of Politics*, MIT Press, Cambridge MA, 1978.

7 – See Edward Said, *Orientalism*, Routledge & Kegan Paul, London, 1978, p. 14: 'we can better understand the persistence and the durability of saturating hegemonic systems like culture when we realise that their internal constraints upon writers and thinkers were productive, not unilaterally inhibiting.'

8 – I have avoided asking the obvious question – how effective was suffrage propaganda? – largely because of the impossibility of answering it. Too many other factors were operative in the course of the campaign, and too many converts were coy about the influences of moral principle, party interest or personal contact that won their support. The women's vote was never the major issue at a parliamentary election, but suffrage propaganda (and militancy) gave it a prominence before 1914 it had never enjoyed before 1906. This in turn prepared the ground for the catalytic effects of the First World War. MPs may not have been converted in significant numbers (the voting figures on particular bills are an unreliable indication, not least because of the impact of militancy and Home Rule), but the burgeoning membership of the chief societies was witness to the effective-

ness of suffrage activity and organisation, as on another level was the formation of the anti-suffrage societies in 1908. The process of 'conversion' is described in memoirs and fictional accounts which accord with Stephen Yeo's description of the conversion to socialism. 'Poverty, religious eclecticism, unresolved guilt, domestic unhappiness, unfocused indignation, scattered activity, wealthy aimlessness, or social unease' helped to prepare the soil in which a book entered, or a meeting, or an individual evangelist, and the 'idea then presented itself as a certain ground for hope, a convincing analysis of what had gone before, a morally impeccable challenge . . . an organised movement demanding commitment, sacrifice' (Yeo, 1977, p. 10).

9 – Robert Cholmeley, 'The Women's Anti-Suffrage Movement', NUWSS pamphlet, London, 1908 (Fawcett Library).

10 – Harriet Taylor Mill (1851), p. 13.

11 – 'On the Admission of Women to the Electoral Franchise', speech to the House of Commons 1867 published as a pamphlet, London, 1867 (Museum of London).

12 – Harrison (1978, pp. 115–17) discusses anti-suffrage sentiment before the formation of the anti-suffrage leagues in 1908. 'An Appeal Against Female Suffrage' appeared in the *Nineteenth Century* in June 1889 with the names of 104 distinguished or well-connected women attached to it. (Readers were encouraged by the editor to detach, sign and send in the adjacent page as evidence of their support.) As Mrs Fawcett pointed out in a rejoinder in the July issue, the list of signatories contained 'a very large preponderance of ladies to whom the lines of life have fallen in pleasant places'. The 'Appeal' rehearsed most of the arguments, under five main headings, which made up the substance of the anti-suffrage case twenty years later. *The Times* (12 June 1908) was defensive about this: 'The arguments as yet put forward by the association have already been denounced by some of the suffragist women as "the old arguments". So they are; they are the old arguments, and they have never been refuted.' Both suffragists and anti-suffragists were eclectic in their arguments, attempting to hit as many targets and touch as many sympathies as possible. It did not matter to them that this produced inconsistencies. Since both camps sheltered a range of positions that had only the cause in common, consistency was in any case unlikely.

13 – Writing in the *Contemporary Review* in 1911, Teresa Billington-Greig deplored the narrowing of a 'rebellion against the general degradation of women', a movement demanding 'a revolution in every department of human life' to 'emancipation by machinery' and 'the winning of the Parliamentary vote'. It was nevertheless the justice of the claim and (in feminist terms) its lack of controversy that unified women of all classes and beliefs in its support ('Feminism and Politics', *Contemporary Review*, vol. 100, November 1911).

14 – Both sides impugned the other's motives and arguments. Almroth Wright (1913) described suffragists as motivated almost exclusively by resentment at men's superior faculties, social position and 'happier physiological conditions', and their cause as without 'moral prestige'. He referred to the 'thick husks of untruth' in the suffrage rhetoric of emancipation and claimed that 'in short, all the ungrateful women – flock to the

banner of Woman's Freedom – the banner of financial freedom for woman at the expense of financial servitude for man. The grateful woman will practically always be an anti-suffragist.' For her part May Sinclair of the Women Writers' Suffrage League claimed that it 'would seem as if almost any old argument were good enough for the man who reads the papers', including a frank appeal to prejudice, a generalised case against a whole sex from a single instance 'painful, intimate and domestic', or the suppression of all evidence unsuited to the argument at hand (May Sinclair, *Feminism*, The Women Writers' Suffrage League, London, undated [1913]).

15 – Harriet Taylor Mill (1851), p. 5. More specifically, suffragists argued that there should be no taxation without representation, that individuals should have a say in the laws that governed them and the right to be tried by their peers. Any or all of these points might be conceded by those who did not support the notion of 'natural rights'.

Rover (1967), Rosen (1974), Harrison (1978) and Hume (1982) all offer summaries of the main debates with different emphases. See also Aileen Kraditor, *The Ideas of the Woman Suffrage Movement 1890–1920* (Columbia University Press, New York, 1965), for the American campaign. I have attempted to retain the flavour of original sources but my own account is of necessity a rather brutal précis which falls short of the '101 points in favour of Women's Suffrage' published in the *Vote* during 1910. I have drawn in part on a large number of leaflets published by the suffrage and anti-suffrage societies which it would not be practicable to list in detail (chiefly from the Museum of London, the Fawcett Library and the John Johnson Collection of printed ephemera in the Bodleian Library, Oxford). Kraditor (for the US campaign) and Hume (for the NUWSS) argue a shift in emphasis from 'rights' to 'expediency' in the 1890s, as a result of developing social consciousness in the campaign and among the groups to which it was increasingly directed.

16 – See the NLOWS *Handbook* (1912), p. 53: 'The vote is not a natural possession of a human being. It is a device invented in the course of men's banding themselves into social states for purposes of defence, advancement, and trade, and to enable them to decide which among them had the power to direct these activities of the organisation in the way they desired.' Also p. 53: 'All that taxation gives a right to is that protection of life and property, and amelioration of conditions which women enjoy equally with men.'

17 – House of Commons Debate 27/4/92, col. 1513, quoted Pugh (1980), p. 6. Asquith also raised questions of expediency, putting to the House on 6 May 1913 'in one sentence' the 'gist and core of the real question'. 'Would our political fabric be strengthened, would our legislation be more respected, would our domestic and social life be enriched, would our standards of manners – and in manners I include the old-fashioned virtues of chivalry, courtesy, and all the reciprocal dependence and reliance of the two sexes – would that standard be raised and refined if women were politically enfranchised?' (quoted in Stephen Koss, *Asquith*, Allen Lane, London, 1976, p. 132).

18 – Tennyson, *The Princess* (1847), part v, ll. 437–41. Rover

(1967, p. 173) quotes Edith Milner's letter to *The Times* (29 October 1906) which cites Ruskin to the effect that each sex has what the other lacks, and argues that when women undertake duties for which men are constitutionally better fitted they are still *less* fitted for it, and women's work remains undone. The 'separate spheres' of men and women were understood as moral (they involved the exercise of different virtues), psychological (men and women had different temperaments) and practical (different activities were appropriate to each).

19 – 'Female Suffrage', *Saturday Review*, 28 March 1868, quoted in Stella Mary Newton, *Health, Art and Reason: Dress Reformers of the Nineteenth Century*, John Murray, London, 1974, p. 64. Harriet Taylor Mill (1851) had predicted that 'the dispute is more likely to turn on the fitness of politics for women' than the fitness of women for politics, and had discussed the principal arguments under this heading.

20 – 'Female Suffrage: A Letter from the Right Hon. W. E. Gladstone to Samuel Smith MP', 1892, quoted Rover (1967), p. 120.

21 – Harrison (1978, p. 160) remarks that the antis displayed an uncharacteristically 'majoritarian' stance on the question because they believed they could win a referendum. No previously enfranchised group had been required first to demonstrate its unanimity. The Acts of 1867 and 1884 had resulted from a combination of vigorous pressure with the careful negotiation of party interest (Gladstone remarked of the agricultural labourers that he was not concerned as to whether they *wanted* the vote: the state wanted it for them).

22 – '. . . and which has hitherto been her chief protection': 'Lord Curzon's Fifteen Good Reasons Against the Grant of Female Suffrage', NLOWS leaflet (Fawcett Archives, Box 298). See also 'The Danger of Woman Suffrage: Lord Cromer's View', NLOWS leaflet (Box 298).

23 – Mary Taylor had dismissed the notion of influence in *The First Duty of Women* in 1870: 'I should like to see a human being, man or woman, whose main business was in influencing people. How do they make a business of it? What time does it begin in the morning? And how do they fill, say, a few hours every day, in the doing of it? Not commanding or teaching, but influencing' (1870, p. 14; quoted in Janet Horowitz Murray, *Strong-Minded Women and Other Lost Voices From Nineteenth-Century England* (1982), Penguin Books, London, 1984).

24 – Violet Markham in the *Anti-Suffrage Review*, November 1910, p. 9; Curzon (see note 22); the *Anti-Suffrage Manifesto* (Fawcett Archives, Box 298).

25 – Roger Fulford (*Votes for Women: The Story of a Struggle*, Faber & Faber, London, 1958, p. 82) quotes Eliza Lynn Linton's response to the formation of the Primrose League and the Women's Liberal Federation from the *National Review*, 1889: 'Think of our imperial policy directly influenced by the local genteel spinsters and small shop-keepers whose mental range reaches as high as the curate and as far as the school feast.'

26 – Sir Almroth Wright (1913, p. 47) went further in claiming that 'the belief of men in the inherent inferiority of women in the matter of intellectual morality, and in the power of adjudication,

has never varied.' Wright's position was considered eccentric (and female antis were obliged to dissociate themselves from it – as Mrs Humphry Ward put it in a speech on the founding of the Women's National Anti-Suffrage League in 1908: 'Difference, not inferiority – it is on that we take our stand'). But it might be said that Wright articulates what politer texts merely gloss.

27 – Harrison (1978), p. 73. (Harrison offers a detailed discussion of the 'physical force' argument – see especially pp. 73–78.)

28 – Both quotations from Curzon, see note 22. See also *The Times*, 22 June 1908, on the suffrage processions of the 13th and 21st. The editorial acknowledged the evidence that 'a great many women are for the time being eagerly desirous of the franchise,' but insisted that 'it would weaken the moral fibre of the nation if the supreme decisions of the State were determined, partly by women who could not feel the same responsibility for seeing them carried through as men . . .'

29 – Harrison (1978), p. 75. Edward Said has pointed out that 'political societies impart to their civil societies a sense of urgency, a direct political infusion as it were, where and whenever matters pertaining to their imperial interests abroad are concerned' (*Orientalism*, 1978, p. 11). This view (derived from Gramsci) is borne out by the appearance of variants of the 'physical force' argument, not just in concern about German re-armament and the state of British military preparedness, but in moral and cultural debates of the late Victorian and Edwardian period. For imperialists like Curzon and Cromer the British state was a virile state, and in that virility the Empire was secured. (No doubt an array of associated investments, repressions and anxieties about 'feminisation' was active here too.) As Almroth Wright put it: 'there cannot be two opinions on the question that a virile and imperial race will not brook any attempt at forcible control by women . . . no military foreign nation or native race would ever believe in the stamina and firmness of purpose of any nation that submitted even to the semblance of such control' (1913, p. 33). John Mackenzie (*Propaganda and Empire: The Manipulation of British Public Opinion 1880–1960*, Manchester University Press, Manchester, 1984) discusses the relationship between imperialism, moral regeneration and the ideology and institutions of militarism from 1880 to 1914. Samuel Hynes (*The Edwardian Turn of Mind*, Princeton University Press, Princeton, New Jersey, 1968, pp. 26–27) discusses the connection with Baden-Powell and the Boy Scouts.

30 – Curzon, see note 22.

31 – NLOWS pamphlet, no. 15 (Fawcett Archives, Box 298).

32 – Professor A. V. Dicey, quoted in Rover (1967), p. 45.

33 – Almroth Wright (1913), p. 60; and in its most extreme form, pp. 11–12: assumptions that men and women, men and men, Europeans and natives should live side by side with equal rights are based on 'a quite artificial equality' . . . 'we have here a principle which, consistently followed out, would make of every man and woman *in primis* a socialist; then a woman suffragist; then a philonative, negrophil, and an advocate of the political rights of natives and negroes; and then, by logical compulsion, an anti-vivisectionist, who accounts it *unjust* to kill animals for

food; and finally one who, like the Jains, accounts it *unjust* to take the life of even verminous insects.' Suffragists never campaigned for the right of women to become MPs, and the possibility first arose as an unlooked-for consequence of the Representation of the People Act in 1918. But it suited the antis to alarm their public by claiming that this was the true aim of the suffrage movement. See also Mrs Humphry Ward, 'Women's Suffrage and After', WNASL pamphlet, no. 2, 1909 (Museum of London).

34 – Robert Cholmeley, 'The Women's Anti-Suffrage Movement', NUWSS pamphlet, 1908 (Fawcett Library). The anti-suffrage manifesto claimed that because 'the spheres of men and women, owing to natural causes, are essentially different ... their share in the management of the State should be different': a sentence pounced on by Cholmeley not only because it contained 'no less than three premisses to one conclusion' but because it left the argument just where it was before.

35 – Harriet Taylor Mill (1851), p. 20.

36 – Eunice Murray, 'The Illogical Sex?', WFL, undated (Fawcett Library).

37 – Cicely Hamilton, *Marriage as a Trade* (1909), The Women's Press, London, 1981, p. 84. 'At its best, such a code of behaviour is a meritorious attempt to atone for advantage in essentials by self-abnegation in non-essentials; at its worst, it is simply an expression of condescension.'

38 – Almroth Wright (1913), p. 20. For an account of the notion of 'chivalry' and its impact on Victorian culture see Mark Girouard, *The Return to Camelot: Chivalry and the English Gentleman*, Yale University Press, New Haven and London, 1981.

39 – House of Commons Debate, 11 July 1910, col. 143, quoted Harrison (1978), p. 72. See also Emmeline Pethick-Lawrence's speech at the Albert Hall meeting following the Women's Coronation Procession of 1911, 'We had the Vision' (printed in *Votes for Women*, 23 June 1911), with its humanitarian claims for the women's vote underpinned by the tradition of nineteenth-century female philanthropy.

40 – *The Times*, 22 June 1908.

41 – The *Common Cause* editorial, 15 April 1909.

42 – Robert Cholmeley (1908), who adds that 'it really ought not to be necessary at this time of day to refute the Mind-the-Baby argument. It has even dropped out of the repertoire of the omnibus-driver.'

43 – In the collection of the Division of Political History, The National Museum of American History, Smithsonian Institution, Washington DC.

44 – *Women Do Not Want the Vote*, A. M. K. (Alice Kidd), The Private Publishing Bureau, undated (Fawcett Archives, Box 298): '[Women] have left to men the responsibilities *which long ago they ought to have shared*. What wonder if, single-handed, men have failed to maintain right and equal standards of morality, and have grown selfish in their legislation.'

45 – Mill had argued in his speech to the House of Commons in 1867 that women's exclusion from the franchise, unlike that of other groups, was 'absolute': prisoners could serve their sen-

tence, children come of age, the poor improve their incomes, and lunatics recover their reason. Images of rational, virtuous (and middle-class) women slighted in such company were intended to convey their sense of grievance. Antis like Almroth Wright responded by claiming that since their exclusion was different in kind, women manufactured such grievances for themselves. Other groups forfeited their right to the vote. Women were neither suited for it nor burdened with it. Suffragists countered that whatever the *grounds* for their exclusion, the effect was the same, that in this important respect they were denied a voice in the legislative processes of the state.

46 – Quoted in Rossi (1973), p. 238.

47 – Balfour's 1892 speech was reissued as a pamphlet (Museum of London). See p. 5.

48 – *The Times* and the *Westminster Gazette*, 15 June 1908. See also Dora Meeson Coates's cartoon in the *Women's Franchise*, 17 September 1908: all would-be male voters have to take on the boxer Jim Jones before entering the polling booth. There are endless variants in suffrage imagery on the theme of the voteless female shouldering the burdens of the enfranchised but invalid male.

49 – Israel Zangwill, 'Old Fogeys and Old Bogeys', 7 June 1909, printed as a pamphlet and published by the (N)WSPU (Fawcett Library).

50 – According to the 1901 census, 5,309,960 women were employed in paid labour out of a total female population of 21,356,313, compared with 12,951,186 male workers (quoted Rover, 1967, p. 17). Census figures tend to underestimate women's work which is not always registered for home-working, wives assisting their husbands, and 'invisible' or undeclared means of augmenting the family income, such as taking in lodgers or laundry (see Sally Alexander in Mitchell and Oakley (eds), 1976).

51 – See Lady Chance, quoted in *Votes for Women*, 21 April 1911: 'It is, or should be, humiliating to any educated woman to be *used* as an instrument of political warfare; to be implored to cajole, to charm, to educate, in fact, to influence in any way, legitimate or illegitimate, the male voter, and then to be thrust aside when this part of her work is done, and to be told that her political judgement is of less value than that of the men she has influenced. It would be no small gain to the national character if all women ceased to hold these semi-oriental views of their function in the body politic.' It suited the antis to claim a positive plank in their platform; that is, to urge women to make greater use of the municipal vote, rather than to present an entirely negative case. But the distinction between municipal and national politics was increasingly hard to maintain in practice and gave them a Canute-like status which artists were quick to exploit. The 'thus far and no further' stance caused Israel Zangwill to dub them the 'hithertos'. They were defending a crumbling status quo and trying to make a virtue of it, but the lines they drew were too obviously arbitrary and subject to revision.

52 – 'Two Voices' in the St Andrew's Hall, Glasgow. Refutation by Lord Lytton, suffragist (9 December 1912), of the arguments of Lord Curzon, anti-suffragist (1 November 1912), published

by the Edinburgh Branch of the Conservative and Unionist Women's Franchise Association (Fawcett Library).

53 – Karl Marx, *The Eighteenth Brumaire of Louis Bonaparte* (1852), Progress Publishers, Moscow, 1954, p. 106. (I intend the double meaning of visual, as well as parliamentary, representation, which Marx did not.)

54 – Mary Phillips, 'A Typical Suffragist', *Votes for Women*, December 1907, p. 35.

55 – Mary Phillips, as above.

56 – Quoted by Gillian Sutherland in the *Times Literary Supplement*, 10 July 1981, p. 792.

57 – From 'Women and Fiction', reprinted in *Virginia Woolf, Women and Writing*, The Women's Press, London, 1979, p. 49.

58 – See 'The Rhetoric of the Image' in *Image–Music–Text*, pp. 46–47; and also Volosinov, *Marxism and the Philosophy of Language*, Seminar Press, New York, 1973.

59 – House of Commons Debate, 11 July 1910, col. 99, quoted in Harrison (1978), p. 138. In a middle-class family magazine like *Punch* the sentiment, like the draughtsmanship, is more refined, but an obsession with what it coyly termed 'the fair sex' is similarly marked. *Punch* became more sympathetic to women's suffrage towards the end of the nineteenth century. 'Strong-minded' women, prominent in issues from the 1870s and 1880s, go at least as far back as John Leech's caricatures of the bloomer costume in 1851.

60 – George Orwell, 'The Art of Donald McGill', *Horizon*, September 1941, vol. IV no. 21. Orwell isolates the characteristics of comic postcards – the 'small change' of the revue and music-hall stage – as an overpowering vulgarity, hideous colour, an ever-present obscenity, a low mental atmosphere, a grotesque and staring quality of drawing, grinning and vacuous faces and monstrously parodied women. They 'stand for the worm's eye view of life' (the male worm's, surely, if worms were sexed), 'something as traditional as Greek tragedy, a sort of sub-world of smacked bottoms and scrawny mothers-in-law which is part of western European consciousness'.

61 – Sigmund Freud, *Jokes and their Relation to the Unconscious* (1905, English translation 1916). My references are to the edition published as vol. 6 of the Pelican Freud Library, Penguin Books, London, 1976. These quotations are from p. 147 and p. 140 respectively.

62 – 'On the Universal Tendency to Debasement in the Sphere of Love', Pelican Freud Library, vol. 7, 1977, pp. 247–60.

63 – *Jokes and their Relation to the Unconscious*, p. 144.

64 – *Jokes*, p. 147: 'We are now prepared to realize the part played by jokes in hostile aggressiveness. A joke will allow us to exploit something ridiculous in our enemy which we could not, on account of obstacles in the way, bring forward openly or consciously; once again, then, the joke *will evade restrictions and open sources of pleasure that have become inaccessible*. It will further bribe the hearer with its yield of pleasure into taking sides with us without any very close investigation . . .' (original italics).

65 – 'No woman has ever yet been a caricaturist, in spite of the fact that her femininity befits her pre-eminently for the part. That she has desisted is a mercy for which man may be devoutly thankful.' Quoted in Houffe (1978), p. 113.

66 – *Jokes and their Relation to the Unconscious*, p. 183.

67 – *Punch*, 17 June 1871 and 14 March 1874. See also the unprepossessing women in the front row of 'Mrs Lyon Hunter's drawing-room, during a lecture on "Women's Rights"' (1875).

68 – See for example 'Vanoc', 'Concerning Spinsterhood: The Wrongs of the Unmated' in the *Referee*, 14 March 1909, and Almroth Wright (1913).

69 – Graphically depicted in *Punch*: see 'An Ugly Rush', 28 May 1870.

70 – Marie Corelli, *Woman, or – Suffragette?* (1907), p. 38.

71 – See *Punch*, 'Essence of Parliament', 3 May 1871, on the debate on Bright's women's suffrage bill.

72 – Cf. Miss Miniver in H. G. Wells's *Ann Veronica*, who has glasses, a drab green dress, a whimsically petulant mouth, a pinched nose, and straight hair 'out demonstrating and suffragetting upon some independent notions of its own'. For Ann Veronica, who dislikes Miss Miniver's 'physical insufficiency and her convulsive movements', it 'does seem germane to the matter that so many of the people "in the van" [are] plain people, or faded people, or tired-looking people' (1909, reprinted Virago, London, 1980, pp. 27, 107, 30, 118).

73 – On the dress reform movement see Stella Mary Newton, *Health, Art and Reason: Dress Reformers of the Nineteenth Century*, John Murray, London, 1974. She discusses the type of the 'Strong-Minded Woman', pp. 59–69. The 'Strong-Minded Woman' became the bridge between the traditional spinster and the 'Women's Rightist', and in 1907 Mary Gawthorpe recalled how: 'Pictures of women with short hair, billycock hats, and other articles of masculine attire, were paraded as another argument against giving women the vote' (*Votes for Women*, December 1907). The implication was not only that these were the women who wanted the vote, but that the vote would *make* women flat-chested, big-footed, large-handed and thin-lipped. Images like these are common in anti-suffrage propaganda. American feminists embraced the term 'strong-minded', and for some time its connotations in the *Revolution* (edited by Susan B. Anthony and Elizabeth Cady Stanton) were entirely positive, if not quite those of *Punch*.

In America the bloomer was briefly adopted by feminists such as Amelia Bloomer (after whom it was named) and Elizabeth Cady Stanton in 1851. In Britain there were few connections between dress reform and the suffrage campaign. Medical supporters of rational dress were often motivated by a thoroughly conservative desire to improve women's physical efficiency in their traditional roles as childbearers. Aesthetes were devoted to picturesque costume but not necessarily to the suffrage cause, although there was some overlap in the area of the Arts and Crafts Movement (Henry Holiday was a noted dress reformer and suffragist). Rationalists were the most likely group to support other emancipatory causes, to point out that fashionable female dress was restricting and inconvenient, and to base their arguments on the need for a change in women's roles. The name that links the suffrage campaign most closely with that of dress reform is Florence Harberton's. Viscountess Harberton, co-founder of the Rational Dress Society in 1881 and subsequently its president, was a member of the WSPU when she died in 1911. Her obituaries in the suffrage press were carefully worded to avoid too close an association between sartorial eccentricity and votes for women (*Votes for Women*, 5 May and the *Common Cause*, 11 May 1911). The suffrage movement naturally attracted women impatient of social convention, but appearances were a matter of propaganda and not just of individual principle or taste. *Votes for Women* (30 July 1908, p. 348) noted that the suffragette was dainty and precise in her dress, 'for the honour of the cause she represents'. See also Cicely Hamilton, *Life Errant*, Dent, London, 1935, pp. 75–76: 'A curious characteristic of the militant suffrage movement was the importance it attached to dress and appearance, and its insistence on the feminine note. There was no costume-code amongst non-militant suffragists, but in the Women's Social and Political Union the coat-and-skirt effect was not favoured; all suggestion of the masculine was carefully avoided, and the outfit of a militant setting forth to smash windows would probably include a picture-hat ... I have heard Mrs Pankhurst advise very strongly against what she considered eccentricity in the matter of dress; her reason being that it would shock male prejudice and make the vote harder to obtain. After the vote was won, she said, we could do as we liked in the matter of garments – but till then ...' Charlotte Despard's age, dignity, and well-known record of public service seem to have deflected criticism from the obvious eccentricity of her dress. In the poverty of Wandsworth it went unremarked, and on demonstrations and at public meetings it became her trademark. (She is instantly recognisable in photographs and illustrations with her white hair beneath a lace mantilla, her plain black dress like a secular habit, and open sandals on her feet.) She once outlined to the press a proposed boycott of hats and unnecessarily expensive clothing which led to the WFL being dubbed 'the hatless brigade' (see Andro Linklater, *An Unhusbanded Life*, Hutchinson, London, 1980, p. 154).

74 – Ethel Smyth, *Female Pipings in Eden*, Peter Davies, London, 1933, p. 197.

75 – Sylvia Pankhurst (1931), p. 219. Against the accusation that women were extravagant in dress, Sylvia Pankhurst argued that it was primarily men who profited from the (exploitative) clothing trade, and that many suffragists spent 'more money on clothes than they can comfortably afford, rather than run the risk of being considered *outré*, and doing harm to the cause' (*Votes for Women*, 23 September 1910, p. 825).

76 – Emmeline Pethick-Lawrence (1938), p. 162.

77 – Fanny Johnson in the *Vote*, 13 April 1912. This was also the point of Cicely Hamilton's Pageant of Great Women (1909), of the banners carried on suffrage demonstrations, and of illustrations in the suffrage press and in *Beware Women* (by C. Hedley Charlton, Mary Lowndes and Dora Meeson Coates), which challenged the stereotypes and stressed diversity. Suffragists were alive to the power of representation and indignant at having to negotiate its effects. Maud Arncliffe-Sennett, for example, despaired of the fact that she could not persuade the Eastbourne shopkeepers to stock suffrage postcards, when one woman who '*shrank* from them' stocked a selection of misogynist seaside postcards without a qualm (Maud Arncliffe-Sennett

albums, vol. 3, 1908, pp. 74–75, British Library. She includes the postcards.)

78 – Quoted by Michael Holroyd, 'George Bernard Shaw: Women and the Body Politic', *Critical Inquiry*, Autumn 1979, p. 20. The source is George Bernard Shaw's ghostwritten introduction for a lecture by H. M. Walbrook on 'The Women in Bernard Shaw's Plays' (1911).

79 – Craig Owens, 'The Medusa Effect or, The Spectacular Ruse' in *We won't play nature to your culture*, catalogue of an exhibition of works by Barbara Kruger at the ICA, London, 1983 (p. 7).

80 – Mrs Lynn Linton devoted more energy than any other journalist to the description and classification of feminine types, but there are numerous accounts, both pro and anti, at all levels of the popular and serious press. See Herbert van Thal, *Eliza Lynn Linton: The Girl of the Period*, George Allen & Unwin, London, 1979.

81 – Foucault discusses the importance of the gaze to clinical scrutiny in *The Birth of the Clinic: an archaeology of French medical perception*, Tavistock, London, 1973. Phrenology claimed to read character from cranial formation and physiognomy from the detail of facial features. Jeanne Fahnestock (see note 85 below) gives a useful and concise review of the literature. See also David de Giustino, *Conquest of Mind: Phrenology and Victorian Social Thought*, Croom Helm, London, 1975. (I owe this reference to Lynda Nead.) Both phrenology and physiognomy aimed to decipher the truth of human character as it was written across the body and encouraged the analysis of criminal, racial and pathological 'types' as they were later constituted in the discourses of eugenics and anthropology. David Green (see note 89) reproduces Francis Galton's composite photographs of criminal and Jewish types (1883, 1885) and an illustration from Havelock Ellis, *The Criminal* (1890).

82 – I have borrowed the reference from Richard Sennett, who uses it as part of his discussion of the decoding processes necessary to Victorian social life in *The Fall of Public Man*, Cambridge University Press, Cambridge, 1976, p. 169 ('Detectives are what every man and woman must be when they want to make sense of the street'). He argues that in contrast with the easy-going public life of the *ancien régime*, 'as people's personalities came to be seen in their appearances, facts of class and sex ... became matters of real anxiety' (p. 167). It would seem to have been a matter of particular anxiety for unaccompanied women to escape the voyeuristic and controlling gaze of men on the public streets – something which made their organisation into political demonstrations all the more difficult and remarkable.

83 – See Mary Cowling, 'The artist as anthropologist in mid-Victorian England: Frith's *Derby Day*, the *Railway Station* and the new science of mankind', *Art History*, vol. 6 no. 4, December 1983.

84 – In *Realizations: Narrative, Pictorial, and Theatrical Arts in Nineteenth-Century England* (Princeton University Press, Princeton, New Jersey, 1983, pp. 33, 294, 396), Martin Meisel discusses the relation between oil painting and pictorial journalism in the work of artists employed by the *Graphic* such as Herkomer and Fildes.

85 – See Jeanne Fahnestock, 'The Heroine of Irregular Features: Physiognomy and Conventions of Heroine Description', *Victorian Studies*, vol. 24 no. 3, Spring 1981.

86 – Laycock's lectures were published in the *Medical Times & Gazette*, January–June 1862. The *Punch* drawings are reproduced 1 March 1862, p. 207. I am very grateful to Ludmilla Jordanova who kindly provided this reference.

87 – The vitality of the illustrated press as it developed in the 1830s and 1840s derived from a rich heritage of eighteenth-century draughtsmanship: of type and character (rooted in medieval illustrations of the different 'humours'), and political and social caricature (a satirising of the tradition of exaggerated sixteenth-century Italian portrait sketches). See Houffe (1978), pp. 28–29.

88 – The *Daily Mirror*, 25 May 1914, p. 5. See also an unidentified press cutting re the 1913 Pilgrims from 'A Man in the Street' dated 19 July 1913 (Fawcett Archives, Box 298): 'They would and do affect the dress and manners of men; they are losing their attractive softness of manner and its grace, which has especially attached to women. Their hard, strenuous exercises and thought are affecting their facial expression, in that they are hardening and becoming more livid and strained; in a word, they are attempting to attain a position for which they are physically unfit ... This so-called enfranchisement of women is having its effect on the home, on obedience, on ordinary laws of decency and dress, all tending not to the betterment of the race, but to its deterioration.' See also Margaret Lonsdale, 'Platform Women', the *Nineteenth Century*, March 1884, pp. 409–15: 'The mental and moral condition which the modern platform woman herself exhibits is the surest proof of the mischief which public speaking is working by her agency on the community at large – the gradual hardening of the countenance and of the external manner and address, indicating too surely the real repression going on within of much that is lovable and admirable in a woman.'

89 – The term 'eugenics' was introduced by Francis Galton (*Inquiries into Human Faculty*, 1883) to define the study of inherited mental, moral and physical differences, and such measures of social control as would ensure the improvement of the species. I am indebted here to David Green's 'Veins of Resemblance: Photography and Eugenics', *Oxford Art Journal*, vol. 7 no. 2, 1984 (p. 9). See also J. W. Burrow, *Evolution and Society*, Cambridge University Press, Cambridge, 1968, and D. R. Oldroyd, *Darwinian Impacts*, Open University Press, Milton Keynes, 1980, on social Darwinism; and for eugenics D. Mackenzie, 'Eugenics in Britain', *Social Studies of Science*, 6, 1976, pp. 499–532; and G. R. Searle, 'Eugenics and Class', in C. Webster (ed.), *Biology, Medicine and Society 1840–1940*, Cambridge University Press, Cambridge, 1981.

90 – The analogy with the decline and fall of the Roman Empire was widely touted: see Hynes (1968), pp. 24 ff.

91 – Philip Abrams, *The Origin of British Sociology*, University of Chicago Press, Chicago, 1968, quoted in Green (1984), p. 15.

92 – Richard Dyer, 'Stereotyping', in R. Dyer (ed.), *Gays in Film*, British Film Institute, London, 1977 (pp. 28–29). There is a considerable sociological literature on stereotypes – Dyer,

Perkins and Gilman give references. See also Steve Neale, 'The Same Old Story: Stereotypes and Difference' in *Screen Education*, 32/33, Autumn/Winter 1979/80.

93 – T. J. Clark (1984), p. 8.

94 – T. E. Perkins, 'Rethinking Stereotypes' in Michele Barrett, Philip Corrigan, Annette Kuhn and Janet Wolff (eds), *Ideology and Cultural Production*, Croom Helm, London, 1979.

95 – Craig Owens (1983), p. 7.

96 – Perkins in Barrett, Corrigan, Kuhn and Wolff (eds), 1979.

97 – Sander Gilman, *Difference and Pathology: Stereotypes of Sexuality, Race and Madness*, Cornell University Press, Ithaca and London, 1985, p. 31.

98 – Perkins in Barrett, Corrigan, Kuhn and Wolff (eds) (1979), p. 148.

99 – Dyer (1977), pp. 28–29. See also p. 37: social types and stereotypes are linked to psychological categories, sorts of personality; member types are linked to historically and culturally specific social groups or classes.

100 – Norman Bryson, *Vision and Painting: The Logic of the Gaze*, Macmillan, London, 1983, p. 155.

101 – Bryson (1983), p. 156. See also Catherine Belsey, *The Subject of Tragedy: Identity and Difference in Renaissance Drama*, Methuen, London and New York, 1985, p. 165: 'the construction of stereotypes cannot ensure permanent stability, not only because the world always exceeds the stereotypical, but also in so far as the stereotypes themselves are inevitably subject to internal contradictions and so are perpetually precarious.'

102 – From the speech by Eva Gore-Booth, 19 May 1906, on the suffrage deputation to the Prime Minister (quoted Liddington and Norris (1978), p. 203). There are useful extracts from the nineteenth-century literature on women's work in Hollis (1979) and Murray (1982).

103 – See the cover of *Votes for Women*, 26 May 1911. The seamstress had been the principal trope of sweated labour and blighted womanhood ever since the publication of Thomas Hood's poem *The Song of the Shirt* in the Christmas issue of *Punch* in 1843.

104 – Hynes (1968), p. 55. These titles included the seventeen volumes of Charles Booth's *Life and Labour of the People in London* (1889–1903); B. Seebohm Rowntree's *Poverty: A Study of Town Life* (1901); C. F. G. Masterman's *From the Abyss* (1902) and *The Condition of England* (1909); L. G. Chiozza Money's *Riches and Poverty* (1905); Will Reason's *Poverty* (1909); Sidney and Beatrice Webb's impressive *Minority Report of the Poor Law Commission* (1909); Seebohm Rowntree and Bruno Lasker's *Unemployment: A Social Study* (1911); W. H. Beveridge's *Unemployment: A Problem of Industry* (1912); Philip Snowden's *The Living Wage* (1912); and A. L. Bowley and A. R. Burnett-Hurst's *Livelihood and Poverty* (1915).

105 – There is a useful summary of the census figures from 1861 to 1911, and much information of interest in Lee Holcombe, *Victorian Ladies at Work: Middle-Class Working Women in England and Wales, 1850–1914*, David & Charles, Newton Abbot, 1973. I am indebted to her account. Holcombe comments on the unreliability of the census figures for vaguely defined groups like nurses in her appendix. Sally Alexander,

Anna Davin and Eve Hostettler discuss the inadequacy of statistical accounts for an understanding of the nature and extent of women's work in 'Labouring Women: A Reply to Eric Hobsbawm', *History Workshop Journal*, no. 8, Autumn 1979. Clara Collet ('Prospects of Marriage for Women', the *Nineteenth Century*, April 1892) estimated that 31 per cent of women in paid employment belonged to Booth's 'poor', 51 per cent to the artisan class, and 18 per cent to the middle and upper classes. Class boundaries were blurred in new 'white blouse' work in the Post Office or the retail trades. And the term 'middle class' is remarkably elastic, embracing not just the bourgeoisie but, as Patricia Branca has reminded us, the small household with one servant and an income of £200–£300 a year.

106 – See Barbara Drake, *Women in Trade Unions*, Labour Research Department, London, 1920, p. 44.

107 – For example in match-making, in potteries (which used lead glazes) and in the lead industry where women suffered paralysis, blindness and miscarriage from the lead poisoning that could also kill them. See R. H. Sherard, *The White Slaves of England*, J. Bowden, London, 1897.

108 – On the 'pit-brow lasses' who unloaded and sorted coal at the pit head see Angela V. John, *By the Sweat of Their Brow: Women Workers at Victorian Coal Mines*, Croom Helm, London, 1980. Chainmaking and pit-brow work, more than any other kinds of female labour, were subject to repeated attempts at regulation during the nineteenth and early twentieth centuries. Both were arduous and unrewarding, but both seem to have been thrown into prominence because they were seen as degrading and 'unwomanly'. The pit-brow women often wore trousers, which seems to have provoked some prurient attention.

109 – Maud Royden's 'Votes and Wages: How Women's Suffrage Will Improve the Economic Position of Women' (NUWSS 3rd edition, July 1912, Fawcett Library) puts most of the main points. There are numerous other pamphlets including Violet Shillington, 'Women Wage-Earners and the Vote' (NUWSS, undated), 'Parliament and Women's Needs', reprinted from the *Women's Trade Union Review*, 'Will the Vote help the Industrial Woman?', 'Easier to Starve', 'Women's Suffrage and the Protection of Women Workers', 'Parliament and Women in Industry', 'Some Reasons Why Working Women Want the Vote' (all in Fawcett Library).

Clementina Black had pointed out in 1887, as secretary of the Women's Trade Union League, that there were worse stories than those of the Black Country chainmakers in the sufferings of trades no one dreamed of forbidding, like needlework and matchbox-making: 'men never propose to interfere with these trades. Why not? There is no need to ask. Men do not work at these trades and suffer nothing from the competition of women.' The *Women's Suffrage Journal*, November 1887, quoted in Liddington and Norris (1978), p. 37.

110 – The *Anti-Suffrage Review*, February 1911: 'The Working Woman and the Suffrage' by 'D', pp. 24–25.

111 – Robert Gray, 'Bourgeois Hegemony in Victorian Britain' in Jon Bloomfield (ed.), *Class, Hegemony and Party*, Lawrence &

Wishart, London, 1977, p. 81. See Liddington and Norris (1978), pp. 240–41. On the Factory and Workshops Acts see Wanda Neff, *Victorian Working Women*, Columbia University Press, New York, 1966, and Lee Holcombe (1973).

112 – Beatrice Webb, *Women and the Factory Acts*, Fabian Tract, no. 67, 1896.

113 – See Sally Alexander *et al.*, 'Labouring Women', *History Workshop Journal*, no. 8, Autumn 1979, p. 178. Weavers, spinners and miners were beginning to adopt the demand for a family wage by the mid-nineteenth century. Liddington and Norris (1978, p. 53) suggest that Ruskin's ideas (as in 'Of Queens' Gardens') found a strong response in working-class men; and that the ideology of 'separate spheres' had become working-class orthodoxy by the 1890s.

114 – Henry Broadhurst at the Trades Union Congress, September 1877, reported in the *Women's Union Journal*, October 1877 and quoted in Barbara Drake (1920, p. 16), articulates this. See the following pages for further extracts from the 1877 Congress and subsequent conflicts between the TUC and the Women's Trade Union League. As Hobsbawm remarks (*History Workshop Journal*, no. 6, Autumn 1978, p. 132): 'The paradox of the labour movement was thus that it encouraged an ideology of sexual equality and emancipation, while in practice discouraging the actual joint participation of men and women in the process of labour as workers.'

115 – The Women's Protection and Provident League was founded by Emma Paterson in 1874. For the history and prehistory of women's trade unions see Barbara Drake (1920). Sally Alexander ('Labouring Women', p. 180) notes that the reports and journals of the Women's Trade Union League and the National Federation of Women Workers indicate that there were persistent attempts to unionise women pottery and textile workers, needlewomen, chainmakers, rope and sailcloth makers, from the 1870s.

116 – Eva Gore-Booth begged the labour movement to consider the plight of 5 million working women 'who have to go out the same as a man goes out on Monday mornings to their work for the same number of hours, but at the end of the week they come home with far less wages ... the very poorest of the poor, the poorest of your own class' (quoted in Liddington and Norris, 1978, p. 238).

117 – There were approximately 1 million 'surplus' women. Clara Collet estimated that one woman in six, or one woman in five in London, would remain unmarried ('Prospects of Marriage for Women', the *Nineteenth Century*, April 1892).

118 – Maud Royden (1912), p. 6. Royden claimed there were more than 5 million women earning their living in England; that the average weekly wage for a female industrial worker was 7s. to 7s. 6d. per week and for a homeworker probably 4s. 6d. per week (according to evidence before the Select Committee on Home-Work, 1907).

119 – The penny magazine *M.A.P.* published some pungent criticism from the left by an unidentified 'representative' in 1910. The author had recently returned from an 'inquiry into the condition of women's labour in the provinces' which left him appalled 'at the complexity and immensity of the problems

surrounding the question of female labour and the paucity of effort directed towards their solution'. Suffragists (by whom he seems to have meant the WSPU) 'would be well advised to study sociological questions of the deepest national importance at first hand rather than organise costly processions reminiscent of a circus rather than of a serious movement'. He draws on the WSPU Annual Report to contrast the £5000 spent on salaries and the £330 on the drum and fife band by 'the richest association connected with womanhood in England', with the condition of 'thousands of women [who] are not sufficiently nourished to feed their babies at their breasts'. The discrepancy was everyone's business, he argued, 'once platform speakers state in their speeches that the gift of the suffrage means the bettering of the working and sweating millions'. But his logic was faulty insofar as the WSPU claimed to act on the *cause* of suffering, rather than on the amelioration of its condition (*M.A.P.*., 8 October 1910, Fawcett Archives, Box 147).

120 – See Marion Holmes, 'The ABC of Votes for Women', WFL, *c.* 1910, pp. 4–5; and 'Will the Vote help the Industrial, Woman?' (Fawcett Library). On government employment and the Fair Wages Committee of 1907, see Drake (1920), pp. 44–45.

121 – *Power and Responsibility*, MLOWS, no. 53 (Fawcett Library).

122 – See Sally Alexander, 'Women's Work in Nineteenth-Century London: A Study of the Years 1820–50' in Mitchell and Oakley (eds), 1976: 'Most women workers in London were domestic servants, washerwomen, needlewomen or occupied in some other sort of home work. Many married women worked with their husbands in his trade. These traditional forms of women's work were quite compatible with the Victorian's deification of the home, and so passed almost unnoticed' (p. 63). They are also unnoticed in the work even of labour historians, a contemporary 'blindness' remarked by Sally Alexander, Anna Davin and Eve Hostettler in 'Labouring Women: a reply to Eric Hobsbawm', *History Workshop Journal*, no. 8, Autumn 1979, p. 174.

123 – 'Better and Happier; An Answer from the Ladies' Gallery to the Speeches in Opposition to the Women's Suffrage Bill', 28 February 1908, by Lady McLaren, T. Fisher Unwin, London, 1908 (Fawcett Library). The emphasis on domestic labour is significant and finds little parallel in suffrage imagery, perhaps because it was less emotive and seemed so 'natural'. Although the numbers were declining (33 per cent of women workers in 1901, 27 per cent in 1911), more women were employed in domestic service than in any other occupation before the First World War.

124 – See E. J. Hobsbawm, 'Man and Woman in Socialist Iconography', *History Workshop Journal*, no. 6, Autumn 1978; and Sally Alexander *et al.*, 'Labouring Women: a reply to Eric Hobsbawm', in no. 8, Autumn 1979.

125 – See Drake (1920), chapter IV, 'The National Federation of Women Workers and the Modern Women's Trade Union Movement 1906–14', for an account of women's industrial unrest and increasing unionisation in this period. The female membership of all trade unions, which rose from 166,000 to 183,000 between 1906 and 1910, almost doubled between 1910 and 1914.

126 – Maud Royden, editor of the *Vote*, was typically discreet in her pamphlet on 'Votes and Wages': '[Homeworkers] are getting 6s. and 5s. and less. They are supported, for the rest, on the rates, on charitable doles, and on the price for which they may sell themselves in the street. Those who keep straight – and there are many – are heroines. Those who do not – and they are not few – which of us shall blame?' See in this context the Atelier postcard, 'The Scylla and Charybdis of the Working Woman'.

127 – Jean Finot from *La Revue*, November and December 1910, translated and abridged in *Votes for Women*, 10 February 1911. His article was also cited in the *Vote*, 24 December 1910, which pointed out that he drew on the sociology of Lester Ward to argue against the permanence of sexual characteristics and in favour of women's evolutionary pre-eminence.

128 – Holbrook Jackson, *The Eighteen Nineties*, Grant Richards, London, 1913 (cited from Harvester edition, Brighton, 1976, pp. 21–22). On the New Woman see A. R. Cunningham, 'The "New Woman" Fiction of the 1890s', *Victorian Studies*, December 1973; Elaine Showalter, *A Literature of Their Own: British Women Novelists from Brontë to Lessing* (1977), Virago, London, 1978, (chapter VII); Gail Cunningham (1978); and Rosalind Rosenberg (1982, chapter 3), all of whom cite further sources.

129 – This is Showalter's point (1978, p. 184). For the American version see *The New Woman*, a play by Sydney Grundy (1894); Sarah Grand, 'The New Aspect of the Woman Question', *North American Review*, March 1894; and Caroline Ticknor, 'The Steel Engraving Lady and the Gibson Girl', *Atlantic Monthly*, July 1901.

130 – The *Saturday Review*, 8 February 1896, quoted by Gail Cunningham (1978), p. 117. Cunningham takes as her epigraph the winning verse from a competition in *Woman*, 26 September 1894, for the best definition of the New Woman: 'She flouts Love's caresses / Reforms ladies' dresses / And scorns the Man-Monster's tirade; / She seems scarcely human / This mannish New Woman / This Queen of the Blushless Brigade.'

131 – Cunningham (1978, p. 49) cites mental breakdown, madness and suicide as the common penalties for flouting decorum in 'New Woman' novels, even those written by feminists, who thereby demonstrated the crippling force of social convention.

132 – Millicent Fawcett's review of *The Woman Who Did* appeared in the *Contemporary Review*, LXVII, 1895, p. 630 (quoted in Showalter, 1978, p. 185). There was a marginal strand within the feminist movement committed to 'free love' (by which they meant voluntary unions outside of wedlock, not promiscuity). It was centred on *The Freewoman*, edited by Dora Marsden who was briefly a member of the WSPU, but the social purity position dominated feminist discussion of sex in the years before 1914.

133 – Showalter (1978), p. 182.

134 – For one of many written descriptions see 'Character Note: The New Woman' in the *Cornhill Magazine*, 1894,

p. 365. 'Novissima' is dark ('fairness usually goes with an interest in children, and other gentle weaknesses'). She dresses in manly and simple tailor-mades, strides from the hip, and holds her elbows out from her sides. 'With mild young men she is apt to be crushing. She is anti-prettiness, and not pretty herself.' She has a long, sallow face, a discontented mouth, and a nose 'indicative of intelligence but too large for feminine beauty as understood by men'.

135 – Rheta Childe Dorr, *A Woman of Fifty*, Funk & Wagnalls, New York, 1924, p. 101 (Dorr spent some time associated with the British campaign and ghosted Mrs Pankhurst's *My Own Story*, Eveleigh Nash, London, 1914).

See also Arnold Harris Mathew, *Woman Suffrage*, in the Social Problems Series, no. 5, T. C. & E. C. Jack, London, 1907. 'This is a new era in many respects, and the title "new woman" has not been thrown out in vain. The woman of to-day differs from the woman of past generations in the fact that she has a clearer consciousness of her own personality; she has more liberty than has ever, hitherto, been allowed to her sex; she is better educated; she is wider awake in all senses; she has broken down many barriers of custom; and as she takes stock of her position she recognises that she has gained, in all respects, by the change. How, then, can we stop her onward progress . . . ?'

136 – See for example Elizabeth Chapman, *Marriage Questions in Modern Fiction*, John Lane, London, 1897, foreword: 'I believe that these [feminist aims] have been obscured to a rather serious extent of late by the interminable flood of gaseous chatter to which the invention of a journalistic myth known as the "New Woman" has given rise, and that it has become necessary sharply to emphasise the distinction between this phantom and the real reformer and friend of her sex and humanity whom I would call the "Best Woman"' (cited in Cunningham, 1978, pp. 11–12).

137 – Paul Thompson, *The Edwardians: The Remaking of British Society*, Weidenfeld & Nicolson, London, 1975, p. 41.

138 – Patricia Branca, *Silent Sisterhood: Middle-Class Women in the Victorian Home*, Croom Helm, London, 1975, chapter 8 (and p. 145). It could be argued that the 'modern' epithet is most applicable to middle-class women in the Edwardian period. See also Alex Inkeles, 'The Modernization of Man' in Myron Weiner (ed.), *Modernization and the Dynamics of Growth*, Basic Books, New York, 1966; and Ester Boserup, *Women's Role in Economic Development*, Allen & Unwin, London, 1970. The 'modernity' of the Victorian woman did not extend to the freedom of the streets and its concomitant freedom to *look* (essential attributes of the *flâneur*, hero of the literature of modernity). See Janet Wolff, 'The Invisible *Flâneuse*: Women and the Literature of Modernity', *Theory Culture and Society*, vol. 2 no. 3, 1985.

139 – See for example *Punch*, 30 October 1912, 'The Split' ('Are you a Peth or a Pank?') – two suffragettes discussing the Pethick-Lawrences' split with the WSPU in the local tea-rooms. Leonore Davidoff points out that by the turn of the nineteenth century there was 'beginning to be provision for respectable women to meet in public places outside their homes' and that

'cafés, the growth of tea-rooms, the use of buses, even the provision of public lavatories for women, were as important in freeing middle-class women from strict social ritual as the slow erosion of chaperonage' (see *The Best Circles: Society, Etiquette and The Season*, Croom Helm, London, 1973, p. 67).

140 – Branca (1975), p. 145. Branca notes that the ability of the middle-class woman to 'modernise' was enhanced 'by an unusually nucleated family structure and by the ability to forge a standard of living above subsistence level'. She was 'the only woman who both needed and could afford the advances in technology' (the working-class woman was too poor and the upper-class woman had a retinue of servants). At the same time there were ambiguities in 'modernisation' for women, particularly in the contradiction between modern notions of personal autonomy and modern notions of attentive motherhood.

141 – See Ludmilla Jordanova, 'Natural facts: a historical perspective on science and sexuality' in Carol MacCormack and Marilyn Strathern (eds), *Nature, Culture and Gender*, Cambridge University Press, Cambridge, 1980, p. 61. The whole essay is particularly lucid and helpful.

142 – Almroth Wright (1913), p. 40. In 1894 Charles Harper (*Revolted Woman: Past, Present and to Come*) had already credited 'the Women's Rights frenzy, the Girl of the Period furore, and the Divided Skirt craze' with creating 'the writings and doings of the pioneers of the New Woman, who forget that Woman's Mission is Submission' (p. 2).

143 – 'The Decline and Fall of the British Empire', published anonymously by a young Tory pamphleteer called Elliott Mills in 1905 (p. 22). The analogy with Roman decadence was subsequently taken up elsewhere, notably in Baden-Powell's *Scouting for Boys* of 1908. I am indebted to Hynes (1968) who discusses it together with Balfour's 1908 address on 'Decadence' and other sources related to the supposed physical and moral deterioration of the population, in his second chapter, 'The Decline and Fall of Tory England'. Weeks (1981, p. 125) points out that 'degeneration' was evoked in the 1880s as an explanation for the consequences of urban change. ('Behind it was a fear, particularly among the urban middle class, that Britain might have taken a wrong turn in becoming an urban, industrial society.') The concern with *moral* decline was enhanced by the trial of Oscar Wilde in 1895, and the publication in the same year of the English translation of Max Nordau's *Entartung* as *Degeneration*. Nordau argued that all characteristically modern art showed evidence of the decadence threatening the human race.

144 – 'Social Darwinism' is the conventional term for a variety of applications of evolutionary theory to social theory, in the period between the 1870s and the First World War. The term 'eugenics' was coined by Darwin's cousin, Francis Galton, in 1883. Eugenic theories were also influenced by the work of the social philosopher Herbert Spencer, who had first used the expression 'the survival of the fittest' in 1864. I came belatedly to Lorna Duffin's interesting essay 'Prisoners of Progress: Women and Evolution' (in Sara Delamont and Lorna Duffin (eds), *The Nineteenth-Century Woman: Her Cultural and Physical*

World, Croom Helm, London, 1975), having written this section from other primary and secondary sources. I was gratified but also chastened to discover myself in accord with her much earlier and more detailed account. Raymond Williams has a chapter on 'Social Darwinism' in *Problems in Materialism and Culture*, Verso, London, 1980. There is useful introductory material on social Darwinism and the impact of eugenics in Jeffrey Weeks, *Sex, Politics and Society: The regulation of sexuality since 1800*, Longman, London and New York, 1981 (see chapter 7, 'The population question in the early twentieth century'); and in Jane Lewis, *Women in England 1870–1920*, Basil Blackwell, Oxford, 1984, pp. 81–111. I am indebted to David Green's 'Veins of Resemblance: Photography and Eugenics', *Oxford Art Journal*, vol. 7 no. 2, 1984; and have found generally stimulating Rosalind Rosenberg, *Beyond Separate Spheres: The Intellectual Roots of Modern Feminism*, Yale University Press, New Haven, 1982; and Gillian Beer's marvellous *Darwin's Plots: Evolutionary Narrative in Darwin, George Eliot and Nineteenth-Century Fiction*, Routledge & Kegan Paul, London, 1984. See also J. W. Burrow, *Evolution and Society*, Cambridge University Press, Cambridge, 1968; D. R. Oldroyd, *Darwinian Impacts*, Open University Press, Milton Keynes, 1980; Greta Jones, *Social Darwinism and English Thought*, Harvester Press, Brighton, 1980; G. R. Searle, *Eugenics and Politics in Britain 1900–14*, Noordhoft International Publications, Leyden, 1976; and Janet Sayers, *Biological Politics: Feminist and Anti-Feminist Perspectives*, Tavistock, London, 1982.

145 – Hynes (1968), p. 197. See also Weeks (1981, pp. 125–26) on the differential birth rate. Karl Pearson argued that 25 per cent of the population was likely to produce 50 per cent of the next generation, to the detriment of the racial stock, since the birth rate was highest among unskilled labourers. On the increased emphasis on motherhood in the Edwardian period (which was expressed in new state interventions in the regulation of maternal duties, and in a number of unofficial bodies directed towards working-class mothers), see Anna Davin, 'Imperialism and Motherhood', *History Workshop Journal*, Spring 1978; Jane Lewis, *The Politics of Motherhood: Maternal and Child Welfare in England 1900–39*, Croom Helm, London, 1980; and Carol Dyhouse, 'Working-Class Mothers and Infant Mortality in England, 1895–1914', *Journal of Social History*, vol. 12, 1978.

146 – Quoted in Janet Sayers (1982), pp. 16–17.

147 – Karl Pearson (socialist and social Darwinist), *The Woman Question* (1885), p. 16, quoted in Lewis (1984), p. 84. It was also argued that feminists and their supporters set out to damage Britain's imperial interests. 'Whatever tells against the dignity and integrity of our empire they advocate. They eulogise and uphold the pronounced enemies of our country. They would give the keys of our foreign possessions into the hands of Russia or France; they brand patriotism as jingoism; and they . . . ridicule our national traditions . . . dishonour our national flag.' (Eliza Lynn Linton, 'The Partisans of the Wild Women', the *Nineteenth Century*, vol. 31, 1892, pp. 455–64; and see also Mona Caird's spirited 'A Defence of the so-called "Wild Women"', in the same issue, pp. 811 ff.

148 – See Rosenberg (1982), pp. 14–15: 'Paradoxically, Darwinism provided the biological affirmation of female uniqueness that antifeminists needed to oppose change and that feminists relied on to defuse the threat of change.'

149 – Lewis (1984, p. 84) points out that when it was found that women's brains were heavier than men's in proportion to their body weight, scientists began to search for other measurements of difference. See also Elizabeth Fee, 'Nineteenth-Century Craniology: the Study of the Female Skull', *Bulletin of the History of Medicine* 53, Fall 1979; Sayers (1982), p. 86; and Rosenberg (1982), pp. 8–9, who cites further references. Women were supposed to have a lower metabolic rate than men, to be weaker and less intelligent. Motherhood increased these disadvantages by forcing them into dependence on the male. Protected, as Rosenberg puts it, from the full force of natural selection, they were also partly immune from its progressive influence (p. 7).

150 – Henry Maudsley in Rosenberg (1982), p. 11. See also Maudsley, quoted in Brian Easlea, *Science and Sexual Oppression* (1981), p. 143: 'for it would be an ill thing, if it should so happen that we get the advantages of a quantity of female intellectual work at the price of a puny, enfeebled and sickly race'; and Harper (1894, p. 27): 'it is not to be supposed that even the prospect of peopling the world with stunted and hydrocephalic children will deter this modern woman from her path, even though her modernity lead to the degradation and ultimate extinction of the race.'

151 – Patrick Geddes, *The Evolution of Sex* (1889, p. 247) quoted by Jill Conway in Martha Vicunus (ed.), *Suffer and Be Still: Women in the Victorian Age*, Indiana University Press, Bloomington and London, 1972, p. 146.

152 – Lewis (1984, p. 104) points out that even Olive Schreiner, in *Woman and Labour* (1911, p. 109), argued that working mothers would improve the race: 'parasitical mothers' produced 'softened sons'.

153 – Both quotations from Lady Sybil Smith, 'Woman and Evolution', pamphlet published by the Women's Freedom League, undated (Fawcett Library). She speculated that domestic labour might become at the same time more specialised and more collective. 'Such a possibility is not necessarily incompatible with home life, for each family might according to some such plan inhabit adjoining houses or separate sets of rooms in one building, meals could be sent or fetched from a common restaurant, and each block might contain a general laundry and creche. However, as yet all this exists only in the speculations of theorists, though the trend of civilisation towards the economic independence of women seems to point in some such direction.' It is not clear whether men would share in this collectivised domestic labour (as in Edward Carpenter's *Love's Coming of Age*, 1896) or not (as in Robert Blatchford's *Merrie England*, 1893). She also argued that the development of machinery would make an impact on sexual selection. 'It is noticeable that bodily strength and prowess in man still appeal above all other characteristics to women of primitive type. But with her growing independence woman begins to demand different qualities in her mate, qualities such as sympathy,

gentleness and self-control, and in obedience to Nature's laws, man will become modified accordingly.'

154 – This view was encouraged by a feminist reading of works like Patrick Geddes's and J. Arthur Thomson's *The Evolution of Sex* (1889), which argued that sex differences were physiologically based, but which celebrated women's separate and complementary sphere as the basis of 'civic' or 'social' motherhood. Geddes's most significant populariser in America was Jane Addams, who claimed that women were the agents of moral change and the guardians of 'city housekeeping'; but arguments for 'social motherhood' were common in England too. See Conway, 'Stereotypes of Femininity in a Theory of Sexual Evolution' in Vicunus (ed.), 1972.

155 – See Frances Swiney, *The Bar of Isis: or, The Law of the Mother*, C. W. Daniel, London, 1907. Swiney developed a theory of women as biologically, 'racially' and intellectually superior to men. She described them as the major force in evolutionary development, but as martyrs to an 'organised and systematic sexual wrong-doing' on the part of men (p. 38).

156 – Thomas Johnston, *The Case for Woman's Suffrage and Objections Answered*, The Forward Printing and Publishing Co. Ltd, Glasgow, *c.* 1907, p. 13. Feminisation could be seen as a positive (civilising) or a negative (polluting or enfeebling) influence. Feminists argued for the first, of course, but under conditions in which women's emancipation freed and strengthened them for their evolutionary role.

157 – Amy Bulley, 'The Political Evolution of Women', *Westminster Review* LXXXIV, 1890, quoted in Showalter (1978), p. 186.

158 – See *Theory of the Leisure Class* (1899), Mentor Books, New York, 1958 (the comparison was also drawn by Mary Wollstonecraft). Veblen commented that 'among the women of the well-to-do classes' there was 'a demand, more or less serious, for emancipation from all relations of status, tutelage, or vicarious life . . . The grievance of the new woman is made up of those things which . . . [a] typical characterisation of the movement urges as the reasons why she should be content. She is petted, and is permitted, or even required, to consume largely and conspicuously – vicariously for her husband or other natural guardian. She is exempted, or debarred, from vulgarly useful employment – in order to perform leisure vicariously for the good repute of her natural (or pecuniary) guardian. These offices are the conventional marks of the un-free, at the same time that they are incompatible with the human impulse to purposeful activity' (pp. 231–32).

159 – Rachel Bowlby discusses the appeal of the 'new commerce' to women in *Just Looking: Consumer Culture in Dreiser, Gissing and Zola*, Methuen, London, 1985. As she points out (p. 18), psychoanalysis was not the only enterprise at the turn of the century to be interested in the answer to Freud's famous question, 'What does a woman want?'

160 – The sense of a long women's history as it was constructed in the suffrage press, and by the banners and tableaux in their processions, was intended to have this effect. In anticipation of the Historical Pageant in the Women's Coronation Procession of 1911, *Votes for Women* (2 June 1911, p. 581) hoped that the windows of Piccadilly would be filled 'with elderly relations accustomed to raise their hands in horror at the "modernness" of their nieces and daughters', and that as the pageant passed it would dawn on them 'that theirs is really the modern point of view, dating from no further back than the simpering artificialities of the early eighteenth century'.

161 – Israel Zangwill, opening quotations from a speech at the Albert Hall, 11 December 1909, reported in the *Vote*, 16 December 1909; and 'Take women away from the coal-pit . . .' from 'Old Fogeys and Old Bogeys', speech delivered at the Queen's Hall, 7 June 1909, printed as (N)WSPU pamphlet (Fawcett Library). 'Old Fogeys' begins: 'Ladies and gentlemen, the time is fast coming – coming at motor speed – when in no civilised country will be seen cars without electricity or women without votes.' Mrs Chapman Catt, in her presidential address to the International Woman's Suffrage Alliance in 1909, pointed out that anti-suffragists were often the beneficiaries of campaigns to which they had not contributed. 'Yet these modern anti-suffragists are educated women, and some possess a college degree, an opportunity and an achievement which other women won for them in the face of universal ridicule; they are possessed of property which is theirs today as the effect of laws which other women have laboured for a quarter of a century to secure; they stand upon public platforms where free speech for women was won for them by other women amid the jeers of howling mobs, not infrequently armed with rotten eggs; they adopt the right of organisation, now an established custom among women, but which was established as the result of many a heart-ache and many a brave endeavour when the world condemned it as a threat against all moral order. They accept with satisfaction every political right which has hitherto been accorded by their government . . . [but] they turn upon the last logical step in the movement which has given them so much, and with supreme self-satisfaction say: "Thus far shalt thou come and no farther."'

162 – Simon Patten, 'The Evolution of a New Woman', *The Annals of the American Academy*, vol. 56, November 1914, pp. 111–21 (New York Public Library). Patten argues that women are changing physically, 'that the so-called womanly woman was in fact a retarded type', and that with their emancipation women's health and intellectual vigour will increase. He draws on a distinction between the physiognomies of 'lower' and 'higher' races (common in social Darwinism) to predict that the emancipated or evolved woman will have an oval face with a strong profile, a prominent nose and high cheekbones. Unfortunately young men are continuing to make conventional choices influenced by the 'Madonna faces' in paintings and magazines, and a crisis is developing as a result of their inability to recognise that it is 'the driving forceful girls about them' who would make the best mothers.

163 – Laurence Housman to Janet Ashbee, 14 June 1908 (Ashbee Journals, King's College, Cambridge). See also Teresa Billington-Greig, 'Suffragist Tactics: Past and Present', WFL, undated (Fawcett Library), for the identification of the militant suffragist as a new female type.

164 – Strachey (1931, pp. 63–64) quotes a letter from Mrs

Fawcett in which she refers to the disparaging remarks of an MP whom she later encountered at dinner. Amused at his discomfort she remarked that what he had said was after all 'very mild compared to Horace Walpole's abuse of Mary Wollstonecraft as a "hyena in petticoats"'. The phrase is quite well known, but until Claire Pajaczkowska drew my attention to 'Hyena Myths and Realities' I had not realised how richly connotative it was. Stephen Jay-Gould (in *Hens' Teeth and Horses' Toes*, Pelican, London, 1983) writes on the three myths about hyenas which 'helped to inspire the loathing commentary of ancient texts': that they were scavengers and carrion eaters; hybrid animals and not a true species; and hermaphrodites, bearing both male and female organs. It is apparently the case that the sexual organs of young female hyenas are superficially indistinguishable from those of the male (they have a peniform clitoris and false scrotum). I am very grateful to Claire Pajaczkowska for her comments on an earlier draft of this section.

165 – Eliza Lynn Linton in the *Saturday Review*, 19 March 1870; Florence Bright, 'An Outsider's View of the Women's Movement', WSPU, 1907, p. 5. In 1909 Lord Curzon described the suffrage movement as made up of talented and intellectual leaders at one end of the scale and 'female howling dervishes' at the other (quoted in *Votes for Women*, 21 May 1909).

166 – Stephen Heath, *The Sexual Fix*, Macmillan, London, 1982, p. 26 and p. 31: 'it names and dispenses with a whole realm of the "emotional", any reaction that falls outside the convention of the "reasonable", and it talks about and contains the relation of women and sexuality, and it is always there with a history and a context of medical seriousness and credit that underlies and guarantees its general extension, supporting and maintaining the basic representation: of women as *the female sex.*' For a vivid instance of this see the magistrate's comments on Sarah Bennett, who held a suffrage meeting on the doorstep of the Secretary of State for Scotland (in his absence): 'Mr Plowden observed that she appeared to take a pride and even glory in her conduct, and her attitude almost made him think that he ought to remand her for medical examination . . . Miss Bennett retorted sharply, "I am not insane." Mr Plowden – "Oh no, no; but there is such a thing as hysteria and being out of health"' (undated newscutting, c. February 1908, Maud Arncliffe-Sennett Collection, vol. 2, p. 59). Almroth Wright's letter to *The Times* was published on the morning of the reading of the second Conciliation Bill, and may have influenced the vote. It provoked a correspondence that continued into April. There was much discussion of 'insurgent hysteria' in the press around March 1912, provoked by WSPU window-breaking and encouraged in some quarters by a concern to discredit the Conciliation Bill.

167 – Michel Foucault, *The History of Sexuality*, vol. 1: *An Introduction* (Paris, 1976), Allen Lane, London, 1979. See especially p. 104: 'A *hysterisation of women's bodies*: a threefold process whereby the feminine body was analysed – qualified and disqualified – as being thoroughly saturated with sexuality; whereby it was integrated into the sphere of medical practices, by reason of a pathology intrinsic to it; whereby, finally, it was placed in organic communication with the social body (whose regulated fecundity it was supposed to ensure), the family space (of which it had to be a substantial and functional element), and the life of children (which it produced and had to guarantee, by virtue of a biologico-moral responsibility lasting through the entire period of the children's education): the Mother, and her negative image of "nervous woman", constituted the most visible form of this hysterisation.'

168 – *Charles Kingsley: His Letters and Memories of His Life edited by His Wife*, H. S. King, London, 1877, vol. II, p. 247; quoted in Heath (1982), p. 25.

169 – *The Times*, 28 March 1912.

170 – Almroth Wright (1913), p. 71. Hysteria (and therefore feminism) was associated with varieties of uterine disorder unnatural in the healthily menstruating and reproductive wife. Marriage and motherhood became medical as well as social norms in this prescription, but *all* women remained at the mercy of their reproductive systems.

171 – J. Laplanche and J-B. Pontalis, *The Language of Psycho-Analysis*, Hogarth Press, London, 1980, p. 195. The standard history is Ilza Veith, *Hysteria: The History of a Disease*, University of Chicago Press, Chicago and London, 1965. I am indebted also to Heath (1982), chapters II and IV. See also Elaine Showalter, *The Female Malady: Women, Madness and English Culture 1830–1980* (Virago, London, 1987) which appeared too late for inclusion in my text.

172 – Heath (1982), pp. 29–30.

173 – Foucault's attempt to map an economy of discourses on sexuality is a very different project from that of measuring the plimsoll line between an acceptable 'sexuality' and one that is unacknowledged or repressed. He argues that there was a proliferation rather than a repression of discourses on sexuality during the nineteenth century. See also note 167.

174 – Two prominent women anti-suffragists, Violet Markham and Mrs Humphry Ward, wrote to *The Times* to dissociate themselves from Almroth Wright's letter published on 28 March 1912. But the National League for Opposing Woman Suffrage, of which Mrs Ward was an official and Violet Markham a leading member, continued to circulate complimentary copies despite their objections.

175 – Heath (1982), p. 31; Weeks (1981), p. 43. The hormonal pattern for the menstrual cycle was not discovered until 1928.

176 – The complexities set up in the 'reality and the *force* of hysteria' are outlined in Heath (1982), pp. 30–31. Exceptionally, Jews and aliens were 'hysterical' too: see George Sims (ed.), *Living London* (3 vols), Cassell, London, 1906, vol. 1, p. 52 on 'Sweated London', which refers to the 'nervous hysteria' and 'high-pitched voices' and screams of a downtrodden people.

177 – Laplanche and Pontalis (1980), p. 195.

178 – See Hynes (1968), pp. 138, 164. Hynes notes that the London Psycho-Analytical Society was founded in 1913 with nine members, only four of whom were practising analysts. 'In 1911, when Dr David Eder presented the first paper on clinical psychoanalysis to be read at a British Medical Association meeting, the chairman waited until he had finished and then stalked out of the room without a word, followed by the entire

audience.' The *British Medical Journal* consistently opposed Freud's theories, and the medical establishment was openly hostile to psychoanalysis until the application of analytic therapies to shell-shock cases during the First World War.

179 – Foucault (1979), p. 53. There were 212 women doctors in 1901 (and 22,698 men), and 495 in 1911 (and 25,048 men), including those classed as retired. See the *Census of England and Wales* for 1901 (HMSO, London, 1902), Appendix A, Table 33.

180 – Harrison (1978), pp. 67–68, discusses the hostility of the medical profession. It should be stressed that the relationships between middle-class women and their doctors were complicated by various factors including the ambiguous social standing of the local practitioner, described by Davidoff (1973, p. 87) as half-way between front and back door status. Lewis (1984, p. 86) remarks that the 'female patient/doctor relationship is particularly difficult to interpret' in this period. Feminists like Frances Power Cobbe complained of the doctor's influence and priest-like role ('The Little Health of Ladies', *Contemporary Review*, January 1878), but Jacques Donzelot and Patricia Branca have argued that middle-class women forged alliances with doctors and found their status enhanced as educators and medical auxiliaries within the family. See also Jean L'Esperance, 'Doctors and Women in Nineteenth-Century Society: Sexuality and Role', in John Woodward and David Richards (eds), *Health Care and Popular Medicine in Nineteenth-Century England, Essays in the Social History of Medicine*, Croom Helm, London, 1977 (one of many references I owe to Jeffrey Weeks). This remains a different question, however, from that of the power of medical *discourse* to dominate the discussion of (especially female) sexuality, and to determine the frame of reference within which feminists could respond. On the related issue of medicine and female education see J. N. Burstyn, 'Education and Sex: The Medical Case Against Higher Education for Women in England, 1870–1900', *Proceedings of the American Philosophical Society*, vol. 117 no. 2, 10 April 1973; Rita McWilliams-Tullberg, *Women at Cambridge: A Men's University – though of a Mixed Type*, Gollancz, London, 1975; and Rosenberg (1982).

181 – The *Weekly Dispatch*, 13 April 1913: part of its objection to the 'disgusting nonsense which has been put forward in the name of medical science' (reprinted in the *Suffragette* on 18 April). The power of the medical profession to determine norms of sexual behaviour made the support of doctors (and the presence of women doctors on suffrage processions) all the more significant. See for example 'Normal Women Not Neurotic' by Dr Frederick Peterson in the *New York Times*, 15 February 1914 (reprinted by the National Woman Suffrage Publishing Co. Inc., New York, 1914), in reply to an interview with Professor Sedgewick on feminism and women's suffrage: 'It is an affront to the great body of able and dignified women who are supporting this movement for the betterment of the whole race to stigmatise their efforts as "insane restlessness" and to speak of them as "masculine women", "wild women" and "idle women . . . in search of sex adventure".'

182 – Juliet Mitchell, *Women: The Longest Revolution*, Virago, London, 1984, p. 117. Carroll Smith Rosenberg argues that hysteria was not only the product of role conflict but, within limits, a chosen resolution of it, in 'The Hysterical Woman: Sex Roles and Role Conflict in Nineteenth-Century America', *Social Research*, vol. 39 no. 4, Winter 1972. See also Charles Rosenberg, *No Other Gods: On Science and American Social Thought*, Johns Hopkins University Press, Baltimore, 1976, chapter 2, 'The Female Animal: Medical and Biological Views of Women' (with Carroll Smith Rosenberg).

183 – Cicely Hamilton, *Marriage as a Trade* (1909), The Women's Press, London, 1981, p. 127.

184 – The *Common Cause*, 15 April 1909, p. 1. See also the artist Marie Brackenbury's reminiscences in *Gateway*, January 1932, pp. 37–38 (Museum of London): 'Gentle, cultured, women handing notices of meetings became quite used to such expressions as "You ought to be beaten and then dragged round Trafalgar Square by the hair on your head".' Similar points were made by May Sinclair in her pamphlet on 'Feminism' (Women Writers' Suffrage League, 1912) published in refutation of Almroth Wright; and by Emmeline Pethick-Lawrence in her autobiography (1938), p. 191.

185 – Emmeline Pethick-Lawrence, 'The New Crusade', WSPU pamphlet, 1907 (Museum of London). Cf. Juliet Mitchell's comment (1984, p. 120): 'Indeed feminism, then, as now, inevitably oscillated between asserting that feminine emotion (hysteria) was valid but undervalued, and claiming that the demands for equality were not emotional but rational.'

186 – Pierre Janet, *The Major Symptoms of Hysteria*, Macmillan, New York, 1920, p. 10.

187 – Eliza Lynn Linton, 'The Partisans of the Wild Women', the *Nineteenth Century*, vol. 31, 1892, p. 463. The clinical picture of the 'hysterical personality' stressed the egocentric, narcissistic, unpredictable, highly suggestible, exhibitionist (but often frigid) qualities of such women. These traits are clearly evident in representations of the suffragists by their opponents.

188 – House of Commons Debate, 12 July 1910, cols. 266–67, quoted Harrison (1978), p. 193.

189 – Sylvia Pankhurst (1931), p. 454. The idea that women's political agitation was hysterical and that hysteria was somehow contagious helped to explain the inexplicable for those who refused the political argument. 'Just fancy, too,' J. St Loe Strachey wrote to Violet Markham on 11 October 1909, 'Connie Lytton being arrested for throwing stones at Runciman's car like any street cad. You probably know her and what a gentle harmless creature she is in normal circumstances' (Markham papers 26/30, British Library of Political and Economic Science, London School of Economics).

190 – Heath (1982), p. 20.

191 – Harrison (1978), p. 191; Rover (1967), p. 92.

192 – Teresa Billington-Greig, *The Militant Suffragette Movement*, London, 1911, p. 142, quoted Harrison (1978), p. 192.

193 – Harrison (1978), pp. 192–93.

194 – Quoted in Fulford (1958), p. 250.

195 – Harrison (1978), p. 193.

196 – 'Suffragist Hysteria', *Daily Chronicle*, 16 November 1908.

197 – And with eighteenth-century traditions of political cari-

cature in which aristocratic women might be lampooned as invective peasants or fishwives: see Gillray's caricature of Lady Cecilia Johnston, 'Billingsgate Eloquence', reproduced in Houffe (1978).

198 – How was 'hysteria' to be represented? Hysteria as a clinical condition involves physical symptoms produced in the repression of mental ideas. This process cannot be observed and the symptoms themselves may, or may not, be visible. This did not deter Charcot's attempt to chart the passage of hysterical convulsion across the body of its victim in his famous *Photographic Iconography of the Salpêtrière*, but it is generally allowed that psychoanalysis and the sophisticated treatment of hysterical disorders begin together, with the displacement of looking by 'the talking cure'. It remained the popular view that psychic states were inscribed on the surface of the body, and specifically that the militants' 'hysterical ecstasy' always betrayed itself 'unmistakably in the expression of the face' (*Daily Mirror*, 25 May 1914). Anti-suffrage imagery shared with Charcot, if unscientifically and with a much more elastic and vernacular concept of the 'hysterical', the impetus to produce the *signs* of feminine deviance, but as instances of social, as well as individual, pathology. Here indeed are the 'elements of a fantastic spectacle of women' (Heath, 1982, p. 34), but perhaps what they speak to most directly are the fears and anxieties of men. Bernard Partridge's 'The Shrieking Sister' in *Punch* (17 January 1906) is a good example of the way in which class-based codes of appearance and decorum were used to evoke the distinction between the 'womanly' and the 'hysterical' woman. There was a double irony in this. First, because the suffrage movement was (wrongly) accused of having no substantial working-class following; and second, because 'hysteria' was widely recognised as a disorder predominantly of middle-class women. (See for example Samuel Ashwell, *A Practical Treatise on the Diseases Peculiar to Women; Illustrated by Cases, Derived from Hospital and Private Practice*, Samuel Highley, London, 1844; a reference I owe to Lynda Nead, together with that from *The Lancet* in note 199.)

199 – 'Checks to Population', *The Lancet*, 10 April 1869, p. 500. The hysteric was already accounted deficient or frustrated in her sexuality, and this encouraged her identification with the lesbian, the virago, the ugly and embittered spinster or the menopausal wife.

200 – 'Frenzied Femininity: Shall Maenads Govern?', the *Referee*, 19 July 1914. I have had no hesitation in referring to 'Vanoc' as 'he'.

201 – Heath (1982), pp. 46–47.

202 – The effectiveness is evident in later accounts, such as Anthony Ludovici's *Enemies of Women: The Origins in Outline of Anglo-Saxon Feminism*, Carroll & Nicholson, London, 1948 (which blames the progress of feminism on male degeneracy); and Ronald Pearsall's description of Annie Kenney as 'Thin, haggard, hysterical . . . the stuff of which disciples are made' (*Edwardian Life and Leisure*, David & Charles, Newton Abbot, 1973, p. 168).

203 – Maud Arncliffe-Sennett papers, vol. 3, p. 53 (British Library). See also vol. 3, p. 1: 'Please note that in all the

Allegories the woman is omnipotent and politically imposing – in *Real Life* – she is politically helpless and impotent.'

204 – William Gass, 'Monument/Mentality', *Oppositions*, p. 138; I have borrowed this reference from Marina Warner, who uses it in *Monuments and Maidens: The Allegory of the Female Form*, Weidenfeld & Nicolson, London, 1985, p. 12.

205 – Emmeline Pethick-Lawrence, 'An Army with Banners', *Votes for Women*, 15 July 1910, p. 689.

206 – Christabel Pankhurst quoted in Emmeline Pethick-Lawrence (1938), p. 151.

207 – J. St Loe Strachey to Violet Markham, 15 March 1911 (Markham Papers 26/30, British Library of Political and Economic Science, London School of Economics).

208 – See especially the *Daily Mirror* photographs, 15 May 1914.

209 – The American suffragist Anna Shaw on the Congressional Union, 27 July 1916 (NAWSA papers, Library of Congress), quoted in Rosen (1974), p. 233. Mrs Pankhurst wrote to Ethel Smyth on 29 May 1914: 'On Sunday it was reported that I was dead and I don't think McKenna would have been sorry if that had been the result of the horrible bear's hug that huge policeman gave me when he seized me. Fortunately for me I have "young bones" or my ribs would all have been fractured. After it I suffered from a form of nausea just like very bad sea-sickness . . .' (Ethel Smyth, *Female Pipings in Eden*, Peter Davies, London, 1933, p. 233).

210 – The Victoria Memorial, richly embellished with female personifications by Thomas Brock, was unveiled in 1911; the Victory in a four-horse chariot on top of the Wellington Arch – a silhouette of enormous panache by Adrian Jones, captain of Hussars and qualified vet – in 1912. Edwardian London was full of these monuments; and the implications of the allegorical female figures that crown them or swoon on their pediments are discussed in detail in Warner (1985). Thomas Thorneycroft's Boadicea (1902) in a two-horse chariot on Westminster Bridge was a suffrage favourite. Copies of a drawing after the sculpture by J. Blake Wirgman (which added a banner, the scales of Justice, and an angel crowning her with laurel) were presented to each guest at the dinner presided over by Mrs Fawcett on 11 December 1906 to welcome ten released prisoners of the WSPU. (There is a copy in the Museum of London.) Dora Montefiore said she had always wanted to hold a meeting there, 'as Boadicea in her chariot always appeared to me to be advancing threateningly on the Houses of Parliament, and she was therefore a symbol of the attitude towards Parliament of us militant women' (*From a Victorian to a Modern*, E. Archer, London, 1927, p. 109).

211 – Emmeline Pankhurst, 'Why we are Militant', speech delivered at Madison Square Garden, 21 October 1913, printed by The Women's Press, London, 1913 (Fawcett Library).

212 – Reproduced in colour in John Gorman, *Images of Labour*, Scorpion Publishing, London, 1985, p. 162. Chivalric elements were conspicuous in the language and imagery of social purity movements, militant feminism and socialism, all of which used the term 'crusade'. See Gorman (1985).

213 – Maurice Agulhon discusses the same issue as it arose in the French Revolution and its aftermath in *Marianne into Battle: Republican Imagery and Symbolism in France 1789–1880* (1979), Cambridge University Press, Cambridge, 1981. See especially pp. 168, 172.

214 – See Sherry Ortner, 'Is female to male as nature is to culture' in M. Z. Rosaldo and L. Lamphere (eds), *Woman, Culture and Society*, Stanford University Press, Stanford, 1974; and for a more nuanced discussion Ludmilla Jordanova, 'Natural facts: a historical perspective on science and sexuality' in Carol MacCormack and Marilyn Strathern (eds), *Nature, Culture and Gender*, Cambridge University Press, Cambridge, 1980.

215 – Warner (1985, p. 368, note 81) notes a prescription in *Iconology* (London, 1832) that Friendship should be 'the figure of a woman, simply dressed in white, with flowing hair, and crowned with a garland of myrtle and pomegranate flowers; her breast is uncovered and her feet bare.' This casts the goddess of Socialism in a rather different light, as the embodiment of comradeship. On labour imagery see Gorman (1973 and 1985) who gives further references, and a series of articles in *History Workshop Journal* in 1978–79: Eric Hobsbawm, 'Man and Woman in Socialist Iconography', no. 6, Autumn 1978; Tim Mason, 'The Domestication of Female Socialist Icons: a note in reply to Eric Hobsbawm', no. 7, Spring 1979; Maurice Agulhon, 'On Political Allegory: a reply to Eric Hobsbawm', and Sally Alexander, Anna Davin and Eve Hostettler, 'Labouring Women: a reply to Eric Hobsbawm', no. 8, Autumn 1979. There is a riot of allegorical females in Great War imagery (Mercy, Justice, Compassion, the Great Mother, various personifications of national identity), as well as depictions of 'real' women making munitions or bidding their husbands to the front.

216 – The *Suffragette*, 9 May 1913. *Votes for Women* informed its readers of the impending beatification of Joan of Arc on 16 April 1909. The ceremony took place in Rome on the 18th, and was reported in *The Times* on the following day. Emily Wilding Davison had laid a wreath at the foot of a statue of Joan of Arc the day before she ran out on to the Derby racecourse.

217 – John Masefield, quoted by Christabel Pankhurst (1959), p. 231.

218 – G. Vaughan, *Votes for Women*, 14 April 1911.

219 – Christabel Pankhurst, the *Suffragette*, 9 May 1913. See Mrs Fawcett, quoted in Strachey (1931), p. 232: 'I never believe in the possibility of a sex war. Nature has seen after that; as long as mothers have sons and fathers daughters there can never be a sex war. What draws men and women together is stronger than the brutality and tyranny which drives them apart.'

220 – Evelyn Sharp, *Votes for Women*, 23 April 1909.

221 – Marina Warner, *Joan of Arc: The Image of Female Heroism*, Weidenfeld & Nicolson, London, 1981. I am indebted to her account.

222 – Christabel Pankhurst, the *Suffragette*, 9 May 1913.

223 – *History Workshop Journal*, no. 6 (1978), p. 135: see note 249. There are endless references to, and images and personifications of, Joan of Arc in the militant campaign.

224 – Christabel, however, did not take kindly to a constitutionalist interest in 'our patron saint', and in 1914 produced a scathing review of the appreciation published by Mrs Fawcett in 1912. Unstinted praise of the 'warrior saint', she wrote, came oddly from the lips of one who had just signed a public manifesto against militancy. See 'An Anti-Militant on Joan of Arc', the *Suffragette*, 26 June 1914. (Mrs Fawcett's pamphlet had stressed the 'special wonder' of Joan's nature, derived from the androgynous union of male and female, strength and tenderness.)

225 – *Manchester Guardian*, 17 July 1908. The Bugler Girl was borrowed for the Women's Party in the American campaign. Other figures with banners and trumpets appear in American imagery, such as the hand-painted silk banner of The Woman Suffrage Party of Manhattan. Inez Mulholland rode as Joan of Arc in processions in New York.

226 – See NUWSS Executive Committee minutes, particularly 31 July, 18 September and 16 October 1913 (Fawcett Archives, Box 83). Numerous alternatives were suggested. Mrs Watts wrote recommending G. F. Watts's painting of Faith sheathing her sword, but Mrs Fawcett did not consider it suitable.

227 – The *Common Cause*, 14 November 1913.

228 – Warner (1985), pp. 250–51.

229 – Quoted from the Pelican Freud Library, vol. 7 (1977), p. 251.

230 – For a discussion of the Amazon, the archetypal warrior woman, as a patriarchal construction and an equivocal resource for women, see Mandy Merck, 'The City's Achievements: The patriotic Amazonomachy and ancient Athens', in Sue Lipshitz (ed.), *Tearing the Veil*, Routledge & Kegan Paul, London, 1978. There are several articles on historically or mythically militant women in the suffrage press: see for example S. D. Shallard, 'Warrior Women', *Votes for Women*, 3 March 1911 (which had a drawing of Bellona, the goddess of war, on its cover). The militants sought to honour as heroines those whom *The Times* described as maenads and hysterics. Their imagery grants women the power of violence in a just cause, which offered an imaginary compensation both for the 'maiming subserviency' of upper-class womanliness and for their vulnerability on the streets. As Viscountess Rhondda recalled 'Black Friday': 'I watched the police deal with one woman in particular, twisting her arms with violence till she cried out with the pain. It was horrible. I suddenly found myself swearing aloud in the street' (*This Was My World*, Macmillan, London, 1933, pp. 166 ff.); 'maiming subserviency' is from Lady Constance Lytton's description of herself as one 'of that numerous gang of upper-class, leisured-class spinsters, unemployed, unpropertied, unendowed, uneducated ... economically dependent entirely upon others', quoted in Sylvia Pankhurst (1931), p. 332.

231 – Eliza Lynn Linton, *The Girl of the Period and Other Social Essays* (2 vols), Richard Bentley & Sons, London, 1883, vol. II, p. 110.

232 – Laurence Housman, 'What is Womanly' from *Articles of Faith in the Freedom of Women*, A. C. Fifield, 2nd ed. 1911, p. 38 (Museum of London).

233 – Louisa Thomson-Price, 'The Womanly Woman', the *Vote*, 8 October 1910, p. 286.

234 – Almroth Wright (1913), *passim*.

235 – See Ivy Pinchbeck, *Women Workers and the Industrial Revolution 1750–1850* (1930), Virago, London, 1981. Also Catherine Hall, 'The butcher, the baker, the candlestick maker: the shop and the family in the Industrial Revolution', in E. Whitelegg *et al.* (eds), *The Changing Experience of Women*, Martin Robertson, Oxford, 1982; Catherine Hall and Leonore Davidoff, 'The Architecture of Public and Private Life: English Middle-Class Society in a Provincial Town, 1780–1850' in Anthony Sutcliffe (ed.), *The Pursuit of Urban History*, Edward Arnold, London, 1983; and for the United States, Nancy Cott, *The Bonds of Womanhood: 'Woman's Sphere' in New England, 1780–1835*, Yale University Press, New Haven, 1977. Leonore Davidoff and Catherine Hall have published *Family Fortunes: Men and Women of the English Middle Class 1780–1850* (Hutchinson, London, 1987) since the completion of my text.

236 – Mary Wollstonecraft, quoted in Alice Rossi (ed.), *The Feminist Papers: From Adams to de Beauvoir* (1973), Bantam Books, New York, 1974, p. 45. The character of the ideal woman is discussed in Rousseau's *Emile* (1762), book 5.

237 – See Robert Gray, 'Bourgeois Hegemony in Victorian Britain' in Jon Bloomfield (ed.), *Class, Hegemony and Party*, Lawrence & Wishart, London, 1977.

238 – Quoted in Hall (1979), p. 29. Françoise Basch discusses the contradictory features of womanliness as both submissive and inspirational in *Relative Creatures: Victorian Women in Society and the Novel 1837–67*, Allen Lane, London, 1974 (part 1, chapter 1). Kate Millett and Carol Christ see womanliness as chiefly repressive (respectively 'The Debate over Women: Ruskin vs Mill' in Martha Vicunus (ed.) (1972); and 'Victorian Masculinity and the Angel in the House' in Vicunus (ed.), *A Widening Sphere: Changing Roles of Victorian Women*, Indiana University Press, Bloomington, 1977). For an opposing view see David Sonstroem, 'Millett versus Ruskin: A Defense of Ruskin's "Of Queens' Gardens"', *Victorian Studies* 20, 1977.

239 – John Ruskin, *Sesame and Lilies* (1865), Everyman edition, Dent, London, 1907, p. 60.

240 – Elsie Clews Parsons, *Social Rule: A Study of the Will to Power*, Putnam, New York, 1916, p. 54, quoted in Rosenberg (1982), p. 173. Parsons was on to something. The relation of 'womanliness' to shifting definitions of masculinity is important and underestimated. In *Orientalism* (p. 3) Edward Said remarks that 'European culture gained in strength and identity by setting itself off against the Orient as a sort of surrogate and even underground self.' The same could be said of nineteenth-century bourgeois masculinity. Fears for women's masculinisation (by work, by higher education or by the vote) masked fears for men's concomitant feminisation (see Peter Gabriel Filene, *Him/Her/Self: Sex Roles in Modern America* (1974), Mentor, New York, 1976, pp. 72–77). Weeks (1981, p. 40) refers to the 'construction of recognisable, and still current, definitions of masculinity' which proceeded rapidly in the last decades of the nineteenth century, with an increasing emphasis on sport and will-power in the militaristic public schools.

241 – See Ruth Bloch, 'Untangling the Roots of Modern Sex Roles: A Survey of Four Centuries of Change', and Nancy Cott, 'Passionlessness: An Interpretation of Victorian Sexual Ideology, 1790–1850', both in *Signs*, vol. 4 no. 2, Winter 1978 (and both of which give detailed references); Mary Poovey, *The Proper Lady and the Woman Writer*, University of Chicago Press, Chicago and London, 1984; and Catherine Hall, 'The Early Formation of Victorian Domestic Ideology' in S. Burman (ed.), *Fit Work for Women*, Croom Helm, London, 1979.

242 – See F. K. Prochaska, *Women and Philanthropy in Nineteenth-Century England*, Clarendon, Oxford, 1980. Lynda Nead discusses the visual construction of 'womanliness' in works such as George Elgar Hicks's 'Woman's Mission' in *Representation and Regulation: Women and Sexuality in English Art c. 1840–1870*, PhD thesis, University College London, 1985. See also Deborah Cherry, 'Picturing the Private Sphere', *Feminist Art News*, no. 9, 1983.

243 – See Cynthia White, *Women's Magazines 1693–1968*, Michael Joseph, London, 1970; and Marjorie Ferguson, *Forever Feminine: Women's Magazines and the Cult of Femininity*, Heinemann, London, 1983.

244 – Strachey (1928), p. 78.

245 – Sarah Lewis, 'Woman's Mission' (1839) in Janet Horowitz Murray *Strong-Minded Women and Other Lost Voices from Nineteenth-Century England*, Penguin, London, 1984, pp. 23–24.

246 – Jane Harrison, 'Homo Sum: Being a Letter to an Anti-Suffragist from an Anthropologist', NUWSS, c. 1912, p. 6 (Fawcett Library).

247 – Hamilton (1909), 1981, p. 86.

248 – George Gissing, *The Odd Women* (1893), Virago, London, 1980, p. 136.

249 – Louisa Thomson-Price, the *Vote*, 8 October 1910, p. 286. The metaphor, which Wollstonecraft uses in the *Vindication*, is a familiar one in Victorian imagery.

250 – Laurence Housman, *Articles of Faith in the Freedom of Women*, A. C. Fifield, 2nd ed. 1911, pp. 40, 42.

251 – Elsie Clews Parsons, *Old Fashioned Woman* (p. 210) and *Social Rule: A Study of the Will to Power* (p. 55), quoted in Rosenberg (1982), p. 172.

252 – The *Vote*, 8 October 1910, p. 286.

253 – Quoted by Herbert van Thal in *Eliza Lynn Linton: The Girl of the Period*, George Allen & Unwin, London, 1979, pp. 46–47. The womanly woman 'knows that she was designed by the needs of the race and the law of nature to be a mother; sent into the world for that purpose mainly; and she knows that rational maternity means more than simply giving life and then leaving it to others to preserve it . . . she thinks a populous and happy nursery one of the greatest blessings of her state' (*The Girl of the Period*, quoted Hollis, p. 20). See also Marie Corelli: 'Shall we sacrifice our Womanhood to Politics? Shall we make a holocaust of maidens, wives and mothers on the brazen altars of Party? Shall we throw open the once sweet and sacred homes of England to the manoeuvres of the electioneering agent? Surely the best and bravest of us will answer No! – ten thousand times no!' ('Woman – or Suffragette: A Question of National

Choice', Arthur Pearson, London, 1907, Museum of London).

254 – *Emile*, book 1 (1762), quoted Rozsika Parker, *The Subversive Stitch*, The Women's Press, London, 1984, p. 128.

255 – See Walkowitz (1980), p. 117.

256 – See pamphlet 'Mother's Day Sunday May 14th Normal Park Presbyterian Church, Chicago' (Museum of London). On social or 'civic' motherhood see Lewis (1984), pp. 92–97.

257 – Mrs Fawcett, letter in the *Daily Graphic*, undated cutting from her scrapbook in the Fawcett Library.

258 – Mrs Gerald Paget, 'Good Motherhood', *Votes for Women*, 13 January 1911. She lists four needs: the interests of the mother first, not last, in the state; the triple burden of the woman worker lightened; adequate protection for young girls; and the rescue of home and nursery from legislative domination by one sex.

259 – The *Vote* (13 May 1911) quoted with approval the slogan on a New York suffrage banner: 'We prepare children for the world; let us prepare the world for the children'. Arguments like these were intended to refute the claims of antis such as Almroth Wright ('the happy wife and mother is never passionately concerned about the suffrage') and Professor A. V. Dicey (that women's private virtues were defects in public life; see A. V. Dicey, *Letters to a Friend on Votes for Women*, John Murray, London, 1909). '[Ours] is also the demand that the mother-half of humanity should be given its proper place: that the preserver and producer of life, the maker of men, should be as highly honoured as the destroyer of life, the maker of things' (the *Common Cause*, 15 April 1909).

260 – 'The ABC of Women's Suffrage', the *Common Cause*, 12 September 1913. More than anything else, and especially on processions, feminists had to bear the brunt of calls to get the dinner / mind the baby / make the old man's tea. These rose spontaneously, and out of a sexual indignation so strong that the humour in a London cabbie instructing the mature and dignified figure of Lady Strachey, seventy years old and mother of ten, to go home and mind the baby was often lost on the assembled crowds. The Museum of London has an anti-suffrage postcard addressed to 'Miss Pankhurst and her Crew' inscribed, 'You set of sickening fools – if you have no homes no husbands – no children – no decent [crossed out] relations – why dont you drown yourselves out of the way?' (sic).

261 – Annie G. Porritt, 'Votes and Babies', 1912 (New York Public Library, SNSP vol. 11 no. 17). See also Annie G. Porritt, 'The Political Duties of Mothers', National American Woman Suffrage Association (New York Public Library SNS p vol. 11 no. 26); and NUWSS leaflets B44 'Women in the Home' (undated), B105 'Parliament and Wives and Mothers' (1913), B106 'Parliament and Moral Reform' (1913) (Fawcett Library), E3 'Votes for Mothers' (1913) (Bodleian Library, John Johnson Collection).

262 – In *Life Errant* (Dent, London, 1935), Cicely Hamilton claimed that she worked for the vote not because she believed in counting female noses at elections, but because the agitation would inevitably shake the foundations of a 'normal' (maternal, dependent) femininity.

263 – See Steve Neale, 'Propaganda', *Screen*, Autumn 1977, p. 34 note 4: 'Generally speaking, propaganda is produced as an intervention from a particular apparatus . . . [in this case the constituent organisations of the suffrage campaign]. The "we" – "you" structure of its address is thus frequently one in which the "we" is identified with a particular apparatus, which in turn claims to represent "you", the audience.' What I am arguing here is that 'we' represented not 'suffragists' but womanliness.

264 – 'The Home or the Street Corner for Women', Tom Harper, reproduced by Paula Harper in H. Millon and N. Nochlin (eds), *Art and Architecture in the Service of Politics*, MIT Press, Boston, 1978.

265 – Quoted from *The Times*, 1871, by Walter Arnstein in 'Votes for Women: Myths and Reality', *History Today* 8, 1968, p. 533.

266 – See Annie Porritt, 'The Political Duties of Mothers' (note 262), for a formulation of the suffrage demand entirely within the bounds of domesticity. 'The newer suffrage movement . . . has its origin in the home. It is the demand of the normal home-making woman for a chance to do her duty effectually and fully. It is not so much a demand for woman's rights as it is a demand for opportunity that she may perform her duty. It is not a demand put forward for the sake of exceptional or abnormal women; it is a demand of the mother, the wife, the home-maker – of the normal woman doing the work that throughout the ages has been held to be peculiarly the province of womanhood. It is true that the modern suffrage movement, like the earlier movement, is a movement of discontent and dissatisfaction. It is an uprising of the women in the homes against conditions which degrade the home, and make the fulfilment of home duties extremely difficult and sometimes impossible. But it is not a movement of discontent with home life or with home duties in themselves. It does not represent any desire of women to desert the home, and it does not indicate any feeling of antagonism between women and men, or any desire of women to encroach on any department of life which is essentially masculine. The modern suffragist is far more emphatic than her "anti"-sister in asserting that the place of the women is the home, and that the work and functions of men and women are different. It is upon these two facts that she bases her claim to a vote.'

267 – On angels see Fritz Saxl, 'Continuity and Variation in the Meaning of Images', *A Heritage of Images: A Selection of Lectures by Fritz Saxl*, Peregrine Books, London, 1970, pp. 21–26, and Warner (1985), especially p. 138; and on virtues, Warner (1985), chapter 4.

268 – The *Suffragette*, 26 December 1913. The Sistine Madonna was no casual invocation of maternal womanliness: phrenology had already claimed to connect the features of a Raphael madonna with the attributes of an idealised femininity. 'The head of the Virgin is a perfect model of female loveliness. The anterior lobe is fully developed, the lower ridge and middle-perpendicular portions (constituting the observing and practical organs) predominating. The coronal (or moral) region is large . . . [there is] a large development of the organs of Adhesiveness and Philoprogenitiveness, with small Amativeness . . .' George Combe, *Phrenology Applied to Painting and Sculpture*, Simpkin, Marshall & Co., London, 1855.

269 – Class was one of the points at issue, since the features of womanliness were linked with a middle-class ideal and, to some extent, with the privileges of a middle-class life. The poor both looked different and were perceived as different: they tended to be smaller, more toil-worn, with cast-off clothing that fitted badly. Leonore Davidoff has drawn attention to the late-Victorian health visitor who noted that cast-offs fitted even worse because the rich *perceived* the poor as having large hands and feet. They therefore passed on boots that were too large, and so their perceptions appeared to be confirmed (Davidoff, 'Class and Gender in Victorian England' in Judith Newton, Mary Ryan and Judith Walkowitz (eds), *Sex and Class in Women's History*, Routledge & Kegan Paul, London, 1983, p. 69 note 74). The classed distinction between womanliness and unwomanliness is evident in Bernard Partridge's 'Shrieking Sister' for *Punch* (17 January 1906). Uncouth and ungainly hands and feet are prominent in anti-suffrage depictions of feminists who are at the same time unsexed and declassed: 'And You, in this disconsolate London square / Flaunting an ill-considered purple hat / And mud-stained, rumpled, bargain-counter coat, / You of the broken tooth and buttered hair, / And idiot eye and cheeks that bulge with fat, / Sprawl on the flagstones chalking for a vote!' (T. H. Crosland, 'Votes for Women', 1908, quoted in C. Willett Cunnington, *Women*, Burke, London, 1950, p. 218). The heroic peasants of Sylvia Pankhurst's WSPU membership card were intended to serve against the depiction of working-class women as parodies of womanliness on the one hand or as womanly victims on the other.

270 – The *Vote*, 12 March 1910, p. 237: 'The new series . . . will, we believe, fill a long-felt want. The man-in-the-street who, with hoarse reiterance, tells us to "go home and mind the baby", to "do the washing", to "get the dinner", and to indulge in other domesticities is now provided with an opportunity of seeing us engaged in these labours.' The photographs appeared between March and May 1910.

271 – Dr William Acton, *Prostitution*, John Churchill, London, 1857, p. 1, citing the *Quarterly Review*, September 1848, p. 359.

272 – On the politics of sexuality in the Edwardian period see Weeks (1981), especially chapters 7–10; Lucy Bland, '"Cleansing the portals of life": the venereal disease campaign in the early twentieth century' and Frank Mort, 'Purity, feminism and the state: sexuality and moral politics, 1880–1914' in Mary Langan and Bill Schwarz (eds), *Crises in the British State 1880–1930*, Hutchinson, London, 1985; and Lucy Bland, 'Marriage Laid Bare: Middle-Class Women and Marital Sex *c.* 1880–1914' in Jane Lewis (ed.), *Labour and Love: Women's Experience of Home and Family 1850–1940*, Basil Blackwell, Oxford, 1986. (I am very grateful to Lucy Bland and to Frank Mort for letting me see their papers in typescript.) Lynda Nead has written extensively on high art representations of sexuality in the Victorian period. Her use of 'moral panic' theory seems to me quite as applicable (and possibly more so) to the years before 1914. See 'A Definition of Deviancy: Prostitution and High Art in England *c.* 1860' in *Block* 11, Winter 1985/86, which draws on Stanley Cohen, *Folk Devils and Moral Panics* (MacGibbon &

Kee, London, 1972), to argue that the prostitute functioned as a 'folk devil' on to whom anxieties provoked by social crises could be displaced.

273 – On the Contagious Diseases Acts and the campaigns surrounding them, see Judith Walkowitz's excellent study, *Prostitution and Victorian Society: Women, Class and the State*, Cambridge University Press, Cambridge, 1980. The Contagious Diseases Acts of 1864, 1866 and 1869 'were introduced as exceptional legislation to control the spread of venereal disease among enlisted men in garrison towns and ports' (pp. 1–2). By 1869 they had provided the impetus for new medical institutions, and new precedents for police and medical intervention into the lives of the 'unrespectable' poor (p. 88). They were suspended in 1883 and repealed, after a sixteen-year campaign, in 1886. Walkowitz outlines (p. 117) the relations between the repealers and other feminist campaigns of the 1870s and 1880s; and summarises (p. 255) the importance of the example of the repeal campaign for Edwardian suffragists.

274 – Linklater (1980, pp. 160–62) summarises the findings of the WFL watch committees on the courts (one man received nine months' jail for the manslaughter of his wife and another received four months for baby battering – the baby died; while a woman received three years' penal servitude for stealing a watch and chain). He also quotes a remark by the Recorder of Sandwich suggesting that an attack on a little girl was not an ordinary crime like theft but one which 'the most respectable man might fall into'. The exposure of such inequalities was one of the suffragists' strongest weapons against the argument that men's chivalry was adequate protection for women. See also Sheila Jeffreys, *The Spinster and Her Enemies: Feminism and Sexuality 1880–1930*, Pandora Press, London, 1985, pp. 54–65; and the 1913 NUWSS pamphlet 'Parliament and Moral Reform' (Fawcett Library) which claimed that indecent assault on children under sixteen was treated more lightly than offences involving property of the value of £2 and upwards.

275 – Dora Marsden, a disillusioned member of the WSPU, provided the impetus behind the *Freewoman*, which first appeared in November 1911, and which became the principal outlet for minority feminist debates on women's personal freedom and sexual autonomy. It was co-edited by Dora Marsden and Mary Gawthorpe. There is an advance notice for it in Fawcett Archives Box 148. See also Ellen Carol Dubois and Linda Gordon, 'Seeking Ecstasy on the Battlefield: Danger and Pleasure in Nineteenth-Century Feminist Sexual Thought', *Feminist Studies*, vol. 9 no. 1, Spring 1983. 'Slow atrophy' is from F. Stella Browne, 'Some Problems of Sex', *International Journal of Ethics*, July 1917.

276 – The *Suffragette*, 25 July–26 September 1913. Discussed in Rosen (1974), and more sympathetically in Jeffreys (1985), and Bland in Lewis (ed.) (1986). *The Great Scourge* was a less isolated text in 1913 – in content and tone – than it has since appeared. Discoveries made around the turn of the century indicated that venereal disease, particularly gonorrhoea which was often undiagnosed in women, was the cause of widespread ill-health in wives infected by their husbands. Christabel claimed medical authority for the assertion that 75 per cent to

80 per cent of men had contracted gonorrhoea and 20 per cent to 25 per cent syphilis before marriage, and that 'out of every four men there is only one who can marry without risk to his bride.' Cooler perspectives like Cicely Hamilton's still presented *Marriage as a Trade* (1909), and prostitution as the paradigm for the condition of economically dependent women within it.

277 – Emmeline Pankhurst, 'Why we are Militant', a speech delivered in New York, 21 October 1913, printed by The Women's Press (Fawcett Library).

278 – Teresa Billington-Greig, 'The Truth about White Slavery', *English Review*, June 1913, quoted by Frank Mort in Langan and Schwarz (eds) (1985), p. 222.

279 – On the White Slave Traffic see Edward Bristow, *Vice and Vigilance: Purity Movements in Britain since 1700*, Gill & Macmillan, Dublin, 1977, pp. 171–94; Walkowitz (1980); Banks (1981), chapter 5; Mort (note 273). The 1913 NUWSS pamphlet 'White Slave Traffic' defined it as 'a world-wide trade in young girls for immoral purposes, out of which enormous profits are made'. The picture it painted was one of seduction or entrapment of young British girls, 'girls just like your own daughters', sold into foreign brothels and condemned to violence, sickness, and an early grave. This was almost certainly exaggerated, but it owed a great deal to the details of white slavery and child prostitution scandals as they had been rehearsed in social purity crusades since the early 1880s and particularly to W. T. Stead's articles on 'The Maiden Tribute of Modern Babylon' published in 1885.

280 – Sylvia Pankhurst (1931), pp. 522–23.

281 – Walkowitz (1980), chapter 1.

282 – William Tait, quoted in Walkowitz (1980), p. 13. On the prostitute in high art see Lynda Nead (*Oxford Art Journal*, vol. 7 no. 1, 1984; PhD thesis 1985; *Block*, no. 11, Winter 1985–86).

283 – Ruskin, *Sesame and Lilies* (1865), 1907, p. 59. Coventry Patmore's 'Angel in the House' (1855–56) sold a quarter of a million copies in forty years.

284 – George Barlow, 'Why I Oppose Woman Suffrage' (Fawcett Archives, Box 298).

285 – Nina Auerbach, *Woman and the Demon: The Life of a Victorian Myth*, Harvard University Press, Cambridge MA, 1982, p. 218.

286 – See Cicely Hamilton (1909), p. 122: 'Economic pressure and the law of self-preservation produced the "womanly woman"; now, from the "womanly woman" economic pressure and the law of self-preservation are producing a new type . . .'

287 – Jordanova (1980), p. 64.

288 – Frank Burton, *Official Discourse: on discourse analysis, government publications and the state*, Routledge & Kegan Paul, London, 1979, p. 19.

5 EPILOGUE

1 – Pugh, *Electoral Reform in War and Peace 1906–18* (1978), chapter X, is excellent, and detailed on parliamentary developments. I am indebted to his account. Rosen (1974), Hume (1982) and other histories of the campaign offer concluding chapters on 'the war and after'. See also Arthur Marwick, *The Deluge: British Society and the First World War*, New York, 1965, pp. 87–94, and Marwick's *Women at War 1914–1918*, Fontana, London, 1977 (though there are some inaccuracies).

2 – Circular letter from the NUWSS Executive, 6 August 1914 (quoted Hume, 1982, p. 222), and LSWS *Annual Report*, 1914 (quoted Hume, 1982, p. 222).

3 – See the NUWSS leaflet *War-Time Work in the National Union* (Fawcett Library) for details; information on the Women's Emergency Corps (involving Emmeline Pethick-Lawrence and Mrs Kineton Parkes, late of the Women's Tax Resistance League) in the Maud Arncliffe-Sennett collection, vol. 24, between pp. 50 and 51; 'Women's Service' organised by the LSWS (leaflet in the Fawcett Archives, Box 145), which appeals for a further £10,000, in part to develop the Women's Service workshops to train educated women in elementary education and oxyacetylene welding (Mary Lowndes was involved in establishing these and Ray Strachey reproduces a photograph of the Women Welders' School in *Women's Suffrage and Women's Service*, London and National Society for Women's Service, London, 1927); the NUWSS *Annual Report and Statement of Accounts*, 1916; Ray Strachey, *Millicent Garrett Fawcett* (1931), pp. 276 ff., and the *Annual Report of the Play Department of the Actresses' Franchise League*, 20 October 1916 (Fawcett Library). John Grigg notes that fewer than 400,000 additional women took jobs in industry in the first year of the war, but that between July 1915 and the end of the war another 1,250,000 were recruited, most strikingly in industries with no recent tradition of female employment (*Lloyd George: From Peace to War 1912–16*, Methuen, London, 1985).

4 – Sylvia Pankhurst (1931), p. 593; Liddington and Norris (1978), p. 253. The Women's Freedom League, the United Suffragists and Sylvia Pankhurst's Workers' Suffrage Federation continued – discreetly – to work for the vote.

5 – Sylvia Pankhurst (1931), pp. 592–95 (quotation p. 595).

6 – Copies of this circular letter have survived in various collections, including that of the Imperial War Museum. It is reprinted in Mackenzie (ed.) (1975), p. 282. It emphasises at the same time the 'feminine' virtues that will end bloodshed once they are incorporated into the state, and the militant *feminist* attributes of patriotism, courage and endurance that will win the current war.

7 – The WSPU was quick to adapt its militant and crusading rhetoric to a new enemy and realign itself with the men of its own nation, who were offered the chance to redeem themselves in battle. Christabel announced in the *Suffragette* on 7 August 1914 that, 'This great war is nature's vengeance . . . God's vengeance upon the people who held women in subjection'; and in a speech at Plymouth on 17 November 1914 Mrs Pankhurst remarked that, 'The war has made me feel how much there is of nobility in man, in addition to the other thing which we all deplore' (quoted Pugh, 1978, p. 137). Joan of Arc, 'The Great Militant' on the cover of the *Suffragette* in 1914, had become Joan 'The Great Patriot' by 1915 (a shift to which David Doughan of the Fawcett Library first drew my attention).

8 – Sylvia Pankhurst (1931), p. 595: '"Women would stand for

peace!" How often, how often had they and all of us averred it!'
9 – Ada Nield Chew, quoted in Liddington and Norris (1978), p. 257.
10 – Broadly speaking, the WSPU leadership and members loyal to it, together with Blatchford and Hyndman among the socialists, allied themselves with the government in the active prosecution of the war. The leadership of the WSPU became 'The Women's Party' from its announcement in *Britannia* on 2 November 1917 (for its programme, a curious blend of national socialism and reactionary, anti-trade-union elements, see 'The Women's Party: Victory, National Security and Progress', Fawcett Library). Sylvia Pankhurst and the Workers' Suffrage Federation, Mrs Pethick-Lawrence, a breakaway group from the WSPU, and those who seceded from the NUWSS in April 1915 joined the Women's International League for Peace and Freedom or were committed to pacifism as individuals. (From 1917 Charlotte Despard decided to work for the Women's Peace Crusade, but her executive committee was anxious to distinguish this from the official stance of the WFL.) Mrs Fawcett and the remaining members of the NUWSS adopted a middle road. The NUWSS dissociated itself from anti-war propaganda, but also from the militant stance of the WSPU. Pugh (1978) argues that, 'It was greatly to the advantage of the women that during the first three years of the war no major branch of their movement had become associated with the cause of a negotiated peace, though many individual members had devoted themselves to it. Anti-suffragists in Parliament were only too anxious to deploy the argument that women as voters would hinder governments from waging war.'
11 – Cited in Pugh (1980), p. 30 and Pugh (1978), p. 144. He suggests that the extent of women's war work was easily exaggerated in the press, which looked to it for copy, and that the most dramatic increase was in munitions factories. The important point for the campaign, however, was precisely that of press representation and its impact on the public mind. The NUWSS *Annual Report and Statement of Accounts* for 1916 (Fawcett Archives, Box 152) noted with satisfaction 'speaking generally the press has made a complete *volte face*': 'The virtues of the woman war worker have been extolled to the skies, notably the munition workers; every "new" occupation which women have taken up has been carefully recorded, and papers which were formerly anti-feminist in tone have vied with each other in pointing out the value and the necessity of women's work to the nation' (p. 32). It instanced the articles on 'Women in Industry' in *The Times* on 24, 26, 31 May and 7 June and a second series on 'Women and War Work' on 3, 4 and 5 October 1916, as well as publications from the War Office and the Ministry of Munitions.
12 – *Daily Sketch*, 23 March 1915, p. 4: 'We cannot doubt that it is part of the German policy to hold and maintain a low conception of the status of women . . . The German is all for the man-State.'
13 – Lloyd George papers D/17/5/2 (quoted Rosen (1974), p. 252).
14 – Christabel Pankhurst (1959), pp. 289–91.
15 – See the *Programme* of the procession (Fawcett Library):

'The motive is an inspiring one, and its appeal includes women who are not actively concerned with the question of "women's rights" in ordinary circumstances.' Rosen (1974, pp. 253–54) notes that there were protests by some members and ex-members of the WSPU against the use of its name and platform in this connection.
16 – Christabel Pankhurst (1959), pp. 289–91.
17 – Imperial War Museum f/EMP/13/2. Lord Northcliffe, a belated convert to the women's cause, gave the plans for the procession valuable publicity.
18 – The following account is drawn from contemporary press reports, chiefly those in *The Times, Daily Telegraph, Daily Chronicle, Daily Mail, Daily News* and *Manchester Guardian* (all 19 July 1915), the *Observer* (18 July 1915) and the *Weekly Dispatch* (18 July 1915). See also the *Suffragette* (16 July 1915) and the *Souvenir of the Programme. Women's Great Patriotic Procession and Route in London. For the Right to Work* (Fawcett Library).
19 – *Manchester Guardian.*
20 – *Daily Telegraph.*
21 – *Manchester Guardian. The Times* remarked that it 'was a strange sight to see Mr Lloyd George fraternizing with Mrs Pankhurst; it was as if Daniel had invited the lion to his den.'
22 – *Observer.*
23 – *Daily Telegraph* and the *Daily News*. Lloyd George's powerful turn of phrase was widely reported: 'The women of this country can help, and help enormously. I believe they can help us through to victory. Without them victory will tarry, and victory which tarries means victory whose footprints are the footprints of blood' (*Daily Chronicle*).
24 – *The Times.*
25 – The *Herald*, 24 July 1915. On another page of the same issue the *Herald* reprinted a letter from Margaret Llewelyn Davies to the *Daily News* which exposed the unequal reality behind the 'women of every condition united' canvassed by the 'Right to Serve' procession.
26 – In a speech at the London Pavilion on 5 October 1915, Mrs Pankhurst insisted that 'in a time of national crisis like this, all the old prejudices must go and all the old rules and regulations must go' (quoted in Mackenzie, 1975, p. 294).
27 – In September Lloyd George issued a statement from the War Office urging employers to further efforts in the training and employment of women. In a chilling euphemism he drew their attention to the 'necessity of replacing wastage in our Armies' which would 'eventually compel the release of all men who can be replaced by women' (quoted in Mackenzie, 1975, p. 306).
28 – Strachey (1928), p. 340, points out that the Annual Reports of the Chief Inspector of Factories and Workshops, the Report of the War Cabinet Committee on Women in Industry, and the Home Office Report on the Substitution of Women for Men during the War 'justify the use of superlatives'. But see Laurence Housman (1937), p. 297: 'Voteless women, we were told, were not responsible for the mess men had made of things in a man-governed world; and would, when political power was

given them, guide our feet into the way of peace . . . All that went in a day.'

29 – And traditional representations of women as wives and mothers continued to be used alongside the newer and less familiar images: 'Women of Britain Say "Go"' and 'The Great Mother'.

30 – Mrs Fawcett, quoted in Liddington and Norris (1978), p. 253.

31 – Sylvia Pankhurst (1931), p. 601; Pugh (1978), p. 143.

32 – The *Anti-Suffrage Review*, quoted Pugh (1978), p. 139.

33 – See the N U W S S *Annual Report and Statement of Accounts* for 1916, pp. 32–33 (Fawcett Archives, Box 152). Also Violet Markham's letter to Lord Cromer, 2 November 1916: 'I cannot pretend that the experience of the war has left me unmoved as to the principle of women's suffrage. Even without the modifications of opinion which have answer in my own mind I should not be optimistic as to the practical possibility of sustained opposition in the future' (Markham papers, British Library of Political and Economic Science).

34 – 14 August 1916, quoted in Rosen (1974), pp. 258–59.

35 – Pugh (1978, p. 74) gives the membership of the Speaker's Conference and its various allegiances, together with an account of its deliberations and report.

36 – 28 March 1917, quoted in Rosen (1974), pp. 262–63.

37 – The women did not wish to compromise their success in capturing the 'patriotic' stance by raising the divisive question of female suffrage, and the government was equally anxious to avoid the resurrection of militant or any other activity that might threaten national unity.

38 – Sylvia Pankhurst (1931), p. 607.

39 – Strachey, *Millicent Garrett Fawcett* (1931), pp. 315–16.

40 – By which point women in New Zealand (1893), Australia (1902), Finland (1906), Norway (1913), Denmark (1915) and the U S S R (1917) already had the vote. Canada (1918) and Germany, Austria, the Netherlands, Poland and Czechoslovakia (1919) followed. A number of American states beginning with Wyoming (1869) had granted women the vote before the passage of a Federal Amendment in 1920.

41 – Sylvia Pankhurst (1931), p. 608.

42 – N U W S S *Programme*, 13 March 1918 (Bodleian Library, John Johnson Collection, Women's Suffrage, Box 1). See also Fawcett Archives, Box 152, which contains Mary Lowndes's proposals for decorations to celebrate the granting of the equal franchise in 1928 (dated 30 November 1927).

43 – Or the hotly debated question of the part their war work played in gaining it. Newspaper placards announced the passage of the bill with the phrase 'The Nation Thanks the Women', and the war was the reason most often given by opponents who changed their minds. It could be said to have been the catalyst which precipitated a whole series of factors, which operating together with the gains of the pre-war campaign transformed the climate in which women's suffrage became a parliamentary issue once more. The suffragists had come close to attaining their goal on several occasions before 1914, and the obstacles which baulked them then – party divisions, Asquith's intransigence and competition from the struggle with the Lords or for

Home Rule – were more effectively smoothed by factors outside the campaign than they were amenable to suffrage leverage directly. Pugh (1978) argues that in 1918 'the suffragist majority of what was still the Parliament of 1910 was at last harnessed to a measure which the government wanted to enact.' Others (including Lord Fenner Brockway) believed that women would have won the vote in the new Parliament due to be elected under normal circumstances in 1915 (largely because of the dedicated propaganda activities of the N U W S S). The W S P U version assumed that 'by its pre-war crusade for the Vote, followed by its patriotic stand and national service during the War, [the W S P U] has won the greatest political victory on record' (circular letter from the Women's Party, 23 February 1918, with the names of Flora Drummond and Annie Kenney, Fawcett Archives, Box 226); but then the W S P U was engaged in a struggle not only for the vote but for priority in the suffrage campaign and pre-eminence in its histories.

44 – Sylvia Pankhurst (1931), p. 608.

45 – In the Imperial War Museum, Suffrage and Politics, Box III 148/13, together with letter from Edith How-Martyn to Miss Conway, 18 June 1919.

46 – In a reprise of its cartoon of 'The Angel in the House' (1884), *Punch* apologised for the vinegary spinster of its predictions ('The Penitent', 10 December 1919). The wealthy, stylish and attractive Lady Astor was not *that*.

APPENDIX 7

1 – On the American campaign see Ida Husted Harper, *A History of Woman Suffrage*, vol. 5: 1900–1920 (1922), Arno and the *New York Times*, New York, 1969; Eleanor Flexner, *Century of Struggle: The Woman's Rights Movement in the United States*, Atheneum, New York, 1974; and Aileen Kraditor, *The Ideas of the Woman Suffrage Movement, 1890–1920*, Columbia University Press, New York, 1965. See also Harriot Stanton Blatch and Alma Lutz, *Challenging Years: The Memoirs of Harriot Stanton Blatch*, G. Putnam's Sons, New York, 1940; Inez Haynes Irwin, *The Story of the Woman's Party*, Harcourt Brace, New York, 1921; and Doris Stevens, *Jailed for Freedom*, Liveright Publishing Co., New York, 1920.

2 – At the 1903 N A W S A convention, Edwin Merrick spoke of the crime of enfranchising 'a horde of ignorant Negro men when at that time there were nearly 4 million intelligent white women keenly alive to the interests of their country to whom the ballot was denied' (quoted in Harper, 1969, p. 80).

3 – Mrs Pankhurst (1914, p. 37) claimed that the founding of the W S P U in 1903 was partly inspired by a visit of Susan B. Anthony to Manchester in 1902. She made three highly publicised trips to the United States in 1909, 1911 and 1913. Elizabeth Robins, the American actress and writer on the W S P U committee, provided introductions to her sister-in-law Margaret Dreier Robins, the head of the Women's Trade Union League (see Jane Marcus, 'Transatlantic Sisterhood: Labor and Suffrage Links in the Letters of Elizabeth Robins and Emmeline Pankhurst', *Signs*, vol. 3 no. 31, 1978). Robins herself published essay after essay on British militancy in the

American press, many of which are collected in *Way Stations*, Hodder & Stoughton, London, 1913.

4 – Carrie Chapman Catt referred to England as the 'storm-centre' of the movement in her presidential address to the Congress of the International Woman Suffrage Alliance in London in 1909 (Fawcett Library, Personal Authors A–C). So did Alice Paul, who spoke on 'the English situation' at the annual NAWSA convention of 1910.

5 – Sylvia Pankhurst (1931), pp. 346–50.

6 – See the NUWSS Executive Committee minutes, 15 October 1913 (Fawcett Archives, Box 301).

7 – Banners designed by the Artists' Suffrage League in commemoration of Elizabeth Cady Stanton, Susan B. Anthony and Lucy Stone were carried in the 1908 procession. Carrie Chapman Catt had wanted to produce a version of the Pageant of Women's Trades and Professions in New York.

8 – Reported in the *Vote*, 13 May 1911: 'A large number of very beautiful banners were carried at the head of the various contingents, the first in the parade bearing the words, "We prepare children for the world; let us prepare the world for the children".' There are (chiefly typographical) banners in the Smithsonian Institute and in the Schlesinger Library at Radcliffe College; and an important collection of 'professional' banners, appliquéd in felt, in the Connecticut State Library, Hartford.

9 – Harriot Stanton Blatch (1940, p. 136) describes how the name of her organisation was changed in 1910 to the Women's Political Union, and 'the usual yellow of suffrage organisations' changed to purple, white and green, to 'show the public there was to be a change in suffrage method'. The colours were to stand for new techniques 'such as pageants and parades, outdoor meetings – in short, for all those picturesque forms of propaganda the origin and development of which we owe entirely to the militants of England' (p. 204). The colours of NAWSA were blue and gold. Those of Alice Paul's National Women's Party were purple, gold and white.

10 – Laurence Housman (1937, pp. 269–70) gives an amusing account of how Alice Paul padded herself against rough handling by the police on a London demonstration, and of how 'the buttons (strained beyond endurance) broke from their moorings in swift succession, and the padding like the entrails of some woolly monster emerged roll upon roll.'

11 – The National Women's Party papers are in the Library of Congress Manuscript Division. They include a great deal of correspondence and the detailed plan of march for the Washington demonstration (3 March 1913), together with papers relating to the 'disgraceful and riotous scenes' that disrupted it and the inactivity of the police (NWP Correspondence 1877–1916, Box 1 Folder 12). Hundreds of costumes were designed for the occasion by an experienced suffragist (Mrs Patricia Street), and manufactured at two dollars a piece by John Langley Lanzilotti, who made costumes for the Manhattan Opera Company. There are photographs of various American demonstrations in the Smithsonian Institute (Department of Political History), the Library of Congress and the New York Historical Society.

12 – Harper (1969, p. 367) quotes Lucy Burns's report to the NAWSA convention of 1913: 'We are "news" as we have never been before.' Relations between NAWSA and its Congressional Committee were strained despite the success of the demonstration, and by 1913 Alice Paul had made the Congressional Union (later the National Women's Party) a separate, and militant, organisation.

13 – See the *Catalogue and Price List of Woman Suffrage Literature and Supplies*, NAWSA (undated, Smithsonian Institute, Division of Political History 1979.0939), which offers a dozen imported English posters ($1.25 each) and a dozen postcards (three cents each, $1.50 per 100). A very wide range of suffrage literature and imagery produced in England has settled into American collections as a consequence of donations and bequests.

14 – See letter to the author from Rebecca Reyher, 9 October 1984: 'Posters or printed material were expensive and were not often issued – except to announce specific meetings.' (Rebecca Reyher entered the suffrage campaign about 1916–17 and became head of the New York Office of the National Women's Party. I am grateful to her for replying to my queries, and to Amelia Fry for putting me in touch with her.)

15 – NAWSA had an Art Publicity Committee and Mrs Grace Thompson Seton reported on its work to the convention of 1916 (Harper, 1969, p. 493): '[She] told of the prizes that had been offered for posters and slogans and the cooperation of men and women prominent in the literary, artistic and social world; of the "teas" given at the national headquarters ... of the beautiful banners and costumes designed for the suffrage parades and other features of this somewhat neglected side of the work for woman suffrage.' Harper also mentions a poster competition in 1917 (p. 532) which closed with an exhibition that opened at NAWSA headquarters and toured other cities. About 100 posters were submitted and $500 awarded in prizes.

16 – The closest parallels are between images like 'American Woman and her Political Peers' (1893, reproduced in Harper, 1975, fig. 11) and Edwyn Llewellyn's '*This* is allowed to vote ...' (1907, John Johnson Collection, Bodleian Library). 'Polling Station' is discreet in its comparison of middle-class women and working-class men, and 'It is Time I Got Out of this Place' probably less contentious in placing the graduate among her convict and lunatic 'political peers'.

LIST OF ILLUSTRATIONS

BLACK AND WHITE ILLUSTRATIONS IN THE TEXT

1 Sylvia Pankhurst in her studio. (Pankhurst Collection, Institute for Social Research, Amsterdam)
2 Marion Wallace Dunlop carrying the stamp with which she printed part of the Bill of Rights on the wall inside the House of Commons, 21 June 1909. (Nurse Pine Collection, Museum of London)
3 'Political Help': winner of the NUWSS/Artists' Suffrage League poster competition in 1907. Designed by Dora Meeson Coates, printed by Weiners, published by the NUWSS in 1908. (Library of Congress)
4 Drawing for 'Handicapped': one of a series in Duncan Grant's sketchbook for 1909. (By kind permission of Richard Shone)
5 The Suffrage Atelier Broadsheet, 1913. (Museum of London)
6 Edith Craig. (Private collection)
7 'Votes for Women (Bogies)': poster, anon., Suffrage Atelier. Undated. (Museum of London)
8 Sylvia Pankhurst, WSPU membership card, c. 1905. (Museum of London)
9 Sylvia Pankhurst working on the murals for the Prince's Skating Rink Exhibition, 1909. (Communist Party Archives)
10 'Franchise Villa': poster, anon., Suffrage Atelier. Undated. (Museum of London)
11 'Asquith, Traitor to Liberal Principles': poster, designed by Jessica Walters of the Suffrage Atelier, c. 1913. (Museum of London)
12 Walter Crane, 'A Garland for May Day 1895'. (Courtesy of Isobel Spencer [Johnstone])
13 Sylvia Pankhurst's designs for the walls of the WSPU exhibition at the Prince's Skating Rink in 1909. (Institute for Social Research, Amsterdam)
14 'Is your Wife a Suffragette?': postcard, Burlesque Series, postmarked 1908. (Collection of Patricia Leeming)
15 Lunatic Asylum visitor: postcard designed by Lawson Wood. (Collection of Rosemary Hards)
16 'A Bird in the Hand': poster and postcard designed by Pamela Coleman Smith for the Suffrage Atelier, 1909. (Museum of London)
17 'In the Dim and Speculative Future': poster designed by Gladys Letcher of the Suffrage Atelier, 1909, and reproduced in the Women's Franchise, 29 July 1909. (Fawcett Collection)
18 The Common Cause, 3 February 1910 (anti-suffrage 'types' by the suffragists).
19 'This is Allowed to Vote': postcard designed by Edwyn Llewellyn, 1907. (Bodleian Library, John Johnson Collection: Postcards: Women's Suffrage)
20 'John Bull's Horse': postcard, anon., Suffrage Atelier. Undated. (Museum of London)
21 'Justice Demands the Vote': poster, anon., published by the Brighton and Hove Society for Women's Suffrage and available from the Artists' Suffrage League in 1909. (Library of Congress)
22 'Votes for Women' ('The People, not the Commons . . .'): poster and postcard designed by A. Patriot (Alfred Pearse) on behalf of the WSPU who used it in the General Election of December 1910. It was based on a well-known advertisement for Ripolin paint, as Votes for Women acknowledged when it was reproduced on 2 December 1910.
23 'Mrs Partington' ('Coming in with the Tide'): poster designed by Emily J. Harding Andrews, printed by Carl Hentschel and published by the Artists' Suffrage League. Undated. (Fawcett Collection)
24 Advertising Votes for Women in Kingsway. (National Museum of Labour History)
25 Mrs Fawcett opening the Suffrage Shop in Kensington before the 1908 march. (Fawcett Collection)
26 The NUWSS committee rooms during the Oldham by-election. (Fawcett Collection)
27 & 28 'Pro' and 'anti' cards from the BB series of twelve, 'The House that Man Built'. (Museum of London)
29 'The Suffragette Not at Home': postcard, C. W. Faulkner and Co. (Collection of Patricia Leeming)
30 'Beware of Suffragists', E. Dusédau, Jersey: a card postmarked 1909. (Collection of Patricia Leeming)
31 WSPU procession, 18 June 1910. (Museum of London)
32 Page from the Illustrated London News, 20 June 1908, reporting the NUWSS demonstration of 13 June. (Fawcett Collection)
33 Electrical trades union banner: woman as angel. (Photograph from the John Gorman Collection)
34 National Union of Vehicle Workers (Aldgate Branch) banner: woman as widow. (Photograph from the John Gorman Collection)
35 Banner of the Oxfordshire, Buckinghamshire and Berkshire Federation of the NUWSS, probably designed and executed by the Artists' Suffrage League. (Fawcett Collection)
36 'Caroline Herschel' banner: designed and worked by the Artists' Suffrage League, 1908. (Fawcett Collection)
37 WSPU banner-making for the procession of 23 July 1910. (Museum of London)
38 The banner of the Hampstead branch of the 'Church League for Women's Suffrage' (founded 1909): worked by Clemence Housman to a design by Laurence Housman. (The drawing is in Street Public Library, Somerset; the banner belongs to the Museum of London)

39 Incidents from the Mud March, 9 February 1907. Published in the *Daily Mirror*, 11 February 1907. (Suffrage Album, Fawcett Collection)

40 The Mud March. Supplement to the *Graphic*, 16 February 1907. (Communist Party Archives)

41 NUWSS members with Artists' Suffrage League banners, 13 June 1908. (Fawcett Collection)

42 Cicely Hamilton and members of the Women Writers' Suffrage League with the Writers' banner in 1910. (Fawcett Collection)

43 Mary Lowndes's 'Scriveners'' design, made up by the Artists' Suffrage League in 1908 as the Writers' banner. (The design is in Mary Lowndes's Album in the Fawcett Collection; the banner is in the Museum of London)

44 View of the Albert Hall decorated with banners at the end of the NUWSS procession. From the *Daily Graphic*, 15 June 1908. (Suffrage Album, Fawcett Collection)

45 WSPU wall poster showing the platforms in Hyde Park, with portraits of the twenty women chairing them on 21 June 1908. (Photograph by Oppé, courtesy of the Mansell Collection)

46 Mrs Drummond addressing MPs on the terrace of the House of Commons, a few days before the WSPU demonstration of 21 June 1908. (Fawcett Collection)

47 Mrs Pankhurst with Mrs Wolstenholme Elmy, in front of the WSPU banner donated by Emmeline Pethick-Lawrence, 21 June 1908. (Fawcett Collection)

48 Christabel Pankhurst with Emmeline Pethick-Lawrence on the militant demonstration of 21 June 1908. (Fawcett Collection)

49 A section of the crowds in Hyde Park, 21 June 1908. (Fawcett Collection)

50 & 51 Painters, Nurses and Midwives from the Pageant of Women's Trades and Professions, 27 April 1909. The emblems were designed by Mary Lowndes and executed by members and associates of the Artists' Suffrage League. (Fawcett Collection)

52 'English Inquisitors': poster, anon., Suffrage Atelier, *c.* 1912. (Fawcett Collection)

53 'The Prevention of Hunger Strikes': postcard, R. F. Ruttley, Suffragette Series. (Collection of Patricia Leeming)

54 'Feeding a Suffragette by Force': postcard, National Series. (Collection of Patricia Leeming)

55 'The Right Dishonourable Double-Face Asquith': poster and postcard designed by A. Patriot (Alfred Pearse), 1909, on behalf of the WSPU for use in the General Election of January 1910. Reproduced in *Votes for Women* (10 December 1912) and available from the Women's Press in two sizes at 6d and 3d. (Library of Congress)

56 'Who's Afraid? Not I!': postcard and poster, anon., Suffrage Atelier, *c.* 1911–12. (Museum of London)

57 WSPU procession, 18 June 1910, with Hunger Strikers' banner. (Photograph, Fawcett Collection; banner, Museum of London)

58 WSPU procession, 23 July 1910. Artists from the Suffrage

Atelier with palettes and ribbons. (Nurse Pine Collection, Museum of London)

59 Laurence Housman's 'From Prison to Citizenship' banner, carried by the prisoners' contingent on 23 July 1910. (Museum of London)

60 Horsewomen riding astride at the head of the west procession designed by Edith Craig and Laurence Housman, in the WSPU demonstration of 23 July 1910. (Fawcett Collection)

61 Processionists with emblems of prison gates, 23 July 1910. (Nurse Pine Collection, Museum of London)

62 The Women's Coronation Procession, 17 June 1911. (Fawcett Collection)

63 The Pageant of Empire from the Women's Coronation Procession, 17 June 1911. (Museum of London)

64 The Welsh contingent in 'national dress', 17 June 1911. (Fawcett Collection)

65 Mrs Despard in front of the Women's Freedom League banner, 17 June 1911. (Fawcett Collection, which also has the banner)

66 The Actresses' Franchise League, 17 June 1911. (Museum of London, which also has the banner)

67 'Political Conjuring': postcard designed by Hope Joseph for the Suffrage Atelier, and advertised in the *Vote*, 6 July 1912. (Fawcett Collection)

68 'Now Ain't That a Shame': postcard, Donald McGill. (Collection of Rosemary Hards)

69 'McKenna's Cat "Bill"': poster, anon., Suffrage Atelier, *c.* 1913. (Fawcett Collection)

70 The funeral cortège of Emily Wilding Davison passing through Piccadilly Circus, 14 June 1913. (Museum of London)

71 A WSPU guard of honour salutes its martyr as Emily Wilding Davison's coffin is carried into St George's Church, Bloomsbury. (Museum of London)

72 Advertisement from the *Common Cause*, 20 June 1913.

73 Cyclists at Clayton on the Brighton Road, on the NUWSS Pilgrimage in the summer of 1913. (Fawcett Collection)

74 Mrs Fawcett addressing the crowds in Hyde Park at the culmination of the Pilgrimage, 26 July 1913. From the *Common Cause*, 1 August 1913.

75 'John Bull: Excuse Me If I Laugh': designed by Harold Bird and printed by the National Press Agency for the National League for Opposing Woman Suffrage, 1912. Reproduced in the *Anti-Suffrage Review*, February 1912. (Bodleian Library, John Johnson Collection: Posters: Women's Suffrage)

76 'How the Law Protects the Widow': poster designed by 'MaC' for the Suffrage Atelier, 1909. (Fawcett Collection)

77 'How the Law Protects the Widower': poster designed by 'MaC' for the Suffrage Atelier, 1909. (Fawcett Collection)

78 'What a Woman May Be . . .': poster and postcard, anon., Suffrage Atelier, *c.* 1912. (Museum of London)

79 'Twentieth Century Robbery!': postcard and poster designed by Gladys Letcher for the Suffrage Atelier and advertised in the *Vote*, 6 July 1912. (Museum of London)

80 Miss Gander Bellwether ('At Mrs Lyon Chacer's "Small and Early"'), *Punch*, 14 March 1874. (*Punch* Picture Library)
81 'The Suffragette, Number 1 in a series on Present Day Types', the *Bystander*, 31 December 1913. (Mansell Collection)
82 'A Woman's Mind Magnified': poster. (Collection of Patricia Leeming)
83 'The Suffragette Face: New Type Evolved by Militancy', *Daily Mirror*, 25 May 1914.
84 'Waiting for a Living Wage': postcard and poster designed by Catherine Courtauld for the Suffrage Atelier, *c.* 1913. (Museum of London. There are two studies for the print among Catherine Courtauld's surviving papers.)
85 'Votes for Mother': postcard (and four-colour poster) produced by the Artists' Suffrage League and advertised in the *Common Cause*, 24 November 1910. Probably by Joan Harvey Drew. (Fawcett Collection)
86 'Women Underpaid, Men Out of Work': postcard, anon., Suffrage Atelier, *c.* 1913. (Museum of London)
87 'The Comfortable Women': poster, anon., Suffrage Atelier, 1912. (Fawcett Collection)
88 'The Scylla and Charybdis of the Working Woman': postcard designed by M. Hughes for the Suffrage Atelier. Undated, but probably *c.* 1912. (Museum of London)
89 'Polling Station': poster, anon., printed and published by the Suffrage Atelier. Undated, (but the little owl stamp and the Stanlake Villas address suggest *c.* 1912. (Museum of London)
90 'The ASS as Scientist': card by Catherine Courtauld for the Suffrage Atelier. (Bodleian Library, John Johnson Collection: Postcards: Women's Suffrage)
91 'The Antysuffragyst', the *Vote*, 26 September 1913.
92 'A Little Behind the Times': postcard designed by Joan Harvey Drew, printed and published by the Artists' Suffrage League, *c.* 1909. (Fawcett Collection)
93 'Time to shut up shop', *Votes for Women*, 4 July 1913.
94 'No Votes Thank You': poster designed by Harold Bird for the NLOWS, *c.* 1912. (Museum of London)
95 'Her Mother's Voice', Harold Bird, *Anti-Suffrage Review*, January 1912.
96 'The Shrieking Sister', Bernard Partridge, *Punch*, 17 January 1906. (*Punch* Picture Library)
97 'Votes for Women' ('Always make room for a lady'), postcard published by Archibald English and Edward Wise, postmarked 1910. (Collection of Patricia Leeming)
98 'Even Strong-Minded Suffragists have their Weak Moments': postcard, Suffragette Series. (Collection of Patricia Leeming)
99 Arrest of Miss Helen Tolson, 8 August 1909. (Nurse Pine Collection, Museum of London)
100 'Are We Down-Hearted?': postcard, Donald McGill, published E. S., London. (Collection of Patricia Leeming)
101 'Slow March Constable': postcard, Bamforth and Co., postmarked 1916. (Collection of Patricia Leeming)
102 'The Scarem Skirt' ('Not in these trousers'): postcard. (Collection of Rosemary Hards)
103 'Come Over Here': postcard. (Collection of Rosemary Hards)
104 *Votes for Women*, 24 May 1912: 'Prisoners of War'
105 Mrs Pankhurst arrested by Inspector Rolfe outside Buckingham Palace, 21 May 1914. (Museum of London)
106 *Votes for Women*, 13 August 1915: Britannia: 'A Vote! For the Child's Sake'.
107 Miss Annan Bryce as Joan of Arc, 17 June 1911. (National Library of Scotland)
108 'The Appeal of Womanhood': poster and postcard designed by Louise Jacobs of the Suffrage Atelier and advertised in the *Vote*, 6 July 1912. (Museum of London)
109 'The Prehistoric Argument': poster and postcard designed by Catherine Courtauld of the Suffrage Atelier and advertised in the *Vote*, 6 July 1912. (Museum of London)
110 'Modern Culture' by 'Cynicus' (pseudonym of Martin Anderson, a popular cartoonist of the period), postcard published by the Cynicus Publishing Co. (Collection of Patricia Leeming)
111 'I Pray for All the Grown-Ups' ('The Votes for Women Prayer'): postcard designed by C. Hedley Charlton, a professional illustrator associated with the Artists' Suffrage League. Undated. Published in America by the *Women's Journal* and the Massachusetts Woman Suffrage Association as 'The Land of Counterpane'. (Museum of London)
112 'Mummy's a Suffragette': commercial anti-suffrage postcard. (Museum of London)
113 'Won't You Let Me Help You John?': poster designed by Joan Harvey Drew of the Artists' Suffrage League, printed and published by David Allen and Son, *c.* 1909. (Library of Congress)
114 'Mrs How-Martyn Makes Jam': postcard number 3 in a series of 'Suffragettes at Home' published in the *Vote* and independently by the Women's Freedom League. (Museum of London)
115 Advertising *The Great Scourge*, 1913. (Museum of London)
116 Signing up for munitions work on 17 July 1915. (Nurse Pine Collection, Museum of London)
117 The Women's War Work procession passing through Piccadilly Circus, 17 July 1915. (Nurse Pine Collection, Museum of London)
118 'Belgium' from the Pageant of the Allies in the Women's War Work procession of 17 July 1915. (Nurse Pine Collection, Museum of London)

COLOUR PLATES *between pages 50/51 & 210/211*

I 'Handicapped': joint winner of the ASL poster competition in 1909. Designed by Duncan Grant, printed by Carl Hentschel, published by the Artists' Suffrage League. All ASL posters are professionally printed chromolithographs. (Library of Congress)
II 'Votes for Workers': joint winner of the ASL poster competition in 1909. Designed by W. F. Winter, printed by

Carl Hentschel, published by the Artists' Suffrage League.
(Library of Congress)
III 'Factory Acts' ('They've a Cheek'): poster designed by
Emily Ford, printed by Weiners, published by the Artists'
Suffrage League. (Library of Congress)
IV 'Convicts and Lunatics': poster designed by Emily Harding
Andrews, printed by Weiners, published by the Artists'
Suffrage League, c. 1908, reprinted 1910. (Library of
Congress)
V 'Justice at the Door': poster designed by Mary Lowndes,
published by the NUWSS, 1912. (Fawcett Collection)
VI 'Cat and Mouse': poster, anon., printed and published by
David Allen and Son for the WSPU, 1914. (Museum of
London)
VII 'Modern Inquisition': poster designed by A. Patriot
(Alfred Pearse) and published by the WSPU for the January
1910 General Election. (Museum of London)
VIII 'The Bugler Girl': poster designed by Caroline Watts
and published by the Artists' Suffrage League, originally to
advertise the NUWSS procession of 13 June 1908. (The
Schlesinger Library, Radcliffe College)
IX a. 'Spiritual Militancy', b. 'Joan of Arc', c. 'Florence
Nightingale' and d. 'North Berwick': four designs for banners
from Mary Lowndes's album. (Fawcett Collection). The Joan
of Arc banner (designed by Barbara Forbes) and the Florence
Nightingale banner (now in very poor condition) are also in the
Fawcett Collection. Both date from 1908; the others may be
later.
X Banner in appliquéd velvets designed by Mary Lowndes for
the Women Writers' Suffrage League, executed by Mrs
Herringham of the Artists' Suffrage League for the NUWSS

procession of 13 June 1908. (Museum of London)
XI a. 'Deeds not Words': the banner of the Hammersmith
branch of the WSPU. (Museum of London)
b. Design for a banner for the Conservative and Unionist
Women's Franchise Association, by the Fabian suffragist
Caroline Townshend. (Collection of Martin Harrison)
XII a. 'Cambridge Alumnae': banner designed by Mary
Lowndes and worked by the students of Newnham and Girton
for the Cambridge contingent in the NUWSS procession of
13 June 1908. (Reproduced by permission of the Principal and
Fellows, Newnham College, Cambridge)
b. Newnham and Girton staff and students with the
Cambridge banner. (Collection of Patricia Leeming)
XIII The Artists' Suffrage League banner, designed
presumably by Mary Lowndes, c. 1908. (Museum of London)
XIV a. 'Physical Education', b. 'The Office', c. 'Mary Moser',
d. 'Boadicea'. Banners executed by the Artists' Suffrage
League for the NUWSS procession of 1908. Probably designed
by Mary Lowndes. (a. and b., Museum of London: c. and d.,
Fawcett Collection)
XV 'A Suffragette's Home': designed by John Hassall, printed
by Miles Litho, and published by the National League for
Opposing Woman Suffrage, 1912. (Bodleian Library, John
Johnson Collection: Posters: Women's Suffrage)
XVI a. 'A Perfect Woman': postcard designed by John Hassall
for the NLOWS, 1912. (Fawcett Library)
b. 'Votes for Women': anon. (Bodleian Library, John Johnson
Collection: Postcards: Women's Suffrage)
c. 'We Want the Vote': postcard, anon. (Museum of London)
d. 'Hear Some Plain Things': postcard, anon. (Collection of
Rosemary Hards)

INDEX

Page numbers in italics refer to illustrations.
Colour plates are in italic roman numerals.

Actresses' Franchise League, 24, 67
  surviving banners of, 254
  taking part in Women's Coronation
    Procession, *131*
  war work of, 229
Adkins, Harriet S., 243
Advertisement of clothing 'For the
  Pilgrimage', *142*
Advertising *The Great Scourge and How
  to End It*, *224*
Advertising *Votes for Women* in Kingsway
  46
Albert Hall decorated with banners,
  87
Allen, David (printers), 18
Allen, Grant, 183
American suffrage movement, 266–7
Anderson, Sara, 19
Andrews, Emily J. Harding, 243
Anthony, Susan B., banner of, 254
Anti-Suffrage League, 99–100, 130
Anti-suffrage posters, surviving, 253
Anti-Suffrage Review, 177
anti-suffragists, 98–100, 154–6
'Antysuffragyst', *189*
'Appeal of Womanhood' – poster, *214*
'Are We Downhearted?' – McGill
  postcard, *202*
Arncliffe-Sennett, Maud, 88, 111
arson campaign, 135–6
Artists' Suffrage League, 15, 18–21, 37,
  43, 48, 50, 67, 80, 130, 211
  banners designed by, 69, 70
  foundation of, ix, x, 16
  poster production by, 44–5
  produce postcards for 1910 General
    Election campaign, 109
  supply Californian campaign, 266
  surviving banners of, 254, *xiii, xiv*
  surviving posters of, 250
Ashbee, Janet, 192
Asquith, H., 6, 9, 55, 79–80, 98, 235
  becomes Prime Minister, 80
  in suffrage imagery, 34
  receives deputation of suffragists, 148
'Asquith, Traitor to Liberal Principles'
  – poster, *31*
'ASS as Scientist' – card, *187*
Astor, Nancy, elected to Parliament,
  237
Austen, Jane, banner of, 254
Australia, Commonwealth of, banner of,
  255

Balfour, Arthur, 79

Balfour, Lady Frances, 4, 56, 69, 111,
  123
  leads Mud March, 75
banners, 60–73
  and banner-making, 262–4
  surviving, 254–61
  see also ix, x, xi, xii, xiii and *xiv*
Barker, May, 243
Bar-Las, Katherine, banner of, 254
Bartels, Mary, 243
Beggarstaff Brothers, 30
Belfort Bax, E., 6
Belloc, Hilaire, 162
Bell, Vanessa, 13
Besant, Annie, 130
'Beware of Suffragists' – postcard, *52*
Billing, Clara, 243
Billington-Greig, Teresa, 9–10, 38,
  201, 224
  banner of, 254
Bird, Harold, 249
'Bird in the Hand' – poster, *35*
birthrate, drop in, 186
Black, Clementina, 123
Black Agnes of Dunbar, banner of, 254
'Black Friday', 121
Blackwell, Elizabeth, banner of, 254
Blatch, Harriot Stanton, 266
Boadicea, 126, 128, 207; banner of,
  254, *xiii*
Bodichon, Barbara, 4, 15
Boucherett, Jessie, 4
Brackenbury, Georgina, 15, 243
Brackenbury, Marie, 15, 243
British Women's Temperance
  Association, 74
Browning, Amy Katherine, 243
Browning, Elizabeth, banner of, 211,
  255
Bryce, Annan, *210*
'Bugler Girl, The' – poster, 211–12, *viii*
Bulley, Amy, 190
Burney, Fanny, banner of, 255
Butler, Josephine, banner of, 255
by-elections, 48

Caird, Mona, xi, 183
Cambridge Alumnae, banner of, 255, *xii*
Campbell-Bannerman, Sir Henry, 9
Canute, King, 39, *41*
caricature, 161–7
Carroll, Lewis, 39
'Cat and Mouse' Act (*see*) Prisoners'
  Temporary Discharge for Ill
  Health Act

'Cat and Mouse' – poster, *vi*
  see 'McKenna's Cat "Bill"' – poster
Central Society for Women's Suffrage,
  74
Charlton, C. Hedley, 30, 243
Chartism, 3
Christian Commonwealth, 130
Church League for Women's Suffrage
  Hampstead Branch banner, *72*
  takes part in June 1910
    demonstration, 114
  takes part in Women's Coronation
    procession, 130
Civil Service, banner of, 255
Clews, Elsie Parsons, 216, 217
Clitheroe Society, banner of, 255
Coates, Dora Meeson, 16, 244
  background of, 19–20
colours, suffrage, 265, 293
'Come Over Here' – postcard, *203*
'Comfortable Women' – poster, *181*
Common Cause, 6, 10, 14, 16, 18, 21, *36*,
  43, 49, 143, 146, 157, 158, 211
  and the Women's Coronation
    procession, 123
  on Joan of Arc, 212
  reports: Pageant of Women's Trades
    and Professions, 102–103;
    Women's Pilgrimage, 144, 145
  sold on Women's Pilgrimage, 143
Conciliation Bill, 111, 112, 119–120,
  131–3
  killed by Parliament, 115
  redraft of, 121–2
Conciliation Committee, 110
Conservative and Unionist Women's
  Franchise Association, 128
  banner, *xi*
Conservative Party, 6
Contagious Diseases Acts, 197, 223
'Convicts and Lunatics' – poster, *iv*
Copsey, Helen Dorothy, 244
coronation of George V, 56–7
Corrupt Practices Act (1883), 5
Courtauld, Catherine, *175*, 244
*Cosmic Procession, or the Feminine
  Principle in Evolution*, 190
Craig, Edith, 24, 244
  designs banners for July 1910
    demonstration, 117
  designs banners for June 1910
    demonstration, 112
  Portrait of, *24*
Crane, Walter, *31*, 32
Curie, Marie, banner of, 255

Curzon, Lord, 160
  on a political role for women, 155,
  156

Daily Chronicle
  reports: 'hysteria', 203; NUWSS
  demonstration, 89
Daily Express
  reports: June 1910 demonstration,
  114; WSPU demonstration, 96
Daily Graphic, reports on NUWSS
  demonstration, 90
Daily Herald
  reports: funeral of Emily Wilding
  Davison, 140; 'Right to Serve'
  demonstration, 234
Daily Mail, 59, 81
  coins word 'suffragette', 8
  reports Women's Coronation
  procession, 126
Daily Mirror, 59
Daily News
  reports: on forced feeding, 105;
  NUWSS demonstration, 87–8;
  Women's Pilgrimage, 146
Daily Sketch, 59, 230
  advocates mobilisation of women, 231
  reports Women's Coronation
  procession, 130–1
Daily Telegraph, 58, 82
  reports: Pageant of Women's Trades
  and Professions, 101; 'Right to
  Serve' demonstration, 231;
  Women's Pilgrimage, 147
Dallas, Hilda, 244
Darwin, Charles, 186, 188, 189
Davies, Emily, 4, 123
Davison, Emily Wilding, 136–40
  funeral cortège of, *139*
'Deeds not Words' (Hammersmith
  WSPU banner), 260, *xi*
demonstrations, use of, 58
Descent of Man, 186, 188, 189
Despard, Charlotte, 9, 10, 25, 112
  leads WSPU on Mud March, 75
  takes part in NUWSS demonstration,
  84
Dickinson, Willoughby, 79
Dimmock, Edith, 111
Douglas, James, 88
Downing, Edith E., 15, 27, 244
  designs procession for July 1910
  demonstration, 119
  organises Women's Coronation
  procession, 125–6
Drew, Joan Harvey, 19, 244
Drummond, Mrs, addresses MPs from
  steam launch, *92, 94*, 112, 125
Dunlop, Marion Wallace, 15, *15*, 27,
  244
  designs procession for July 1910
  demonstration, 119

imprisonment of, 104
organises Women's Coronation
  procession, 125–6
Dyer, Richard, 172

East London Federation of
  Suffragettes, 229
'Edgerton, George', 183
Edgerton, Giles, 13
Edgeworth, Maria, banner of, 255
Education banner, 255
Edwardian, period, xii, 38, 48, 51, 99,
  151, 152, 166
Electoral Reform, 131
Electrical Trades Union banner, *64*
Eliot, George, 71; banner of, 255
Elizabeth banner, 256
Embroidery, 73
Enfield banner, 256
'English Inquisitors' – poster, *106*
Englishwoman, reports Women's
  Pilgrimage, 146
eugenics, 186
Evangelicalism, 3, 215–16
'Even Strong-Minded Suffragists have
  their Weak Moments', *199*
Exhibition of banners (1908), 70–1,
  80

Fabian Women's Group, 67, 130
Factory Act (1895), 177
'Factory Acts' – poster, *iii*
fashion among the suffragettes, 166
Fawcett Collection, 18, 68, 69, 250
Fawcett, Henry, 4
Fawcett, Millicent, 4–5, 6–7, 47, 56,
  59, 80–1, 86
'Feeding a Suffragette by Force' –
  postcard, *108*
Femininity
  imagery of, 182–3
  representations of types, 174–226
  stereotypes of, 161–2
feminism, 3, 153, 183
Ferguson, Rachel, 60
finance, 42–5, 62–3
Florence, Mary Sargant, 19, 244–5
  banners designed by, 69
'Florence Nightingale', banner of, *ix*
Forbes, Barbara, 18–20, 50, 245
forced feeding, 104–7
Ford, Emily S., 15, 19, 124, 245
  designs banners for Women's
  Coronation procession, 130
'For the Pilgrimage' – advertisement,
  142
Foucault, Michel, 196
Franchise, 4–5
'Franchise Villa' – poster, *31*
Free Churches banner, 256
Freud, Sigmund, 163, 200, 196–7,
  212–3

'From Prison to Citizenship' – banner,
  112
  being carried, *118*
'From Prison to Citizenship' – postcard,
  51
Fry, Elizabeth, banner of, 256
Fry, Roger, 20
Fulleylove, Joan E. A., 245
fund raising, 115

'Garland for May Day' – poster, *31*
Garrard, Violet, 19, 245
Geddes, Patrick, 188
General Election (January 1910),
  109–10
General Election (December 1910), 121
George V, King, coronation of, 56–7
Gilman, Sander, 172
Girl of the Period, 213
Gissing, George, 183
Gladstone, Herbert, 79
Gladstone, W. E., 4
  on a political role for women, 155
graduates, women, 220
Graduates of London University
  banner, 256
Gramsci, Antonio, x
Grand, Sarah, 183
Grant, Duncan, 16, 18, 245
Graphic, 180
Great Scourge and How to End It, 223, *224*
Great War (1914–1918), 229–35
Green, David 170
Grey, Sir Edward, 122

Hamilton, Cicely, xii, 14–5, 24, 81, *85*,
  86, 158, 198, 216
Hammersmith WSPU banner, 260, *xi*
Hampden, John, banner of, 256
Hampstead Church League for
  Women's Suffrage banner, *72*, 256
*Handbook of the Daily News Sweated
  Industries' Exhibition*, 175
'Handicapped' – poster, 16, *17*, 18, *i*
Hardie, Keir, 6, 158
  tables parliamentary question on
  forced feeding, 105
Hardy, Thomas, 183
Harrison, Jane, 216
Hassall, John, 249
'Hear Some Plain Things' – postcard,
  xvi
Heath, Stephen, 194, 205
Hentschel, Carl (printers), 18
'Her Mother's Voice', *195*
Herringham, Mrs, 245
Herschel, Caroline, banner of
  68, 256
Hobsbawm, Eric, 211
Hockin, Olive, 15, 136, 245
Holloway WSPU banner, 260
Home-Makers banner, 256

Home Rule Bill, 135
Housing Question banner, 256
Housman, Clemence, 245
  background of, 22
  banner-making by, 69, 71
Housman, Laurence, 21, 47, 192,
  245–6
  background of, 22
  banners designed by, 69, 94
  designs banners for July 1910
    demonstration, 117
  on womanliness, 213
How-Martyn, Edith, 10
  makes jam – postcard, 221
  stands for Parliament, 237
'How the Law Protects the Widower' –
  poster, 157
'How the Law Protects the Widow' –
  poster, 157
hunger strikes, 104–7
Hyndman, H. M., 6
'Hysterical Woman, The', 192–205

iconography, 152
  of banners, 67–9
Ilford WSPU banner, 260
Illustrated Chronicle, reports funeral of
  Emily Wilding Davison, 138
Illustrated London News, 61
Independent Labour Party, 8, 9, 57, 73
Inter-Departmental Committee on Physical
  Deterioration, Report of, 186
International Delegates banner, 256–7
International Suffrage Alliance, 18, 100,
  123
'In the Dim and Speculative Future' –
  poster, 35
'invented traditions', 56–7
'I Pray for All the Grown-Ups' –
  postcard, 218
Irish Women's Franchise League, 114
'Is your Wife a Suffragette?' – postcard,
  34

Jackson, Holbrook, 183
Jacobs, Louise R., 246
Joan of Arc, 208, 211, 212, 234
  and Militant Woman, 209–11
  Annan Bryce as, 210
  surviving banner of, 81, 257, ix
John, Augustus, 20
'John Bull: Excuse Me If I Laugh' –
  poster, 149
'John Bull's Horse' – postcard, 39
Jopling, Louise (Louise Jopling-Rowe),
  15, 34, 246
Joseph, A. E. Hope, 246
'Justice at the Door' – poster, v
'Justice Demands the Vote' – poster,
  40

Kauffmann, Angelica, 13

Kenney, Annie, 8, 94
Kennington, T. B., 50
Kingsley, Mary, banner of, 257

Labour Party, 6
  NUWSS form alliance with, 133
  Women's Social and Political Union
    breaks with, 8
Labour Representation Committee, 6
Ladies' Ecclesiastical Embroidery
  Society, 73
Laycock, Thomas, 169
Lear, Edward, 39
Lewisham WSPU banner, 260
Liberal Association, Women's, 5
Liberal Party, 4, 6, 9
  NUWSS's disillusionment with, 133
  support of, 80
Lind, Jenny, banner of, 257
Linton, Eliza Lynn, 213, 217
'Little Behind the Times' – postcard,
  191
Lloyd-George, David, 109, 233–4
London banner, 257
London Society for Women's Suffrage,
  18, 59
  takes part in NUWSS demonstration,
  84
Lowndes, Mary, 14, 19, 20, 37, 58, 101,
  246
  and banner-making, 63, 66, 67, 73
  and the Women's Coronation
    procession, 123–4
  background of, 18–19
  design of banners by, 71
  designs banners for Pageant of
    Women's Trades and Professions,
    101–2
  war work of, 229
  See also Artists' Suffrage League and
    Appendix 5
'Lunatic Asylum Visitor' – postcard, 35
Lytton, Lady Constance, 107

MacDonald, Ramsay, 175
McGill, Donald, 162
McKenna, Reginald, 136
'McKenna's Cat "Bill"' – poster, 137
Macclesfield banner, 257
Madame Tussaud's, wax portraits of
  suffragettes in, 93
Manchester & Salford banner, 257
Manchester Guardian, 211
  reports Women's Pilgrimage, 146
Markham, Violet, 155
Markievicz, Countess, elected to
  Parliament, 237
Married Women's Work, 175
Married Working Woman, 175
Marsh, Charlotte, 112
Men's League for Opposing Woman
  Suffrage, 179

Men's League for Women's Suffrage,
  19–20, 23
Men's Political Union, 130
  surviving banner of, 257
Meredith, George, 183
'Militant Woman, The', 205–13
militancy and hysteria, 192–205
Mill, Harriet Taylor, 3, 153, 154, 157
Mill, John Stuart, 3, 4, 153
Mills, Ernestine, 246
'Miss Gander Bellwether', 165
Mitchell, Juliet, 197
'Modern Culture' – postcards, 218
'Modern Inquisition' – poster, vii
Modern Parisienne, 13
'Modern Woman, The', 182–92
Montgomerie Beddow, A., banner of,
  254
Moore, George, 183
More, Hannah, 215
Morning Leader
  reports: NUWSS demonstration,
    88–89; Pageant of Women's
    Trades and Professions, 102
Morris, May, 247
  banner designed by, 69
Morris, William, 27, 32
Moser, Mary, 13
  surviving banner of, 257
motherhood and the vote, 217–219
'Mrs How-Martyn Makes Jam' –
  postcard, 221
'Mrs Partington (Coming in with the
  Tide)' – poster, 41
Mud March, 18, 74, 76–7, 78
  impact of, 181
  organisation of, 74
'Mummy's a Suffragette' – postcard,
  219
Municipal Franchise Act (1869), 5
Museum of London, 68

National Association of Women Civil
  Servants, banner of, 257
National League for Opposing
  Woman Suffrage, 99
  surviving posters of, 253, xv
  See also anti-suffragists
National Union of Societies for Equal
  Citizenship, 237
National Union of Vehicle Workers'
  banner, 65
National Union of Women's Suffrage
  Societies, 6, 7, 8, 10, 16, 18, 43, 58
  avoidance of militant imagery, 211
  becomes National Union of Societies
    for Equal Citizenship, 237
  demonstration (1908), 80–91
  denounce militancy, 132
  dispute with WSPU, 107–9, 111
  Glasgow banner, 258
  influence on MPs, 80

National Union of Women's Suffrage
  Societies – *cont.*
  Partick banner, 258
  Pilgrimage (1913), 141–7
  Procession Committee set up, 80
  processions organised by, 74
  propose July 1910 demonstration,
    115–16
  struggle to maintain identity, 212
  support Women's Enfranchisement
    Bill, 79
  surviving banners of, 258
  take part in Women's Coronation
    procession, 122–31
  war work of, 229
  See also Mud March
National Union of Women Teachers,
  banner of, 257
National Union of Women Workers,
  take part in NUWSS demonstration,
  84
National Woman Suffrage Association,
  (USA), 266
New, Edmund Hort, 71, 247
New Age, 100
Newcombe, Bertha, 19, 247
New English Art Club, 13
Newport banner, 257–8
New Woman, concept of, 182–184
Nicholson, William, 30
Nightingale, Florence, banner of, 258, *ix*
'North Berwick', banner, *ix*
Northern Franchise Demonstration
  Committee, 75
Northern Men's Federation, banners of,
  258
'No Votes Thank You' – poster, *193*
'Now Ain't That a Shame' – McGill
  postcard, *134*

Office banner, 258
Oldham by-election, NUWSS committee
  rooms during, *49*
Omega Workshop, 20
Order of Universal Co-Freemasonry, 130
Origin of the Species, 186
Orwell, George, 163
Oxfordshire, Buckinghamshire &
  Berkshire Federation of the NUWSS
  banner, *67*, 258

Pageant of Empire from the Women's
  Coronation procession, *127*
Pageant of Great Women, 24
'Pageant of the Allies', *233*
Pageant of Women's Trades and
  Professions, 18, 100–4
pageantry, 57–8
Pall Mall Gazette, reports on NUWSS
  demonstration, 90–1
Pankhurst, Adela, 8
Pankhurst, Christabel, 8, *95*, 223

correspondence with Arthur Balfour,
  79; with Herbert Asquith, 98
stands for Parliament, 237
Pankhurst, Emmeline, 6, 9, 23
  arrest of, *207*
  background of, 8
  war work of, 230, 231
Pankhurst, Sylvia, xi, 8, 20, 26, *29*, 57,
  91, 220, 247
  artistic talent of, 27–9
  banners designed by, 69
  design for Prince's Skating Rink
    Exhibition, 1909, *33*
  income of, 43
  visit to United States, 266
Parliament Act (1911), 131
Parliamentary Committee for Women's
  Suffrage, 78
Paul, Alice, 266
Pearse, Alfred, 27, 247
Perkins, T. E., 172
Pethick-Lawrence, Emmeline, ix, 8, 9,
  42, 55, 94, 98, 111, 166, 205
  and banners, 71
  selects colours for WSPU, 93
Pethick-Lawrence, Frederick, 39, 115
  organises advertising for WSPU
    demonstration, 91
Phipson, Edith Pechey, banner of, 258
Physical Education banner, 258
physiognomy, 169–170
Pilgrimage. *See* NUWSS
Pocock, Isobel, 247
'Political Conjuring' – postcard, *132*
'Political Help' – poster, 16, *17*
'Polling Station' – poster, *187*
postcards 50–2
  humorous, 53, 162
  publication of propaganda, 50
poster parades, 47
posters
  as objects of connoisseurship, 48
  circulation of, 45–50
  party political, 50
  production of, 44–5
  surviving, 250–3
Post Office, monopoly on postcard
  production, 50–1
Power and Responsibility, 179
'Prehistoric Argument' – poster, *215*
Pre-Raphaelitism, x, 15, 28, 32, 220
'Present Day Types – The Suffragette',
  168
Press coverage of NUWSS demonstration
  (1908), 86–91
'Prevention of Hunger Strikes' –
  postcard, *108*
Primrose League, Women's Council of,
  5
Prisoners' Temporary Discharge for Ill
  Health Act ('Cat and Mouse' Act),
  15, 38, 39

introduction of, 136
propaganda and art, purpose of, x–xi,
  151, 161
propaganda training, by Suffrage
  Atelier, 20, 21
prostitution, 222, 225
Pryde, James, 30
psychoanalysis and hysteria, 197
Punch, 164, 169, 180, 184, 220
  satirises militants, 205

Referee, 59
  reports on 'hysteria', 204
Reform Acts (1832) (1867) (1884), 4, 5,
  7
Reform Bill, withdrawal of, 132, 134,
  135
Representation of the People Act
  (1918), 236
Ridley, Ada Paul, 247
'Right Dishonourable Double-Face
  Asquith' – poster, *109*
Rights and Wrongs of Women, 217
'Right to Serve' Demonstration (1914),
  231–233
Robins, Elizabeth, 14, 71
Rokeby Venus, slashing of, 134, 135
Roosevelt, Theodore, 266
Round About a Pound a Week, 175
Rowbotham, Sheila, 3
Royal Academy, 13, 16
Royal College of Art, 28
*Royal Commission on the Care and Control
  of the Feeble Minded, Report of*, 186
Royden, Maud, 176

St Catherine of Siena banner, 258
St George banner, 258
St Teresa of Spain banner, 258
Sanderson, Annie Cobden, 9
Saturday Review, 183
'Scarem Skirt' – postcard, *202*
'Scriveners'' banner, *85*
'Scylla and Charybdis of the Working
  Woman' – postcard, *182*
Sex Disqualification Removal Act
  (1919), 237
sexuality, 223
  in literature, 183–4
sexuality and hysteria, 195–6
Sharp, Evelyn, 210
Shaw, Rev. Anna, 81
Shaw, George Bernard, 81, 86, 94, 159,
  167, 183
Shore, Bethia, 19, 247
Shorthand Writers banner, 259
'Shrieking Sister', *198*
'Shrieking Sisterhood', 192–205
Shute, E. L., 247
Siddons, Sarah, banner of, 259
'Signing up for munitions work 1915',
  227

silk banners, 261
Sinclair, May, 183
'Slow March Constable' – postcard, 202
Smith, Pamela Coleman, 247–8
Snowden, Philip, 6, 130
Social Darwinism, 186–90
Social Democratic Federation, 6
socialism, 3
social types, 173
Society for Promoting the Employment
    of Women, 174
Somerville, Mary, banner of, 259
Speaker's Conference (1917), 235–6
Spectator, 126
Spencer, Herbert, 170, 188
Stanger, Henry York, 79
status of women in society, 209
stereotypes, 173–4, 226
Stevenson, R. A. M., 23
Stone, Lucy, banner of, 259
Strachey, Lady Julia, 16
Strachey, Philippa, 20, 111, 124
Suffrage Annual and Women's Who's Who,
    16, 18, 190
Suffrage Atelier, 15, 20–1, 24–5, 50,
    67
    artistic influences on, 30, 32
    banner-making and, 69, 71
    Broadsheet, 22
    constitution, 21–2, 241–2
    function, ix, x
    poster production by, 44, 45
    surviving posters of, 250–2
    takes part in June 1910
        demonstration, 112, 114
    takes part in July 1910 demonstration,
        119
    takes part in Women's Coronation
        procession, 130
Suffrage Conference (1916), 235
Suffrage Shop, Kensington, 46
'suffragette', 8
Suffragette, 47
'Suffragette Face: New Type Evolved
    by Militancy', 171
'A Suffragette's Home' – poster, xv
'Suffragette *Not* at Home' – postcard,
    52
suffragists, stereotypes of, 167–72
Surrey Sussex & Hants banner, 259
Swiney, Frances, 190

'*This* is Allowed to Vote' – postcard, 37
'This is the House that Man Built' –
    postcards, 51
Thompson-Price, Louisa, 248
Times, 58, 98, 157, 158
    Liberal Manifesto published in, 109
    on exhibition of banners, 80
    publishes articles against Conciliation
        Bill, 115

reports: 'hysteria', 192, 204; June
    1910 demonstration, 114; July
    1910 demonstration, 119; Mud
    March, 75; NUWSS Demonstration,
    86, 90–91; 'Right to Serve'
    Demonstration, 234; Women's
    Pilgrimage, 146; on women's war
    work, 235; WSPU demonstration,
    94, 96
'Time to Shut up Shop', 191
Tolson, Helen, arrest of, 201
Trades Union Congress, 6
    Parliamentary Committee of, 176
trade union banners, 69
trade unions, 177, 178
Tribune, 75, 78
Tuck, Raphael & Sons, 51
Tuke, Mabel, 122
Tutill, George, banner maker, 62–3, 66
'Twentieth Century Robbery!' – poster
    and postcard, 159

United States, British propaganda in,
    266–7
United Suffragists' banner, 259
Uzanne, Octave, 13

Velázquez, 134
Victoria, Queen and Mother banner,
    259
Vindication of the Rights of Women, 3
visual imagery, 161–2
Vote, 6, 22, 25, 130, 157
    reports Women's Coronation
        procession, 128
'Votes for Mother' – postcard, 179
Votes for Women, 6, 42, 47, 60, 66, 91, 98
    'Britannia', 208
    on Joan of Arc, 210–11
    plan of campaign published in, 79
    'Prisoners of War', 206
    reports: June 1910 demonstration,
        115; July 1910 Demonstration,
        116; WSPU Demonstration, 96
'Votes for Women (Always make room
    for a lady)', 199
'Votes for Women' – postcard, see 'We
    Want The Vote'
'Votes for Women (Bogies)' – poster, 26
'Votes for Women' – poster, 41
'Votes for Women and Chastity for
    Men', 223
'Votes for Workers' – poster, 16, ii

wages, low, 178
'Waiting for a Living Wage' – poster and
    postcard, 175
Walters, Jessica Lloyd, 248
Ward, Mrs Humphry, 99–100
war service, women urged to register
    for, 230
Watts, Caroline M., 80, 248

'We Want the Vote' – postcard, xvi
Webb, Beatrice, 177
Weiners of Acton (printers), 18
Wells, H. G., 34
Welsh contingent at Women's
    Coronation procession, 128, 129
West Ham WSPU banner, 260
West Midlands banner, 259
Westminster Gazette, 160
'What a Woman May Be . . .' – poster
    and postcard, 159
Wheelhouse, Mary V., 19, 248
White Slave Traffic Bill (1912), 224
'Who's Afraid? Not I!' – poster and
    postcard, 110
Wigan, Bessie, 15, 19, 248
Willis, E. B., 20, 248
Wilson, E. Hartley, 248
Wimbledon WSPU banner, 260
Windsor & Eton banner, 259
Winter, W. F., 16, 248
Wollstonecraft, Mary, 3, 4, 153, 213, 215
    banner of, 259
'Woman Militant', 61
'Woman Offering Her Gifts at Her
    Country's Door' – poster 220
'Womanly Woman, The', 213–26
'Woman's Mind Magnified' – postcard,
    169
Women in the Printing Trades, 175
Women's Co-operative Guild, 9, 74
    takes part in NUWSS demonstration,
        84
Women's Coronation procession, 57,
    71, 122–31
Women's Council of the Primrose
    League, 5
Women's Employment Defence
    League, takes part in NUWSS
    demonstration, 84
Women's Freedom League, 6, 10, 24,
    25, 38, 47, 55, 111
    banners, 129, 259–60
    in 1910 General Election campaign,
        109
    income of, 42
    take part in June 1910 demonstration,
        112
    take part in NUWSS demonstration, 84
    take part in Women's Coronation
        procession, 128
Women's Industrial Council Enquiry,
    175
Women's International League for
    Peace and Freedom, 229
Women's Liberal Association, 5
Women's Liberal Federation, 74
Women's National Anti-Suffrage
    League, 58
    formation of, 99
Women's Peace Conference (1915),
    229

Women's Rights Convention, New
    York, 266
Women's Service Bureau, 229
Women's Social and Political Union, ix,
    6, 8–9, 10, 24, 26–7, 38, 48,
    57
banner-making by, 70
cost of banners used by, 63
demonstration organised by, 91–100
dispute with NUWSS, 107–9
embark on militant campaign,
    133–5
income of, 42
membership card, 28
militancy in, xii, 205
'Moral Crusade' by, 223, 225
organise 'Right to Serve'
    demonstration, 232–4
poster production by, 44
processions organised by, 73–4
procession with drum and fife band,
    53
produce postcards for 1910 General

Election campaign, 109
seek to maintain image of militant
    woman, 201
surviving banners of, 260
surviving posters of, 252–3
take part in funeral of Emily Wilding
    Davison, 138
take part in June 1910 demonstration,
    112, 113
taking part in July 1910
    demonstration, 116, 117
take part in Women's Coronation
    procession, 122–31
violence by, 120–1
wall poster in Hyde Park, 92
Women's Tax Resistance League, 24,
    67
take part in July 1910 Demonstration,
    119
take part in Women's Coronation
    Procession, 130
Women's Trade Union League, 177
Women's War Work procession, 232

Women's Work and Wages, 175, 176
'Women Underpaid, Men Out of Work'
    – postcard, 179
Women Writers' Suffrage League, 119
    banner, x
take part in Women's Coronation
    procession, 130
'Won't You Let Me Help You John?',
    – poster, 221
Woodward, Alice Bolingbroke, 248
Woolf, Virginia, 13
work force, women in, 176
'Working Woman, The', 174–82
Wright, Sir Almroth, 34, 42, 156, 158,
    161, 185–6, 197
on hysteria, 192, 194
Writer's Suffrage League, take part in
    June 1910 demonstration, 114

YMCA Overseas Friends' banner, 260

Zangwill, Israel, 160, 192